The Encyclopedia of
Herbs and Herbalism

The Encyclopedia of Herbs and Herbalism

Edited by
Malcolm Stuart

ORBIS · LONDON

First published in Great Britain by Orbis Publishing Limited 1979
Reprinted 1982, 1984
Reprinted 1986 by
Orbis Book Publishing Corporation
A BPCC plc Company
Greater London House, Hampstead Road, London NW1

Printed in Italy
ISBN: 0-85613-067-2 (hardback)
ISBN: 0-85613-700-6 (paperback)

Half-title page: The pomegranate (Punica granatum) *from Duhamel's nineteenth-century herbal,* Traite des Arbres *(Michael Holford)*

Title page: English Lavender (Lavandula spica) *(Jane Burton/Bruce Coleman)*

Right: Some of the ingredients for making pot-pourri (Leslie Johns)

Contents

Introduction

Herbalism has long been thought to consist almost exclusively of the light-hearted study of early printed works which dealt with the supposed medicinal action of plants or their use in cookery. The study of herbs has only recently begun to lose its association with quack medicine and become part of the return to a more natural way of life with the rediscovery of our pre-industrial heritage. The study of herbs cannot be slotted into a narrow botanical niche, either, since the development of man's relationship with plants has always been inextricably linked with economics, religion and science.

In defining the term 'herb', 'herbaceous' plants are those which lack a woody stem and die down to the ground at the end of their growing season, or life if the plant is an annual. Yet this definition cannot accommodate some of the first herbs that come to mind such as Sage, Rosemary or Lavender. These are among the most commonly used herbs which are woody and do not die down. As the dictionary restricts our study to the use of stems and leaves from plants whereas herbalism can involve the use of lichens, fungi and innumerable other plants whose fruit, roots, bark and gums are of value to us, we must simply define herbalism as the study of those plants which are of use to man. The definition of a herb is further complicated by the inclusion of such plants as certain onions, beetroot, celery, olives and chicory, which we now term vegetables. Originally herbs were divided into three different types: pot herbs, which included onions, for example; sweet herbs, such as thyme, which we now call culinary herbs; and salad herbs such as wild celery. In the seventeenth century pot herbs began to be called vegetables since they were no longer thought of as suitable only for the pot but were also used at table. The horticultural breeding of these plants led to the development of their structure and their flavour away from the wild plant to the larger and less bitter modern equivalents.

Left: The old-world charm of a formal herb garden showing the use of a focal point and plants with foliage of various colours (Gaulden Manor, near Taunton, England).

Until comparatively recently herbs were an integral and quite clearly a necessary commodity in life. In medieval Europe, for instance, their cultivation, collection and distribution were essential to the smooth maintenance of any household. In the kitchen Ash twigs (*Fraxinus excelsior*) and Horsetail (*Equisetum arvense*) served respectively as egg whisks and brushes. Such herbal implements are to be found today only in exclusive chandlers. Soapwort or Bouncing Bet (*Saponaria officinalis*) was used as a soap for delicate fabrics, and Pennyroyal (*Mentha pulegium*) as a flea-repellent. Mullein (*Verbascum thapsus*) and other herbs served as tapers or emergency candles, and almost every daily task involved one herb or another. For cheesemaking Lady's Bedstraw (*Galium verum*) provided a juice which acted as the rennet. Herbs still play a vital role in the tobacco and brewing industries, in the manufacture of wine and liqueurs, as

Above: This ancient painting of healing drugs was used to illustrate a book by Galen, whose accounts of botanical drugs were undisputed until the Middle Ages.

Below: A page from an eleventh-century herbal. It illustrates an Ivy and describes the herb's medicinal applications. (This one was written at Bury St Edmunds, England.)

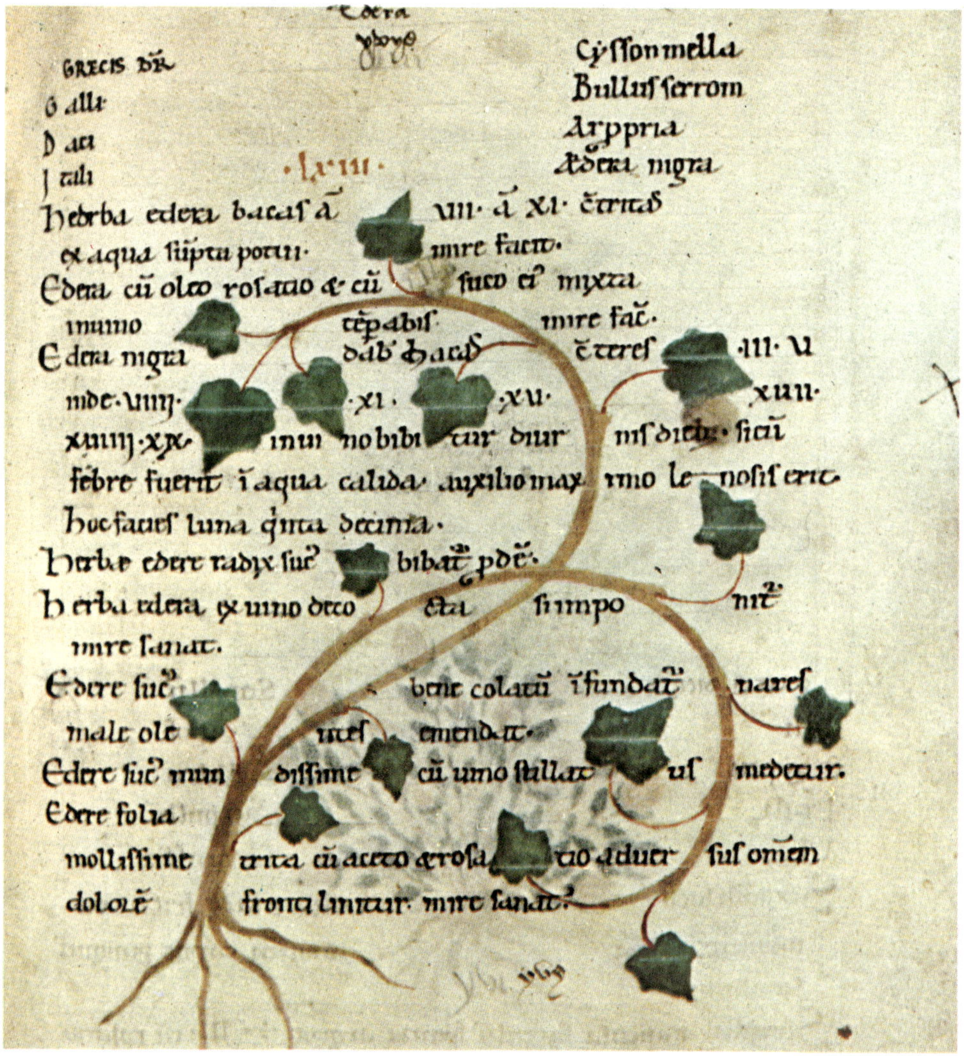

flavourings and colourings in the confectionery trade and in the manufacture of dyes. With their lovely natural scents and oils, herbs are once again becoming as essential to the modern cosmetic business as they have always been to perfume manufacturers.

In order to understand the present revival of herbalism, the development of man's relationship with plants through the centuries should be examined. History from the emergence of Homo sapiens to the present day can be divided into three broad epochs: the hunter-gatherer period, the agricultural period and the present agricultural-industrial period with its beginnings some four hundred years ago.

Our knowledge of the very early history of man and his evolution is still very vague. We can know very little for certain about early man's diet and way of life, and our assessment of his dependence on plants must, therefore, be a combination of surmise and deduction from the remains discovered by archaeologists. While tools and artifacts commonly survive to give an indication of economics and technology, plants and foods are only preserved in ideal conditions, such as particularly dry regions and, often, caves. Plant remains comprise a variety of forms, mostly seeds, some flower and fruit stalks and leaves. A skilled botanist can identify plants from these remains, and even fossilized faeces can provide clues.

As a hunter-gatherer, man hunted animals, fished, gathered wild fruits and leaves and grubbed up the edible roots of wild plants. He may or may not have reacted instinctively in his rejection of poisonous plants. Certainly he must have experimented with and come to know the many plants within the limits of his nomadic wanderings. Most were innocuous and bland; some nourished him; a handful were particularly pleasant to taste and some equally unpleasant. By trial and error he discovered that some could relieve pain, some proved fatal and a few had a strange unearthly effect on his mind and body. In this period man was able to develop techniques for neutralizing or rendering palatable the parts of plants which he discovered to be of any value to him.

Plants were chopped, leached, dried, roasted and cooked. There is even some evidence that the hunter-gatherer may have experimented with fermentation.

Right: Marjoram was cultivated in medieval times not only as a food flavouring but also for its medicinal qualities, particularly as an antiseptic.

Maiorana.

The hunter-gatherer period was the longest clinical trial in history which eventually produced the herbs that provided the best foods, the poison to destroy enemies, the finest fuels and weapons, soporific drinks, medicines, the plants that produced colour for body and cave paintings, and the 'magic' plants which carried primitive man away from reality.

This last group consists, of course, of those herbs causing visual, auditory, tactile, taste or other hallucinations. They are variously described as hallucinatory, psychedelic, narcotic or psychoactive, and their effect can vary from mild euphoria to the inducement of artificial psychoses. Their importance cannot be overemphasized since the effects they have on the human mind and body led to the powerful role they played in primitive society. To early man such herbs offered temporary relief and an escape from the severity of his environment. When sick they provided a direct palliative or cure for his ills, though often we must suppose that the psychic effects of these plants were of more importance than their purely physical effects. This is especially significant when we consider that to early man the modern divisions between science, medicine, art and religion would not have had any meaning. Sickness, in primitive societies, is often attributed to supernatural forces entering the body and from the earliest times, therefore, medicine was linked with the supernatural.

The early doctors and herbalists were invested with an appropriately high social status and indeed, they often enhanced their social position by guarding the 'secrets' of their herbal remedies and stage-managing superstition. Mandrake, a herb with anciently appreciated anaesthetic and purgative properties, was imbued with many forbidding superstitions. In the first century A.D., Josephus the Jewish historian said that Mandrake had the power to expel evil spirits from sick persons but that it was certain death to uproot it casually. The Paeony, too, had to be dug at night, for if a woodpecker caught a gatherer by day, woe to his eyes! Hallucinatory herbs and their products have been used for thousands of years in all civilizations. Today their abuse is a topic of much contention in what is known as the drug problem. Opium, hashish, cannabis, morphine, and cocaine are the most frequently misused. The long historical associations of such herbs with the supernatural and primitive religion have been incorporated into modern attitudes to herbalism. Much of the valuable knowledge our ancestors accumulated about herbs has been dismissed because of superstitious contamination.

The second period in history witnessed the birth of agriculture, not as was once supposed in the fertile valleys of Mesopotamia, but in the Near East. One of the earliest archaeological sites is at Jarmo in Iraq where excavations have revealed evidence of wheat and barley which have been dated at 6750 B.C. Agriculture began a few thousand years later in the New World and probably started independently. Maize, gourds, beans and squashes have been found in early sites in Mexico. The discovery of agriculture or the Neolithic revolution, as archaeologists term it, was to change man's whole existence. Whereas the hunter-gatherer needed a good deal of land to sustain him, agriculture meant that relatively smaller areas of land under cultivation could sustain a whole community. Man began to make permanent settlements and the prerequisites for the growth of science commenced. Instead of subsisting man could open up the forests to make suitable environments for the herbaceous sun-loving crops he favoured.

By 3500 B.C., the Egyptians were making ropes from Papyrus and palm fibre, they had begun to make cosmetics and

Left: The frontispiece of a compendium of plants, which was published in France in 1774. It describes the plants' range of uses to man.

Right: Many aquatic herbs are still important as medicinal or aromatic plants – Papyrus, the best known aquatic herb, was used by the Egyptians 5000 years ago.

perfumes and in their treatment of disease they became less reliant on magic. By 2700 B.C. the Chinese had started to cultivate tea and to approach healing with the use of herbs on a more scientific basis. Everywhere those species most useful or highly prized for domestic, medicinal or religious employment were brought into cultivation, planted nearer to human dwellings and stored. The Persians gave man the first gardens by planting aromatic and scented herbs together with shade-offering trees in beautiful and peaceful sites. In some early cities like Nineveh, municipal herb gardens were planted for popular use. State-run medicinal herb gardens can be seen in Nepal.

Slowly scholarship and trade developed and flourished. Ideas were exchanged as communication grew and with the great civilizations of Greece and Rome the foundations of modern science and medicine had been laid. The classical works of the Greeks and Romans provided standard reference sources right up to the seventeenth century, but nevertheless the most useful herbs included in them can be traced back to the hunter-gatherers and Neolithic man. Herbalism and our understanding of the benefits of plants did not stop developing with the Greeks and Romans, however, neither has its study been limited to Europe. The discovery of the New World brought many new plants which were added to European herbals and pharmacopoeias. But even so we only have records of a mere fraction of the world's 342,000 estimated species of plant life. Wild products and plants are still gathered in large quantities even in the most economically advanced countries; new species of wild plants are still being taken into cultivation in exactly the same way as the first agriculturalists did, while more uses are being found for well-known plants.

Yet our initial enthusiasm for the chemical and synthetic alternatives to herbs made available by modern science has had the effect of blindfolding us to our real and continued need for herbs. Removed from the basic processes of production, we now know little or nothing about the raw materials or stages involved in the commodities we buy – we cannot tell whether the dye in blue jeans is from Indigo or India. Efficiency had dictated that of the 200,000 species of flowering plants, only 12 or 13 are widely cultivated, and most of us have a far more restricted vegetable diet than the Roman conquerors of Europe. Sadly, industrialization has meant the loss of much of the valuable herbal knowledge of our ancestors and the misconception that we can manage without herbs.

This is clearly a very great misconception if one thinks of the massive quantities of crude herbs used today even in the most sophisticated of societies.

After a decline of about two hundred years, herbalism is now experiencing a revival of both public and professional interest. The professions which so ridiculed medical herbalism as ineffective and superstitious 'old wives' tales' are once again turning to nature in an attempt to discover methods and materials free from the undesirable side-effects frequently experienced with the modern 'chemically tailored' synthetic drug. New methods of reappraisal are being used to judge the beliefs produced by centuries of practical experience. There are signs that the revival of interest in herbs will be extremely profitable to man and the herbal practices of our ancestors are being increasingly vindicated. By careful studies it has been shown that a good proportion of the beliefs of the old herb physicians were right, and that, for example, plants do indeed possess different properties if harvested at different times of the day or year and that certain combinations of plants are more active than the individual herbs used separately.

There has also been a revival of popular interest in herbs. Enthusiasm has been aroused for the charm and serenity of the old fashioned herb garden with its associated culinary and aromatic herbs which somehow suit the requirements of modern times. Herb gardens provide useful materials and yet remain attractive with a minimum of maintenance, for herbs do not require special soils or complex horticultural skills. Herbs provide the vitamins and minerals increasingly sought after for a healthy diet. They provide an ideal starting-point for a range of home-made products such as cosmetics, ales, wines, scented sachets, pot-pourris and dyes. Not only are herbs cheap and easy to use, but those in general use have the advantage of being free from the dangers to health often contained in man-made commodities, be they drugs, food colourings or hair dyes.

Herbalism has become part of the new concern in our society for an ecological balance and an unpolluted 'natural' way of life. This late twentieth-century appreciation of herbs and their immense value in food and medicine truly represents the rediscovery of old wisdom indicating that the biblical expression 'all flesh is grass' is as true today as it always has been.

The history of herbalism

Who first used plants we do not know. But someone – more probably, many different people – in the earliest mists of history, long before the earliest records that now survive, discovered that some plants are good to eat and that others have healing properties. This was the first step in a lengthy process of trial and error by which early man in different communities slowly built up a corpus of knowledge about plants. To this gradual process was added, no doubt, experience handed down from generation to generation by word of mouth and a measure of intuition.

Why and how a plant should have been capable of curing sickness must have remained a mystery to those early communities. (Indeed, only the development of sophisticated techniques of chemical analysis in the last century or so has at last begun to provide the solution.) So those who took a special interest in the healing qualities of plants and became especially skilled in their application gradually gained an honoured place in society. Their skills and knowledge singled them out from the mass as medicine men. Because there were no readily comprehensible explanations of how plants healed, primitive communities tended to attribute the process to a god or gods, as indeed they did any phenomenon that puzzled them. Thus the earliest medicine men became associated with the whole structure of religious belief in a community. Many were priests who acted as instruments of the gods, receiving their powers of healing from them.

Left: A dog uprooting the 'shrieking' Mandrake. For centuries it was thought that if humans dug up the plant it meant certain death.

This much is assumption. But it is valid assumption, given our understanding of human nature in general and our knowledge of the earliest communities that archaeologists have been able to trace. It also accords with the first medical records that we have, from India, China, Egypt and Assyria.

This very vagueness about the first herbalists points to an important dichotomy in our knowledge of herbs and those who used them. The story that follows inevitably recounts what might be termed the 'official' aspect of herbalism – the only one for which records remain. We can only suppose – but none the less with every confidence – the existence of an 'unofficial' side to herbalism, a succession of ordinary country men and women skilled and knowledgeable about the herbs of their area and their uses – medicinal, culinary and in the preparation of dyes, perfumes and cosmetics. Only rarely do these people emerge in the 'official' story. Finally, in the nineteenth-century industrial revolution in the western world, urbanization and the increasing division of labour gradually caused such rural wisdom to die out.

We know little of the origins of medicine in China and in India. It is thought that the Emperor Chin Nong composed a herbal in about 2700 B.C. and that some 60 years later another Emperor, Huang-ti, wrote a treatise on medicine. In India, the Rig Veda, one of the sacred books of the Brahmins, mentions the use of medicinal plants. The scarcity of knowledge about ancient medical practice in these countries should not, however, lead us to assume that no developed system existed there, nor that ideas, beliefs and practices may not have passed across Asia, between these ancient civilizations, in a process of cross-fertilization of which we now know nothing. Lack of evidence means that we can only point to China and India and state that a tradition of medicine as old as that of Europe does exist there, perhaps one that is even older, and that plants were undoubtedly used as remedies. As a result, an account of the history of herbalism is confined to describing the gradual development of medical knowledge in Egypt and Mesopotamia, its spread first to the countries of the eastern Mediterranean and Persia and Armenia, to ancient Greece and then throughout Europe and – two thousand years later – to the New World.

For many centuries botany and medicine were closely linked, and plants were central to medical practice. They provided the chief, if not the only, remedies other than surgery, and many medical theories were built around them. In addition, many ordinary people will have put their faith in the long line of herbalists who sold their patent remedies made up from different herbs in towns and villages, successful because they were cheaper than doctors and physicians and perhaps also because they appealed to the always very potent traditions of folklore and magic. Only since the eighteenth century have the paths of botanists and medical scientists divided; at the same time medical treatment has become available for everyone, and the old herbal remedies have died out.

EGYPT

The Egyptian civilization is the first of which we have any extensive medical knowledge. Much of that is somewhat imprecise, as is illustrated in the case of Imhotep, the first Egyptian physician whose name survives. He served Zoser, a 3rd Dynasty Pharaoh, in about 2980 B.C. and was renowned as an astrologer and magician as well as for his healing powers. His reputation lived on after he died; legends grew up about his work and he was eventually transformed into a god of healing. For the Egyptians some two millennia later, whether Imhotep had actually lived or not would have been unimportant; in fact, his reality would not have been questioned in such terms. Just as a contemporary healer would have been regarded as a priest and instrument of the gods because of his healing skills, Imhotep, who had been the subject of legends handed down for many centuries, would have been regarded as a god.

The ground becomes rather firmer by about 2000 B.C. Various medical papyri – most important among them being the famous Ebers Papyrus – discovered by archaeologists in the last 100 years list a series of medical prescriptions in use after about 1800 B.C. Mineral substances and animal products were included, but about five-sixths of the ingredients were of vegetable origin. Each prescription describes the symptoms of the disease and gives instructions on how the cure is to be administered and prepared. One typical prescription, intended 'to empty the belly and clear out all impurities from the body of a sick person', required field herbs, honey, dates and *uah* grain to be mixed together and chewed by the patient for one day.

These same papyri demonstrate the central role of the gods in Egyptian medicine – and, of course, in the entire life of Egyptian society. Osiris was worshipped as a god of vegetation. Isis, his twin sister

Left: Imhotep (c.2980 B.C.), the first known Egyptian physician. A celebrated sage among his contemporaries, he was worshipped as a god after his death. Imhotep was the patron of the sciences and of doctors. For ordinary people he was regarded as the god of healing.

and mother, was one of the most ancient goddesses of Egypt. She held it in her power to renew life and was reputed to have transmitted the secrets of healing to mankind. As such a powerful magician and healer, it was to her that the Egyptians prayed for deliverance from disease. Thoth was believed to have formulated each healing prescription. He is represented as holding in his left hand the symbol of life and in his right a staff around which a serpent is coiling itself – a symbol of the physician to this day.

So the picture that comes down to us from Egyptian sources is of increasing medical skill confined as it were within a framework of magic. A herbalist carried with him both a casket of medicines and a magician's wonder-working rod; before treatment could begin, the gods had to be called on to cast out the devil which possessed the patient. We shall find this association between medicine and magic continuing in ancient Greece. How much both there and in Egypt it was a result of a genuine belief in the power of the gods, how much because of a desire on the herbalist's part to keep his skills secret through a process of mystification we cannot now distinguish. But before we turn to Greece – which also saw the beginnings of objective medical science – we must look at the civilizations of Mesopotamia and their approach to medicine.

MESOPOTAMIA

The Sumerians believed that sickness was the manifestation of devils and evil spirits that had attacked the human body. Magic and medicine went hand in hand, and many of the gods were believed to be physicians. The similarity of these beliefs to those of Egyptians is clear. Whether the Egyptians influenced the Sumerians or vice versa is not known. Quite probably, they both borrowed from a common Asian source in a process of cultural contact all trace of which is now lost.

The earliest Sumerian herbal dates from some time after 2500 B.C. and has come down to us in the form of a copy dating from the seventh century B.C. Later Assyrian inscribed tablets are much more informative. Tablets from the library of Ashurbanipal, King of Assyria between 668 and 626 B.C., reveal that knowledge of herbs and their medicinal properties must have been considerable. Some 250 vegetable drugs are mentioned, as well as 120 mineral drugs and some 180 that remain unidentified. This wealth of information makes it reasonable to assume that gardens where medicinally useful plants were cultivated must have been established. Whether physic gardens in the sense that the term came to be used in the Middle Ages ever existed is uncertain. But we do know that gardens and parks were laid out round the royal palaces and that in one at least herbs were grown.

Language is an obvious indicator of the origin and spread of ideas, and it is significant that a number of the names by which plants are known today are derived from the Sumerians, having passed through the Greek and Arabic languages. These include Apricot, Saffron, Cumin, Turmeric, Myrrh, Mandrake, Almond, Poppy, Mulberry and Sesame.

ANCIENT GREECE

The civilization of classical Greece took much from the Egyptian world and from Mesopotamia, including, of course, its knowledge of the practice of medicine. It took much, but it added even more. It also began, perhaps most important of all, to establish a scientific basis for medicine.

Above: Tablet depicting Ashurbanipal, King of Assyria, at work on his herbal. Ashurbanipal was very interested in herbs and their medicinal properties, and large numbers were grown in the royal gardens for his use.

Aesculapius

Like the Sumerians and Egyptians, the Greeks believed that the gods were the first herbalists and physicians and that they had taught the art of healing to man. Aesculapius was the first, and probably the greatest, of them. Historians now believe that he actually lived, but whether he did or not is of little importance. Aesculapius must have been a healer whose skills and successes brought him renown and about whom after his death legends gradually grew up. His significance lies in those legends. They tell that Aesculapius was the son of Apollo and Coronis. Born in Epidaurus in about 1250 B.C., he was slain by Zeus, who was jealous of his success in healing the sick and raising the dead. His daughter was Hygieia, the goddess of health. Another tradition provides a closer link with Egypt by claiming that Aesculapius was born in the Egyptian city of Memphis and emigrated to Greece, bringing with him Egyptian medical techniques and knowledge.

The root-gatherers

The link with the Egyptian association of healing with magic and mystery is clear. It is also demonstrated by the rhizotomists – root-gatherers who wandered from place to place gathering roots and herbs used in medical prescriptions. For the most part, they were uneducated and would follow a complex ritual as they went about their work – complex in all likelihood, again, to protect their trade from inquisitive outsiders. Certain prayers and chants had to be spoken as the plants were gathered, and specific times were appointed for the task. The rhizotomists sold their plants to pharmacopolists, who prepared drugs and other healing remedies for sale in village markets. The rhizotomists and pharmacopolists of ancient Greece together form the start of a long tradition of what might best be described as dealers in herbs, usually itinerant and always referring to magic and mystery to justify their products. Such people could still be seen in the markets and fairs of Europe in the early part of this century.

Hippocrates

Despite the traditional framework of religious belief, it was in ancient Greece that scientific medicine (as we now understand the term) was first developed. Hippocrates (460–377 B.C.), who was born and practised on the island of Cos, is known as the father of medicine. He earns this description because he was the first person to establish and set down a scientific system of medicine. Much of his learning he took from Egyptian sources. But he dropped the elements of mystery and magic and, recognizing disease as a natural phenomenon, established for the first time a system of diagnosis and prognosis. Hippocrates used about 400 drugs, mostly of vegetable origin, but he never wrote a herbal.

The Hippocratic Oath, to which all doctors until very recently had to swear before they could practise, is of course named after Hippocrates. Its opening words – 'I swear by Apollo, the Physician, by Aesculapius, by Hygieia and Panacea and by all the Gods and Goddesses that to the best of my power and judgment . . .' – demonstrate a close and fascinating link between modern medical practice and the beliefs of the earliest medical scientists.

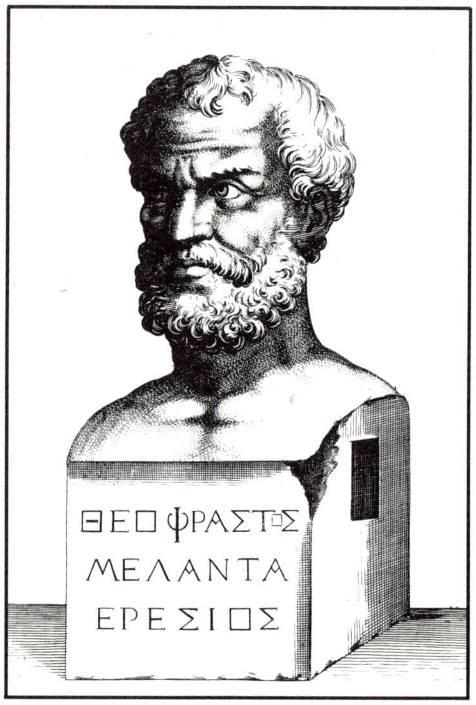

Above: Aesculapius, the Greek god of medicine.

Left: Hippocrates, the most important physician of the classical world. He wrote a number of medical works distinguished for their scientific content, much of which is still valid. The Hippocratic Oath is a memorial to his ethical philosophy.

Left: Theophrastus (c.372–286 B.C.), the Greek philosopher, was a pupil of Aristotle and the first scholar to attempt to establish a scientific classification of plants. He is reputedly the author of 227 works.

Right: Hygieia, the Greek goddess of health and daughter of Aesculapius. She is usually depicted with him and others of the family such as her sister Panacea.

The first Greek herbals

The earliest Greek herbal of which anything is known was written by Diocles Carystius, who was born some time in the first half of the fourth century B.C. He listed plants, noted their habitats and briefly described their medicinal properties. Nothing is now left of Diocles' writings.

It was Theophrastus of Eresus (*c.*372–286 B.C.), on the island of Lesbos, who was the first person to try to establish any scientific system of plants. Theophrastus was Aristotle's friend and pupil and was bequeathed Aristotle's garden on the latter's death. His two treatises, *Historia Plantarum* and *De Causis Plantarum* (*Inquiry into Plants* and *Growth of Plants*), which between them listed some 500 plants, were based on Aristotle's botanical writings. These he supplemented with his own observations made during his travels and with the reports of foreign travellers and merchants.

The Alexandrian School

It was after the foundation of Alexandria – named after the Greek Emperor Alexander the Great – in 331 B.C. that Greek medicine really began to flourish. A school of medicine was rapidly set up – commonly referred to as the Alexandrian School – which attracted the foremost scientists and botanists from all over the Near East. Gradually a body of knowledge and experience was built up, based on the observations of contemporary writers, but also drawing on Egyptian knowledge and practices and on the beliefs of the Sumerians and Assyrians. In addition much information was brought back from Alexander's campaigns into western Asia. The Alexandrian School thus brought together beliefs and practices from many different sources and developed and extended them through research and writing, so forming a tradition that was eventually transmitted to medieval Europe through the writers and scholars of the Arab world.

The written herbals produced during the Alexandrian period were mainly the works of physicians. Of these, Herophilus (first half of the third century B.C.), Mantias (*c.*270 B.C.), Andreas of Karystos (d.217 B.C.) and Appolonius Mys (*c.*220 B.C.) were perhaps the most important. Later, in the second century B.C., Nikander produced a work on poisons and their antidotes.

Mithridates

Experimental work was also carried out under the aegis of the Alexandrian School and was encouraged by Mithridates, who was Eupator (king) of Pontus between 120 and 63 B.C. Mithridates was especially interested in poisons and their antidotes. His name is commemorated in the word 'mithridate', which came to mean any concoction used as an antidote against poison. Up to the eighteenth century every physician would be equipped with his personal mithridate. Mithridate's rhizotomist, Kraetus, was more intelligent and sensitive than most of his calling. He not only collected plants but wrote about them and – most significant of all – illustrated the entire plant, including its roots. Each drawing was accompanied by the name of the plant and by a description of its medicinal uses.

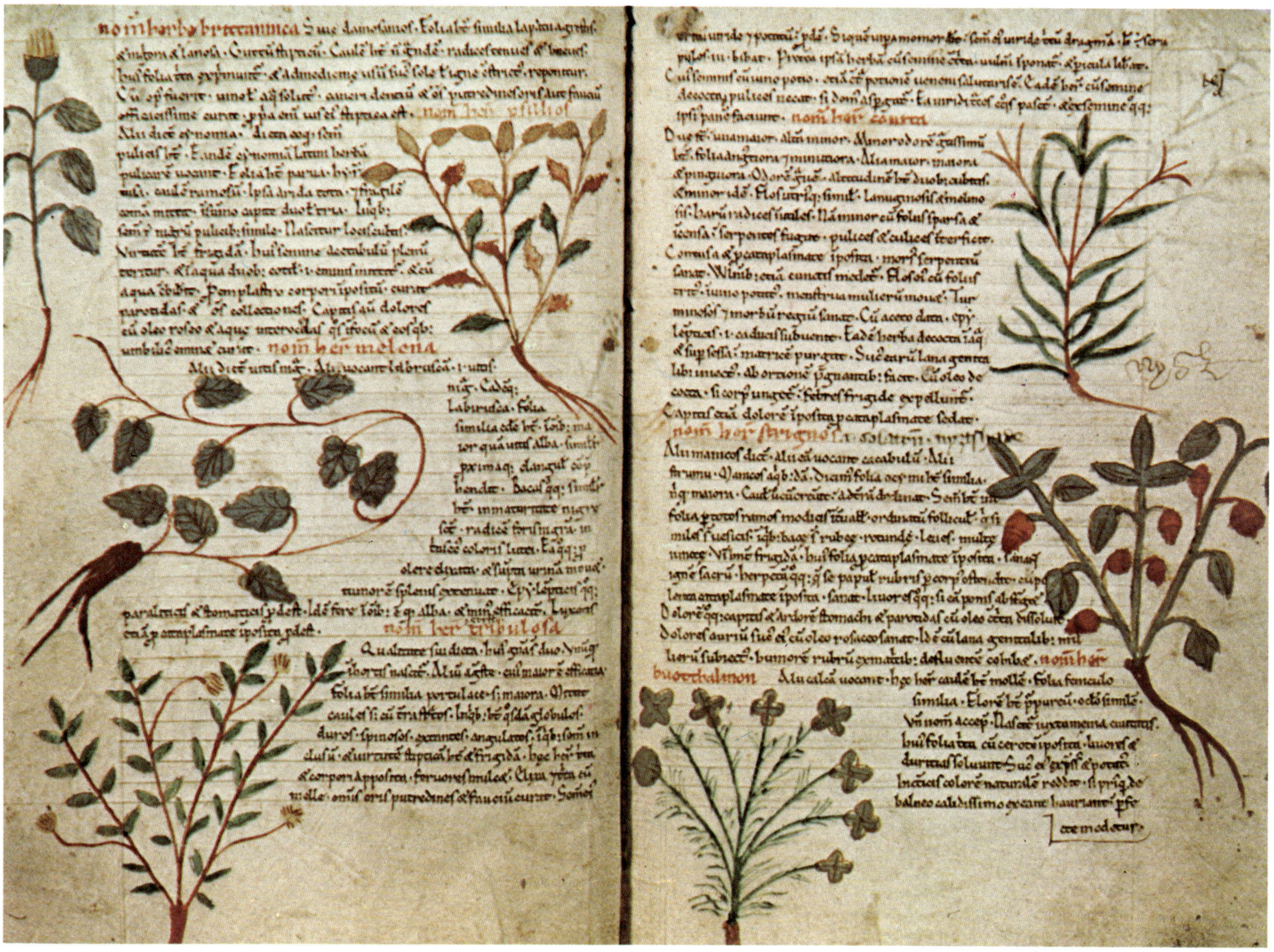

Above: Pages from an illustrated Latin version of Dioscorides' writings made in the twelfth century. Beautiful though the illustrations may be, they have little or no scientific value.

Below: Galen, philosopher, teacher and physician. The theories and diagnoses he proposed in his extensive medical works remained, in essence, unchallenged until the Renaissance.

Dioscorides

Thus the picture at the beginning of the first century A.D. is one of increasing experimentation and knowledge. One man, the Greek physician Dioscorides, drew this knowledge together and assembled it in one vast work, *De Materia Medica*. Dioscorides was a physician with the Roman army and much of his information came from first-hand observation in the Near East, France, Spain, Germany and Italy. He supplemented this with material taken from Hippocrates – about 130 of the plants known to Hippocrates are mentioned by Dioscorides – Theophrastus, Andreas, Kraetus and many others. His work mentions some 600 plants. Each entry names the plant, describes it and its habitat, notes how it should be prepared for medicinal use and the effect it has.

Dioscorides was without doubt the first real medical botanist. For 1500 years his *Materia Medica* was the standard reference work on the medical application of plants and most later herbals were closely modelled on it. Indeed, many of the plants he mentions still gain a place in modern pharmacopoeias such as Aniseed, Chamomile, Cinnamon, Dill, Ginger, Marjoram, Pepper, Rhubarb and Thyme.

Other Greek herbalists in the early Christian era were Pamphilos, who arranged the plants in his herbal in alphabetical order, Menecrates, physician to the Emperor Tiberius (reigned A.D. 14–37), and Andromachos of Crete.

ANCIENT ROME

Pliny was the most important writer on plants in ancient Rome. He devoted seven of the 37 volumes of his *Historia Naturalis* (*Natural History*), composed in A.D. 77, to their medical uses. Pliny's writing was uncritical, his information unverified, and thus his work is now of little value. It was during this time, however, that the Doctrine of Signatures, later to become of such significance in Paracelsus' hands, originated.

Galen

Much more significant are the writings of Galen (A.D. 131–201), perhaps the greatest physician after Hippocrates. Galen was Greek by birth; he travelled extensively in the Near East and had an enormous output of books, which earned him a great reputation as a philosopher, teacher and physician. His herbal, which forms part of *De Simplicibus*, contains information on each plant and its habitat, usually together with a note about its use in medicine.

THE DARK AGES

With Galen, the Greek herbal tradition, which, as we have seen, embraced the much older traditions of Egypt and Mesopotamia, comes to an end. Though the dark ages after the fall of the Roman Empire no longer seem so dark to the historian, scientific research and writing stopped. Six centuries or so must pass before we can point with any confidence in the evidence to a resumption of interest in herbs and, indeed, in botany and medicine in general.

What happened in the intervening time can only be sketched in outline. In Europe, only the monasteries kept alive the literature of medical and herbal practices. Monks were often physicians and care for the sick was seen as part of a Christian's duty. In another way, too, the monasteries preserved knowledge, for it was there that scribes copied manuscripts by hand. Outside the cloister walls, folklore became very influential; travelling bone-setters and herb women treated the sick, and ritual and magic were resorted to, much as they had been in ancient Egypt.

THE ARAB WORLD

In contrast, the highly sophisticated culture of the Arab world maintained and added to the legacy of the Greeks. By about A.D. 900 or a little after, all the surviving Greek medical works had been translated in the great cultural centres of Damascus, Baghdad and Cairo. Knowledge of them spread with the advancing Arab armies across North Africa and into Spain, almost all of which had fallen under Moslem rule by the end of the eighth century. The greatest physicians of this Arab empire drew on the works of the Greek physicians and writers as well as on what one writer on medieval Spain has described as the 'accumulated botanical and pharmacological lore of the entire Orient' and on their own observations. Among them were Rhazes (865–925), a Persian employed as a royal physician in Baghdad, whose investigations into clinical practice gave a considerable impetus to knowledge, and Avicenna (980–1037), whose *Canon Medicinae* brought together information about the diseases, drugs and medical theories known in the Arab world. In Spain, in particular, where the Cordoban physician Abulcasis (d.1013) practised, especially high standards were reached, and wealthy men came from all over Europe for treatment.

Above: Avicenna, A.D. 980–1037, possibly the greatest physician and scientist of the Moslem world. His Canon Medicinae *was translated into Latin and kept its place as a standard university textbook until as late as the seventeenth century.*

ANGLO-SAXON HERBALS

Although it was the Arab world that preserved the main tradition of medical learning, it should not be supposed that all writing came to a halt in northern Europe. The Anglo-Saxon inhabitants of England, for instance, were very interested in herbs, and a number of manuscripts have survived. The earliest of these is the *Leech Book of Bald*, compiled between 900 and 950 by a scribe named Cild under the direction of Bald, who is thought to have been a friend of King Alfred of England. This is the first book on herbs written in the vernacular and also the first which did not base itself directly on Greek texts. The knowledge it displays of herbs is remarkable. Another such manuscript is the *Lacnunga*, thought to have been written in the late eleventh or early twelfth century. It consists chiefly of a poem in praise of the nine sacred herbs of the Nordic god Woden. Ritual and magic still played an enormous role in the herbalist's work, just as they had in ancient Egypt: Waybroad, for instance, one of the nine sacred herbs, was believed to cure a headache if it were gathered, untouched by iron, before sunrise and its roots bound round the sufferer's head with a red ribbon.

THE REVIVAL OF KNOWLEDGE

Greek medical theory – supplemented as we have seen by Arab observation and practice – was restored to western Europe at the end of the dark ages by two main routes. In Spain, a school of translators grew up in Toledo (which had fallen to Christian forces in 1085) in the twelfth century. The work generally went in two stages, first from Arabic to Romance (a form of old French), then from Romance to Latin, the universal language of scholarship in medieval Europe. In Italy,

Constantine the African (*c.*1020–1087) translated a number of Arabic philosophical, scientific and medical works into Latin. Constantine remains a shadowy figure of whom little is known except that he was an Arabic-speaking Christian who became a monk and spent the last years of his life at the Benedictine abbey at Monte Cassino, where he composed most of his translations. His work spread rapidly throughout Europe.

*Above: Constantine the African (*c.*1020–1087), an Arabic-speaking Christian, translated a number of Arabic medicinal and scientific works into Latin. These new ideas marked the end of the dark ages.*

The work of the monks

Both these cultural channels, as one might describe them, centred upon monasteries (the school of translators at Toledo had been established under the patronage of Archbishop Raymond, a member of the Cluniac order). And the monasteries played a vital role in medieval Europe in the spread of medical knowledge and writing. Many monks were skilled copyists and until the invention of printing were the most important (in early medieval times probably the only) source of books. Others were horticulturalists; again, they were secure in their monasteries and had both time and opportunity to cultivate herbs and other plants; contacts with other monasteries in their order throughout Europe no doubt led to an interchange of information and of actual plants. Care of the sick was another part of their work, and in many areas only the monks possessed any medical skills. At Barnwell Abbey in England, the *infirmarius* (the monk in charge of the pharmacy) was required always to have 'ginger, cinnamon, penny and the like, ready in his cupboard, so as to be able to render promptly assistance to the sick if [they were] stricken by a sudden malady'.

The study of medicine

Two of the most important schools of medicine were at Salerno, where Constantine the African's translations were particularly influential, and at Montpellier, founded by Gerald of Cremona (1114–1187), who had translated Avicenna's *Canon Medicinae.* The *Canon* became a standard work at the University and was still a prescribed textbook as late as 1650. These schools and others – for instance at St Gall, Bobbio, Reichenau and Fulda – produced numerous influential medical works. Two emanating from Salerno were the *Liber de simplici medicina*, a herbal compiled by Matthaeus Platearius during the middle of the twelfth century, and the *Regimen Sanitatis Salerno*, thought to have been assembled by Arnold of Villa Nova, a Catalan who studied at Salerno for a time. The *Liber de simplici medicina* (usually known by its opening words, *Circa instans*) was concerned with the medicinal use of plants and was compiled from both Latin and Arabic sources. It had considerable influence throughout the Middle Ages.

Despite increasing medical studies from the twelfth century onwards, the framework within which writers and physicians worked and thought had remained unaltered since Galen's day. There was

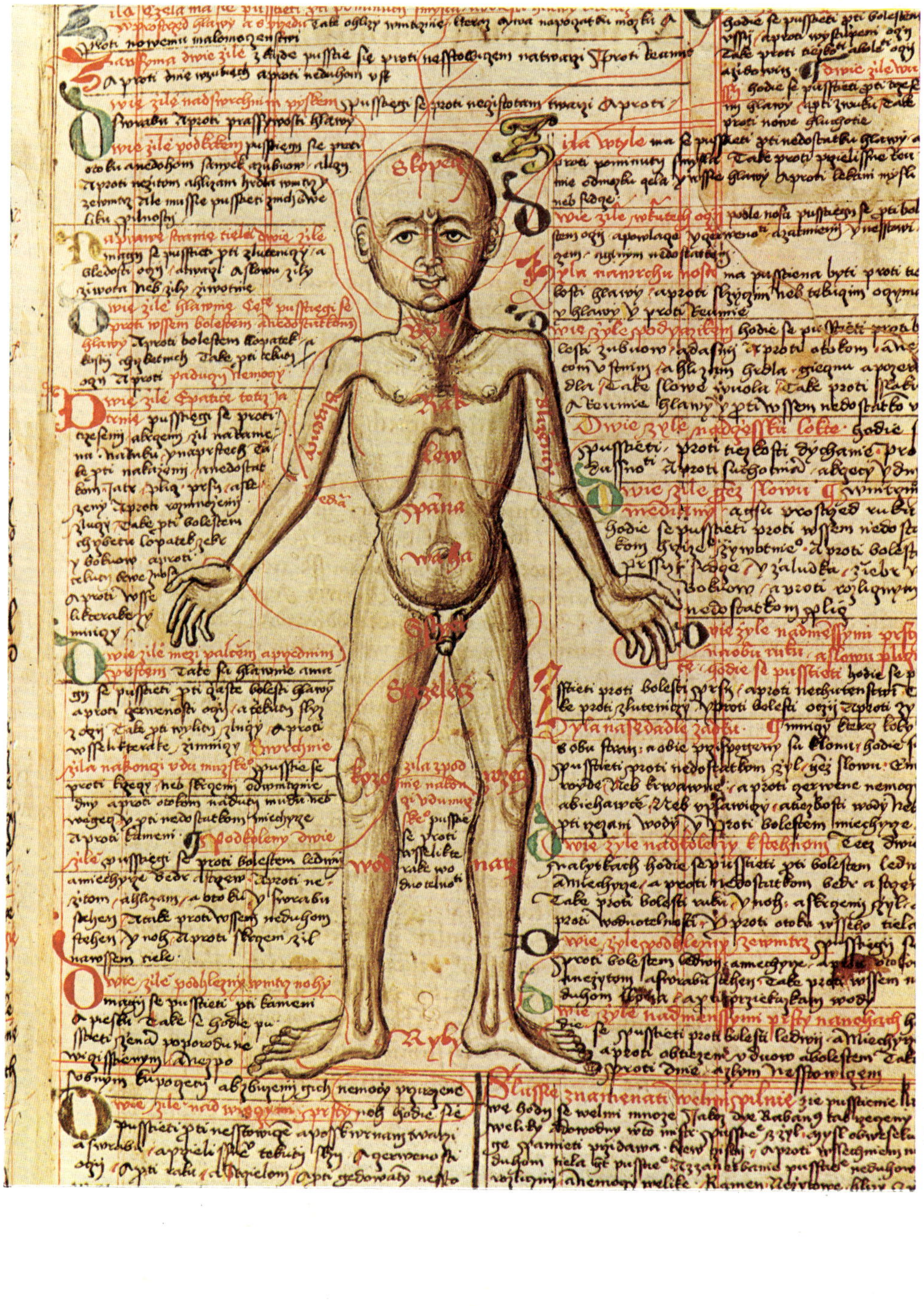

Right: Page from the Trattato de Pestilentia, *a fourteenth-century work on the human body and the diseases to which it is subject. Almost all medical writing at this time was derivative and theoretical; practical experimentation of any consequence was not to begin until several centuries later.*

little new observation or research. What there was was confined within galenic ideas; there was little questioning of basic premises – certainly no attempt to overthrow them – and most medical writers were content to base their writings on the works of Greek physicians which, as has been shown, had been translated into Arabic and then further into Latin. This cumbersome process had led to numerous errors; illustrations of plants often bore little or no resemblance to the original plants and were useless from any scientific point of view; often the names of the plants themselves had become altered because of errors of transcriptions made by scribes. The development of medicine had stultified, and it was to take a complete revolution in methods and outlook before any genuine progress was made. Even the foremost medieval scientist Albertus Magnus (*c.*1200–1280), who based his writings on plants on first-hand observations and refused to accept without question the statements of earlier writers, failed to break out of the galenic mould.

The birth of the herbals

As the Middle Ages progressed, increasing interest began to be taken in herbal remedies. The first major work in English on botanical medicine was the *Rosa Medicinae* (also known as the *Rosa Anglica*), written between 1314 and 1317 by a monk known as John of Gaddesden. His work combined Greek, Arabic, Jewish and Saxon medical writings and herbal lore but also included observations based on personal experience. Other vernacular herbals – among them the *Book of Nature* by Konrad von Megenberg (1309–1374), which was written in German – contributed to the process. So, too, did the increasing number of exotic herbs and spices from the East available in western Europe.

For much of the Middle Ages Venice was the European centre of this trade, and Venetian merchants grew rich from the commodities that eventually reached Europe after the long journey across Asia from India and China.

Dissemination of knowledge

The whole intellectual revolution of the Renaissance had of course a profound effect on medical science. The old galenic preconceptions gradually fell away; observation and experiment flourished, drawing on the works of ancient writers but soon soaring beyond their preconceptions. More particularly, the invention of printing in the mid-fifteenth century gave a tremendous boost to herbalism, as indeed it did to all forms of knowledge. Herbals could be circulated in far greater numbers. The first to be printed had previously been available in manuscript form, but by the early sixteenth century original works were being reproduced. These were vast improvements on their immediate predecessors, both in their scope and organization and in the quality of their woodcuts, which depicted the plants described accurately and in detail rather than as mere decoration, which had previously been the case. Hieronymus Tragus' *Kreuterbuch*, first published in Germany in 1539, gave precise descriptions of all the plants included. In England, William Turner, the first part of whose *New Herball* appeared in 1551, was the first person to study plants scientifically. He travelled widely throughout Europe and grew herbs in his garden at Kew, coincidentally on the site of the present Royal Botanic Gardens. Three years later in the Low Countries, R. Dodoens published his *Cruydboeck*, in which he grouped plants according to their properties and affinities rather than alphabetically. Later a French translation was published, and in 1578 an English version. John Gerard's *Herball*, first published in 1597 and extended and

*Left: Illustration of Coltsfoot (*Tussilago farfara*) from an illuminated Greek copy of Dioscorides'* De Materia Medica. *In his commentary Dioscorides wrote that the leaves could be dried and then smoked through a reed to clear mucus and catarrh – a remedy that has now been used for over two thousand years.*

Below: Title page of the first edition of John Gerard's Herball. *Gerard was the best-known herbalist in Elizabethan England; he had his own garden in London, where he grew plants assembled from all over the world. He was also gardener to Lord Burghley for over 20 years. Gerard's herbal is based entirely on the work* Pemptades, *written in 1583 by the Flemish physician Dodoens. But it is in fact the later editions of Gerard's* Herball, *which were considerably extended by Thomas Johnson in 1633, that are most valuable.*

revised by Thomas Johnson in 1633, proved extremely popular. By this time herbals had become authoritative and comprehensive, covering practically every plant then known; one which appeared in 1640 mentioned 3800 plants, whereas von Megenberg's *Book of Nature*, the first printed edition of which had appeared in 1475, had dealt with just 89.

THE DOCTRINE OF SIGNATURES

Despite what, to use a twentieth-century term, might be called a 'boom' in herbals, not all of them consisted of what we today would describe as 'objective' information. In the sixteenth century in particular, the Doctrine of Signatures held sway over many writers. It was promoted by Paracelsus (1493–1541), a physician whose controversial opinions and manner (not for nothing was his second name Bombastus!) caused him to lead an unsettled existence in many of the cities of central Europe. According to this dogma, every plant acted in effect as its own definition of its medical application, resembling either the part of the body afflicted or the cause of the affliction. William Coles, an English herbalist who published the *Art of Simpling* in 1656, wrote that God had not only 'stamped upon them [plants] (as upon every man) a distinct forme, but also given them particular signatures, whereby a Man may read even in legible Characters the Use of them. Heart Trefoyle is so called not only because the Leafe is Triangular like the Heart of a Man, but also because each Leafe contains the perfect Icon of an Heart and that in its proper colour.' Nicholas Culpeper (1616–1654), too, was an influential exponent of the Doctrine of Signatures, as well as of various astrological theories, by which herbs were set under the domination of the sun, the moon or one of the five planets then known. His herbal, published in 1652, was immediately successful and was reprinted many times. He was perhaps the first herbalist to write directly for ordinary people who might collect and use herbs during the course of their daily lives.

THE APOTHECARIES

The increasing number of herbals being produced and their growing scope and accuracy (Culpeper being the last important adherent to the Doctrine of Signatures) reflected the widening interest in herbal remedies and the developing status of the apothecary. Originally, apothecaries had merely sold drugs – the root of the word comes from the Greek for a store – but gradually they had absorbed skills and knowledge and had come to prepare and compound drugs, as well as sell them. In England they had been associated professionally with the Grocers' Company since 1378, a body of general traders who also sold herbs and drugs. (Interestingly enough, the Grocers themselves had their origin in the twelfth century in one of the early City of London guilds, the Guild of Pepperers, a reminder of the importance of the spice trade in medieval times.) Apothecaries purchased herbs and roots collected in the countryside by wandering 'green men and women' (the term is one of many used to describe rural herb collectors), the descendants, nearly two thousand years later, of the rhizotomists of ancient Greece, and also imported drugs and spices from abroad. They also established their own physic gardens, so serving as a link between horticulture and medicine by growing their own medicinal herbs.

By the late sixteenth century in England the apothecaries were trying to dissociate themselves from the Grocers and establish their own guild. Their work demanded specific professional skills, and there had been allegations that grocers were selling adulterated drugs. Then, in 1586, came an attempt by the College of Physicians to set up their own physic garden. The apothecaries thought that this was their prerogative – for by that time the practice was for physicians to diagnose and prescribe, while the apothecaries dispensed medicine and attended the patient. Although the apothecaries failed to prevent the physicians establishing their garden, they did in 1617 succeed in forming the Worshipful Society of Apothecaries of London, with 114 members. At the same time a law was passed forbidding medicines to be sold by surgeons or grocers.

THE PHYSIC GARDENS

The origins of physic gardens can be traced back several centuries. The monastic communities, as we have seen, kept alive interest in herbs and their healing potential during the dark ages and the early part of the Middle Ages, and it seems fairly certain that the first herb gardens were established behind monastic walls. The monastery at St Gall in Switzerland probably had 16 herb beds as early as 830, and twelfth-century plans for a monastery at Canterbury indicate a small piece of ground set aside for a herb garden. But the first garden intended to provide plants for the purpose of study (until then, students had worked from herbals alone) was not established until 1545, at the medical school of the University of Padua in Italy. Botany and medicine – hitherto studied as one subject – were from then on taught separately. Pisa followed almost immediately and also set up a herbarium (in which pressed and dried plants are preserved on paper). Within two decades, Florence, Rome and Bologna had started their own gardens. Nor was the rest of Europe far behind. By the end of the seventeenth century, physic gardens had been laid out at

Above: Portrait of Nicholas Culpeper and, right, illustrations from his herbal. Culpeper's theories rested on his belief in astrological influences: herbs were placed under the dominion of one of the five planets, the sun or the moon; different parts of the body were themselves governed by the planets. He also believed that plants resembled either the part of the body or the ailment which they were intended to treat. His Herball *and* A Physical Directory *both enjoyed an enormous sale.*

Above: Carl Linnaeus (1707–1778), the founder of modern botany. The system of plant classification he developed opened the way for the precise identification of plants and their properties at a time when new plants were being discovered at a great rate throughout the world. Although Linnaeus's system has been continually modified, it remains the basis of today's internationally applicable system.

Right: The botanical garden at the University of Uppsala, Sweden. Founded in 1655 and destroyed by fire in 1702, the garden was revived by Carl Linnaeus who arranged the plants according to his system, and described it in Hortus Upsaliensis.

Heidelberg, Leiden, Montpellier, Strasbourg, Oxford, Paris (the garden there is now the famous and popular Jardin des Plantes), Uppsala and Amsterdam, to name only a few. All of them were linked with universities where medicine was taught. In London, the Chelsea Physic Garden was founded by the Worshipful Society of Apothecaries in 1673; it still flourishes on the same site today.

THE BEGINNINGS OF TRADE

One consequence of the age of exploration, inaugurated by Christopher Columbus' discovery of central America in 1492, was an increase in the number and variety of imported herbs and spices available in Europe. The English in India and Ceylon and the Dutch in the East Indies were the main suppliers, and London became the centre of the world spice trade, keeping this position until the early years of the twentieth century, when New York superseded it. Nor were herbs, spices and plants of all kinds the only imports from the New World; great interest was taken in the remedies practised by the native inhabitants. Nicholas Monardes, a physician from Seville, was one of the first to describe these. His three books, published in Spain in 1569, 1571 and 1574, were translated into English as *Joyfull Newes out of the Newe Founde Worlde* in 1577, as well as into Italian, French, Flemish and Latin.

Interest in the plants of the New World continued for a long time. In the eighteenth century in particular, numerous botanists made the transatlantic journey; plants were even more frequent passengers – one way of packing them was to wrap them in an ox bladder half filled with wet moss and the plant's natural soil – and form the basis of the North American collections in many European botanic gardens.

By the early eighteenth century the heyday of herbalism was passing. William Salmon's *Botanologia: The English Herbal* (1710) was the last herbal of any importance to be published. The curative properties of plants still, of course, played a vital role in medicine, but over the next two centuries the skills of the herbalists were slowly replaced by medical techniques that owed more to the scientific laboratory than to traditional wisdom.

CLASSIFICATION OF PLANTS

The system of plant classification established by Carl Linnaeus in his *Genera Plantarum* and *Critica Botanica* of 1737 was a harbinger of the new attitudes. Linnaeus in effect formalized a new scientific language – botanical Latin. Each plant was described by two separate names: one, the generic name (given first), identified the class to which the plant belonged, that is, a group with common structural characteristics; the second name, of the individual species, distinguished the plant from all its fellows within the same class. In his *Philosophica Botanica* of 1751 Linnaeus defined a genus as a group of species possessing similarly constructed organs and arranged in a similar way; later he published rules for the formulation of a generic name. Though changes have since been made in the bases upon which the classifications are made, the principle of Linnaeus' system is still in operation. Indeed, it is now obligatory throughout the world.

Thus by the mid-eighteenth century, it was possible for the first time to distinguish specific plants in a scientific manner. Before, different writers might have given the same plant widely differing names. For instance, the Autumn Crocus, used as a remedy against gout, was given no less than seven Latin names by different herbalists during the sixteenth century. In addition, it was known by at least half a dozen names in English and by a similar number in most of the different European languages. The new system made it impossible, at least for trained botanists, to confuse different plants. More important, it also identified many previous mistakes and misconceptions, thus enabling herbalists to refine and extend their skills and knowledge.

Although herbalists of course benefited from Linnaeus' work, in as much as it helped all those associated in one way or another with plants, in another, wider, sense it helped to speed the decline of the herbal tradition and to establish the

division between botany and medicine. Botanists were interested in all aspects of plants, rather than merely those that had value as herbs. From the late eighteenth century, and especially throughout the nineteenth, plant-collecting expeditions were mounted, and plant-hunters – usually out of the best scientific motives, but sometimes spurred on by desire for commercial gain – roamed over many previously unknown, or at least uninvestigated, parts of the world, sometimes accompanying, on other occasions only a few steps behind, many famous explorers. They – and other botanical writers at home – produced flora rather than herbals, scientific studies of all the plants of an area rather than merely of those thought to have medical value.

THE ROOTS OF MODERN MEDICINE

At the same time, medical science was moving in quite different directions. The slow development of chemical and biochemical techniques during the eighteenth and nineteenth centuries gradually enabled scientists to isolate and then to manufacture the chemical substances previously administered in plant form. Plant material was never entirely rejected, but nevertheless it came to be considered old fashioned and in some way second class. None the less, even today, the orthodox medical profession relies on substances extracted from plants – digitoxin from the Foxglove and morphine from the Opium Poppy, for example. During the First World War, tincture of Valerian was frequently administered as a sedative for shell-shock. It was the Second World War, however, during which traditional sources of plant drugs dried up (quinine from Malaysia for malaria, for example), that provided the impetus for the search for alternative chemical synthetic drugs.

After the war, an enormous programme of research and development, much of it carried out by international drug companies, gave us the wide range of antibiotics available today.

Even the most dedicated and skilled herbalist found himself gradually denied a role as the work of modern medicine slowly came to be divided among the drug companies, which became ever larger from the mid-nineteenth century onwards, who manufactured, doctors, who

Above: Stripping the bark of the Cinchona tree to obtain quinine, which is used to treat malaria – in the 300 years between its introduction to western medicine and the First World War it was the only effective remedy. The tree is found principally in tropical South America, as well as in Asia.

prescribed, and chemists, who dispensed. In some countries herbalists were forbidden to practise (although, no doubt, in remote country areas, remedies continued to be dispensed – part of the continuing 'unofficial' tradition of herbalism), in others their work was frowned on and came to be dismissed as in some way 'cranky' (though schools of homeopathy thrived and, in the United States, a school of physiomedicalism flourished in the latter part of the nineteenth century).

MEDICINE IN THE TWENTIETH CENTURY

Today, in the last quarter of the twentieth century, the dominance of what might be termed chemical medicine is indisputable. None the less the medical profession – and, beyond it, an increasingly concerned and informed lay public – is taking a growing interest in the old herbal remedies and is slowly realizing that they have by no means been entirely superseded by medical science. To begin with, actual plant material is still used to a far greater extent than many people are aware – in 1968, some 3 per cent (over 41 million items) of prescriptions in the United States contained crude herbs. Conferences have examined the role of traditional medicine in contemporary society, and increasing notice is being taken of the experience of the Third World, both in regard to those nations' own medical development and to its application in the industrialized world. In this context, Chinese practice is especially interesting: acupuncture is practised alongside western medicine, neither tradition dominating at the expense of the other. In herbaria throughout the world, a vast store of information – much, no doubt, merely native folklore but some surely of enormous importance – noted by plant-collectors is only now being gradually tapped and collated (it took researchers four and a half years to survey the collection at Harvard University; they ended with almost 6000 notes of interest, revealing new information of value not only to medical scientists but also to those active in the fields of nutrition and plant taxonomy and entomology). In England, the Herb Society has started to build up a national herb centre with a botanical garden which will eventually provide data for a computerized collection of literary and scientific references to herbs. Research centres have also been established in China, Germany, Holland, Poland and the United States.

This then points to the way ahead. No one suggests that the clock should be turned back and the advances of modern science be ignored, nor that the old folklore remedies have any credibility merely by virtue of their longevity. Yet – despite all the mystery and charlatanism that have surrounded herbalists and their work – surely we should not ignore the wisdom accumulated and found effective over many centuries.

Right: Interior view of a pharmacy or apothecary's shop at Dubrovnik, Yugoslavia, thought to be one of the oldest in Europe. Such shops flourished in medieval Europe and dispensed a wide variety of medicines. Between the fifteenth and seventeenth centuries they were the centres of medical practice. Doctors would meet their patients at the pharmacy where the drugs they prescribed would be made up and sold by the apothecary. The word 'pharmacy' comes from the Greek word for drug.

The biology and chemistry of plants

Most herbs belong to the relatively highly developed class of living organisms known as flowering plants, but nearly all the divisions of the plant world include at least a number of herbs. They are different from other plants only in that they are beneficial to man – being nutritious to eat, good flavouring agents or effective medicines because they happen to contain certain 'active constituents'. This section sets out the evolutionary interrelationships of the plant kingdom and explains the basic plant anatomy and physiology which is essential for an understanding of herbs.

THE BIOLOGY OF PLANTS

There are two classes of living things on this planet – animals and plants. Both owe their existence to the presence of an extremely complicated chemical substance known as deoxyribose nucleic acid (DNA) which has the remarkable ability of being able to replicate itself from smaller chemicals in its vicinity. This material is said to house the genes, and it controls, as we shall see later, all the activities of the organism. The DNA molecules of all living things are essentially similar, and the minute variations in the composition of this material determine the type of organism that results.

Life, then, is literally dependent on the presence of this DNA. The original oceans contained millions of organic and inorganic substances formed by the action of heat, light and electric storms on the air and minerals. The first living thing may be looked upon as the first strand of DNA which happened to be formed in the 'primeval soup' and then replicated itself. This single molecule subsequently developed into a unicellular organism by enclosing its own controlled environment around itself, within a cell-wall. There are still present today a number of unicellular organisms exactly like those original ones from which all living things evolved. We know that there have been two main routes of evolutionary development, one resulting in plants and the other in animals. As will be explained later, the fundamental difference between the two classes is the way in which they obtain their food, but first we should examine the way in which a plant grows.

In considering the basic biology of herbs, we are concerned mainly with the higher plants. They can be recognized by the greenness of their aerial vegetative parts: this characteristic separates chemically the higher plants from the lower, and plants themselves from animals – the possession of chlorophyll. Chlorophyll is the catalyst which enables plants to build up their body of cells from inorganic elements. Each body will vary in size, depending upon the species, from microscopic algae to the huge Californian redwoods which are certainly the biggest living things on earth. Growth depends upon cell enlargement and division, both of which are made nutritionally possible by the actions of roots and the leaf activity.

Left: As this Bumble Bee collects nectar from a Scottish Thistle, pollen rubs off onto its legs which become involuntary pollinators.

The cell structure of plant leaves is largely open with wide intercellular spaces. Filtering through them is a constant stream of air brought in through small pores or stomata which are normally situated on the undersides. Young green stems also possess stomata. Oxygen is taken from the air for the respiration process characteristic of all living things. The green chlorophyll, however, which is in all leaf cells apart from the upper and lower epidermal layers, promotes reactions, enabling the small amount of carbon dioxide in the air to be utilized. This is combined with the water brought up from the soil to produce usable foods in the form of carbohydrates. The process is known as photosynthesis, literally 'building up in the presence of light'. The simplified process, upon which all plant nutrition (and hence ultimately animal foods as well) is based, can be shown as:

$$6\,CO_2 + 6\,H_2O \xrightleftharpoons{\text{light}} C_6H_{12}O_6 + 6\,O_2$$

carbon dioxide, water → glucose (a sugar), oxygen

The energy needed to power the process comes from sunlight. Certain species of plants are adapted to live in shady habitats and this is usually reflected in their larger, thinner leaves which can utilize the weaker energy source. Once made the simple sugars can be translocated around the plant or stored in some form – often starch – in roots or tubers. The enormous variation in plant forms can thus be seen as a response to habitat and what it offers in soil nutrients and climate (that is, temperature, availability of water and especially light).

Greenness, then, is typical of the more highly evolved members of the plant kingdom and, at the same time, essential for their existence. Plants which are not green fall into two main categories: those where the chlorophyll, although present, is masked by the presence of another pigment – Purple Sage and Purple Basil are typical examples – and those which have developed a cuckoo-like existence by living either on the decomposing remains of their fellows (saprophytes) or directly, as parasites upon other living plant or animal hosts. All fungi come into these two categories: mushrooms are in the former group while others, such as various diseases, fall into the latter. Some of these, as facultative parasites, have the extraordinary ability to live saprophytically on the remains of the host they have themselves parasitically killed. Those that die with the host (which they themselves have probably killed) are described as obligate parasites.

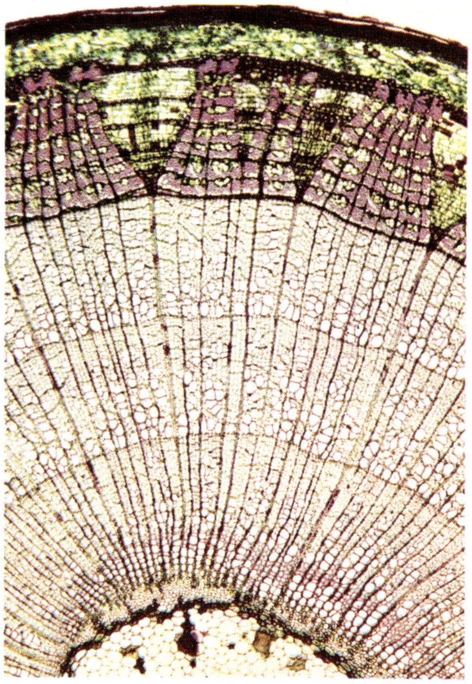

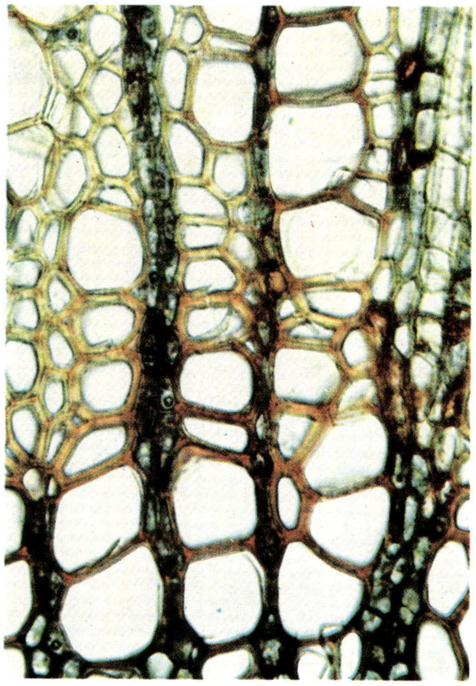

Above: A differentially stained, transverse section of a tree trunk (left), magnified 30 times, shows the outer cork (at the top), the phloem (dark pink) and the inner xylem (mauve). The layers in the xylem are known as annual rings. The main water-conducting elements of the wood – the vessels (right), magnified 375 times.

The range of plants alive today and the number of species that have become extinct are the products of that unceasing search for efficiency and effectiveness in any given habitat which must accompany success as an organism. 'Survival of the fittest' is no mere Darwinian catchphrase but a basic fact of life compounded upon competition. This teeming diversity within the plant kingdom has been a part of man's existence from the earliest times, notably as a basic source of food, but even at a very early stage man recognized that certain plants had the power to heal and others to harm. As a knowledge of plants with medicinal powers became of more than local importance, a comprehensive popular knowledge developed which has come down to us from classical times.

This produced the beginnings of classification and nomenclature which are still developing today. Both aspects might seem to be of only academic interest but this is far from the case. Unless it is possible to refer individually to the approximately 342,000 different species of flowering plants and to the 6000-odd species of ferns, or to the almost innumerable algae, fungi and mosses, no knowledge can be successfully disseminated and all reference must be suspect.

CLASSIFICATION AND NOMENCLATURE

The first attempt to classify living things was made by Theophrastus in the fourth century B.C. He classified plants as either herbs, shrubs or trees. The word 'herb' here does not, of course, have present-day implications but merely relates to the overall size of the plant. A very significant step in classification was made with the publication in 1753 of *Species Plantarum* by Carl Linnaeus. His system, largely restricted to the flowering plants, noted differences in the form of flowers. This classification was 'artificial' in as much as variation of one particular character, namely flower structure, often does not necessarily indicate any real or 'natural' affinity. It was not until the publication of Darwin's theory on evolution that the idea was fully conceived that living organisms might be related to each other by descent, that is to say that certain present-day organisms share common ancestors. We have seen already that all living things have arisen from similar DNA molecules and as modifications were made to these original molecules, so branching of the evolutionary tree occurred. Some of these primitive organisms developed the ability to produce certain photosynthesizing pigments, notably those organisms known now as the blue-green algae. Many simple green algae survive in fresh and salt waters today and there is evidence from fossils of the Pre-Cambrian period that similar plants existed over one thousand million years ago. Certain of these original organisms gradually acquired the ability to live outside their first environment – the oceans – and slowly began to colonize estuaries and mud-flats and then finally became land-living. Profound structural and physiological changes were required and such developments were concerned mainly with the conservation of water.

Modern classification

A classification based on ancestry will obviously yield considerably more information about the relationships between plants than one based on similarities of certain morphological characters, and the former is the main criterion used in modern systems of classification. Morphology is not completely disregarded, however. Indeed, with modern analytical instruments, such as the electron microscope, fine structural differences may be of use in clarifying certain relationships. Similarly, recent advances in techniques of chemical analysis have made it possible for the presence or absence of certain chemical substances in plants to be used for classification purposes. Such taxonomic knowledge may help in the search for more useful herbs; if, for example, a medicinally useful plant is known to possess a certain type of chemical constituent as its active ingredient, a search in closely related plants, which probably also contain similar (though not necessarily identical) substances, may lead to the discovery of a plant with similar useful pharmacological actions, but, for example, less undesirable side-effects. Classification has come a long way from Theophrastus and is undergoing constant revision as more and more data comes to light.

A current classification of the plant kingdom has 17 initial divisions. It begins with the bacteria which are the simplest and therefore probably evolutionarily the most primitive, and it proceeds in ascending order (in developmental and hence evolutionary terms) to the flowering plants. The latter group, although the most obviously visible and valuable to man, by no means encompasses all plant life.

The bacteria possess neither chlorophyll nor an obvious nucleus in their unicellular bodies, and their relationship with the animal kingdom is very close. The next eight divisions make up what we generally term the seaweeds. These are the algae, varying from single-celled organisms that can move around by movements of their special whip-like outgrowths called cilia, to the green covering on tree bark or to the incredibly diverse marine flora, some of which can be almost as large as terrestrial trees. A connection

*Left: Mistletoe (*Viscum album*) is a semi-parasite and gains some of its nourishment by sending its own roots directly into the tissue of the host, either deciduous or evergreen, which is in this case a Silver Maple (*Acer saccharinum*).*

A Classification of the Plant Kingdom

Divisions

- **Algae**
  - Bacteriophyta (9 orders)
  - Cyanophyta (4)
  - Pyrrophyta (4)
  - Euglenophyta (1)
  - Chrysophyta (6)
  - Chlorophyta (11)
  - Chlorochytridiales
  - Phaeophyta (Brown Seaweeds) [Gelidium]
  - Rhodophyta (Red Seaweeds)
- **Fungi**
  - Myxophyta
  - Acrasiophyta
  - Lichenes [Cetraria]
  - Mycophyta (4 Classes, 33 Orders) [Yeasts, Ergot, Fomes]
- **Liverworts and Mosses** — Bryophyta
  - Hepaticae (5)
  - Musci (15)
- **Ferns and fern allies** — Pteridophyta
  - Lycopsida (club-mosses) [Lycopodium]
  - Psilotinae
  - Sphenopsida
  - Equisetinae (Horsetails) [Equisetum]
  - Filicopsida (true ferns) [Dryopteris, Ophioglossum]
- **Seed-bearing plants** — Coniferophyta (Gymnospermae)
  - Cycadopsida
    - Cycadales
    - Ginkgoales
  - Coniferopsida
    - Coniferales (5 fams) [Pinus, Juniperus]
    - Taxales (2 fams)
    - Gnetales (3 fams) [Ephedra]
- **Higher flowering plants** — Magnoliophyta (Angiospermae)
  - Magnoliopsida (Dicotyledons) — 44 orders — over 300 Families
  - Liliopsida (Monocotyledons) — 10 orders — over 60 Families

Herb examples in [ ]

can be noticed immediately: these simple plants are not able to conserve moisture well and so must live in water or in damp, shady places.

The Mycophyta – moulds, mildews and mushrooms – are all fungi. Unlike the algae they cannot photosynthesize because they do not contain any chlorophyll, which accounts for their parasitic or saprophytic modes of existence.

Lichens have an unusual position in the classification order in that each species is a symbiotic combination of an alga and a fungus. We see them usually as grey, yellow or brown circles on rocks, and, in areas of the world where humidity is high, lichens can attain considerable proportions.

The many types of mosses and liverworts follow next. These are still humble plants needing, in most cases, much moisture to survive. They comprise the Bryophyta and are the lowest generally noticed level in any community of plants.

Higher in the evolutionary order and usually in stature, too, come the ferns and fern-allies: the Pteridophyta. They can be tiny plants or as large as some trees (though the trunks of tree-ferns are not composed of real wood, but compressed

Left: Each main division of the plant kingdom is divided into classes, orders, tribes, families and genera. Such a classification reflects origins, relationships and evolutionary progress from the most primitive algae to the higher flowering plants.

Below from left to right: Different small fungi – fruiting bodies of a Penicillium; *a young root tip in symbiotic association with a mycorrhizal fungus;* Mucor, *a black saprophytic mould.*

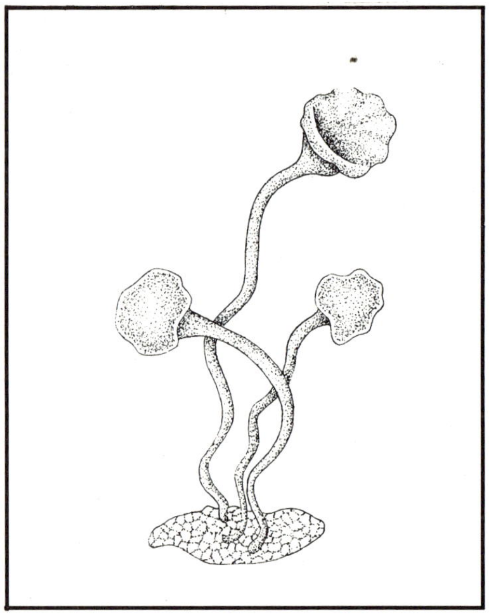

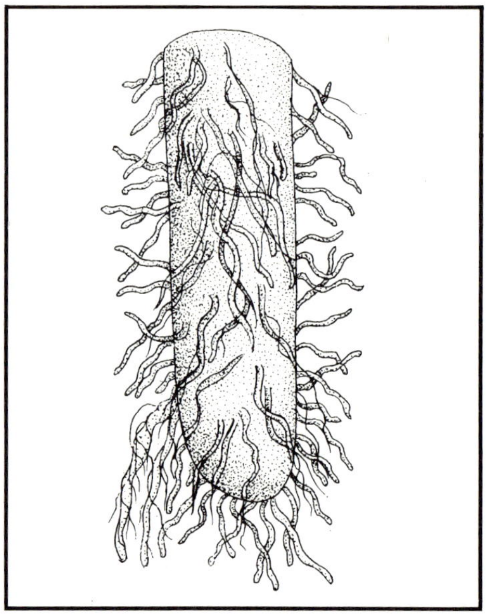

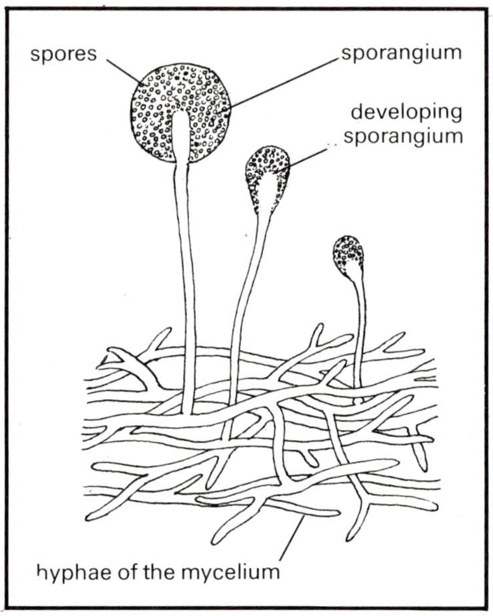

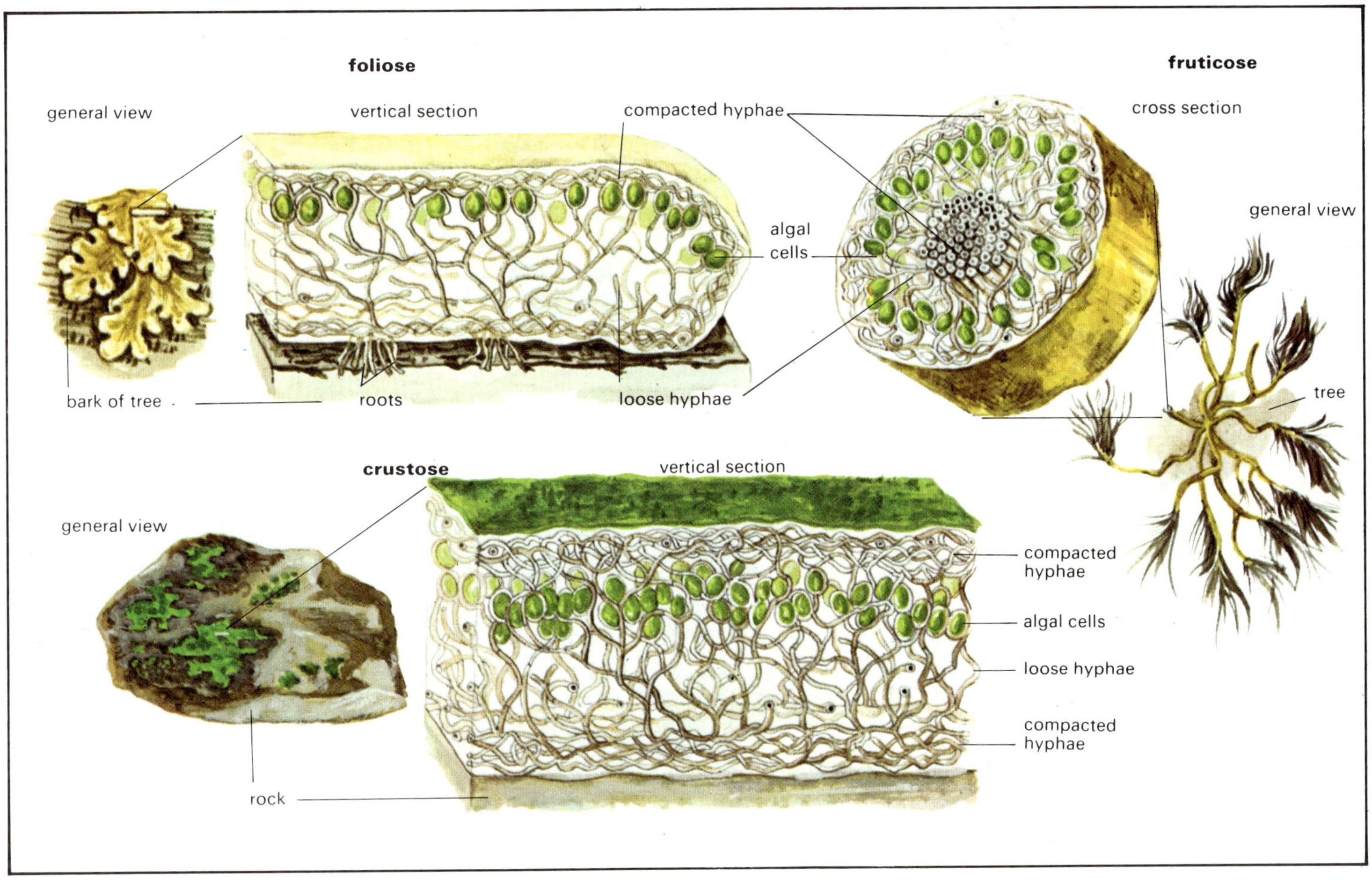

frond-bases and root-like growths) and are invariably leafy in habit.

Of the earlier groups only one or two useful fungi – mushrooms and yeasts – are cultivated by man. Although few ferns are of use as foods or in any other utilitarian way (*Dryopteris filix-mas* which is used as a treatment for worms is an exception) many are grown as objects of beauty. Bacteria, algae and bryophytes can usually reproduce themselves by a vegetative process – by fragmentation – as well as by sexual means; this helps in their classification. Ferns, however, have a special method of reproduction involving a rather complicated life-history. The spores which develop and are shed like dust from underneath the fern-fronds germinate, not into a recognizable fern plant, but into a flat plate of green tissue which resembles a liverwort. This prothallus in turn produces male and female sexual organs, the combination of whose gametes (reproductive cells) eventually develops into a typical fern of the species.

All the plant groups so far mentioned, although succeeding in their damp, if not actually watery, habitats, are not very highly evolved. This implies that they have not developed the range of organs with specific functions within the organism as have higher plants, and so their world is greatly circumscribed by external factors. A similar rough comparison may be made within the animal kingdom – molluscs with mammals, for instance.

The last two major groups of this plant kingdom classification are visually and economically by far the most important to man – though the interdependence of all plant and animal communities should never be forgotten, as no one group can be disregarded just because it seems to have no immediate economic relevance. These two groups, the Gymnosperms and the Angiosperms, are the seed-bearing plants. Gymnosperms include cycads (a few tropical palm-like trees) but mainly consist of the invaluable conifers so named because the majority develop their seeds, not in flowers, but in the axils of woody 'cones' – those of Pine, Cedar, Spruce and Fir are very familiar. Less obviously 'coniferous' are Yew (*Taxus baccata*) and the Maidenhair tree (*Ginkgo biloba*) with their berry-like fleshy fruits.

Angiosperms are the highest (evolutionarily speaking) flowering plants whose development has in many ways been conditioned by the need to ensure pollination of the flowers with consequent reproduction and continuation of the species. The diversity of this group is legion and is discussed later.

Above: Lichens consist of two plants, an alga and a fungus living in partnership. The green alga makes food for the fungus which in turn provides moisture and shelter for the alga. Foliose lichens are leafy, fruticose lichens are shrubby while crustose lichens form flat crusts on rocks or trees. Each type consists of strands, called hyphae, of fungus which enclose the algal cells in the upper layers of the lichen.

Each of the 17 groups in the plant kingdom possesses many, usually thousands, of different organisms. Since Darwin, the belief that each was an individual creation has not held credence. As we have seen, each plant is the product of its genetic background affected, gradually, over millions of years, by its environment. The necessity to classify and to slot each into the divisions already described requires a continuation into smaller and smaller related groups through subdivisions, classes, sub-classes, orders, sub-orders, tribes, sub-tribes and families. Such hierarchical placings have been built upon study and research over centuries but as classification depends utterly upon nomenclature (it has to be possible to refer to something by name for discussion to follow) it is now universal practice to go back only as far as the eighteenth century to Linnaeus. In his *Species Plantarum*, as well as offering a form of classification, he also introduced a method for the naming of plants which has been adopted as standard. His book listed and described all the plants known at that time. He gave a two-part name to each, one for its genus (the generic name) followed by a species name (specific epithet). The two make up the plant's name, for example, the Green Hellebore is *Helleborus* (genus) *viridis* (species). A plant (or animal) species can thus be referred to by a combination of words which belong to it and it alone. Universality was and still is assured by the use of Latin. To be absolutely correct, such botanical names are followed by the names of the botanist who first described the species. Thus the Green Hellebore should properly be referred to as *Helleborus viridis* Linnaeus (often abbreviated to L).

All the plants which we would recognize as being identical – all the Green Hellebores, to retain our example – thus have the same binomial. Other plants, for example the Stinking Hellebores, are similar enough to the green ones to be placed in the same genus (*Helleborus*) but have their own species name – *foetidus*. Still more plants have enough similar characteristics to be placed in the same family (the next highest ranking in the hierarchy) as the hellebores but not in the same genus, such as Monkshood (*Aconitum napellus*) and the Common Buttercup (*Ranunculus acris*). All these plants are in the family Ranunculaceae.

By a similar process of comparison, this time with other families, these Ranunculaceous plants are placed in the order Tubiflorae, along with 25 other families, and the order Tubiflorae in the class Sympetalae. Sympetalae is a class within the subdivision Dicotyledones, in the division Angiospermae.

Cultivar is the term for a category, within the same species, of distinct cultivated sorts. They are usually referred to as varieties in seed catalogues. Hybrids between species of the same or even different genera occur and these are indicated by an × sign, for example, *Tilia* × *europaea*, being the hybrid derived from *T. cordata* and *T. platyphyllos*. An international system of rules now governs nomenclature.

The necessity for this seemingly very complicated system of nomenclature is that correct botanical names are thus consistent worldwide.

THE STRUCTURE OF PLANTS

A prime factor in the success of the flowering (and hence of the seed-bearing) plants lies in their extraordinary diversity of form. The number of species, although great, cannot compare with that of the lower plant groups but their dominance in most habitats is paramount. This will be discussed more fully when the adaptation of plants to their environment is considered. Some aspect of diversity of form is exhibited by almost every species. Indeed, it is largely these differences of form which, as we have seen, have been used to give a plant its specific status. Even though every plant specimen is a living individual and as such is subject to biological variation, each individual of a single species maintains enough characteristics of that species to be able to breed successfully with others of the same species among its community.

The destiny of an organism lies in its part in the successful continuance of the species. *Atropa belladonna* is a herb which grows best on calcareous soils in the half-shade. Under these ideal conditions a strong healthy plant is formed (that is, the conditions are good for the health of the plant as an individual), but, concomitant with this, the plant makes luscious black berries which contain the seeds which will germinate to provide the next generation of the plant species. What is good for the individual must also be good for the species. Breeding or reproduction is the end to which all life-cycles, plant or animal, are conditioned.

Below: Parts of a generalized plant. All flowering plants have the same general arrangement of their parts, but individual modifications to their organs vary enormously.

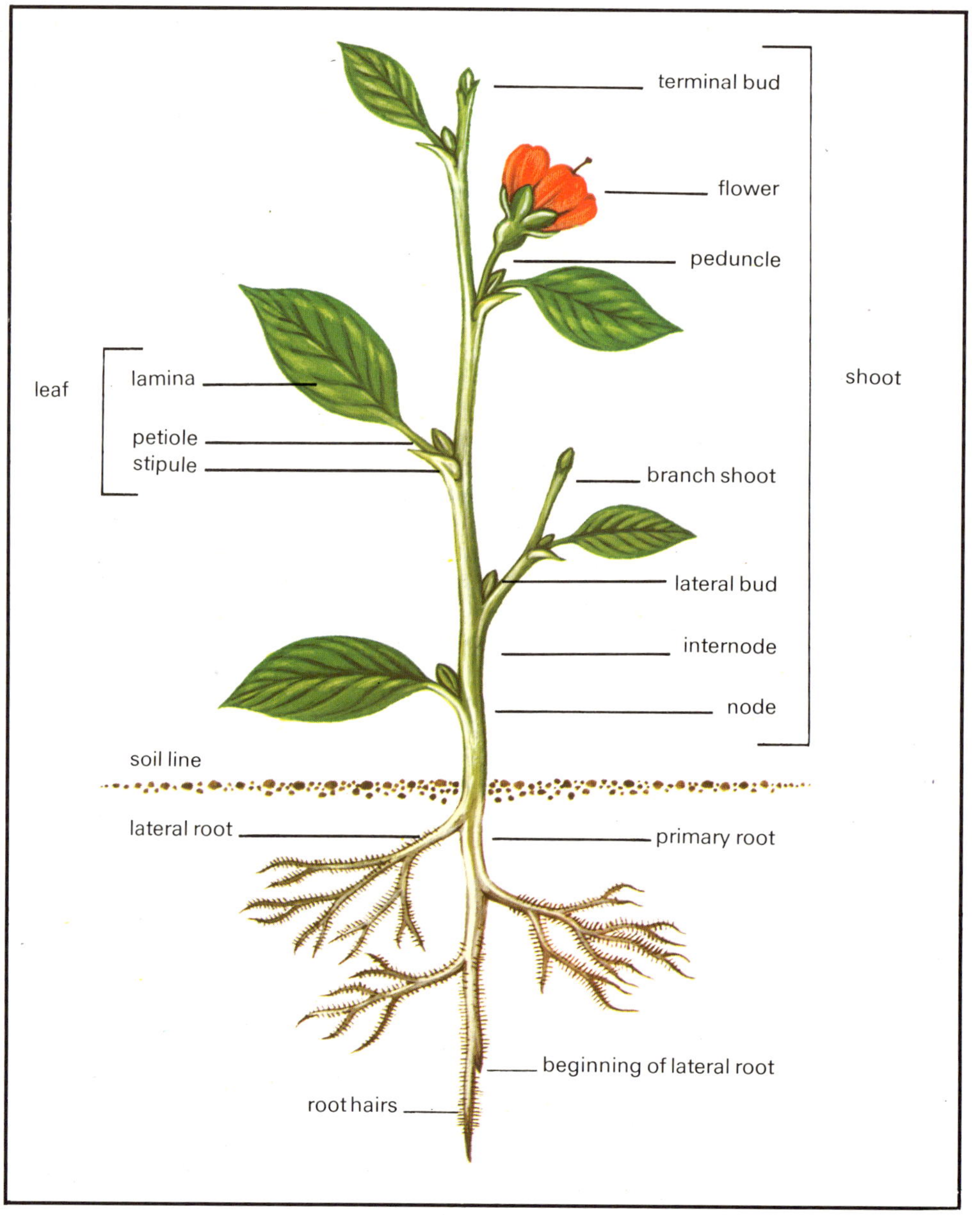

The life-cycle of a flowering plant begins with the seed. Already diversification is apparent. A seed may be a huge coco-de-mer of the Seychelles weighing several kilograms, the mustard-seed used in the Bible to illustrate a tiny measure, or the even smaller dust-like seeds of certain orchids and begonias. Each seed, regardless of its size, contains the vital ability to continue its species for a further generation. It bears the full genetic complement of its parents, making it what it will be, similar to, but not necessarily identical with, those parents. Any slight differences that do occur take their chance in the race for life. A variant that helps, however infinitesimally, an individual to survive better in its habitat than its otherwise identical fellows stands a better chance of continuing into a subsequent generation, and in so doing gradually changes the characteristics of the species – this is the process of evolution. A debilitating variant is less likely to survive to reproduce. Variegated plants, for example, have reduced photosynthetic capabilities and only the efforts of gardeners in propagating them vegetatively keep them alive.

Once the seed has found a suitable environment the new generation can begin to grow. The seed-coat opens and a first root emerges to give initial anchorage, and then a shoot appears to reach for the light. By the time this happens unicellular root hairs are abstracting water and salts in solution from the soil. As it breaks above ground, the shoot's greenness develops and photosynthesis begins. The energy for this first growth-spurt is obtained from the food-store within the seed itself, produced while the seed was still developing within the fruit on the parent plant. From this moment the plant develops and eventually attains maturity. As with any living organism its life is beset with dangers and difficulties: problems of competition, availability of food, unpredictability of weather, inevitability of predators. Yet if only because of the sheer number of any one species generally involved, success for that species is assured. Only geological cataclysms and man's interference – now a greater danger than ever before – are likely to cause extinction.

Structure of the typical plant

Depending upon the species concerned vegetative growth continues by extension of the primary shoot and root structures (all growth, of course, is by continual cell elongation and division) which branch and branch again. In a 'typical' plant aerial growth is paralleled by that underground growth which cannot be seen. But

Right: The object of these methods of seed dispersal is to prevent young plants from growing too close to their parents but rather to colonize new ground.

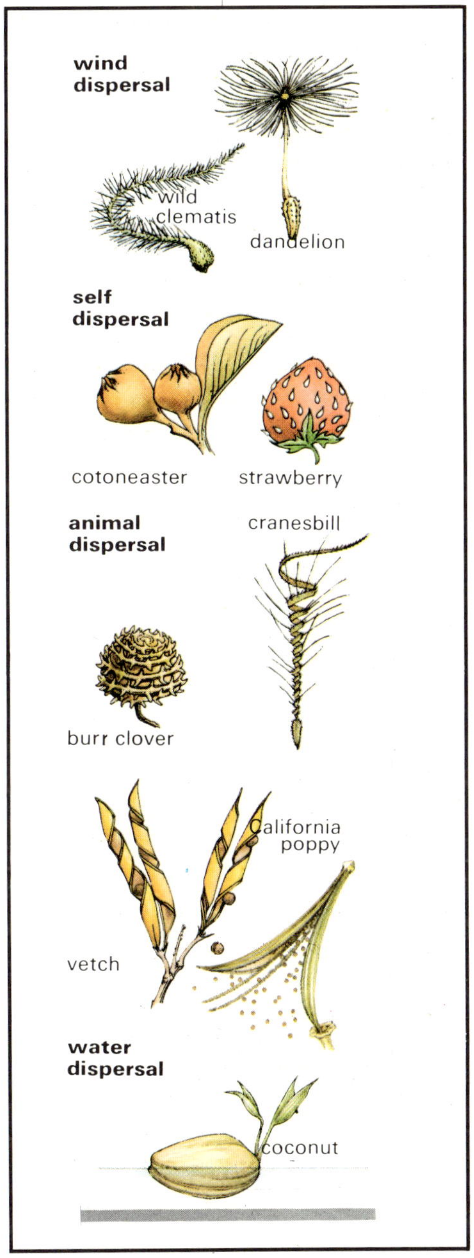

although diversity of form is extreme the basic parts have the same functions. The organs of an angiosperm may be classified as vegetative or reproductive. Vegetative organs are those structures of the plant which are concerned with growth, maintenance and development such as roots, stems and leaves. Those parts of the plant which are concerned with the production of the next generation are classified as the reproductive parts and include the flowers which give rise to the seed-containing fruits.

The root of an angiosperm is typically a subterranean organ whose functions are to anchor the plant to its growing medium and to take up water and other nutrients from the soil. These absorbed materials are either utilized in the roots themselves or conducted via the vascular tissue to other parts of the plant. In addition, they may have certain specialized functions: food storage, especially as starch (as in *Taraxacum officinale*, the Dandelion), or as aerial roots they may serve to support the plant either by growing downwards at an angle from the stem to the soil (maize, for example) or by being especially modified as climbing roots to anchor stems to walls and rocks (*Hedera helix* (Ivy), for instance). Further, some species such as *Viscum album* (Mistletoe) have parasitic roots which penetrate the vascular tissues of a plant host.

The stem is that part of the plant which rises above the ground and, together with the leaves, forms the shoot. Most stems are erect aerial organs but some remain underground and still others creep along the surface. The stem typically serves as a mechanical support for the leaves, flowers and fruits; a pathway for conduction of newly made food to other parts of the plant, perhaps for storage, and of stored food to its required site; a site for the manufacture of the food itself (in green stems); and as a potential reproductive structure. Certain underground stems may be used for food storage as tubers, rhizomes, bulbs and corms. Modifications to aerial stems include stolons, tendrils and thorns.

Leaves, the characteristic photosynthetic organs of higher plants, have their size, shape and structure expressly designed to promote maximum contact with light and air. Another important leaf activity is transpiration, the loss of water vapour through the leaves.

Leaves, like stems and roots, vary in many respects – for example, in their shape and size, their arrangement on the stem and their vein patterns. Certain basic features are, however, distinguishable. The leaf blade or lamina is attached to the stem by means of a continuation of the stem itself, the stalk or petiole. At the base of the petiole are axillary buds which produce secondary branches or flowers or both. Sometimes small leaf-like structures, called stipules, are found. In some leaves, leaf petioles are absent and the leaves are said to be sessile. The blades of some leaves are deeply indented at the margins or edges while others are completely separated into individual parts called leaflets. If the lamina remains in one piece even though deeply lobed, the leaf is referred to as a simple leaf. Complete segmentation of the blade into leaflets produces a compound leaf. There are many different examples of both types.

Flowers are specialized branched stems with lateral appendages. The flower is supported by a stem or pedicel which enlarges terminally to give a receptacle, to which the floral parts are attached. The sepals (collectively forming the calyx) are joined to the receptacle and within them are found the petals (or corolla). Together the calyx and corolla are termed the perianth. The next group of appendages are the stamens (the male parts, collectively called the androecium) each consisting of a narrow filament, topped by an anther which produces the pollen. Within these, at the centre of the flower, is the female reproductive structure, the gynoecium. The basic unit of this is the carpel. At the base is the ovary containing the ovules which develop into the seeds. The ovule is surmounted by a style culminating in a stigma. Extraordinary variation of the relative size and arrangement of these structures is observed. Some flowers – so-called perfect flowers – have both male and female parts, but other plants have male flowers which are distinct from the female ones. When both types of flowers are found on one plant, the plant is said to be monoecious (for example, Cucumber); when they are on separate plants, the species is known as dioecious (for example, Holly).

After fertilization, the flower structure develops into a fruit containing the fertilized ovules or seeds. The embryo within the seed consists of a short axis with one or two seed-leaves or cotyledons which are food stores. After germination, sometimes the seed-leaves stay below ground (hypogeal germination), but in other species they break through the soil surface to act as the primary photosynthesizers (epigeal germination). Monocotyledonous plants produce only one cotyledon, dicotyledonous two. In addition the mature embryo contains a plumule which gives rise to the shoot and the radicle which becomes the root system. The seed is surrounded by a testa or seed-coat.

The wall of the immature ovary gives rise to the main structure of the fruit-wall – the pericarp – which is generally divided into three, more or less distinct, layers: the exocarp, the mesocarp and the endocarp. A very wide range of seeds and fruits exists. The variation in form and character of each of the organs is useful in identification and a brief description of each main type will be found in the glossary.

It will be realized that every plant is perfectly adapted to its habitat. The available resources of nutrients derived from the soil (both of organic and inorganic origins) restrict or promote the success or dominance of certain groups. So, too, do the amounts of water and the vagaries of climate. Because they are plants they are able to harness air and sunlight. Herbs, as they have come to be defined, are plants used by man in a number of different ways: only in a few cases does this detract from their efficiency as organisms. Their botanical classification, however, is not necessarily determined by human usage. Certain plant families contain relatively large numbers of herb plants. The Umbelliferae, which includes Parsley, Dill, Caraway, Coriander and Angelica, and the Labiatae with Sage, Thyme, Mint, Savory, Rosemary, for example, have many culinary herbs. The Solanaceae include a disproportionate number of drug plants (Mandrake, Stramonium, Belladonna and Henbane).

PLANT GROWTH

The basic necessities for plant growth are light, water, warmth, air and nutrients. We will see shortly how plant forms develop in response to the search for these basic requirements, so making maximum use of the available resources. Air is the only essential factor for every phase of growth of the higher plants except in the short initial stage of seed germination. In normal conditions the ramifying root system possesses myriads of root hairs in contact with the soil. Each soil 'crumb' is surrounded by a film of water in which inorganic salts (the product of the continual weathering of inorganic rocks and decomposing organic remains) are dissolved. The root-hair wall acts as a membrane through which water and certain dissolved salts can pass. Osmosis, the process by which two solutions (in this case cell sap and soil water), separated by a semi-permeable membrane (here, the root-hair wall) attempt to equalize each other, means that weaker solutions flow into stronger ones. In this case, the cell sap is the more concentrated and hence water (and salts) from the soil are drawn into the root hair. Its contents are now weaker than those of the adjoining (inner) cells and so the osmotic flow proceeds inwards until it reaches the conducting

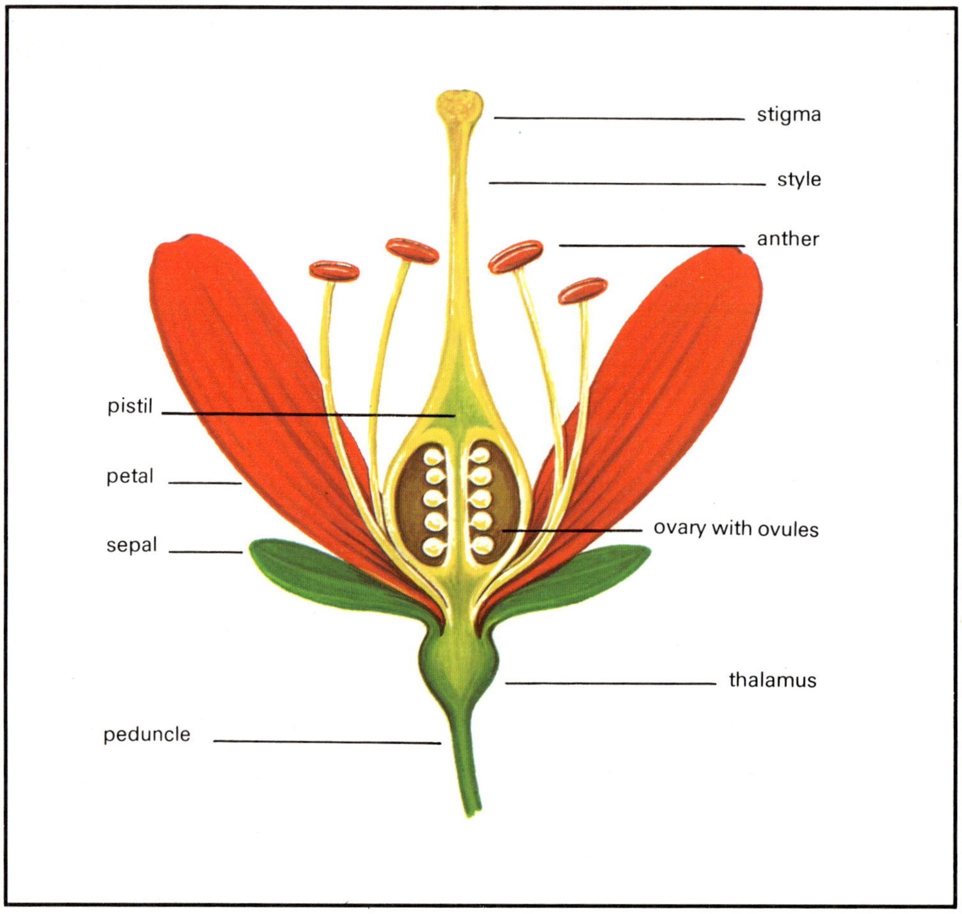

Right: Diagram of a generalized flower (all flowering plants have the same general arrangement), which may be defined, simply, as a specialized branched stem with a number of modified lateral appendages. The enormous variations in size, shape and colour are often attributable to the plant's adaptation to a particular method of pollination.

tissues. These are groups of specialized cells extending throughout the plant whose function it is to convey water and dissolved minerals to all part of the plant (both the nutrients and the products of photosynthesis in the green parts). The sophistication of these tissues is a feature of the morphology of the higher plants. The conducting or vascular tissues are capable of permitting nutrient movement in both directions (that is, both to and from the roots). In young roots and stems there are separate strands of xylem (taking nutrients up from the roots) and phloem (bringing the products of photosynthesis down). There is considerable variation in the form of these conducting elements (vessels and tracheids are examples) and this diversity may be used for identification purposes. In more developed (older) plants, these tissues exist as rings which develop as the stems and roots enlarge.

Above: This courgette seedling has been kept in the dark and so has developed a long stem with small leaves – a good example of a plant growing without light, one of the necessities for healthy growth.

The nutrition of plants

For efficient growth plants require a wide range of nutrients in solution, the main elements being nitrogen, phosphorus and potassium. To these are added calcium, sulphur, magnesium and a large number of trace elements such as boron, iron, copper, zinc and molybdenum which are equally essential but in minute quantities only. Deficiencies of these minor or trace elements show as physiological diseases; in excess, however, they can be positively toxic.

Nitrogen is a basic constituent of all proteins but also of the vitally important chlorophyll, hence a lack of this element produces weak, yellowish plants. An excess of nitrogenous fertilizers results in lush, sappy growth which is prone to disease. Surprisingly, although nitrogen is a major constituent of the air with which most plants are in constant contact, only a relatively small number of them can make direct use of this source. Most nitrogen has to be obtained from nitrogenous compounds in the soil – hence we apply ammonium nitrate or sodium nitrate as fertilizers to supplement what is already there. But members of one plant family in particular, the Leguminosae, have developed a symbiotic (or mutually beneficial) relationship with certain bacteria (notably *Bacillus* species or *Rhizobium radicicola*) which are able to 'fix' this atmospheric nitrogen. The bacteria live in small nodules grown by the roots of the plant host and provide it in return with nitrogen. This is why crops of peas or beans, for example, positively benefit the soil provided that the underground parts are left in the ground after the crop has been harvested. Decomposition of the root system with the nodules and the bacteria they contain releases useful nitrogen-containing compounds into the soil, so becoming available for the next season's crop. This is in contrast with most crops which deplete soil nitrogen. The nodules are clearly visible on any carefully lifted legume root. Alders and a few subtropical trees such as Casuarinas also display this adaptation.

Plants lacking phosphorus appear stunted with a reddish tinge. Phosphorus transfers energy through photosynthesis and respiration, and without it both reactions in the plant body fail to take place properly. Potassium seems to have a special part to play in carbohydrate metabolism and a deficiency shows as poor general development in many parts of the plant. Potassium also contributes to resistance against disease and frost.

It is not necessary to list all the roles of the inorganic nutrients which plants obtain through their roots to appreciate the importance of a healthy root system growing in a balanced soil. The vital part played by water as a pathway to nutrient availability is also clear. Water is also essential to all the biochemical processes in the plant, including photosynthesis. Most plants, however, take up more water than they actually require for these processes because the essential materials are generally only present in the soil in very dilute solution, so that a lot of water has to be taken into the plant for it to obtain enough of its dissolved salts. This excess water is transpired from the surface of the leaf or young stems. Vast amounts of water pass through the plants in this way: a summer crop of grass, for example, has been estimated to have transpired some 500 tons of water per acre (1255 tonnes per hectare) between May and July.

The warmth needed for plant growth relates directly to the species naturally occurring in any one climate. Plants are seldom killed by cold in their own habitats. When a range of exotics is grown in a cold climate, however, it can be seen that the ability to withstand frost is not necessarily inherent. Among primitive plants much greater extremes appear possible. Certain unicellular algae, for example, have been recorded in Antarctica, while some species of bacteria may live at 77°C (171°F). In higher plants the life-cycle is also seen to be directly related to seasonal temperatures. A similar relationship is observed, in the higher or lower latitudes, according to the amount of daylight available. Flowering plants grow rapidly and seeds germinate in response to increased temperature and day-length. These growth patterns of vegetative development leading to flowering and seed production have evolved to capitalize upon or to work within the conditions that exist in their native habitats. The stimulus for activity may not, however, be a direct one, such as this. Winter-hardy cereals, for example, flower

*Left: Tangles (*Laminaria digitata*), with a smooth stalk and a strap-like blade which is slit into several sections, is one of the oar-weeds. These are brown algae which are specially adapted to live only in particular zones along the seashore.*

in the warmth of the early summer because their seedlings have been subjected to winter cold. Chrysanthemums only flower in autumn as the night-length increases sufficiently to allow production of the various plant hormones which in turn cause the buds to develop. That we now accept as normal the permanent availability of chrysanthemums, and other crops, out of season, is an indication of man's success in providing, particularly in the highly controlled environments of greenhouses, the exactly right amount of the basic necessities for growth. Air is enriched with higher concentrations of carbon dioxide to accelerate photosynthesis, extra light is provided or denied, temperature is controlled, optimal amounts of water and concentrations of nutrients are given. All these factors must be contrived to create the balanced regime that may accelerate, but cannot fundamentally alter, the growth pattern of the plant species concerned.

ADAPTATION TO ENVIRONMENT

Plants, no less than animals, are the result of each species' evolutionary response to its environment. Yet plants complement and add to their environment in a way that animals cannot.

A climate which permits forest as a vegetation climax (so called because this represents the peak of plant growth and development) is itself aided by the continual transpiration of water vapour from the highest branches of the trees that form a forest canopy. The soil which enables the trees to attain maturity is enriched by annual leaf-fall (even from evergreen species) and protected from erosion by being held in the root network of the plants. Within such woodland a stratification of other plants, from shrubs to mosses, is encouraged and helps to develop its associated fauna. A fully developed habitat encourages a great richness of plant and animal life. Yet the natural ecological balance is very sensitive to man's interference. The aridity of the Sahara desert today, and the pollution of much of the Mediterranean coastal areas, is a reminder of the hazards of careless human exploitation.

Not all natural environments, however, permit the attainment of the woodland climax and yet in the areas of the earth which are able to provide even a minimum of the necessary requirements for plant growth, some such growth is always present. Its form reflects the availability of the basic necessities and the external factors that may limit their utilization.

It seems probable that terrestrial life moved in very slow evolutionary stages from watery habitats, and thus in plants the ability to withstand drought can be seen as a highly developed (and late) stage of this evolution. Thus the world of plants may be seen as an unbroken continuum from lake or even sea to desert. Each main habitat characteristic compels plant species to adapt to it (although the plants which are successful in this adaptation may be of widely differing families and of diverse evolutionary origin and age). This similarity of form in response to the conditions prevailing in a particular habitat is known as convergent evolution.

In watery habitats the simpler, non-flowering plant divisions are predominant. Flowering plants which now live in water have probably moved back to it from the land to cope with excessive terrestrial competition and have, therefore, had to develop very specialized structures. The floating leaves of water-lilies have stomata on their upper sides, not mainly on the lower ones as do most aerial plants. The cells of the largely submerged water plants, hydrophytes, are large with wide intercellular spaces, for air is at a premium. If a plant is to succeed each problem has to be solved. The swamp cypress of the Florida Everglades, *Taxodium distichum*, grows snorkel-like structures, known as pneumatophores, which protrude above the water level and so help in obtaining enough air. The mangroves of most tropical swamps have developed an invaluable seed-dispersal method: seeds just dropped would fall into the sea and probably be carried away with little chance of germination. Seeds of several species thus germinate on the parent plant, producing a heavy torpedo-like first root; the seedling falls, slicing through the water to stick into, and so grow in, the mud below.

Bog plants have no difficulty in finding enough water so long as it is not brackish, but aeration at the roots presents more of a problem. The plants of the saline marshes, halophytes, suffer from physiological drought. Water is available all around, yet because of its high salt concentration osmotic intake is difficult. Water-loss must thus be avoided at all costs and halophytes exhibit similar water-conserving characteristics to desert plants, where all water is scarce.

Plants which grow best in normal soils are known as mesophytes. They are included in a broad band of morphological types reflecting every sort of habitat and micro-climate throughout the world. The great majority of herbs are mesophytic. In cultivation, however, the individual requirements of each species have to be considered: semi-shade and a moist soil suits Angelica and Sorrel, for example, while Sage and Basil like full sun and perfect drainage. In general all aromatic herbs thrive in warmth and sunlight. In areas of high humidity where plant growth is at its most concentrated, such as the equatorial jungles, trees will be covered with flowering plants and ferns which have adapted themselves to enjoy an aerial life. These so-called epiphytes are especially represented in the Orchidaceae (for example, Vanilla) and Bromeliaceae (Pineapple) families.

The typical plants of desert regions are the cacti. They are generally leafless with thick moisture-retaining stems and deeply sunken stomata to reduce water-loss. Cacti are good examples of the extreme xerophytic condition, and are native only to the New World. The problem of water retention and excessive water-loss (leading of course to wilting, desiccation and ultimately death) is, however, worldwide. It may be a seasonal problem, as in the Arctic where although there is always plenty of water, it is unavailable to the plant in the winter because it is locked away in the form of ice. Plants have developed a vast number of ways of minimizing such dangers. Leaves (always the most vulnerable of organs) may have thick, waxy cuticles such as the Bay Laurel. The woolly covering of many grey-leaved shrubs (and their colour) also helps to reflect excessive sunlight. Leaves may be greatly reduced (as in Lavender and Rosemary) or be completely missing (Ephedra, for example). Succulent leaves (Purslane) indicate their increased capacity for water storage.

Variation in morphology is also clear in the type of life a species is programmed to live, and every possibility exists. Ephemerals such as Corn Salad rush through their life-cycle (that is to say, the seed germinates, develops into the adult plant which flowers and produces a new generation of seeds) in only a few weeks, when suitable conditions are available. Annuals require a full summer season. Biennials, on the other hand, take two years for the full cycle: during the first year the seed germinates and develops into a vegetative 'body' and an underground storage organ. The stored food is used the following summer to produce a flowering spike which then produces fresh seed. Many vegetables and herbs do this, for example, Carrot, Parsnip and Parsley.

Perennial plants, which live from three to four years to several thousands, have bifurcated into the herbaceous, which retire to a resting bulb, bud or some other root-stock in inclement seasons (either excessively hot or cold), or the woody. Shrubs, and especially trees, increase their vegetative body yearly, and this in its turn has demanded the production of special strengthening tissues to support the enormous weight of the tree trunks. Similarly, in these cases, special water-conducting mechanisms within the plant (to convey water and nutrients from below soil-level to the tips of the highest branches – which may be a hundred metres above) have had to be developed.

Whatever the form of body and of lifestyle a species has evolved, it must be seen as a preliminary to flowering and sexual reproduction. The range of flower types has evolved in parallel with the diversity of fauna which are available to pollinate them. Colour, scent, size and season are geared to the animate visitors such as insects and birds and the inanimate wind and rain. Efficiency is all and the fact that a plant succeeds in the wild is proof that the methods adopted, however bizarre, actually work.

Only distribution of the seeds remains to be considered and the methods are as varied as those employed for pollination. The individual species demonstrates by its existence the efficiency of the whole organism. Each has reached success and continues to succeed in its ecological niche by a constant process of adaptation over many thousands of years.

The range of species that man has used as herbs throughout the world – as food, medicine or dyes – is enormous. As already indicated, almost all of the major plant groups include suitable species which by trial and error have been discovered to possess useful properties. The alkaloids which are now used from such species as *Datura stramonium* (Thorn Apple) and *Hyoscyamus niger* (Henbane) may be by-products of the plant's normal metabolic processes or defence mechanisms. It would seem that the volatile oils of Rue or Rosemary are in fact intended as a discouragement to browsing animals. Man, ironically, finds them attractive and both collects them in the wild and cultivates them.

It is significant that few herbs are the product of intensive breeding or, indeed, selection. They are species that have been first collected, then cultivated, and now even farmed with the development of horticulture. They have not, however, been changed genetically from their original wild form.

*Above: Swamp cypress (*Taxodium distichum*), seen here in autumn coloration, shows adaptation to its marshy environment by having modified roots known as pneumatophores which come above wet soil or water for air, and a special method of seed germination which avoids losing the seeds in the sea where they may fail to develop.*

THE CHEMISTRY OF PLANTS

We know that some plants are useful in treating certain diseases or in cooking, but it is not sufficient to say that we know that they work or that they impart pleasing odours and flavours to food. The reason for their various actions is that they contain certain active chemical substances and it is these compounds that produce various effects. This section is concerned with a consideration of what these active materials are, how and why the plant makes them and how we can best use them. Before discussing the active substances, however, it is necessary to look at the chemistry of plants in general.

There are a number of similarities between plants and animals – both are composed of cells, for example. The typical mature plant cell is a very small (about 0.01 to 0.001 cm or 0.004 to 0.0004 ins in diameter), many-sided compartment enclosed by a cell-wall. Within this wall is contained the cytoplasm (in which most of the life-giving processes occur) and the nucleus (which houses the genes and controls all activities of the cell). Most of the cell is occupied by a cavity or vacuole containing a watery sap. Some of the most important components of the cytoplasm are the chloroplasts in which the plant assimilates its food. This is the fundamental point of difference between plants and animals. The latter take in large molecules such as starches, proteins and fats (which contain many carbon atoms), and gradually break them down in a sort of controlled combustion process, thus obtaining their contained energy (required for growth, for example) in small definite quantities rather than all at once as in a fire. They then reassemble these small fragments of the original food molecules to form their own substance. Plants, on the other hand, take in from the air a very small molecule, carbon dioxide, as their source of carbon and bring together several (sometimes many) of these single carbon units, combined with water from the soil, to make up their own substance, releasing back oxygen into the air in the process. The energy required for this conversion is provided by sunlight which is trapped by the green pigment, chlorophyll, contained in the chloroplasts. Other pigments, usually yellow, trap light of slightly different wavelengths so increasing the efficiency of the conversion of solar to chemical energy. The initial product of these photosynthetic reactions is a simple sugar containing six carbon atoms, glucose, which may then be used in other reactions or stored as starch.

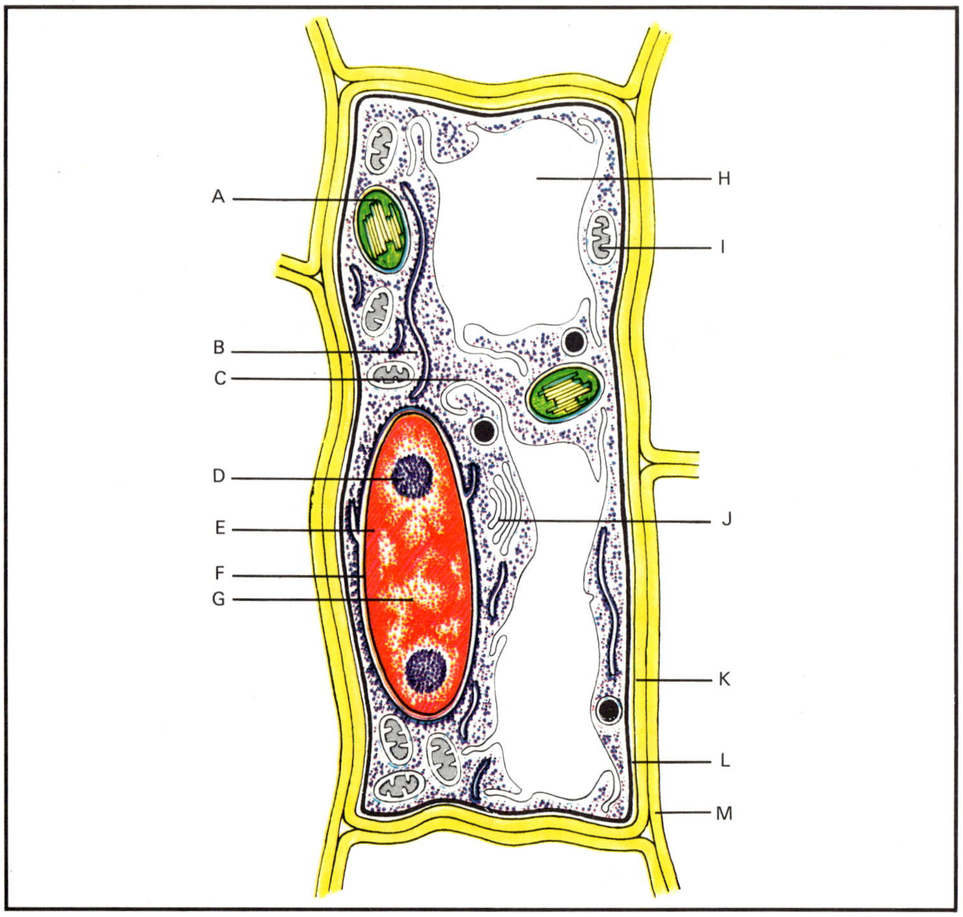

Enzymes

Plants are very efficient at carrying out this process because unlike in the chemical laboratory when a great deal of energy (usually heat) has to be supplied to cause a chemical change to take place (which is very wasteful), reactions in living systems are controlled by complex protein catalysts called enzymes. These work by drastically lowering the energy required for each stage in a complicated sequence of reactions (like the process of converting carbon dioxide to glucose). The protein of most enzymes is combined in some way with a metal atom such as iron or manganese which explains why small quantities of these materials are essential for healthy growth. If that metal is absent, the particular enzyme of which it forms a part cannot be produced, and the reactions which that enzyme catalyzes cannot proceed so that the chemical constitution of the plant, hence its development, is impaired or even stopped. A little energy is still required for enzyme-catalyzed reactions and this energy is stored in special chemical bonds (high-energy phosphate bonds), hence the requirement for phosphorus. Enzymes are highly specific materials which can promote only one small reaction in a complicated sequence and the overall change from carbon dioxide to glucose requires the presence of hundreds of closely related enzyme molecules. The absence or malfunction of just one of these means that the reactions cannot proceed normally. They are also extremely dependent, among other factors, on temperature (the optimal temperature is usually 37°C or 98°F).

The sugars produced by the green tissue in the first stages of photosynthesis may be further metabolized in the same cell or transported, via the vascular tissue, to other parts of the plant. They may then

Left: Parts of a typical rigid-walled plant cell. (The cell-wall material is mainly cellulose but may be impregnated with other materials such as lignin.)

A *choroplast*
B *endoplasmic reticulum*
C *cytoplasm*
D *nucleolus*
E *chromatin*
F *nuclear membrane*
G *nucleus*
H *vacuole*
I *mitochondrion*
J *Golgi membrane*
K *cell membrane*
L *plasma membrane*
M *thickened cell-wall*

Right: The enzyme (1) combines with certain substrate molecules (2) to form an activated complex (3). This breaks down to give the products (4) and regenerates the enzyme. Only some molecules will exactly 'fit' on the enzyme surface which explains their high specificity.

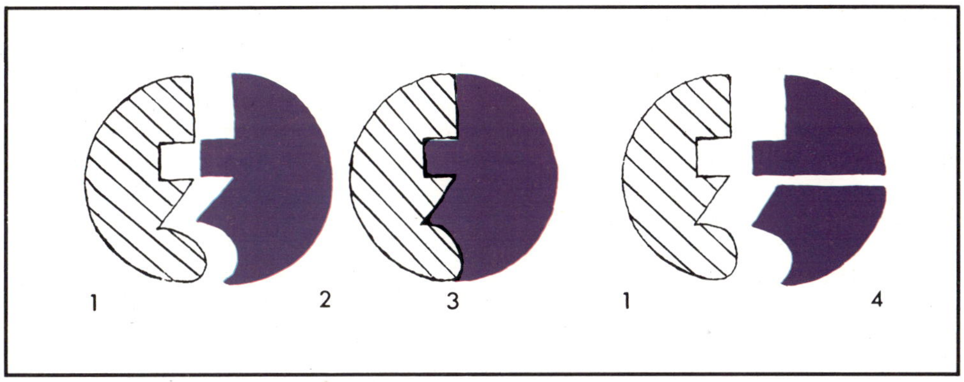

be assimilated to give, for example, cellulose (the main constituent of plant cell-walls) or starch (an important food storage material), or they may be used in the synthesis of other important biochemicals such as proteins (some of which may be used to make more enzymes), nucleic acids (which make up part of the genetic material of the cells – the chromosomes) and fats.

A plant increases its substance, or grows, either by enlargement of the existing cells of which it is comprised or by division of certain of these cells to produce two further cells which may subsequently enlarge and divide themselves. Both enlargement and division are influenced by the environment as has been mentioned previously but it is at the biochemical level that control really takes place.

Seeds, for example, germinate as a result of increased temperature in the spring because the warmth activates certain enzymes which produce chemical substances whose function it is to initiate growth by acting directly on cells which are to become important centres of division. An increase in the length of stems and roots (as in germination), in the development of their branching systems and in the development of lateral growths (such as leaves, flowers and root hairs) is known as primary growth. The regions of extremely active, dividing cells which give rise to these growths are called primary meristems. Secondary meristems also occur and the most important of these is known as the cambium. It usually occurs as a continuous, annular layer of small cells from just above the root tip to just below the stem apex. Lateral division of these cambial cells inwards (towards the centre of the stem) produces xylem cells, which conduct water upwards from the roots. Outward division in the same manner produces phloem cells, which convey nutrients to all parts of the plant. All cell division and elongation requires the utilization of energy and the energy stored as 'active' phosphate groups may be released (and so become available for carrying out other processes) by a sequence of reactions which is essentially the reverse of photosynthesis – the breaking down of large molecules to much smaller ones in the process which is known as respiration.

Above: A lack of potassium in the soil produces browning and death of the leaves of this Paeony plant. Other deficiencies also give rise to different diseases but all may generally be rectified by application of the appropriate fertilizer. The soil must be well tilled or the fertilizer will be unable to benefit the plant.

Light, vital as an energy source, exerts an obvious chemical influence on chlorophyll production as well as inducing indirect chemical changes which promote flowering in the Chrysanthemum, for example, as has already been mentioned. In an established plant, cell division and thus elongation of the stem or branch occurs at the apical bud because it produces certain growth-retarding substances (hormones) which suppress activity at the other buds lower down the stem. If the apex, and hence the hormones, are removed – by pruning, for example – growth may proceed at other levels and eventually one of the previously inhibited laterals takes over as the main growth point.

Primary and secondary metabolism

All these fundamental, literally life-giving, processes (the assimilation of food, its digestion, respiration and hence growth) are common to most plants, and their biochemical control is essentially identical in all cells (whether they are on the surface of a leaf or deep inside a root) of all species from microscopic, floating seaweeds to the giant redwoods. For this reason they are known as primary metabolic processes and the compounds involved as primary metabolites.

Most plants, however, make other substances in addition to those they require

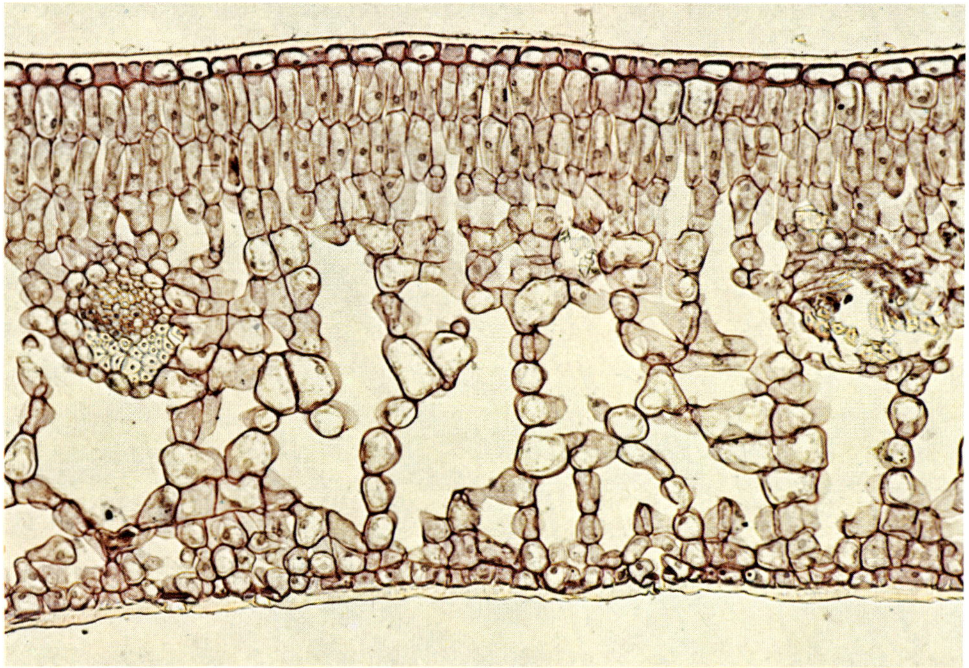

Above: This section through a holly leaf shows the 'open' structure of leaves with large air-spaces to promote good circulation of gases. Holly, an evergreen, possesses a modification to enable it to withstand drought conditions in winter by having a thick outer cuticle.

merely to exist and these are often of very complicated structure. They can sometimes be unique to a single species or a group of very closely related species. Despite their wide diversity of character and distribution they all have one thing in common and that is that their function in the plant, if they have one at all, is very poorly understood. It is these secondary metabolites, sometimes present in an extremely minute concentration, which exert the physiological or pharmacological effects on man and are responsible for the strong flavours and odours of some species and it is obvious that it is on these substances that an account of the chemistry of herbs should concentrate.

Biosynthesis

The secondary metabolites which may be regarded as 'end-products' of metabolism have an extremely wide range of chemical structure but their functions are largely unknown. Some coloured compounds have an obvious reproductive role in that they are responsible for the colour of flowers (the red flavonoids of roses and the yellow carotenes of sunflowers are good examples) and hence attract insects which pollinate and cross-fertilize. Others may have a role in growth regulation – the hormones already mentioned – while still more may serve a protective function. Some compounds are extremely toxic (even in very low concentrations) and a bird, for example, which eats a berry which contains these substances and as a result becomes ill soon learns to avoid the fruit from that particular species; the chances of survival of the plant are thus increased.

Some evidence that these secondary substances are concerned, however indirectly, with vital processes is given by the fact that not all parts of those plants which contain these materials have the same concentration of them. They may, for example, be concentrated in the bark (as in the Buckthorn) or the fruits (for example, Caraway). Their concentration, furthermore, varies with the season (and this has obvious important consequences regarding the collection of some medicinal plants and herbs which will be referred to later) and even with the time of day. The concentration of active principles in the medicinally useful plants of the family Solanaceae (particularly the Deadly Nightshade) for instance show marked diurnal variation. Another example in which secondary metabolites may play a role in fundamental metabolism is given by the so-called 'pink flush' of lettuces. When growth and photosynthesis is very active, in young seedlings for example, high concentrations of sugars build up increasing the osmotic pressure of the cell sap to dangerously high levels. If allowed to proceed the cells could literally explode; at this point certain enzymes are activated which divert the metabolism to break down these sugars to aromatic compounds with low osmotic pressures called flavonoids, which happen to be red. A pink colour thus develops in the leaves. After some time when the plant has grown and so needs and can accommodate more sugar, the red substances are removed by reconversion into useful sugars so that the pink hue gradually disappears.

The main types of metabolites

The 'active constituents' of plants may be categorized according to their chemical structure:

Alkaloids are distinguished chemically by the fact that they contain a basic nitrogen atom. An alkaloid-containing plant almost never contains just one alkaloid but rather a whole range of closely related chemical components. Thousands of alkaloids are known and they are very widespread in the plant world being present even in certain fungi. Some of the best known are the Solanaceous group (atropine and hyoscine, for example) from, among other species, Deadly Nightshade and Thorn Apple. Another much more complex group which includes morphine is found in certain species of poppy.

Glycosides are compounds which consist of two parts: a sugar portion attached via a special linkage to a non-sugar residue. They may be split by enzymes or by the action of dilute acid. Probably the most important group are those which exert a powerful physiological effect on heart muscle – the cardio-active glycosides – which are special steroids found, among other plants, in the Foxglove and Lily-of-the-Valley. Second only to the cardiac glycosides are those compounds based on anthraquinone, the purgative substances of Cascara, Rhubarb, Buckthorn and Senna.

Saponins are special glycosides which form stable froths or foams when shaken in water. Their physiological action depends on the fact that they break up red blood cells (haemolysis). The Primula is one of the herbs containing saponins.

Essential oils are complex mixtures of quite small molecules which are volatile and generally have a pronounced odour. They are responsible for the flavours of many culinary herbs (for example, the umbelliferous fruits including Dill, Caraway, Fennel and Anise and the leaves of certain species of Labiatae including Peppermint and Thyme). In addition, some oils have a therapeutic effect – for example, oil of Clove is antiseptic.

Mucilages and *gums* consist of large molecules made up of several hundred individual sugar units linked together to form chains. They have the special property of being able to form gels with water and thus exert a soothing effect on inflamed tissue. They may also act as laxatives by increasing the bulk of the contents of the intestines and hence induce peristalsis. A good example is Marshmallow root.

Tannins are complex phenols which react with protein. Just as a tannin solution is used to prevent putrefaction of animal hides by converting them to leather so may an extract of the Oak (which is high in tannin content) be used to promote wound healing by encouraging the formation of new tissue under the leathery layer formed on broken mucosal surface by the action of tannins. Because of their astringent properties these compounds also have a marked effect on flavour – as in tea, for example.

Bitters as the name implies have a strong bitter taste but do not belong to any one special chemical class. They are generally used to stimulate the appetite – Gentian, for example, is included for this purpose in a number of aperitifs.

It can be seen that all these different classes of substances have very different chemical properties. Because of these differences, the methods used in the preparation of extracts of plants also vary. The extraction procedures obviously depend on the types of constituent present and it is worthwhile examining the various procedures in detail.

Above: The volatile oil of certain plants being extracted. The oil (seen as yellow droplets) is driven off mixed with steam and condenses in the upper right-hand arm of the apparatus.

MAKING EXTRACTS OF PLANTS

Although it is desirable for all purposes to have as fresh material as possible it is not always feasible, and it is thus necessary to preserve the plant in as near the fresh state as possible and sometimes, though not always, profitable to extract from it the active constituents.

It is important to choose the appropriate part of the plant, for not all plants contain their active ingredients distributed evenly throughout each organ. The active materials in Bearberry, for example, are concentrated mainly in the leaves while the useful parts of Chamomile are the flower-heads.

After collection the procedure for handling the material depends on the species, part of the plant, active ingredients and whether or not the plant is to be used at once or stored. Fresh plant material contains a high proportion of water (leaves and flowers usually lose up to about 85 per cent of their weight on drying) and for this reason the fresh materials are rarely used in the preparation of extracts. A more concentrated extract may be obtained if the plant is first dried, which has the added advantage that drying is also the simplest method of preservation. The fresh plant material is spread out in thin layers (or in certain cases hung up in bunches) and kept in a dry, well-ventilated place. Tubers and roots will obviously take longer to dry than flowers and leaves even though the former are sometimes cut up into small pieces. Selection of the correct drying temperature is also vital. Too high a temperature may cause loss of active ingredients (volatile oils, for example, as their name suggests vaporize readily at temperatures above about 40°C (104°F) or some chemical degradation may occur as in *Digitalis* and most other glycoside-containing plants). On the other hand, too low a temperature may actually accelerate decomposition by promoting enzyme activity within the plant itself.

Once dried the plant material should be stored in a dark, cool place in containers that are as near airtight as possible. Some deterioration is bound to occur with time, however, and it is advisable to use only material which has not been stored for longer than two years. The material is usually reduced to a moderate powder by grinding just before use.

Purification of the extract

The next problem is the extraction of the active substances. There are two major difficulties: the first is to choose a method which will extract the desired compound in a high yield and the second is to ensure that as few unwanted impurities as possible are removed from the plant at the same time. As has been seen already the active principles have very different chemical, and hence solubility, characteristics depending on the class of compound to which they belong. Since, for example, oils are insoluble in water, water or solvents containing a high proportion of water cannot be used in their isolation. Alkaloids are soluble in organic solvents such as chloroform but so are the highly coloured pigments such as chlorophyll and carotenes. Glycosides are water-soluble but a great many other substances formed in plants such as the sugars and acids also dissolve in water. Thus it is extremely difficult to prepare an extract which contains a reasonably high concentration of the desired material and that material alone. A fairly satisfactory compromise may be achieved, however, by the use of dilute ethyl alcohol. Ethyl alcohol contains enough of the properties of water to dissolve the sugars and acids, which are polar compounds. It also behaves sufficiently like a non-polar (organic) solvent such as petrol to cause the larger organic molecules, such as polypeptides and steroids, to dissolve. This has the advantage in that in most herbal remedies the compounds actually responsible for the reported action are either not known or they are only, or sometimes more, effective in combination with other substances (either closely related or not) which are found in that particular plant. This last phenomenon, known as synergism, is discussed in the next chapter. The various ways of making extracts follow.

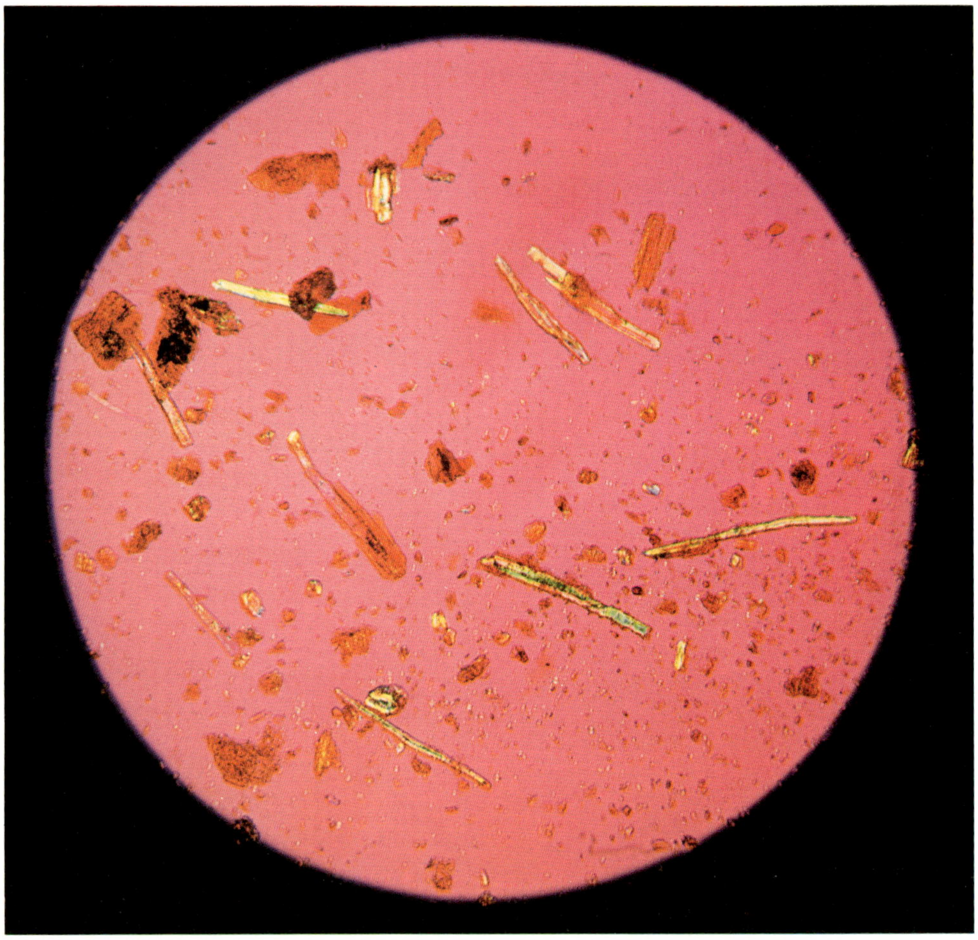

One of the simplest ways of using herbs is as herbal teas or tisanes, which involves simply extraction of the plant with water. If the active ingredients are very soluble in water, it may be sufficient to macerate the powder with water for several hours at room temperature. Maceration at higher temperatures (as in the case of some hard barks) is called digestion. If the drug is boiled in water for half an hour or so the result is a decoction; but probably the best method is to place the plant in a pot, cover with water that is just boiling for about a quarter of an hour and strain the resulting infusion.

Not all plant constituents are soluble in water under these circumstances, however, and it may be necessary to leave the plant material in contact with the water for several days or longer. This may either be by maceration in a closed vessel with occasional shaking or stirring or by a process of percolation which involves packing the drug into a glass column and slowly pouring water through, over the drug. The active ingredients dissolve in the water which may be collected and passed through the column a second time. Concentration by evaporation results in a thick residue known as an extract. If alcohol is used the percolate is called a tincture.

Volatile oils may be extracted in a rather pure state by a process known as steam distillation. This method involves heating the powdered drug with boiling water which causes the oil to vaporize into the steam. The oil and the steam are collected together by condensation. The oil, being lighter than the water, floats on the surface and may then be collected.

METHODS OF IDENTIFICATION

As the activities of plants are very diverse and even quite closely related species often have completely different effects, it is important to ensure that the correct species is being used and that it is of good quality.

This is relatively straightforward when the plant is in the whole, fresh condition either by direct comparison with an authentic specimen or by the use of books of plant descriptions (floras). Many recognizable characteristic features may be lost on drying, however, and certainly in the powdered condition further work is required and this is best achieved by a microscopical investigation.

Microscopical examination

Although most plants contain essentially the same sorts of cells (cork, for example, or the elements in the xylem, the conducting tissue) which have broadly the same form in all species, the fine, microscopic structure of these cells is often highly individual. Examination of a powder under the microscope and the observation of xylem vessels shows that the powder contains wood, but from the fine structure it may be possible to identify the source plant. Even the size of the individual cells may be important: the width of the fibres enables powdered Cinnamon (*Cinnamomum zeylanicum*) to be distinguished from the closely related Cassia (*Cinnamomum cassia*).

The botanical source of the plant is not necessarily a sufficiently strong criterion

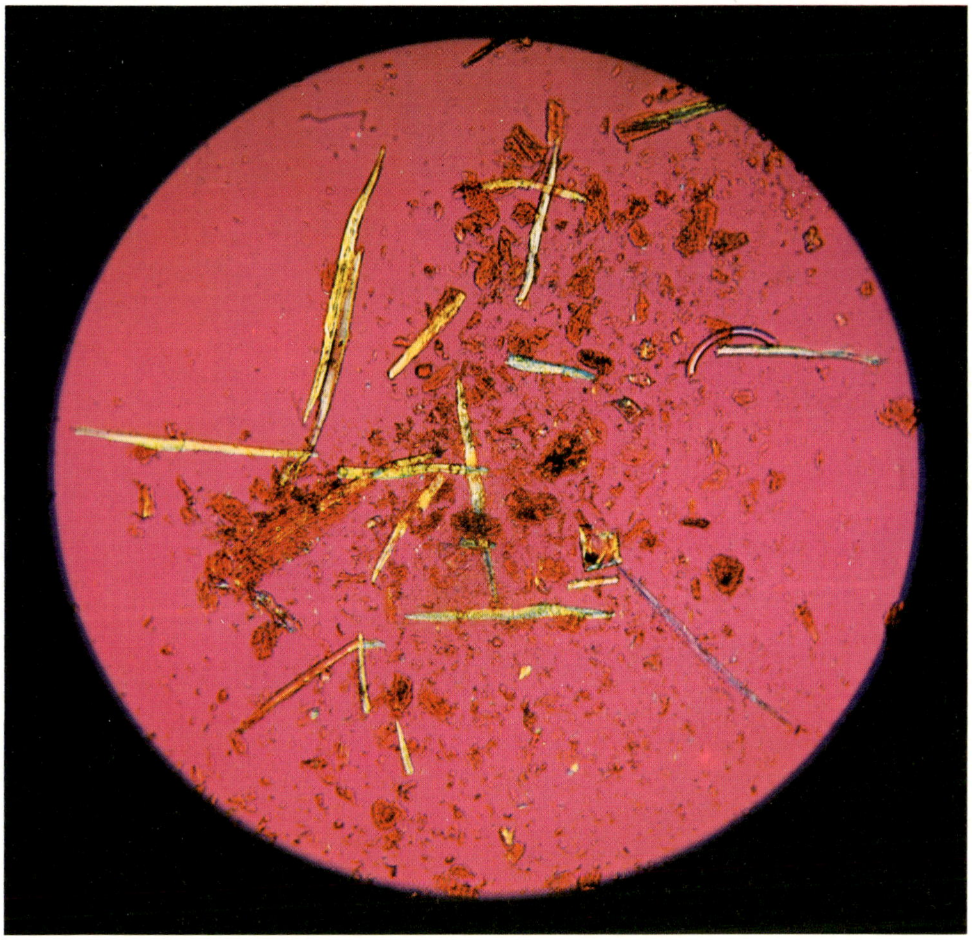

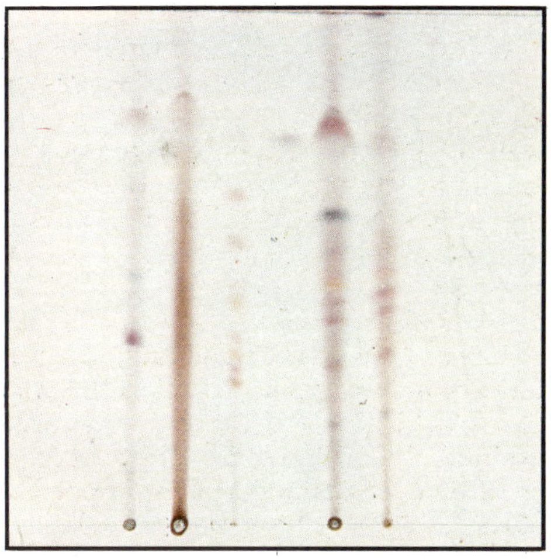

Above: In this chromotagraphic separation, the various constituents of the plant react with the spray reagent to produce coloured spots. Unknown extracts of plants may thus be compared with those of authentic specimens.

Left: Closely related plants in the powdered state are often indistinguishable to the eye but may be easily identified microscopically. Fibres in powdered Cinnamon (near left) are rarely greater than 30 micrometres in diameter, while those in Cassia *(far left) are usually between 30 and 40 micrometres.*

of identity. Certainly such techniques may not be applied to the examination of extracts or tinctures which contain no plant material. Some further means of control is obviously desirable, but the problem is complicated by the fact that although many plants have been thoroughly investigated and their biological activity referred to one particular or more than one group of constituents, many have not and we still have very little idea of which components are the physiologically active ones. If we did, it should be possible to purify the crude extract and actually isolate the active substances so as to fully characterize them chemically. This is not possible in the majority of cases, however, and the solution to the problem may be approached in two ways. One is the application of certain chemical tests. If an extract under investigation is suspected to be of, for example, Blueberry, which is known to contain tannins, a simple chemical test with a dilute solution of ferric chloride (which gives a blue-black colour with such substances) would rapidly tell the investigator if tannins were present or not. But it would certainly not tell him if the extract were truly of Blueberry because generally all tannins (from whatever source) would give a similar colour.

Chromatography

The second technique, which has been known for about 30 years but only recently applied to the study of plant extracts, is called chromatography. This enables very small quantities of material to be examined and separated into individual components. Several techniques are available but essentially all involve placing a small amount of the sample on a sheet of paper or glass plate covered with a suitable adsorbent. The paper or plate is then placed in a tank which contains a solvent. This solvent gradually rises up the support by capillary attraction and as it does so the individual components of the mixture applied to the bottom of the plate move as well, but at different rates depending on their affinity for the solvent and the adsorbent. When the solvent reaches the top of the plate, the plate is removed and dried. Coloured compounds are visible directly, but the plate is usually sprayed with a detecting reagent which reacts with colourless compounds to give coloured spots. The pattern of spots produced by this technique is characteristic for a particular plant extract under a particular set of operating conditions. Although the compounds which give rise to the spots may not be those which are actually responsible for the pharmacological activity of the plant, the pattern of spots produced is none the less characteristic and if these patterns are compared with those produced by an authentic specimen, obtained under identical conditions, reasonably certain identification may be made. Extra evidence may be obtained by comparing the patterns made using different chromatography solvents.

By this technique small differences in biochemical make-up of plants may be detected and this is important both from the quantitative and qualitative points of view – the amount of extract of a certain plant which is low in active ingredient required for a particular pharmacological effect may be very different from the quantity of extract required from an apparently identical plant which contains a high concentration of active material. Such variations could lead to serious overdoses. Only chemical examination would show these differences. Qualitative differences will also be shown up by chromatography. The chemical assessment of a herb must take into account crucial variables such as the habitat, time of collection and the fact that plants of the same species can have completely different active constituents.

Vierdt Theyl
Cornelbaum. Cap. vij.
Welschkirsen.
Natur oder Complexion.
Von Bäumen vnd Stauden.
LXXVIII
Krafft vnd Wirckung.
Pfersingbaum. Cap. viij.
Natur oder Complexion.
Krafft vnd Wirckung.

The medicinal uses of plants

Until the last 150 years crude plant use has been central to medicine and there is little doubt that herbs are man's most ancient therapeutic aids. We are still heavily dependent on plants in the western world as sources of starting materials for semi-synthetic drugs or as the drugs themselves. Because there are still many conditions we are unable to treat significantly, and because synthetic drugs sometimes cause side-effects, there is a growing tendency to reconsider the traditional systems of healing as alternative medical treatment, and one such system is herbalism.

Herbalism is now understood to be a collection of different methods for using plants in healing: some of these methods use poisonous plants, some do not; some employ mixtures of herbs, others believe in the success of 'simples' or individual plants; others combine different forms of treatment with a healing régime using plants. This situation is reflected in the names given to the various approaches to herbalism – such as eclectic medicine, physiomedicalism, botanic medicine, plant healing, medical herbalism, phytotherapy and flower remedies. Their common denominator, however, is their derivation from the beliefs of folklore and origin in the observations of ordinary people.

*Left: Lonitzer's 'Kreuterbuch', a German herbal published in the sixteenth century, appeared in various editions until 1783. The left-hand page shows the Spindle tree (*Euonymus*), whose berries were once used as a purgative.*

Because plants were so central to medicine throughout history they acquired many of the beliefs of folklore, which sometimes had nothing to do with the intrinsic therapeutic qualities of plants, and in order to re-evaluate the efficacy of herbs, we must, therefore, consider the development of a medicinal plant's usage together with the influence of folklore on that use. All medical folklore converges on a common belief that illness and disease are the result of supernatural spirits, and hence from the earliest times medicine and religion have been closely associated. As soon as primitive societies developed, the man who became the priest also became the magician and medicine man and he started to employ a limited range of therapeutic methods which included predominantly herb-lore and suggestion (psychotherapy). The combination was an important one, and was effective for as long as mankind associated disease with the unknown. Indeed, the success of suggestive methods of treatment is shown to this day in the efficacy of placebos.

In these early days many of the most important plants used were those which acted on the mind – the so-called hallucinogens or narcotics, which temporarily relieved pain and which in combination with the suggestion of medico-religious ritual were probably of material benefit. Numbers assumed an importance which was initially derived from the astrological beliefs of the Babylonians. Seven and nine were believed to be especially powerful; thus plants which carried the sign of these numbers were thought to be particularly

Left: Alchemilla mollis *readily seeds itself and is used only as a decorative plant. Other* Alchemilla *species are of medicinal importance and of these none had a greater reputation than Lady's Mantle (*Alchemilla vulgaris*). It was once used to treat painful menstruation, and in veterinary medicine.*

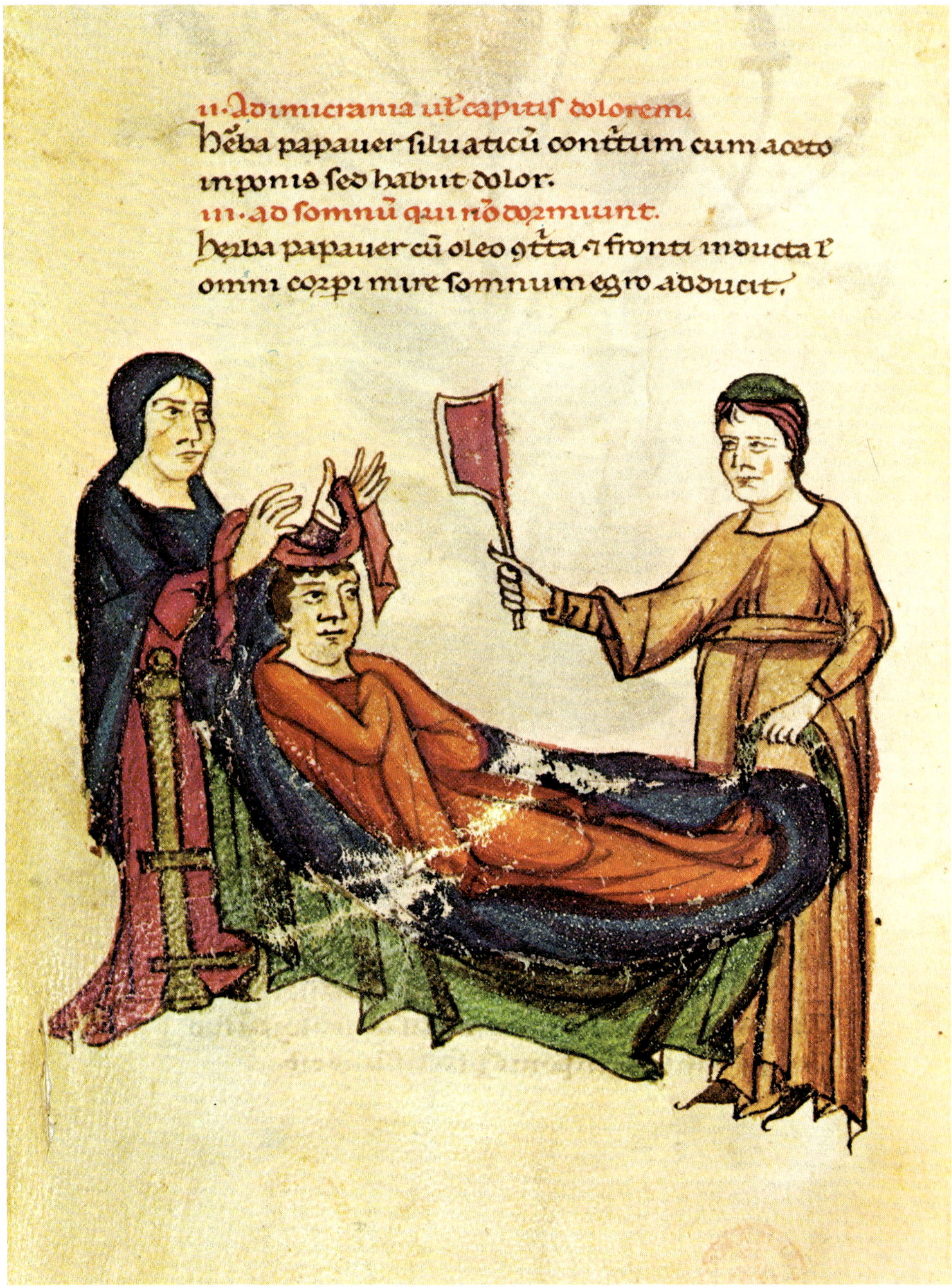

Below: An illustration of early surgery from the anonymous thirteenth-century Pseudo-Apuleius herbal, in which the use of 'herba papauer' or the Opium Poppy is described. Several herbs with the ability to lessen pain were known to early surgeons, and of these the Opium Poppy and the Mandrake were undoubtedly the most important.

beneficial. Lady's Mantle with its nine lobes on the leaves is one such plant with numerical power; alternatively, plants with seven or nine roots or berries or seeds would be prescribed.

These and many similar folklore beliefs must have already become associated with plants by the time the Egyptian physicians began to formulate their healing remedies because it was probably the Egyptians who began the orthodox rejection of magic in medicine. It is evident that by 1550 B.C. the orthodox physicians had begun to specialize, for it seems that the Egyptian doctors then restricted their treatment to one disease or one part of the body. Thus there arose the two levels of healing which have continued through the ages to the present day – those we now call orthodox, which initially represented the efforts by physicians to introduce logic and experimentation into medical practice, and unorthodox, which represented a continuation of very old, traditional and often magical beliefs, but which until two centuries ago largely represented the medical treatment available to rich and poor respectively.

Whether the unorthodox medicine of the Egyptians was conducted by the herb women who characterized so much of later history we do not know. But we do know that much of the knowledge of Egyptian medicine was passed on to the Greeks – Hippocrates (460–377 B.C.) learned much from their works – and that the close association between medicine and religion was continued by the Greek physician priests. Hippocrates, however, began the process of careful observation which characterized the birth of science, and he laid down the laws which deemed him the 'father of medicine' and which founded modern medicine. Information had largely been localized to this point but one of the first important movements of medicinal plant knowledge began with the establishment of Alexandria in 331 B.C. and with it the Alexandrian School.

This signalled the introduction of Greek medicine into Egypt, Mesopotamia and Syria, and ultimately it led to the fusion between Arabic, Graeco-Alexandrian and Oriental medicine that emerged in Europe at the end of the dark ages.

It was in Alexandria that the best recorded experiments with poisons were conducted, and there Mithridates in the second century B.C. formulated both poisons and antidotes which remained famous as the 'theriacs' and 'mithridates' of succeeding centuries.

The works of Mithridates and all before

him were distilled into four books dealing with the 600 best known plants by the greatest figure in the history of herbalism, Pedacius Dioscorides. Following the collapse of Corinth in 146 B.C. Greek physicians moved to Rome, and from there as an army surgeon under Nero (54–68 A.D.) Dioscorides travelled widely and described the herbs he saw in use in what was the first 'materia medica' or 'pharmacopoeia'. Without doubt he was the first real medical botanist, and his work was for 1500 years the standard reference for the medical application of plants.

Galen (A.D. 131–201) – whose name gave rise to the term galenical, meaning botanical drug – also had enormous influence until the seventeenth century, but Galen was a physician, and his major contribution to plant therapy was the introduction of a system of 'polypharmacy' or mixing herbal preparations to treat specific conditions; some forms of herbalism still retain this type of therapy.

Following Galen and Dioscorides, and the decline and fall of the Roman Empire, European medicine entered a stagnant period which was to last several hundred years. To a large extent the moral ethics of physicians were replaced with greed, envy and quackery, and the old incantation and magic of previous ages resurrected.

Folklore rose to the surface again, and individuals either treated themselves with family recipes, visited travelling bone-setters and herb women, or were helped by those in religious orders. Even the medical work of monks, however, was stopped by the Papal decrees which were issued regularly for a century, from that of Clermont council (1130) to the council of Le Mans (1247). In early Germany medicine fell largely into the hands of 'wise women' or 'wild women' who employed herbal remedies, magic and amulets, and to the lêkeis who were the equivalent of the Anglo-Saxon leech-men.

In Russia the position was similar with the 'wolf-men' or volkhava employing herbs and spells, while the Celtic order of Druids and Druidesses did likewise. The Druids favoured seven magic herbs of which the Mistletoe held pride of place.

In the dark ages, however, between the ninth and twelfth centuries, Arabic medicine rose on the tide of Mohammedanism, and physicians of the standing of Rhazes, Haly ben Abbas and Avicenna, and the Jewish physician Avenzoar, combined the previous Greek work with their own observations and studies of botanical drugs and pharmacology. Much of this work was recorded in the thirteenth-century compilation of Ibn Baitar whose materia medica described 1400 drugs.

The proximity of Arabia to the East led Arabian pharmacists (or sandalani) to the study of a wide range of plants and plant products which became of immense importance to later European medicine; they developed the use of Cassia, Senna, Rhubarb, Camphor, Myrrh, Cloves, and used the flavouring ability of rose-water, orange and lemon peel and other aromatics to mask unpleasant tastes in medication.

Before the advent of printing in the mid-fifteenth century there had already begun the internal wrangling in the medical profession – to be exacerbated by the printed word – which continued until the late nineteenth century. Initially this concerned the relative status of surgeons and barbers; the latter being increasingly persecuted by the surgeons who tried to prevent them from treating wounds. In England in 1368 the Master Surgeons formed a separate guild, and in 1421 joined forces temporarily with the Physicians, although even these two bodies treated each other with suspicion. This move forced the barbers to obtain a separate charter (1462) and led to the beginning of barber-surgery or surgery of the common people. Similar events took place in France and Germany. Under

Above: An Arch Druid in full judicial costume. The Druids had an excellent knowledge of the medicinal application of local herbs, and considered some to possess magical qualities. Of all plants, the Mistletoe held pride of place.

Henry VIII's act of 1511 English physicians and surgeons became the only licensed practitioners, and all others were excluded from practising medicine, but by 1542 the greed shown by the profession caused another act to be passed to allow those common people having knowledge of herbal and folk medicine to minister to the poor.

Below: The sumptuous interior of a sixteenth-century apothecary. As some apothecaries charged very high prices, people sought the services of herbalists.

While herbal traditions based on folklore continued, the effect of printing was to mark the beginning of the Renaissance and the continuation of the scientific method started by Dioscorides. The sixteenth century was marked by the emergence of both 'proto-botany' books and herbals, although the herbal did not reach its peak in England until 1633 when Thomas Johnson improved and enlarged the herbal of John Gerard, itself mostly derived from a translation of Dodoens. This period also saw the beginning of printed works devoted to those substances employed by apothecaries; the 'materia medicas', pharmacopoeias and dispensatories (the first edition of the London Pharmacopoeia, for example, appeared in 1618).

Apothecaries were originally drug and herb traders, who managed to develop a special relationship with the medical fraternity. In England they had been associated from 1378 with the Grocers' Company who also sold herbs and drugs, and who were the original drug vendors. Both the grocers and apothecaries purchased herbs and roots collected from the

countryside, and they also imported drugs and spices from abroad. The apothecaries frequently established their own physic gardens and thus served as a link between horticulture and medicine by growing their own medicinal herbs. The Worshipful Society of Apothecaries of London was incorporated in 1617 and the apothecaries soon began to diagnose and prescribe without associating with a physician. They continued to do so until 1886 when medical registration was finally only granted to those candidates qualifying by examination in surgery, medicine, and pharmacy.

By the middle of the seventeenth century therefore, herbs were being used in many different ways by physicians, apothecaries, manufacturers of proprietary medicines and a host of traditional country herbalists and town quacks. During the eighteenth and early nineteenth centuries, although herbs continued to play an important role in medicine, their importance slowly declined. The botanic writers who amassed details of plant use included information from a host of sources – the Greeks, the Arabs, folklore, early botany, and information received by the grocers or apothecaries from foreign lands. In some cases the identity of plants mentioned was uncertain, and while the real advances of medicine such as anatomy, physiology and clinical diagnosis were progressing, plant-lore became increasingly confused with an assortment of chemical compounds, mixtures, electrical and magnetic treatment, and blind faith in tradition.

By the beginning of the nineteenth century scientific investigation was growing apace, and with it came the realization that specific effects could be demonstrated when particular, isolated or purified substances were applied to living systems. This study, known as pharmacology, owes much to the work and inspiration of Justus von Liebig (1803–1873), the father of physiological chemistry, who introduced the concept of 'metabolism', and carried forward the development of organic chemistry which had already produced such important isolated substances as morphine (1806) from the Opium Poppy, strychnine (1818) from *Strychnos nux-vomica* and quinine (1820) from Cinchona bark.

This approach is the modern rationale to medical therapeutics: the effect of specific substances on specific cells, and in the excitement of the nineteenth-century development of organic chemistry the orthodox practitioner was as eager as the research worker to move away from crude plants to the more 'exact', isolated chemical. Notable exceptions to this in the West were the introduction of homeopathy by Samuel Hahnemann (1755–1843) and the work of American physicians of the early nineteenth century known as physiomedicalism, a branch of herbalism. Homeopathy is a system of healing based on the supposition that infinitesimally small quantities of a given substance, such as a medicinal plant, will cure a condition in which symptoms exist that would be identical to the symptoms produced in a healthy person who is given large quantities of the same substance.

Many American doctors had an open approach to medicine which was unfettered by the historical trappings of their colleagues in the Old World; certainly the early settlers took with them their traditional remedies when they left Europe, but they soon adapted to the rigours of their new life by adopting some of the remedies of the North American Indians. All these remedies were in continuous use by an oral culture, rather than a culture which depended upon written (and, therefore, often erroneous) records, and were therefore found to be reliable. This led to many reliable drugs being incorporated into the first American materia medicas and dispensatories.

One group of physicians, led by Samuel Thompson, decided not to interest themselves in the isolation of active ingredients of plants, as was being done elsewhere in America and Europe, but simply to administer tinctures of the whole plant, a system which became known as the physiomedical concept, and which was concerned with assisting the natural power of tissue regeneration which the body possesses. Schools specializing in physiomedicalism flourished for a while, mainly in Chicago, but by the beginning of the twentieth century their influence declined and this concept is now only retained in some forms of unorthodox herbalism.

Herbalism as a system of healing exists today in name only as there are various approaches which range from the use of all types of plant material to the use of non-poisonous herbs only. In the West the orthodox employment of medicinal plants is largely restricted to those with strong

Left: The less opulent interior of the Swiss rural pharmacy of Michael Schuppart, an eighteenth-century apothecary. He is examining the urine of the patient who is sitting in front of him.

Right: The Opium Poppy (Papaver somniferum). *The latex, which is obtained by excision of the immature capsules, contains 25 different alkaloids of which morphine – indispensable to modern medicine – is the strongest pain reliever (analgesic).*

pharmacological action, such as Opium Poppy, Foxglove and their derivatives. The great dependence of Third World nations on traditional plant use has, however, recently stimulated the beginnings of a modern medical appraisal of herbs, and it is possible that future scientific reassessment will lead to the wider orthodox utilization of ancient herbal remedies and the discovery of new ones.

MYTHS AND TRADITIONS

Many magical and religious ideas associated with plants have survived almost unaltered to the present day. In Crete the fat onion-like bulbs of the Sea Squill (*Urginea maritima*) are hung up by farmers at the entrances to their vineyards to protect the ripening grapes from harmful influences, a superstition which seems pointless but which is explained by tracing the Squill back to the days when it was sacred to the god Pan who protected mortals from evil spirits. Similarly, in some parts of central Europe villagers still plant the succulent Houseleek (*Sempervivum tectorum*) on the roof tiles to prevent their houses from being struck by lightning. The Romans called it *Iovis caulis* or Jupiter's plant because they believed Zeus or Jupiter had given it to man to protect his property from the destructive bolt of lightning he wielded.

Some plants were carried on the person for the benefit of their protective qualities. A leaf of Betony (*Stachys officinalis*) carried in the pocket or purse was said to offer protection from witchcraft. A sprig of Mugwort (*Artemisia vulgaris*) worn inside the shoe was thought to prevent a traveller from becoming tired, an old practice which, surprisingly, persisted in East Anglia until the beginning of this century. In southern Europe walking-sticks cut from the boughs of the Chaste tree (*Vitex agnus-castus*) were carried by pilgrims because they believed they were magical and could protect them from both robbers and the bites of venomous creatures.

These primitive beliefs in the talismanic qualities of plants are, however, by no means confined to the ancient cultures of the world; they abound today in Third World countries, and you can still be stopped in the heart of London by gypsies hawking sprigs of 'lucky heather'.

In ancient times, and even today in some parts of the world, many of these plants were thought not only to protect man from the dangers of the outside world, but also to preserve him from disease and ill health, so it was considered logical to wear a magical plant with protective properties or better still to drink an infusion of it.

The Houseleek, which was believed to protect the thatched roofs of medieval houses from fire from the sky, was also considered to be effective against fire in the body – medicine in the Middle Ages still classified diseases into hot and cold, wet and dry. So William Salmon, writing on the medicinal virtues of the Houseleek as late as the end of the seventeenth century was able to say – 'Herba iova is Glutinative and Segnotick; it quenches thirst, allays heat, stops fluxes and abates the violence of cholerick Fevers, being given in a spoonful or two of Wine, or the juice mixt with Sugar. Outwardly in a Balsam it cures burns, scalds, shingles, pains of the gout, creeping ulcers and hot inflammations.'

All these therapeutic indications are concerned with 'heat' in some form or other, and the example demonstrates vividly how the magical 'primary' use of the plant dictated its 'secondary' or medical use. We now know that the Houseleek's principal active constituents are tannins, malic acid and mucilages, and while they may have some minor effect in treating superficial burns and diarrhoea they are completely ineffective in shingles, gout and fevers.

The history of medical botany or herbalism is full of myths and false ideas, and this is partly due to the fact that early writers on the subject received their information by hearsay or accepted without criticism what they read in the works of other authors. This early attitude led to the publication of a large number of accounts of plants which did not even exist, such as the 'Scythian Lambe' described by John Parkinson, and the 'Fountain tree of water' which Lewis Jackson maintained grew on the Canary Islands. There was even thought to be a 'Barnacle tree' that bore fruit which eventually hatched into live geese. Of the plants which did actually exist, many were attributed with medicinal properties because of their association in previous ages with a god or goddess who governed a particular disease. One of the best examples is the common Myrtle (*Myrtus communis*).

Myrtle was known to the Greeks as 'myrsini' and was sacred to the goddess Aphrodite (who was also known as Myrsini), the goddess of fertility, simply because the pointed elliptical leaves of this plant closely resembled the shape of the female genitalia. As a result of this association the Myrtle was chiefly employed in Greek medicine as a herb for treating female complaints – a practice which was not discredited until the nineteenth century.

Another medicinal plant which earned its reputation by association with the Greek gods was the Black Hellebore (*Helleborus niger*), a plant sacred to the 'kthonoi' or gods of the underworld. These deities, whose number included cave spirits and the souls of the dead and deified physicians, belonged to an older and darker cult than the celestial Olympian deities. It was believed that they possessed the power to inflict enormous suffering on mankind in the form of disease and madness. Black Hellebore, which became linked with their worship, was considered to be the specific remedy for the diseases for which they were held responsible, and the root was used for treating epilepsy, melancholia, hysteria and other neurological disorders. In Shakespeare's time and beyond it continued to be used for 'the falling sicknesses' (epilepsy), 'all melancholicke diseases' and 'convulsions', besides being employed as a poison, an abortive and a local anaesthetic. Modern examination, however, has suggested that Black Hellebore does assist in the general neurological conditions for which the Greeks employed it, and today a homeopathic tincture is prepared from the rhizome and used to treat epilepsy, certain psychoses, eclampsia (convulsion associated with pregnancy), meningitis and encephalitis.

After a period in which herbal medicine was regarded with the greatest suspicion by the medical profession, many of the claims of herbalism are now being substantiated by scientific observation and reinstated.

THE INTAKE AND ACTIONS OF MEDICINAL PLANTS

Plants are very complicated structures composed of millions of cells many performing extremely specialized functions and each contributing to the existence of the organism as a whole. Organisms are 'alive' because of the many chemical reactions which are carried out in each of these cells; thus life is essentially a series of highly controlled chemical changes which consist of building up (anabolism) or breaking down (catabolism) processes (collectively known as metabolism); these changes are initiated by chemical catalysts. All these reactions are under the direct influence of the genetic material found in the nucleus of each cell.

Animals, including man, are very similar to plants in this respect, the fundamental difference between the two groups being in the way in which they obtain their food. Plants build up their own food from small molecules whereas animals take in large molecules and break them down. All materials ingested by the animal are treated in exactly the same general way: the food is digested in the gastro-intestinal tract, the small molecules so formed are absorbed through the gut wall and transported via the blood to other parts of the body where they are used to build up new enzymes or cell material or act as essential catalysts in these reactions. Certain foodstuffs contain ingredients such as minerals and vitamins which are essential for some enzymic process to occur. A deficiency of these in our diet is likely to lead to an impairment in some of our basic metabolic functions, just as mineral deficiencies in plants lead to visible abnormal symptoms such as spots and yellowing.

The digestive and transportation processes described above are not capable of discriminating between materials which find their way into the gut from different sources. Thus certain plants are 'good' foodstuffs because they are rich in starch or protein and some plants are 'toxic' because they contain substances which after absorption enter certain biochemical

*Above: The evergreen Myrtle (*Myrtus communis*) is now of little importance, but it was once sacred to the Greek goddess Aphrodite. In the Middle Ages Myrtle berries were used as a condiment, like pepper. It was also used in the treatment of female complaints.*

*Below: The Christmas Rose or Black Hellebore (*Helleborus niger*) contains powerful substances which act on the heart rather like Digitalis. These make the plant much too strong for modern herbal use.*

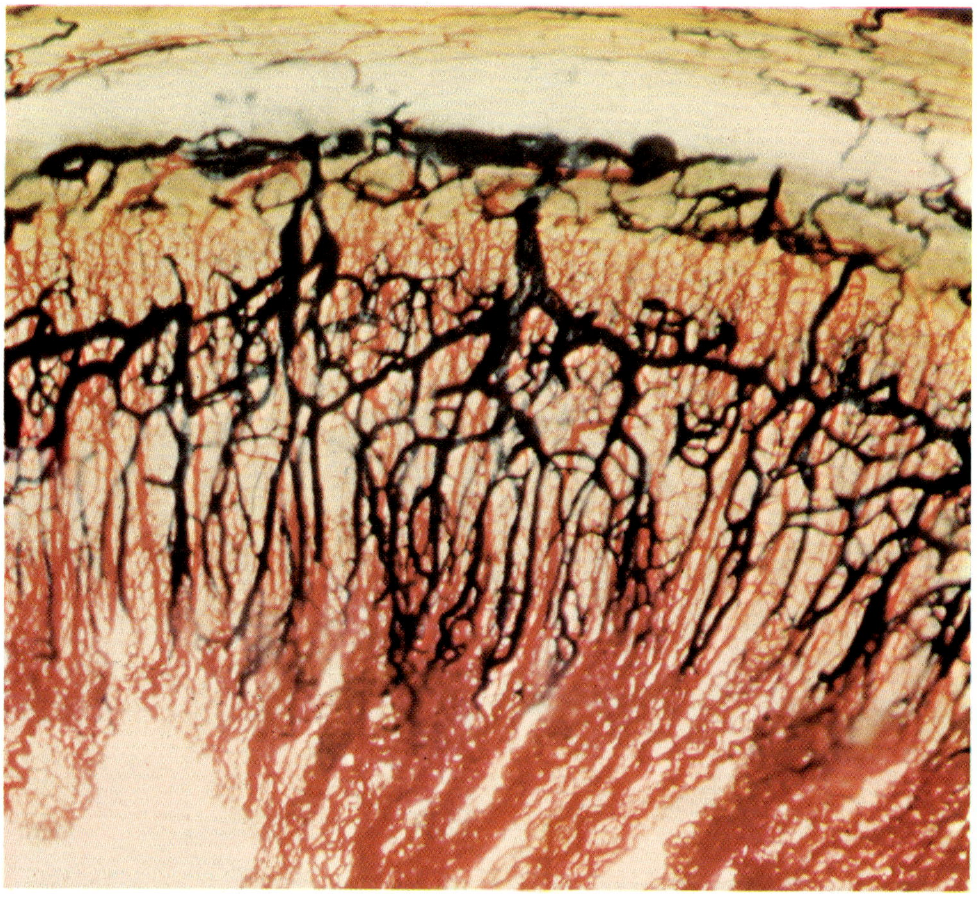

Right: A magnified section through the wall of the small intestine showing the folded mucous membrane (top, pink) through which food and drugs are absorbed. The rate of absorption depends on the nature of the food or drug molecule and on the other substances present in the tract.

processes and disrupt them. Similarly the plants which are medicinally useful contain materials which act in some beneficial way on the fundamental processes in animal cells, either by promoting certain reactions or inhibiting other processes which may be abnormal. The practice of medicine with herbal products in this respect is in no fundamental chemical way different from treatment with synthetic drugs. Both act by the introduction of a foreign molecule into the body (sometimes at a more or less specific site) so that it may exert its effect. The concept of herbalism does, of course, differ theoretically from the orthodox in that herbal medicine attempts to treat the patient as a whole, rather than the condition in isolation.

Pharmacology

Pharmacology is the study of the manner in which the functions of living organisms can be modified by chemical substances. Since living cells are very complex, many of the factors which control their activities are completely unknown. For this reason a new science, pharmacokinetics, has been developed to study the factors affecting the absorption, distribution and eventual elimination of drugs from the body and it largely employs mathematical models.

A theory which has been advanced from simple experimental evidence and has found considerable success in explaining why drugs exert their effects is the receptor theory. It was proposed originally by Paul Ehrlich who believed that mammalian cells possessed side chains which contained receptors (reactive chemical groupings) which combine with another active group on the drug molecule (in a more or less reversible way) to cause the drug effect. This proposal was a great advance and much modern research is based on a modified form of the theory. Simply, drugs can be considered as precisely cut keys, and the receptors on the cells as locks which may be opened only by the appropriate keys. When the key turns the lock (that is when the drug reaches and combines with the receptor on the cell) processes are initiated which cause chemical changes and so induce the drug to exert its effect on the cell, and hence on the body. This goes a long way to explaining the highly specific nature of some drug actions, as well as why some compounds possess powerful, often dangerous, side-effects, since some drugs may by chance interact with more than one type of receptor.

Routes of drug administration

The oral route is the one most frequently used because it is cheap, easy and convenient and the patient can administer himself tablets which can be manufactured to contain an exact dose. However, if the medicine is in the form of a liquid or powder, and most herbal preparations are, the dosage is likely to be inaccurate. The drug will also be diluted by the contents of the stomach and intestine. Since the stomach juices are strongly acid and those in the intestine alkaline this may lead to decomposition of the active ingredients. Absorption through the gastro-intestinal tract may be slow or irregular due to the presence of the partly digested or undigested food, thus delaying the effect.

Some materials are given as suppositories and the active ingredients are absorbed through the delicate lining (mucous membrane) of the rectum. This may be particularly useful for giving substances which would cause vomiting if given orally, or which would decompose in the acid stomach juices. Other routes which involve passage of active materials through a mucosal layer are those via the vagina or urethra. Drugs may also be administered by slowly dissolving a lozenge under the tongue (sublingually) or as snuffs (whereby absorption is effected through the nasal mucosa).

When a local effect is required application is made to the surface of the skin in the form of a cream, paste, ointment, lotion or liniment. In these cases some absorption may occur by penetration through to the subcutaneous tissues. Sterile solutions may, of course, be injected directly into the bloodstream which removes the initial absorption step.

The rate and efficiency of absorption of a material from the gut is largely dependent on its chemical nature but also on the method of formulation (how it is presented for administration). The most obvious factor is the solubility of the substance in the gastro-intestinal contents. No substances can be absorbed from the fluid in the gut unless they are soluble in the first place. Secondly, the barriers to the passage of drugs (that is the intestinal cell walls) consist largely of fatty substances, hence drugs which dissolve well in fats are absorbed more rapidly and completely than those which do not. There are some exceptions to this and these depend on the existence of a specific transport mechanism for a particular type of chemical. In addition, some drug molecules contain acidic or basic groupings which may be ionized (electrically charged) in aqueous solution. Since only non-ionized or electrically neutral molecules are fat-soluble, absorption is also governed to some extent by this factor.

Finally, the presence of substances in whole plants other than the active ingredients may considerably modify not only the physiological effect of the active substances themselves but also their solubility and hence absorption.

The active materials, once absorbed, are transported throughout the body via the blood and the compounds that permeate freely through cell membranes become more or less evenly distributed in all parts of the body. Some, however, tend to concentrate at particular sites. Compounds are often bound to carrier molecules – for example, proteins in the blood plasma – or become strongly attached to specific binding sites in tissues. Where such active transport processes exist, the ordinary physico-chemical principles no longer apply. One particularly effective mechanism is known as the blood-brain barrier which prevents the passage of most molecules from the bloodstream into the central nervous system and the cerebro-spinal fluid.

Metabolism

When a drug enters the body, it is acted upon by enzymes which usually change its chemical structure into substances which have less effect (pharmacological activity) on the body. This is why the effects of drugs wear off gradually. These enzymatic reactions are known as detoxification processes, and the most important organ concerned is the liver.

This does not always happen, however. Pharmacologically active metabolites (products that have been produced by the breakdown of the drug) may be formed from an inactive substance (a precursor or 'pro-drug'), or sometimes the metabolites may have a type of activity which differs from that of the 'active' ingredient in the drug originally administered. The principal route of excretion of drugs and their detoxified metabolites is the urine. This may be facilitated by metabolic changes in as much as the detoxification reactions generally produce compounds which are more soluble in water (hence in urine) than in fat. Alternatively, drugs may be excreted into the intestinal tract via the bile and so eliminated in the faeces. Minor routes of elimination include the lungs, saliva, tears, sweat and milk.

It will now be apparent that when one takes a dose of herbal medicine many processes intervene before and after the drug exerts its effect. Not only the active ingredients but also the 'ballast' substances which may exert a modifying effect on the 'active' substances have first to be made soluble, then absorbed and distributed (perhaps via an active binding process) throughout the whole body, to reach their active site (receptor) before they can produce an action. Later they are usually metabolized to inactive substances and then excreted.

Biological variation

Repeated measurements of the same quantity do not always give identical results. While this may be due to variations in accuracy, with living systems it is more likely to be the result of biological variation – by its very nature biological material is variable. This produces problems in the quantitative biological evaluation of all medicines, and these difficulties are particularly severe in the case of medicinal plants and their extracts. Medicinal plants are usually administered as tinctures of the whole plant, which will consist of solutions in dilute alcohol of many different chemical substances, only some of which are active pharmacologically. Not only may the presence of the so-called inactive substances modify the absorption of the active ones (mixtures are in general more soluble than pure compounds), but they may actually modify the pharmacological activity of the active ingredients, either in a potentiating way or oppositely as retardants. The former is known as the synergistic effect or synergism.

The modifying substances need not necessarily come from the same plant. It is sometimes found that the effect of one particular plant extract is considerably altered by the presence of greater or smaller amounts of extracts of other plants. This is of paramount importance in herbal medicine where combination therapy, often quite complex, is the rule rather than the exception. This is the fundamental difference between herbal and orthodox medicine. Whereas the latter is often symptomatic in approach, the former essentially treats the patient as a whole rather than as a collection of isolated conditions. Hence preparations containing several different plant extracts are administered with the intention that each component will exert its own specific effect which will produce an overall combined effect. One of the problems of this herbal combination therapy is that haphazard administration of different plant extracts can produce undesired effects. For this reason orthodox medical authorities sometimes consider such herbal practices as unscientific and inexact.

Above: Magnification of secretory cells of the stomach, which secrete the fluid which helps digestion.

Evaluating herbal medicines

In recent attempts at the scientific evaluation of this approach it has been realized that some of the compounds present in minute concentration in plants – often so low as to be undetectable by standard techniques – may themselves by extremely potent pharmacological agents. This phenomenon is often referred to as the effect of ballast material.

It must be emphasized that everything ingested by the body can be considered as a drug. This is an easy concept to accept when an active material exerts a pronounced, readily observable pharmacological effect on the body such as producing anaesthesia, but some compounds may act in a more subtle way, for example, by promoting efficient working of certain enzymes or by encouraging the development of a good immunological defence system. Plants producing these effects belong to the group about which we currently know least: traditionally they were the panaceas or tonics – Ginseng being the best-known example. Today they are known as adaptogens.

All these problems have led to great difficulty in deciding how herbal preparations should be examined, tested and standardized and this has contributed to the current scepticism about the efficacy of the herbal approach. When these difficulties have been overcome this scepticism will undoubtedly decline and some aspects of plant medication will assume an even more important role in medicine.

Having described briefly the uptake and actions of herbs, four groups of diseases, including their physiology and their treatment with medicinal plants, are now examined. The plants mentioned have found use both in orthodox and herbal methods and no distinction is made between them – the examples simply emphasize the importance of plants in medicine as a whole.

DISEASES OF THE HEART AND CIRCULATION

The cardiovascular system is concerned with the circulation of blood. It consists essentially of a pump, the heart, and a system of tubes, the arteries, veins and capillaries – comprising the blood vessels. Circulation involves two joined systems: one in which blood passes from the heart to the lungs where it is oxygenated, and then back to the heart; and another in which this oxygen-rich blood is pumped to the furthest parts of the body, gives up some of its oxygen to the tissue's cells, and then returns to the heart.

Besides oxygen, which all tissues need for certain of their biochemical reactions, the blood carries foodstuffs absorbed from the alimentary tract, and is also responsible for carrying the waste products of metabolism to sites of excretion, such as the kidneys.

The treatment of disorders

Cardiovascular diseases are concerned with disorders of the heart and blood vessels. The commonest disorder of the blood vessels is *arteriosclerosis* (resulting in narrowing of the arteries), the commonest site being the blood vessels supplying the heart (coronary arteries). This leads to a reduced oxygen supply for the action of the heart, especially during exercise, resulting in chest pain (*angina pectoris*). The coronary blood supply is sometimes so drastically obstructed that a portion of the heart wall dies, and this is known as *heart attack*. Another common disorder is *hypertension*, in which the blood pressure is abnormally raised, causing excessive strain on the heart, rupture of cerebral (brain) blood vessels causing a stroke, and damage to the kidneys.

Both coronary artery disease (of which arteriosclerosis is one) and hypertension may cause *heart failure:* this is when the pumping action of the heart is unable to cope with the work load; this results in shortness of breath, tiredness, and retention of salt and water (causing ankle swelling, for example) due to a reduced blood-flow to the kidneys. Other causes of heart failure include rheumatic fever, congenital defects, diseases of the valves (which separate the chambers of the heart), infections and chronic respiratory disease.

The treatment of heart failure includes oxygen, cardiotonic substances (which improve the function of the heart) and diuretics (substances which cause an increased excretion of salt and water by the kidneys). The leaf of the Foxglove (*Digitalis purpurea*) is an effective cardiotonic for the treatment of heart failure and millions of people throughout the world are still treated with this material today (or its derivatives). The active principles of the Foxglove are complex steroidal substances known as cardiotonic glycosides or cardenolides. Many very closely

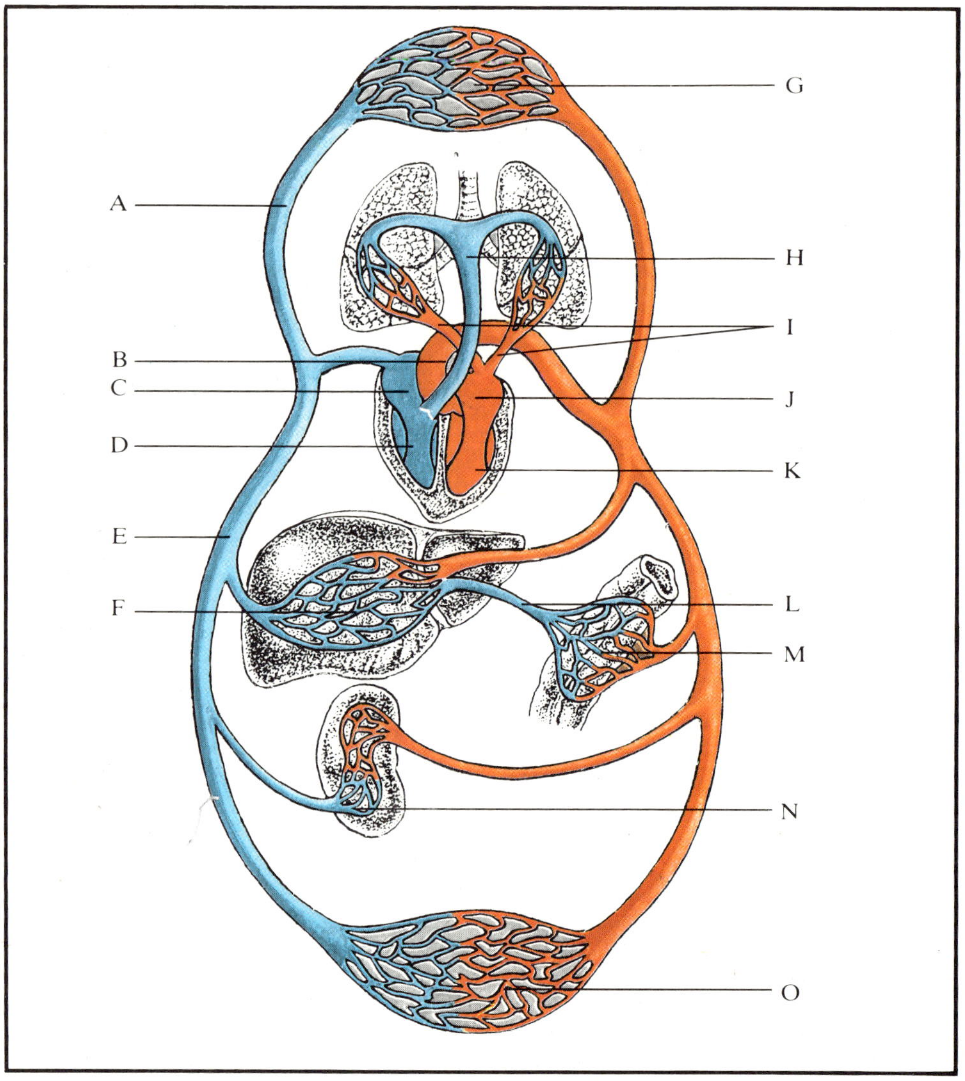

Left: Diagrammatic representation of the cardiovascular system:
A Superior vena cava
B Aorta C Right atrium
D Right ventricle E Inferior vena cava
F Blood exchange in the liver
G Blood supply within the upper part of the body especially the brain
H Pulmonary vein
I Pulmonary arteries
J Left atrium
K Left ventricle L Portal vein
M Blood exchange in the intestine
N Blood exchange within the kidneys and
O within the lower parts of the body.
Areas of blood exchange consist of arterioles and venules which meet at the smallest subdivisions or capillaries.

related compounds of this type are present in the plant and some of these have a pronounced strengthening effect on the failing heart. They bind to heart muscle and increase the force of contraction of the heart at each beat without increasing its need for oxygen; the heart thus pumps more efficiently.

The need for cardiotonic substances is enormous and much modern research is concerned with the chemical modification of these active molecules in order to produce better drugs. The major glycosides of *Digitalis purpurea* (digitoxin) and of *D. lanata* (digoxin) are often isolated from the dried leaves by complex and costly chemical procedures to enable administration to the patient in the form of tablets, but better results, however, are sometimes obtained by treatment with the whole powdered leaf. It is found that the combined effect of the highly active glycosides together with the less potent compounds found in the crude drug may provide therapy which is less harsh, more easily controlled, and therefore safer than the use of isolated active compounds alone. Another explanation may be that certain compounds present in the leaf in minute concentration may completely alter the physiological effect of the glycosides – this is a good example of synergism.

*Below: The Woolly Foxglove (*Digitalis lanata*) which contains 63 different steroidal glycosides. The most important of these substances is digoxin, often used in modern medicine to treat heart failure.*

A major problem with Foxglove therapy is that the therapeutic dose (the dose required to produce the desired effect) is almost as high as the toxic dose (the dose at which undesirable and sometimes dangerous side-effects occur). This may be overcome to some extent by the use of the whole dried leaf, as mentioned above.

Similar cardiotonic activity is found in the closely related *D.lanata* and the Yellow Foxglove, *D.lutea*. Hedge Hyssop (*Gratiola officinalis*) which belongs to the same family as the Foxgloves, the Scrophulariaceae, has also been shown to possess cardiotonic action, but it is considered too toxic to use medically. Almost identical compounds are present in certain Apocynaceae (including members of the genera *Strophanthus*, *Nerium*, and *Acokanthera*), which possesses more genera containing cardiac glycosides than any other so far studied. Similar compounds have been identified in members of the Ranunculaceae, the Nymphaeaceae, the Celastraceae and the Bignoniaceae.

Digitalis glycoside-like active principles are also found in the morphologically far removed monocotyledonous families, the Liliaceae and Cactaceae. *Convallaria majalis*, of the Liliaceae Family, is in fact the most powerful of all the cardiac glycoside-containing plants growing in temperate zones, and has an important place in both the folk and orthodox medical treatment of arrhythmia (lack of a regular heart beat), especially in eastern Europe.

In exactly the same way that the Foxglove glycosides promote regular beating of the heart so does quinidine – an alkaloid isomeric with quinine, the antimalarial substance from the same source, the bark of the Cinchona tree. This discovery was made quite by chance when it was noticed that patients being treated with Cinchona bark for malaria were free from arrhythmias.

As well as cardiotonic agents, diuretics are essential in the treatment of heart failure and a very large number of medicinal plants possess some diuretic action. Although this is often not very powerful there are several herbs, notably those with certain volatile oil contents, which are effective in diuresis. The ripe fruit of Juniper (*Juniperus communis*), for example, contains up to two per cent of a volatile oil plus resins and a bitter principle which, together, act directly on the kidneys. Juniper, however, is too powerful to be used when the kidneys are inflamed, and it can in this case be replaced with Buchu leaves (*Agathosma betulina*) which contains volatile oil and diosphenol, Wild Carrot (*Daucus carota*) which contains both volatile oil and an alkaloid, daucine, or Dandelion (*Taraxacum officinale*) which possesses several active substances that make it one of the most effective of all plant diuretics. Dandelion also has the advantage of containing large quantities of potassium salts – substances which are often lost from the body during the process of diuresis, and which need replacing.

Several medicinal plants may be used in the treatment of hypertension, some of which have been shown to be remarkably effective. Hypertension has long been treated in Asia by the root of a shrub, *Rauvolfia serpentina*, but it was not until the 1930s that the agent largely responsible, reserpine, was isolated. This compound acts on the central nervous system by depleting the stores of a vital transmitting substance called noradrenaline (or norepinephrine as it is known in the United States); without this material nerve impulses cannot travel and the resultant loss of smooth muscle tone in the walls of the blood vessels causes their relaxation and so reduces blood pressure, thus acting as a hypotensive.

Rauvolfia alkaloids act synergistically with other hypotensives such as the alkaloids from *Veratrum* species, and this potentiation of the combined effect (synergism) is very useful since it enables relatively low doses of both materials to be used – an important fact since both substances may cause side-effects when used on their own.

New Treatments

Many other herbs have similar histories in that only recently has detailed investigation of their activity been started. This has shown the presence of other chemical groups in plants which have a beneficial effect on the cardiovascular system. The plants under current investigation include the Hawthorn (*Crataegus monogyna*), which is widely used in the treatment of angina pectoris, arteriosclerosis, heart failure, hypertension and coronary thrombosis. Its major constituents are flavonoids.

Buckwheat (*Fagopyrum esculentum*) also contains substances beneficially affecting the cardiovascular system, as well as vitamin P. Hawthorn and Buckwheat are often combined in the treatment of hypertension; they are frequently also combined with *Tilia* × *europaea* (Lime tree) and *Viscum album* (Mistletoe). Many herbs with cardio-active properties contain alkaloids. The hypotensive *Veratrum* contains several, of which the most important are protoveratrin A and B. Broom (*Sarothamnus scoparius*) possesses the alkaloid sparteine and is employed to raise the blood pressure in cardiac insufficiency. Motherwort (*Leonurus cardiaca*), however, contains alkaloids which assist in lowering the blood pressure, and help in angina pectoris.

With further detailed study of traditional remedies, it is possible that new groups of compounds will be discovered or certain plant combinations will prove to be useful in cardiovascular disease.

DISORDERS OF THE DIGESTIVE SYSTEM AND LIVER

The digestive system consists of the alimentary canal and the accessory digestive organs. Food passing along the tract is broken down by enzymes into small units which are then absorbed into the blood stream by passage across the gut cell-wall. Some substances in the diet need no digestion before absorption – for example, water, certain vitamins and minerals – but the most important foodstuffs – fats, proteins and carbohydrates – all require extensive degradation before they may be absorbed.

Some dietary constituents, however, such as the cellulose of plant cell-walls are not digested at all by man because the appropriate enzymes are lacking, and so these pass through the gut to be expelled unchanged in the faeces; their inclusion in the diet is none the less important because they add bulk to the intestinal contents and improve peristalsis – the rhythmic contractions which propel the contents from one end of the gastro-intestinal tract to the other.

The digestive system

The alimentary canal comprises the mouth, pharynx, oesophagus, stomach, small intestine, large intestine, rectum and anus. Although digestion begins in the mouth while the food is being chewed, since saliva contains the enzyme ptyalin which breaks down starch into sugars, by far the most important digestive organs are the stomach and small intestine.

The stomach produces a secretion which provides the optimal degree of acidity for the operation of the enzyme pepsin, also secreted in the stomach. The partly digested food passes to the small intestine where it meets an alkaline secretion composed of juices provided by two glands – the bile from the gall-bladder and the digestive juices from the pancreas.

Below: A schematic representation of the human digestive system which consists principally of a hollow tube about 9 metres (30 feet) long from the mouth to the anus. Each part, with its specialized structural or cellular form, plays one or more roles in the processes of mastication, maceration, digestion and absorption of foodstuffs, processes which all contribute to the eventual elimination of unwanted waste matter from the body.

Bile, produced initially by the liver, not only facilitates digestion but is also an important route for the elimination of certain waste products in the faeces. The pancreas, in addition to producing a digestive juice which is discharged into the gut, also releases directly into the blood-stream a hormone, insulin, which regulates the blood-sugar level. The condition where insufficient insulin is produced is known as diabetes.

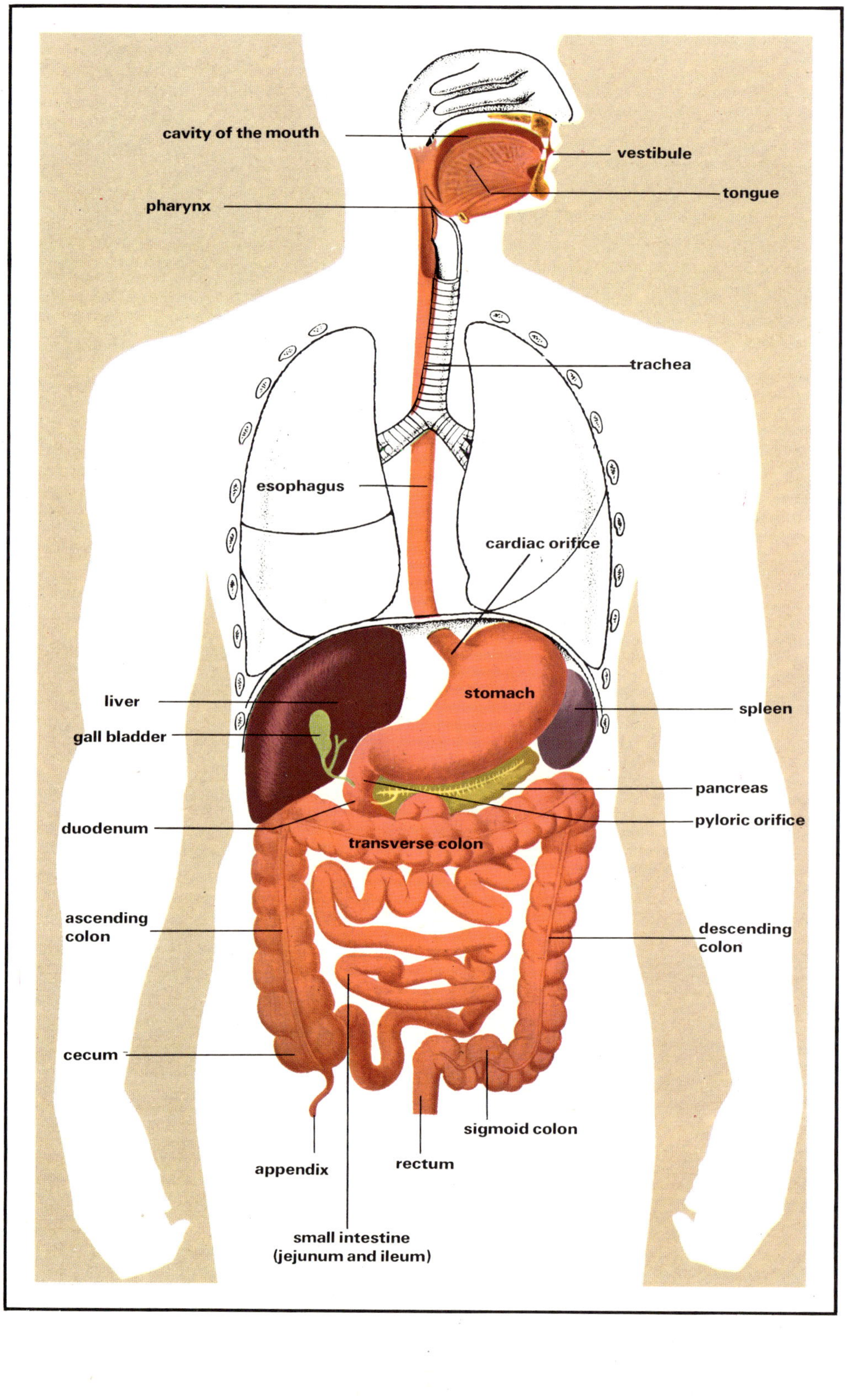

Digestion is thus completed in the small intestine and most of the small molecules so produced – amino-acids, sugars, fatty acids, and glycerol – are absorbed by the time the mass of food (bolus) has reached the far end of the small intestine.

Overactive acid-producing cells in the stomach initially produce heartburn and indigestion. If the excessive secretion of gastric hydrochloric acid is prolonged, peptic ulcer of the wall of the stomach or the duodenum may result. Here a small portion of the delicate mucosal lining is digested away, exposing the lower layers together with their associated nerve-endings, which are irritated by the acidic gastric contents to produce pain.

Ulcers have long been treated with Liquorice (*Glycyrrhiza glabra*) and a semi-synthetic derivative of its major constituent, glycyrrhizin, has been introduced with useful results.

Plants used for indigestion include Hops (*Humulus lupulus*) which was the traditional remedy of North American Indians, and *Carlina acaulis* (Stemless Thistle). In Europe a favourite is Meadowsweet (*Filipendula ulmaria*) which is often combined with *Althaea officinalis* (Marshmallow). The latter contains up to 20 per cent mucilage, which protects the stomach lining, acting in a similar way to the natural mucus. For the same reason the mucilage-rich *Cetraria islandica* (Iceland Moss) is similarly employed.

During convalescence or in the elderly it may be desirable to stimulate the appetite. Usually the agents used for this purpose are bitter tonics containing bitter principles, which increase glandular secretions. Many plants have a history of this use and the most popular come from the family Gentianaceae (which characteristically contain bitter principles), for example, *Gentiana lutea*, the best known and most widely used bitter tonic, *G. macrophylla, G. punctata, G. purpurea, Menyanthes trifoliata* (Buckbean) and *Sabatia angularis* (American Centaury).

Because the tone of the muscle in the gastro-intestinal tract as well as the secretion of the digestive juices is controlled by nervous as well as chemical stimulation, an increase in nervous activity may lead either to gastric hyperacidity or spasm in all parts of the intestine, known as colic. Many members of the Solanaceae family contain simple tropane alkaloids, such as atropine and hyoscine, which are powerful antispasmodics. Good examples are *Atropa belladonna, Hyoscyamus niger* and *Datura stramonium*. More gently acting herbs include certain gentians and mints, *Acorus calamus, Alpinia officinarum* and Wild Yam root (*Dioscorea villosa*). Emesis (vomiting) may be induced in cases of poisoning by administration of the tincture of Ipecacuanha (*Cephaelis ipecacuanha*). Other plants have been used in this respect but their effect was due mostly to their toxicity – the body simply reacts to the presence of a noxious substance in the stomach and removes it by the most rapidly effective means.

Anti-emetics include some herbs containing anticholinergic properties which act by inhibiting the overactivity of the vomiting centre in the brain. Some of these are found in the family Solanaceae. Their action is drastic however, and often associated with side-effects. *Ballota nigra* is safer and effective, especially in vomiting during pregnancy and is often combined for this purpose with *Filipendula ulmaria, Chamaemelum nobile* and Peppermint (*Mentha × piperita*).

Purgatives The major use of herbal preparations for digestive problems concerns constipation. Purgatives may be divided into three main classes: bulk purgatives, which simply increase the volume of the intestinal contents and so

Below: The liver performs several important functions besides producing bile for use in the digestive process: the removal of waste products from blood, the destruction of worn-out blood cells, and the vital detoxification of drugs and harmful substances.

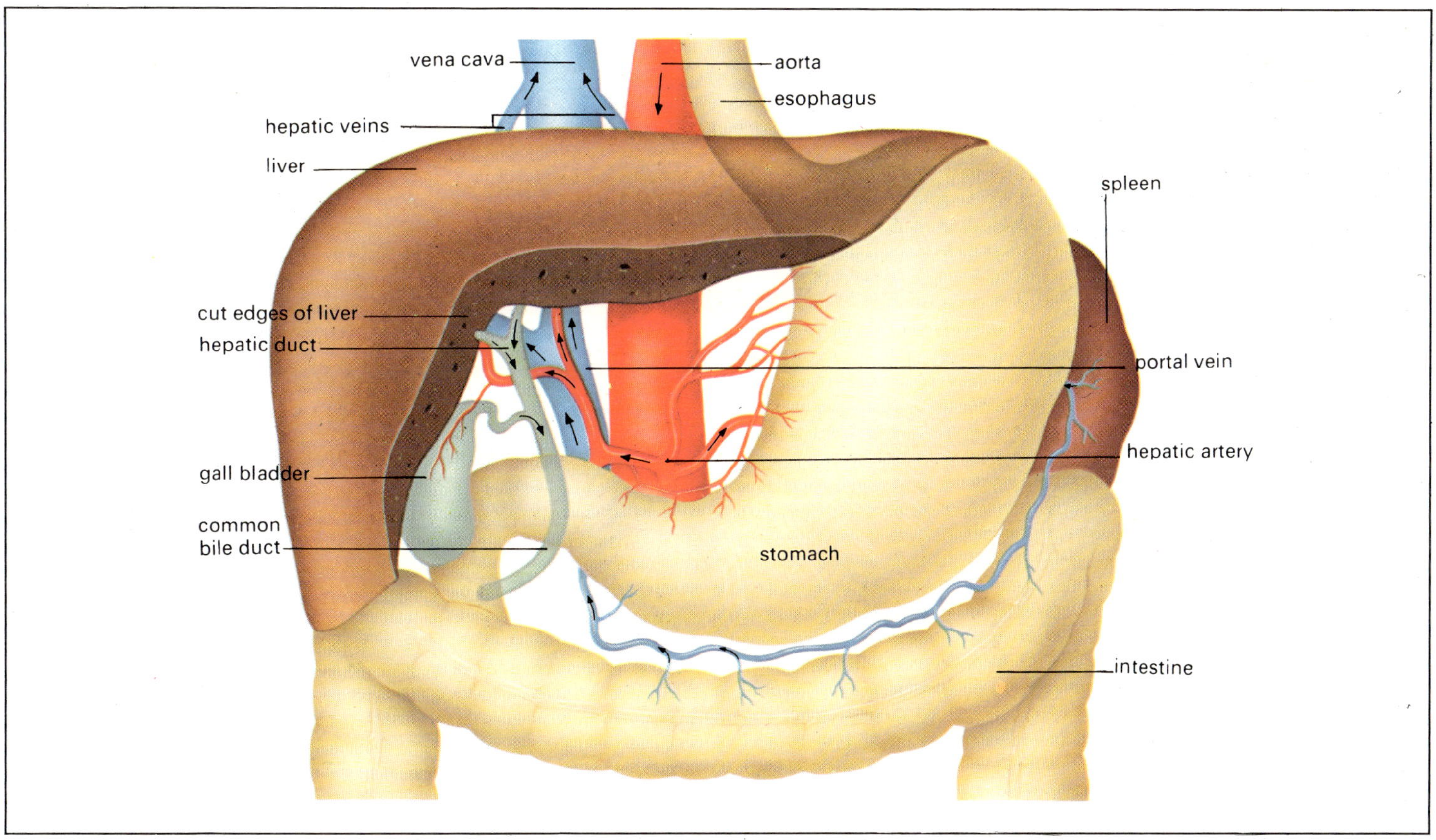

promote a 'natural' peristalsis and hence defaecation; lubricant purgatives, which act by generally loosening and softening the impacted faecal mass; and irritants, which exercise a localized irritant action on the wall of the large bowel, inducing reflex evacuation.

Foods which contain a high proportion of indigestible cellulose or 'roughage' such as bran or seeds of *Plantago* species are not destroyed by digestion and swell by absorbing water; when they reach the lower intestine, therefore, they act as bulk purgatives.

As the name suggests, lubricant purgatives include mucilages and oils which are extracted from a variety of plants, including the *Psyllium* species, *Athaea officinalis*, *Ricinus communis* (Castor Oil Tree) and *Olea europaea* (Olive Tree).

Irritant purgatives are used either because they are toxic hence causing a violent reaction to the presence of the poison, for example, *Ricinus communis* seeds (Castor oil) and certain *Podophyllum* species, or for some specific physiological action. Toxic irritant purgatives are seldom used because they are dangerous.

Of those which cause a specific physiological action, the most effective are the species which contain glycosides based on the anthraquinone nucleus. The main examples are Senna (*Cassia angustifolia* and *C. acutifolia*), Aloes (*Aloe ferox*, for example), Rhubarb (*Rheum* spp) and certain members of the Rhamnaceae such as *Rhamnus frangula* (Alder Buckthorn) and *Rhamnus purshiana* (Cascara).

Injection of extracts of these plants results in purgation in about 30 minutes but orally they take eight hours or more to exert their effect. This is because the active principles are in the form of inactive glycosides. These are well absorbed from the small intestine and are then hydrolyzed by enzymes in the blood to give the active aglycones. These latter compounds are excreted into the colon where they irritate the mucosa to produce evacuation. This process takes several hours and for this reason extracts of such plants are best taken at night.

Diarrhoea, an increase in the fluidity and frequency of the stools, has usually been treated with plants which predominantly contain astringent tannins. The action of these compounds is to coagulate protein in a thin layer of the gut lining thereby stopping its secretory action. Common examples of such herbs are *Potentilla* species, *Agrimonia* species, *Quercus* species, *Rubus idaeus*, *Polygonum bistorta* and *Ulmus campestris*.

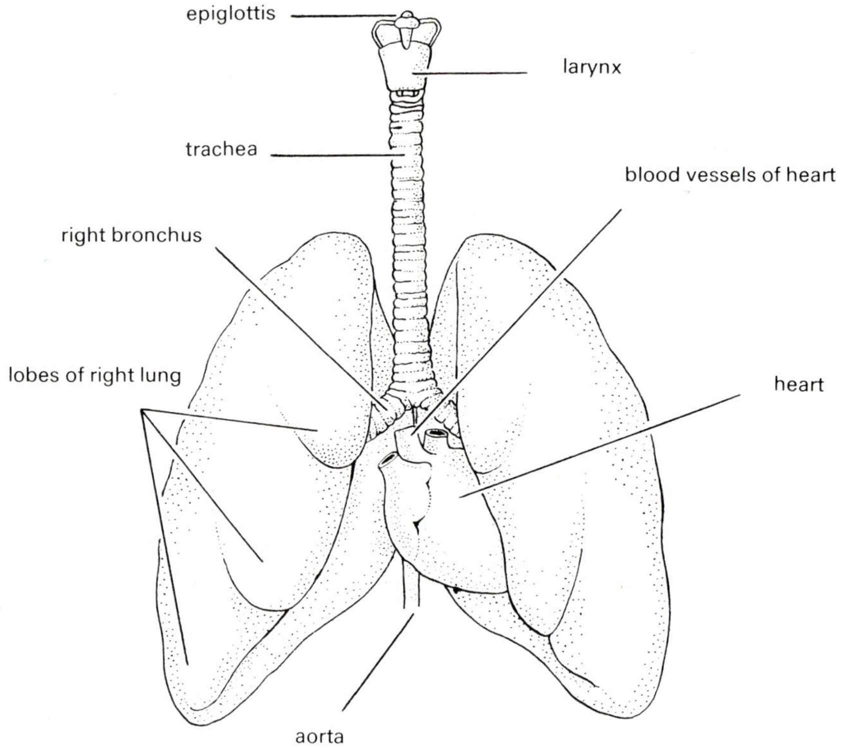

Diseases of the liver may lead to the impairment of the metabolism of all kinds of foods and, since the liver is the main organ of detoxification in the body, to an accumulation of waste products.

As the liver is closely associated with the gall-bladder problems of these organs are usually considered in association. Hence some herbs are accredited with both choleretic action (stimulating the production of bile, and thus working directly on the liver itself), and cholagogue action (increasing the release of bile from the gall-bladder). Important cholagogues are *Berberis vulgaris* (Barberry), *Chelone glabra* (Balmony) and *Taraxacum officinale* (Dandelion).

The Dandelion also possesses choleretic action and is one of the most useful plants for treating liver disease. It is employed in jaundice, cholecystitis (inflammation of the gall-bladder), and cholelithiasis (stones in the gall-bladder or bile duct); it may also relieve the first stage of cirrhosis.

Another important choleretic is *Cynara scolymus* (Globe Artichoke) which has also been shown to promote liver regeneration, following damage by poisons.

Flatulence can be treated with the carminative plants which contain volatile oils. Important here are the aromatic Umbelliferae such as Anise, Fennel and Dill, and certain Labiatae (Mint and Rosemary, for example).

DISORDERS OF THE RESPIRATORY SYSTEM

When we breathe, air is taken first into the nasopharynx and then into the chest via the windpipe, or trachea. This divides into two bronchi (one for each lung) and then further into smaller tubes, bronchioles. The bronchioles branch further into very fine tubules known as alveolar ducts, each leading to an alveolar sac. These alveoli are small hollow spheres and they comprise the main body of the lung itself. They have very thin cell-walls which are well supplied with minute blood vessels called capillaries.

The respiratory system

Oxygen from the air contained in the alveoli diffuses across the cell-walls into the blood and in exchange waste products, notably carbon dioxide, are expelled into the air. This exchange of gases is known as respiration. At every breath the air contained in the lungs is partially exchanged for fresh air from the atmosphere.

Oxygen is required for nearly all the biochemical processes which occur in the

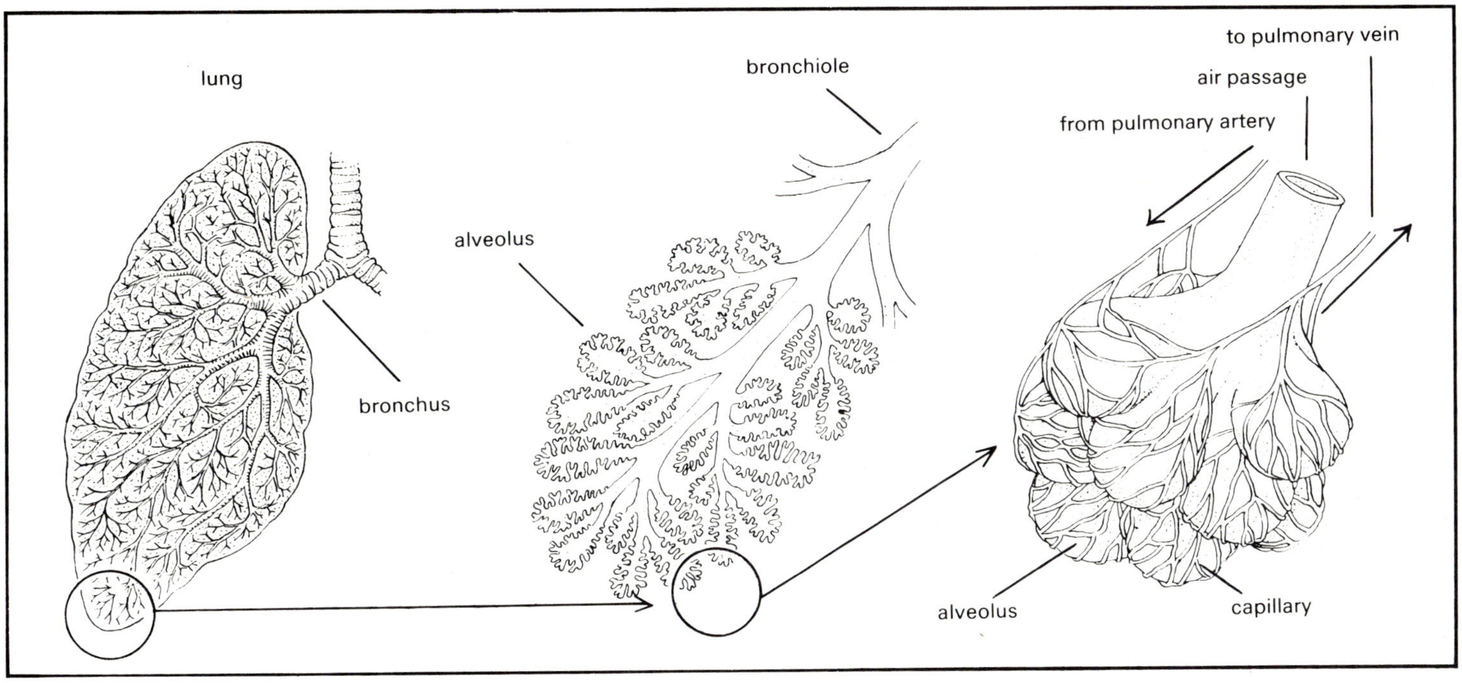

Left: Diagrammatic representation of the respiratory system. Increasing magnification of a portion of one lung (above) to show its internal structure, and the relationship between blood vessels and alveoli, which allows the exchange of oxygen in the air with waste carbon dioxide in the blood.

body, and the maintenance of a high oxygen level in the blood is therefore vital. The rapid removal of carbon dioxide is equally important because high blood or tissue concentrations of this substance may depress many enzyme processes.

Most of the oxygen in the blood is not simply dissolved in the body fluid but is actively bound to a special molecule called haemoglobin, found within the red blood corpuscles. This is a complex organic molecule, rather like the light-absorbing chlorophyll of green plants in its structure, but instead of containing an atom of magnesium (as in chlorophyll) it is bound to iron. This is the main reason that our diet should contain an adequate quantity of this element, for a deficiency of iron or its inefficient utilization in the body leads to anaemia.

As blood passes around the organs of the body, oxygen from the oxygenated haemoglobin passes into the cells to be used up in their chemical processes, and each cell exchanges its waste carbon dioxide.

The commonest chronic disorder of the respiratory tract is chronic bronchitis (inflammation of the bronchi), which may be associated with emphysema (enlargement of the alveoli). This may be caused by recurrent episodes of infection which lead to an increased number of the mucus glands and therefore an increase in viscous secretions. Smoking and air pollution also contribute to an increased activity of these glands. There may, in addition, be spasm of the muscle in the walls of the bronchi adding to the obstruction.

Another condition of the bronchial system which causes considerable suffering is asthma. This is frequently of allergic origin, that is to say that attacks (pronounced constriction of the bronchi and excessively viscous secretions which lead to the characteristic wheezing of asthma sufferers) are induced by the inhalation of a specific foreign substance, often a particular type of pollen. Treatment consists of the relaxation of the bronchi using bronchodilators, and some of the best known of these are *Ephedra* species, which contain ephedrine. Ephedra has been used for 5000 years by the Chinese to treat this condition.

Lobelia inflata is effective in chronic bronchitis and bronchial asthma for which purpose the North American Indians smoked the leaves. In India the related *L. nicotianaefolia* is used in the same way. The following plants are also commonly employed in both asthma and bronchitis often in combination with each other: *Drosera rotundifolia, Euphorbia hirta, Grindelia camporum, Sanguinaria canadensis, Polygala senega, Symplocarpus foetidus* and *Urginea maritima.*

A relatively new treatment for asthma depends on the administration of a semi-synthetic substance which is a derivative of khellin, a compound isolated from the mediterranean umbelliferous plant *Ammi visnaga* – a plant which has a long history as an anti-asthmatic agent among the Arabs.

Cough is a natural reflex to help clear the respiratory system of secretions and foreign materials. Anti-cough or anti-tussive agents may be needed to facilitate rest and promote sleep. Cough is controlled by a reflex from a centre in the central nervous system, and many anti-tussives (like alkaloids from Opium, the dried latex of *Papaver somniferum*) act by suppressing this reflex. They are thus widely used in cough syrups.

Also used are extracts of Wild Cherry bark (*Prunus serotina* or *P. virginiana*) which was once frequently used with a complex bitter compound produced by the Greater Prickly or Wild Lettuce (*Lactuca virosa*); the combined action is sedative as well as anti-tussive.

For difficulty in clearing the chest of phlegm a class of agents known as expectorants may be used. These act either by inducing cough or by increasing the fluidity of an excessively viscous bronchial secretion. The best-known irritant or cough-inducing expectorant is tincture of syrup of Ipecacuanha used in a much weaker concentration than that for promoting emesis. Other expectorant herbs include Cowslip (*Primula veris*), Soapwort (*Saponaria officinalis*), Mullein (*Verbascum thapsus*) and Snakeroot (*Polygala senega*), all of which contain saponins (detergent-like substances) that aid dissolution of sputum. *Viola odorata* is also employed as an expectorant; it contains a glycoside, violarutin, as well as saponins.

Primary infection of the upper respiratory tract is in 90 per cent of cases caused by minute living particles called viruses. These may be highly infectious (demonstrated by the occurrence of the common cold), and so far few plants have been shown to possess specific anti-viral activity. General resistance to these and other infections in the body may be increased, however, by employing *Phytolacca americana*, which stimulates the immunological defence system. Where primary viral infection is followed by bacterial infection a number of plants are used, although few possess the power of antibiotics (originally isolated from minute plants, the moulds). Garlic (*Allium sativum*) is strongly antibacterial as are Cone flower (*Echinacea angustifolia*), and Elecampane (*Inula helenium*).

DISORDERS OF THE NERVOUS SYSTEM

The nervous system controls and integrates all the activities of the body. There are two main parts: the central nervous system consisting of the brain and spinal cord, and the peripheral nervous system comprising the major nerves which connect the spinal cord with the minute nerve-endings in every part of the body. The peripheral system conducts messages from the organs to the central nervous system and also conveys controlling impulses in the reverse direction.

The nervous system

That part of the peripheral system which is under active control is called the voluntary system and is concerned with the skeletal muscles while the involuntary (or autonomic) system acts on the muscles of the organs and glands which cannot be controlled by will, such as the heart or the bladder.

Messages are conducted by changes in the electrical balance of the nerve cells or neurones concerned. More than one cell is involved with each pathway, and the electrical change is transmitted from one cell to another by the release of tiny amounts, or quanta, of a special chemical substance called a transmitter.

This process can be illustrated with a specific example. When you burn your hand, temperature-detecting cells in the skin activate nerve-endings. This message is passed along afferent or sensory nerve fibres to the spinal cord by electrical changes. When the message arrives at the spinal cord, a chemical transmitter passes it across the synapse (the junction between two cells) and activates another neurone in the spinal cord. The 'message' is transmitted up the spinal cord to the cerebral cortex in the brain. The pain is 'perceived' and as a result an impulse passes down the spinal cord and then down the efferent or motor nerve to the muscles of the arm and hand – which is withdrawn involuntarily from the heat.

Function of organs (autonomic activities) are controlled in distinct regions of the spinal cord and brain by two sets of nerve cells – the sympathetic and the parasympathetic – which, generally speaking, act in opposite ways. The parasympathetic nervous system is responsible, for example, for increased blood-flow to the digestive system after a meal, and the decrease in size of the pupil in bright sunlight. The transmitting substance for these nerves is known as acetylcholine.

The sympathetic nervous system, which uses mainly adrenaline and noradrenaline as its transmitter compounds, comes into effect in conditions of stress such as fear and anger, and acts antagonistically to stimulation of the parasympathetic system. Thus sympathetic stimulation causes increase both in pupil size and heart-rate but, at the same time, constriction of the blood-vessels in the skin and abdominal viscera. All these actions prepare the body for intense activity.

At a higher level of activity functions such as consciousness, thought, memory,

Below: The autonomic nervous system, showing the opposing actions of the parasympathetic and sympathetic parts on various organs of the body. Most organs receive nerves of both systems and are controlled by impulses from each.

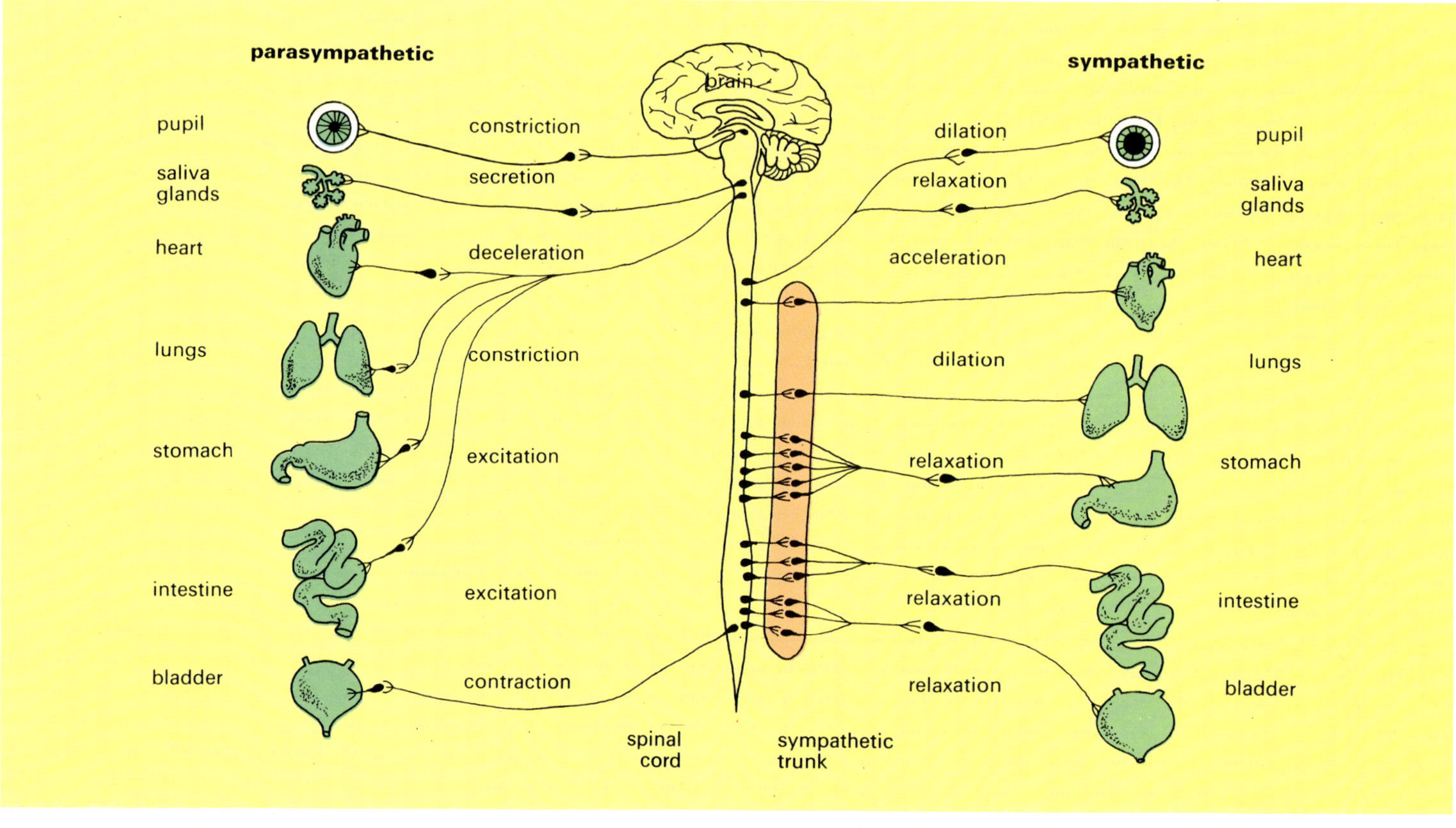

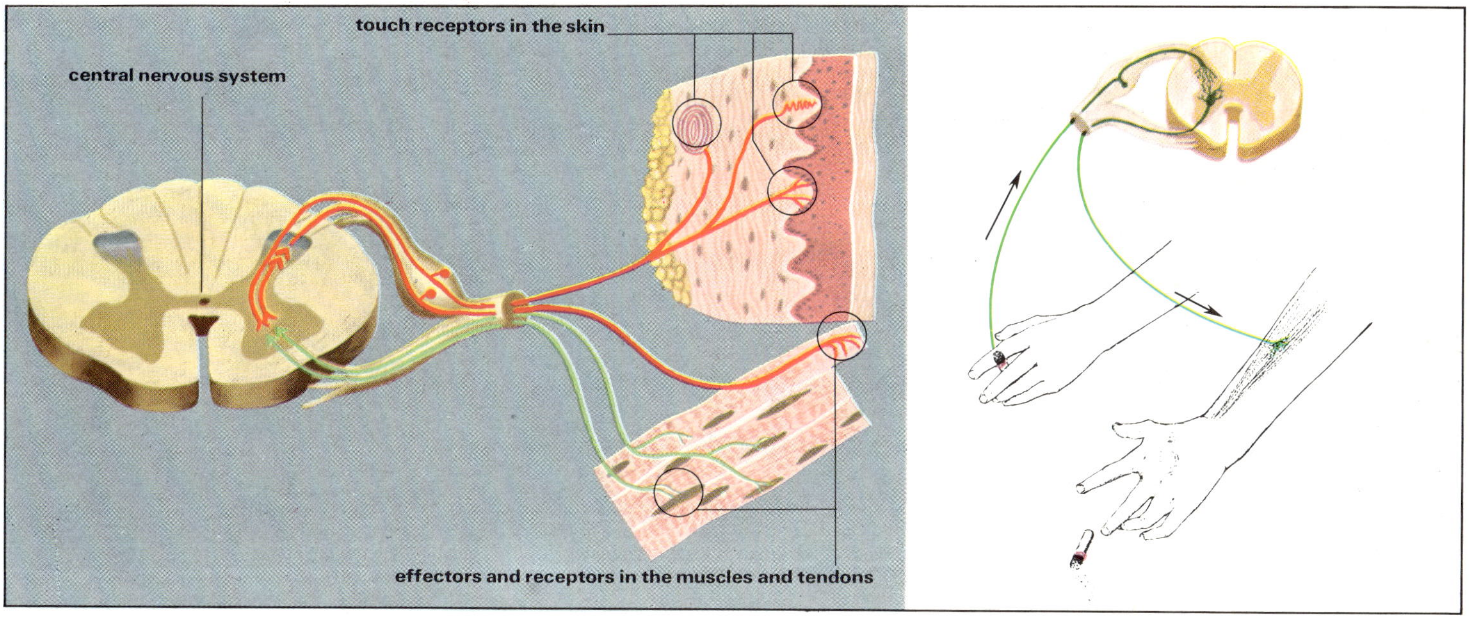

and reasoning reside in the superficial layer of the cerebral cortex in the brain. In man, with his high intellectual capacity, these portions of the brain dominate all others. Co-ordination of the reflexes is carried out in a smaller region of the brain called the hypothalamus. The mid-brain and medulla are concerned with the maintenance of the wakeful state (and hence also sleep), temperature regulation, respiratory regulation and maintenance of blood pressure.

Treatment of nervous disorders

The most widely used drugs which act on the central nervous system are those which relieve pain, the analgesics, and the strongest of these known in the plant kingdom are derived from the Opium Poppy (*Papaver somniferum*).

Historically the best-known pain-killer is Mandrake root (*Mandragora officinarum*) which, like Henbane (*Hyoscyamus niger*), contains the alkaloids hyoscyamine and scopolamine. Both were used during early surgery. Other analgesics include *Boswellia serrata*, *Chrysanthemum anemifolium*, *Ervatamia dichotoma* and many herbs which contain certain essential oils, such as *Gaultheria procumbens* (Wintergreen) whose oil comprises mainly methyl salicylate.

Other central nervous system drugs include the depressant group comprising the anaesthetics, hypnotics, sedatives and tranquillizers; and, conversely, the stimulants such as antidepressants and hallucinogens. A well-known depressant is tincture of Valerian (*Valeriana officinalis*); its active ingredients are terpenoid compounds called valepotriotes, present in the fresh root-stock. The Indian species *V. wallichii* is even more effective. Extracts of the Passion-flower (*Passiflora incarnata*) which contain the alkaloids passiflorine, harmol, and harmine, are also used as sedatives. Other popular medicinal plants in this category include Lady's Slipper (*Cypripedium pubescens*), also known as American Valerian; and *Tilia* species.

Drugs acting on the peripheral nervous system may be divided into two groups depending on whether they exert their effect on the sensory or motor neurones. In the first class fall the local anaesthetics (such as cocaine from the South American shrub, *Erythroxylum coca*), and counter-irritants from, for example, the seed of Mustard and the oil of Wintergreen.

Drugs which act predominantly on the cholinergic nerves (that is those in which the chemical compound, acetylcholine, is the physiological transmitter) of the autonomic system include stimulants which act like an excess of acetylcholine (such as nicotine in the leaves of *Nicotiana tabacum*), pilocarpine (from *Pilocarpus jaborandi*) or eserine (isolated from the beans of *Physostigma venenosum*).

Drugs which act on the parasympathetic autonomic nervous system in the opposite way, that is by inhibiting or antagonizing the effects of acetylcholine, include the tropane alkaloids from many species of the family Solanaceae, for example, *Atropa belladonna* and *Hyoscyamus niger*.

Adrenergic drugs, or those acting on the sympathetic neuromuscular junction, include stimulants such as ephedrine (from *Ephedra* species) and drugs acting in the opposite way (antagonists) such as reserpine (from both *Rauvolfia serpentina* and *R. vomitoria*) and ergotamine (from *Claviceps purpurea*).

Above and left: A reflex consists of the stimulation of a receptor neuron and an involuntary muscle movement. The diagrams show the reaction to the pain of a cigarette burn, and the receptor pathway (red) linking with the effector pathway (green) via the central nervous system. The reflex response causes the cigarette to be dropped.

*Below: Henbane (*Hyoscyamus niger*) is rarely used today since it contains many powerful substances but, historically, it has been very important.*

SELF-HELP WITH HERBS

Throughout history both the mainstream medical profession and unorthodox practitioners have tended to dissuade ordinary people from treating themselves or obtaining the means or information for doing so.

This opposition was often concerned with the profit motive and, equally, no doubt because of the need for secrecy to conceal lack of knowledge, ineffective remedies or even outright charlatanism.

The strongest argument today against self-medication is the danger of mis-diagnosis. Certain commonplace symptoms, such as vomiting, stiff neck, headache, fever or earache, may seem in themselves trivial complaints. But, considered in the perspective of other associated symptoms and the patient's predispositions and case history, such symptoms may indicate a much more serious problem.

Since any complaint is best treated immediately, it is important to remember that if symptoms do not disappear very quickly, proper qualified advice must be sought. Children must never be treated with herbal remedies, or with any other form of home medication; in children ordinary symptoms such as those of the common cold may develop into a potentially serious condition in as quickly as 24 hours.

Apart from mis-diagnosis, some individuals do not tolerate certain plant material either because of an intrinsic allergic problem, or because an organ or system in the body is malfunctioning to some extent. Juniper berries, for example, are frequently described as a diuretic, but they must not be used where there is a kidney inflammation. Similarly, some herbs may raise the blood pressure in a person already suffering from hypertension, and there are some plants which must never be taken internally by pregnant women.

Left: There are many different ways of preparing herbal remedies but for the purposes of self-care, only three methods need be employed. Infusion *involves the extraction of water-soluble substances from the less dense parts of a herb, such as its leaves, stems or flowers.* Decoction *is best for hard plant parts which will release their water-soluble parts only after being soaked in hot water.* Poultice *simply means the use of a fresh plant by bruising or crushing it into a pulp, which is then mixed with a moistening material, such as small quantities of hot water, in readiness for application directly to the body surface. The variety of containers and implements assembled here indicate all three methods, and include a saucepan and kettle, a good mortar and pestle, a fine strainer, lots of wooden spoons, storage jars, and, most importantly, a wide range of dried and fresh herbs. (Other methods of preparing herbal remedies require a greater knowledge of pharmacy and are best left to the experts.)*

There is also the question of correct dosage: how and when the dose should be administered, and the length of time for which a remedy should be taken. Lack of knowledge of correct herb combinations, and the use of incorrect doses, can produce adverse effects.

Simply because herbs are natural products it does not follow that their use in medicine is any easier than the use of synthetic substances – in many ways, indeed, it is more complicated.

It is for these reasons, therefore, that self-medication cannot be recommended and why so many popular modern 'herbals' may be considered with interest, but not as medical manuals. In this chapter some examples have been given of plants medically effective in disturbances of the cardiovascular, nervous, respiratory and digestive systems to demonstrate the effectiveness of herbal medicine as administered by a properly qualified practitioner. Some of these plants are poisonous even in only moderate doses. There are, however, many simple conditions which can be treated at home so long as the warnings above are fully considered.

PREPARATIONS

Herbal remedies may be prepared in several different ways. Some methods are directly related to their form of administration – poultices, ointments, creams and salves, for example, are obviously for external application only.

Other methods are related to the extraction of specific groups of active materials from a plant, so that alcoholic solutions may be needed to remove therapeutic chemicals which would not be released or solubilized in water.

Still other methods are related to the physical nature of the herb itself; pouring boiling water over a thick hard root may extract only a fraction of its constituents, whereas the same procedure is perfectly satisfactory for most leaves and flowers.

A complete understanding of all the different methods of preparation of herbal remedies requires a knowledge of pharmacy, and is thus not relevant to self-care. For this purpose only three methods need be employed, namely infusion, decoction and poultice. These should always be made fresh before use, and never kept for more than 12 hours as they may deteriorate. Even under ideal conditions herbs lose their activity: leaves, flowers and fruit should be used within one year; seeds, roots and rhizomes within three years.

In both infusions and decoctions the weight of remedy used is 30 g. For those remedies containing more than one herb, the combined weight is still 30 g.

Infusion Used to extract the water-soluble substances from the less dense parts of herbs such as the leaves, stems and flowers, the method is also sometimes employed on thin, small or chopped roots and fruits.

The method consists of pouring 500 ml of boiling water on to 30 g (or 1 oz to 20 fl ozs) of the finely cut material contained in a porcelain, stone or glass vessel, fitted with a tight lid. The lid keeps in the volatile substances which would otherwise be lost during the 10 or 15 minutes normally required for infusion. After straining the liquid is allowed to cool to just below blood heat before the dose is taken, or it may be allowed to cool completely. The normal dose is up to one cup of infusion taken three times a day, usually before meals.

Decoction Hard plant parts such as roots, rhizomes, bark, seed, and wood release their water-soluble constituents only after more prolonged hot water treatment. This requires adding 30 g of the herbal remedy to 500 ml (or 1 oz to 20 fl ozs) of cold water in an enamel or glass vessel and allowing it to soak for 10 minutes. The temperature is raised to boiling point and the mixture then simmered for 10 to 15 minutes; this is followed by a further 10 minutes steeping. During the entire process the vessel should be kept covered. After straining and cooling the dose may be taken; this is usually one cup (or slightly less) three times a day before meals.

Poultice This method may utilize either fresh plant material which is bruised and crushed to a pulp, and then mixed with a small quantity of hot water; or dried herbs which are softened by mixing with host pastes, which act as a suspending material, made from flour, bran, corn meal or other suitable vehicles. If the latter method is employed 60 g of dried herbs are mixed with 500 ml (or 2 ozs to 20 fl ozs) of fairly loose paste. Both fresh and dried plant poultices are best applied indirectly to the skin by sandwiching the paste between thin cloth prior to application to the affected part of the body surface.

Left: Herb farms, such as the one shown here, can supply the herbs used in the following recipes.

Below: The dosage is for adults – children must not be treated. Herbal remedies should be taken daily for two to three weeks. No medication should be taken continuously; it is sometimes better to vary the formulations. The figures indicate the proportionate parts by weight.

Key

bk	*bark*	*fl*	*flower*	*pt*	*petals*
by	*berry*	*ft*	*fruit*	*rs*	*resin*
bd	*buds*	*hb*	*herb*	*rt*	*root*
bl	*bulb*	*lf*	*leaf*	*sd*	*seed*
cl	*clove*				

ACIDITY see Dyspepsia

ANAEMIA

Chives
Comfrey
Dandelion
Nettle
Iceland Moss
Spinach
Watercress
As salad herbs, or vegetables: frequently

Nettle lf
Infusion: 2 cups per day

2 Nettle lf
1 Birch lf
1 Walnut lf
1 Sage lf
Infusion: 2 cups per day

2 European Centaury hb
1 Thyme hb
1 White Horehound lf
1 Hyssop hb
Infusion: 2 cups per day

1 European Centaury hb
1 St Johns Wort hb
Infusion: 2 cups per day

ANTISEPTIC (external use)

1 Garlic cl
1 Rosemary hb
1 Echinacea rt
1 Juniper by
Poultice or Decoction

1 Onion bl
1 Myrrh rs
1 Melilot hb
1 Thyme hb
Poultice or Decoction

1 Golden Rod hb
1 Wintergreen lf
1 Rue hb
1 Southernwood hb
Poultice or Infusion

1 Golden Seal rt
1 Myrrh rs
Decoction, use diluted

APPETITE (lack of)

Agrimony hb
Infusion: 1 cup 1 hr before meals

1 Wormwood hb
1 Angelica rt
1 Peppermint lf
Infusion: ½ cup 1 hr before meals

1 Gentian rt
1 Sweet Flag rt
1 Caraway sd
Decoction: ½ cup ½ hr before meals

1 Agrimony hb
1 Gentian rt
1 Calumba rt
1 European Centaury hb
Decoction: ½ cup 1 hr before meals

1 Bogbean hb
1 Blessed Thistle hb
1 Mugwort lf
Infusion: ½ cup 1 hr before meals

1 Globe Artichoke lf
1 Gentian rt
Decoction: ½ cup 1 hr before meals

BAD BREATH see Halitosis

BILIOUSNESS see Nausea

BLEEDING

Plantain lf
Poultice

1 Cranesbill rt
1 Raspberry lf
1 Bistort rt
Decoction: as a poultice or wash

Witch Hazel, distilled water of
Apply on cotton wool

BRUISES

Hyssop hb
Arnica fl
Cowslip lf
Oak lf
Cabbage lf
Marigold fl
Black Bryony hb
Comfrey lf
St Johns Wort hb
Linseed sd
Cuckoopint lf
Lime bk
Herb Robert lf
Rue hb
Fenugreek sd
Sanicle hb
Hemp Agrimony hb
Apply hot poultices of any of the above, alone or in combination. Renew at least 4 times a day

BURNS

1 Cucumber ft
2 Comfrey lf
1 Oak bk
1 Marigold fl
2 St Johns Wort hb
Poultice: renew frequently

1 Marigold fl
1 Sanicle hb
1 Plantain lf
2 Comfrey lf
2 Lady's Mantle hb
Poultice: renew frequently

1 Chickweed hb
2 Golden Seal rt
1 Irish Moss hb
Poultice: renew frequently

Burdock rt
Marigold fl

Coltsfoot lf
Plantain lf
Hound's Tongue lf
Lady's Mantle lf
Sweet Flag rt
Willow lf
Elm bk
Avens rt
Tormentil rt
Decoction: wash carefully with any of the above, alone or in combination

CHILBLAINS

2 Blessed Thistle hb
1 Rue hb
1 Mugwort hb
2 Horseradish rt
Poultice

2 Blessed Thistle hb
1 Mallow lf
1 Sage lf
1 Coltsfoot lf
1 Walnut lf
Poultice

4 Slippery Elm bk (powder)
1 Cayenne (powder)
2 Blessed Thistle hb
Poultice

2 Angelica rt
2 Lady's Mantle hb
2 Golden Rod hb
2 Yarrow hb
1 Hawthorn fl
Infusion: 2 cups a day

4 Slippery Elm bk (powder)
1 Blood Root rt
Poultice

COLDS

1 Yarrow fl
1 Elder fl
1 Peppermint lf
Infusion: 3–4 cups per day

1 Hyssop hb
1 White Horehound, hb
Infusion: 3 cups per day

1 Elder fl
1 Lime fl
Infusion: 3 cups per day

1 Bayberry bk
1 Ginger rt
Infusion: 2 cups per day, in small doses

4 Boneset hb
4 Elder fl
4 Yarrow fl
1 Ginger rt
Infusion: 3 cups per day

1 Liquorice rt
2 Elder fl
1 Meadowsweet hb
2 Violet fl
1 Garlic cl
Decoction: 2 cups per day

1 Rosemary hb
1 Peppermint lf
1 Sage lf
1 Marjoram lf
1 Eucalyptus lf
1 Garlic cl
Pour on boiling water and inhale the vapour

CONJUNCTIVITIS

Eyebright hb
Infusion: apply as lotion or eyewash

1 Marigold fl
1 Fumitory hb
1 Eyebright hb
Infusion: apply as lotion or eyewash

1 Golden Seal rt
1 Rose pt
1 Elder fl
Decoction: dilute 1:5 with water and apply as lotion or eyewash

1 Chamomile fl
2 Plantain lf
1 Cornflower fl
1 Melilot fl
Infusion: dilute 1:3 with water and apply as lotion or eyewash

1 Fennel sd
1 Rue lf
Decoction: apply as eye compress

CONSTIPATION Mild

Fruit juices, especially prune
Cabbage
Figs
Dates
Prunes
Rhubarb
Raisins
Bran
Spinach
Apples
The above should be incorporated in the diet, or their intake increased

1 Psyllium sd
1 Alpine Plantain sd
Decoction: do not strain, drink 3 cups per day

1 Liquorice sd
1 Fennel sd
1 Linseed sd
Decoction: 3 cups per day

1 Turnera hb
1 Yellow Dock rt
1 Dandelion rt
Decoction: 3 cups per day

2 Alder Buckthorn bk
1 Ash lf
1 Alder fl
1 Peppermint lf
Infusion: 1 cup before retiring to bed

1 Couch-grass hb
2 Borage lf
2 Dandelion lf
1 Angelica rt
1 Alder Buckthorn bk
Infusion: 1 cup before retiring

Severe

3 Senna lf
1 Marjoram lf
2 Chamomile fl
1 Sweet Flag rt
1 Peppermint lf
Decoction: 1 cup before retiring

4 Senna lf
1 Ginger rt
4 Sweet Flag rt
2 Rhubarb rt
Decoction: 1 cup before retiring

COUGHS Suppressant

2 Elecampane rt
1 White Horehound, hb
1 Coltsfoot lf
2 Fennel sd
Decoction: 3 cups per day

1 Sundew hb
1 Thyme hb
1 Aniseed sd
Infusion: 3 cups per day

2 Irish Moss hb
1 Thyme lf
4 Elecampane rt
2 Aniseed sd
4 Liquorice rt
4 Lungwort lf
1 Fennel sd
Decoction: 3 cups per day

Expectorant

2 Coltsfoot lf
1 White Horehound, hb
1 Liquorice rt
Decoction: 3 cups per day

2 Cowslip fl
1 Marshmallow rt
2 Soapwort hb or rt
1 Mullein hb
1 Balm of Gilead bd
Infusion: 2 cups per day

1 Sage lf
1 Marshmallow rt
1 Coltsfoot lf
1 Comfrey lf
Infusion: 3 cups per day

CUTS see Bleeding

DIARRHOEA

Tormentil rt
Agrimony hb
Ground Ivy hb
Oak bk
Bilberry ft
Bistort rt
Elm bk
Yarrow hb
Lady's Mantle hb

Cranesbill rt
Decoctions of any of the above, alone or in combinations. Up to 2 cups per day taken in small doses

1 Jambul ft
1 Oak bk
2 Raspberry lf
1 Sweet Flag rt
Decoction: 3 cups per day, in small doses

2 Plantain hb
2 Tormentil rt
1 Thyme hb
1 Ginger rt
Decoction: 3 cups per day, in small doses

DYSPEPSIA

Meadowsweet hb
Infusion: 3 or more cups per day

1 Meadowsweet hb
1 Lemon Balm lf
1 Marshmallow lf
Infusion: 3 cups per day

1 Sweet Flag rt
1 Meadowsweet hb
Decoction: 3 cups per day

1 Gentian rt
1 Chamomile fl
1 Angelica rt
1 Lemon Balm lf
Decoction: 3 cups per day

1 Wormwood hb
2 Coriander sd
2 Sage lf
1 Liquorice rt
Infusion: 1 cup per day

EXPECTORANTS see Coughs

FLATULENCE

4 Sweet Flag rt
1 Ginger rt
2 Meadowsweet hb
Decoction: 3 cups per day

2 Peppermint lf
2 Caraway sd
1 Garlic cl
1 Yarrow fl
Infusion: 2 cups per day

1 Lemon Balm hb
1 Chamomile fl
1 Peppermint lf
Infusion: 2 cups per day

1 Caraway sd
1 Fennel sd
1 Mugwort hb
1 Anise sd
Decoction: 3 cups per day

1 Winter Savory hb
1 Angelica rt
1 Lovage rt
1 Cumin sd
1 Thyme hb
Decoction: 2 cups per day

GARGLE

1 Red Sage lf
1 Myrrh rs
1 Marigold fl
Decoction: as required

1 Cleavers hb
1 Peppermint lf
2 Blackberry lf
2 Marigold fl
Infusion: as required

1 Marshmallow rt
1 Sage hb
1 Herb Robert hb
Decoction: as required

1 Sanicle hb
1 Lavender fl
1 Thyme hb
1 Tormentil rt
Infusion: as required

1 Golden Seal rt
1 Herb Robert hb
1 Sage lf
1 Sea salt
Decoction: as required

HALITOSIS

Anise sd
Cardamom sd
Clove
Angelica rt
Fennel sd
Peppermint lf
Parsley lf
Sweet Flag rt
Tarragon lf
Dill sd
Chew a little of any of the above, alone or in combination. Consider the need for a laxative, dental care, treatment of flatulence or stomach acidity.

1 Caraway sd
1 Anise sd
1 Fennel sd
1 Orris rt
Decoction: gargle frequently

2 Lavender fl
2 Sage lf
1 Myrrh rs
Decoction: gargle 3 times per day

HEADACHE

1 Lime fl
1 Lemon Balm hb
1 Rosemary hb
Infusion: as required, 1–4 cups per day

1 Catmint hb
1 Rosemary hb
Infusion: 3 cups per day

1 Vervain hb
1 Scullcap hb
Infusion: 3 cups per day

1 Yarrow fl
1 Scullcap hb
Infusion: 2–3 cups per day

1 Valerian rt
2 Chamomile fl
1 Lavender fl
Infusion: 2 cups per day

1 Hops hb
1 Valerian rt
Infusion: 2 cups per day

2 Blessed Thistle hb
1 Rosemary hb
Infusion: 3 cups per day

INDIGESTION

Peppermint lf
Infusion: 1 cup as required, not to exceed 4 cups per day

2 Dandelion lf
1 Meadowsweet hb
1 Lime fl
1 Marshmallow rt
Infusion: 4 cups per day

1 Parsley hb
1 Sage lf
1 Fennel sd
Decoction: 2 cups per day

1 Sweet Flag rt
1 Ginger rt
Decoction: $\frac{1}{2}$ cup as required, not to exceed 2 cups per day

1 Fennel sd
1 Gentian rt
1 Peppermint lf
1 Woodruff hb
Decoction: 2 cups per day

1 Wormwood hb
1 Chicory rt
2 Basil hb
1 Sweet Flag rt
Infusion: 2–3 cups per day, taken in small doses

2 Sarsaparilla rt
1 Turnera hb
1 Cola ft
1 Ginger rt
Decoction: $\frac{1}{2}$ cup as required, not to exceed $1\frac{1}{2}$ cups per day

INFLAMMATIONS

Apple	Irish Moss
Carrot	Chickweed
Coltsfoot	Borage
Linseed	Cucumber
Houseleek	Slippery Elm
Oats	Purple Loosestrife
Onion	White Pond Lily
Parsley	Okra
Comfrey	Lungwort
Pumpkin	Marshmallow
Watercress	Iceland Moss

Any of the above may be crushed and pulped with a little hot water to produce a poultice suitable for application to inflammations or swellings

INFLUENZA see Colds

INSECT BITES

Houseleek lf
Rue lf
St Johns Wort lf
Marigold fl
Parsley lf
Leek bl
Olive oil
Plantain lf
Pennyroyal lf
Comfrey lf
Crush the fresh plant of any of the above and rub on the sting

Repellent

Oil of Lavender
Oil of Pennyroyal
Elder lf (crushed)

INSOMNIA

Valerian rt
Hops hb
Lime fl
Chamomile fl
Fennel sd
Aniseed sd
Passion flower hb ($\frac{1}{4}$ cup only)
Lavender fl
Woodruff hb
Thyme hb
Infusions of any of the above; 1 cup at night

1 Dill sd
1 Fennel sd
1 Peppermint hb
Decoction: 1 cup at night

1 Lime fl
1 Hops hb
1 Lemon Balm hb
1 Valerian rt
Infusion: 1 cup at night

LARYNGITIS (see also Gargle)

8 Coltsfoot lf
4 Blood Root rt
4 Balm of Gilead bd
1 Poke Root rt
Decoction: gargle

Hedge Mustard hb
Infusion: 4 cups per day

Garlic cl
Eaten raw; 2 per day

1 Mallow fl
1 Mullein hb
1 Coltsfoot lf
1 Marshmallow rt
1 Liquorice rt
Infusion: 3 cups per day

LAXATIVES see Constipation

NAUSEA

Black Horehound hb
Infusion: 2 cups per day

1 Galangal rt
1 Marshmallow rt
1 Black Horehound hb
Decoction: 3 cups per day

1 Sage hb
1 Black Horehound hb
1 Vervain hb
1 Pennyroyal hb
Infusion: 3 cups per day (not during pregnancy)

1 Raspberry lf
1 Ginger rt
1 Peppermint hb
1 Lemon Balm hb
Infusion: 2 cups per day

Clove
Chew one slowly

SCALDS see Burns

SEDATIVES

1 Betony hb
1 Scullcap hb
Infusion: 3 cups per day

1 Lady's Slipper hb
1 Oats sd
1 Scullcap hb
Infusion: 3 cups per day

1 Lady's Slipper hb
1 Oats sd
1 Hops hb
Infusion: 3 cups per day

1 Hyssop hb
1 Lemon Balm hb
1 Lavender fl
Infusion: 4 cups per day

2 Valerian rt
1 Mistletoe hb
2 Scullcap hb
Infusion: 2 cups per day, in small doses

2 Mistletoe hb
4 Lime fl
1 Hawthorn ft or fl
Decoction: 2 cups per day, in small doses

1 Lavender fl
1 Orange fl
1 Lemon Balm hb
1 Basil hb
1 Hops hb
1 Valerian rt
Infusion: 2 cups per day. Or take any one alone, 2 cups per day

SORE THROAT

1 Golden Seal rt
1 Thyme hb
2 Sage lf
1 Myrrh rs
Decoction: gargle

1 Bistort rt
1 Balm of Gilead bd
1 Sanicle hb
Decoction: gargle

Garlic cl
Eaten raw: 2 per day

1 Golden Rod hb
1 Meadowsweet hb
Infusion: gargle

Summer Savory
Infusion: gargle

Red Sage lf
Infusion: gargle

Bayberry bk
Decoction: gargle

TONICS

1 Dandelion lf
1 Chicory rt
2 Dog Rose ft
1 Peppermint lf
Infusion: 3 cups per day

1 Hibiscus fl
1 Dog Rose ft
1 Sage lf
Infusion: 4–5 cups per day

1 Turnera hb
1 Saw Palmetto by
1 Cola ft
1 Oats sd
Decoction: 2 cups per day, in small doses

TOOTHACHE

Mallow lf
Soften, and chew gently

Clove oil
Apply to tooth cavity, but avoid gums

Chamomile fl
Infusion: repeatedly rinse mouth

VOMITING (see also Nausea)

2 Peppermint hb
2 Spearmint hb
2 European Centaury hb
2 Chamomile fl
1 Wormwood hb
Infusion: sip as required, to 3 cups per day

1 Chamomile fl
1 Lemon Balm hb
1 Peppermint hb
1 Fennel sd
1 European Centaury hb
Infusion: as required

During Pregnancy

1 Iceland Moss hb
1 Black Horehound hb
Decoction: 2 cups per day

1 Chamomile fl
1 Meadowsweet hb
1 Black Horehound, hb
Infusion: 2 cups per day

Herbs in the kitchen

Herbs and spices have had an important rôle in cooking for more than 5000 years. No doubt herbs were eaten for their flavour long before it was recognized that they possessed various other beneficial properties. An organized international trade in spices already existed by about 1550 B.C. The Ebers Papyrus, an Egyptian medical work, contained references to Indian spices as well as locally grown plants. In about 950 B.C. King Solomon was visited by the Queen of Sheba who brought gifts of Arabian spices and herb seeds. Ancient Babylon already grew its own Bay, Saffron, Thyme, Cumin and Juniper. In 450 B.C. Herodotus described Indian spices then known in Greece. It was from the mediterranean regions that many plants came to northern Europe as the Roman empire expanded. Native herbs were augmented by Roman favourites such as Mustard, and spices were imported. South Indian Pepper was the most popular import and this pungent spice was sprinkled liberally over dishes both sweet and savoury. Even today freshly milled pepper is sometimes added to strawberries to heighten their flavour. Ginger was next in popularity in the cuisine of first-century Rome and was used in many spiced mixtures, sauces and stuffings as a digestive and laxative.

Biblical references to herbs and spices, and oils obtained from them, abound in both the Old and New Testaments. In Proverbs (xv:17), we find 'Better is a dinner of herbs where love is, than a stalled ox and hatred therewith'. Classical literature is similarly rich in references to herbs and spices. Theophrastus, born in Greece in 372 B.C. and a student of Plato and Aristotle, includes many descriptions of herbs in his writings. Pliny, born in A.D. 23, included natural history in his writings and referred to the custom of sprinkling egg-brushed bread dough with Poppy-seeds prior to baking.

In A.D. 812 the Emperor Charlemagne issued an edict instructing his people to grow certain herbs and vegetables in their gardens – probably the earliest 'permitted list' of herbs. Perhaps the Emperor's best tended garden, stocked according to his plan, was in the Benedictine monastery at St Gall in Switzerland.

In Britain, the Guild of Pepperers was in existence in 1180. The guild then became the Mistery of Grossers, Pepperers and Apothecaries, later the Guild of Grocers and finally the Grocers' Company. From the fourteenth century the guild acted as a watchbody, controlling the quality of spices, which could easily be adulterated with spent or low grade material. Adding water was another means of defrauding the buyer. Only in 1875 did the necessary legal machinery come into the hands of the law with the Sale of Food and Drugs Act, which rendered the watchdog powers of the guild less vital.

The fifteenth-century term 'peppercorn rent' arose from the occasional practice of paying rents to landlords in

Left: Herbs, bread and eggs – simple materials that can provide cooks with all the variety they need.

Above: Herbs have been used for hundreds of years, and it is only in recent times that they have been neglected. Here a cook seasons one of his dishes – illustration from a cookery book published in 1507. For the medieval cook herbs were an essential part of cooking, most often for their preservative powers.

Right: Ginger, Black Pepper, Caper and Cayenne: four spices that have been used in kitchens for many centuries.

specified weights of peppercorns. A peppercorn rent signified a trivial amount, but realistic rents paid in pepper consignments meant that the landowner's annual pepper expenditure could be avoided. Rent paid in peppercorns was often preferred because it held its value better than unstable coinage – suggesting problems with inflationary currency even in those days!

The staff of monastic gardens, kitchens and distilling rooms, the cultivators of the farms of the Knights of St John of Jerusalem and church missionaries (often selected because of their botanical acumen) all played important rôles in promoting the knowledge and use of herbs and spices. The Arab conquest of Spain meant that Arabian spice traders operated from Spain to the borders of China. At about the same time Greek, Levantine and Arabian traders were busy establishing trading stations and factories along the west coast of India.

The period between 1100 and 1290 saw the blossoming of the North Italian spice trade centres. In 1486 Bartholomew Diaz navigated the Cape of Good Hope and trade was transformed, the legendary overland caravan routes being replaced by sea journeys. In 1492 Columbus made his first voyage to the New World and six years later Vasco da Gama landed in Calicut. In 1510 the Portuguese established a base in Goa and a year later they entered Malakka in the Spice Islands. In 1517 the Portuguese established a base in Colombo, Ceylon. In 1600 the British East India Company was founded. The Dutch formed a similar trading company two years later, the Danes following in 1616. In 1651 the Portuguese were driven out of Malakka, in 1658 out of Ceylon, and for some 200 years London was the leading spice market.

As trade in spices slowly developed, references to their culinary use were gradually documented. The fourteenth-century book *Forme of Cury* published in England is evidence of the widespread use of herbs in cookery. The plays of Shakespeare are liberally sprinkled with references to herbs. To quote just one extract, from *A Midsummer Night's Dream* (II.ii.249): 'I know a bank whereon the wild thyme blows, where ox-lips and the nodding violet grows; Quite over-canopied with lush woodbine, With sweet musk roses and with eglantine.'

The sixteenth and seventeenth-century writers such as Andrew Boorde, Gervase Markham and John Evelyn made frequent references to culinary plants. The indulgent use of herbs and spices may well have been necessary to mask the taints of partially rotten and rancid food (storage and preservation techniques were primitive, to say the least), and to add greater variety to the flavour of basic foods. Today, though methods of food storage and preservation may be technologically sophisticated, factory and battery-farming methods of rearing cattle and poultry leave much to be desired in terms of flavour. Even certain fruit and vegetable crops (notably apples and potatoes) have come under fire, and the plant breeder is often reproached for breeding uniform, unblemished items, designed to suit the packer's boxes rather than to delight the consumer's palate. Once again, herbs and spices are coming to the cook's aid.

Herbs are often associated with specific dates, often religious festivals. The earliest Shrove Tuesday pancakes were tansy-flavoured; bitter herbs still symbolize the Jewish Passover; on Good Friday (traditionally free of devilish influence) cuttings of Bay, Lavender, Sage, Rosemary and Thyme are planted to ensure their healthy growth; on 1 May the German *Mai-Bowle* – a white wine cup flavoured with Woodruff and early Strawberries – is prepared. August crayfish parties in Sweden and Finland would not be traditional without the flavour of Dill and decorative Dill heads which are used to garnish the mounds of succulent red shellfish previously boiled in a Dill bath.

HERBS AND DIET

As a source of nutrients herbs and spices are usually consumed in too small quantities to enter the calculations of the dietician concerned with daily recommended intakes. The contribution of vitamin C to the diet from a particular plant is only significant if a bowlful is consumed. Used as a garnishing herb, the same plant may contribute little in nutrient terms but a good deal in visual and palate appeal, thereby playing an essential role in stimulating the appetite and aiding digestion.

Certain plants, however, are known to be rich sources of nutrients. For example, vitamin C is present significantly in Rosehips, Sweet Peppers, Nettles and in Watercress. Nutritional claims are made for certain herbs: for instance, Comfrey and Alfalfa shoots provide an essential source of vitamin B12 in the vegan diet. Deficiency of this component of the vitamin B complex can be a dietary hazard in vegan diets.

The function of herbs and spices may be transient in dishes which are quickly prepared, served and eaten, such as a herb omelette, Elder flower fritters or a bowl of salad decorated with Nasturtium blooms; herbs have more of an effect on diet if, for instance, they are used in stored pickles, chutneys, preserves, wines, vinegars, honeys and oils.

AVAILABILITY OF HERBS

Most herbs are grown and harvested in rural settings such as country gardens, though nowadays many flourish in town plots and window-boxes or pots. For those without access to the fresh form, the cool cabinets of some chain-stores now have a limited range of freshly packed containers or freeze-dried herbs in jars and ring-pull aluminium cans. Until relatively recently, when the upsurge of interest in herbs began, many cooks were using herbs which were not always packaged and stored in the best manner. Often they were too old, and so generally poor results were obtained. Today the situation has much improved. There is more interest in growing fresh herbs and the home freezer enables the grower to store herbs much more effectively.

Adding herbs to dishes needs experience, judgment and care. The nature of the herb itself, whether it is in the fresh or dried state, and the method and time of the cooking process are all important factors. Steeping, distilling, infusion, or addition at just the right moment may be necessary. The dish may be needed for immediate consumption, or for freezer storage or (as in the case of certain pickles, chutneys and wines) it may need time to mature.

Four main botanical families supply the majority of culinary herbs, the Umbelliferae which include Angelica, Caraway, Dill, Fennel and Parsley, the Labiatae (the Mints, Basil, Sage and Thyme), the Compositae (Chamomile, Tansy and Yarrow) and the Cruciferae (Mustard).

Gathering fresh herbs

Pick or snip the young leaves or whole sprigs from the ends of stems if the plant is large enough. Avoid over-picking too many leaves from one stem or from very

Below: This flourishing herb bed contains Marjoram, Lemon Balm, and two types of Fennel, together with many other plants used by man, which together provide an attractive kitchen garden. (The table on page 123 lists some herbs suitable for a cook's garden.)

Left: Garlic, onions and chillies on sale – these are three of the best known and most popular herbs used in the kitchen. Garlic and onions belong to the same family and both have a very wide culinary use, ranging from soups to meat. Chillies are an integral part of Indian cooking and are responsible for that distinctively hot, spicy taste.

young plants. Use at once or wrap in foil and keep in the refrigerator. Sprigs of Mint (*Mentha* spp) and Parsley (*Petroselinum crispum*) may be kept in a jar of water for a few days.

Picking and drying

Herbs are usually harvested when the flowers are just coming into bloom as they are then richest in aromatic oils. Inevitably a certain amount of loss of these oils occurs during drying and storage. Some herbs are harvested when in full bloom, namely Hyssop (*Hyssopus officinalis*), Lavender (*Lavandula* spp), Rosemary (*Rosmarinus officinalis*), and Thyme (*Thymus vulgaris*). Sage (*Salvia officinalis*) is harvested when the earliest buds are seen. Pick just after the dew has gone and discard any yellow or damaged herbs. Handle with care and only rinse to remove obvious dust or soil. Pat the herbs dry gently with kitchen paper. Dry them in an airing cupboard or in a barely warm oven, leaving the oven door open. The temperature should not exceed 34°C (95°F). Lay the herbs on wire cooling racks covered with muslin, cheesecloth or nylon net. When dry the herbs are brittle and crumbly. Put the dried herbs into storage jars, preferably of tinted glass, and cover with a plastic screw cap. Should signs of condensation appear inside the jar, the herbs are incompletely dried and should be returned to the drying cupboard or oven.

Long-stemmed herbs may be dried by hanging them in a warm, dry, airy place for a few days. Tie in small bunches in a loose fashion. Cover the bunches with dark paper if direct sunlight is liable to reach them. Crumble and store the dried herbs as above.

Avoid purchasing large quantities of dried herbs as shelf-life is limited and avoid paper-packaged brands. Choose containers made of dark glass or plastic with well-fitting lids so that direct light and air do not shorten the storage life. Do not store over a warm cooker but in a dry cool spot. When the herb loses its aroma it is of doubtful use in cooking and should be replaced.

Freezing herbs

Perhaps the most satisfactory domestic method of storing herbs is in the freezer since variable results are obtained by drying and not all herbs dry well – Chives (*Allium schoenoprasum*) and feathery Dill (*Anethum graveolens*) and Fennel (*Foeniculum vulgare*), for example. Freeze the clean herbs in small quantities suitable for use in average size dishes. Blanching may be dispensed with if the freezer storage time is to be brief, say six to eight weeks. For longer storage, blanch the herbs by immersing them in boiling water for about 45 seconds, then plunge them into chilled water, drain, and pack in freezer wrapping material or freezer bags. An alternative method of blanching herbs is to steam blanch them by placing the sprigs in a steamer above rapidly boiling water. Allow about $1\frac{1}{4}$ minutes blanching time. The recommended freezer life for blanched frozen herbs is six months. Whole sprigs may be crumbled while frozen.

Frozen herbs can be added to many dishes without thawing. Defrost before using in salads and spreads or for garnishing. Bouquets garnis and portion-wrapped sprigs of herbs can be protected in the freezer by placing the labelled foil- or polythene-wrapped parcels in covered plastic boxes or screw-top jars.

Chopped herbs can be mixed with soft breadcrumbs and frozen for use as toppings or in stuffings and dumplings. Place the chopped herbs in ice-cube containers and top up with stock. Transfer the frozen cubes to freezer bags for storage. Likewise, you can put small sprigs of tiny Mint leaves in ice-cube trays, top with water and freeze for use in wine cups and some aperitifs. Chopped herbs can be mixed with butter, rolled into cylindrical rolls or flat blocks ready for slicing and served with grilled meat or fish, or as part of a sandwich filling. Herbs commonly used in such savoury butters are: Parsley (*Petroselinum crispum*), Basil (*Ocimum basilicum*), Chives (*Allium schoenoprasum*), Tarragon (*Artemisia dracunculus*), Watercress (*Nasturtium officinale*), Chervil (*Anthriscus cerefolium*), Garlic (*Allium sativum*), Capers (*Capparis spinosa*), Dill (*Anethum graveolens*), Horseradish (*Cochlearia armoracia*) and Mustard (*Brassica nigra*). Lemon juice and salt may also be added. Similarly, store Rose petals (*Rosa* spp) in butter and spread on sweet scones for tea. Remember that ready-prepared dishes stored in the freezer should be seasoned more lightly than dishes for immediate consumption. Herbs and other aromatic seasonings become more pronounced in flavour during freezer storage.

USING HERBS IN COOKING

Fines herbes are mixtures of three or four chopped herbs used to flavour particular dishes, the classical mixture consisting of Parsley (*Petroselinum crispum*), Chervil (*Anthriscus cerefolium*), Tarragon (*Artemisia dracunculus*) and Chives (*Allium schoenoprasum*). Fines herbes are used in soups, sauces, omelettes and cream cheese.

Herb bouquets are small bunches of herbs added to food usually only for the duration of cooking. They can easily be removed if they are tied together with white cotton thread or bound in cheesecloth. A bouquet simply consists of a few sprigs of Parsley (*Petroselinum crispum*) and a few Chives (*Allium schoenoprasum*), chopped and added to sauces, salads or cream cheese. A bouquet garni is made of two Parsley stalks (*Petroselinum crispum*), two sprigs of Thyme (*Thymus vulgaris*), (one sprig of Marjoram (*Origanum onites*), optional) and half a Bay leaf (*Laurus nobilis*). Such bouquets may be added to stocks, soups and stews or put into roasting birds. Ready-made sachets of the dried herbs are easily obtainable.

Left: Making a bouquet garni which includes Parsley, Thyme, Marjoram and a Bay leaf. This makes a delicious addition to soups, stews and casseroles. If tied together with white cotton thread or string, for example, the herbs can be easily removed when the food is cooked.

Generally speaking, herbs and spices should be used carefully and sparingly. There are exceptions to this rule; for example in the use of fresh Dill sprigs (*Anethum graveolens*) in the preparation of dill-marinaded salmon when liberal amounts of the herb bring the best results. Herbs and spices play a major rôle in enhancing rather than overpowering natural food flavours in the various foods and dishes to which they are added.

The addition of one tablespoon of chopped fresh herbs usually suffices in a four-portion dish. Correspondingly less of the dried herb is used ($\frac{1}{2}$ to $\frac{3}{4}$ teaspoon if coarsely chopped, $\frac{1}{4}$ to $\frac{1}{2}$ teaspoon if ground). This last amount also applies to ground spices. Freshly ground spices are more flavoursome than those purchased ready-ground particularly if they have been stored for some time. Commercially prepared freeze-dried herbs, such as Chives and Dill, are almost the equal of fresh herbs in colour and flavour. They are expensive to buy but excellent in quality. Store at room temperature in well-sealed containers.

Dried seeds are usually bruised prior to use to help to release their flavour. Frozen herbs retain most of the flavour if used within the recommended storage period. In frozen foods the flavours of herbs and spices tend to become stronger during storage, so use them with discretion in dishes destined for the freezer. Some herbs, however, must be used in the fresh state to obtain good culinary results, and these are listed in the table on pages 90–91.

HERB TEAS

The terms tea and tisane are often used synonymously, but the distinction is of vital importance. A tea is a drink made by adding boiling water to the fermented leaves and stalks of one or more plants. A tisane is made by adding boiling water to the fresh or dried – but unfermented – plant material (normally in the form of green leaves). The resulting drinks have completely dissimilar tastes, the action of fermentation producing quite different flavours.

Whether you plan to make teas or tisanes, you should always pick the herbs just before they come into full flower. This will ensure the very best aroma and flavour.

Individual sachets of herb teas are readily available and convenient to use. The range includes Rosehip, Rosehip and Hibiscus, Fennel, Peppermint, Chamomile, and Green Buckwheat.

Tisanes

Simply pack the herbs loosely on a wire rack in the airing cupboard or any other warm, airy place out of direct sunlight for about 48 hours. When they are completely dry and brittle, store them in airtight jars made of dark glass. They should last for about a year.

Do not use an ordinary tea-pot when making a tisane, as the tannin deposits it will inevitably contain will mar the delicate flavour of many herbs. Take about two to three teaspoons of fresh herbs (or one teaspoon of dried) to each 140ml (5 fl oz). Pour on boiling water, infuse for three to ten minutes, strain and serve hot or cold.

Tisanes are drunk without milk. They can be sweetened with a little sugar or honey according to taste. Some people like to add a little lemon juice, and sometimes spices as well.

Among those herbs which are most suitable for use as tisanes are Lime, Peppermint, Garden Thyme, Rosehip, Angelica, Bergamot, Green Buckwheat, Hibiscus, Chamomile, Lemon Balm, Sage and Marjoram. Certain herbs, such as Bergamot and Lemon Balm for example, need to be boiled for at least a few minutes to extract the full flavour.

Aromatic seeds may also be used in the preparation of infusions. They need to be bruised and crushed and then simmered gently for at least ten minutes to draw out their full flavour. Use four teaspoons of seeds to every 560ml (20 fl oz). Strain and serve hot.

Teas

The characteristic flavour of Tea (including herb teas) results from the high tannin content of the leaves used; the aroma is not naturally present in the fresh leaves but is formed during the process of fermentation.

Due to their high tannin content the best herb teas include Lady's Mantle, Strawberry, Raspberry, Blackberry and Rose-bay Willow herb. The leaves should

	For Fragrant Enjoyment	Stomach Soothing	Stimulating and Uplifting	Cosmetic and Skin-refreshing	Pain-killing	Antiseptic	Sweat-inducing	Diuretic	Coughs and Colds	Fever-allaying	Anti-bilious	Sleep-inducing	Tonic
Agrimony									●	●			
Angelica leaves		●											
Aniseed	●											●	
Anise leaves		●											
Bergamot (red)									●				
Borage			●							●			
Burdock	●						●	●					
Caraway	●	●											
Celery seed								●				●	
Chamomile		●		●	●								
Clove pinks (Gilly flowers)			●										
Coltsfoot									●				
Comfrey					●				●				
Cowslip												●	●
Cumin		●											
Dandelion					●			●			●		
Dill	●	●		●									
Elder flowers	●						●		●	●			
Fennel	●	●				●			●				
Hibiscus	●												
Hops					●							●	
Hyssop				●		●				●			
Jasmine	●												
Lemon Balm		●	●				●		●				
Lime	●			●			●						
Lovage		●								●		●	
Maté	●												●
Marjoram			●			●	●						
Mints		●		●		●							●
Mugwort											●		
Nasturtium						●							
Nettle				●									●
Orange-flower	●												
Parsley								●					
Pennyroyal		●							●				
Peppermint							●		●				
Primrose													●
Raspberry leaf										●			
Red Rose petals	●		●										
Rose-Geranium	●												
Rosehip	●												
Rosemary		●		●									
Saffron													●
Sage						●			●			●	●
Salad Burnet													●
Savory		●											
Sorrel													●
Sweet Cicely		●							●				
Tansy				●							●		
Thyme			●			●	●		●				
Vervain										●			
Violet			●						●				
Watercress						●							
Wild Strawberry								●					
Woodruff			●										
Yarrow							●		●		●		

Left: Most people think of just the everyday Chinese and Indian varieties when making tea. There are a great number of plants, however – such as Aniseed, Dandelion, Lovage and Vervain – that can make a refreshing drink. Many of them are also medicinally beneficial, while others possess cosmetic properties.

*Right: Yerba Maté (*Ilex paraguariensis*) being gathered in Paraguay. Once gathered, the leaves are dried on a wooden frame, placed over a fire and then pounded. The tea made from the leaves contains both caffeine and tannin. Maté tea should not be prepared in advance but drunk when freshly brewed. It is an effective tonic and mild stimulant.*

be collected from the time they start to unfold until they begin to flower. It is necessary to use large quantities of the leaves as small amounts will ferment only with difficulty.

Leave the fresh leaves in the shade for 12 to 24 hours. The temperature should be sufficiently high to make them wilt but not so high that they dry out. Then bruise them with a rolling pin, spreading them out in thin layers. Fold the bruised leaves in a cloth. Store the cloth in a warm place (20–45°C, 68–113°F) for 24 to 48 hours; during this time the leaves will start to generate their own heat. Finish the process by drying the leaves in the shade at a temperature of not more than 54°C (129°F). The tea leaves should be more or less brown.

Much the best way of producing satisfactory herb teas is by experiment, both with the fermented leaves of different plants and with different blends. Take about one teaspoon of the dried leaves to each 140ml (5 fl oz). Pour on boiling water, infuse for 3 to 10 minutes, strain and serve hot or cold. As with tisanes, a little lemon and honey or sugar may be added. Some established blends are as follows:

1 Blackberry 8 parts
  Strawberry 4 parts
  Raspberry 2 parts
  Peppermint 2 parts
2 Blackberry 8 parts
  Raspberry 4 parts
  Thyme 2 parts
3 Blackberry 8 parts
  Rose-bay Willow herb 4 parts
  Raspberry 4 parts
  Lime (flowers) 2 parts
4 Lady's Mantle 8 parts
  Raspberry 8 parts
  Peppermint 2 parts
  All parts by weight

SOUP DISHES

Gazpacho

Serves 4

half a cucumber
1 medium-sized onion
1 green pepper
2–3 large ripe tomatoes
1–2 cloves Garlic (according to taste)
3 tablespoons olive oil
1 tablespoon superfine or castor sugar
4 tablespoons wine vinegar
280ml (10 fl oz) tomato juice
25g (1 oz) fresh Parsley
salt and white pepper

Peel and dice the vegetables. Cut the cucumber lengthwise and remove the seeds. Using a sieve or an electric blender, mix the vegetables with the olive oil, sugar, wine vinegar and a little of the tomato juice. Add the oil and vinegar sparingly, making sure that the mixture becomes neither too oily nor too sharp. Pour into a bowl, add the remaining tomato juice and seasoning to taste. Stir together and put in the refrigerator. Serve chilled sprinkled with Parsley.

Pea Soup

Serves 4–8

450g (1 lb) dried split peas
50g (2 oz) diced salt pork or ham
170g (6 oz) chopped celery
170g (6 oz) chopped onion
2l (70 fl oz) cold water
1 ham bone
1 Bay leaf
6 Parsley stalks
10 whole Allspice
1 piece blade Mace
salt and pepper
2 tablespoons chopped Parsley

Soak the dried peas in cold water overnight. Rinse and drain. Brown the pork or ham in a heavy saucepan adding a little oil if the meat is lean. Add the celery and onion and cook for a few minutes. Add the cold water, drained peas, ham bone and the herbs and spices tied in muslin. Simmer for about 2 hours. Remove the ham bone and the muslin bag. Taste and adjust the seasoning. Serve sprinkled with Parsley accompanied by fresh bread.

Norwegian Caraway Soup

Serves 4

25g (1 oz) butter or margarine
15g (½ oz) plain flour (unbleached, enriched)
1 litre (35 fl oz) good veal stock
225g (8 oz) chopped Caraway leaves
1 egg yolk
2 tablespoons cream
salt
ground black pepper
4 poached eggs or 2 hard-boiled eggs, sliced
2 tablespoons finely chopped Caraway leaves

Melt the butter or margarine in a saucepan. Stir in the flour. Gradually add the stock, stirring constantly, and bring to the boil. Add the Caraway leaves and simmer gently for 5 to 10 minutes. Beat the egg yolk and cream together and add a spoonful of the soup to this mixture before pouring it into the rest of the soup. Keep the soup hot but do not let it boil once the cream has been added. Taste for seasoning and adjust if necessary. Garnish each serving with a poached egg or slices of hard-boiled egg. Sprinkle with chopped Caraway leaves, serve with buttered toast.

Garlic Soup
Serves 6

6 tablespoons whole Garlic cloves
25g (1 oz) butter
4 tablespoons olive oil
1 litre (35 fl oz) chicken stock
3 egg yolks
salt
pinch Cayenne and ground Mace
6 rounds French bread (fresh or toasted)
2 tablespoons chopped Parsley

Peel the Garlic cloves carefully. Heat them in a heavy pan in the butter and a tablespoon of the olive oil over a low heat for about 15 minutes. Avoid browning the cloves. Pour on the stock. Bring to the boil and simmer for 20 minutes.

Beat the egg yolks with a whisk until they thicken. Add the rest of the oil drop by drop. Stir a few spoonfuls of the soup into the egg-oil mixture, then add this mixture very slowly to the saucepan stirring constantly. Heat but do not boil. Rub through a sieve into a warmed pan or tureen. Season to taste and add the spices. Place a slice of French bread in each warmed soup bowl and pour the soup over. Sprinkle with Parsley and serve.

Sorrel Soup
Serves 4–6

450g (1 lb) French Sorrel leaves
450g (1 lb) spinach
50g (2 oz) onion
40g ($1\frac{1}{2}$ oz) margarine
40g ($1\frac{1}{2}$ oz) plain flour (unbleached, enriched)
1 litre (35 fl oz) chicken stock
black peppercorns and salt
2 tablespoons lemon juice
140 ml (5 fl oz) sour cream
finely snipped Chives

Trim and wash the Sorrel and spinach very thoroughly. Put the leaves into a large saucepan and cook until tender. Drain and purée in a blender or rub through a fine sieve. Peel and chop the onion and fry in the margarine until softened and clear. Add the flour and stir to blend. Remove from the heat and stir in the stock. Return to the heat and bring to the boil gently, stirring constantly. Season with pepper and salt. Simmer for 3–5 minutes. Stir in the puréed vegetables and lemon juice. Check seasoning – adjust with a little sugar if preferred. Pour into bowls and divide the sour cream between them. Sprinkle Chives on the cream. Serve hot or chilled.

Above: Garlic, one of the most popular herbs of all. It is most often added to meat dishes.

MEAT AND POULTRY DISHES

Chicken Legs Hunter's Style
Serves 4

225g (8 oz) button mushrooms
50g (2 oz) margarine
1 small onion
8 chicken legs
2 tablespoons plain flour (unbleached, enriched)
7 tablespoons dry white wine
420ml (15 fl oz) chicken stock
2 tablespoons tomato purée
$\frac{1}{2}$ teaspoon salt
$\frac{1}{4}$ teaspoon ground black pepper
1 teaspoon chopped fresh Chervil or
$\frac{1}{4}$ teaspoon dried Chervil
1 teaspoon chopped fresh Thyme or
$\frac{1}{4}$ teaspoon dried Thyme and 1 Bay leaf
1 tablespoon finely chopped Parsley

Rinse and chop the mushrooms and fry them in half the margarine in a heavy saucepan. Lift the mushrooms out of the pan and fry the chopped onion and the chicken legs in the rest of the margarine until golden brown. Sprinkle the flour over the chicken and onion and fry gently. Pour on the wine and stock and add the tomato purée, salt, pepper, Chervil, Thyme and Bay leaf. Cook gently for 20 minutes or until the chicken is tender, stirring occasionally. Add the mushrooms and simmer for a further couple of minutes. Stir in the Parsley just before serving. Serve with boiled rice and haricots verts or a green salad.

Chicken with Rosemary
Serves 4

1 chicken, about 1kg ($2–2\frac{1}{4}$ lb)
25g (1 oz) margarine
1 tablespoon chopped Rosemary or
1 teaspoon dried Rosemary
200ml (7 fl oz) sour cream
2 tablespoons tomato purée
1 pickled cucumber, finely chopped
salt and pepper

Heat the oven to 425°F (215°C) or Gas Mark 7. Divide the chicken into quarters. Place them in a fireproof dish and brush them with melted margarine. Season with

salt, Pepper and Rosemary. Roast the chicken in the oven for about 45 minutes until the meat is thoroughly cooked and nicely browned. Mix the sour cream, tomato purée, Cucumber and seasoning if required. Serve the sauce with the chicken accompanied by boiled potatoes and a salad.

Chicken Paprika
Serves 4

4 or 5 chicken pieces
salt
25g (1 oz) margarine or butter
25g (1 oz) lard
3 onions, chopped or sliced
4 teaspoons Hungarian Paprika
560ml (20 fl oz) stock
2 teaspoons cornflour (cornstarch)
280ml (10 fl oz) carton sour cream

Sprinkle chicken pieces with salt. Melt the margarine and lard in a skillet or covered frying pan. Add onions and cook gently until they start to brown. Add Paprika and stock. Bring to the boil and add the chicken. Cover pan and simmer until tender, about 1¼ hours. Stir the cornflour into the sour cream and stir into the pan. Cook gently for a few minutes, but do not bring to the boil. This dish can also be made with turkey breasts.

Above: Goose baked in a moderate oven with Rosemary, Garlic and Bay leaves is an unusual way of serving this bird; this combination of herbs brings out to the full the delicious flavour of the meat, while at the same time masking the slightly fatty taste which tends to be a characteristic of goose. Chicken may be used instead of goose in this recipe and will be just as delicious.

Goulash
Serves 4

675g (1½ lb) lean stewing beef cut into cubes
2½ large onions, sliced
50g (2 oz) dripping
1 heaped tablespoon Hungarian Paprika
salt
1 teaspoon Caraway seeds
1 teaspoon Marjoram
2 crushed cloves of Garlic
stock
550g (1¼ lb) potatoes (optional)

Fry the onions and Garlic in a casserole or pan for a few minutes in dripping. Add the Paprika, salt, Marjoram and Caraway seeds and cook briefly. Add the meat and cover with stock. Cover the pan and cook in a slow oven for at least 3 hours. Half an hour before serving add the potatoes.

Turkish Lamb
Serves 4

900g (2 lbs) best end of neck of lamb
3 large onions
225g (8 oz) carrots
4 fresh or canned tomatoes
1 green pepper
4 diced potatoes
1 teaspoon Fennel or Dill
1 teaspoon Sage
2 Bay leaves
2 chopped cloves Garlic
700ml (25 fl oz) stock
50g (2 oz) lard
flour
salt and pepper

Melt the lard in a thick pan. Peel and roughly chop the onions and fry them with the Garlic until they are golden. Divide the meat into chops, coat them in seasoned flour and fry them for a couple of minutes on each side. Add the carrots, tomatoes, green pepper, Bay, Sage, Fennel or Dill, stock and seasoning. Cover the pan, bring to the boil, skim and simmer for 1¾ hours. Add the diced potatoes and chopped onions and Garlic and simmer for a further 45 minutes.

FISH DISHES

Fish au Poivre Vert
Serves 5

280–340g (10–12 oz) plaice, flounder or any white fish fillets, fresh or frozen
7 tablespoons double or whipping cream
7 tablespoons sour cream
2 teaspoons salt
1½ teaspoons chopped green peppercorns
1½ teaspoons chopped Chervil or Parsley
1½ teaspoons chopped Basil

Thaw frozen fillets under running cold water. Fold them and place them in a shallow pan. Whip together the cream, sour cream, salt and herbs and pour the sauce over the fish. Cover with a lid and simmer for 5 minutes. Serve with freshly cooked vegetables and boiled potatoes.

Potted Shrimps
Serves 4

225g (8 oz) freshly cooked peeled shrimps (or frozen)
110g (4 oz) butter
pinch ground Nutmeg
pinch ground Mace
pinch Cayenne Pepper
salt

Clarify the butter by adding small knobs of it to boiling water in a small saucepan. When the butter has all dissolved, remove

Above: Fennel stalks and leaves make a delicious vegetable dish, while the seeds are a pungent flavouring.

the pan from the heat and let it cool. Lift off the solid butter, dry the undersurface on kitchen paper and divide the butter into two equal portions.

Heat half the butter in a frying pan together with the spices. Add the peeled shrimps and toss them in the butter. Transfer to small pots and allow to cool. Melt the rest of the butter and pour over the shrimps to seal them. Chill before serving with hot toast.

Sea-Bream (Porgy) with Fennel
Serves 6

1 sea-bream or porgy, about 1kg (2–2¼ lb)
a few sprigs green Fennel or
slices of Fennel root
salt
black pepper
2–3 tablespoons olive oil
4 tablespoons Pernod

Gut and scrape the sea-bream thoroughly to remove the scales. Rinse and pat the fish dry with kitchen paper. Fill the fish with Fennel sprigs or chopped Fennel root and place it on a large sheet of aluminium foil brushed with the oil. Warm the Pernod, set it alight and pour it over the fish. Season the fish with salt and pepper and wrap in the foil parcel and place it on a baking dish. Bake at 350°F (180°C) or Gas Mark 4 for 30 minutes, turning the fish parcel after the first 15 minutes.

Check that the fish is thoroughly cooked before serving with boiled potatoes and a green salad.

If sea-bream is not available use bass or haddock.

Soused Fish
Serves 4

boiled or left-over fish (approx 450g [1 lb])
280ml (10 fl oz) fish stock
280ml (10 fl oz) vinegar
4 Fennel leaves
3 Bay leaves
2 Cloves
12 peppercorns and salt
3 slices of lemon

Place the pieces of fish in a deep dish. Boil up the fish stock with the vinegar and the herbs, lemon and salt. Pour over the fish and leave so that the fish becomes thoroughly saturated. Refrigerate and serve with thin slices of brown bread.

Pickled Mackerel
Serves 4

4 mackerel
280ml (10 fl oz) malt or distilled vinegar
140ml (5 fl oz) water
6 Bay leaves
1 teaspoon Allspice
salt and pepper
12 peppercorns

Clean and wash the fish and remove the bones. Place in a baking dish, sprinkle with salt and pepper, add Bay leaves, peppercorns, Allspice, vinegar and water. Bake in a cool oven for about an hour. Allow the fish to cool and serve in the liquor.

EGG DISHES

Parsley and Garlic Eggs
Serves 2

2 eggs
25g (1 oz) butter
½ tablespoon chopped fresh Parsley
1 clove Garlic, chopped
salt and pepper

Melt half the butter in a heavy-bottomed saucepan. Break the eggs into the butter and sprinkle with salt and pepper. Leave over the heat until the whites of the egg have almost whitened and formed, then remove. Meanwhile cream the remaining butter with the Garlic and Parsley and a pinch of salt and drop this mixture in small lumps over the eggs. Serve at once. This is a delicious and unusual dish to start a meal.

Herb Omelette
Serves 2

4 large eggs
1 medium-sized onion
1 clove Garlic, chopped
1 medium-sized boiled potato
2 tomatoes
1 teaspoon chopped Lovage
1 teaspoon chopped Chives
1 teaspoon Tarragon
1 teaspoon Thyme
1 teaspoon Marjoram
1½ tablespoons olive oil
salt and pepper

Roughly chop the onion, Garlic, potato and tomatoes. Heat the oil in a frying pan and gently fry the onion and Garlic until soft. Add the tomatoes and potato and cook for a few minutes. Break the eggs into a mixing bowl and beat them, adding the herbs according to taste and season. Mix quickly with the vegetables in the pan and cook until the underside is setting. Then finish the omelette under a hot grill.

Oregano Flan
Serves 4

Pastry
140g (5 oz) whole wheat flour
70g (2½ oz) mixed fats (butter or margarine and lard)
salt

Filling
1 × 400g (14 oz) can Italian peeled tomatoes
110g (4 oz) grated Cheddar cheese
1 small can anchovies
50g (2 oz) black Olives
6 teaspoons chopped fresh Oregano or
2 teaspoons dried Oregano

Mix the whole wheat flour, salt and fats together in a bowl, adding water to make a stiff dough. Knead the pastry lightly and chill for 15 minutes. Roll the mixture out on a pastry board and cover the base and sides of a flan case with it. Drain the tomatoes and chop all but one in half. Place the whole tomato in the centre of the case and distribute the halves throughout the case. Drain the anchovies and lay them like the spokes of a wheel across the case. Scatter the cheese, Olives and Oregano over the flan. Bake for 45 minutes, for the first 15 minutes at 400°F (200°C) or Mark 6. For the last 30 minutes lower the heat to 350°F (180°C) or Mark 4.

PASTA DISHES

Spaghetti Rosmarino

Serves 4

450g (1 lb) spaghetti
110g (4 oz) butter
6 tablespoons chopped fresh Rosemary or
2 tablespoons of dried Rosemary

Cook the spaghetti in a large pan of boiling, salted water. Meanwhile, melt the butter in another pan. If dried Rosemary is used, fry it gently in the butter for a minute or two. Drain the spaghetti well and toss it thoroughly in the Rosemary and melted butter before serving.

Herb Rice

Serves 4

450g (1 lb) rice
2 Bay leaves
4 Cloves
25mm (1 in) Cinnamon stick
4 peppercorns
4 crushed Cardamom seeds
20–30 blanched almonds
20–30 sultanas (or raisins)
50–85g (2–3 oz) butter
2 tablespoons cooking oil
2 teaspoons salt (less if salted butter is used)
2 teaspoons sugar
560ml (20 fl oz) water
onions
hard-boiled eggs
tomatoes

Wash the rice and soak in cold water for about 1 hour. Heat the oil in a thick saucepan and fry the Bay leaves, Cloves, Cinnamon, peppercorns, Cardamom, almonds and sultanas for a few minutes. Add the butter. When it has melted add the drained rice and fry for a few minutes, stirring to prevent it sticking to the base of the pan. Then add the water, salt and sugar. Bring to the boil and reduce the heat to just above the minimum. Cover the pan and let it simmer for 5 to 10 minutes. The water will evaporate and the rice will cook without being stirred or disturbed in any way. Test the rice by eating a few grains, but do not lift the pan lid during the first 5 minutes. Decorate the rice with slices of tomato, hard-boiled egg or fried onions

VEGETABLES AND SALADS

Aubergines (Eggplants) with Herbs

Serves 4

4 aubergines (eggplants)
3 slices of streaky bacon
2 small cloves Garlic
1½ teaspoons chopped fresh Basil and Marjoram mixed or
½ teaspoon of dried Basil and Marjoram mixed
4 tablespoons olive oil
salt and pepper

Wash but do not peel the aubergines. Cut two slits lengthwise in each. Chop the Garlic, mix with herbs, pepper and salt. Dice the bacon and fill the slits in the aubergine with bacon and Garlic. Pour the oil over the vegetable. Bake slowly in a shallow, covered dish for 1 hour.

Below: Spring Risotto, an Italian dish with herbs to taste such as Basil, Oregano and Summer Savory.
Overleaf: You can select suitable herbs for each dish you cook from the chart on the following two pages.

	Alecost	Allspice	Angelica	Aniseed	Basil	Bay	Bergamot	Blackcurrant leaves	Black Pepper	Borage	Burnet	Capers	Caraway seeds	Cardamom seeds	Cayenne	Chervil	Chicory	Chives	Cinnamon
Alcoholic beverages	●	●	●	●						○	○		●						
Apples				●									●	●					●
Apricots																			●
Artichokes, globe						●													
Artichokes, Jerusalem									●										
Asparagus									●										
Baked goods		●	●	●						○			●	●					●
Beans, Broad					●														
Beans, French					●				●										
Beef				●	●		○					●	●	●	●				
Beetroots					●								●	●					
Brussels sprouts				●					●										
Cabbages		●											●						
Carrots			●		●					○			●					●	
Cherries		●																	●
Chocolate														●					●
Citrus fruits								●		○									
Cocoa														●			●		●
Coffee														●			●		
Condiments						●					○				●	●		●	
Cream												●			●			●	
Cucumbers					●								●					●	
Currants																			●
Dairy foods				●	●		○				○	●	●		●	○		●	
Eggs					●	●						●	●		●	●		●	
Fish	●	●	●	●	●	●				○		●			●	●		●	
Game													●						
Gooseberries																			
Lamb	●	●		●								●	●		●				
Marinades	●	●			●	●				○			●			●		●	
Mayonnaise												●			●			●	
Onions		●				●													
Pasta sauces					●	●			●			●	●		●			●	
Peaches		●																	●
Pears			●											●					●
Peas					●														
Pickles		●				●				○	○	●		●	●	●		●	●
Pork	●				●	●	○				○		●			●		●	
Potatoes		●					○					●		●				●	
Poultry	●				●	●							●					●	
Pumpkins		●																	●
Rhubarb			●																●
Salad dressing	●				●	●				○			●		●	●		●	
Salads	●		●		●		○			○	○	●	●			●	●	●	
Savoury rice						●			●					●		●			
Soups	●	●			●	●			●				●		●	○		●	
Spinach					●				●										
Stews					●	●							●					●	
Swedes (Rutabagas)									●										
Sweet sauces														●					●
Tea	●	●	○				○			○	○		●						
Tomatoes	●				●											○		●	
Turnips													●					●	
Veal	●										○					●		●	
Vinegars						●				○	○					●		●	●

	Cloves	Coriander	Cowslips	Cumin	Curry powder	Dandelion	Dill	Elder berries	Elder flowers	Fennel	Garlic	Ginger	Globe artichokes	Hops	Horseradish	Hyssop	Jasmine	Juniper	Lemon Balm
Alcoholic beverages	●			●		●		●	●				●	●				●	
Apples	●	●								●		●							
Apricots	●															●			
Artichokes, globe							●				●								
Artichokes, Jerusalem																			
Asparagus																			
Baked goods	●	●	●		●				●	●		●							
Beans, Broad							●			●									
Beans, French																			
Beef										●		●			●				
Beetroots		●		●						●									
Brussels sprouts																			
Cabbages				●			●											●	
Carrots																			
Cherries	●																		
Chocolate	●																		
Citrus fruits																			
Cocoa	●																		
Coffee						●													
Condiments		●					●			●	●								●
Cream							●												
Cucumbers							●												
Currants	●																		
Dairy foods		●		●	●		●			●	●			●	●				
Eggs				●	●		●			●	●								○
Fish					●		●			●	●	●			●	●		●	○
Game					●					●								●	
Gooseberries									●			●							
Lamb							●				●							●	
Marinades						●	●				●					●		●	●
Mayonnaise					●								●		●				
Onions	●																		
Pasta sauces							●				●								
Peaches	●																		
Pears	●	●										●							
Peas																			
Pickles	●	●		●	●	●	●			●	●				●				●
Pork		●						●				●							
Potatoes	●						●				●							●	
Poultry				●	●		●			●		●						●	
Pumpkins	●											●			●				
Rhubarb												●							
Salad dressing					●	●	●				●				●	●			●
Salads						●	●			●			●						
Savoury rice		●		●	●														
Soups				●		●					●		●						
Spinach																			
Stews										●									
Swedes (Rutabagas)																			
Sweet sauces	●											●							
Tea						●	●		●	●				●		●	●		●
Tomatoes						●	●												
Turnips		●								●									
Veal							●												
Vinegars		●					●			●	●	●		●				●	●

○ *indicates herb must be used fresh* ● *indicates herb may be used fresh or dried and sometimes candied*

	Lovage	Mace	Marigold	Marigold petals	Marjoram	Mint	Mustard	Nasturtium	Nutmeg	Orange	Oregano	Paprika	Parsley	Pepper	Pine Nuts	Poppyseeds	Purslane	Rose petals	Rosemary	Saffron	Sage	Salad Burnet	Savory	Sesame seeds	Sorrel	Spice mixtures	Sunflower seeds	Sweet Cicely seeds	Tansy	Tarragon	Thyme	Turmeric	Vanilla	Vanilla pods	Violets	Watercress	Wormwood	Yarrow leaves
Alcoholic beverages			●										●					●	●																○		●	○
Apples									●																	●								●				
Apricots																																		●				
Artichokes, Globe											●		●																			●						
Artichokes, Jerusalem									●				●		●															●								
Asparagus																																						
Baked goods	●		●						●		●					●		●	●	●	●			●		●	●	●					●	●	○			
Beans, Broad													●								○		●							●						○		
Beans, French																																						
Beef				●	●		●						●	●									●								●							
Beetroots																															●							
Brussels sprouts									●																													
Cabbages		●				●										●					●						●											
Carrots		●				●			●				●										●							●	●					○		
Cherries									●																								●					
Chocolate		●							●																								●					
Citrus fruits						●																																
Cocoa									●																								●					
Coffee																																						
Condiments	●				●	●	●							●							●						●			●								
Cream							●		●			●	●	●		●									●					●								
Cucumbers												●	●																							○		
Currants						●																																
Dairy foods	●	●	●		●	●	●	●	●		●	●	●	●	●				●	●	●			●						●	●					○		
Eggs	●				●	●	●		●		●	●	●	●	●	●			●	●	●	●	○							●	●	●						
Fish	●	●	●		●	●	●		●		●	●	●	●					●	●	●		○	●	○				●	●	●	●				○		
Game							●					●	●	●					●		●		●							●	●							
Gooseberries																																						
Lamb					●	●	●				●		●	●	●				●		●		●								●							
Marinades	●					●	●				●			●					●		●	●								●								
Mayonnaise					●		●						●	●																●								
Onions									●		●			●	●						●										●							
Pasta sauces	●		●		●	●			●		●		●	●	●				●		●		●								●							
Peaches									●																								●					
Pears																																	●					
Peas						●																									●							
Pickles	●	●			●	●	●														●						●			●								
Pork	●					●	●				●	●	●	●	●					●	●		●	●												○		
Potatoes		●				●			●			●	●	●		●					●		●	●						●	●	●						
Poultry									●		●	●	●	●	●					●	●		●	●						●	●							
Pumpkins		●							●																													
Rhubarb						●																																
Salad dressing	●				●	●	●				●	●		●		●			●		○	●	○							●	●				○			
Salads			●					●					●	●			●					●		●	○		●			●					○	○		●
Savoury rice				●					●		●	●	●	●	●	●				●				●							●	●						
Soups	●	●	●		●				●		●		●	●					●	●	●		●					●		●	●					○		
Spinach		●							●																				●									
Stews	●		●		●						●		●	●					●	●			●							●	●							
Swedes (Rutabagas)		●							●																													
Sweet sauces									●																									●				
Tea	●		●		●	●				●			●					●	●		●				●	●		●	●		●					○	●	○
Tomatoes											●			●									●						●									
Turnips																																						
Veal							●					●	●	●					●		●		●								●							
Vinegars	●				●	●	●	●						●				●	●		●					○	●			●								

Cinnamon Spinach
Serves 4

2kg ($4\frac{1}{2}$ lb) spinach
50g (2 oz) butter
$2\frac{1}{2}$ tablespoonfuls cream
Cinnamon
salt
sugar
lemon rind

Trim and prepare the spinach and wash several times in a lot of cold water. Place in a saucepan with very little water and salt to taste. Boil for 5 to 10 minutes until tender.

Strain and press the spinach until free of water. Over a low flame, melt the butter in a frying pan. Add the cream, a pinch of sugar and salt and Cinnamon to taste, and a teaspoon of grated lemon rind. To this add the spinach and stir well. Serve at once.

Sweet and Sour Tomato Salad
Serves 4

6 tomatoes
1 medium-sized onion
Chives
Basil
malt or distilled vinegar
2 tablespoons granulated sugar
water
freshly ground black pepper

Wash and dice the tomatoes and place in a bowl with the finely chopped onion. Add a few sprigs of freshly chopped Chives and a few torn Basil leaves. Prepare the dressing by combining equal parts of vinegar and hot water with the sugar. Pour over the tomatoes, sprinkle very lightly with freshly milled black pepper and place in the refrigerator. Serve slightly chilled.

Mushrooms à la Grecque

450g (1 lb) mushrooms
1 large onion
1 large carrot
2–3 dozen Coriander seeds (according to taste)
2 or 3 Bay leaves
3–4 sprigs Parsley
3 large tomatoes
Thyme
salt
black pepper
280ml (10 fl oz) white wine
140ml (5 fl oz) olive oil

Chop the onion finely and lightly fry in the olive oil until it is beginning to turn golden. Dice the carrot and add it to the onion, frying for a further 5 minutes. Add the salt, black pepper and Coriander seeds and cook briefly. Pour the wine into the pan and cook slowly until the mixture is bubbling gently. Peel and roughly chop the tomatoes, wash the mushrooms and halve them if they are the field variety (button ones can be left whole). Chop the Parsley stems. Add the mushrooms, tomatoes, Bay leaves, Parsley stalks and a sprinkling of Thyme to the mixture in the pan and cook uncovered for about 15 minutes. The mushrooms and carrot should be tender but still crisp. Put in the refrigerator and serve slightly chilled, sprinkled with finely chopped Parsley.

Mint and Grapefruit Cocktail
Serves 4

1 400g (14 oz) can grapefruit segments or 3 fresh grapefruits
gin to taste
chopped fresh Mint

Chop the grapefruit into small segments and place in a bowl. Add a little gin, about 1 tablespoon will be sufficient. Sprinkle with chopped mint and serve chilled. This makes a delicious hors d'oeuvre.

SAUCES AND DRESSINGS

Franco's Dip

2 large bunches of Parsley, chopped
$\frac{1}{4}$ medium-sized red pepper, cleaned and chopped
a small can of anchovy fillets, drained and chopped
olive oil
fresh breadcrumbs
vinegar or lemon juice

Chop the Parsley, red pepper, and anchovies as finely as possible, and then mix them all together thoroughly. Add enough olive oil and breadcrumbs to make a fairly stiff 'dip'. Then add a very small amount of vinegar or lemon juice but not enough to make it tart. Season to taste.

This is delicious eaten with really good old fashioned home-baked bread. Don't put butter on the bread.

Herb Butter

110g (4 oz) butter or margarine
3 tablespoons finely chopped celery leaves
3 tablespoons finely chopped Chives or spring onion greens
1 tablespoon lemon juice
$\frac{1}{4}$ teaspoon salt
$\frac{1}{2}$ teaspoon Basil

Mix the ingredients in a blender or with a pestle and mortar. Use in sandwiches or on hot French bread or with grilled fish or meat.

Horseradish Sauce

25g (1 oz) Horseradish
140ml (5 fl oz) double or whipping cream
pepper and salt
prepared English Mustard
vinegar
superfine or castor sugar

Wash, peel and grate the Horseradish. Whisk the cream lightly. Fold the Horseradish into the cream and add the seasonings, sparingly, to taste. Serve with boiled fish, beef, tongue or as a garnish to cheeses such as Edam.

Poppyseed Sauce

50g (2 oz) butter or margarine, melted
2 teaspoons Poppyseeds
1 tablespoon lemon juice
$\frac{1}{4}$ teaspoon freshly chopped Marjoram or Thyme
pinch Paprika
$\frac{1}{2}$ teaspoon salt

Mix the ingredients in a small heavy saucepan over a gentle heat. Serve as an accompaniment to hot cooked carrots, cauliflower or peas.

Herb Dredge

Fennel seeds
Coriander seeds
Cinnamon
sugar
breadcrumbs
flour
(quantities to taste)

Grind the Fennel and Coriander seeds and mix together with the Cinnamon and sugar to taste. Add a few breadcrumbs and a very little flour. Score the side of a joint of pork or lamb and rub this seasoning in before roasting.

Aïoli Provençal Garlic Mayonnaise

4–6 Garlic cloves
ground black pepper
1 teaspoon salt
2 teaspoons French Mustard
3 egg yolks
olive oil
wine vinegar or lemon juice

Pound the Garlic cloves with a pestle in a mortar together with the Pepper, salt and Mustard until smooth. Add the egg yolks and mix well. Add the oil, drop by drop at first. If the sauce becomes too thick add a little vinegar or lemon juice or a teaspoon of hot water. When the aïoli has reached a firm consistency pour it into a bowl and serve chilled with fresh vegetables, eggs or fish.

Herb Sauce

1 tablespoon of grated Horseradish
2 finely chopped shallots
a few sprigs each (or 1 teaspoon of dried) Winter Savory, Basil, Marjoram, Thyme, Tarragon.
6 Cloves
thinly peeled rind and juice of 1 lemon
280ml (10 fl oz) strong vinegar
560ml (20 fl oz) water

Wash the Horseradish and remove stalks from the herbs. Put all the ingredients into a saucepan and simmer gently for 20 minutes. Strain. When quite cold pour into bottles for storing. Make sure they are securely corked.

Below: The traditional ingredients of Provençal cooking: artichokes, tomatoes, Garlic, black and green olives, olive oil, Parsley and wine and, of course, a variety of aromatic flavouring herbs including Marjoram, Basil and Bay.

Forcemeat

4 tablespoons grated suet
8 tablespoons white breadcrumbs
2 teaspoons chopped Parsley
1 teaspoon powdered mixed herbs
$\frac{1}{2}$ teaspoon Nutmeg
$\frac{1}{2}$ teaspoon grated lemon rind
1 egg
milk
salt and pepper

Mix all the dry ingredients together. Add egg and enough milk to moisten. Season with salt and pepper. This is suitable for pork, duck or veal.

Mustard Dressing

$2\frac{1}{2}$ tablespoons olive or cooking oil
$2\frac{1}{2}$ teaspoons dry English Mustard
juice of $\frac{1}{2}$ lemon

Add the Mustard to the oil, beating until all the lumps have vanished. Add the lemon juice and mix thoroughly. The ingredients of this dressing can be varied according to taste. It is especially tasty on a salad of lettuce alone.

Above: Basil leaves provide one of the most distinctive flavours.

Sage and Onion Stuffing

3 medium-sized onions
10 Sage leaves
110g (4 oz) breadcrumbs
40g ($1\frac{1}{2}$ oz) margarine or dripping
1 egg yolk
salt and pepper

Peel the onions, put into boiling water and simmer for 10 minutes. Just before you take the onions out, put the Sage leaves in for $\frac{1}{2}$ minute. Chop the onion and Sage leaves very finely and then add the breadcrumbs, seasoning, margarine or dripping, and egg yolk. Mix together.

Pesto

3–5 small bunches Basil, washed and dried
25g (1 oz) strong Cheddar cheese, finely grated
25g (1 oz) Parmesan cheese, finely grated
25g (1 oz) Pine nuts
50ml (2 fl oz) olive oil
2 cloves of Garlic, finely chopped
pinch of salt

Chop the Basil into very fine pieces. Crush the Pine nuts in a pestle and mortar. Combine all the ingredients with the olive oil. Let it stand for 2 hours before using. Pesto is used as a sauce with spaghetti.

Left: Gathered from the hedgerows, rosehips – from the plant Dog Rose – can be used to make a tasty dessert soup, as well as rosehip syrup and rosehip wine.

Herb Vinegars

Most herbs can be added to white wine (or cider) vinegar for use in salad dressings and marinades. Pour the warmed vinegar onto the chosen herbs (560ml or 20 fl oz vinegar to 8 tablespoons herbs). Cover the container and allow to infuse for 14 days in a warm place. If the flavour is strong enough, strain the vinegar, bring to the boil and pour into suitable hot, sterilized bottles, adding a decorative and identifying sprig of the appropriate fresh herb. Cap tightly and store in a cool place. Popular vinegars include French Tarragon, Basil, Thyme, Marjoram, Rosemary Mint and Sage. Garlic may also be infused. Use 140g (5 oz) peeled, bruised Garlic cloves to 1l (35 fl oz) hot white wine vinegar. Cloves, peppercorns and Caraway seeds may also be added. Strain after one week.

DESSERTS

Christmas Day Pudding
Serves 4

1 pkt raspberry jelly (3 oz pkt gelatin)
50g (2 oz) crystallized Ginger
110g (4 oz) glacé cherries
110g (4 oz) well-drained pineapple pieces
170g (6 oz) mixed dried fruit
50g (2 oz) chopped walnuts
Cinnamon and Nutmeg
whipped cream
4 tablespoons medium dry sherry
1 can unsweetened orange juice

Soak the dried fruit in orange juice and a little water overnight. Make the jelly with half the usual amount of hot water. Chop the Ginger and soak it in a little hot water for 5 minutes. As the jelly is about to set, pour the dried fruit and orange juice, pineapple, walnuts, Ginger, glacé cherries and sherry into it and sprinkle with Cinnamon and Nutmeg. Wet a mould and turn the jelly into it. Chill and serve with cream.

Elder flower Fritters

170g (6 oz) plain flour (unbleached, enriched)
25g (1 oz) melted butter
2 tablespoons vegetable oil
pinch salt
1 egg, separated
140ml (5 fl oz) lukewarm water
oil for frying
superfine or castor sugar
Elder flower-heads (flat parts)

Place the flour and salt in a mixing bowl. Put the egg yolk in the centre and a little of the water. Mix to a batter with a wooden spoon or fork, gradually adding the rest of the water. Mix in the melted butter. Fold in the stiffly beaten white of egg. Dip the flower-heads into the batter and fry in hot oil. Drain on kitchen paper. Serve immediately sprinkled lightly with castor sugar.

Rosehip Soup
Serves 6–8

1kg (2¼ lb) Rosehips
3 litres (105 fl oz) water
50g (2 oz) cornflour (cornstarch)
25g (1 oz) almonds
sugar
cream
sweet rusks

If possible, collect the Rosehips following an overnight frost. They should be well ripened and have a good red colour. Trim off the stalks and rinse the Rosehips thoroughly. Simmer the hips for a couple of hours in the water, strain and return the liquor to the heat. Add sugar to taste. Cream the cornflour with a little cold water then whisk it into the soup, beating constantly. Cook for 3 to 5 minutes. Scald the almonds and remove the skins. Slice the nuts lengthwise and add to the soup. Serve with cream and sweet rusks.

Ginger Jelly
Serves 4

1 pkt lime jelly (3 oz pkt gelatin)
4 to 6 pieces Ginger preserved in syrup, drained and sliced

Reconstitute the jelly according to the instructions on the packet and allow to cool. When almost set, stir in the Ginger and leave in a cold place until fully set. Serve chilled, decorated with whipped cream and crystallized Violets.

Gooseberry Fool
Serves 4

450g (1 lb) gooseberries
6 tablespoons water
2 tablespoons chopped Mint
1 piece fresh green Ginger
110g (4 oz) sugar
280ml (10 fl oz) custard sauce (preferably made with eggs and Vanilla sugar)
140ml (5 fl oz) double or whipping cream, whipped
4 pieces crystallized Ginger, chopped
4 young Mint sprigs

Rinse the gooseberries. Simmer gently with the water in a heavy, partially covered pan with the chopped Mint and peeled, chopped green Ginger. Stir in the sugar. Rub through a nylon sieve or cool and purée in an electric blender. Stir in the custard. When cold fold in the cream and chopped crystallized Ginger. Pour into chilled glasses and decorate each with a tiny sprig of fresh Mint.

BREAD AND CAKES

Whole Wheat Herb Bread
Makes about 675g (1½ lb)

225g (8 oz) each whole wheat and plain white (unbleached, enriched) flours
10g (¼ oz) lard, rubbed in
2 teaspoons each salt and sugar
1 teaspoon Dill seed
2 teaspoons chopped fresh Savory or
1 teaspoon dried Savory
1 teaspoon chopped fresh Dill weed or
½ teaspoon dried Dill weed
15g (½ oz) fresh yeast or
2 teaspoons dried yeast
280ml (10 fl oz) warm water

To make the dough with fresh yeast, mix the flours, lard, herbs, salt and sugar together in a bowl. Blend yeast in the water and add all at once. Mix to a soft scone-like dough (adding more blended flour if necessary) so that it leaves the bowl clean.

To make the dough with dried yeast, dissolve a teaspoon of the sugar in a cup of the hand-hot water. Sprinkle the dried yeast on top. Leave for about 10 minutes until frothy. Add with the rest of the water to the flours, containing rubbed-in lard, herbs, salt and the rest of the sugar. Mix to a soft scone-like dough.

Knead the dough thoroughly on a lightly floured board. Half-fill two well-greased loaf tins. (The inside of the pots may be sprinkled with cracked wheat after greasing.) Place the tins inside a large, oiled polythene bag, tie loosely and allow the dough to rise until it doubles in volume.

Remove bag. Bake on the middle shelf of a hot oven at 450°F (230°C) or Gas Mark 8 for 30 to 40 minutes. Serve hot with soup or salad and cheese.

Gingerbread

110g (4 oz) margarine
170g (6 oz) black treacle
50g (2 oz) golden syrup
140ml (5 fl oz) milk
2 eggs
225g (8 oz) plain flour (unbleached, enriched)
50g (2 oz) sugar
1 teaspoon mixed spice
1 tablespoon ground Ginger
1 teaspoon bicarbonate of soda

This quantity is suitable for the following tins: 18cm (7 in) or 20cm (8 in) round cake tins; two 18cm (7 in) square tins, 2.5cm (1 in) deep; two 18cm (7 in) loaf tins.

Using a large saucepan, warm together the margarine, treacle and syrup. Add milk and allow to cool. Beat eggs and blend with cooled mixture. Sieve dry ingredients into a bowl, add the cooled mixture and blend with a tablespoon. Turn into prepared tins and bake on the middle shelf of a slow oven 300°F (150°C) or Gas Mark 2 for 1½ hours depending on the size of the tin.

Above: Freshly baked bread decorated with Sesame seeds. Sesame seeds may also be used in combination with Cinnamon, for example, to flavour bread. Many other herbs can be used as a flavouring, notably Garlic with or without some finely chopped green herbs such as Parsley.

Cardamom Cake

fresh breadcrumbs
340g (12 oz) self-raising flour
1 level teaspoon baking powder
110g (4 oz) butter or margarine
200g (7 oz) granulated sugar
3 teaspoons ground Cardamom or Cinnamon
140ml (5 fl oz) cream
90ml (3 fl oz) milk

Topping
25g (1 oz) flaked almonds
25g (1 oz) granulated sugar
2 teaspoons Cinnamon

Grease a 900g (2 lb) loaf tin and line with fresh breadcrumbs. Mix the flour and baking powder together. Cut the butter or margarine into the flour and rub in with the fingertips until the mixture resembles fine breadcrumbs. Mix in the sugar and Cardamom. Add the cream and milk and stir well until the mixture forms a stiff dough. Spread the mixture out in the prepared tin and level the top. Sprinkle evenly with topping. Bake at 400°F (200°C) or Gas Mark 6 for approximately 1 hour.

Onion Küchen

225g (8 oz) white bread dough
225g (8 oz) onions, peeled and sliced
50g (2 oz) butter or margarine
15g (½ oz) plain flour (unbleached, enriched)
140ml (5 fl oz) milk
¼ teaspoon Garlic salt – optional
1 teaspoon Poppyseeds
salt and pepper

Grease and flour a 20cm (8 in) sandwich tin. Roll out the dough on a lightly floured board to fit the tin. Place in the tin, cover with a lightly oiled polythene bag and allow to rise until double in size (30–45 minutes at room temperature).

Cook the onions in the butter or margarine in a saucepan until just tender. Stir in the flour and cook for one minute. Add the milk and bring to the boil stirring, boil for 1 minute. Stir in the salt, pepper and Garlic salt. Spoon the onion mixture onto the risen dough base and sprinkle with Poppyseeds. Bake on the middle shelf of the oven at 375°F (190°C) or Gas Mark 5 for 30 minutes.

Garlic Bread

1 French stick or Vienna loaf
85g (3 oz) butter creamed with 1–2 cloves Garlic

Slice the loaf obliquely and chunkily, leaving the base layer intact. Spread both sides of each slice with the creamed garlic butter. Spread garlic butter over the crust of the loaf. Wrap the loaf in aluminium foil and heat in the oven at 400°F (200°C) or Gas Mark 6 for 10 minutes. Serve this delicious bread crusty and hot either with soups, cheese or salads.

HERB AND FLOWER CONFECTIONS

The leaves, stems, flowers and buds of many herbs and fragrant flowers can be attractively preserved using sugar syrups and then dried to retain their original colour and shape making delicious and decorative confections. Additional colouring and flavouring can occasionally be added, and the crystallized, as opposed to the candied, forms are encrusted with a surface layer of fine sugar crystals.

The leaves, stems and newly opened flowers or buds should be good specimens – young and unblemished. A sugar-boiling thermometer is a useful aid in candying. A syrup is boiled to soft ball stage (234°F or 94°C). Use 450g (1 lb) of sugar to 280ml (10 fl oz) water. Add a few of the leaves or the flowers at a time and boil (at 234°F or 94°C) for one minute. Drain using a frying spoon and transfer to a tray covered with aluminium foil. Allow to dry thoroughly in a warm atmosphere such as a barely warm oven (not more than 100°F (38°C) or Gas Mark $\frac{1}{4}$).

Candied Angelica

This method requires the use of a hydrometer. Use green tender young stems picked in April or May. Trim the stems and cut them into 7cm (3 in) lengths. Soak for 15 minutes in cold water. Rinse and boil in water for 5 to 10 minutes, until tender. Drain and scrape off the outer skin. Prepare a syrup by boiling 450g (1 lb) of sugar with 560ml (20 fl oz) of water. (If you use a Beaumé hydrometer, the strength should be 25°, or 46° when a Balling or Brix hydrometer is used.) Cyril Grange in his book *The Complete Book of Home Food Preservation* (Cassell) prescribes the following eight-day sugar-boiling programme for Angelica. Each day more sugar is added and the syrup is boiled to the prescribed degree of strength, and the stems are soaked for the prescribed time.

Day	Soaking Time	Beaumé Reading	Balling Reading
1	24 hours	25	46
2	24 hours	27	50
3	24 hours	28	51
4	24 hours	30	55
5	24 hours	32	60
6	3 days	35	65

Remove and drain the Angelica (*Angelica archangelica*) stems on a wire cake tray. Dry on foil-covered baking trays in a barely warm oven at about 100°F (38°C) or Mark $\frac{1}{4}$. Store in covered jars in a cool dark cupboard.

Herb honeys

Bruised fresh herbs and spices may be added to warmed honey (clover or orange blossom). Pour the warmed honey containing the bruised herbs, spices or flower petals into jars. Cool and cover. Stand in a warm place for one week before use. The following brief list gives a few of the possible additions to honey: Lemon Balm (*Melissa officinalis*), Bergamot (*Monarda didyma*), Borage (*Borago officinalis*), Cardamom *Elettaria cardamomum*, Cinnamon (*Cinnamomum zeylanicum*), Cloves (*Syzygium aromaticum*), Coriander (*Coriandrum sativum*), Fennel (*Foeniculum vulgare*), Ginger (*Zingiber officinale*), Mints (*Mentha* spp), Poppyseeds (*Papaver somniferum*), Rose petals (*Rosa* spp), Sage (*Salvia officinalis*), Savory (*Satureia hortensis*), Sesame seeds (*Sesamum indicum*), and Thyme (*Thymus vulgaris*).

Below: Coriander (left) and Cinnamon (right) plants. Both of these herbs can be used for flavouring honey and mulled wine. Coriander and Cinnamon have both been used for thousands of years.

Herb and spice sugars

Vanilla sugar is made by inserting a piece of Vanilla pod into a jar of superfine or castor sugar. Seal the jar during storage. It is delicious in ice cream, egg custard, cakes and biscuits. Ground Cinnamon and Cardamom may be mixed with sugar for use in puddings. Sprigs of Lemon Balm (*Melissa officinalis*) can be infused in sugar for use in fruit dishes.

HERBS IN ALCOHOL

Herbs have always provided alcoholic beverages with much of their specific flavour and properties. It is surprising to realize just how many of the drinks that we prize most and reserve for special occasions owe their desirable taste and smell to the judicious use of certain herbs – although they may not always be immediately identifiable. Some of the most popular alcoholic drinks, ranging from sweet mead to mulled wines and exotic liqueurs, derive their special qualities from herbal additives.

American iced juleps are made of bourbon whisky, sugar, Mint sprigs and ice and American cobblers and coolers are similarly flavoured with pleasantly additive herbs. Pimms No. 1 is decorated with Borage sprigs (*Borago officinalis*) and Mint (*Mentha* spp). Spices such as Cinnamon sticks (*Cinnamomum zeylanicum*), Cloves (*Syzygium aromaticum*), Cardamom seeds (*Eletaria cardamomum*) and sometimes root Ginger (*Zingiber officinale*) are added to mulled red wines and Swedish glögg. Many aperitif wines owe their characteristic flavours to herbs. Wormwood (*Artemisia absinthium*) is used in vermouth and absinthe production, Anise (*Pimpinella anisum*) in Pernod, bitter herbs in Campari, and globe artichokes (*Cynara scoly-*

mus) are used in Italian Cynar. Mead is flavoured with herbs such as Rosemary (*Rosmarinus officinalis*) and spices such as Cinnamon (*Cinnamomum zeylanicum*), Mace, Nutmeg (*Myristica fragrans*), Cloves (*Syzygium aromaticum*) and Ginger (*Zingiber officinale*). Liqueurs are flavoured with herbs. Crême de Menthe, for example, is flavoured with Mint oils (*Mentha* spp), Kümmel is Cumin (*Cuminum cyminum*) and Caraway flavoured (*Carum carvi*) and Green Chartreuse may contain over one hundred different plant flavours. Aquavit is Cumin-flavoured (*Cuminum cyminum*) and gin is flavoured with Juniper (*Juniperus communis*).

Alcoholic beverages

Herb beers and ales can provide the amateur beer-maker with new experimental lines based on herbs such as Meadowsweet (*Filipendula ulmaria*), Raspberry leaves (*Rubus idaeus*), Chamomile (*Chamaemelum nobile*), Burdock (*Arctium lappa*) root and leaves, Betony (*Stachys officinalis*), Agrimony (*Agrimonia eupatoria*), Dandelion (*Taraxacum officinale*) leaves, Nettles (*Urtica dioica*), Hops (*Humulus lupulus*), Dock (*Rumex crispus*) and Horehound (*Marrubium vulgare*) leaves. Ground Ginger (*Zingiber officinale*) is often used to flavour the brew. A typical recipe for **Botanic Beer** is:

50g (2 oz) Meadowsweet
50g (2 oz) Betony
50g (2 oz) Agrimony
50g (2 oz) Raspberry leaves
25g (1 oz) Hyssop
1.2kg (2½ lb) sugar
9 litres (2 galls) water
ale yeast

Boil the leaves in the water for 15 minutes. Strain. Add the sugar. When tepid add a little ale yeast and bottle.

Nettle Beer

1kg (2¼ lb) young Nettles (tops only)
2 lemons
1 teaspoon ground Ginger
4.5l (1 gall) water
450g (1 lb) demerara or light brown sugar
25g (1 oz) cream of tartar
20g (¾ oz) fresh baker's yeast or
1 teaspoon dried yeast

Bring the rinsed Nettle tops, the peel of the lemon and the Ginger to the boil in the water in a large pan. Simmer for 20 minutes, strain onto the sugar and cream of tartar in another large clean vessel. Stir and allow to cool. Add the lemon juice and yeast. Cover with linen tea towels and leave in a warm place for three days. Transfer to a cold place for a further two days. Strain and bottle using robust flasks. Screw the tops down firmly only when fermentation has ceased. Store for about one week only. It is not a brew for long storage.

Mrs Tritton's Dandelion Beer

225g (8 oz) Dandelion plants with taproot
450g (1 lb) demerara or light brown sugar
15g (½ oz) crushed root Ginger
juice of 2 lemons
liquid ale yeast
water to 4.5l (1 gall)

Boil the washed roots in some of the water, cool and add the rest of the ingredients. Ferment until most of the sugar has gone, then bottle.

Herb wines

The upsurge in home wine-making facilitates the herb wine-makers task since equipment for fermentation and storage is readily available. A wide range of plant material may be used in herb wine-making such as Cowslip flowers (*Primula veris*), Dandelion flowers (*Taraxacum officinale*), Elder flowers (*Sambucus nigra*), Comfrey root (*Symphytum officinale*), Coltsfoot flowers (*Tussilago farfara*), Lemon Balm (*Melissa officinalis*), Rosemary (*Rosmarinus officinalis*), Rose petals (*Rosa* spp), Rhubarb (*Rheum rhabarbarum*), Burnet (*Poterium sanguisorba*) and Bramble tips. (Note that measurements in wine-making are usually by volume. Do not press the herbs down in the jug but firm them by 'bumping' the jug once or twice.)

Dandelion Wine

2.3l (4 pts) Dandelion flowers
4.5l (1 gall) water
2 large oranges
1 large lemon
50g (2 oz) raisins
2 tablespoons yeast
1.6kg (3½ lb) sugar

Put the flowers into the water in a large pan and bring to the boil. Add the orange and lemon rinds and sugar and boil for one hour. Strain, cool until tepid then add the yeast. Next day add the orange and lemon juices and raisins. Bottle. Cork loosely about a month later when fermentation has ceased.

Elder flower Wine

560ml (1 pt) Elder flower-heads (tightly packed into the measure)
2 lemons
4.5l (1 gall) boiling water
1.4kg (3 lb) sugar
15g (½ oz) yeast (preferably champagne yeast activated two days before being added, but baker's yeast creamed with some of the sweetened must and a pinch of tartaric acid will suffice).

Put the flower-heads and thinly peeled lemon rinds into a large bowl. Pour on the boiling water and stir. Cover and leave for three days, stirring occasionally. Stir and bring to the boil, adding the sugar. Simmer for about 10 minutes. Allow to cool until tepid. Decant into a fermentation flask. Add the lemon juice and yeast. Stir to mix. Bottle after four months, tying the corks down.

Marigold Wine

2.3l (4 pts) Marigold flowers
2 oranges
1 lemon
1.4kg (3 lb) sugar
4.5l (1 gall) water
15g (½ oz) baker's yeast

Put the flowers, the thinly pared orange and lemon rinds and the juice of the orange and lemon into a large bowl. Pour on the water which has been brought to the boil with the sugar. Allow to cool. Add the yeast. Stir thoroughly, cover and leave in a warm place for one week. Strain into a fermentation jar, cover and leave in a warm place until fermentation ceases. Store in a cool place for three to four weeks before bottling.

Right: Elder flowers in the wild.

Overleaf: The chart shows the tremendous variety of uses for your herbs, and may well give you new ideas for flavouring and garnishing.

	Stocks Soups Chowders	Sauces and Stuffings	Salads and their Dressings	Vegetable Dishes	Savoury Rice and Pasta Dishes	Dairy Foods	Egg Dishes	Fish and Shellfish Dishes	Meat Dishes	Poultry and Game Dishes	Sweet Dishes and Puddings	Baking	Jams, Jellies, Syrups and Sweetmeats	Vinegars, Pickles, Chutneys and Ketchups	Teas	Wine, Liqueurs, Beer, Ale and Mead	Garnishing
Agrimony															●	●	●
Alecost (Costmary)	●	●	●					●	●	●					●	●	●
Allspice (Pimento, Jamaica Pepper)	●	●		●				●	●	●	●	●		●	●	●	
Angelica leaves			●	●				●							●		
Angelica root								●			●	●	●		○		
Angelica seeds											●		●			●	
Angelica stems			●	●							●	●	●		●		●
Anise	○		○														
Aniseed	●			●		●		●	●	●	●	●				●	
Balm, Lemon		○	●				○	○	○	○	○			●	●		
Basil	●	●	●	●	●	●	●	●	●	●	●						
Bay	●	●	●	●	●		●	●	●	●	●			●			●
Bergamot			○			○									○		○
Borage	○	○	○	○	○			○			○	○		○	○		○
Burnet (Salad Burnet)	○		○	○		○								○	○		○
Capers		●	●			●	●	●	●					●			●
Caraway	●	●	●	●	●	●	●		●			●			●	●	
Caraway seeds	●	●	●	●	●	●	●		●	●		●		●	●		●
Cardamom					●				●		●	●	●	●			
Cayenne (Pepper, Tabasco)	●	●	●	●	●	●	●	●	●	●				●			●
Celery	●	●	●	●		●	●	●	●	●							
Celery salt	●	●	●	●	●	●	●	●	●	●				●			
Celery seed	●	●	●	●	●	●	●	●	●	●				●	●		
Chamomile														●	●		
Chervil	○	●	○	●	○	○	●	●	●	○				●			○
Chili powder	●	●	●	●	●	●		●	●	●				●			
Chives	●	●	●	●	●	●	●	●	●	●				●			●
Chive salt	●	●	●	●	●	●	●		●	●							●
Cicely seeds	●	●	●	●					●						●		
Cicely, Sweet	●	●		●					●			●			●		
Cinnamon, ground											●	●	●	●			
Cinnamon stick											●	●	●	●			●
Clove Pinks (Gillyflowers)											●		●				
Cloves (whole or ground)		●							●		●	●	●	●		●	●
Coriander leaves	○		○	●	○	○			○			●		●			
Coriander seeds	●		●	●	●	●			●		●	●		●			
Cumin seed	●	●		●		●	●		●					●	●		
Cumin, ground (Jeera)	●	●		●	●	●	●		●	●				●		●	
Curry powder	●	●	●	●	●	●	●	●	●	●		●		●			
Dandelion	●		●	●										●	●	●	
Dill	●	●	●	●	●	●	●	●	●	●				●	●		●
Dill seed, ground	●	●	●	●		●		●									
Dill seed, whole	●	●	●			●		●						●	●		
Elderflower									●		●	●			●	●	
Elderberry									●							●	
Fennel	●	●	●	●		●	●	●	●	●				●			●
Fennel seed	●	●				●	●	●	●		●	●		●	●		
Garlic	●	●	●	●	●	●	●	●	●	●				●			
Garlic powder	●	●	●	●	●	●	●	●	●	●							
Garlic salt	●	●	●	●	●	●	●	●	●	●				●			
Geranium			○								○	○	○		○	○	○
Ginger, ground	●								●	●	●						
Ginger, root				●			●	●	●	●	●	●		●		●	
Hops						●									●	●	●
Horseradish			●			●		●	●	●				●			
Hyssop	●	●	●					●	●	●	●				●		

○ *indicates herb must be used fresh* ● *indicates herb may be used fresh or dried and sometimes candied*

	Stocks, Soups, Chowders	Sauces and Stuffings	Salads and their Dressings	Vegetable Dishes	Savoury Rice and Pasta Dishes	Dairy Foods	Egg Dishes	Fish and Shellfish Dishes	Meat Dishes	Poultry and Game Dishes	Sweet Dishes and Puddings	Baking	Jams, Jellies, Syrups and Sweetmeats	Vinegars, Pickles, Chutneys and Ketchups	Teas	Wine, Liqueurs, Beer, Ale and Mead	Garnishing
Jasmine															●		
Juniper				●				●	●	●				●		●	
Lavender	●		●						●	●	●	●	●	●	●		
Leek	●	●	●	●	●		●	●	●	●							●
Lime															●		
Lovage	●	●	●	●	●	●	●	●	●	●				●	●		
Lovage seeds	●							●	●	●		●					
Mace, whole	●	●						●	●					●			
Mace, ground	●	●		●		●		●	●	●	●		●	●			
Marigold	●		●		●	●		●	●			●	●		●	●	●
Marjoram	●	●	●	●	●	●	●	●	●	●				●	●		
Mints	●	●	●	●	●	●		●	●		●		●	●	●		●
Mushrooms, dried	●	●	●	●	●		●	●	●	●				●			
Mushrooms, fresh	○	○	○	○	○		○	○	○	○				○			○
Mustard, dry			●					●	●					●			
Mustards, prepared		●	●			●	●	●	●	●							
Mustard seeds	●	●	●					●	●					●			
Nasturtium leaves and flowers			○			○											○
Nasturtium seed pods			○											○			○
Nettle			●	●											●	●	
Nutmeg	●	●		●	●	●	●	●	●		●	●	●				●
Onion	●	●	●	●	●		●	●	●	●		●		●			●
Onion powder	●	●		●	●		●	●	●	●		●		●			
Onion salt	●	●	●	●	●	●	●	●	●	●		●		●			
Oregano (Wild Marjoram)	●	●	●	●	●	●	●	●	●	●							
Paprika		●	●	●	●	●	●	●	●	●				●			●
Parsley	●	●	●	●	●	●	●	●	●	●					●	●	●
Pepper, green	●	●			●			●	●	●				●			
Pepper, ground	●	●	●	●	●	●	●	●	●	●	●			●			●
Pepper, whole	○	○	○	○	○		○	○	○					○			
Poppyseeds			●	●	●	●	●				●	●					●
Rose petals											●	●	●		●	●	●
Rosehips											●		●		●	●	
Rosemary	●	●	●	●	●	●	●	●	●	●					●	●	●
Saffron	●	●	●	●	●	●	●	●	●	●	●	●	●	●	●		
Sage	●	●	○	●	●	●	●	●	●	●				●	●		
Savory	●	○	○	●	○		○	○	●	●							
Sesame seed	●		●	●	●	●		●			●	●					●
Shallot	●	●	●	●	●		●	●	●	●				●			
Sorrel	○	○	○	○				○							●		
Spring Onions	●	●	●	●	●	●	●	●	●	●							●
Tamarind	●	●												●	●		
Tansy				●				●			●				●		
Tarragon	●	●	●	●		●	●	●	●	●				●			
Thyme	●	●	●	●	●	●	●	●	●	●					●		
Thyme, Lemon	●	●	●	●	●	●	●	●	●	●	●				●		
Turmeric		●			●		●	●						●			
Vanilla											●	●	●				
Verbena		○						○	○	○	○		○		○		○
Vervain															●		
Violet flowers			○								○		○			○	
Violet leaves			○								○		○			○	○●
Watercress	○	○	○	○		○		○	○						○		○
Woodruff															●	●	●
Wormwood															●	●	
Yarrow			●												●	●	

The domestic and cosmetic uses of herbs

The multitude of uses man has found for plant material – including medicinal, domestic and culinary – demonstrates his close association with nature.

Apart from their traditional use for all man's ills and ailments, herbs have proved invaluable in many other different ways in the domestic context. They have provided shelter, floor coverings, fire, weapons and utensils; imparted colour, flavour and decoration to a great variety of commodities; proved beneficial to health and been used to enhance man's natural beauty. And so it has been since the very earliest times.

HERBS IN THE HOME

Reeds, grasses, heather and turf have all been used as roof coverings, while a variety of plants, many of them still to be found growing wild, have been found to be useful in the home itself. Birch twigs (*Betula* spp) still make the strongest and most effective broom or garden besom, though Heather and Ling (*Calluna vulgaris*) are equally long-lasting and effective. Broom itself (*Sarothamnus scoparius*) received its common name from being used as such. Birch bark can be fashioned into a waterproof tray or basket. The North American Indians made household dishes and trays from Birch bark, which they stretched into shape and decorated around the edges with grasses. It was also the Indians who used Birch bark rolls as roofing materials, and formed small rolls into funnels which could be used for pouring. Bamboo (*Phyllostachys* spp) has always been basic to oriental economy and employed in a variety of ways, from bridges to buildings and furnishings, for utensils, vehicles and decoration.

Left: Herbs form the basis of an infinite variety of beautiful natural dyes, producing a range of subtle and vibrant colours. These garments have been dyed with different plants, each of which imparts its own individual fragrance.

Often the vernacular names of plants provide a clue to their use. The many applications of Equisetums or Horsetails are belied by their prehistoric appearance. Large quantities of the abrasive material, silica, are deposited in their stalks rendering them invaluable for polishing and scouring. Dutch Rush (*Equisetum hyemale*), formerly exported from the Netherlands, has been known as Scouring Rush or Pewterwort. It will clean pewter and form a substantially effective scourer for saucepans, baking utensils and wooden kitchen surfaces. It will also polish because of its abrasive action. Several fresh Horsetails tied together form an effective whisk in the preparation of food and washing materials – but do not use the dried plant since pieces are liable to fall off the stem. Plants of a high acid content such as Rhubarb (*Rheum palmatum* or *Rheum officinale*) and Sorrel (*Rumex acetosa*) can be boiled in water and used as pan cleaners, often bringing a high polish to the surfaces; but do not leave a strong rhubarb solution in aluminium pans as it may burn a hole through the bottom.

Soapwort (*Saponaria officinalis*), also known as Latherwort, is almost self-

Above: Soapwort, as its name implies, has traditionally provided an effective cleansing agent; however, it has a somewhat astringent lather.

explanatory. It is useful as a cleaning agent, especially for old or delicate fabrics that require gentle treatment. The leaves, and to a lesser extent the root, produce a somewhat astringent green soapy solution when decocted (covered and boiled) in hot water which restores old fibres and vegetable dyes to their former strength and clarity. The green coloration soon washes out in the rinsing process. Soapwort has been specifically employed in the restoration of valuable tapestries and brocades.

CANDLES

Chandling has long been a home craft, the simplest of candles being created from kitchen by-products, such as beef fat or marrow bone grease (obtained after boiling). The low melting-point of tallow demands a rather larger wick and this is best obtained from rushes.

Rush dipping can be mastered with a little practice. It is best to use the soft Rush (*Juncus effusus* or *Juncus conglomeratus*). Both grow fairly abundantly in wet pasture, bogs and damp woodland, especially on acid soils. After gathering, soak the rushes for a few hours and then dry out of doors, preferably in the sunshine. Strip the outer husk away and then hang the pithy centre part to dry before dipping in hot tallow or wax. Dip repeatedly, drying the tallow or wax before each operation.

When using reeds as candles, secure them safely as they are longer in length

Above: Rushlights were once the most economical source of domestic lighting in many rural areas. The rushes are gathered (above). Then fat – in this case mutton fat – is shown being melted (left). The rushlight is dipped once only into the fat (below left), and finally (below) it is placed in a traditional holder. One rush candle will last for about an hour indoors. They provide a lovely soft light and have the particular advantage of not dripping any wax.

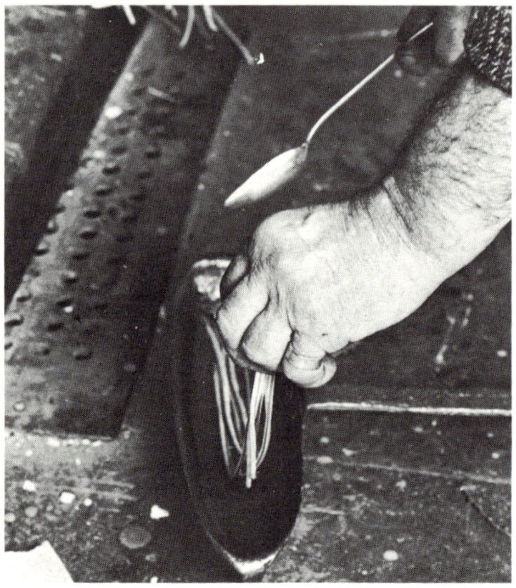

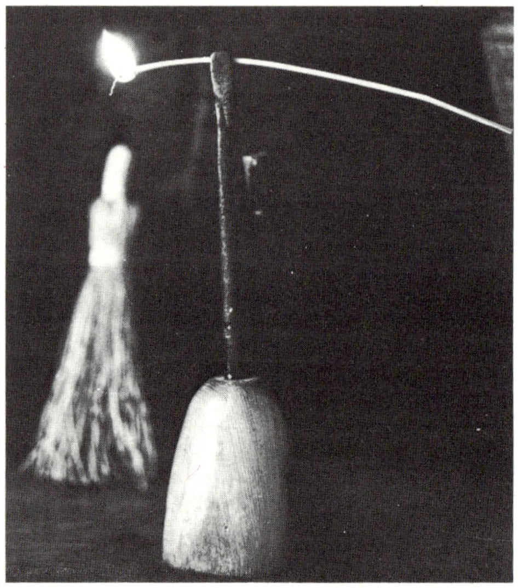

and less stable than household candles, but they have the advantage of not dripping wax. They are best contained in special holders which take several at one time and can be adjusted as they burn down. They can be burned indoors or outdoors without excessive guttering. One candle will last approximately one hour when used indoors; outside any breeze will reinforce the burning but will probably cause flickering.

Some nuts with a fleshy kernel such as Coconut (*Cocos nucifera*) can be threaded onto a reed wick and burned to provide light. Though adequate, they will smoke and smell fairly strongly, however, so they should be kept for barbecues or summer evenings when this will not matter. For such festive occasions, the reeds can be coloured before they are dipped. Either one colour may be used, or bands can be created along the length of the reed.

A modest range of various tallows and waxes is available from most craft shops, but it is far more satisfying to manufacture all the raw materials from plant matter.

TO SWEETEN THE AIR

Sweet rushes, evergreens such as Juniper (*Juniperus communis*), Lavender (*Lavandula spica*) and Santolina (*Santolina chamaecyparissus*), as well as the tough, resilient Tansy (*Tanacetum vulgare*), were traditionally strewn about the house to act as sweet-smelling and absorbent floor coverings. Their scent helped counteract the fetid atmosphere of less hygienic days.

Air fresheners have always been popular because of the alleged antiseptic properties of certain herbs and their use was promoted to counteract disease. There were many different methods: some were held in the hand; others placed among linen and clothing; many simply placed in bowls around the house.

The subtle scents of Sandalwood (*Santalum album*), Cedarwood (*Cedrus* spp), Lavender (*Lavandula spica*) and Lime flowers (*Tilia* × *vulgaris*) scattered in a closed cupboard permeate the contents and maintain freshness. Even the common custom of bringing fresh flowers into a sickroom not only delights the eye but freshens the atmosphere as well. Sweet Woodruff (*Asperula odorata*) scattered behind books will dissipate mustiness, while sachets, pomanders, lavender bags and nosegays of dried herbs such as Pennyroyal (*Mentha pulegium*) and Southernwood (*Artemisia abrotanum*) keep closed drawers fresh and pleasant, while at the same time discouraging insects. Of all of them, however, pot-pourri is the traditional favourite.

POT-POURRI

This is essentially a homogeneous mixture of dried sweet-scented flowers and leaves with aromatic spices and stabilizing agents or fixatives – the most usual of which are common salt or bay salt and Orris root (*Iris germanica*). These fixatives are the key to the long life of pot-pourri. When making up the fixative, use twice as much common salt or bay salt as Orris. Rose petals traditionally comprise the greater bulk, but the other ingredients invest the mixture with a lasting individual fragrance, and any combination of attractive scented leaves, flowers and flower buds can be used. No single perfume should predominate.

There are two kinds of pot-pourri, the dry and the moist. The former is easier to make, and quicker too, but is not as enduring or as fragrant as the moist variety. The materials for both need to be assembled over a period, and this is why the recipes are intentionally flexible. Generally, the flowers should be gathered as dry as possible immediately prior to being fully blown and if, like Honeysuckle (*Lonicera periclymenum*), there is a time of day when they are at their most fragrant, that is the time for harvesting.

For moist pot-pourri pull apart the petals and scatter them on trays or flat boxes covered with foil, then cover with sheets of greaseproof paper or cheesecloth. If it is not too windy, dry them out of doors in a shaded position; otherwise a shed or spare room is ideal. Once the petals are limp and leathery, they can be used to make the moist pot-pourri.

Dry pot-pourri

The petals must be dried thoroughly until they are papery but not brittle; they should still retain some colour and, of course, their scent. Drying time varies according to the moisture content of individual petals. Carnations (*Dianthus caryophyllus*) and Roses (especially *Rosa rugosa*, *Rosa damascena* and *Rosa gallica*), for example, take longer than Lavender (*Lavandula spica*) or Rosemary (*Rosmarinus officinalis*).

Ingredients to choose from

Flowers
Carnations *(Dianthus caryophyllus)*
Elder flowers *(Sambucus nigra)*
Honeysuckle *(Lonicera periclymenum)*
Jasmine *(Jasminum)*
Lavender *(Lavandula spica)*
Lily-of-the-Valley *(Convallaria majalis)*
Philadelphus spp
Pinks *(Dianthus plumarius)*
Rosemary *(Rosmarinus officinalis)*
Rose (scented) spp
Stocks *(Matthiolas)*
Sweet Peas *(Lathyrus odoratus)*
Thyme *(Thymus vulgaris)*
Wallflowers *(Cheiranthus)*
(Thick-petalled flowers such as Lily *(Lilium* spp*)* and Hyacinth *(Hyacinthus* spp*)* are not really suitable.)

Aromatic leaves Rub leaves through a sieve or grind them in an electric blender after drying
Bay *(Laurus nobilis)*
Bergamot *(Monarda didyma)*
Choisya *(Choisya ternata)*
Coriander *(Coriandrum sativum)*
Lavender *(Lavandula spica)*
Melilot *(Melilotus officinalis)*
Rosemary *(Rosmarinus officinalis)*
Sage *(Salvia officinalis)*
Sweet Woodruff *(Asperula odorata)*
The scented-leaved Geraniums such as *Pelargonium quercifolium* and *P. crispum*
The sweet-scented Artemisias such as *Artemisia abrotanum*
Thyme *(Thymus vulgaris)*
Verbena *(Verbena officinalis)*

Seeds and Spices Grind very coarsely the following seeds and spices in any combination, in a coffee grinder.
Alexanders *(Smyrnium olustratum)*
Allspice *(Pimenta dioica)*
Aniseed *(Pimpinella anisum)*
Cassia *(Cinnamomum cassia)*
Cinnamon *(Cinnamomum zeylanicum)*
Cloves *(Syzygium aromaticum)*
Coriander *(Coriandrum sativum)*
Nutmeg *(Myristica fragrans)*
Parsley *(Petroselinum crispum)*
Vanilla *(Vanilla planifolia)*

Fixatives These are substances which retain the aroma of the pot-pourri components and help to release them slowly into the air. All are themselves fragrant materials and they are essential for a successful pot-pourri.
Gum Benzoin *(Styrax benzoin* and *Styrax* spp*)*
Orris root powder *(Iris germanica)*
Storax *(Liquidamber orientalis)*
Sweet Flag powder *(Acorus calamus)*
Violet root powder *(Viola odorata)*

Note: Ground citrus peel can be added as above, or a whole Orange *(Citrus sinensis)* or Lemon *(Citrus limon)* can be stuck with Cloves (*Syzygium aromaticum)* and immersed in the pot-pourri mixture to absorb the scent.

The dry recipes can be mixed as the season progresses and, provided they are not left uncovered for too long, will retain their fragrance for up to two years. Though some varieties will lose some of their strength, others containing coumarin, such as Woodruff (*Asperula odorata*) and Melilot (*Melilotus officinalis*), develop a scent like new-mown hay. Dry pot-pourri can be improved by the addition of both these herbs. Use any combination of scented leaves and flowers you wish.

Moist pot-pourri

The moist recipes are usually superior because they last longer and ingredients can be accumulated over the growing season. Once petals are dry and leathery, store them in a mixture of common salt, coarsely ground sea salt or bay salt and Orris root (*Iris germanica*) in a wide-necked jar. Pack a layer of petals in the base of the jar, then sprinkle with a generous layer of fixative, to cover the petals to a depth of 6 mm (¼ in). Repeat in layers until the jar is full. Place a weight on the top and then cover to exclude light and air.

Treat aromatic leaves in exactly the same way, harvesting them prior to the plant flowering – this is when the essential oils are at their peak. As the season draws to a close, assemble all the dried plant matter, checking that they bear no hint of mustiness.

Below: Orris. The dried powdered root is used with other herbs in pot-pourris and some dry shampoos.

Keeping pot-pourri

The dry recipes for pot-pourri will generally last for about two years. The moist varieties last longer and need not be stored in covered containers. They can be revived very quickly by adding a few drops of essential oils, such as oil of Bergamot (*Citrus aurantium* var. *bergamia*), Ylang-Ylang (*Cananga odorata*) or Spike Lavender (*Lavandula spica*). Once the drier kind fades, however, the mixture cannot be restored to its former fragrance.

Use one of the many specially designed porcelain bowls or jars for storing pot-pourri. The lids of these are pierced with holes or slits to release the scent, and sometimes there is an inner lid with a fitted cover to keep in the fragrance.

Connoisseur's pot-pourri

Mix a jug full of dried Rose petals with one handful of common salt or bay salt, and then leave for several weeks. Store dried Lavender (*Lavandula spica*), Rosemary (*Rosmarinus officinalis*), Pinks (*Dianthus plumarius*) and Wallflowers (*Cheiranthus*) in separate containers, together with a little salt or bay salt and some scented leaves. Prepare wedges of citrus fruit peel by sticking them all over with Cloves (*Syzygium aromaticum*) and allowing them to dry naturally for a few weeks.

When all the ingredients are ready, thoroughly mix the petals with the leaves. Add the citrus fruit and Cloves whole or grind them in an electric blender and add handfuls to equal the quantity of salt used. Add a teaspoon of Cinnamon (*Cinnamomum zeylanicum*) and another of Allspice (*Pimenta dioica*). Mix well and leave overnight. Then add a few drops of essential oils: Lavender (*Lavandula spica*), Bergamot (*Monarda didyma*) and Geranium (*Pelargonium* spp). Store in a closed container for eight to ten weeks.

Traditional pot-pourri

9 litre (2 gall) bucket of Roses
340g (12 oz) common salt
225g (8 oz) finely powdered bay salt
85g (3 oz) Allspice (*Pimenta dioica*)
85g (3 oz) Cloves (*Syzygium aromaticum*)
50g (2 oz) brown sugar
110g (4 oz) Gum Benzoin (*Styrax benzoin*)
50g (2 oz) Orris root (*Iris germanica*)
½ cupful of brandy
Several handfuls of dried fragrant flowers and leaves such as Carnations (*Dianthus caryophyllus*), Pinks (*Dianthus plumarius*), Wallflowers (*Cheiranthus*) and Jasmine (*Jasminum*).

Place the Rose petals and salt in a jar in layers, then add the other ingredients and mix well. Store in closed jars. Open and stir occasionally when the room is to be perfumed. If the pot-pourri appears to dry out too much, moisten with a few drops of brandy.

An Elizabethan recipe

A quarter of a 9 litre (2 gall) bucket filled with Rose petals
85g (3 oz) common salt
50g (2 oz) fine rubbed bay salt
50g (2 oz) Allspice (*Pimenta dioica*)
50g (2 oz) Cloves (*Syzygium aromaticum*), coarsely ground
50g (2 oz) brown sugar
5g (¼ oz) Gum Benzoin (*Styrax benzoin*)
50g (2 oz) Orris root (*Iris germanica*)
2 tablespoons brandy
110g (4 oz) Lavender heads (*Lavandula spica*)
110g (4 oz) Verbena leaves (*Verbena officinalis*)
50g (2 oz) Rose-Geranium leaves (*Pelargonium graveolens*)

Sprinkle the fresh Rose petals with the common salt and leave for three days. Stir in the remaining ingredients, then place the mixture in a stone pot. Stir every three days for two weeks, adding a few drops of brandy if the mixture appears too dry and lacking in scent. A moist pot-pourri like this will have a more lingering perfume.

A quick pot-pourri

Throw together handfuls of dried Rose petals and dried Lavender (*Lavandula spica*), Honeysuckle (*Lonicera periclymenum*), Carnations (*Dianthus caryophyllus*), Rosemary (*Rosmarinus officinalis*) and Sweet William (*Dianthus barbatus*) flowers. Ensure that you have twice the bulk of the flowers in Rose petals. Add some powdered Cinnamon (*Cinnamomum zeylanicum*), Nutmeg (*Myristica fragrans*), Cloves (*Syzygium aromaticum*) and some dried Lemon peel (*Citrus limon*), at the ratio of about one teaspoon of the mixed powders to every two handfuls of flowers. Add a few drops of brandy and/or pot-pourri reviver, and then store the mixture tightly packed for a month or so before using.

Using pot-pourri

An attractive alternative to putting pot-pourri into an open container is to tuck it into a porcelain pomander and hang it in a cupboard or wardrobe. You can make sachets of the sweet-smelling mixture using scraps of light, pretty fabrics, cutting them to the size and shape required, and then embroidering them or adding beads, lace or ribbon.

Cut two pieces of fabric to shape and

Above: Sweet-smelling Lavender may be dried and used wherever its aroma will enhance the household – as scented accessories to aid sleep, as a fragrant pot-pourri or placed with clothes.

size, place them together, right sides facing, then stitch all round leaving a small opening for stuffing. Turn to the right side, clipping the seam allowances around any curves and cutting across corners to achieve an even shape. Tack any trimming into the seam before stitching.

Turn to the right side, stuff with pot-pourri and slip stitch the opening to close. Trim the edges afterwards if preferred. Place among linen or among clothes where it will remain effective for up to two years.

LAVENDER BAGS

You can make similar sachets with Lavender (*Lavandula spica*). It is best to gather the flowers just before they open so that they are still firm. The drying process will not alter the shape of the flowers and you will find them easier to handle when making up the bags.

Hang up the stalks in bunches in a dry place for a week or so; once dry, rub the flowers from the stalks. It is advisable to wear a mask of some sort over the mouth and nose as Lavender is a powerful sneezing agent.

Lavender dollies

The stalks of Lavender dry out so well and smell so good that it is a pity not to use them. As they remain fairly soft, try plaiting them to make Lavender dollies, in exactly the same way as you would make corn dollies.

Incorporate a narrow ribbon in a pretty colour as you work, not only to add decorative interest but to help hold the dolly together; or weave small capsule-shaped cylinders and fill them with dried Lavender flowers for an even more powerful aroma.

HERB PILLOWS

Historically, herb pillows are an extension of the idea of stuffing mattresses with sweet-smelling grasses and aromatic herbs. They are usually small and cushion-like in appearance and are mainly used today to add fragrance to bedclothes. Many people believe that if a herb pillow is tucked under a pillow proper or used as a neck rest, the fragrance of the herbs will encourage a deep and restful sleep; if trimmed with lace and made up in pretty prints, herb pillows make delightful bedroom accessories and charming gifts.

You can use almost any fragrant and aromatic leaves or petals, and assemble them in any combination that is personally pleasing. Make a pillow slip in a plain cotton, stuff with the mixture and then make a separate cover in an attractive cotton fabric, decorated to taste.

Choose from dried petals, flower-heads or leaves of Rosemary (*Rosmarinus officinalis*), Lavender (*Lavandula spica*), Roses, Lemon Verbena (*Aloysia triphylla*), Thyme (*Thymus vulgaris*), Marjoram (*Origanum vulgare*) and Rose-Geranium (*Pelargonium graveolens*), enhancing their scent with spices, ground citrus peel and a drop or two of an aromatic oil such as Neroli (*Citrus aurantium*), Lavender (*Lavandula spica*), Patchouli (*Pogostemon patchouli*). The most widely used herb pillow to promote sleep is one containing dried Hops (*Humulus lupulus*) and it is certainly effective providing the Hops are replaced every four to six months after which they lose their strength.

Rosemary herb pillow

Mix a sufficient quantity of herbs in the following proportions:

4 cups dried Rosemary leaves (*Rosmarinus officinalis*)
1 cup dried Lemon Verbena leaves (*Aloysia triphylla*)
1 cup dried Pine needles (*Pinus*)
1 tablespoon crushed Orris root (*Iris germanica*)
2 crushed Cloves (*Syzygium aromaticum*)

Note: When adding the Pine needles to the mixture, be sure that you make the pillow slip of strong, closely woven cotton, otherwise your sleep might be interrupted by their prickly escape into the bed.

Fragrant herb pillow

Mix together:

1 cup dried Rose petals
1 cup dried Lavender (*Lavandula spica*)
1 cup dried Lemon Verbena leaves (*Aloysia triphylla*)
1 cup dried Rosemary leaves and flowers (*Rosmarinus officinalis*)
1 cup other dried flowers, for example, Carnation (*Dianthus caryophyllus*), Honeysuckle (*Lonicera periclymenum*), Lily-of-the-Valley (*Convallaria majalis*), Jasmine (*Jasminum*)
Ground citrus peel from 2 Lemons (*Citrus limon*) and 2 Oranges (*Citrus sinensis*)

Note: The Lemon peel is added as a fixative. Alternatively, add two teaspoons powdered Orris (*Iris germanica*), or Sweet Flag (*Acorus calamus*) root or 3 drops of oil of Bergamot (*Citrus aurantium* var. *bergamia*).

OTHER SCENTED ARTICLES

The number of ideas for creating other scented articles is wide ranging. Here are just a few suggestions to stimulate enthusiasm for making your own home-made gifts and accessories.

Clove oranges

These are surprisingly easy to prepare and will last well when hung in wardrobes or on a Christmas tree for a spicy festive atmosphere. Use thin-skinned Oranges (*Citrus sinensis*) preferably and make slits around the fruit working in both directions – top to bottom and left to right. These will hold the ribbon in place for hanging the finished article.

Dry the Orange for a day or two above a stove or domestic boiler, then push Cloves (*Syzygium aromaticum*) into the entire surface of the skin so that the heads almost touch. If you find them hard to push in, make holes first with a sharp needle or bodkin.

Roll the Orange in a powder made up of equal parts of Cinnamon powder (*Cinnamomum zeylanicum*) and Orris powder (*Iris germanica*), then leave wrapped in the powder for two weeks. Remove the wrapping after this time, shake off the surplus powder, tie a ribbon or cord in place and hang so that its spicy scent fills the room or cupboard.

Below: A pomander makes a delightful gift. First the orange is cut so that the ribbon can eventually be tied on. The cloves are stuck into the orange (below). It is then rolled in powdered Cinnamon bark and Orris root and left to dry, wrapped in greaseproof paper, in a warm place (such as an airing cupboard or above a stove). Finally, the ribbon is tied on (below right), making an attractive and fragrant pomander (bottom).

Tussie-mussies

The name 'tussie-mussie' has been known in a multitude of different forms since the fifteenth century when it appeared as 'tumose of flowrys or other herys'. Basically, it is a sweet-scented nosegay, small enough to carry around, its origins being in the posies carried by judges and travellers in the Middle Ages to ward off bad odours and infection.

Collect fragrant leaves and flowers, and form a tiny Victorian posy-like bunch. Use a Rose-bud (*Rosa* spp) or a feather of Artemisia foliage as the centrepiece, and arrange the other leaves and flowers around it. Tie or bind with a ribbon and back with a paper frill or doily for an especially pretty finish.

Give them away as presents, tuck into cupboards or drawers, or place in a small vase to decorate a dressing table.

Lavender-scented pomander beads

By making up beads of herbs and flower materials and then stringing them together, you can wear your memories of summer around your neck or wrist right through wintertime.

2 level tablespoons dried Lavender flowers (*Lavandula spica*)
1 tablespoon Sweet Flag root powder (*Acorus calamus*)
1 tablespoon ground Gum Benzoin (*Styrax benzoin*)
2 teaspoons Sandalwood powder (*Santalum album*)
6 drops essence of Lavender (*Lavandula spica*)
3 drops essence of Ambergris
1 teaspoon powdered Gum Tragacanth (*Astragalus gummifer*)
8 teaspoons Orange-flower water
Lavender oil

Grind the dried Lavender flowers to a fine powder and sift into a bowl with the Sweet Flag, Gum Benzoin and Sandalwood powders. Mix them all together thoroughly, then add the essence of Lavender and Ambergris.

Make a mucilage of Gum Tragacanth by mixing one teaspoon of the Tragacanth with eight teaspoonfuls of Orange-flower water. Then use the mucilage to mix all the ingredients into a paste. If you find the powder does not form a paste easily, add a drop or two more of Orange-flower water.

Moisten your hands with a few drops of Lavender oil and break the paste into small equally sized pieces. Roll each one into a round, oval or cylindrical shape. Pierce with a large needle. Either string immediately and place in a dark cupboard or drawer for about a week, or dry the beads first and string later.

Aromatic beads

1 level tablespoon finely ground Gum Benzoin (*Styrax benzoin*)
1 level tablespoon Orris root powder (*Iris germanica*)
1 heaped tablespoon Sweet Flag root powder (*Acorus calamus*)
1 heaped tablespoon Mace powder (*Myristica fragrans*)
1 heaped tablespoon Nutmeg powder (*Myristica fragrans*)
1 heaped tablespoon dried powdered Basil (*Ocimum basilicum*)
4 finely ground Cloves (*Syzygium aromaticum*)
2 drops oil of Cedarwood (*Cedrus* spp)
1 drop oil of Spike Lavender (*Lavandula spica*)
3 drops essence of Ambergris
Gum Tragacanth (*Astragalus gummifer*)
Rose-water

Pass all the powdered herbs and spices through a fine sieve and blend thoroughly in a bowl. Add the oil of Cedarwood, Spike Lavender and Ambergris. Incorporate all these oils into the mixture. Make a thick mixture of Gum Tragacanth and the Rosewater, add to the other ingredients and stir thoroughly to form a paste.

Lubricate your hands with a fragrant oil, pull off a small piece of the paste about the size of a cherry pip and roll into a ball. Before it becomes too hard, pierce with a bodkin or large needle, then thread on a string. Lubricate the piercing instrument and the string with oil to make both jobs easier. If the paste hardens before you have strung all the string, soften it by warming.

Moth bags

You can protect your clothing and linen by making up small bags or sachets to hang in wardrobes and scatter in drawers. The perfume will deter insects.

Mix equal quantities of dried Cotton Lavender (*Santolina chamaecyparissus*) leaves with dried Tansy (*Tanacetum vulgare*) or Costmary (*Chrysanthemum balsamita*) leaves. Put them all in a grinder or chop and pound together in a mortar. Make up as required – their effectiveness will last for about three to six months. To increase effectiveness, add a small quantity of Pyrethrum powder or, even better, Pyrethrum flowers (*Chrysanthemum cinerariifolium*).

TEXTILE DYES

Natural dyes are the pigments obtainable from plant matter. They are soluble in water and have the capacity of imparting colour to fibre.

Fibres of animal origin such as wool and silk are essentially protein-based, while those from vegetable sources such as cotton and linen are predominantly cellulose in structure. The former take natural dyes especially well, as the structure of the fibres expands when the temperature of the dye-bath is raised, thus providing an increased surface area for the dye to permeate with colour.

Mordants are generally employed in the natural dyeing process. These are chemical substances that combine with the dye and fix the dyestuff in the fabric or fibres, and they can also be used to control the colour, either by shade or strength.

The range of chemicals suitable for use as mordants is as follows:

Alum (Aluminium potassium sulphate) – this is usually combined with cream of tartar in the ratio of three parts alum to one part of tartar.

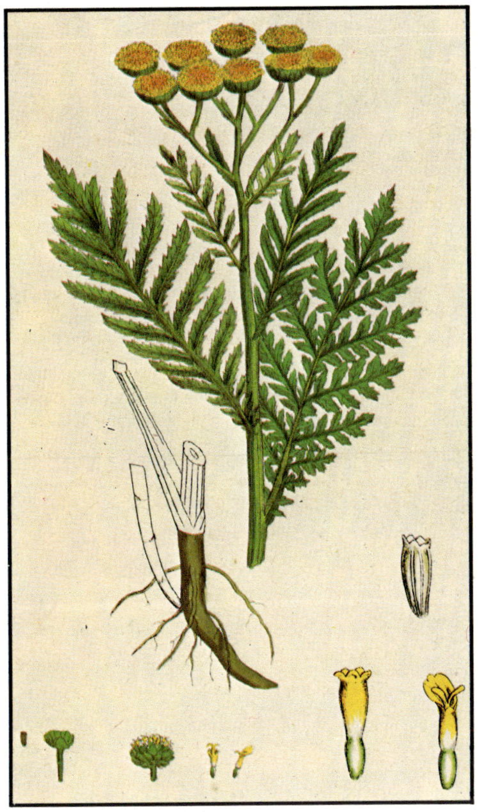

Above: The use of Tansy as an insecticide was once essential as part of the day-to-day running of a home. It can be hung up in bunches and will effectively repel flies and other insects.

Below: A procession of Buddhist monks in Sri Lanka. Their robes have been dyed with different plants to achieve the colours shown here. Saffron, for example, has been used to produce the deep, rich yellow tones. (See the table overleaf for dyeing at home.)

Tin (Stannous chloride) – a brightening agent used to brighten colours.

Iron (Ferrous sulphate) – usually called a 'saddening' agent because of its dulling and darkening effect on colours.

Chrome (Potassium dichromate) – deepens colours and creates a more lasting dye.

Copper sulphate or blue vitriol – adds a blue-green tinge to a colour.

Household ammonia – the clear kind – and white vinegar can also be used as mordants, providing an alkaline or acid medium respectively, as required.

The chart suggests some plants suitable for dye extractions, plus the effects you can expect to obtain when various mordants are added. The acid or alkaline content of the dye-bath will affect the fastness of the colour when the fabric is washed later. An alkaline fixed dye, for example, can be washed very successfully with soap which is alkaline based.

Dyes are extracted from herbs by boiling or soaking; the plant matter is then removed and the textiles or fibres to be dyed immersed in the dye-bath together with the mordanting agent. Work to a general guideline of 1 litre (35 fl oz) of liquid dye for each 25g (1 oz) of woven textile or yarn. A common failing is to try to cram too much textile into the dye-bath, resulting in patchy colouring. Spread the material out – especially wool – so that the fibres are completely immersed in the liquid and stir constantly to ensure even dyeing.

Natural dyeing is not usually cheaper and certainly not easier than using commercial dyes, but the colours are beautifully subtle and impart a delicious fragrance to woven or natural yarns.

Guide to natural dyeing

Colour	Plant	Mordant
Grey	Horsetail (*Equisetum sylvaticum*) st	alum
Black	Onion (*Allium cepa*) sk	chrome (on bleached wool)
	Meadowsweet (*Filipendula ulmaria*) rt	iron
Dark brown	Onion (*Allium cepa*) sk	chrome
	Coreopsis fl	chrome
	Madder (*Rubia tinctorum*) rt + lf	chrome
Chocolate brown	New Zealand Flax (*Phormium tanax*) rt	alum and washing soda
Mid brown	*Rhododendron* spp lv	chrome and iron
Warm brown	Madder (*Rubia tinctorum*) rt + lf, rt/lf	alum
	Madder (*Rubia tinctorum*) rt/lf	chrome
Light golden brown	New Zealand Flax (*Phormium tanax*) rt	tin and cream of tartar
Shades of brown	New Zealand Flax (*Phormium tanax*) fl + bd	iron and copper sulphate
Copper	*Pseudocyphellaria thouarsii* wp	tin and vinegar
Apricot shades	New Zealand Flax (*Phormium tanax*) fl + bd	tin and cream of tartar
Orange	Tansy (*Tanacetum vulgare*) ft	chrome and cream of tartar
Orange yellow	Dyer's Greenweed (*Genista tinctoria*) lv	chrome
Gold	Coreopsis fl	alum and tin
Golden yellow	Onion (*Allium cepa*) sk	alum
	Onion (*Allium cepa*) sk	alum and iron
	Tansy (*Tanacetum vulgare*) ft	alum
	Dyer's Greenweed (*Genista tinctoria*) lv	tin
	Pseudocyphellaria thouarsii wp	ammonia and washing soda
Bright yellow	Onion (*Allium cepa*) sk	alum and tin
Clear yellow	Marshmarigold (*Caltha palustris*) fl	alum
	Coreopsis fl	none
	Dyer's Greenwood (*Genista tinctoria*) lv	alum
	Carrot (*Daucus carota*) lv	alum
Creamy yellow	Birch (*Betula* spp) lv	alum
Acid yellow	*Pseudocyphellaria thouarsii* wp	ammonia
	Evernia spp wp	chrome and tin
Bright lemon yellow	Coreopsis fl	alum or iron
Pale lemon	*Rhododendron* spp lv	alum and tin
Greenish yellow	Dyer's Greenweed (*Genista tinctoria*) lv	iron
	Carrot (*Daucus carota*) lv	chrome
Murky yellow	*Evernia* spp wp	copper sulphate and ammonia
Dark green	*Rhododendron* spp lv	alum and iron and copper sulphate
	Pseudocyphellaria thouarsii wp	tin and copper sulphate
Bright green	Carrot (*Daucus carota*) lv	copper sulphate
Pale green	*Rhododendron* spp lv	iron
Blue-green	*Evernia* spp wp	copper sulphate
Soft murky blue	Elder (*Sambucus nigra*) rfr	none
Lavenders and purple	Elder (*Sambucus nigra*) rfr	alum and salt
Rich rose purple	*Umbilicaria* spp wp	alum and ammonia
Purple	Dandelion (*Taraxacum officinale*) rt	tin and vinegar
Red	St John's Wort (*Hypericum maculatum and H. perforatum*) fl + bd	tin
Rusty red	Bedstraws (*Galium verum and G. mollugo*) rt	none
Chestnut red	Madder (*Rubia tinctorum*) rt + lf rt/lf	alum and tin
Brownish red	St John's Wort (*Hypericum maculatum and H. perforatum*) ft (dried)	alum and cream of tartar
Magenta	Dandelion (*Taraxacum officinale*) rt	alum
Rose	*Umbilicaria* spp wp	tin
Pink	New Zealand Flax (*Phormium tanax*) lv	alum and iodized salt
	Dandelion (*Taraxacum officinale*) rt	none
Rose pink	*Umbilicaria* spp wp	ammonia
Pink-fawn	Madder (*Rubia tinctorum*) rt + lf rt/lf	none
	New Zealand Flax (*Phormium tanax*) fl + bd	alum or aluminium and washing soda

PAPER AND INK

New techniques have transformed the making of paper from an ancient craft to a modern industry, but the basic processes remain the same.

The Chinese are attributed with the invention of paper in about A.D. 105, though papyrus and parchment had been comparable forerunners. The Chinese used bark fibre and Flax (*Linum usitatissimum*), steeping the raw materials in water and beating them to a paste with stones and hammers to produce a sheet that was then dried in the sun. Some 700 years later, the Japanese perfected the process of making hand-made paper from the wood of the Paper Mulberry (*Broussonetia papyrifera*), the fibre being known as *kozo* in Japan.

Many plants have fibres substantial enough to provide the basic ingredient for making paper in the home, such as Nettle (*Urtica dioica*), Flax (*Linum usitatissimum*) and Pineapple (*Ananas sativus*). Pineapple fibres are used extensively in the production of textiles, but the waste from this material is excellent for making paper.

Woods such as Magnolia (*Magnolia* spp) and Poplar are also used, particularly *Populus tremula, P. alba* and *P. italica*. The Cotton plant (*Gossypium hirsutum*) offers another suitable fibre.

Plants of the grass family (Gramineae) which possess long, straight, conductive cells are excellent too. Suitable species range from tall-growing bamboos to cultivated cereals – the Common Oat (*Avena sativa*), Barley (*Hordeum sativum*), Common Wheat (*Triticum vulgare*), Rye (*Secale cereale*), Maize (or Indian corn) (*Zea mays*), Esparto (*Stipa tenacissima*), and the Danube Weed (*Phragmites communis*) can all be used with good results.

Prior to 1800, when chlorine bleaching was invented, pulped fibre was treated with a range of animal and vegetable glues during the process of sizing to prevent wetting and the penetration of the paper by inks and paints. The Chinese first painted on paper with a short stick of hardened Pine wood (*Pinus* spp) using a mixture of soot and glue, which was rubbed on an inkstone with a drop or two of water to produce the required consistency.

Left: A dyer's chart to facilitate the selection of the right herb, or specific part of it, together with the mordant which will combine to produce the specific colour required from a plant.

Key	
sk	*skin*
lv	*leaves*
fl	*flowers*
ft	*flower tops*
rt + lf	*root and leaf*
rt/lf	*root or leaf*
st	*stalks*
rfr	*ripe fruit*
wp	*whole plant*
ft (dried)	*dried flower tops*
fl + bd	*flower and buds*

Above: A section from the ancient Egyptian Book of the Dead. *The Egyptians wrote on the material they obtained from Papyrus, an aquatic herb which grows along the banks of the Nile. The writing material was made from the pith of this strong, reed-like plant, and ink was applied to it with reed pens. The word paper comes from papyrus.*

The Romans used reed pens, the Egyptians made use of rushes for writing, while styli of all kinds have been fashioned from wood through the centuries. Today, the best quality artist's charcoal is made from the Willow (*Salix* spp).

A writing ink has been made in Europe since the Middle Ages from the Bullet Gall or Oak nut. These are not the commonly known Oak Apples, but galls, formed by insects, which mature in August and remain on the tree throughout the winter long after the insects have left the tree. They are to be found on the Pedunculate Oak (*Quercus robur* and *Q. pedunculata*), and the Sessile Oak (*Quercus petraea* syn. *Q. sessiliflora*), both commonly to be found in the scrubland, copses and hedgerows of Europe. On the whole, northern European-grown galls do not contain enough tannic acid to make really successful ink, but they are certainly worth a try. Alternatively try some of the scented inks suggested in later recipes.

Black ink

450g (1 lb) bruised galls
4.5 litres (1 gall) boiling water
155g ($5\frac{1}{2}$ oz) ferrous sulphate
85g (3 oz) Gum Arabic (*Acacia Senegal*) previously dissolved in a few drops of antiseptic such as a five per cent carbolic acid solution, or Tincture of Myrrh (*Commiphora molmol*).

Macerate the galls by steeping for 24 hours, then strain and add to all the other ingredients. The ink is then ready for bottling and use.

Lemon Verbena scented ink

You can use this basic recipe with other herbs and flowers such as Rosemary (*Rosmarinus officinalis*) and Lavender leaves (*Lavandula spica*).

$\frac{1}{2}$ cup tightly packed and crushed Lemon Verbena leaves (*Aloysia triphylla*)
55 ml (2 fl oz) bottle of ink
$\frac{1}{2}$ cup cold water

Place the Lemon Verbena leaves in a small saucepan with the cold water. Bring to the boil rapidly, and then simmer for 10–30 minutes with the pan covered. Do not let the water evaporate completely; when it becomes opaque and brownish in colour, remove the pan from the heat.

Strain the liquid, allow it to cool, then add to a bottle of ink. The resultant aromatic ink will vary in potency according to the freshness of the dried leaves.

Above: Tobacco leaves drying in the sun. As nicotine and tar-rich tobacco has now been shown to be harmful, the traditional practice of mixing and blending plant smoking mixtures has once again become popular. A large number of the herbal smoking mixtures commercially available today are based on Coltsfoot.

Scented notepaper

This is easily made by storing several sheets of paper in a box with a liberal sprinkling of either dried pot-pourri or one of several powdered aromatic substances. Use Orris root (*Iris germanica*), Sweet Flag root (*Acorus calamus*), and Violet root (*Viola odorata*); or even powdered Allspice (*Pimenta dioica*), Aniseed (*Pimpinella anisum*), Cinnamon (*Cinnamomum zeylanicum*), Tonka beans (*Dipteryx odorata*), Vanilla pods (*Vanilla planifolia*) or Sandalwood (*Santalum album*). A crinkled effect is achieved by spraying an aromatic water (Rose-water or Rose-Geranium water, for example) by means of a fine hand spray, and then hanging the sheets to dry in the sun before storing.

LEISURE AND PLEASURE

The knowledge of Tobacco (*Nicotiana tabacum*) and its uses derives from the Americas where, in 1492, a party of Columbus's men reconnoitring Cuba reported seeing men carrying lighted firebrands and perfumed herbs. Tobacco chewing was also observed on the coast of South America in 1502. On Columbus's second visit from 1494 to 1496, he noted that snuff – a derivative of Tobacco – was in popular use.

Smoking

The American Indians used to call their smoking pipes 'tabaco'. These pipes were Y-shaped and hollow, the two points being inserted into the nostrils to inhale smoke from burning Tobacco. So closely identified with Tobacco has smoking become that the word now describes any variety of plant matter which is smoked for pleasure.

Herbs such as Coltsfoot (*Tussilago farfara*) are rendered into a smoking mixture by a process similar to the commercial production of Tobacco. This involves drying or 'curing' the leaves, and then mixing or blending them with other materials. Smoking tobacco mixtures include Liquorice (*Glycyrrhiza glabra*), salt, saltpetre and sugar. Herbal mixtures can be blended with other leaves and seeds. Coltsfoot tobacco is rubbed in the hands much as a pipe smoker prepares his tobacco.

Contemporary thinking blames the smoking of Tobacco for chest complaints and cancers, but it should not be forgotten that many 'poisonous' plants are quite harmless when used correctly. The smoking of leaves to relieve pulmonary congestion and coughs has been recommended since the days of Dioscorides, 2000 years ago, when he smoked through a reed.

'British Herb Tobacco', of which Coltsfoot is a principal ingredient, also includes Buckbean (*Menyanthes trifoliata*), Eyebright (*Euphrasia officinalis*), Betony (*Stachys officinalis*), Rosemary (*Rosmarinus officinalis*), Thyme (*Thymus vulgaris*), Lavender (*Lavandula spica*), and Chamomile flowers (*Matricaria recutita*). In France, *tabacs des Vosges* or *tabacs des Savoyards* is a pleasing herbal smoking mixture made up of the leaves and roots of Arnica (*Arnica montana*). Both Yarrow (*Achillea millefolium*) and Mallow (*Malva sylvestris*) can be used for herbal tobaccos too.

Snuff

In 1715, the British Parliament acted to 'Prevent the Mischiefs by manufacturing leaves and other things to Resemble Tobacco, and the Abuses in Making and Mixing of Snuff'. The bill notes that 'It is found by experience that of late Several Evil Persons have Cut, Cured, Manufactured and Sold Wallnut-Tree-Leaves, Hop leaves, Sycamore Leaves and other Leaves, Herbs, Plants and Materials resembling Tobacco.'

Snuff is made by a complicated and intricate process of fermenting Tobacco with salt, Liquorice (*Glycyrrhiza glabra*); Tonka bean (*Dipteryx odorata*) and other ingredients, many of which are closely guarded secrets. After fermentation has taken place, the mixture is dried and ground, and then sometimes fermented a second time to enrich the flavour even further.

Whether of the dry or moist variety, snuff needs to be kept damp, though not too damp. Throughout the nineteenth century flavours were refined to newer heights of sophistication, and today an enormous range of blends exists, and the habit is again becoming popular. Many incorporate such plants as Mints (*Mentha* spp), Jasmine (*Jasminum* spp), Rose (*Rosa* spp), Bergamot (*Monarda didyma*), Violet (*Viola odorata*), Geranium (*Pelargonium* spp) and Carnation (*Dianthus caryophyllus*). Most powders ground from Tobacco are so fine that a moistening agent is required to prevent the powder blowing away.

GUMS AND GLUES

Fairly simple glues can be made from powdered gums such as Gum Arabic (*Acacia Senegal*), Gum Tragacanth (*Astragalus gummifer*), Ghatti Gum (*Anogeissus latifolia*) and Carob Gum (*Ceratonia siliqua*). Karaya or Katira Gum (*Cochlospermum gossypium*) is especially effective and is still used in some countries to attach colostomy bags to the body.

The quantity of powdered gum to water varies according to your requirements and the gum used. Usually half a teaspoon of gum to half a cup of water is sufficient.

Several plants contain natural mucilages which can be used as simple gums. The berries of Mistletoe (*Viscum album*) and the bulbs of the Bluebell (*Endymion nonscriptus*) are examples.

In the Middle Ages small birds were caught on sticks coated with birdlime, a practice which is still carried on in such countries as Portugal and Italy. Today the glues are obtained from the petro-chemical industry, but 400 years ago one of the most effective birdlimes came from the Holly tree (*Ilex aquifolium*).

The Holly's young bark was stripped from the tree, soaked and boiled, and the inner layer allowed to ferment – sometimes this was done by burying the material in a closed container. This fermentation produced a mucilaginous mass, which was then ground, washed and refermented, finally being mixed with a fatty substance to produce an extremely effective sticky paste.

Birdlime from Holly is a useful glue in greenhouses or animals' quarters, and can be incorporated in fly papers.

Below: A number of herbs can be used in the garden to deal with pests and have the advantage of not producing the side-effects of chemical insecticides. The Mole Plant repels moles, Clover is a good fertilizer, and Quassia is an excellent pest deterrent. It makes much better sense, ecologically, to use herbs such as these judiciously in the garden.

GARDEN AND VETERINARY

Plants – and herbs in particular – have a number of parts to play in the natural cycle. Some decompose to form valuable fertilizers; others control pests or act as insecticides; and there are some plants that seem to affect other plant and insect life without there being any known scientific basis to their success.

A quick guide to successful gardening

Fertilizers	Lucerne (*Medicago sativa*)	green manure
	Clover (*Trifolium pratense*)	green manure
	Wrack (*Fucus vesiculosus*)	mulch manure
Insecticides	Pyrethrum (*Chrysanthemum cinerariifolium*)	controls: aphids, leaf-hoppers, spider mites, etc
	Derris (*Derris elliptica* and *D. malaccensis*)	controls: aphids, leaf-eating caterpillars, mosquito larvae
	Quassia (*Picraena exelsa*)	controls: mealybugs, leaf-hoppers, thrips, slugs
	Nicotine (POISONOUS) (*Nicotiana tabacum*)	controls: aphids, leaf-hoppers, thrips, spider mites, whitefly
Traps and controls	Cucumber (*Cucumis sativus*) skins, left on floor 3–4 nights	repels: cockroaches, woodlice in sheds and greenhouses
	Angelica (*Angelica archangelica*) – scatter pieces of the hollow stem among herbaceous plants	traps: earwigs
	White Hellebore (*Veratrum album*) – chop root into pieces and scatter over the garden	disperses: rodents
	Mole Plant (*Euphorbia lathyrus*)	repels: moles
	Onions (*Allium cepa*) planted among salad crops	discourages: rabbits
Plant associations from folklore	Parsley (*Petroselinum crispum*)	repels: Rose beetle
	Garlic (*Allium sativum*) or Chives (*Allium schoenoprasum*) – near Roses	repels: blackspot, mildew, aphids
	Garlic (*Allium sativum*) or Chives (*Allium schoenoprasum*) – near lettuce or peas	repels: aphids
	Hyssop (*Hyssopus officinalis*) – near beans	repels: blackfly

COMPOST ACCELERATOR

Home-made compost is a valuable asset to the gardener, making use of green waste and enriching the soil. Some herbs decompose more quickly than others and can be made into an accelerating material that rapidly breaks down waste.

Mix equal parts of Valerian (*Valeriana officinalis*), Nettle (*Urtica dioica*), Dandelion (*Taraxacum officinale*), Chamomile (*Matricaria recutita*), Yarrow (*Achillea millefolium*) and Oak bark (*Quercus* spp). Use whole plants, leaves or bark to form thin layers, and then alternate with any green garden rubbish and soil, dampening the pile with water as it is made. Compost manufacture is greatly assisted by a warm temperature, and a well-ventilated compost box or bin is essential.

ANIMAL CARE

Animals benefit from medicinal herbs in the same way that humans do, and there are many substances which are effective but considered too powerful for human use. Examples include some of the stronger plant purgatives and vermifuges used to expel worms.

Many plants have been employed through history as food supplements. White Bryony (*Bryonia dioica*), for example, has been used traditionally to supplement horse and cattle fodder to condition their coats. The dried root of the same plant can be used directly to polish the coat, while tanners use it to thicken hides. It can also be used as a purgative.

Fleas and lice in animal coats can be treated very easily and successfully with a decoction of Walnut (*Juglans regia*) leaves or Stavesacre (*Delphinium staphisagria*) seed, soaked overnight. Pyrethrum (*Chrysanthemum cinerariifolium*), Derris (*Derris elliptica*) or Wormwood (*Artemisia absinthium*) each mixed with water are also very effective. Soak the coat thoroughly with the liquid, then brush and comb well once dry. If used in large quantities, use as a dip rather than a lotion.

Horseheal or Scabwort (*Inula helenium*) has been used in veterinary medicine in the effective treatment of sheep scabs.

HERBS FOR BEAUTY

The health and appearance of the skin reflects the inner physical and psychological health of an individual. Healthy skin and hair cannot be obtained by cosmetic use alone and attention should be paid to well-balanced diet and adequate exercise, rest and general health.

Herbal or natural cosmetics are, however, of material benefit to the body especially if used on a regular basis.

HERBAL BATHS

The scenting of water is a long practised custom, and it renders the water refreshing for bathing. The Romans threw Lavender (*Lavandula* spp) into their baths, not only to scent the water, but to act as a disinfectant. In fact, the name *Lavandula* is from the Latin *lavare*, meaning to wash. Herbal baths are taken today for one or more of several reasons. They stimulate the action of the pores, relax the muscles and soothe the joints, and perfume the water.

Bath bags

The best results are to be obtained by using a herb sachet. A square or circle of either cheesecloth or muslin should be filled with herbs and tied securely. Fix the bag under running hot water, agitating and wringing it out to release the oils and perfume, then allow it to steep in the bath water.

Oatmeal can be mixed together with the herbs to help soften the water and impart smoothness to the skin. Use in the proportion of twice the amount of finely ground oatmeal to the amount of herbs. The herbs can be chosen from what is available or they may be mixed according to personal preference. Some herbs have a stimulating effect, while various others are relaxing.

Herbs for the bath

Stimulating
Basil *(Ocimum basilicum)*
Bay *(Laurus nobilis)*
Fennel *(Foeniculum vulgare)*
Lavender *(Lavandula spica)*
Lemon Verbena *(Aloysia triphylla)*
Lovage *(Ligusticum officinale)* – also considered to act as a deodorant
Meadowsweet *(Filipendula ulmaria)*
Mint *(Mentha* spp*)*
Pine *(Pinus* spp*)*
Rosemary *(Rosmarinus officinalis)*
Sage *(Salvia officinalis)*
Thyme *(Thymus vulgaris)*

Relaxing
Catnep *(Nepeta cataria)*
Chamomile *(Matricaria recutita)*
Jasmine *(Jasminum officinale)*
Lime flowers *(Tilia* x *europaea* or *T.* x *vulgaris)*
Vervain *(Verbena officinalis)*

Healing
Comfrey *(Symphytum officinale)*
Lady's Mantle *(Alchemilla vulgaris)*
Marigold *(Calendula officinalis)*
Mint *(Mentha* spp*)*
Yarrow *(Achillea millefolium)*

Left: This chart details the properties of various herbs which can be infused and added to the bath. Herbal baths are taken for many reasons: they stimulate the action of the skin's pores, relax muscles and soothe joints, and, additionally, impart a pleasant perfume.

Above: Yarrow is particularly efficient as an astringent for oily skin and is an ingredient of many 'natural' facial cleansers.

Tonic baths

Herbs will only yield their essential oils when subjected to heat, so those rich in fragrant oils are especially effective when used in a sauna: try Basil (*Ocimum basilicum*), Chamomile (*Matricaria recutita*), Elder flowers (*Sambucus nigra*), Lime flowers (*Tilia x europaea* or *T. x vulgaris*), Sage leaves (*Salvia officinalis*), Thyme (*Thymus vulgaris*) and Verbena leaves (*Verbena officinalis*) or Eucalyptus (*Eucalyptus globulus*).

If it is a real tonic that is required – after winter, for example, when the skin tends to look really dingy and tired – Blackberry (*Rubus*) leaves will prove invaluable. Collect new young shoots and leaves, and dry and crush them with a rolling pin. To each 560 ml (20 fl oz) of water, add 170g (6 oz) of plant matter, and then heat the two together to a temperature of 45°C (115°F). Allow to infuse for three to five minutes, and then strain and add the liquid to the warm bath.

Similar tonics are easy to make using Nettle (*Urtica dioica*), Dandelion (*Taraxacum officinale*) or Daisies (*Bellis perennis*). Allow 450g (1 lb) of dried plant matter to every 3–4 litres (6–8 pts) of water. Allow the flowers or herbs to steep in the liquid for 30 minutes, then strain and add to a warm bath.

Bath oils

Very few oils will disperse completely in water, so if you do not want to emerge glistening from top to toe, use a specialist oil. Castor oil (sometimes sold as Turkey Red oil) from the Castor Oil plant (*Ricinus communis*) disperses and does not leave a dirty ring around the bath. Mix it with your favourite aromatic oil in the proportion of half a cup of Castor oil to ten drops of aromatic oil such as Rosemary (*Rosmarinus officinalis*), Pine (*Pinus* spp) or Sandalwood (*Santalum album*). Pour into a jar, screw on the lid, shake to mix thoroughly and then store until required. Shake each time before using – one teaspoonful of the oil is sufficient for the bath.

Aromatic oils can be used, of course. Just a drop or two will prove sufficient since pure plant oils are powerful and some may cause headaches. It is, therefore, advisable to experiment with small quantities of various essential oils until you find ones which suit you. The different fragrances are supposed to affect the emotions differently, a theory which is practised by aromatherapists who use essential oils in the treatment of a number of physical and emotional conditions.

Bath salts

You can add a handful of bath salts to turn the routine bath into a luxurious experience. The soda base of the salts neutralizes the acids secreted by the skin so that the perfume clings to the body afterwards, and it softens even the hardest of waters at the same time.

Mix the following ingredients together:
140g (5 oz) Bicarbonate of Soda
85g (3 oz) powdered Orris root (*Iris germanica*)
A few drops of essential oils such as oil of Neroli, oil of Rosemary or oil of Lavender

Once mixed together, pound in a pestle and mortar, and then store in an airtight tin. They will keep for about three months so long as the container is firmly sealed.

After-bath cologne

Use this fragrant cologne as a friction rub after a bath.

½ cup fresh flower petals – Roses (*Rosa* spp), Carnation (*Dianthus caryophyllus*), Jasmine (*Jasminum officinale*) or any other strongly scented species.
½ cup deodorized alcohol*
1½ cups very hot water
3 tablespoons ground citrus peel
1 tablespoon dried Basil (*Ocimum basilicum*) or Lemon Verbena (*Aloysia triphylla*) (crushed)
1 tablespoon Mint (*Mentha* spp) or Thyme (*Thymus vulgaris*) (crushed)

**Note:* In many countries customs and excise regulations make it difficult to obtain certain alcohols normally used in cosmetics. As a substitute use food-grade isopropyl alcohol which can be obtained from most chemists.

Soak the flowers in the alcohol for one week in a tightly closed jar. On the sixth day, make an infusion of the citrus peel and herbs in the hot water, then allow to stand for 24 hours.

Strain through cheesecloth or muslin; then drain the petals. Combine the two resulting liquids in a jar or bottle with a screw top and shake well. Use a little whenever required.

Soap balls

Perfumed or medicated balls of soap were extremely popular in the seventeenth and eighteenth centuries before soap-making was industrialized. The most sophisticated kinds were made in Italy and incorporated exotic perfumes and a wide range of aromatic powders. Soap balls were made in most homes, either in the still-room or pantry, and the traditional recipes can be adapted to modern day requirements very easily.

Use Castile or simple (unperfumed) soap as a base. After grating it, add a variety of perfumed petals, leaves or powdered roots. The following traditional recipe can be followed very easily: 'Take a pound of fine white Castile Sope, shave it thin in a pinte of Rose-water, and let it stand for two to three days, then pour all the water from it, and put to it halfe a pinte of fresh water, and so let it stand for one whole day, then pour out that, and put half a pint more, and let it stand a night more, then put to it halfe an ounce of powder called Sweet Marjoram, a quarter of an ounce of powder of Winter Savory (*Satureia montana*), two or three drops of Oil of Spike, and the Oyl of Cloves, three grains of Musk, and as much Ambergris, work all together in a fair Mortar, with the Powder of an Almond cake dryed, and beaten as small as fine flowre, so roll it round in your hands in Rose-water.' (Ambergris and Musk can be substituted by three drops of essence of Ambergris and the same of oil of Musk. The almond cake could be replaced by a macaroon or ratafia biscuit.)

Right: Summer Savory is of great practical value in the home. Apart from its use in salads, sauces and as a complement to broad beans, it also has medicinal properties. Applied to a bee sting, the crushed fresh leaf of Summer Savory relieves pain, and it can also be added to aromatic bath mixtures.

Modern washballs

1 large bar simple soap or Castile soap
¼ cup of Rose-water (*Rosa* spp)
3 drops oil of Lavender (*Lavandula spica*)

Grate the bar of soap into a suitable container, then pour the Rose-water over it. Allow the soap to stand in the liquid for 15 minutes, and then transfer to an electric blender or pestle and mortar, adding the oil of Lavender, one drop at a time.

Once smoothly blended, pour the mixture into a basin, then allow to stand for a day or so. Form into small balls by breaking off pieces and rolling them in your hands. Allow the soap to dry and harden. To obtain a smooth and attractive finish, moisten your hands with Rose-water and roll the balls into shape in the palms of your hands.

EYE BATHS

A quick and simple remedy for eye strain requires placing a slice of Cucumber (*Cucumis sativus*) over each eye and resting in a darkened room for five to ten minutes. For those with more time, try either of the following recipes, noting that they have to be used fresh and stored no longer than 12 hours. Decomposition takes place after this period of time and can cause even greater irritation to the eyes.

15g (½ oz) Plantain (*Plantago lanceolata*) leaves
15g (½ oz) Cornflowers (*Centaurea cyanus*)
15g (½ oz) Melilot flowers (*Melilotus officinalis*)
420ml (15 fl oz) boiling water

Make an infusion of the herbs in the boiling water. Allow to stand for an hour, then strain and use when tepid. A few drops in the eyes will relieve tiredness, while it can also be used as an eye bath to soothe soreness and inflamed eyelids.

15g (½ oz) Cornflowers (*Centaurea cyanus*) or Eyebright (*Euphrasia rostkoviana*)
420ml (15 fl oz) water or rain-water

Infuse the flowers in the water by boiling. Strain and allow to cool. The resulting liquid will add sparkle and vitality to tired, sore eyes.

BODY POWDERS

The best known of all the body powders is Talcum powder. The word 'talcum' is from the Persian *talk*, and strictly means powdered Hydrated Magnesium Silicate. This soft greasy powder was first introduced to European toiletry in the sixteenth century. The term 'talcum powder' is now used rather loosely, and often includes mixtures containing Corn starch (*Zea mays*), precipitated chalk (light Calcium Carbonate) and various other substances.

It is relatively easy to make a range of toilet, face, scented, cosmetic and talcum powders, either using a chemical base, a powdered herbal material or a combination of the two – the latter is often best.

Above: The oil of this plant, Bergamot Orange, can be added to a dry pot-pourri to enhance the fragrance or to revive an old mixture; it is often used in body powders, perfumes and sun-tan lotions.

Traditionally, a cosmetic powder known as *poudre de chipre* was made by macerating Oakmoss in running water for two to three days. It was then dried and reduced to a powder. Oakmoss is now rarely available, and the most common plant powder bases are either Orris root (*Iris germanica*) or Corn starch (*Zea mays*).

Chemical base:
30% French chalk; 30% Corn starch; 40% precipitated chalk.

Herbal base:
60% Orris root; 30% Corn starch; 10% Rice flour.

(These percentages refer to weight.)

All the ingredients must be reduced to as fine a powder as possible. Combine these chemical and herbal bases in any proportion you wish, or use them separately. Experimentation will reveal the best type of powder for your skin type.

Poudre à la Mousseline

450g (1 lb) base (chemical or herbal as described)
170g (6 oz) powdered Coriander seed (*Coriandrum sativum*)
50g (2 oz) powdered Mace (*Myristica fragrans*)
25g (1 oz) powdered Cloves (*Syzygium aromaticum*)
25g (1 oz) powdered Cassia (*Cinnamomum cassia*)
25g (1 oz) powdered Sandalwood (*Santalum album*)

Frangipani aroma

1.2kg (2½ lb) base (chemical or herbal, as described)
110g (4 oz) powdered Sandalwood (*Santalum album*)
110g (4 oz) powdered Vanilla (*Vanilla planifolia*) beans
50g (2 oz) powdered Tonka (*Dipteryx odorata*) beans
4 drops Neroli oil (*Citrus aurantium*)
4 drops Bergamot oil (*Citrus aurantium* var. *bergamia*)
4 drops Rose-Geranium oil (*Pelargonium graveolens*)

Lavender

450g (1 lb) base (chemical or herbal, as described)
450g (1 lb) powdered Lavender flowers (*Lavandula spica*)
50g (2 oz) powdered Gum Benzoin (*Styrax benzoin*)
25ml (1 fl oz) Lavender oil

Simple scented powder

450g (1 lb) base (chemical or herbal, as described)
8 drops of any one of the following essential oils:
Bergamot (*Citrus aurantium* var. *bergamia*)
Patchouli (*Pogostemon patchouli*)
Frangipani (*Plumeria rubra*)
Lavender (*Lavandula spica*)
Ylang-Ylang (*Cananga odorata*)
Lime (*Tilia × europaea* or *T. × vulgaris*)
Lemon grass (*Andropogon* spp)
Neroli (*Citrus aurantium*)
Rose-Geranium (*Pelargonium graveolens*)
Aniseed (*Pimpinella anisum*)
Bay (*Laurus nobilis*)

Add the essential oil to the base drop by drop and mix thoroughly, using a pestle and mortar for the best results.

Supplement with powdered aromatic seeds or herbs to a proportion of two parts base to one part additional ingredients. Experiment with different aromas.

Foot powder

Foot care is important, both for their health and to relieve general soreness. This powder will reduce friction between the toes and so eases walking.

½ cup Talc
½ cup Corn starch (*Zea mays*)
½ teaspoon Peppermint (*Mentha × piperita*) extract
1 teaspoon rubbing alcohol (or food-grade isopropyl alcohol)

Mix all the ingredients together thoroughly, then keep in a jar with a tight-fitting lid. Use after drying the feet thoroughly.

Tooth powder

A simple and very effective tooth powder is made by mixing 4 teaspoons Sage leaf (*Salvia officinalis*), 3 teaspoons rock salt or sea salt and 1 teaspoon Myrrh (*Commiphora molmol*). Place the mixture on an open tray and heat in the oven for about 30 minutes at a medium temperature. Remove and allow to cool for ten minutes then grind very finely in a pestle and mortar or electric grinder. Press the mixture through a fine sieve and store the resulting powder; throw away any lumps left in the sieve.

This is gently abrasive at first (until the components dissolve in the mouth) as well as being an effective antibacterial. Use it with a soft action on the teeth with an ordinary toothbrush.

CLEANSING THE SKIN

Everyone knows the importance of keeping the pores of the skin unclogged and clean. This often requires more than a quick wash with soap and water, and steaming the face is the quickest and cheapest way to improve the cleanliness of the skin.

Provided your skin is fairly normal –

not too dry or sensitive, with no thread veins visible – begin by making an infusion of herbs in a large bowl. Use three tablespoonfuls to two litres ($3\frac{1}{2}$ pts) of boiling water. Choose between Sage (*Salvia officinalis*, Peppermint (*Mentha × piperita*), Chamomile flowers (*Matricaria recutita*) or Lime flowers (*Tilia × europaea* or *T. × vulgaris*) for the best results.

Place a towel over your head, lower your face until it is just above the bowl and allow the vapour to rise to meet your skin. The towel forms a tent that traps the vapour, and you should allow the treatment to continue as long as you can bear the heat; ten minutes is about the right length of time.

After steaming, the skin will be pink and glowing. Splash with tepid and then cold water to close the pores, or use an astringent lotion dabbed on with cotton wool or tissues. Stay indoors for an hour or so after steaming, and do not repeat the treatment for at least three days.

Herbal butter-milk cleanser

No beauty routine should be without a lotion to cleanse the skin at the end of the day. This recipe is gentle in its action, but most effective.

140ml (5 fl oz) butter-milk
2 tablespoons Elder flowers (*Sambucus nigra*) or Lime flowers (*Tilia × europaea* or *T. × vulgaris*).

Heat the butter-milk, add the flowers and boil gently for approximately half an hour. Leave to infuse for two hours. Strain before using; apply to the face with cotton wool and remove all traces of dirt, grease and make-up with gentle movements.

Fragrant cleansing lotion

420ml (15 fl oz) warm Rose-water
2 handfuls dried Rose petals (preferably *Rosa gallica*)
5g (1/16 oz) Gum Benzoin (*Styrax benzoin*)

Mix the warm Rose-water with the dried Rose petals in an earthenware jar. Leave to infuse for one to two hours, and then strain off the liquid. Leave a day or so before adding the Gum Benzoin. Use to cleanse the skin as in the previous recipe.

Blackheads

Blackheads are a problem even on a relatively unblemished skin. If rubbing the affected spot with a slice of Tomato (*Lycopersicon esculentum*) or Marrow (*Cucurbita pepo* var. *ovifera*) and then rinsing in tepid water does not work, give the face a steaming treatment as described, then try gently pushing out the blackheads with a tissue and clean fingertips. Steaming should unblock the pores – a blackhead is only a blockage of grease (sebum) secreted by glands under the surface of the skin, with a layer of dirt trapped on top. Excessive pressure may cause local skin damage, and the formation of spots or pimples. If this happens, add 50g (2 oz) Burdock root (*Arctium lappa*) to 560ml (20 fl oz) cold water. Bring to the boil and simmer for 15 minutes. Allow to cool, strain and apply to the infected spot.

MASKS FOR OILY SKIN

Most people have at least some oily areas of skin on their face, and blackheads and whiteheads tend to congregate where there is an excess of grease. Steaming is one method of attack, but there are others: masks and packs, for example, that are designed to clear this grease away.

Oatmeal (*Avena sativa*), Almond meal (*Prunus dulcis*) and Corn starch (*Zea mays*) are all substances that when mixed with Lemon (*Citrus limon*) juice, cider vinegar, water or tepid milk or butter-milk, and then rubbed over the face, will act as cleansing agents. Beaten egg white and/or yoghurt can be used to control grease, either applied directly to the face or combined with any one of the agents described above, together with herbs such as Yarrow (*Achillea millefolium*), Chamomile flowers (*Matricaria recutita*), Elder flowers (*Sambucus nigra*), Sage (*Salvia officinalis*) or Lady's Mantle (*Alchemilla vulgaris*). Yarrow tea – made by infusing two tablespoons of dried Yarrow in a glass and a half of boiling water – is especially recommended for clearing excessively oily skins.

The action of a face pack rids the skin of impurities by drawing them to the surface. It also tightens the skin and stimulates the circulation, thus encouraging the skin to glow. The use of masks on drier skins should be undertaken with care. Although they can humidify the skin and restore natural oils, masks must be blended carefully to fulfil these functions.

There are a wide range of herbs and fruits that can be utilized for making packs for the face and neck. Milk, yoghurt, egg white or egg yolk, Oatmeal (*Avena sativa*), honey or Fuller's earth are all spreading or thickening agents, though quite simple treatments exist such as rubbing the skin with fresh Cucumber (*Cucumis sativus*) or Strawberry (*Fragaria vesca*).

The usual method for using a face mask is to fasten back the hair or protect it in some way, lie down on a bed or lean back in a chair and spread the pack over the face and neck. Avoid the skin around eyes and lips as these areas are too delicate to be stimulated in this way. Raise the level of your feet above your head, then rest for 10 to 15 minutes. The mask should then be washed away using tepid water and tissues or cotton wool.

Above: A woman from Mozambique wearing a herbal face paint. Though valued as a cosmetic, it also protects her skin.

Below: An oatmeal face pack is used on its own to draw out impurities from the skin, or as a binding agent in combination with other cosmetic herbs.

Right: The most renowned gentle astringent of all is the common Cucumber. It also provides a quick remedy for eye strain – a slice of Cucumber placed over each eye has a cooling and soothing effect.

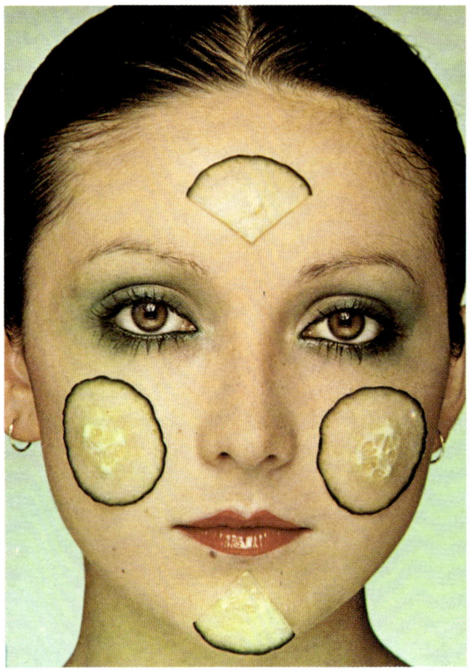

Astringent mask for oily skin
Blend together equal amounts of Tomato juice and the pulp of a Lemon. As an alternative, you can steep the Tomato juice in the pulp of the cut halves of the Lemon, and then scrape away the combined pulp. The end result is exactly the same, whichever method you use. Splash the mixture on your face, paying particular attention to the greasy areas, then wash off with tepid water after the allotted time.

Egg white and cucumber mask
Egg white is renowned for tightening the skin and temporarily firming away lines and lifting sagging skin. It works most powerfully on ageing, oily skin with large pores – known as 'orange-peel' skin.

Mix together:
2 egg whites
1 Cucumber (*Cucumis sativus*)
1 teaspoon Lemon juice (*Citrus limon*)
¼ teaspoon Peppermint extract (*Mentha ×piperita*)
1 teaspoon 50% rubbing alcohol (or isopropyl alcohol)
ice cubes

Whip the egg whites, then blend together with all the other ingredients in an electric blender. Anything left over can be stored in your refrigerator.

Dab the mixture on to your face and leave for approximately eight minutes. If there is an excessive tingling effect before this time, remove the pack with tepid water and tissues or cotton wool and splash the skin once more with tepid water afterwards, or omit the alcohol.

MASKS FOR DRY SKIN

It is not advisable to use any drying treatment on skin that is either naturally dry or ageing. Egg white is particularly damaging, since it dries on the face and becomes a powerful astringent.

Use fatty substances such as egg yolk as a spreader, and incorporate such agents as Sunflower (*Helianthus annuus*) or Wheat germ (*Triticum vulgare*) oil, Almond (*Prunus dulcis*) or Linseed (*Linum usitatissimum*) oil. Other ingredients such as Apple (*Malus* spp) juice, Peach (*Prunus persica*) or Pear (*Pyrus communis*) juice, mixed with ground Almonds (*Prunus dulcis*) will help revitalize the skin by stimulating the pores to secrete more natural oils.

Yeast face mask
1 teaspoon honey
1 tablespoon brewer's yeast
1 teaspoon Comfrey infusion (*Symphytum officinale*)
1 teaspoon milk or yoghurt
1 teaspoon Marigold infusion (*Calendula officinalis*)
1 teaspoon skin oil – this can be a favourite proprietary oil or Sunflower oil (*Helianthus annuus*), Avocado (*Persea americana*), Olive oil (*Olea europaea*) or Peanut (*Arachis hypogaea*) oil

Combine the honey with a few drops of very hot water. This will thin the honey down and make it easier to use. Blend in the yeast, then add the milk or yoghurt and the herb infusions. Stir until it becomes a thick paste.

Pat your face with the oil, and then spread a layer of the paste. Allow to set for approximately 15 minutes, then wash off with tissues and splash with tepid water.

Oatmeal facial
For dry skins, Oatmeal makes a nourishing and somewhat bleaching base when mixed with a favourite flower water – Rose-water, Elder flower-water, for example.

Work the ingredients into a paste, then pat onto the face and neck. Allow to dry for up to 15 minutes, then wash off with tepid water or clean off with tissues and pat with a damp face flannel.

Fruit sundae special
This is a recipe to try in the height of summer when there is a glut of your favourite fruit. Incorporate Strawberry (*Fragaria vesca*), Peach (*Prunus persica*), Water Melon (*Citrullus lanatus*), Pineapple (*Ananas sativa*) and Cucumber (*Cucumis sativus*) with or without the white of an egg and reduce all to a pulp in a blender or pestle and mortar. The flesh of the fruit should be as smooth as possible. Spread over the face and neck, relax for a few minutes, then wash off.

NOURISHING THE SKIN

Some skins require nourishing, especially when exposed to the drying effect of weather. All the recipes that follow are for use on normal skin. If your skin is sensitive or has a tendency to blemishes, do not use before seeking medical advice.

Almond oil
Almonds are well known for their healing, nourishing and soothing effect on the skin and were used extensively in ancient Greece for facial and hand creams.

40g (1½ oz) ground almonds
1 litre (35 fl oz) Rose-water or rain-water
1 teaspoon sugar
½ teaspoon tincture of Benzoin (*Styrax benzoin*)

Mix the almonds with the Rose or rain-water until the mixture resembles a fine paste. Then filter through fine muslin. Add sugar and a few drops of tincture of Benzoin (*Styrax benzoin*) and bottle ready for use.

Cucumber oil
This is also cooling in effect and is an excellent protection against sunburn.
You will need:
2 ripe Cucumbers (*Cucumis sativus*)
1 litre (35 fl oz) cold water
1 litre (35 fl oz) rain-water
2 dessertspoons glycerine
½ teaspoon tincture of Benzoin (*Styrax benzoin*)

Cut the Cucumbers into small pieces, including their rinds. Put them in a pan with the cold water. Bring to the boil gradually and simmer for 20 minutes. Strain and squeeze through fine muslin or a jelly bag. When cold, mix with the rain-water, the glycerine and tincture of Benzoin. Apply to the skin as required.

Cold cream
A little of this applied every night before sleep will feed and revitalize your skin.

70g (2½ oz) spermaceti
25g (1 oz) fresh beeswax
340ml (12 fl oz) sweet Almond oil

40ml (1½ fl oz) glycerine
40ml (1½ fl oz) Rose-water
40ml (1½ fl oz) Cucumber juice

Melt the spermaceti in a double boiler with the fresh beeswax and the sweet Almond oil. Stir continually with a wooden spoon or spatula. Once the ingredients have melted and amalgamated, add the glycerine, Rose-water and Cucumber juice.

Stir until the cream is quite cold. *Note:* Cold cream derives its name from the very fact that it is stirred until it is cold. It is at the point when it sets that it becomes ready for use.

Alternative cold cream recipe

110g (4 oz) spermaceti
50g (2 oz) fresh beeswax
435ml (15½ fl oz) Almond oil
25ml (1 fl oz) glycerine
25ml (1 fl oz) Rose-water
10 drops Rose essence (or any other fragrance preferred)

Melt the spermaceti, beeswax and Almond oil in a double boiler. Pour into a basin and mix with a wooden spoon or spatula. Leave to set in the refrigerator.

Pound for 45 minutes in a mortar, or blend in an electric mixer until it turns into a thick white cream, add the glycerine and Rose-water. Blend again for two to three minutes to emulsify the cream. Add the Rose essence and mix again for one minute. Refrigerate until it solidifies, and then bottle until required.

Night cream

Use this very rich and nourishing cream every night to keep your skin looking youthful and to help smooth out lines. It contains lanolin which is a waxy substance obtained from wool grease and is used widely in cosmetics for its moisturizing effect on the skin.

2 teaspoons beeswax
2 teaspoons lanolin
4 teaspoons Almond oil (*Prunus dulcis*)
2 teaspoons distilled water
pinch of borax or 3 drops of tincture of Benzoin (*Styrax benzoin*)
2 capsules (1 teaspoon) Wheat germ oil (*Triticum vulgare*)

Warm the beeswax, lanolin and Almond oil in a double boiler until they have melted and combined. Dissolve the borax in the warmed distilled water, then allow both liquids to cool. Mix them together, then beat in the Wheat germ oil.
Note: Add infusion of Comfrey (*Symphytum officinale*) or Marigold (*Calendula officinalis*) to assist cell regeneration.

Anti-wrinkle lotion

Drop 15 to 20 Poppy (*Papaver rhoeas*) petals into 280ml (10 fl oz) boiling water and allow them to infuse for approximately ten minutes. Filter or strain and then allow the liquid to cool before bottling. Use night and morning; it is especially kind to dry skin.

Cocoa-butter neck smoother

1 tablespoon Cocoa butter (*Theobroma cacao*)
1 tablespoon lanolin
½ cup Wheat germ oil (*Triticum vulgare*) or Corn (*Zea mays*) or Peanut (*Arachis hypogaea*) oil
4 tablespoons water (optional)

Melt all three oils in a double boiler until completely dissolved. (The addition of water makes the cream easier to spread.) Allow to cool, place in jars and refrigerate. Shake before use. The mixture may be cloudy but this in no way impairs the power of the cream.

HAIR HEALTH

Throughout the centuries, man has improved the health and beauty of his hair through the use of a variety of herbal preparations.

Hair is a dead substance made up of a protein called keratin. It cannot be rejuvenated. No amount of wishful thinking will bring it back to life, though massage will encourage healthy growth by stimulating the circulation.

The majority of proprietary herbal hair products have a synthetic basis, an attractive perfume, delightful packaging and a pretty name. However, purely herbal shampoos, among other things, have been made in the past, and even today herbalists still base their range of hair cosmetics and medicaments on completely natural substances. Apart from shampoos, you will find that they stock hair and scalp conditioners, rinses and dyes. If you make them yourself, you will derive far more satisfaction and save money, too.

Shampoos

Pure herbal shampoos of the past relied on certain plants which contained soapy substances called saponins. One of the best sources of these substances is an attractive flowering perennial bush called Soapwort (*Saponaria officinalis*). This type of shampoo produces very little foam and gives a dry astringent wash. It was last produced commercially in 1930. Those with greasy hair will find a decoction of Soapbark (*Quillaja saponaria*) very effective.

Manufacturers of commercial hair products have classified the general public into three categories: those with dry, greasy or normal hair. The herbal trichologist, however, claims that all hair is normal – normal to the individual that is – and that dryness and greasiness should not be treated as an isolated condition, but as part of a larger problem.

Anyone who feels they have severe problems with their hair, either with an excess of oil or hair that is so dry that the ends are badly split, should consider their general health. Greasy hair can be associated with diet, while those with dry hair should look first to their shampoo: it could be far too strong. Synthetic shampoos leave the hair unnaturally clean, the acidic balance of the hair being upset by their action.

On the other hand, a natural shampoo always leaves a certain amount of grease, and therefore dirt, on the hair. By modern standards, of course, this would not be considered clean enough.

The first step towards using herbs for hair health is to get a good shine – nothing else may be necessary. Make an infusion of Rosemary (*Rosmarinus officinalis*), Nettle (*Urtica dioica*), Chamomile (*Matricaria recutita*) or any herbs you particularly favour. Measure 560ml (20 fl oz) of water to each 25g (1 oz) weight of herb. Boil the water. Place the herbs in a suitable container such as a jug or basin and pour the

Below: Although hair is composed of a dead substance, keratin, its health depends upon the condition of the scalp and underlying cells. The top diagram shows a hair in the normal position (left) and 'frightened' (right). The bottom diagram shows how a new hair is produced from the follicle.

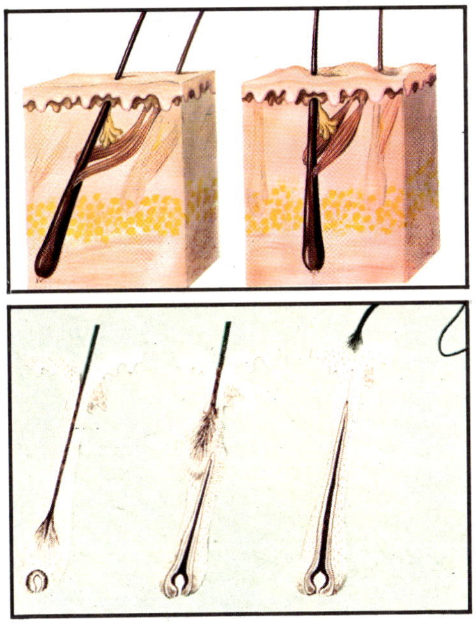

Left: An Indian lady displays the palms of her hands which have been delicately painted with Henna. Henna was also used to dye nails red.

boiling water over them. Allow the herbs to steep for 30 minutes. Strain through muslin or cheesecloth. Allow to cool. Mix the infusion with your usual shampoo and wash your hair in the normal way.

In cases of illness or an unexpected occasion where hair washing is ill-advised or timed, try a dry shampoo. These can be purchased in the form of a white powder, ground from Orris root (*Iris germanica*), Arrowroot (*Maranta arundinacea*), Rosemary (*Rosmarinus officinalis*) or Quassia chips (*Picraena exelsa*), and each designed to remove grease from the hair by absorption. Brush it into the hair, and then out again.

Powdered Orris root was also used as a sweet-scented hair powder in the eighteenth century. Wheat (*Triticum vulgare*) and lichens were used to whiten wigs and in 1748, the year of the Great Famine, a quarter of a million pounds weight of hair powder was used to indulge fashion while most of the populace starved.

Hair and scalp conditioners

These are usually acidic in reaction, containing Lemon (*Citrus limon*), vinegar, Verbena (*Verbena officinalis*) or Lemon Verbena (*Aloysia triphylla*). They are all designed to rid the hair of residual alkaline after shampooing, or to restore the natural acidic balance of the skin.

Rinses for use after shampooing can be made from the juice of all citrus fruits, though Lemon is the most popular. Lemon has traditionally been used, along with vinegar, in a final rinse to remove 'scum', so allowing the hair to shine with a natural lustre. Add a teaspoonful to your last rinse for deliciously scented results. Even better would be white wine, white or cider vinegar.

An infusion of Rosemary (*Rosmarinus officinalis*) can also impart shine to hair. It has the advantage of acting as a mild antiseptic. Steep the spikes in boiling water for 30 minutes, then strain and cool. Use as a rinse as required. Rosemary, incidentally, is one of the major herbs added to commercial natural hair cosmetics.

Another pleasant rinse is one made by gathering equal parts of Chamomile (*Matricaria recutita*), Fennel (*Foeniculum vulgare*), and Lime flowers (*Tila × europaea* or *T. × vulgaris*), together with some Sage (*Salvia officinalis*), Rosemary (*Rosmarinus officinalis*), Nettle (*Urtica dioica*), Horsetail (*Equisetum arvense*) and Yarrow (*Achillea millefolium*). For blonde or light hair add more Chamomile, and for dark hair less Chamomile and more Rosemary.

Place 25g (1 oz) of the mixed herbs into a container and pour 560ml (20 fl oz) of boiling water over them. Steep until cool, then strain in the usual way. Use as a final rinse for general health and lustre.

To condition the scalp, make an infusion of the common stinging Nettle (*Urtica dioica*), and then strain and cool. Apply to the scalp to dilate the blood vessels and so encourage healthy growth. The stimulant plant Jaborandi (*Pilocarpus microphyllus*) from Brazil was once the most popular herbal scalp conditioner and hair restorer, but it is no longer considered safe enough to use. If a massage is preferred, take equal quantities of herbs such as Fennel (*Foeniculum vulgare*), Nettle (*Urtica dioica*), Chamomile (*Matricaria recutita*) and Yarrow (*Achillea millefolium*), or any of those previously mentioned, and steep them in 560ml (20 fl oz) of Sunflower (*Helianthus annuus*) oil. Place in the sunlight if possible to encourage the release of the herbs' oils. Note the results for future reference.

Setting lotions

Vegetable sources can be used to encourage the hair to curl, or at least to hold a curl in place once it is set. Gum Tragacanth, an exudation from an Asiatic plant, *Astragalus gummifer*, is used as the basis for setting lotions and as an additive in certain hair conditioners. More recently, Sodium Alginate, a derivative of seaweeds, has been used to provide a basis for commercial setting lotions.

An excellent naturally based setting lotion can be derived from the Quince (*Pyrus cydonia*). Measure 50g (2 oz) of Quince seed and boil in 280ml (10 fl oz) of water for 15 minutes. Make up the quantity of liquid as it evaporates. Strain and press through muslin, making sure that as much mucilage as possible is squeezed through. The liquid will jellify and set when cold. Apply either hot or warm, as preferred. You can also adapt this recipe to include Kelp (*Fucus vesiculosus*), a seaweed found on many European coastlines.

Brightening and lightening

For three quick and brightening rinses for dull hair, turn to those stalwarts Chamomile (*Matricaria recutita*), Elder berries (*Sambucus nigra*) and Henna (*Lawsonia inermis*). Chamomile is the only herb which really lightens fair hair. It contains a non-volatile oil called apigenin which

Below: Herbs were essential constituents for the hair powders so much in vogue in eighteenth-century Europe. This lady's elaborate coiffure probably contained powdered Orris root and Rosemary leaf. A similar kind of preparation can be used as a dry shampoo.

gives light hair a lighter yellow tone. Dyes containing quick-lime, of a similar nature to the depilatories, were used by Roman women as bleaches, often with disastrous results. To make a Chamomile rinse, make an infusion from 50g (2 oz) of the herb to 560ml (20 fl oz) of water. Steep, strain and use as a final rinse.

Grey hair can be coloured with a rinse made from Elder berries (*Sambucus nigra*). These were used by the Romans as a pack for grey hair and, used in this way, will impart a bluish hue. You can either buy Elder berries pre-dried, or gather your own between September and November when they are ripe and before the birds get to them. Make up an infusion and add a pinch of salt and alum for additional brightness. Use as a final rinse.

And so, briefly, to Henna (*Lawsonia* spp). For those of you with light brown, through red, dark brown to black hair, Henna is the perfect herb to condition, highlight and give shine to your hair. Weigh out 25g (1 oz) of Henna leaf – any type will do – and make an infusion for a final rinse.

Problem hair

Excessive oil or dryness should be regarded as being associated with general health. Dandruff, however, is the flaking-off of the top layer of skin on the scalp. Its cause can also be linked with diet, climate, environment and stress: any one of these factors or several in combination.

Useful remedies include massaging Olive oil or Sweet Almond oil gently into the scalp to soften it; alternatively you could use an infusion of Chamomile (*Matricaria recutita*) or Marigold (*Calendula officinalis*) mixed and whipped into a cream (cold cream) for this. This is then applied to the scalp.

An itchy scalp is a common complaint. This is usually associated with stress rather than with any physical cause. An infusion of Chamomile (*Matricaria recutita*) smells delightful and is a weak sedative, as well as soothing the scalp itself. Itching can also be attributed to lice. Vinegar rinses are often effective in the removal of nits (the eggs of the louse) that cement themselves to the shaft of the hair. Alternatively, an infusion of Poke Root (*Phytolacca decandra*), Quassia chips (*Picraena exelsa*) or Juniper berries (*Juniperus communis*) can be used to rinse the hair; then comb out the corpses. The procedure should be repeated after two weeks, and again two weeks later. Quassia, in particular, has antiseptic qualities that repel lice.

Cures for baldness have been sought and pursued through history, but we have to accept that there is no magic cure for hair loss which can be for any number of reasons. For those who require a potion to protect what they have, make a strong infusion from Rosemary (*Rosmarinus officinalis*) – or preferably the oil – and rub into the scalp four or five times a week.

Colouring and dyeing

Herbs tend to have a slow colouring effect, and none act directly as a bleach. Commercially produced hair dyes and colouring rinses are based on coal-tar by-products and were first used in the nineteenth century. A large range of synthetic organic dyes are now available. Before rinses became commercially available, Henna (*Lawsonia* spp) was used to render brown hair auburn and to help mask greying strands, while acting as a marvellous conditioner at the same time. It is easily absorbed, the colour being assimilated through the cuticle of the hair into the cortex.

The Romans used herbs and spices to colour their hair, of which Saffron (*Crocus sativus*) and Chamomile (*Matricaria recutita*) were popular. Neither penetrate the hair shaft, however, and such sources are therefore used as colouring rinses and shampoos rather than as direct dyes. Sage (*Salvia officinalis*) has been greatly recommended in the past to disguise greying hair, but the infusion needs to be strong (110g or 4 oz to 560ml or 20 fl oz) and the process repeated weekly for several months. Use as a final rinse. Powdered Rhubarb root (*Rheum officinale*) will add attractive golden tone to light brown or fair hair. It should be made into a pack mixed with hot water and applied to the hair for 30 minutes; but care must be taken as it will dry the scalp. Another traditional remedy which is effective in masking grey or white hair is to crush Black Walnut leaves and husks (*Juglans nigra*). Soaking in water will result in a dark brown stain that will add tone to grey or white hair. Other recipes can include Marigold (*Calendula officinalis*) petals to brighten blonde hair, Oak bark (*Quercus robur*) for a reddish tone and Alkanet (*Anchusa officinalis*) for a light pink – for those who want that colour. Many other herbs (and spices) have been tested over the years for their colouring properties and found to be effective in varying degrees. These include Woad (*Isatis tinctoria*), Logwood (*Haematoxylum campechianum*), Saffron (*Crocus sativus*) and Turmeric (*Curcuma longa*).

There is no doubt, however, that the favourite colouring agent is Henna. Henna is the powdered leaf of Egyptian privet and has been in use for over 5000 years. Mummified remains from Egyptian tombs show that a mixture of Henna and Indigo (*Indigofera tinctoria*) shoots, called Henna reng, was used to colour hair and false beards to a youthful blue-black.

Henna is an integral part of the Eastern culture. Arabic women are given a sack of Henna on the eve of their wedding with which they make a thick paste to colour the hair and decorate their hands and feet in intricate patterns. Certain Berber families embalm their dead in Henna, while a hennaed beard has great religious significance for Muslims.

The powdered leaf gives a rich red tone to hair when mixed with water. It is applied for two to three hours and has to be maintained at a regular temperature; cling film or silver foil assist in this. The quality of the Henna and the colour it imparts to the hair depends on its source and country of origin. Persian Henna is the finest, producing a deep rich red;

*Below: A branch from the Egyptian Privet or Henna tree (*Lawsonia inermis*), the powdered leaf of which provides Henna which has traditionally been used as a colouring agent for both hair and body.*

Right: A modern perfumery in France. Herbal oils which were prized and used thousands of years ago are still employed by the most exclusive perfume manufacturers. Ranged in this laboratory are Lavender, Oakmoss, Patchouli and Neroli. There are four methods of extracting the oils from plants: distillation, maceration, absorption and enfleurage.

Egyptian Henna gives more orange results; Chinese is the cheapest, being of inferior quality.

Another major virtue of Henna, making it even more versatile, is that it can be mixed with other organic substances to modify the colour – coffee, wine, eggs, lemon juice and onion skins are modern variations. Traditionalists may prefer to experiment by adding Indigo shoots (for reng), Walnut husks (darkening), Lucerne (*Medicago sativa*) (darkening), Catechu (darkening), the extract that is so rich in tannin from *Acacia catechu*, or Betel nut (*Piper betle*) (reddening).

To henna your hair, select your variety, then weigh out the Henna powder. For a head of short hair, 170g (6 oz) will be sufficient. Shoulder length hair or longer will require 225g (8 oz). For further benefits or to affect the colouring, a modifying agent should be selected. An egg will act as a secondary and nourishing conditioner; a glassful of red wine, or ground coffee or Cloves (*Syzygium aromaticum*) will result in slight variations of colour; while Lemon juice (*Citrus limon*) or vinegar will aid the release of the dye, so increasing the colouring effect. Have ready a couple of old towels, a plastic bag, a saucepan, a pair of rubber gloves and set aside a couple of hours of your time.

Mix the modifying agent with the Henna and sufficient water to mix to a thick creamy paste. Heat to boiling point, then set aside to cool slightly. To protect the scalp, rub vegetable oil into the skin to act as a protective barrier. Wearing rubber gloves, apply the Henna. Do this thoroughly by making numerous partings from one side to the other or from the back to the front or vice versa. Wrap the hair in cling film to seal in the Henna and maintain a warm temperature. Wrap your head in a towel and sit in a warm place to 'cook'. The longer you leave it, the stronger the colour, so only increase the length of time after you have experimented with leaving it for, say, one and a half hours.

Wash thoroughly until the water runs quite clear and then shampoo. Your hair will glow with colour, and it will shine as never before.

PERFUMERY

The word perfume comes from the Latin meaning 'through smoke'. This is probably derived from the custom of making burnt sacrificial offerings to the gods of those times, as practised by the Romans and Egyptians. The latter were especially generous in using perfumed oils, and the Greeks followed the tradition, so gaining an understanding of the many herbs and plants in their own part of the Mediterranean world. As a result, the Romans spread this knowledge to other parts of Europe.

The numerous delights of perfumery disappeared from Europe during the Middle Ages, though Charlemagne tried hard to recreate the luxury enjoyed by the Romans by using sweet-smelling plants and scenting public fountains in the streets for the people's pleasure.

In the late tenth and early eleventh centuries, Avicenna brought the art of making Rose-water from Persia, and the Crusaders brought back phials of Rose-water from Asia together with many other strongly scented products.

By the fourteenth century, it was customary to offer perfumes to guests in any noble house. They were offered after meals for freshening the hands and fingers after eating – without implements of course. During this period, alcoholic perfumes were being tried in Europe and quickly found favour. 'Hungary water' was particularly successful. By the sixteenth century, *les herbes et plantes de senteur pour embaumer les eaux des fontaines publiques* were commonplace in France for festivals.

There are four methods of extracting essential oils from plants: distillation, (from whole plants), maceration, absorption, and finally, expression (of rind or skin) which is a process known as 'enfleurage' which combines maceration and absorption.

Distillation

This is a steam-assisted process, whereby the plant material is placed in containers above water vats so that the steam carries some of the oil away and forms a condensate containing the essential oil.

Because many of the oils in plants are to a greater or lesser degree water-soluble, the distillate is skimmed off and re-distilled. Plants that cannot be treated by the steam distillation process are treated with various substances (mainly alcohols) which, acting as solvents, remove oils, dissolve fats and break down pigments and other cell components.

Maceration

This is literally the steeping of flowers and herbs in water to release the essential oils.

Absorption

This method involves the plant oil being absorbed by fat or grease, traditionally either tallow or lard. It is used for plants which continue producing oils after being picked like Jasmine (*Jasminum* spp) and Tuberose (*Polianthes tuberosa*) and plants whose oils would be damaged by steam or whose odour would be altered by steam, water or volatile solvents.

The usual method is to spread the fats on both sides of a sheet of glass held in a frame called a 'chassis', and then to spread fresh flowers over the grease every morning for a number of days. The chassis are stacked for 24 hours in a darkened room. Over this period, the fat or grease absorbs the flower oils and becomes impregnated with their perfume. The resulting scented grease is called a 'pomade'.

The quality of the pomade can be recognized by the number attached to it. If the flowers are changed 20 times, the pomade is known as 'Pomade 20'; if changed 30 times, 'Pomade 30' and so on. Originally they were used in their greasy form, but it is now usual to extract the perfume from the pomade by means of alcohol, the resulting scents being called 'Extrait 20' or 'Extrait 30'. If the alcohol is than evaporated, an oil residue is left called 'absolue de pomade'.

A simpler method involves immersing plant matter in molten fats at a temperature ranging from 45°–80°C (113°–176°F) for several hours. The plants are then filtered off and the immersion repeated up to 20 times. In this case, the resulting pomade is known as 'Pomade 20' and sometimes sold as such; or an 'absolue' may be produced as already explained.

Expression

This method is a relatively simple technique for extracting the oils from the rinds or peel of fruit and other plant materials. The matter is subjected to mechanical pressure and grinding to release the oil. A more traditional method involves pressing the whole fruit into a sponge, which is then wrung out to yield the oil.

Classifying perfume odours

Perfume is classified according to one or more identifiable odours, and these fall into six categories: floral scents from plants such as Rose (*Rosa* spp), Lily-of-the-Valley (*Convallaria majalis*), Jasmine (*Jasminum* spp), Gardenia (*Gardenia jasminoides*); spicy scents that include Nutmeg (*Myristica fragrans*), Cinnamon (*Cinnamomum zeylanicum*), Clove (*Syzygium aromaticum*) and Carnation (*Dianthus caryophyllus*); woody scents like Sandalwood (*Santalum album*) and Cedarwood (*Cedrus* spp); mossy scents such as those from Oakmoss (*Evernia purpuracea*) (now very rare). Herbal scents are considered not so powerful and pungent, and these are represented by Tobacco (*Nicotiana tabacum*), Clover (*Trifolium pratense*) and sweet grasses. Oriental scents usually combine woody, mossy and spicy perfumes, with Vanilla (*Vanilla planifolia*) and Balsam (*Myroxylon* spp) being considered in this category.

The simplest fragrances to make at home are the toilet waters. Add 15 drops of essential oil to 560ml (20 fl oz) of water and shake the bottle. The most versatile are Rose-water, Orange-flower water and Lavender water, and all three of these can be used to scent the body directly and as an ingredient for many other cosmetic products. The more complex perfumes depend on blending carefully measured amounts of oil with pure alcohol. Pure alcohol, however, is not for sale to the general public, and isopropyl alcohol (which is itself somewhat scented) must be used in the making of toilet waters.

Lavender water

25ml (1 fl oz) oil of Lavender (*Lavandula spica*)
840ml (30 fl oz) isopropyl alcohol

Shake the ingredients together in a large bottle and leave to settle for about 48 hours. Shake well again. After a further 48 hours the liquid can be put into small bottles with tight-fitting lids.

Hungary water

1 tablespoon fresh Mint leaves (*Mentha* spp)
1 tablespoon fresh Rosemary leaves (*Rosmarinus officinalis*)
50ml (2 fl oz) alcohol (isopropyl alcohol)
110ml (4 fl oz) Rose-water
grated peel of Orange and Lemon

Mix all the ingredients together and leave to soak. Cover well and store for a week, shaking each day. Strain into dark bottles which should have tightly fitting lids for storing.

Orange-flower water

25ml (1 fl oz) Orange-flower essence (*Citrus sinensis*)
4.5l (1 gall) distilled water

Mix the two together and allow to age for at least a week. You can make Rose-water in exactly the same way.

Eau de Portugal

420ml (15 fl oz) 45° proof alcohol (isopropyl alcohol)
20ml ($\frac{3}{4}$ fl oz) essence of Orange
6ml ($\frac{1}{4}$ fl oz) essence of Lemon
1 ml ($\frac{1}{16}$ fl oz) essence of Rose
25 ml ($\frac{3}{4}$ fl oz) essence of Bergamot oil (*Citrus aurantium* var. *bergamia*)

Mix all the ingredients together and bottle. The mixture stores well.

Ancient 'spice' perfume

This is not really a 'perfume' at all, but it was traditionally known as such. It has a splendid spicy scent.

2 cups Rose-water (*Rosa* spp)
15g ($\frac{1}{2}$ oz) bruised Cloves (*Syzygium aromaticum*)
2–3 Bay leaves (*Laurus nobilis*)
2 cups wine vinegar

Combine the Rose-water, Cloves, chopped Bay leaves and vinegar, and boil. As it reduces, add water to make up the quantity. Strain and place the liquor aside in a well-sealed jar for several weeks or more before using.

Right: Women in France at the beginning of this century sorting thousands of rose petals in preparation for the manufacture of perfumes.

Cultivation, collection and preservation of herbs

Herb gardens were traditionally attached to monasteries and provided substances for the treatment of ailments, and flavouring for food, and often the colour and the scents of monastic life as well. Over the centuries herbs have been relegated to garden plots, then retrieved for their old-world charm and associations, forgotten again, and now in the twentieth century they are enjoying a revival of interest. In decorative value most of them fail to reach acceptance, but used in conventional herb garden settings which have been exclusively designed, there is an appeal redolent of ancient atmospheres in which an illusion of simple antiquity can be achieved.

Herbs were first used decoratively in Europe in the sixteenth century, where the practice began of growing herbs in knot gardens. But the progression of horticultural practice, the finer achievements of the art of cultivation, and the immense influx of new decorative plant material superseded the lowly herbs. Household economy has continued to know and to need these plants however unassuming though many of them appear to be.

SELECTION AND PREPARATION OF SITE

Herbs are undemanding plants, their stamina is good, and their natural appeal can be strong. Most are at their best in warm, still air on a site adequately protected from prevailing winds, but not shaded. If the land slopes, a south or south-west facing slope is preferred, and without a hedge or wall running across the base of the slope which would form a frost pocket. A soil free of perennial weeds and with good drainage is an essential factor of any site selected for herbs, unless a bog-type herb garden is being planned.

Shaded shrub borders and rock gardens do not usually make suitable sites, except for the limited range of herbs such as Thyme, pinks, violets, Sedums and Arnica that like the sharp drainage of the rock work. A level site is normally best, or perhaps a site on two levels with a retaining wall between the two to accommodate, for example, ferns, Feverfew, Pellitory and Centranthus.

Preparation of site

Time is well spent in first clearing a proposed site thoroughly of perennial weeds and even fallowing (backsetting) if time allows. The crop of eager weeds that appear following soil disturbance can then be eradicated before the herb seedlings and young plants are introduced. Ideally the soil should be fertile, but not too rich, and some form of moisture-retaining material will probably need to be added but not food material such as artificial fertilizer.

Humus can be provided in the form of compost made from garden and kitchen waste and forked in to improve the soil in both texture and composition. Thus adequate moisture and warmth are en-

Left: At the height of the season herb borders, such as this which includes Chervil and Mint, provide an array of both useful and decorative plant material.

Left: The gardens of the sixteenth century provide excellent blueprints for the design of a formal herb garden today. The simple outline of the beds is important and the relationship of one bed to the others should be carefully considered.

sured. Leaf mould, spent hops, peat or animal bedding straw may also be used to produce humus – they are all organic in composition and gradually break down to encourage a friable (crumbly) well-drained soil. Lightly fork or hoe in the material to the surface of the soil and the frosts will do the rest. If this kind of soil improvement cannot be achieved or if the soil is very light or dry and chalky, the gardener must be content to grow those plants that will tolerate a dry, baked soil such as Rosemary, Thyme, Marjoram, Sage, Broom and pinks.

Levelling

On a site of any considerable size levelling has to be carried out properly, especially where two levels are envisaged, and the work has to be done before any planting starts. On a small site, the surface level can be corrected by forking and raking and there are no difficulties in keeping the top soil on the surface. Where there is a marked discrepancy in existing surface levels, the top soil of the entire area has to be removed, the site levelled and the top soil then replaced.

Paths

As with all workable gardens, the herb garden is best served by well-constructed paths which will give a firm, dry access. Gravel, concrete, paving or bricks all provide these requirements and the choice is dependent upon the cost and availability of material and labour. If beds are to be marked out in turf, where the turf will finally provide the paths, it should be well laid and established before beds are cut out.

Marking out the beds

The outline of beds should first be drawn out on paper, then measured carefully on to the site and marked out with pegs and cord – and, even at that stage, again considered before proceeding. Sufficient space should be allowed between beds so that when plants spread towards the path there will still be enough room for easy passage with wheelbarrows and tools.

Left and overleaf: Based on the principles of classic design, this herb garden indicates the immense range of available material. Paving adds simplicity to the overall design and affords ease of maintenance. Repetition of planting patterns ensures unity and allows the design to be used within a small area. The key (overleaf) shows which plants may be used, taking into account their relative habits of growth and colour. This plan can be adapted to meet the requirements of a smaller site, as shown on page 123.

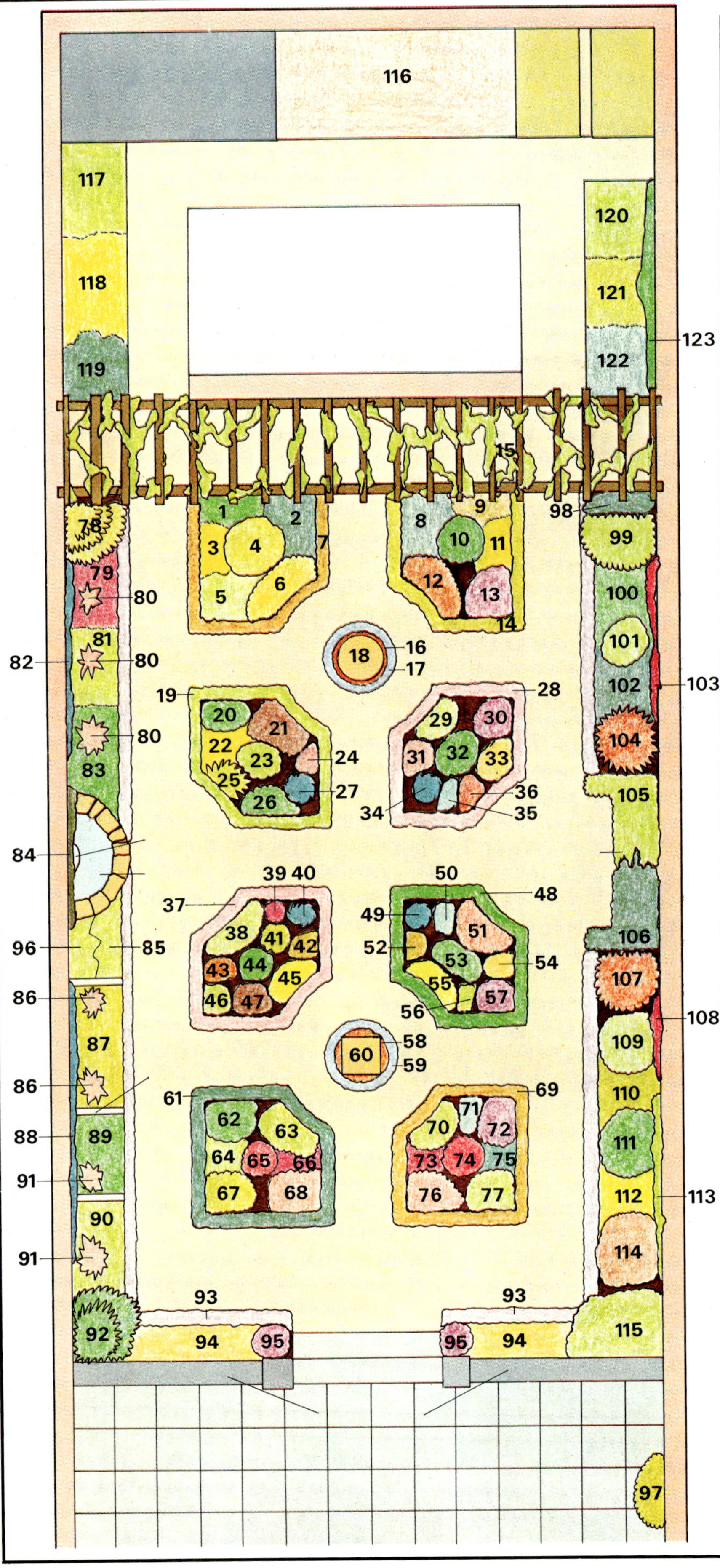

Key to Herb Garden ground plan

Bed A
1 Bergamot or Oswego tea (red)
2 Lamb's Lettuce or Corn Salad
3 Cowslip
4 Lovage
5 Salad Burnet
6 Sorrel
7 Cotton Lavender (border)

Bed B
8 Purslane
9 Bergamot or Oswego Tea (pink)
10 Fennel
11 Cowslip
12 Rue
13 Lavender
14 Parsley (border)
15 Vines (on the pergola)

Bed C
16 Woodruff
17 Wild Thyme (border)
18 Bird bath or tub of plants

Bed D
19 Golden Marjoram (border)
20 French or Pot Marjoram
21 Common Sage
22 Cowslip
23 Tansy
24 Lady's Mantle
25 Sweet Cicely
26 Tarragon
27 Juniper

Bed E
28 Pinks (border)
29 Purple Sage
30 Lavender
31 Lady's Mantle
32 Mallow
33 Hyssop
34 Juniper
35 Bush Basil
36 Clove Carnation

Bed F
37 Pinks (border)
38 Wormwood
39 Violet
40 Juniper
41 Apothecary's Rose (pink)
42 Narrow-leaved Sage
43 Rue
44 Curry Plant
45 Pot Marigold
46 Common Thyme
47 Common Sage

Bed G
48 Lemon Thyme (border)
49 Juniper
50 Bush Basil
51 Clove Carnations
52 Narrow-leaved Sage
53 Rose (red or pink, scented)
54 Hyssop
55 Pot Marigold
56 Golden Sage
57 Lavender

Bed H
58 Woodruff
59 Wild Thyme (border)
60 Sundial or tub of plants

Bed I
61 Chives (border)
62 Chamomile
63 Annual Clary Sage
64 Lavender
65 Rose (red, scented)
66 Violet
67 Golden (wild) Marjoram
68 Clove Carnation

Bed J
69 Cotton Lavender (border)
70 Vervain
71 Bush Basil
72 Lavender
73 Violet
74 Rose (red, scented)
75 Wormwood
76 Clove Carnation
77 Oregano or Garden Marjoram

Left-hand border
78 Bay
79 Violet
80 Foxglove
81 Sweet Woodruff
82 Morello Cherry (on wall)
83 Common Mint or Spearmint
84 Ivy (behind fountain)
85 Apple Mint
86 Foxglove
87 Lily-of-the-Valley
88 Morello Cherry (on wall)
89 Lemon Balm
90 Periwinkle
91 Foxglove
92 Rosemary

End beds and terrace
93 French Marigold (borders)
94 Scented Pelargonium
95 Lavender
96 Myrtle
97 Lemon-scented Verbena

Right-hand border
98 Hop (in angle of pergola)
99 Elder
100 Chervil
101 Winter Savory
102 Borage
103 Rose (on wall)
104 Florentine Iris
105 Honeysuckle (in arbour)
106 Jasmine (mixture of yellow and white)
107 Florentine Iris
108 Rose (on wall)
109 Southernwood
110 Woad
111 Catmint
112 Myrtle
113 Fig (on wall)
114 Rue
115 Tree Germander

Service area
116 Marrows and Courgettes
117 Comfrey
118 French Sorrel
119 Rhubarb
120 Onions
121 Lettuce
122 Garlic
123 Espaliered fruit (on wall)

Above: A traditional garden at Hardwick Hall, Derbyshire. Height is provided by tripods upon which honeysuckles or jasmine can be grown.

SELECTION OF PLANTS

The primary requirement for herbs to grow successfully, as indeed for any plant, is a suitable environment. In the wild state plants select their own location and often indicate the type and condition of the soil, the drainage and the intensity of light. Observation will thus suggest which plants can be expected to flourish in, or at least tolerate, a given situation. While the demands of herbs are few and they can often thrive without much attention, the results will be far more rewarding if some basic requirements are considered before starting to plant.

Number of plants

When a space has been cleared, and the selection of plants has been made, a decision has to be taken as to whether a short or long-term effect is required. In general, ten plants per square metre (one plant per square foot), with the exception of all but the tiniest plants, will give interest in the first year and effect in the second and subsequent years. Where the herb garden is being planted for immediate decorative effect, closer planting needs to be carried out – subsequent judicious thinning is always possible. Small plants, such as Thyme, Pennyroyal, and Chamomile used perhaps as an edging, need to be planted more closely.

On strong or rich soils more growth will be produced than on a poorer soil; similarly, if plants like the soil type they can be expected to establish themselves more easily. The table overleaf indicates the requirements of a number of plants, and by matching a plant to its needs in a selected position greater success can be achieved. The ultimate size of a plant should be considered in proportion to the size of the herb garden.

The type of garden

The second major decision is the sort of herb garden that is required. Is the garden to be decorative or utilitarian? Is it to be a representative collection of medicinal, culinary or scented plants? Once these decisions have been made and the plan drawn up, the plants can be acquired and planting can begin. There is nothing to be gained by haphazard planting; for effect and for usefulness herbs need to be considered with care.

Stocking the garden

The quickest way, but often the most expensive, is to buy plants so that an immediate air of organization can be achieved. It is frequently sufficient to buy one plant each of perennials such as Rosemary, Mint, Tarragon, Lovage and Lemon Balm and propagate them to build up the necessary stock. Many herbs are stem rooters and soon form clusters of roots along their runners and stems, so that new plants can be obtained quite quickly by separating these from the parent plant. In this way it will take two or three years to establish a reasonable stock of plants for an interesting herb garden. There is the added advantage that losses can be replaced, the general plan can be amended, and should any plant prove not to be compatible with its position, no great loss is sustained.

Annuals like marigolds, Dill, Basil, Borage and Summer Savory need to be raised from seed each spring. Some will seed themselves, but often the seedlings appear at the other end of the garden, so where general effect is important they will need to be transplanted as soon as they are sufficiently established to be able to cope with the change. Biennials, such as foxgloves, Verbascum and Angelica do not flower until the second season after sowing, but once established they provide generations of seedlings.

Market stalls and garden centres are the best sources of herb plants, and there are also a number of well-run herb nurseries. Buy the best plants and ensure that they are free from insect and fungus attack. They should be well grown and sufficiently hardened off, if bought during the early spring. A well-grown plant will be short-jointed, of good texture and colour and ought not to be in flower. Buying from herb nurseries and farms may mean buying by mail order, but most establishments have their reputations at stake and are careful to dispatch clean stock. Doubtful specimens ought always to be returned.

A stock of plants can also be made up of snippets and gifts from other gardens – each plant a reminder of a friendly visit. This exchange of plants is one of the most traditional ways of making a plant collection of individuality and interest.

Selection of herbs for the garden

Front of the border, or edging plants

Box (clipped)	Pinks
Catmint	Santolina (clipped)
Chives	Sedum
Feverfew	Sempervivum
Hyssop (clipped)	Thrift
Lavender (dwarf)	Thymes
Lungwort	Violet
Marjoram, golden	Wall Germander
Parsley	

Planting in walls and paving

Alchemilla spp.	Pennyroyal
Catmint	Pinks
Chamomile	Sedums
Feverfew	Sempervivum
Hyssop	Soapwort
Lavender (dwarf)	Thymes
Pellitory	Wall Germander

Hedges

Box
Hyssop
Lavender
Rosa gallica officinalis
Rosemary
Rue
Santolina

Chalky soils

Calamint	Marjoram
Chicory	Mignonette
Chives	Mullein
Hound's Tongue	Periwinkle
Juniper	Pinks
Lavender	Rosemary
Lemon Balm	Sage
Lily-of-the-Valley	Salad Burnet

Light soils

Alkanet	Marjoram
Borage	Marjoram, pot
Broom	Melilot
Bugle	Mugwort
Chervil	Rosemary
Chives	Sage
Garlic	Savorys
Hound's Tongue	Southernwood
Hyssop	Tarragon
Lavender	Thymes
Lemon Balm	Wormwood
Lemon Verbena	

Moist situations

Acorus	Sweet Cicely
Bergamot	Valerian
Bistort	Veratrum
Comfrey	Watercress
Meadowsweet	Yellow Flag
Mints	

Annuals (last 1 year)

Anise	Florence Fennel
Basil	Marigold
Blessed Thistle	Marjoram, sweet or knotted
Borage	Nasturtium
Chervil	Poppy
Coriander	Purslane
Corn Salad	Savory, Summer
Cumin	Sunflower
Dill	
Flax	

Biennials (last 2 years)

Alexanders (common)	Foxglove
Alkanet	Melilot
Angelica	Mullein
Caraway	Parsley
	Woad

Perennials (continue year after year)

Alecost	Lavender
Alkanet (evergreen)	Lemon Balm
Arnica	Liquorice
Artemisias	Lovage
Bay	Lungwort
Bergamot	Marjoram, pot
Bethlehem Sage	Marjoram (wild)
Bistort	Mignonette
Chenopodium	Mints
Chives	Pinks
Coltsfoot	Rhubarb
Cowslip	Rose
Daphne	Rosemary
Dyer's Madder	Rue
Elder	Sage
Elecampane	Santolina
English Mace	Savory, Winter
Fennel	Sorrel
Gentian	Sweet Cicely
Helichrysum	Tarragon
Jasmine	Thymes
Juniper	Wormwood
	Yarrow

SMALL HERB GARDENS

The undemanding qualities of many herbs make them ideal plants for growing in confined and, sometimes, unlikely places. The only real requirements are adequate light, and space for their roots. Small plants like Thyme and Lemon Thyme, Houseleeks, Chamomile, Chives, Dwarf Lavender and Feverfew are ideal for trough or sink gardens. Containers in a wide range of shapes and sizes are obtainable from garden centres; alternatively, very attractive herb gardens can be established in all sorts of disused containers such as wheelbarrows, drinking troughs and birdbaths.

Larger plants like Lavender, Rosemary, Rue and Sage can easily be included in the scheme for containers, such as stone jars, any large pot or even an old bucket, by growing rooted cuttings and either replacing them when they grow out of proportion to the scheme or by judicious pruning and cutting back. Many herbs can be kept in check simply by nipping off shoots as required for the kitchen. A good trick is to leave the rooted cuttings in their

Left: By selecting plants appropriate to a situation, a greater degree of success can be assured. Plants that normally grow on light soils, for example, will thrive best in a garden with sandy or well-drained soil.

Below: Balance of design in one-sided borders is achieved by keeping small plants in front of larger ones and restricting the numbers of plants.

pot, and sink the whole pot below the soil level, and then as the plants grow both pot and plant can be replaced. A variety of containers can be maintained in this way.

Window-boxes

This method of replenishing pots can also be adopted for window-boxes, though good effect and considerable success is possible when plants are grown directly in the soil in the box. The boxes should be about 25 to 30 centimetres (10 to 12 inches) deep and be filled with a moisture-retaining potting compost, such as John Innes No. 2. Drainage is provided by a layer of rough material, such as broken brick rubble, clinker or gravel, being spread over the entire base of the box, which is then covered with about two centimetres (an inch) of rough peat and then with the potting compost. This ensures that the roots of the plants have food, space and drainage. Dampen and firm the compost before planting and in the spring put in rooted cuttings or small plants which were cut back in the previous autumn and have started to break into fresh growth. Most plants can be confined in size by nipping new growth constantly to encourage a bushy growth. The plants selected should be the smaller ones or smaller-growing cultivars (cultivated varieties) – thymes, cuttings of Sage, and Lavender and Rosemary, the smaller mints, Parsley, Tarragon, Marjoram, Chives, Selfheal, scented-leaved geraniums, Dill and Mignonette are all well suited to box cultivation.

Above: Low-growing herbs or rooted cuttings of larger ones can be assembled in an attractive container. Here Angelica, Chives, Sage and other culinary herbs have been tucked into a decorative bowl, which is small enough to be carried from one part of the garden to another.

Patios and balconies

Success with herbs in patio and roof gardening, as with any other plants, depends upon the proper selection of container and of plant material which must be suited to the size and position of the area. A simple effect is always more successful than an elaborate one. Troughs along the base of patio screens are effective and the plants benefit from some shelter, but adequate light must be ensured. Boxes or troughs which are raised or attached to balustrades or walls with firm brackets and hooks are probably the most successful. Hanging baskets, either of the conventional bowl-shaped kind used for summer display or country baskets, and garden trays lined with grey or black plastic to prevent leaking, can make delightful tiny herb gardens to decorate balconies and roof gardens. They require regular attention and occasional replenishment with new plants to maintain the effect.

Bay is one of the most popular choices for patios and balconies and it is usually clipped to a formal shape. It is best to purchase these already trained, and with care they can be expected to last several years. Cold winds are the chief enemy of these potted trees and they appreciate being taken into a porch or light hallway, or even a conservatory during the winter, in all but the mildest districts.

The golden rule for container-grown plants is to try to keep the compost evenly damp, not overwatered – which leads to sourness – and not parched. As most small herb gardens are grown for summer effect and usefulness, watering will be the major task, for it is during the summer months that they require the most water.

Herbs for troughs and containers

Borage
Catmint
Coltsfoot
Chamomile
Chives
Clary
Lemon Balm
Lily-of-the-Valley
Lungwort
Mint (round-leaved kinds)
Pulmonaria
Rosemary (rooted cuttings)
Sage (rooted cuttings)
Thymes
Violet

Herbs for window-boxes

Basil
Black Horehound
Broom (seedlings)
Chives
Corn Salad
Catmint (small divisions)
Clary
Geranium (scented-leaved)
Hyssop
Lemon Balm
Marjoram
Mignonette
Nasturtium
Parsley
Rosemary (rooted cuttings)
Rue (rooted cuttings)
Sage (rooted cuttings)
Savory
Tarragon
Violet

Herbs to plant in a garden for the blind

Scented and textured leaves

Alecost
Angelica
Bergamot
Chamomile (for treading)
Feverfew
Geraniums (scented-leaved)
Hyssop
Lavender
Lemon Balm
Lily-of-the-Valley
Meadowsweet
Mignonette
Mints
Pennyroyal (for treading)
Rosemary
Rue
Sage
Southernwood
Sweet Cicely
Tansy
Thymes (for treading)
Wormwood

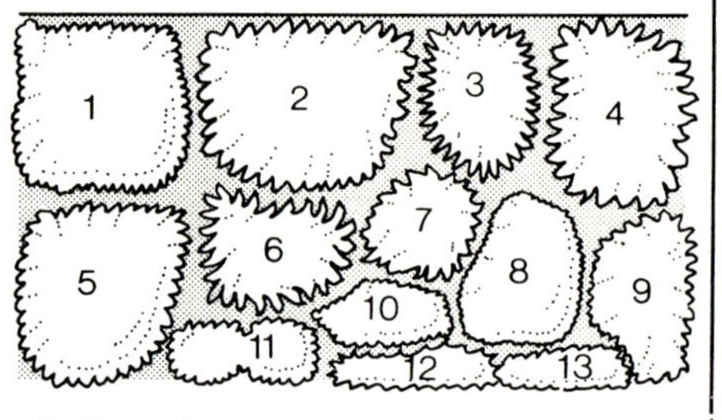

1 Fennel
2 Rosemary
3 French Tarragon
4 Angelica
5 Sage
6 Golden Marjoram
7 Lemon Balm
8 Sorrel
9 Mint
10 Thyme
11 Savory
12 Chives
13 Parsley

Right: A small culinary border can be contained in a run of 3 or 4 metres (about 10 to 15 feet), the design being repeated, or half repeated, where a longer site is available. There is nothing to be gained by making the border deeper, as culinary herbs need to be readily accessible.

In the house

Rooted cuttings grown in pots and decorative containers provide the best method of starting plants for indoor cultivation. Alternatively, as for window-boxes or patio troughs, many plants can be cut back and once the fresh growth starts and the plant has recovered, they can be transferred to indoor cultivation in pots.

Seed can be sown early in the year for Parsley, Cress, Purslane and Clary, while nasturtiums and marigolds can be sown in either spring or autumn. Plants of the right size can be purchased from garden centres and maintained as room plants provided that they are judiciously pruned from time to time.

A large bowl decorated with several small pots of herbs sunk among pebbles, or covered with peat, makes a most attractive, aromatic bedside garden for an invalid.

When grown in the kitchen, plants such as Mint, if cut back and potted up to confine their roots, will provide a long succession of fresh shoots for the cook. Good light is essential and watering must never be neglected.

It is difficult to generalize about plants grown in kitchens, however, because atmospheric conditions vary so widely from one kitchen to the next. As the plants cannot be expected to thrive simply because they are indoors, the right conditions have to be provided for them.

Small herb borders

A square metre (about 10 square feet) of suitable soil can be transformed into a tiny herb plot, but, again, proportion is most important. Small plants grouped together will flourish provided they are not in a draughty passage way or in a shaded corner under dripping trees. A plot so small would usually be used to provide fresh culinary herbs and could well support as much as two clumps of Chives, two plants of Thyme, two of Marjoram, one of Winter Savory, a patch of Mint with its roots confined in an old, deep biscuit tin to prevent it from becoming invasive, one plant of Tarragon and at the back a small Sage bush.

Where small herb borders are virtually part of the vegetable garden and the herbs are grown for culinary use, they are best treated like the remainder of the kitchen garden, and planted in rows. It is then easier to run the hoe along to keep the weeds at bay and to harvest the crop as and when required.

LARGE HERB GARDENS

The name 'herb garden' conjures up a tranquil plot sheltered from troublesome winds, bathed in sunlight and fragrant with delicious scents. All the denizens are humble plants of ancient cultivation, which have no need of flamboyant flowers to advertise their presence. When planning a herb garden it is necessary to have some knowledge of the plants themselves, their requirements and their effect when fully grown.

A herb garden can be formal or informal, there are no salient requirements, but one of formal design has an added atmosphere of authenticity because the herb gardens of the fifteenth and sixteenth centuries were formal plots – usually square. Whatever the details of the design, some form of shelter is needed to enclose the garden; this can be a hedge of Broom, Rosemary or roses, or a dry wall, with Lavender, Hyssop, or Artemisias growing along the top. Best of all, but seen all too infrequently is a walled garden, where roses, Clematis, honeysuckles, Jasmine and other sweet-scented plants can scramble up the walls.

The accompanying plans suggest a simple treatment to achieve formality. Restraint in planting few kinds of plants rather than an extensive range will ultimately give the best result. Further, careful thought needs to be given to the central feature of a formal garden – proportion obviously being the main consideration – for this is what gives each herb garden its individual character. Choose a container-

Herbs for a cook's garden

Alecost	Garlic
Angelica	Lemon Balm
Basil	Lovage
Bay	Marigold
Bistort	Marjoram
Borage	Mint
Caraway	Nettle
Chervil	Oregano
Chicory	Parsley
Chives	Purslane
Coriander	Rosemary
Corn Salad	Sage
Cumin	Savory
Dill	Shallot
Fennel	Tarragon
French Sorrel	Thyme

grown Rosemary or Bay (which will need to be brought into a frost-free place in severe weather) or a sundial, birdbath, fountain, beehive or statuette surrounded by Lavender or Rosemary or Rue – as these are all evergreen they will give an air of permanence. In a larger garden, choose a tree such as Hamamelis, Sambucus or Prunus for the central feature, or make an arbour which can be covered in Jasmine, hops, Ivy and roses. If authenticity is desired, a knot garden should form the central attraction.

Below: This plan, for a culinary herb garden, is based upon the central part of the plan for a large herb garden which is shown on page 117. The central feature can be a sundial or bird bath, for example.

Elizabethan knot gardens

The Oxford English Dictionary defines knot garden as 'a flower bed laid out in an intricate design' – the term was first used in 1494. Designs can be complicated or relatively simple. They are usually symmetrical, and as they are intended to be looked down upon, they should be formed of low-growing plants like thymes, pinks, violets, chives, savories, marigolds, marjorams, Lungwort and Feverfew. The design of each bed needs to be outlined with Box, Santolina, Feverfew or Dwarf Lavender planted closely to form a firm line. Box or Santolina are favourite choices because they are both evergreen and can be clipped.

The site on which the knot garden is to be made must be level. Traditional designs can be copied, or individual schemes may be composed, but it is best to keep designs simple. The design should be drawn on to squared paper, scaled and then drawn out on to the ground.

An original design can be executed quickly from a square piece of graph paper, folded first into two, then into four, then diagonally from the centre. On the paper doily principle, a pattern can be made by cutting away pieces.

Once the design has been transferred to the ground and the outlines of the beds formed by planting Box or whatever has been chosen, the 'colouring' can begin, and the final effect planned. Two or three years are needed for the knot to become effective and, apart from clipping and replacement planting, or attention to annuals, the upkeep is not arduous.

Central beds

A variety of very much simpler central features can be formed on the traditional chequer board design, where a central paved area is broken up into a series of alternating squares like a chess board. All the 'black' squares are paved and each one of the 'white' squares is filled with one kind of plant – so there might be Marjoram in one, Mint in another, and Parsley in a third. Repetition is attractive in this form of garden, but the taller plants such as Fennel and Angelica ought to be avoided.

An even simpler central bed can be made on the cartwheel design, where the rim and spokes of the wheel are picked

Bed D
1 Thymes in variety
2 Pot Marjoram
3 Sage
4 Eau de Cologne Mint
5 Angelica
6 Chives
7 Sweet Cicely
8 Tarragon
9 Parsley

Bed E
10 Thymes in variety
11 Purple Sage
12 Lemon Balm
13 Spearmint
14 Fennel
15 Basil
16 Parsley
17 Winter Savory
18 Apple Mint

Bed F
19 Thymes in variety
20 Golden Marjoram
21 Summer Savory
22 Parsley
23 Purslane
24 Lemon Balm
25 Chives
26 Lovage
27 Apple Mint
28 Poppy
29 Basil

Bed G
30 Thymes in variety
31 Parsley
32 Cumin
33 Corn Salad
34 Pot Marigold
35 Rosemary
36 Narrow-leaved Sage
37 Sorrel
38 Sweet Cicely
39 Bowles' Mint

Bed H
40 Pennyroyal
41 Thrift

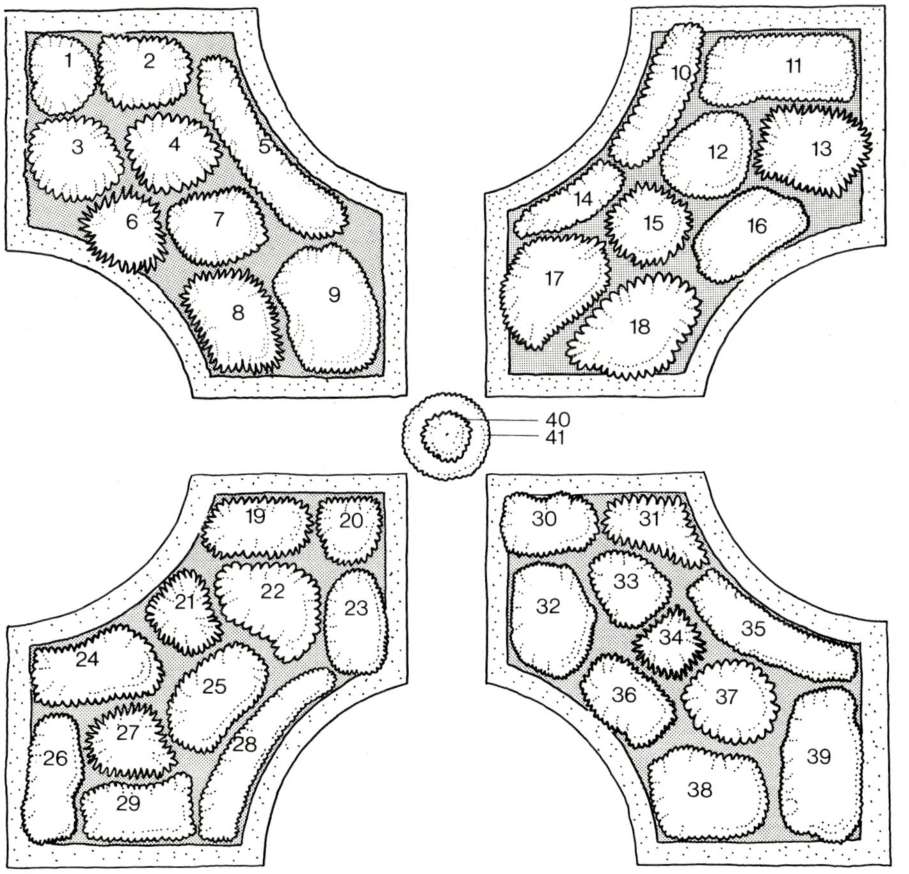

Left: A wide variety of design of knot gardens can be achieved, but the basic concept must be one of geometric symmetry. In their Elizabethan heyday the patterns had delightful names such as cink-foil, trefoyle, crossbow and flower-de-luce, and were often formed of intricately twisted designs. Today simpler patterns are preferred, but the use of compact plants to achieve the general effect cannot be over-emphasized. A level site must be chosen and the smaller the area the simpler the design must be. Some spaces can be filled with shells or coloured pebbles to provide a permanent foil for a range of plants. 1 Crossbow; 2 New knot; 3 Curious fine knot; 4 New knot for a perfect garden; 5 Flower-de-luce; 6 Trefoyle; 7 Flower of Deluce; 8 Good pattern for a Quarter of herbs.

out in clipped Box or Santolina or perhaps even Golden Marjoram and each space is filled with a different herb. Again, the taller growing kinds should be avoided as this destroys the design. For the best results, select plants of different colours.

Informal herb gardens

It is not imperative to have a geometrically planned garden and where the right environment is available an informal herb garden can be very attractive. Visually such a garden is more successful if the Umbelliferae tribe are excluded because they become untidy and many of them seed themselves very easily.

An existing bank may be transformed by working on two levels, or a sheltered corner filled in with a roughly triangular bed. Most successful is a winding grass path between two borders of mixed planting. (See page 126.) The only essential feature in the choice of site is that it is not overhung by trees, because both shade and drip from the trees discourages growth.

Growing herbs commercially

Before starting to grow herbs on any commercial scale several factors need to be considered. Apart from enthusiasm, capital and a suitable site, thought must be given to labour, selection of crops, and the market – whether to market fresh plants or embark upon large-scale drying, and, above all, to the relationship between acreage, yield and profit. Undoubtedly, markets are the most important single factor, for the destination of the crop has to be assured, and the choice of crops is in turn dependent upon the market demand. Are fresh bunches of herbs going to market regularly, or is the whole harvest destined for a distillery? Are herbs to be disposed of fresh or dried, retail or wholesale? How long will it take to establish a paying crop?

Above: A reconstruction of a renaissance-style knot garden at Villandry, France. Clipped Box forms some of the shapes and outlines others. Such patterns are the basis of modern knot gardens and are often symbolic.

Three and a half kilograms (eight lbs) of fresh material should yield 450 grams (1 lb) of the dried herb, and the harvest of fresh material will vary with crop, soil, season and situation. Prevailing local conditions differ, but reasonable averages to expect are up to 500 kilograms per half hectare (half a ton per acre) of say, Angelica or Caraway Seed and three to four tonnes per half hectare or acre of fresh Mint. Lavender bushes in their prime would probably yield a tonne of flower-heads.

Advice should be sought from appropriate government departments and advisory services as prevailing local conditions vary widely. Some experience of herb growing is necessary because the bulk of the harvest could easily be lost – a good case for growing several different sorts of plant.

PROPAGATION AND GARDEN MAINTENANCE

There are several ways in which a supply of plants can be maintained or increased, namely from cuttings, layers or divisions all known as vegetative propagation, or by seed, the sexual method of producing new plants.

Whichever method of propagation is used it is essential to use only disease-free and pest-free stock and to select only typical and not deformed parts of the plant. Knives, pots, boxes and compost should be clean to ensure health of the plants.

Starting with seed

Many herbs can be grown from seed. Some produce their own seeds quite easily, while others need to have special climatic conditions, and some will hybridize so readily with their relatives that the progeny is not necessarily good. The annuals and biennials, or plants cultivated as such, have to be raised from seed. and the time of sowing depends upon the hardiness or frost-sensitivity of each kind of plant. Once the ground has warmed up in spring, seed-sowing can generally begin out-of-doors. An earlier start can be made where greenhouse or frame protection is available, and seeds can be sown in pots. boxes or flats, pricked off, hardened off and later planted out. This earlier sowing does not bring forward the harvest appreciably, but the method can prove convenient in a late spring for such plants as Basil, or where the ground has not been prepared for seed sowing or if it is one in which a good tilth (the texture of cultivated surface soil) cannot be achieved.

Notable exceptions to spring sowing are Cowslip, Chervil, Woad, and Angelica. These seeds need to be sown as soon as ripe to produce a crop of fresh young leaves in late spring. Obviously where winter conditions are unfavourable to seedlings, as in mid-continental gardens, this practice cannot be followed. Self-sown seeds, however, will sometimes germinate quite quickly with the melting snow. General rules for seed sowing include covering the seed lightly with soil, and sowing thinly either in rows or broadcast (scattered). In either instance, the resultant seedlings will need to be thinned out to allow adequate growing space.

Parsley seed is notoriously slow to germinate, but watering the seed drill with boiling water immediately before sowing seems to encourage germination.

Vegetative propagation

Perennial plants with good clump-forming or shrubby habit can be propagated either by cuttings or division or both. Cuttings can be made of hard or soft wood, according to the type of plant, or can be stem cuttings, root cuttings or leaf cuttings. In each case an entirely new plant is formed and each new plant will resemble the parent plant in every way. Broadly speaking, cuttings of such evergreens as Lavender, Rosemary, Santolina and Rue can be taken in spring and struck in a frame, or, if made with a heel of old wood, in open ground in July. (This requires tearing the cutting away, bringing with it a small slip of old wood from the base.)

Cuttings are always best made from non-flowering shoots with the base leaves removed. Trim the stem cleanly below a node (the point at which a leaf stalk joins

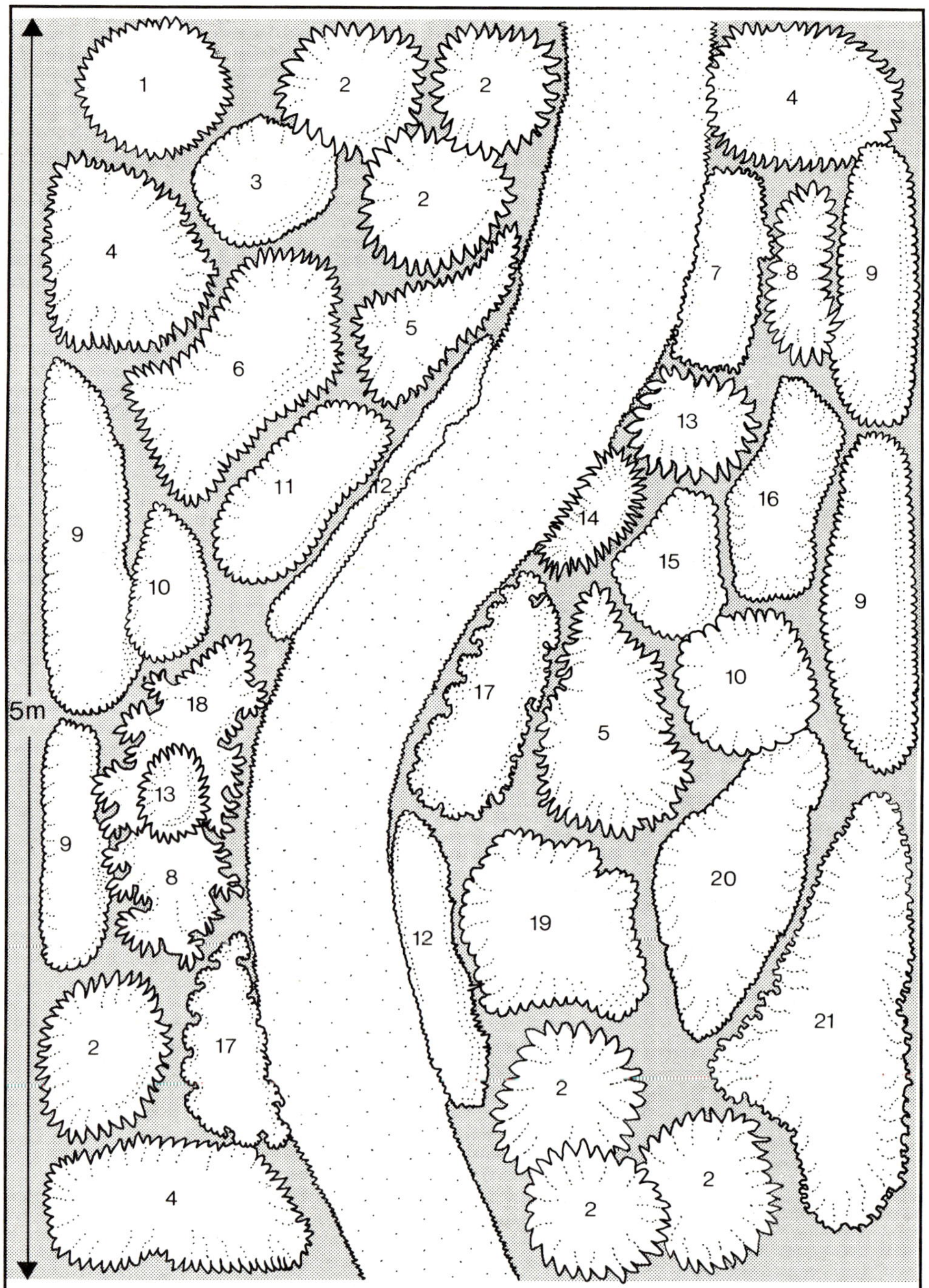

Plan for a decorative herb garden

Key	Number of Plants	Key	Number of Plants
1 Eucalyptus gunnii	1	13 Catmint	6
2 Lavender, Mitcham	7	14 Chives	12
3 Foxglove	12	15 Golden Marjoram	8
4 Rosemary	3	16 Costmary	6
5 Alchemilla	5	17 Pinks	25
6 Bergamot	3	18 Marigold	18
7 Lavender, Dwarf Munstead	6	19 Papaver somniferum	8
8 Mint, Bowles'	6–12	20 Foxglove	12
9 Rosa gallica officinalis	6	21 Brooms	2
10 Artemisias	6		
11 Eau de Cologne Mint	15		
12 Golden Thyme	24		

The chart on pages 132–139 gives further information on each plant

Left: Plan for an informal decorative herb garden for early to midsummer. The planting scheme for the border can be repeated if a greater length is required. Unity of design is achieved by repetition, rather than by introducing a number of new ideas.

Right: The simplest way to increase any perennial plant is to divide the whole crown in spring or autumn. Thus two or more pieces, complete with roots, are obtained (see far right) from one plant. Each piece can be set out separately and will eventually form a new plant.

the stem), dip the tip of the cutting into rooting powder and plant firmly in a proprietary cutting compost or a sharp sandy compost. Where space is limited and pots not available, the base of several cuttings can be packed around with dampened sphagnum moss and firmly folded into a polythene strip, rolled up and held firmly in place by a rubber band or string until the roots have formed.

Increasing stock by cuttings is the only way to perpetuate a specially good form of a plant or a variegation of leaf or some other desirable characteristic of growth. It is by cuttings that the non-flowering forms of those plants like Box, Santolina and Bay which are clipped, resulting in a certain lack of flowering, can be increased. The clippings themselves usually make perfectly adequate cuttings.

Perennials like Mint and Tansy which form good root-stocks can be divided or even torn apart. Each runner with a shoot on it forms an 'Irishman's cutting' and behaves as a rooted cutting.

Division

Division of clumps is a little more demanding and is best carried out when the plant is dormant. Divisions can be made of perennials, and plants that have become thin in the centre of the clump, or too large and bulky. The whole crown of the plant is lifted from the soil, and divided by two forks plunged amid the growth back to back and pulled apart to break up the clump – each of the resultant pieces will eventually bear roots and some growth buds. Replant the pieces in fresh ground, ensuring that the depth of planting is at least as deep as it was before the crown was lifted for division. Firm replanting is vital.

Layers are used as a method of propagation for such plants as Sage in the herb garden, when an old and bare branch is pegged down roots will form at a point in contact with the soil. This shoot can be severed and forms an entirely new plant with the same characteristics as the parent plant. Some plants layer naturally, like the Strawberry and the Raspberry. (The Raspberry is said to form 'tip roots' and the Strawberry layers are called runners.)

Management of the herb garden

The general rules of garden upkeep apply to herb gardens although many herbs are of strong constitution and remarkably tolerant. Weeds need to be kept down, of course, and old flowering shoots and dead or diseased material removed. The latter must be burned and not incorporated into the compost heap as many disease spores survive, or even flourish, in the warmth generated by decaying materials.

Herbs do not require a rich soil, so there is no need to apply fertilizers. Generally known as 'artificials', these give the plants a fillip and generally encourage a spurt of growth. The essential oils of herbs represent their ultimate value, and insufficient is known about the short-term effect of chemical fertilizers on the composition of the plants themselves. Herbs, in any case, often produce larger quantities of oil when grown in poor soils. Garden compost, a so-called organic material, added to the soil and forked into the surface is far more suitable to herbs and will generally improve the quality and texture of the soil. Herb lawns such as non-flowering Chamomile and prostrate Pennyroyal benefit, however, from a late-summer application of fine peat.

Many minor problems in the management of herb gardens can be eliminated by growing plants compatible with prevailing conditions and noting the plants' individual requirements such as watering, protection from wind, and companionship – few plants like to grow in solitary confinement. Many theories have been promulgated for plant associations, but recent experiments have shown that some have little or no scientific justification. Plants respond best when selected according to the habitat available and their idiosyncrasies catered for. Basil, for example, likes to be watered at midday, not in the evening as most plants prefer; Parsley, apart from demanding great patience from the gardener, prefers a humid soil to a dry one otherwise it will soon run away to seed, and Marjoram likes to be left alone during its long seedling stage. Some perennials dislike winter dampness and low temperatures. It is not the freezing temperatures themselves that are responsible for winter damage, but the fluctuations in temperature and the early morning sunshine on frozen plants. A mulch of dry peat, leaf mould, sawdust or

Propagation requirements of selected herbs

Cuttings

Artemisia	Rosemary
Bay	Rue
Box	Sage
Geranium (scented-leaved)	Santolina
	Savory, Winter
Hyssop	Thyme
Lavender	Verbena, Lemon
Mint	

Divisions

Alchemilla	Lungwort
Bergamot	Marjoram
Catmint	Mint
Chives	Periwinkle
Elecampane	Sweet Cicely
Iris	Tarragon
Lemon Balm	Thyme
Lovage	

Seed

Angelica	Lemon Balm
Basil	Marigold
Borage	Marjoram, sweet
Caraway	Parsley
Chervil	Parsley, Hamburg
Clary	Purslane
Corn Salad	Savory, Summer
Dill	Sorrel
Fennel	Verbascum
Foxglove	Woad
White Horehound	

a polythene cover will protect any susceptible plants in cold weather.

Pests and diseases

Garden pests, such as greenfly and blackfly for example, are particularly troublesome on Valerian and Nasturtium and may be cleared by spraying with a pyrethrum or quassia decoction or with soap solution. These sprays, particularly quassia, can also be used against caterpillars and leaf-hopper.

Diseases need to be considered a little more carefully, for their long-term effect is always more serious. Rusts affect mints and violets and the most effective treatment once the disease has got a hold is to scatter straw or wood shavings among the plants in autumn and set light to them. The affected shoots are burned off and the spring growth should be rust-free. Proprietary fungicides are available in spray form for immediate use and are effective, but many growers of herbs, being opposed to anything that is not natural, prefer not to use them.

Below: Aphids or greenfly and blackfly feed on a wide variety of plant by sucking the sap and thus causing deformity to the whole plant. These insects thrive in warm weather. (See the table on page 103 for information on how to control insect attack.)

*Below right: There is a range of rusts and each selects a single type of host plant. This shows the effect of rose rust (*Phragmidium euchronatum*); the rust which attacks violets will be either* Puccinia violi *or* Puccinia aegra, *while that selecting mint will be* Puccinia menthae.

Various leaf spots attack Parsley, pinks, Lavender, Peony and Raspberry. The affected part should be cut away and burned, or if it is summer the plants can be sprayed at three-weekly intervals with Bordeaux mixture.

Occasionally a root rot such as black root rot can attack mints, but by moving the mint beds to fresh soil, preferably a lime-free one, the fungus can be discouraged. Soil treatment with a weak formalin solution (one part formalin to 50 parts water used at the rate of 2.25 litres to 930 square centimetres or half a gallon to a square foot) will usually clear up the trouble.

Renovation

Short-lived plants are best replaced so that a good crop of leaves is assured. Lavender, especially, tends to become leggy after a few years so a supply of rooted cuttings should always be ready to fill in the gaps left when old plants are removed. When Sage has become straggly and bare of growth at the base of the bush, soil can be built up into a mound around the base of the plant. The bare growth should be buried and the tips of growth left protruding. These will soon form roots and can be severed to be used as fresh plants, eventually replacing the mother plant.

COLLECTING FROM THE WILD

It is not now as easy to collect herbs from their wild state as it once was. Perhaps only 150 years ago the 'greenman' roamed the countryside gathering herbs to sell, upon which country people depended for any and every ailment. The endemic flora of Europe generally, as well as that of many parts of North America has undergone drastic changes, particularly during the last 130 years with the development of transport and industry. Since World War II the revolution of mechanized and chemical agricultural practice has destroyed innumerable hedgerow and woodland habitats in which useful plants flourished. Hedges have been removed in England on a vast scale to allow for a longer, and therefore more economical, field run, taking with them the shelter, shade, drainage and microclimates of field verges and hedge bottoms. Many plants, especially those of limited tolerance to environmental factors, have been restricted in number.

The opening up of the landscape in this way and the building of motorways, however, has created new habitats, sometimes relatively temporary ones, where the more ubiquitous plants have colonized.

Herbicides, known and used since the early years of this century, have been employed mainly for weed control since about 1946 when synthetic plant regulator factors such as MCPA and 2,4-D were introduced. The results appear to show that whereas monocarpic annual species of plants (which die after flowering), such as annual grasses and sedges, have been severely reduced in number, the perennials remain and the dicotyledonous annuals have even increased in distribution. This is perhaps most noticeable in *Chenopodium album* (Fat Hen or Goosefoot) and *Stellaria media* (Stitchwort). In short, susceptible species have been reduced and the distribution of immune species has, if anything, noticeably increased.

The devastation of any habitat affects plants directly, but the insect life and the bird life it supports are affected indirectly. Food chains are then radically altered, bringing about a change in balance of the entire habitat. Pollution of sites in contrast to widespread devastation, especially water pollution, tends to affect animal life more easily than plant life, but sewage effluents, detergents and sheep dips, for example, take their toll more slowly on aquatic plant life. Industrial effluents, including highly toxic by-products, are habitually disposed of into rivers, frequently changing not only the chemical content of the water, but the temperature of the whole watercourse.

Excessive water pollution problems exist in many parts of the world and are now far beyond redemption. The water of some of the Swiss lakes will hardly support life at all. The Great Lakes of America, where nitrates drained from farmland are

Right: At Cranborne Manor, Dorset, a small collection of thymes has been made and set out on the old fashioned chequerboard design. Each space is filled with a different thyme. This little herb garden provides a riverside retreat complete in itself, and is the simplest form of herb plot.

overabundant, have the same problem.

Some plants have their own solutions to adverse conditions. The perennials often resort to vegetative survival, and others have built up a tolerance. At first perhaps only a tiny percentage of seedlings was able to survive, but over several generations a resistant strain is built up.

Other plants, however, live quite happily where toxic amounts of, say, salt or metals are present in the soil. Old mine workings, where ore is sometimes exposed, support a number of colonized plants. The plantains and grasses colonize newly disturbed subsoils in this way most noticeably. For centuries man has carved his way over the surface of the earth and nature has always obliterated his traces if left unchecked. But the present level of destruction now far exceeds man's early activities and ignores the vital role of plants in the great circle of life. Their photosynthetic powers are life-giving processes and not infrequently when surface plants have been removed, inland lakes are made to 'replace' the landscape.

It was man, therefore, in his early excursions into the countryside which began from the industrial towns of the nineteenth century – particularly in western Europe – who started the wholesale ravaging of plant life. Collection of primroses, bluebells and cowslips initially provided relaxation, but this led to the clearing of tracks to make roadways which subsequently led, as roads grew ever larger, to the clearing of the road verges themselves, therefore continuing the denudation. The verges were originally cleared by scythe, which took only enough for good hay and encouraged the regeneration of the grass. The scythe has now been replaced by expensive sprays which not only clear the verges but destroy plant life. Man in his disregard of nature has brought about a very serious state of affairs, not only in plant life but in many natural resources.

Conservation, restoration and reconstruction of natural sites, however, have begun. The 1968 Clean Air Act has been responsible for reducing the smoke haze in England which reduced the rate of photosynthesis in plants. The Conservation of Wild Creatures and Wild Plants Act of 1975 not only provides protection for declining plant species in Britain, but prohibits the uprooting of any wild plant. Plants may be uprooted or collected only by the owner of the land or anyone acting with his permission. This is of immense importance to herbalists, for no longer can random collection be made of any plant needed for its roots such as Comfrey, Violet, Valerian, Bistort, Rampion or Dandelion.

Collecting leaves, seeds or flowers from the wild makes several demands on the herb collector. Apart from the general rules for harvesting, the plant must first be identified correctly, and then only harvested from localities in which it is relatively abundant. Cleanliness is difficult to ensure – grit may be removed by washing, though this defeats the objective of trying to harvest when the plants are dry. But toxic sprays, atmospheric pollution by traffic and aeroplanes, and drift from chemical crop dressings are all potential dangers.

Wild plant collecting is easier in most parts of Europe than in England simply because of the greater distribution of plants. The plants can very often be dried out-of-doors without any form of artificial heat. Both the gathering and drying processes are frequently made easier simply by the prevailing lower humidity.

HARVESTING AND DRYING

The care exercised in cultivation can easily be forfeited by incorrect harvesting or inadequate drying. When the part of the plant used is the root, harvesting is carried out at the end of the growing season, the autumn, when the root is mature and is storing as much food as possible. Seeds, too, are harvested when ripe at the end of the season. Knowing the moment to harvest the leaves – or in some instances the entire herb itself – is an ability that comes only with experience. The general rule is to take leaves from the plant just before the flowers are fully open; this is the time when the active principles of the plant are of the best quality. The timing can be critical and care must be exercised to take only the part of the plant required and not so much of it as to impair the metabolism of the whole plant. Take only from clean and representative plants

Left: Herbs may be dried by hanging them in loose bundles along a line in a shaded, draught-free place.

and gather on a dry day when the dew has gone. Keep one kind of plant material separate from another and label it. Lastly, pick amounts that can be handled immediately, for if they are left for an hour or two, they will deteriorate with the resultant loss in value.

Domestic drying

Few households can provide a special room suitable for drying herbs, but a spare room is ideal if the curtains can be drawn against direct sunlight and a continual temperature of 25°C to 34°C (75° to 95°F) can be achieved, perhaps by using an electric convector heater. Attics under a warm roof, airing cupboards, warming drawers of domestic cookers, or even a warm conservatory or garden shed (if it can be shaded) all provide conditions suitable for drying herbs. Ideally, spread the shoots and leaves in a single layer in flat boxes or lids, or on trays or sheets of wrapping paper or newspaper, and during the first day or two turn over the material frequently.

The moisture content of most plants is more than 70 per cent. The aim is to dry them briskly to change the condition of the leaves rather than the chemical content. The temperature in the drying chamber should be 32° to 34°C (90° to 95°F) before the plant material is introduced, and this needs to be maintained for the first 24 hours of drying. Subsequently the temperature may be reduced to 25° to 27°C (75° to 80°F) to complete the process, which should take from three to five days. Material is dry when it snaps easily between the thumb and finger. Fresh material should not be introduced into the chamber before the drying process is complete.

Drying in bulk

The same rules apply where herbs are grown in bulk for drying, but the provision of suitable drying conditions is more difficult. Enough space has to be provided to deal with the amount of material likely to be ready to handle at any one time. Some form of wooden shed can be used where an equable temperature of 32° to 34°C (90° to 95°F) can be maintained together with some form of ventilation to keep the air circulating. The objective should be to remove the moisture-laden air while maintaining the temperature so that the herbs can be dried evenly and quickly. As the moisture from the atmosphere may be reabsorbed if the temperature falls (or if fresh material is added), any new material that has to be brought in should be placed high up.

Plant material for drying in bulk is best handled on trays constructed of plastic mesh, nylon net or hessian stretched over wooden frames. These allow the air to circulate and can easily be stacked if provided with legs or if battens are wedged between them. Where there are large quantities of plant material, racks can be constructed, so that the trays can be stacked.

The dried material obtained will be about one-eighth of the weight of the harvested herb.

Rubbing down

Once the dry herbs are cool the rubbing down process should be carried out in a well-ventilated place. There is no point in trying to do it out-of-doors, for if there is the slightest breeze most of the material will be lost. A kitchen or out-house with the door and windows left open is ideal.

Small amounts can be dealt with satisfactorily by picking the leaves from the stalks, and crushing the leaves with a rolling-pin or in a coffee-mill. The stalks should be discarded. A fine mesh sieve or riddle is useful for the final refinements, especially for culinary herbs.

Treat only one kind of material at a time and wash the utensils each time before dealing with another plant, or else the aroma and flavour will be adulterated and your effort wasted.

Storing

Label each sort of herb and store separately in an airtight container so that moisture cannot be reabsorbed. Wooden boxes or screw-top jars of darkened glass provide the best containers, because the essential oils in herbs will deteriorate if exposed to the light. Plastic bags are obviously unsuitable.

THE HERBARIUM

A herbarium or *hortus siccus* is a collection of plants dried and preserved for use in plant identification. Most botanic gardens and natural history museums of any size have extensive classified collections. There is an obvious advantage in being able to consult a specimen at any time of the year, and perhaps at the same time to compare it with its various relatives.

There are large herbaria at the Natural History Museum, London, and at the Royal Botanic Gardens, Kew, England, and at the Linnean Society, London, which houses the herbarium assembled by Linnaeus. His widow sold it to Dr (later Sir) James E. Smith, a founder of the Linnean Society of London. The collection at the Natural History Museum, London, is based upon eighteenth- and nineteenth-century collections, including those of Sir Hans Sloane and Sir Joseph Banks, and also houses several modern collections. The Kew Herbarium was founded by Sir William Hooker and considerably enlarged by the work of his son, Sir Joseph Hooker, and is rich in colonial flora. A large herbarium at Le Jardin des Plantes in Paris is based upon the collections of Antoine Laurent de Jussieu, his son Adrieu and of Auguste de St Hilaire. There are other important collections in Europe in Vienna, Leiden, Uppsala, Copenhagen and Florence. In the United States of America the chief collections are at Harvard University, formed by Asa Gray, and at the New York Botanic Garden.

A personal herbarium

Plant specimens can be assembled as a satisfying hobby, or as an extension to one's interest in herbs. Essential equipment includes: a notebook and pencil, a hand lens which magnifies up to 10 times, an Ordnance Survey Map and either an old-fashioned vasculum or a series of large plastic bags with wire fasteners, or a portable flower press together with a number of tie-on labels. The map is of considerable importance for it is accepted practice to give the grid reference in addition to the place name when recording the locality for a plant. Notes are made on

Above: A hortus siccus *or collection of pressed plants mounted onto paper is known as a herbarium. Pressed specimens of various trefoils are mounted together for comparison (left). Space is included for information on name, date found and location. A modern herbarium sheet (right).*

the labels as to location, variation in plant features and any other point of special interest, so that no confusion will arise by the time the specimen reaches the flower press. A portable, or even temporary, plant press used out-of-doors ensures that the plants are pressed absolutely fresh.

A plant press

Special presses can be purchased from firms supplying naturalists' equipment and from some department stores, but home-made presses are equally effective and can be made to any size. Sheets of absorbent drying paper are piled together with wooden boards or metal sheets at the top and bottom. These can be strapped or clamped together to hold the papers and plants firmly in position during the drying process. The material to be pressed is first brushed clean and closely examined, identified and then arranged on a sheet of paper in such a way as to display its form as clearly as possible. Leaves and flowers need to be carefully flattened – a small paintbrush is useful for this. Take a second sheet of paper and hold down one edge firmly on top of the sheet with the plant. Slowly roll the top sheet down, taking care not to disturb the specimens. A few hours after insertion, open up the press and rearrange the more tractable material such as the petals.

The time herbs take to dry varies. The paper will need to be changed especially for succulent specimens, and sometimes the process may be hurried by keeping the presses in an airing cupboard or even in the sunshine. The paper may have to be changed at intervals of 6 to 12 hours, and the pressure increased relative to the dryness of the specimen. Drying is complete when the specimen is crisp and does not feel cold when held to the cheek. It should then be mounted on sheets of good cartridge paper, about 43 cm by 28 cm (17 in by 11 in), with all the relevant information added. It is good practice to write this on a label which is stuck to the lower right-hand corner of the paper. Essential information includes: name, date, place (and grid reference) of collection and some note about the habitat.

Mounting the specimens can be done in one of several ways, either by gluing them directly to the paper, or by stitching stems and leaf margins to the paper, or by placing several gummed strips over stems, leaf stalks and leaves to hold the plant in permanent position.

Arrangement of the herbarium

The sheets are usually assembled loosely in large paper or card folders, and when a large number has been collected they should be kept in a cupboard or metal cabinet where dust can be excluded and room temperature maintained. Some authoritative system of classification should be followed, such as the Bentham and Hooker which is still standard in many herbaria. Scatter moth balls with the collection to ward off insect attack.

Overleaf: The following table will enable you to select the herbs you wish to grow according to the conditions of your site.

Abbreviations

Sp	*spring*
E Sp	*early spring*
ES	*early summer*
S	*summer*
LS	*late summer*
M-LS	*mid-late summer*
SS	*second summer*
End S	*end of summer*
A	*autumn*
W	*winter*
LW	*late winter*
AT	*anytime*

SELECTING AND GROWING YOUR OWN HERBS

HERB	TYPE	SOIL	HEIGHT × SPREAD	POSITION
Achillea millefolium (Yarrow)	perennial	well drained, tolerates most	30–65 × 30 cm (12–26 × 12 ins)	tolerant of most
Acorus calamus (Sweet Flag, Rush, Calamus)	perennial, aquatic	very damp, rich	50–140 × 90 cm (20–56 × 36 ins)	bogs, ponds, rich moist soils in full sun
Ajuga reptans (Bugle)	perennial	damp, loamy or dry	10–30 × 30 cm (4–12 × 12 ins)	sun or shade
Alchemilla vulgaris (Lady's Mantle)	perennial	almost any except waterlogged	15–30 × 15 cm (6–12 × 6 ins)	tolerant of most; useful ground cover
Allium cepa aggregatum (Tree Onion, Top Onion)	bulbous, perennial	ordinary, well-drained	30–45 × 15 cm (12–18 × 6 ins) (grow in rows)	full sun
Allium sativum (Garlic)	bulbous, perennial	fertile, well-drained	30–60 × 10 cm (12–24 × 4 ins) (grow in rows)	full sun
Allium schoenoprasum (Chives)	bulbous, perennial	rich and loamy	15–30 × 15 cm (6–12 × 6 ins) (forms clumps)	useful for edging
Anethum graveolens (Dill)	annual	most acidic soils, but not too light	20–90 × 60 cm (8–36 × 24 ins)	full sun
Angelica archangelica (Angelica)	biennial treated as short lived perennial	not too rich, slightly acid	150–240 × 90 cm (5–8 × 3 ft)	back of border where it is cool and moist
Anthriscus cerefolium (Chervil)	annual, sometimes biennial	moist, light, well-drained soils with added compost	40 × 30 cm (16 × 12 ins)	prefers some shade. Mid-border plant
Artemisia absinthium (Wormwood)	perennial	most soils; prefers deeply dug clays	65–110 × 40 cm (26–44 × 16 ins)	back of border or can be used as screen
Artemisia dracunculoides (Russian Tarragon)	perennial	most soils	120 × 50 cm (48 × 20 ins)	full sun
Artemisia dracunculus (French Tarragon)	perennial	warm, rich and well-drained	60–90 × 40 cm (24–36 × 16 ins)	full sun
Artemisia vulgaris (Mugwort)	perennial	most moist soils	90–180 × 40–50 cm (3–6 ft × 16–20 ins)	back of border or mid-border plant
Asclepias tuberosa (Pleurisy Root,	perennial	dry, sandy	90 × 30 cm (36 × 12 ins)	full sun or some shade,
Borago officinalis (Borage)	annual	well-drained poor, dry soils	60 × 40 cm (24 × 16 ins)	full sun; seen to best effect when planted on low wall
Calamintha officinalis (Calamint)	perennial	chalky soils, dryish	30–35 × 50 cm (12–14 × 20 ins) (forms clumps)	dry, not too shaded
Carum carvi (Caraway)	biennial	most well-drained soils	65 × 25–30 cm (26 × 10–12 ins)	full-sun, mid-border

PROPAGATION	EXTRA DETAILS	FLOWER	FOLIAGE	HARVEST
division Sp seed Sp	good light. Tolerates drought	pink or white S	grey-green, feathery, aromatic	leaves before flowering S
division of rhizome Sp, A	only flowers when grown in water	greenish-yellow S	sword-like, plentiful, stout, smelling of tangerine when crushed	rhizome ESp, A
division Sp, A seed Sp	space 30 cm (12 ins) apart, and allow to run together for ground cover	blue; rarely pink or white S	deep green to reddish-purple	whole herb S
division Sp seed ES under glass	spreads fairly rapidly, needs control	yellow ES	pale green, fluted	whole herb S
bulbils Sp, S, A		rarely seen	cylindrical, blue-green	bulbils S leaves LS
bulbs, broken into cloves Sp, A	not shaded	whitish-pink LS	flattish, spiky, odorous when bruised	bulbs LS
bulbs Sp, A seed Sp	seedlings should not be disturbed in first year	rose purple Sp	grassy in clumps	leaves AT
seed, in drills Sp–MS	do not plant close to Fennel. Protect from wind	yellow MS	soft spikes, aromatic	leaves AT seed LS A
seed as soon as ripe Sp	grows better in light shade, produces softer stems. Mature plants cannot be transplanted	yellowish M–LS	soft, fern-like, aromatic	stems Sp leaves Sp, S seed LS root A
seed, sown at 3 week intervals AT	maintain a succession of young plants. Do not transplant	white S	fern-like, dark green, aromatic	leaves before flowering AT
division Sp, A stem cuttings ES seed A	support in LS and cut back in A. Give mulch cover in cold sites	greenish-yellow S	feathery, silvery-green, aromatic	shoots Sp, S
division Sp, A seed LSp–ES	really sunny sheltered position	greenish-white S	pale green, willowy	leaves AT
division Sp cuttings with some heat Sp	really sunny sheltered position; Divide up every 2–3 years. Cut back and mulch in W	greenish-white S	glossy, dark green, aromatic	leaves AT
division Sp, A cuttings S seed Sp	dislikes shade	brownish-yellow S	dark green above, silvery beneath; feathery, aromatic	whole herb S
division A	dry soil	bright orange S	narrow, alternate on short stems	leaves AT rootstock A
seed Sp, MS	only a small seedling may be transplanted. Readily self-sown	blue, pink or white MS	rough, green, aromatic	flowers and leaves AT
cuttings S division Sp		blue, fragrant ES	pale green, light and fragrant	flowers and leaves AT
seed in drills Sp, S, A	prefers cool site. Do not transplant	white SS	soft green, feathery, aromatic	seedheads S leaves AT rootstock of 1st year

HERB	TYPE	SOIL	HEIGHT × SPREAD	POSITION
Chamaemelum nobile (Roman Chamomile)	perennial	well-drained	15–35 × 10–15 cm (6–14 × 4–6 ins)	full sun, or some shade. Useful as lawn
Chenopodium album (Fat Hen)	annual	dryish, rich soils	50 × 300 cm (20 ins × 10 ft)	most positions
Cichorium intybus (Chicory)	perennial	most soils	90–180 × 55 cm (3–6 ft × 22 ins)	sunny position
Cimicifuga racemosa (Black Cohosh)	perennial	rich, loamy	90–270 × 90 cm (3–9 × 3 ft)	rich woodland
Convallaria majalis (Lily-of-the-Valley)	perennial	most fertile, well-drained soils	25 × 10 cm (10 × 4 ins) (spreads slowly)	front of border or among bushes
Coriandrum sativum (Coriander)	annual	fertile, light to average	60 × 30 cm (24 × 12 ins)	protected situation, sunshine needed, mid-border plant
Crocus sativus (Saffron Crocus)	bulbous, perennial	light, rich and well-drained	30–45 cm in height (12–18 ins)	sheltered, full sun
Cuminum cyminum (Cumin)	annual	light, well-drained	30 × 15 cm (12 × 6 ins)	sheltered, full sun
Dianthus caryophyllus (Clove Pink)	perennial, evergreen	well-drained, calcareous	20 × 20 cm (8 × 8 ins)	good edging plant, likes sun
Digitalis purpurea (Foxglove)	biennial	fertile, well-drained	120 × 40–50 cm (48 × 16–20 ins)	full sun, but tolerates shade
Foeniculum vulgare (Fennel)	perennial	fairly rich	40–120 × 60–90 cm (16–48 × 24–36 ins)	full sun, sheltered from wind
Glechoma hederacea (Alehoof)	perennial	light, well-drained	10 × 30 cm (4 × 12 ins) (spreads)	will tolerate shade of hedge
Helianthus annuus (Sunflower)	annual	most soils	90–300 × 90 cm (3–10 × 3 ft)	back of border, allow much space, full sun
Hyssopus officinalis (Hyssop)	perennial, semi-evergreen	light	60 × 20 cm (24 × 8 ins)	sunny situation for best results
Inula helenium (Elecampane)	perennial	any soil, preferably rich and moist	90–180 × 90 cm (3–6 × 3 ft)	needs sun; plant at back of sunny border
Juniperus communis (Juniper)	perennial, coniferous	dry, calcareous	up to 780 × 780 cm (26 × 26 ft) often less	banks in sunny spot, good drainage
Laurus nobilis (Bay)	perennial, evergreen	well-drained	up to 1200 × 1200 cm (40 × 40 ft) often less	sheltered spot, free from wind and frost, good container plant
Lavandula angustifolia (Lavender)	perennial, evergreen	chalky, well-drained, poor soils	90 × 60 cm (36 × 24 ins) (bushy)	not too exposed, prefers full sun
Ledum groenlandicum (Labrador Tea)	perennial, evergreen	wet, rich, sandy or peaty	up to 90 × 90 cm (36 × 36 ins) (forms mat)	some sun or shade on bogs or swampland, not too dry.
Levisticum officinalis (Lovage)	perennial	fertile, acidic, well-prepared	90–210 × 90 cm (3–7 × 3 ft)	Some shade or full sun

PROPAGATION	EXTRA DETAILS	FLOWER	FOLIAGE	HARVEST
division Sp, A cuttings S seed Sp	best when a patch of plants are grown together. Keep soil moist around young plants	white daisy S	pale green fern-grass	whole herb S–LS
seed Sp		mealy-white S	very soft mid-green	shoots Sp
division Sp, A seed Sp		clear blue SS	jagged, green	root A leaves S
seed Sp division Sp, A		yellowish-white S	2–5 wide leaflets	rootstock A
division A	takes time to establish itself, can be grown in pots	white, sweetly-scented ES	mid-green, upright	whole flowers, plant ES
seed (slow to germinate, but usually high germination) Sp	may require support. Do not transplant	pinkish-mauve, sometimes white M–LS	fern-like, green, smells unpleasant just before seeds ripen	seeds End S leaves AT
corm S	divide every 3 years	mauve A	grass-like	stigmas A
seed Sp	water well in drought	pinkish-white S	thread-like, slightly fragrant	seeds End S
pipings or layering S		pink, white and combined arrangement of these colours, very fragrant M–LS	grey, clean, spiky in shape	flowers S
seed Sp, S	protect 1st year seedlings from frost	magenta SS	mid-green, wrinkled, soft	leaves ES
division Sp seed Sp, A	give enough space, and sow in succession	yellow S	thread-like, strongly aromatic	leaves S seed S
division Sp, A	ground cover, allow space, but it may need control	bluish ES	green, marbled with silver, slightly aromatic	leaves S
seed Sp	may need support	bright yellow MS	green, roughish	seed End S
division Sp cuttings ES seed Sp	cut back A or Sp. Replace every 4–5 years	bluish-mauve, pink or white ES–LS	dark green, bushy, aromatic	flowers and shoot tips, when available
division Sp, A seed Sp, A	replace every 3 years	bright yellow MS	large, mid-green	leaves before flowering Sp roots A
cuttings A		greenish-yellow ES	prickly, dark green	berries when ripe
very difficult. cuttings LS	useful as container plant out-of-doors, withstands clipping	creamy-yellow S	smooth dark green	leaves AT
stem cuttings AT seed Sp	regular pruning	mauve, fragrant MS	grey, aromatic	leaves S flowers MS
seeds Sp layering S division Sp, A	suit evergreen borders, but requires shade	cream Sp	short oblong	leaves AT
division Sp, A seed Sp, S	disappears below ground in W, mark the spot to ensure no other plants are too close	yellowish MS	strong green, deeply cut, aromatic	leaves S roots A seed LS

HERB	TYPE	SOIL	HEIGHT × SPREAD	POSITION
Melissa officinalis (Lemon Balm)	perennial	warm, not too dry, poor	60–90 × 40–60 cm (24–36 × 16–24 ins)	full sun or some shade
Mentha aquatica (Water Mint)	perennial	very moist or aquatic	15–90 × 15–20 cm (6–36 × 6–8 ins) (spreads)	will tolerate shade, suitable as a bog plant
Mentha citrata (Eau de Cologne Mint)	biennial	moist and rich	35–45 × 15–20 cm (14–18 × 6–8 ins) (spreads)	full sun or some shade
Mentha × piperita (Peppermint)	perennial	moist, for good results add moisture-retaining material to all soils	50–60 × 20 cm (20–24 × 8 ins) (spreads)	full sun or some shade
Mentha pulegium (Pennyroyal)	perennial	fertile	10–30 × 20 cm (4–12 × 8 ins) (spreads)	can tolerate shade
Monarda didyma (Bergamot)	perennial	moist, and very fertile. Add manure	70 × 30 cm (28 × 12 ins) (forms clumps)	good light, but tolerates some shade
Myrrhis odorata (Sweet Cicely)	perennial	well-drained, fertile and moist	90 × 15 cm (36 × 6 ins)	slight shade
Myrtus communis (Myrtle)	perennial, evergreen	well-drained	300 × 150 cm (10 × 5 ft) (bushy)	needs shelter, dislikes wet soil
Nasturtium officinale (Watercress)	perennial, aquatic	very damp, rich soil, or in shallow water	10–60 cm in length (4–24 ins)	full sun or some shade
Nepeta cataria (Catmint, Catnep)	perennial	fertile, well-drained	50 × 40 cm (20 × 16 ins)	mid-border plant tolerant of most situations
Ocimum basilicum (Basil)	annual	light, well-drained	45 × 15 cm (18 × 6 ins)	full sun
Origanum majorana (Sweet Marjoram)	perennial, usually grown as annual	medium rich, dryish and alkaline	25 × 10–15 cm (10 × 4–6 ins)	full sun
Origanum onites (Pot Marjoram)	perennial	dry, light	50 × 20 cm (20 × 8 ins)	requires sunny position
Petroselinum crispum (Parsley)	biennial, usually grown as annual	rich, fertile with good tilth	30–50 × 20 cm (12–20 × 8 ins)	good edging plant, grow in rows
Portulaca oleracea (Purslane)	annual	light	25 × 20 cm (10 × 8 ins) (forms mat)	sunny spot in herb border or kitchen garden
Poterium sanguisorba (Salad Burnet)	perennial	light, calcareous	30 × 25 cm (12 × 10 ins)	needs damp, grassy surroundings
Pulmonaria officinalis (Lungwort)	perennial	most soils	20 × 20 cm (8 × 8 ins)	front of border, tolerant of shade and shrubs
Reseda lutea (Mignonette)	perennial treated as annual, evergreen	moderately rich, calcareous	90 × 20 cm (3 × 8 ins)	mid-border plant, prefers some shade
Rosmarinus officinalis (Rosemary)	perennial, evergreen	light, well-drained calcareous	60–120 × 180 cm (2–4 × 6 ft)	full sun; good for hedges; prostrate form provides useful ground cover

PROPAGATION	EXTRA DETAILS	FLOWER	FOLIAGE	HARVEST
stem cuttings Sp, S division Sp, A seed ES, A	spreads, needs tidying	creamy-white MS	light green, wrinkled, very fragrant	leaves S
division of runners during growing season	needs confining, otherwise spreads and is invasive	mauve MS	shining green, aromatic	leaves and shoots S, A
division of runners during growing season	needs confining, otherwise spreads	lilac-mauve MS	roundish, green to brown-purple-bronze in dry situations, aromatic	leaves and shoots S, A
division of runners during growing season	needs confining, otherwise spreads and is invasive	lilac MS	dark bronze-purple ranging to black in dry situations, aromatic	leaves and shoots S, A
division of runners during growing season	may need confining. may need protection in severe winters	mauve MS	deep green, sometimes variegated, creeping, aromatic	leaves and shoots S, A
division Sp, A	divide regularly as centre tends to grow bare. Cut back in A	red S	dark green, strongly fragrant	leaves and flowers as required S
seed LS, A root cuttings Sp	requires acidic soil, deeply dug. Very easily self-sown	creamy-white ES	dark green, soft and fern-like	root A leaves Sp, S
cuttings, with heat MS–End S layering MS	often needs wall protection and shelter from winds	white S	light green, smallish	leaves S berries A
division W cuttings of non-flowering shoots Sp, S, A	clean water to grow in	white, very small S	dark green, shiny, plentiful, pungent flavour	whole shoot AT
division Sp, A seed Sp, A		blue spires S	green-grey, soft, aromatic	shoots before flowering Sp
seed under glass ESp outside ES	warmest spot available.	cream S	green, triangular, pungent	leaves AT
seed ES stem cuttings S	tender and not widely cultivated	pink S	soft, mid-green, fragrant	leaves before flowering S
division Sp, A seed Sp		purplish or whitish S	soft green, fragrant	leaves before flowering S
seed Sp, A	long period for germination, assist by pre-soaking seed	creamy-white SS	crisp, curled, bright green, fragrant	leaves S
seed Sp	ought to be thinned	yellow S	light green, smooth with a sheen	leaves S
seed Sp	best sown in drills	reddish-green S	pretty, dark green	leaves AT
division immediately after flowering	appreciates some shade and moisture	pink and blue Sp, ES	rough, silvery marks on dark green	leaves Sp, S
seed Sp, A	does not transplant successfully	spires of reddish-yellow S	mid-green in basal rosette which withers before flowers arrive	whole plant S
cuttings S layering S	withstands clipping. may suffer in cold, exposed, windy sites	pale mauve-blue Sp, ES, often W	highly aromatic, grey-green, narrow	leaves as required

HERB	TYPE	SOIL	HEIGHT × SPREAD	POSITION
Ruta graveolens (Rue)	perennial, semi-evergreen	most soils not damp	50–70 × 60 cm (20–28 × 24 ins) (bushy)	full sun; will tolerate some shade
Salvia officinalis (Purple Sage)	perennial, evergreen	rich, dryish	90 × 90 cm (36 × 36 ins) (bushy)	allow space, prefers full sun
Salvia sclarea (Clary)	biennial or perennial	light and well-drained	90 × 30 cm (36 × 12 ins)	will tolerate a little shade
Sanguinaria canadensis (Blood Root)	perennial	rich, loamy	20 × 30 cm (8 × 12 ins)	cool, moist woodland, under shrubs
Santolina chamaecyparissus (Cotton Lavender)	perennial, evergreen	light, well-drained	40–60 × 40–60 cm (16–24 × 16–24 ins)	good edging plant, likes sunshine
Saponaria officinalis (Soapwort, Bouncing Bet)	perennial	fertile, dampish	30–90 × 30 cm (12–36 × 12 ins)	mid-border or grassy bank, spreading
Satureia montana (Winter Savory)	perennial	light, well-drained	15–40 × 15–40 cm (6–16 × 6–16 ins)	full sun, front of border
Stachys officinalis (Wood Betony)	perennial	ordinary soil, likes some humus	15–90 × 25 cm (6–36 × 10 ins)	full sun, tolerates some shade
Symphytum officinale (Common Comfrey)	perennial	moist, fertile	50–90 × 30 cm (20–36 × 12 ins)	tolerant of shade, likes dampish situations
Tanacetum vulgare (Tansy)	perennial	loam or sand, moist	120 × 90 cm (48 × 36 ins)	full sun or semi-shade
Teucrium chamaedrys (Wall Germander)	perennial	light, well-drained	25 × 20 cm (10 × 8 ins)	needs good drainage, at base of wall or in paving.
Thymus citriodorus (Lemon Thyme)	perennial	light, well-drained, slightly acid	10–20 × 25–30 cm (4–8 × 10–12 ins)	full sun; carpet-forming, needs paving or front of border position
Thymus serpyllum (Wild Thyme)	perennial	light, well-drained	5–10 × 20–40 cm (2–4 × 8–16 ins) (creeps)	full sun; carpet-forming, needs paving or front of border position
Tussilago farfara (Coltsfoot)	perennial	most soils	20 × 10 cm (8 × 4 ins)	dry banks, under shrubs where it can become naturalized
Valeriana officinalis (Valerian)	perennial	rich and moist	135 × 30–40 cm (54 × 12–16 ins)	shaded borders
Valerianella locusta (Corn Salad)	annual	rich	10–20 × 15–25 cm (4–8 × 6–10 ins)	edge of herb bed or kitchen garden
Verbascum thapsus (Mullein)	biennial	dryish, fertile, chalky	90–180 × 25 cm (3–6 ft × 10 ins)	full sun, back of border
Vinca major (Periwinkle)	perennial, evergreen	well-drained	15–40 × 90 cm (6–16 × 36 ins) (spreads)	good for planting on banks
Viola odorata (Sweet Violet)	perennial	well-drained, previously enriched, moist soil	10–20 × 5 cm (4–8 × 2 ins)	some shade, moist banks

PROPAGATION	EXTRA DETAILS	FLOWER	FOLIAGE	HARVEST
cuttings LS seed Sp	needs pruning back every 2nd year	yellow S	grey-green, small, aromatic	leaves S
cuttings S layering S	does not like windy sites	mauve-purple S	grey (some forms variegated or purple), pungent	flowers and bracts S
division Sp, A seed Sp		mauve-blue, rather variable S	dark green, broad	leaves S
division after flowering	keep moist when young	white or pinkish Sp	solitary leaf stem, leaf lobed	rhizome A
stem cuttings S layering A	cut back in Sp. Withstands clipping	yellow S	coral-like, grey bushy growth	leaves AT
division A seed Sp		pink or white, sometimes with red marks M–LS	pale green, soft	leaves and shoots S roots A
stem cuttings S layering S seed (slow) Sp division Sp	lift and divide plants every 3 years. Cut back each A	white or pink S	small, dark, aromatic, enduring subshrub	leaves Sp, S, A
division Sp, A seed Sp		rose-pink S	soft green, aromatic	leaves S
division A root cuttings Sp, A	remove flowers to promote leaves	blue and pink LS–S	large, rough and stiff, pale green	leaves LS–S
division Sp, A seed Sp, A	rampant spreader, needs chopping back, confining and sometimes supporting	yellow buttons S	dark green, fern-like pungent	leaves Sp, S
division A stem cuttings S	trim in Sp	blue-mauve S	dark green, shiny, bushy growth	(decorative plant)
cuttings S division Sp, A layers A	trim back each year	pinkish-mauve S	minute, dark green, aromatic	leaves and shoots S, A
cuttings S division Sp, A layers A	trim back each year	pink S	grey-green, minute, aromatic	leaves and shoots S
division A root cuttings Sp, A	invasive, needs to be confined	yellow – appearing before leaves LW, ESp	dark green, felt-like, grey underneath	flowers ESp leaves Sp
seed Sp, A division of rootstock A	divide and replant every 4 years	pinkish-white LS	green, shiny	rootstock A
seed Sp, A	sow in drills, make successive sowings	mauve S Do not allow to flower if used for salads	pale green, smooth, roughly spoon-shaped; rosette growth	leaves as required
seed Sp, A	lighten heavy soils before sowing	strong yellow SS	felt-like, silver-white	leaves S, A stem A
cuttings S division Sp, A	can be invasive, keep it within bounds	mauve-blue ES	shines, dark green	(decorative plant) leaves Sp–S
runners ESp seed (slow) Sp division after flowering		violet Sp	dark to mid-green	flower Sp

Reference section

The following pages include a detailed list of 420 of the most important herbs, each illustrated with a photograph or drawing and with its characteristics and constituents described in full. The enormous variety and extent of the powers of plants is amply demonstrated in these entries. The practical information included gives ideas on how to cultivate those herbs that interest you, together with a concise indication of their uses, whether culinary, medicinal or otherwise. Once again, however, we must stress that the medicinal use of plants requires expert knowledge. In this respect, the book is a reference work rather than a guide to practical application. Under no circumstances should readers use the information in these pages for home treatment without first taking expert advice.

The cultivation section states whether the species is found in the wild state (as most are), or whether it is found wild only as an escape from cultivation, and also gives details of commercial and horticultural cultivation where applicable. Related varieties which are of greater horticultural importance have been noted, and, in addition, those closely related species that are cultivated as medicinal or economic plants for the same purpose as the species in question are also mentioned.

Left: A mass of different herbs growing in the wild. Many of the herbs described on the following pages – over 420 species – can be collected easily and put to a variety of different uses, which include culinary, medicinal and cosmetic.

Each entry lists the parts of the plant, together with their uses, most commonly employed. In some cases, it has been necessary to list different parts of the plant for different uses, as the effects of different parts of plants can vary widely – to the extent of being contradictory.

The naming of herbs often causes problems. We have used the Latin botanical names of the plants (the most accurate system), followed by the preferred common name in bold type with some of the alternatives. The Latin names have particular significance, and it is as well to know how they are made up. The following example is of a relatively complex name, as the herb is a hybrid, although the principles apply to all other species:

Mentha x *piperita* var. *citrata* (Ehr.) Briq.
LABIATAE
Bergamot Mint Eau de Cologne Mint/ Orange Mint

In this example, *Mentha* indicates the genus and *piperita* the species; (Ehr.) stands for Ehrhart which is the name of the botanist who first classified the species and Briq. (the abbreviation of Briquet) is the name of the person responsible for the accepted reclassification – thus without brackets. Originally this plant was classified by Linnaeus simply as *Mentha piperita*, but it was then reclassified by Ehrhart as *Mentha* x *piperita* var. *citrata*; the x indicates that the plant is a cross between *Mentha spicata* and *Mentha aquatica*, and the 'var.' means that this is a variety of mint which is not sufficiently distinct to be classified as a separate species. Labiatae indicates the family to which the plant belongs.

Abies alba Mill. PINACEAE
Silver Fir
This conifer was once the source of 'Strassburg Turpentine', first described in detail by Belon in *De Arboribus coniferis* (1553). It was retained in the London Pharmacopoeia until 1788. It is now rarely collected, and the leaves, buds and fresh resin are only used in folk medicine.
Description Coniferous evergreen tree to 50 m; trunk straight, branches brownish and pubescent; leaves simple, needle-like, glossy and dark green above, rounded at apex; to 3 cm long. Monoecious, the male cones small; female to 16 cm long, erect, becoming reddish-brown, with deciduous scales. Appearing late spring to early summer.
Distribution Native to central and southern Europe; mountainous regions from 400–2000 m altitude. Introduced elsewhere.
Cultivation Wild. Employed horticulturally, especially the cultivars *Columnaris*, *Compacta* and *Pendula*. Dislikes polluted air.
Constituents Oleo-resin comprising turpentine; essential oil; a sugar, abietite; provitamin A.
Uses (leaves, fresh resin, oil of turpentine occasionally) Antiseptic; diuretic; expectorant; carminative. Employed in the treatment of bronchitis, cystitis, leucorrhoea, ulcers and flatulent colic. The oil is an irritant and can be applied externally, diluted, as a rubefacient in neuralgia.
Contra-indications The oil should only be used externally, and may cause skin reactions.

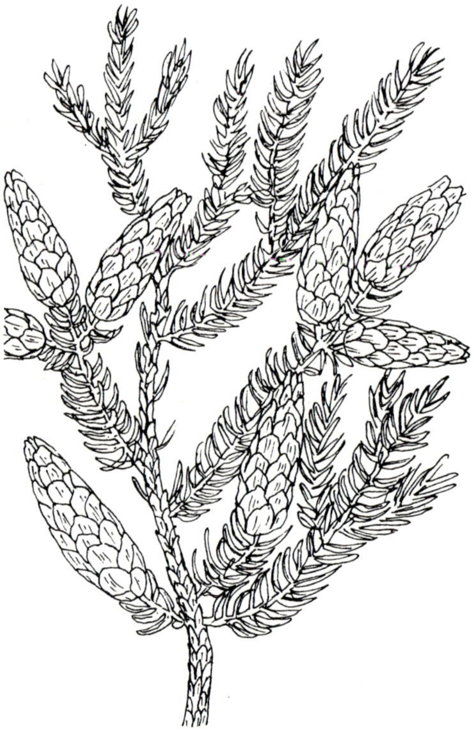

Acacia catechu (L) Willd. LEGUMINOSAE
Catechu Black Cutch/Kutch
This herb was known as *Cacho* or *Kat* and was an important export from India to China, Arabia and Persia in the sixteenth century. It was introduced to Europe in the seventeenth century from Japan. The dark brown extract was not recognized as a vegetable substance

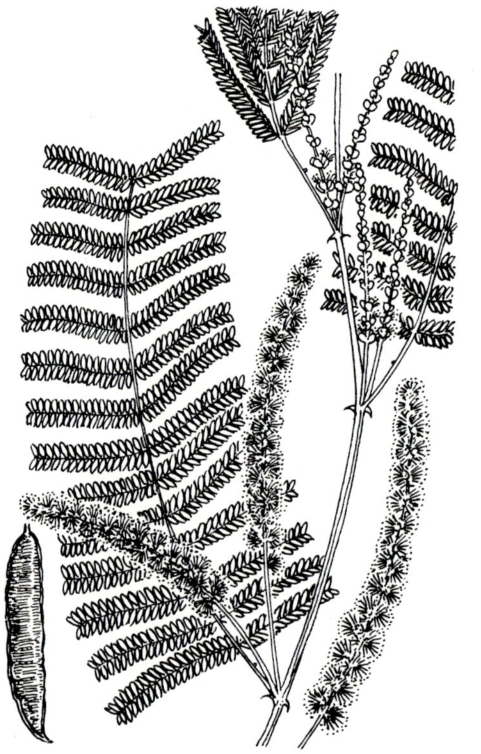

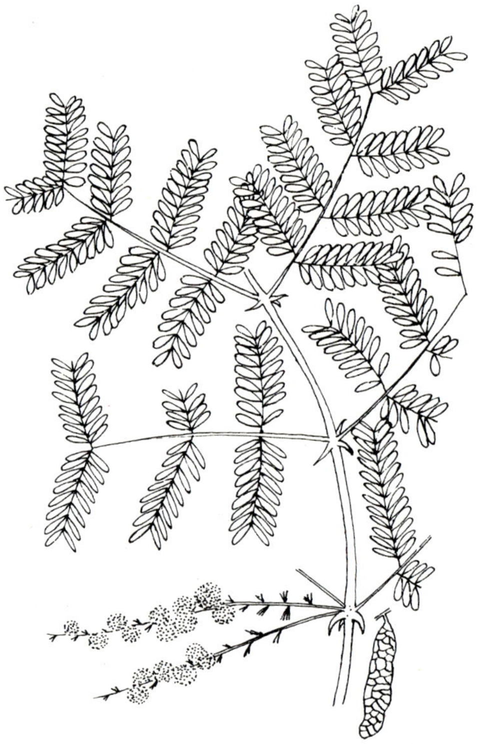

until 1677. It was included in the London Pharmacopoeia of 1721.
Description Moderate sized tree, 9–12 m high; trunk short, not straight, 1.5–2 m in girth; straggling thorny branches; light feathery foliage; rough, dark grey-brown bark; pale yellow flowers.
Distribution Indigenous to eastern India, Burma; common in hotter, drier parts of Ceylon, plains of Burma, forests of tropical east Africa.
Cultivation Not cultivated; trees felled and processed.
Constituents Astringent action due to catechu-tannic acid. Also contains quercetin, catechu red, catechol.
Uses (boiled and strained extract of heartwood chips, forming very dark brown solid mass) Powerful astringent, useful for inflamed conditions of throat, gums and mouth; used diluted as a gargle. Used to treat diarrhoea and externally for ulcers and boils. Wood for posts, heating and charcoal. Catechu and bark for tanning and dyeing.

Acacia Senegal (L) Willd. LEGUMINOSAE
Gum Arabic Acacia Gum/Gummi acaciae
When the Egyptians brought gum from the Gulf of Aden in the seventeenth century B.C., they called it Kami and used it mainly for painting and as an adhesive for lapis lazuli or coloured glass. Theophrastus mentioned Kami, in the fourth century B.C., and Celsus called it *Gummi acanthinum* in the first century B.C. Arabian physicians at the medieval school of Salerno used it and it was liable for customs duty at Pisa and Paris. It reached London by 1521 via Venice. Gum Arabic is still used pharmaceutically.
Description Low tree, 3–6 m high, bending grey branches, grey bark; leaves pale green, smooth; flowers yellowish, fragrant; corolla white.
Distribution Indigenous to east and west Africa. Common in Arabia and India.
Cultivation Not cultivated; trees incised and gum collected early winter.
Constituents Consists mainly of calcium, magnesium and potassium salts of arabic acid (arabin). Forms a mucilage in water.
Uses (dried gummy exudation from stems and branches) Soothing for inflamed tissue. Used in mouth lozenges, cough mixtures, emulsions. Highly nutritious taken as gruel. Adhesive.

Acanthus mollis L ACANTHACEAE
Bear's Breech Brank Ursine
The specific name, Acanthus (from the Greek *akanthos, ake* meaning thorn, *anthos* meaning flowers) occurs frequently in Greek and Roman

writings referring to different prickly plants. The beautiful leaves stimulated designs for the decoration of columns in classical Greek architecture.
Description Hardy perennial; leaves oblong with undulating margins, dark green and glossy, 30–60 cm long; stems straight to 150 cm high; white or lilac pink flowers on spikes, summer.
Distribution Native of southern Europe. Now widely distributed.
Cultivation Tolerates ordinary soil; prefers deep loam, either full sun or partial shade. Propagate by division in spring or autumn; root cuttings, or seed, in spring. May be cultivated as house plant in large pot in full light.
Uses Crushed leaves once used for burns and scalds.

Achillea millefolium L COMPOSITAE
Yarrow Milfoil/Woundwort/Carpenter's Weed
From ancient times this herb has been associated with the healing of wounds and the stemming of blood-flow, hence the generic name; Achilles, for example, was supposed to have cured his warriors with its leaves.
A. millefolium has traditionally had a wide medical use.
Description Aromatic perennial, far-creeping stoloniferous herb; erect furrowed stem, 8–60 cm high; white or pinkish flowers (early summer to autumn) and slightly hairy bipinnate leaves, 2–10 cm long, divided into fine leaflets.
Distribution Widespread in temperate zones; native to Europe; on all but poorest soils.
Cultivation Increase by division spring or autumn. Grows in any soil in sunny position.
Constituents Volatile oil containing azulene; and a glycoalkaloid, achilleine.
Uses (dried aerial parts, including flowers) Diaphoretic; antipyretic; hypotensive; diuretic and urinary antiseptic. Combines with Elderflowers and Peppermint for colds and influenza. Of use in hypertension and coronary thrombosis, dysentery and diarrhoea. Fresh leaf alleviates toothache. Regulates menstrual

periods. Stimulates gastric secretion.
Fresh herb in salads. Can substitute Hops in brewing.
Cosmetic cleanser for greasy skin.
Snuff; tobacco substitute. 'I Ching' sticks.
Contra-indications Large doses produce headaches and vertigo.

Aconitum napellus L RANUNCULACEAE
Aconite Monkshood/Blue Rocket/Wolfsbane
This lethal herb was widely employed as an arrow poison by the ancient Chinese and its generic name comes from the Greek *akontion* meaning a dart. *Napellus* means 'little turnip' – a reference to the shape of its tuberous root.
Aconitum napellus was an important herb among the thirteenth-century Welsh physicians of Myddvai but was not introduced into medicine generally until the eighteenth century.
Description Hardy herbaceous perennial; essentially biennial as roots produced one year, flower the next; stem erect reaching 150 cm; leaves dark green, glossy, 3–8 cm wide, divided; flowers (summer and autumn) violet blue, 2 cm high, helmet shaped, in terminal clusters.
Distribution Indigenous to Alps and Pyrenees; mountainous districts of northern hemisphere. Prefers moist soils in shade.
Cultivation Root division in autumn; selected daughter roots are stored in a warm place and then planted mid-winter in moist loam. Seeds sown in spring flower in 2–3 years. Attractive garden decoration; blue, white and violet cultivars include Blue Spectre, Sparks Variety.
Constituents Sedative and toxic action due to

alkaloid, aconitine. Also contains picraconitine, and aconine.
Uses (dried root tubers, whole plant fresh or dried) Sedative; pain killer; antipyretic. Once used for feverish conditions, now only externally for neuralgia and sciatica.
Contra-indications All parts intensely POISONOUS. To be used only by medical personnel.

Acorus calamus L ARACEAE
Calamus Sweet Flag/Sweet Sedge/Myrtle Flag
Acorus calamus was an ancient herb of the East and is also mentioned in the Bible in the book of Exodus. It was probably introduced into Russia by the Mongolians in the eleventh century, and into Poland by the thirteenth. At the end of the sixteenth century it was widely distributed by the Viennese botanist Clausius.
Description Hardy, vigorous, aromatic perennial; much branched rhizome, 3 cm thick, bearing sword-shaped leaves with wavy margin, 1 m high and 15 mm wide. Small flowers

(early summer), on inflorescence 4–8cm long.
Distribution Indigenous to central Asia, eastern Europe; now native in northern temperate zones, in marshy regions.
Cultivation Needs moist soil and frequent watering, best by water margins. Divide clumps early spring or autumn, cover well. Only flowers in water.
Constituents Bitter, aromatic, volatile oil; bitter principle, acorin.
Uses (dried rhizome) Carminative; vermifuge; spasmolytic; diaphoretic. Stimulates salivary and gastric glands. Slight sedative action on central nervous system. Best used in flatulent colic, dyspepsia.
Beer flavouring and liqueur. Candied rhizomes used as sweetmeats. Young leaf buds in salads.
Insecticide; powder repels white ants.
Perfume additive similar to orris root. Toothpowder, hair-powders and dry shampoos.
Snuff.
Contra-indications Oil of acorus has reputed carcinogenic properties.

Adiantum capillus-veneris L POLYPODIACEAE
Maidenhair Fern Venus Hair
The generic name *Adiantum* is from the Greek word *adiantos* or unwetted, since the foliage repels water and the plant's natural habitat is a wet environment. The specific and common names refer to the hair of the pudenda after the fine, shiny, black petioles. This was once the most important herbal ingredient of a popular cough syrup called *Capillaire* which remained

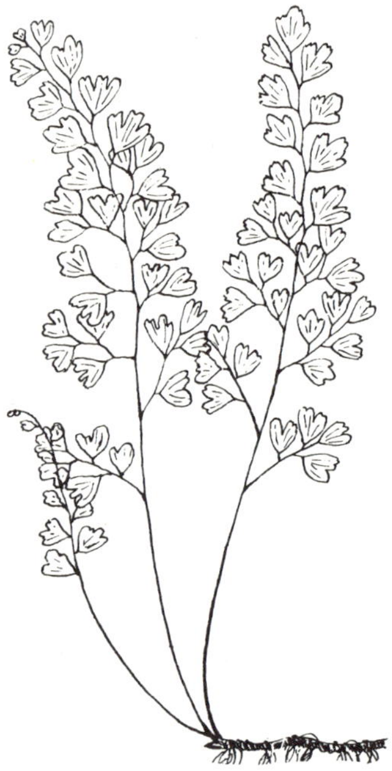

in use until the nineteenth century.
Description Perennial fern 10–40 cm tall; petioles thin, delicate, black and shiny. Leaves ovate to narrowly triangular, finely pinnate, pinnules fan-shaped and toothed; sori reddish-brown on the underside of leaf tips.
Distribution Native to Great Britain, central and south Europe. Now world-wide in temperate and tropical regions. Especially near the sea, in caves, wells, on damp walls; cliffs, on chalky soils; but also to 1300 m altitude.
Cultivation Wild. Cultivated as a pot plant in loam and leaf mould mix; requires moist atmosphere. Propagate by division.
Constituents Mucilage; tannins; gallic acid; sugars; various bitter principles; capillarine; minute quantities of an essential oil.
Uses (fresh, or dried, leafy fronds occasionally) Weak expectorant; bechic; weak emmenagogue; weak diuretic.
Principally employed in chest complaints such as respiratory catarrh, and coughs. Once used in the treatment of both pleurisy and asthma but with little effect in the latter.

Adonis vernalis L RANUNCULACEAE
False Hellebore Pheasant's Eye/Spring Adonis/Ox-eye
The name is derived from the legend of Adonis, who was killed by a wild boar and from whose blood the herb sprang. It is still retained in several European pharmacopoeias. There are two varieties, *A. vernalis* with yellow flowers and *A. annua* with red flowers.
Description Perennial herb, 10–30 cm high; sparingly branched, leaves numerous and much divided; flowers (early spring) solitary, terminal, rich yellow, 3–6 cm wide.
Distribution Central and south-east Europe. Occasionally wild in temperate zones; can be grown in the garden.
Cultivation Grows in moist soils in full sun or shade; flowers best in sunny position. *A. vernalis* suits rockeries. *A. annua* cannot be transplanted.
Some white or double flowered varieties are cultivated.
Constituents Glycosides, including cymarin.
Uses (dried herb) Valuable heart tonic, not cumulative and less toxic than Digitalis. Dilates coronary arteries. Not widely used due to irregular absorption. Vermifuge.
Contra-indications POISONOUS even in very small amounts; to be used by medical personnel only.

Aegopodium podagraria L UMBELLIFERAE
Ground Elder Goutweed/Bishops-weed/Herb Gerard
The name suggests both the leaf shape and the specific use of this herb in ancient times, from the Greek *aigos* meaning goat; *podos* meaning foot and *podagra* the Latin for gout. In the Middle Ages it was cultivated as a pot herb or vegetable.
Description Perennial weed with creeping rootstock; hollow stem reaching 20–40 cm bearing umbels of white flowers (summer), 2–7 cm wide; leaves 10–20 cm long with stalks, subdivided into 3 leaflets.

Distribution Native to Europe, naturalized in eastern North America; often near habitation, hedgerows.
Cultivation Wild; too vigorous for garden cultivation, although *A. podagraria variegatum* is used for edging.
Uses (dried herb, fresh root and leaf) Diuretic; sedative. Traditionally taken as a drink for gout and sciatic pains. Boiled root and leaf in hot poultice applied to joints.
Young fresh leaves cooked in spring as vegetable; taste similar to spinach. Used in salads.

Aesculus hippocastanum L HIPPOCASTANACEAE
Horse Chestnut
Aesculus was the classical name of an oak tree but the origins of the common name are uncertain: it was used extensively in the East as cattle and horse fodder; alternatively the prefix 'horse' may have differentiated it from the edible Sweet Chestnut, *Castanea sativa*.
Description Deciduous tree up to 35 m high; very resinous buds, bark smooth when young and becomes scaly; leaves subdivided into 5–7 leaflets, 8–20 cm long; flowers (early summer) white, pink or yellowish, on erect conical inflorescence; fruit spiny, green, containing brown seed.

Distribution Native to Balkan peninsula; now widely cultivated.
Cultivation Grows in many soils; often self-sown.
Constituents Saponin; aescine; flavones; coumarin; tannins.
Uses (fresh seed without seed-coat, branch bark) Tonic; narcotic; antipyretic. Bark employed traditionally in intermittent fevers. Combined action of constituents of seeds strengthens arteries and veins, preventing thrombosis. Seed extract relieves haemorrhoids. Fruit mash for cattle and sheep fodder.
Contra-indications Seed POISONOUS. To be used by medical personnel only.

Aethusa cynapium L UMBELLIFERAE
Fool's Parsley Lesser Hemlock/Dog Poison
Known to sixteenth-century apothecaries as *apium rusticum*, this is a highly poisonous herb,

as indeed the common names suggest. Care is required when collecting edible plants from the wild. Fool's Parsley, for example, can easily be taken for an edible Parsley.
Description Annual, flimsy looking, rarely more than 30 cm high, thin, hairless, hollow stem; leaves triangular, segments ovate, pinnatifid; umbels of white flowers (summer) 2–6 cm wide with 3 or 4 long pendulous bracteoles.
Distribution Native to Europe; common, widely distributed; weed of cultivated ground.
Cultivation Wild plant.
Constituents Toxic principle an alkaloid, cynopine.
Uses (dried herb) Stomachic; sedative. Once used for gastro-intestinal complaints of children, convulsions, summer diarrhoea.
Contra-indications Very POISONOUS. Small amounts cause pain, confusion of vision, vomiting.

Aframomum melegueta Rosc. ZINGIBERACEAE
Grains of Paradise Melegueta Pepper/ Guinea Grains
The name *Melegueta* is derived from the ancient African empire of Melle which extended over the Upper Niger region. It was originally transported from the African west coast across the desert to ports on the Tripoli coast. It served as a spice in medieval European cuisine and was one of the ingredients of the spiced wine, hippocras. Known as *grana paradisi* because it was imported from distant lands, it was sold at Lyons in 1245. At the same time the Welsh physicians of Myddvai called it 'grawn Paris'.
Description Herbaceous reed-like plant, 1–2.5 m high, long leaves producing delicate wax-like, pale purple flowers, succeeded by pear-shaped scarlet fruit, 6–10 cm long, enclosing pulp and brown seeds, 2 mm wide.
Cultivation Wild; cultivated particularly in Ghana.
Constituents Essential oil; pungent resin.
Uses (seeds) Stimulant. Hot and peppery condiment; used as pepper substitute. Traditionally used in veterinary medicine.

Agathosma betulina (Berg.) Pillans. RUTACEAE
Buchu Bucco/Short Buchu/Round Buchu
One of the few indigenous plants of southern Africa to find a place in both traditional and orthodox western medicine, the use of Buchu was learned from the native Hottentots by the colonists of the Cape of Good Hope. It was first introduced to Europe in 1821. Until recent legislation most of the leaf production was used as a cordial flavouring in the United States. Buchu is still used by herbalists and African tribesmen. Originally classified as *Barosma betulina* (Bergius) Bartl. & H.L. Wendl.
Description A small shrub 1–1.5 m high bearing smooth rod-shaped branches with leathery, glossy, pale yellowish-green leaves 1–2 cm long, 5 mm – 1 cm wide. Young twigs and toothed margins of leaves have conspicuous oil glands. White flowers.
Distribution Cape province of South Africa: mountain-sides and hillsides on dry soil.
Cultivation Wild plant; cultivated on hillsides.
Constituents Volatile oil comprising up to 40% diosphenol; limonene and menthone.
Uses (dried leaf) Urinary antiseptic; of use in cystitis and urethritis. A weak diuretic.
Used to flavour brandy (Buchu brandy).
Used as a blackcurrant flavouring.
Black South Africans use the leaves mixed with oil as a body perfume.

Agave americana L AGAVACEAE
Century Plant Agave/American Aloe
Agave is from the Greek for admirable, after the plant's appearance; the common name refers to the mistaken belief that it flowers only after a hundred years' growth. In many tropical countries the Agave provides one of the cheapest and most effective cattle fences available.
Description Succulent monocotyledon, eventually flowering after 10 years or more, after which it dies, although frequently leaving suckers at the base. Leaves are very thick, 15–20 cm wide, 1–2 m long, grey, smooth, and spiny-edged. Flowers to 3 cm long, pale

yellowish on horizontal branches of a 6–12 m tall stalk.
Distribution Native to tropical America, especially Mexico. Introduced and established in southern Europe, India, central and south Africa, and elsewhere. On arid soils.
Cultivation Wild. Cultivated as an ornamental or hedge plant in tropical countries; propagate from seed or suckers.
Constituents (leaf) acrid volatile oil; agave gum; phloionolic acid; oxalic acid and oxalates; saponoside; cutin; hecogenin, a sapogenin; a sugar, agavose.
Uses (fresh or dried leaf, juice, root, gum) Purgative; emmenagogue; diuretic; insecticide; counter-irritant.
Wide folk-medical use in tropical countries, particularly for external application to burns and contusions.
The juice is fermented to yield the Mexican alcoholic drink, pulque.
Powdered leaf employed as snuff; root used in washing clothes.
Used for fencing in tropical countries.
In veterinary medicine it is only used as a purgative.

Agrimonia eupatoria L ROSACEAE
Agrimony Church Steeples/Sticklewort
The specific name of this herb refers to Mithradates Eupator, ancient king of Persia, who was renowned as a herbalist. 'Agrimony' is a corruption of the Greek word *argemon*, a white speck on the cornea of the eye. This herb was once famous for the healing of wounds, and it was an ingredient of *eau de arquebusade*, used to treat wounds, from the fifteenth-century word for musket or arquebus. Still used in European folk medicine.
Description Perennial herb; erect downy, reddish stems, 30–60 cm high; compound pinnate leaves, up to 20 cm long. Flowers (summer-autumn) yellow, 5–8 mm wide and numerous.
Distribution Throughout Asia, Europe, North America; common on roadsides, waste-ground, hedgebanks.
Cultivation Wild, but easily propagated by root division in autumn. Tolerates varying conditions.

Constituents Tannin; volatile oil; resin. The combination is anti-inflammatory, antibiotic, astringent.
Uses (dried flowering plant) Mild astringent; possibly diuretic. Used for acute sore throats, chronic catarrh, children's diarrhoea, cystitis, and externally as a lotion for wounds. The whole plant yields a yellow dye.

Agropyron repens (L) Beauv. GRAMINEAE
Couch Grass Twitch Grass/Witch Grass
A well-known and troublesome weed to gardeners, Couch Grass has played a long and important role as a medicinal herb, and was promoted by Dioscorides and Pliny. European country people still drink it as a tisane and it is one of the plants eaten by sick dogs to induce vomiting.
Description Perennial grass; long jointed, branching, yellowish rhizome 1–3 mm diameter; erect glabrous stems; bright greenish-grey leaves up to 15 mm wide; small purplish flowers in spikes appearing mid-summer to early autumn.
Distribution Widely distributed native of Europe; naturalized in United States and

troublesome in eastern states. Northern Asia, Australia and S. America. Weed of arable and wasteland.
Cultivation Wild plant.
Constituents Triticin (a carbohydrate which resembles inulin); sugar; inositol; salts of potassium; mucilage; acid malates; a volatile oil with antibiotic properties.
Uses (dried rhizome) Diuretic; urinary antiseptic. Useful in cystitis. Underground parts once used as cattle food.

Ailanthus altissima (Mill.) Seingle
SIMAROUBACEAE
Tree-of-Heaven Copal Tree/Varnish Tree
Introduced to England in 1751 from Nanking in China, and then in 1800 to the United States where it rapidly became a popular ornamental. The medicinal value of the bark was discovered in France in 1859. *Ailanthus* is from the Indonesian for tree of heaven, a name first given to another species. The alternative common names 'copal' and 'varnish' tree are misnomers, as the tree does not provide a varnish (or copal) material.
Description Rapidly growing deciduous tree reaching 10–20 m; leaves 30 cm–1 m long, subdivided into 11–14 oblong, lanceolate or ovate, gland-bearing leaflets 7.5–11.5 cm long. Flowers small, greenish in terminal panicles 10–20 cm long followed by reddish-brown indehiscent winged fruit called samara.
Distribution Chinese native. Naturalized in eastern North America.
Cultivation Wild. Introduced horticulturally to urban areas as a shade-tree due to its rapid growth, and resistance to pollution and disease. Easily grown from seed.
Constituents Fixed oil; volatile oil; gum; oleo-

resin; sugars; oxalic acid; possibly alkaloids and glycosides.
Uses (fresh or dried root and stem bark) Emetic; cathartic; antihelmintic; astringent. Formerly used in the treatment of dysentery and diarrhoea, asthma, epilepsy, palpitations and as a douche in gonorrhoea and leucorrhoea.
The remedy is unpleasant causing nausea, vomiting and debility, and is therefore no longer employed.

Ajuga reptans L LABIATAE
Bugle Common or Creeping Bugle/Bugle Weed
One of the common names of Bugle is the Carpenter's Herb, which reflects its original importance as a plant used to stop bleeding. Known to apothecaries as 'bugula' the herb is rarely used today, but it possesses other

properties which as yet have not been fully researched.
Description Perennial with leafy stolons or runners; basal spatulate leaves form rosette; stem square, hairy on two sides and bearing 6–12 small blue flowers in early to late summer. Occasionally white or pink flowered mutants.
Distribution European native; introduced elsewhere. Common on damp ground in loamy soil, rich in nutrients. Mixed woodland, meadows.
Cultivation Wild plant; horticultural varieties *purpurea* and *variegata*.
Constituents Tannins; unknown digitalis-like substances.
Uses (dried whole herb) Astringent; bitter; aromatic. Formerly used to stop haemorrhages; for coughs, and ulcers. Thought to possess heart tonic qualities.

Alchemilla alpina L ROSACEAE
Alpine Lady's Mantle
The historical associations of Alpine Lady's Mantle are similar to those of *Alchemilla vulgaris*. Traditionally the alpine species was considered more effective although this has not been proven.

Description Perennial herb 10–12 cm high; leaves 3–7 cm in diameter divided into 5–7 leaflets white and silky beneath, glabrous above; small yellow-green flowers in clusters on branched, erect, thin stems. Flowering from mid-summer until early autumn.
Distribution Mountain ranges of Europe and mountain pastures of northern Europe.
Cultivation Wild plant.
Constituents Similar to *Alchemilla vulgaris* (Lady's Mantle).
Uses (dried leaves) As for Lady's Mantle but considered more effective.

Alchemilla vulgaris agg. ROSACEAE
Lady's Mantle Lion's Foot
This is an example of a herb which acquired a

reputation far greater than its therapeutic action would have suggested. Although unknown by ancient classical writers it became an important northern European magical plant on the discovery that overnight dew collected in the funnel-shaped folds of its partly closed nine-lobed leaves. To alchemically minded sixteenth century scientists dew was strongly magical, and so in turn was Lady's Mantle. Hieronymus Bock emphasized this by ascribing the name *Alchemilla* or the 'little magical one' to the herb.
Description Perennial herb, 10–50 cm high, branched stems bearing few round or reniform leaves 3–8 cm in diameter, with 7–11 lobes; flowers not prominent, 3–5 mm in diameter, greenish-yellow, in terminal panicles; upper flowers small and without petals. Appearing early spring to mid-autumn. (At least 11 closely related species are aggregated under the name *Alchemilla vulgaris*).
Distribution Northern Europe and mountainous areas of central and southern Europe. Prefers deep loamy moist soil in meadows, pastures, open grassy woodland, paths. Calcifugous.
Cultivation Wild plant.
Constituents Tannins. Unknown anti-inflammatory substances. Action anti-diarrhoeal.
Uses (dried leaves, rarely dried flowering plant) Astringent and styptic. Prolonged use relieves discomfort of menopause and excessive menstruation.
Used in veterinary medicine for diarrhoea.

Alkanna tinctoria Tausch. BORAGINACEAE
Alkanet Dyer's Bugloss/Spanish Bugloss
Although several colouring plants are now called Alkanets, *Alkanna tinctoria* probably was the first to be used. Its name is derived from the Spanish *alcanna* which came from the Arabic *al-henna*, the well-known Henna dye. Alkanet means the 'little alcanna'. It was exported

from Spain, Germany and France for centuries as a dye for pharmaceutical and cosmetic use. It was also used by victuallers. It is now often replaced by the Evergreen Alkanet, *Pentaglottis sempervirens*, and the Common Alkanet, *Anchusa officinalis*.
Description Thick root up to 10 cm long with purplish root bark, bearing numerous stalks reaching 30 cm high; leaves are long and narrow alternate, somewhat hairy, many clustering around root crown. Attractive funnel-shaped, purple-blue, sometimes white or yellow, flowers; appearing late summer to early autumn.
Distribution Central and southern Europe. At roadsides, dry sandy soil. Calcifugous.
Cultivation Wild plant.
Constituents Possibly an alkaloid poisonous to mammals.
Uses (root, root bark) Not used medicinally. Used variously as a colouring agent. A red colour is released in oils and waxes but not in water.

Alliaria petiolata (Bieb.) Cavara & Grande CRUCIFERAE
Garlic Mustard Hedge Garlic/Jack-by-the-hedge
A common European herb which has never

been of much importance medically. Also known as *A. officinalis* Bieb., the generic name is derived from *allium* or garlic after the smell of the crushed plant.
Description Garlic-smelling biennial or perennial reaching 30–100 cm; stem erect, simple. Leaves thin, pale green, petiolate, coarsely crenate, cordate above, reniform beneath. Flowers small white, 6 mm diameter, in a false umbel; appearing mid-spring to mid-summer.
Distribution European native. In open wasteland, moist woodland, on well-drained nutrient-rich soil.
Cultivation Wild plant.
Constituents Essential oil; a heteroside, sinigrine, which in water yields the aglycone, allyl isothiocyanate.
Uses (fresh, or dried flowering plant occasionally) Antiseptic; vulnerary; stimulant; rubefacient; expectorant; diuretic.
A dilute poultice, applied to ulcers and cuts or abrasions, cleans and aids healing; undiluted, it is of use externally to relieve pain from neuralgia, and rheumatism. Leaf may be used in small quantities as a salad herb, boiled, or in sauces. The crushed seed can be taken as a condiment.

Allium cepa L LILIACEAE
Onion
The Onion has been in cultivation for so long that its country of origin is uncertain and it is now rarely, if ever, found wild.
The plant is recorded in the works of the Chaldeans, Egyptians and Greeks, and as early as A.D. 79 Pliny described in detail its cultivation and the varieties to be used.
Columella in A.D. 42 introduced the word *unionem* from which the common name is derived. Modern classification groups the Shallot, formerly *A. ascalonicum* L, with this species and numerous cultivars of *A. cepa* now exist, including some bred to crop within a limited range of day-length and temperatures. The unusual top Onions, (Egyptian or Tree Onions) were recorded by Dalechamp in 1587, and are usually grown as herb garden novelties.
Description Variable biennial or perennial to 120 cm, characteristically with 4–6 aromatic, cylindrical, hollow leaves and hollow scape. Flowers sometimes absent or replaced by bulbils. When present they are greenish-white, small, numerous, in rounded umbels, appearing late summer.
Distribution Probably native to central Asia or south-west India. Now world-wide.
Cultivation Cultivated plant, or wild very rarely. Numerous cultivars exist which are now subdivided according to major characteristics into 3 groups: the Cepa group, the Proliferum group, the Aggregatum group. The first group contains the common culinary Onion and its members have single bulbs and are usually propagated from seed sown in spring or autumn or from sets sown in summer. The second group contains the Tree Onion and its members produce swollen bulbils in the inflorescence, and are propagated from these bulbils in late spring or late autumn, or by division every 3 years. The last group contains the Shallot, usually sterile but producing a crop of bulbs at the base and grown from these in early spring or late autumn. All onions prefer a very rich, deep soil.
Constituents Similar to those of garlic; also containing glucokinins; pectin; flavonoid glycosides; vitamins A, B_1, B_2, B_5, C, E; nicotinamide.
Uses (fresh bulb, fresh juice) Antibiotic; diuretic; expectorant; hypotensive; stomachic; antispasmodic; hypoglycaemic.
Useful in the treatment of coughs, colds, bronchitis, laryngitis and gastro-enteritis. Reduces the blood pressure and the blood-sugar level.
Used externally as a local stimulant, on cuts, to treat acne, and to promote hair growth.
An important vegetable and flavouring.

Allium sativum L LILIACEAE
Garlic
Garlic, a member of the onion family, is one of the most common flavourings and is used daily in cooking in most of the warm climates of the world. The flavour of the cloves develops best in sunny countries, and may be rank when grown in northern Europe.
It has been cultivated in the East for centuries and was widely employed medicinally by the Egyptians and Romans. The slaves that constructed the pyramid of Cheops were given garlic cloves daily to sustain their strength as were Roman soldiers. The common name is derived from the Anglo-Saxon *leac* meaning a pot-herb and *gar*, a lance, after the shape of the stem.
Description Perennial or biennial; sub-globular bulbs consisting of 8–20 cloves (partial bulbs) surrounded by silky pink-white skin. Several flat, erect, long pointed leaves 1–2.5 cm wide, to 15 cm long arising from base or crown. Unbranched stem (spathe) 7.5–10 cm long, pointed, bearing apical, small, dense umbels of rose-white or greenish flowers, often displaced by sterile pinkish bulbils 4 mm long.
Distribution Asian native; introduced in all warm climates. Prefers rich, light, well-drained soils.
Cultivation This plant has been grown from the Mediterranean to Central Asia for centuries. Several varieties exist including small cloved and giant forms, and white, pink, or mauve skinned forms. Flavour varies from sweet to nutty, mild to strong. Plant individual cloves in spring or preferably autumn in rich, dry soil, in a sunny position, 15 cm apart and 4 cm deep.
Constituents Essential oil, comprising mainly allyl disulphide and allyl propyl disulphide; vitamins A, B_1, B_2, C; antibacterial substances comprising allicin, allicetoin I and II; also an enzyme alliinase.
Uses (fresh bulb) Antibacterial; hypotensive; expectorant; weak anthelmintic; weak fungicide. Employed in the treatment of hypertension and arteriosclerosis; as a carminative and an expectorant in bronchial catarrh. Provides protection against the common cold, amoeboid

dysentery, typhoid and other infectious diseases. Garlic also increases the flow of bile and the fresh juice was once used as an inhalation in the treatment of pulmonary tuberculosis.
Wide culinary use; both fresh and cooked, when the flavour varies. Employed in butters, vinegars and salt. Parsley reduces the aroma on the breath.
Contra-indications May be slightly irritant to the skin.

Allium schoenoprasum L LILIACEAE
Chives
Chives is the only member of the onion group found wild in both Europe and North America, and although used for centuries was not cultivated until the Middle Ages. It cannot be dried with any success but may be quick-frozen and stored.
Description Perennial in clumps; small bulbs produce grass-like cylindrical hollow dark green leaves, 20–30 cm long, 2–3 mm diameter, bearing in the summer an inflorescence of pink or purple flowers in a compact spherical capitulum.
Distribution Native to cool parts of Europe; introduced and naturalized in North America. Tolerates a wide range of conditions from dry, rocky places to stream banks, damp grassland and wood edges.
Cultivation Wild but cultivated commercially

and horticulturally in northern Europe and America. Variable in form depending on the environment. A large leaved type exists. Chinese chives (*A. tuberosum*) is larger, coarser-flavoured and has flat solid leaves. Propagate by sowing seed in mid-spring, or by division of clumps in spring or autumn. An excellent decorative edging plant for herb gardens.
Constituents Very similar to garlic (*Allium sativum*).
Uses (fresh or quick-frozen leaf) Used only for culinary purposes, chopped in sauces, soups, salads and as a garnish.

Alnus glutinosa (L) Gaertn BETULACEAE
Alder English or Common Alder/Owler
The common name derives from an old Germanic word meaning reddish-yellow, since the trunks change from white to reddish-yellow after felling. A supposed colour simi-

larity with blood led to the tradition that felling Alders was unlucky. The tree is an inhabitant of wet environments and coincidentally its main use was as a support under bridges or buildings. Venice is largely constructed on Alder posts.
Description Medium sized tree or large shrub, reaching 25 m; leaves stalked, obovate, 5–10 cm long, downy veins underneath, sticky when unfolding; small flowers appear before leaves in early spring; female catkins referred to as 'berries' almost spherical, formed in autumn.
Distribution North Africa, Europe, parts of Asia. Introduced and locally naturalized elsewhere. Prefers moist, swampy sites beside streams.
Cultivation Wild plant.
Constituents Tannins.
Uses (Bark, leaves) Tonic, astringent. Bark decoctions once used as gargle and for external inflammations. Formally used in bitters.
Used as a wool dye, the bark produces reds and blacks, the young shoots yellow, fresh wood pink and the catkins green.
Once extensively used by tanners.

Aloe vera L *A. perryi* Baker *A. ferox* Miller
LILIACEAE
Aloes Curaçao/Socotrine/Cape
One of the most important crude drugs of history, *Aloe vera* is still extensively used in modern medicine. Known to the Greeks at least as early as the fourth century B.C., a legend claims that Aristotle requested Alexander the Great to conquer the inhabitants of Socotra – the island which produced Aloes – and install Greeks. In the tenth century, however, Moslem travellers reported that Socotra was still the only place cultivating Aloes. Curaçao or Barbados Aloes were offered by London druggists in 1693, and Cape Aloes were exported first in 1780.
Description Several species of succulent liliaceous plants forming clusters of very fleshy leaf blades, usually prickly at the margin and tip; stemless or producing woody branching stems; from 45 cm–15 m tall, bearing erect spikes of yellow, orange or red flowers. Appears most of the year.
Distribution Natives of dry, sunny areas of south and east Africa; naturalized in north Africa, Spain, Indonesia and the Caribbean islands.

Cultivation Wild plant; cultivated commercially in Africa and the Caribbean. Grown as a house plant.
Constituents Barbaloin and isobarbaloin, forming 'crystalline' aloin; 'amorphous' aloin; aloe-emodin; resin; volatile oil. Action on large intestine largely due to purgative effect of aloins and aloe-emodin.
Uses (the brownish crystalline solid, resulting from drying the liquid which exudes from cut leaf blades) Purgative. Used normally in combination with carminatives to prevent griping. Fresh juice used to heal burns.
Contra-indications Excessive use induces haemorrhoids.

Aloysia triphylla Britt. VERBENACEAE
Lemon Verbena
This South American plant was introduced to Europe by the Spaniards and was once used to give a lemon scent to fingerbowls at banquets. The former botanical name *Lippia citriodora* (HBK) and the common name reflect the strong lemon scent of the plant's leaves. Lemon Verbena's modern generic name, *Aloysia* comes from the name Louisa, after Maria Louisa, wife of King Charles IV of Spain. Although half-hardy this herb makes a good indoor plant, as well as providing attractive and aromatic stems and foliage for flower arrangement.
Description Aromatic shrub to 3 m, but rarely more than 1.2–1.5 m in cooler northern temperate zones. Branches striate and scabrous, bearing whorls of 3–4 leaves which are entire, 5–7.5 cm long, short-petioled, glabrous, lanceolate and dotted on the underside with oil-bearing glands. Flowers white or pale lavender, small (6 mm long) in axillary spikes or terminal panicles.
Distribution Native to Chile and Argentina; widely distributed in tropical zones.
Cultivation Wild. Cultivated horticulturally and as a greenhouse plant in temperate zones. Half-hardy in cool temperate countries and requires frost and wind protection; plant against a south facing wall on light, well-drained soil; protect with straw and cut back at the end of the growing season.
Propagate from woody cuttings in early summer or from seed sown under glass in early spring.

Constituents Essential oil, comprising mainly citral.
Uses (fresh or dried leaf) Antispasmodic; stomachic; aromatic.
As a tea it is of benefit in the treatment of nausea, indigestion, flatulence, palpitations, vertigo.
Leaf may be used sparingly as a lemon flavouring in cakes, fruit dishes and sweet foodstuffs, or in drinks.
The dried leaf is employed in pot-pourris and scented sachets.
The oil is used in perfumery.
Contra-indications Prolonged use or large internal dosage may cause gastric irritation.

Alpinia officinarum Hance ZINGIBERACEAE
Galangal East India Root/Galanga
This root was introduced into European medicine by the writings of the Arabic physicians Rhazes and Avicenna; it was first recorded by Ibn Khurdadbah in 869 who listed it with Musk, silk and Camphor as an article of trade from the Far East. It was commonly used in the Middle Ages as a culinary spice with Cloves, Nutmeg and Ginger. The plant from which the root came was not described until 1870, when it was named after Prosper Alpinus the sixteenth-century 'teacher of drugs' at Padua University.
Description Perennial rhizomatous herb of flag-like form; stems reaching 1.5 m, covered with long narrow lanceolate leaves; bearing racemes of orchid-shaped flowers, white and veined red; rhizome 3–9 cm long, 2 cm thick; pleasantly aromatic when dried.
Distribution South China, tropical south-east Asia, Iran.
Cultivation Wild; grown commercially.
Constituents Essential oil and resin, both stimulant. Also galangol; galangin; kaempferide.
Uses (dried rhizome) Carminative, stimulant. Similar to Ginger. Of use in flatulent dyspepsia. Once used for seasickness. Snuff for catarrh. Culinary spice. Vinegar and cordial manufacture; brewing. Popular in east European, Russian and Indian cuisine.

Althaea officinalis L MALVACEAE
Marshmallow Sweet Weed/Schloss Tea/Althea
The name is well known as a confectionery; the original *pâte de guimauve* was a soothing paste containing the powdered root. The plant has a long medicinal and culinary history; the Romans considered it a delicious vegetable, and in the ninth century the Emperor Charlemagne promoted its cultivation in Europe. Today it is widely used both in folk and modern medicine.
Description Erect hardy perennial reaching 1–1.25 m high; stem and leaves hairy, latter with 3–5 lobes or undivided and short petioles; 5-petalled white or pink flowers, 3–4 cm in diameter, clustered in leaf axils, appear in late summer until early autumn.
Distribution Moist places throughout Europe from Norway to Spain; temperate parts of western and northern Asia; Asia Minor, Australia, and eastern North America. Prefers saline areas, salt marshes and damp land near to sea or estuaries. Often wild.
Cultivation Wild and commercially cultivated. Propagation by seed sown spring or summer, or division of root-stocks in spring or autumn. Succeeds on light soil if compost introduced below root level to keep cool.
Constituents 30% mucilage comprising glucosan and xylan; responsible for demulcent action. Also sucrose; lecithin; phytosterol; asparagin.
Uses (dried root, 2 years old; leaves, flowers) Demulcent; emollient. Relieves inflammations of mouth and pharynx, and gastritis and gastric ulcers. Externally as poultice for leg ulcers. Powdered root used to bind active ingredients in pill manufacture. Roots boiled and then fried with butter, or young tops eaten in spring salad.

Althaea rosea (L) Cav. MALVACEAE
Hollyhock Common or Garden Hollyhock
Now a well-known and widely distributed decorative garden plant it first reached Europe from China in the sixteenth century, after which it was used both as a medicinal herb and a pot-herb. Turner gave it the name Holyoke in 1548 indicating the blessed mallow, and Lyte in 1578 called it the 'beyondsea rose'.
Description Tall biennial producing in second year spire-like, hairy, flowering stem up to 3 m tall; large, rough, long-stalked 5–7 lobed leaves, in the axils of which are formed flowers, up to 10 cm in diameter on short peduncles. Colour from pale pink or yellow to purple-black. Flowering mid-summer to late autumn.
Distribution Native of China. Now widespread.
Cultivation One of the oldest cultivated plants;

easily raised from seed. Tolerates most soils.
Constituents Mucilage; volatile oil; tannin and anthocyanin pigment.
Uses (dried double purple flowers) Anti-inflammatory, emollient, mildly purgative. Used as tisane for chest complaints or as a mouthwash. Colours wine.

Amaranthus hypochondriacus L AMARANTHACEAE
Amaranth Love-lies-bleeding/Red Cockscomb
This herb is one of a number of Amaranthus species or varieties which have been taken into horticultural cultivation. Most were native to tropical countries where they are predominantly coarse looking plants usually used as pot-herbs. The name derives from the Greek *amaranton* meaning 'not fading' since the crimson flowers do not fade with the death of the plant, and thus the plant came to symbolize immortality. The bright red colour led to the

belief that the plant stopped all kinds of bleeding – part of the seventeenth-century school of thought known as the Doctrine of Signatures.
Description Tall glabrous annual to 2 m; erect, upper parts branched; leaves dull green, spotted with purple, 3–15 cm long, 15 mm to 1.75 cm wide, on thin petioles; the small greenish or usually crimson flowers, borne on erect terminal clusters, to 20 cm long, appear in late summer.
Distribution Native of tropics and American central states. Prefers waste-grounds, cultivated fields.
Cultivation Wild or grown horticulturally from seed sown in spring.
Constituents Mucilage; sugars.
Uses (dried flowering herb) Astringent. Of use in diarrhoea. Externally as wash for ulcers; as gargle for ulcerated mouth; to reduce tissue swelling, and also as douche for leucorrhoea. Young leaves of Amaranthus species widely used as a vegetable.
The related *A. retroflexus* (L) once used as an alternative to soap, due to high saponin content. It was also used as a vegetable; seeds made into flour.

Anacardium occidentale L ANACARDIACEAE
Cashew Nut
Although only the nut or kernel is widely known this tropical tree provides a wide variety of uses and products, and is of some importance in native medicine in Africa and the Americas.
Description Spreading attractive evergreen tree reaching 12 m, bearing alternate oval leaves 10–20 cm long, 3–10 cm wide, and scented panicles 20 cm long of yellow-pink flowers each 1 cm across. Flowers followed by fleshy edible receptacle (cashew-apple) partly enclosing kidney shaped nut.
Distribution Native to tropical American zones; naturalized and cultivated in tropical countries.
Cultivation Commercially in groves and occurs infrequently in the wild.
Constituents Protein; niacin; magnesium; iron; anacardic acid; cardol.

Uses (nut, oil, tree bark, fruit) Nut or kernel nutritive, high protein content. Tree bark once used in certain malarial fevers and fresh shell juice removes warts and corns. Juice from fruit made into wine and spirit. Milky secretion from incised tree makes indelible marking ink. Non-drying lubricant oil from nut. Ammonium salts of resin form hair dye.
Contra-indications Oil from fresh shell strongly vesicant, causing skin blisters.

Anagallis arvensis L PRIMULACEAE
Scarlet Pimpernel Poor Man's Weatherglass
This is an interesting herb which merits modern research. It was held in high esteem from the time of the earliest Greeks until the nineteenth century and is now rarely used, even in folk medicine. Evidence suggests that it is of benefit in melancholia and diseases of the brain; its Latin name derives from the Greek 'to delight', a term given to the herb by Dioscorides; another common name is 'laughter bringer'. The flowers are sensitive, and close if rain threatens.
Description Annual herb; prostrate creeping

square stems up to 30 cm long, thinner branched ascending stems bearing opposite leaves, ovoid and spotted black on the underside; scarlet flowers, often with purple centre, single, long-stalked, appearing in leaf axil from early summer to early autumn. There are two varieties of *Anagallis arvensis*, one red and one blue.
Distribution Widely distributed in temperate zone, especially Europe. Found in loamy soil with high nutrient content; vegetable and cornfields; rare on wasteland.
Constituents Saponin. Active principles not fully understood.
Use (leaf, whole herb, fresh or dried). Diuretic, diaphoretic. Once used in epilepsy, hydrophobia, depression following liver disease, dropsy, and rheumatic conditions. Leaves once used in salads. Cosmetic herb as 'pimpernel water' for freckles.
Contra-indications POISONOUS; there is evidence the plant causes anaemia. Leaves can cause dermatitis.

Anemone alpina L RANUNCULACEAE
Alpine Anemone
Previously classified botanically as *Pulsatilla alpina* Schrank. and *Anemone acutipetala* Hort., this herb formerly enjoyed only local European folk-medical use, and is not mentioned in either classical or modern works.
Description Perennial on thick rhizome; stems reaching 10–40 cm, soft-hairy. Leaves large, long-petioled, ternate then 2-pinnate. Flowers with 6 sepals, solitary, 5–7.5 cm wide, white tinged with violet; appearing mid-spring to early summer.
Distribution Native to the mountains of Europe. Introduced elsewhere.
Cultivation Wild. The subspecies *sulphurea* (L) Hegi, which is characterized by yellow flowers, is found in alpine collections. Propagate by division or root cuttings in autumn or early spring; or from seed as soon as it is ripe.
Constituents Protoanemonine; anemonine.
Uses (whole, dried flowering plant) Irritant; alterative; anodyne.
Formerly used in the treatment of toothache

and rheumatic pain, but due to its toxicity it has fallen into disuse.
Contra-indications POISONOUS; not be taken internally.

Anemone hepatica L RANUNCULACEAE
Kidneywort American Liverwort
This delicate looking herb possesses individual flowers which last for little more than one week but which in that time have the ability to double in length. Its name comes from the Greek *heparatos* meaning liver; in folk medicine it is still used for treating the liver.
Description Small perennial; much branched root-stock; almost evergreen; produces on

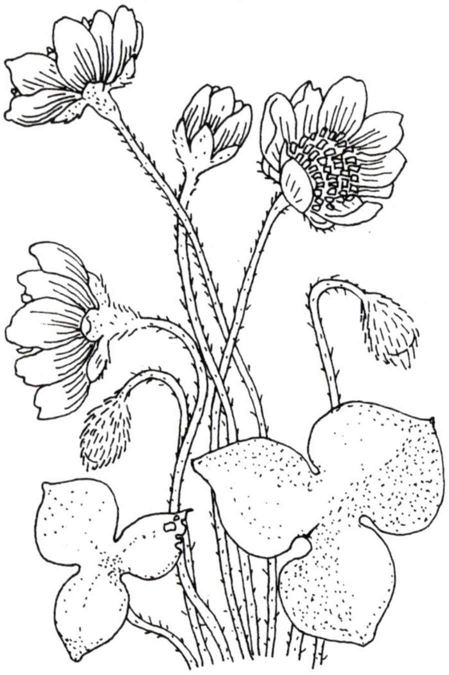

petioles reaching 30 cm kidney-shaped 3-lobed leaves, green above, reddish-purple beneath. Light blue flowers, 4 cm in diameter, born singly on hairy scapes reaching 40 cm; from mid-winter to early autumn.
Distribution North temperate zone; mainly in moist deciduous woodland, preferably calcareous, with loamy soil.
Cultivation Wild plant. Propagate by division soon after flowering; in sheltered position on ordinary soil with good drainage; or from seed gathered and sown in mid-spring. In shade. Seed dispersed by ants.
Constituents Mucilage; tannin; sugar. Action uncertain. Fresh leaf contains the poisonous protoanemonine.
Uses (dried leaves and flowers) Demulcent; pectoral; tonic. Tisane used for liver congestion, kidney, gall-bladder and digestive disorders. Of use as syrup for coughs or bronchitis. Distilled water once used for freckles.
Contra-indications POISONOUS in large doses.

Anemone pulsatilla L RANUNCULACEAE
Pasque Flower Windflower
Legend maintains that anemones only open when a wind is blowing, and the Greek word *anemos* means 'wind'. Certainly this very attractive hairy plant waves about in the slightest breeze, a fact reflected in its specific name *pulsatilla* meaning 'to beat'. Gerard called the herb Pasque Flower as it flowers at Easter. It is still respected in traditional medicine, and is grown widely as a decorative plant.
Description Erect, soft, hairy perennial herb 5–40 cm high, with bi- or tri-pinnate leaves appearing as rosette after solitary flower formed; flowers hairy, dark blue-violet, 6 petals, 3–5 cm long, from late spring to mid-summer.
Distribution Wild on dry, sunny, calcareous slopes throughout Europe. Introduced elsewhere. Prefers well-drained chalky soil, in dry, warm situations.
Cultivation Wild plant. Cultivated by division of rhizomes after flowering or seed sown in shallow tray in spring. Other horticultural varieties are *alba* and *rubra*.

Constituents Fresh plant contains glycoside, ranunculin. This is converted via protoanemonine to anemonine on drying. Action due to anemonine.
Uses (dried aerial parts) Sedative; analgesic; nervine; spasmolytic. Used for headaches, some skin eruptions, earache, painful condition of reproductive organs. Employed homeopathically for measles and also for menstrual pain.
Contra-indications POISONOUS when fresh. Dried herb should only be administered by medical personnel. Overdosage causes violent gastroenteritis and convulsions.

Anethum graveolens L UMBELLIFERAE
Dill Dill Weed/Dill Seed
Dill is mentioned in the Bible and has been in use as a medicinal herb from the earliest times; it is still a constituent of gripe water and is often included in children's medicines. The common name is derived from an old Indo-European word meaning 'to blossom'.
Description Aromatic annual; typically umbelliferous plant, to 1 m tall, with spindle-shaped root, bearing usually one stalk; leaves

feathery, leaflets linear; terminal umbels consisting of numerous yellow flowers in mid-summer.
Distribution Origin southern Europe or western Asia. Wild in cornfields of mediterranean countries. Now widespread garden herb. Tolerates most soils.
Cultivation From seed sown in spring; easily cultivated.
Constituents Oil of Dill comprising, d-carvone; d-limonene; some phellandrine.
Uses (dried ripe fruit, fresh or dried leaf). Carminative; stomachic; slightly stimulant. Excellent as Dill water for digestive problems in children, especially flatulence.
Pickled cucumbers, flavouring for soup, fish, sauces, cakes, pastries. Dill vinegar. Most important in Scandinavian and central European cuisine.
Perfumes soap.

Angelica archangelica L UMBELLIFERAE
Angelica European or Garden Angelica
Now best known as a decorative confectionery made from the candied green stems, Angelica is also an important ingredient of liqueurs and aperitifs. It does not appear to have been used until the fifteenth century, soon after which it acquired a reputation as a plant which gave protection against evil and the plague. The plant's north European origins and its Christianized names hints at its deep association with early Nordic magic.
Description Biennial or perennial; if latter lasting up to 4 years; from 1–2.5 m high, stem hollow, to 6 cm thick, bearing few triangular deeply dentate leaves to 90 cm long. Large spherical umbels of numerous greenish-white flowers, mid-summer to early autumn.
Distribution Native to northern Europe or Asia. Introduced and cultivated elsewhere. Common garden herb; prefers damp meadows, river banks, waste-grounds.
Cultivation Seed rapidly loses viability; sow as soon as ripe in mid-autumn in deep moist soil. Transplant following autumn to 1 m apart, or transplant offshoots from 2 year old plants to

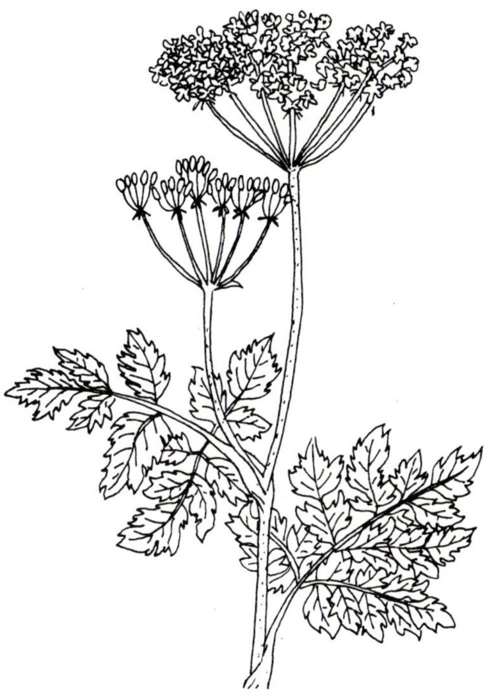

60 cm apart.
Constituents Volatile oil and derivatives of coumarin which stimulate digestive secretions, control peristalsis and increase appetite. Also bitter principles; sugar; valeric and angelic acids.
Uses (dried rhizome and roots, seeds, fresh leaf and stems) Aromatic; stimulant; carminative. Stimulates appetite; of benefit in bronchitis, anorexia nervosa, bronchial catarrh.
Wide culinary and confectionery use. Important constituent of liqueurs such as Benedictine.
Contra-indications Large doses first stimulate and then paralyze the central nervous system.

Antennaria dioica (L) Gaertn. COMPOSITAE
Cat's Foot Life Everlasting/Cudweed
The downy leaves and woolly involucre led to this plant being known as Cotton Weed; its botanical name Antennaria comes from the fact that the pappus resembles antennae. This species was not important even in folk medicine, but much use is made of it in dried flower arrangements. Various related species, however, have been used more than the species *dioica* – for example, an American relative, *Gnaphalium polycephalum* (*A. dioica* previously classified as *Gnaphalium dioicum*) was a favourite Indian remedy for mouth ulcers, and the Chinese herbalists use *G. multiceps* (Wall.) to treat coughs.
Description Stoloniferous, dioecious perennial, 5–20 cm high, on single unbranched erect or decumbent stem. Spatulate basal leaves in a rosette to 2.5 cm long, white and tomentose beneath, green and glabrous above. Linear-lanceolate stem leaves. Flowers 5 mm long in dense terminal involucre, which is woolly at base. White male flowers and pink female appear early summer to early autumn.
Distribution Native to central and western Europe, United States and the North Pacific Aleutian islands; to 2500 m altitude, on semi-dry pasture, light dry woodland and thickets; prefers poor, porous, sandy dry soils.
Cultivation Wild plant.
Constituents Tannin; essential oil; resin; a bitter principle. The combined action promotes the flow of bile.
Uses (dried flowering plant) Astringent; choleretic; weak diuretic.
Once used in mixtures for the treatment of bronchitis and bilious conditions. May be used in diarrhoea, and as a throat gargle.

Anthriscus cerefolium (L) Hoffm. UMBELLIFERAE
Chervil Garden Chervil
Although this is an important culinary herb in France it is not widely grown or used outside that country. It is however one of the best herbs for growing in boxes, and will supply fresh leaf throughout the winter if it is sown regularly in a warm greenhouse.
Description Annual sweet-smelling herb reaching 70 cm high, with pale green delicate leaves, deeply segmented. Stem slightly hairy; flowers white, 2 mm in diameter, in flat umbels, produced mid-summer.
Distribution Native to Middle East, south Russia, the Caucasus. Cultivated in warm and temperate climates. Prefers light soil with degree of moisture.
Cultivation Easily cultivated from seed, lightly pressed into soil at permanent site, early to mid-spring or autumn. Rapid germination and soon runs to seed. May be sown in boxes for winter supply.
Constituents Volatile oil; stimulates the metabolism.
Uses (fresh leaf before flowering) Stomachic. Warm poultice applied to painful joints. Mainly used for culinary purposes; will complement most dishes.

Aphanes arvensis agg. ROSACEAE
Parsley Piert Breakstone Parsley
The common name is derived both from a superficial resemblance to Parsley and from the old French *perce-pierre* signifying a plant which grows through stony ground. The Flemish botanist De L'Obel suggested in 1570 that although the herb was not widely used by herbalists, it was commonly employed by the poor to 'break' stones in the kidney or bladder. Today it is one of the most highly respected plants used in the treatment of kidney stones.
Description Annual; thin branched stem up to 20 cm tall; leaves, 3–5 lobes, wedge shaped; insignificant flowers 1.5–2 mm in diameter borne in axillary clusters; appearing from late spring until late autumn.
Distribution Native British herb, common in parts of Europe on bare soil in dry places, cornfields, wasteland, walls, gravel pits. Calcifugous.

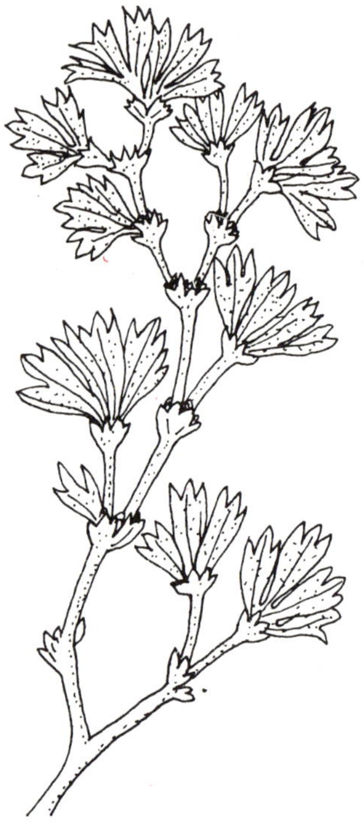

Cultivation Wild plant.
Constituents An astringent principle.
Uses (dried leaf and flowers) Diuretic; demulcent. Considered most effective when freshly collected and dried in the treatment of kidney stones, bladder stones or painful urination.

Apium graveolens L UMBELLIFERAE
Celery Wild Celery/Smallage
Until the seventeenth century all celery flavour was provided by this wild herb, which although somewhat bitter to present day palates, was a favourite of the Romans. The Celery we eat today was developed initially by Italian gardeners on the plain of the Po.
Description Biennial with bulbous fleshy root, producing branched angular stem 30 cm – 1 m high in second year. Leaves opposite, 10–15 cm long, dark green, dentate with fan-shaped leaflets; small grey-white flowers in sparse compound umbels from late summer to early winter. Strong smelling.

Distribution Southern European native. Wild in marshy and salty soils in Africa, Europe, South and North America.
Cultivation Wild plant.
Constituents Volatile oils; apiol.
Uses (fresh or dried plant, seeds) Tonic; appetizer; carminative. Strong diuretic if fresh juice used. Once recommended in treatment of rheumatism, excess weight, loss of appetite. Decoction of seed beneficial in nervousness. Dried leaf may replace celery for soups, sauces, and stocks, although it has a stronger taste than Celery.

Apocynum cannabinum L APOCYNACEAE
Canadian Hemp Hemp Dogbane/Black Indian Hemp
This was one of many North American plants introduced to settlers by native Indians. No longer used in medicine.
Description Perennial to 2 m high, stems erect, branched only at top, bearing ovoid leaves

with hairy lower surface, to 7.5 cm long; flowers small, whitish-green in terminal clusters, followed by thin double pods 10–15 cm long. Flowers late summer. Root up to 2 m long.
Distribution North America, near streams, open ground, forest borders, in gravel or sandy soil.
Cultivation Wild plant.
Constituents Apocynamarin, a cynotoxin; symarin; apocynin and derivatives; phytosterols. Action of a heart stimulant, dilates renal arteries.
Uses (dried rhizome, roots, bark) Diuretic; powerful emetic; laxative. Used in folk medicine in North America to treat worms and fever. Powerful heart stimulant. The fibrous bark employed as substitute for hemp in manufacture of nets and twine.
Contra-indications POISONOUS; greatest caution needed in usage.

Aquilegia vulgaris L RANUNCULACEAE
Columbine European Crowfoot
Columbine is from the Latin *columba* meaning dove. In the Middle Ages it was referred to as aquilinae and ackeley after the Latin *aquila* meaning eagle – both terms referring to the

flower shape.
The herb's antiscorbutic effect was recorded in the Württemberg Pharmacopoeia of 1741, but in the nineteenth century *A. vulgaris* fell from official use.
Description Stout perennial with pubescent stems branched at the top; 60–80 cm tall. Basal leaves long-petioled, biternate, upper leaves sessile. Leaflets 3-lobed, crenate. Flowers few to many, nodding on long peduncles, violet-blue or white, 5 cm diameter; appearing early summer.
Distribution Native to Europe. Naturalized in eastern North America, and introduced elsewhere. In mixed woodland, mountain forest on rich calcareous soils to 2000 m altitude.
Cultivation Wild. Frequently grown as a garden ornamental, especially the double-flowered cultivars *Alba Plena* and *Flore Pleno*. Propagate by seed or by division in spring.
Constituents Cyanogenic glycoside; vitamin C; lipid; an uncharacterized alkaloid.
Uses (Root, flowers and leaves) Antiseptic; astringent; weakly sedative.
No longer employed internally; once used in homeopathy to treat nervous conditions. Only the root may be used, externally, for the treatment of ulcers.
Contra-indications POISONOUS. Seeds may be fatal to children. Most parts have a similarly poisonous effect as Monkshood (*Aconitum napellus L*). Medical use only.

Arachis hypogaea L LEGUMINOSAE
Peanut Ground-nut
Although the Peanut is now one of the best known and universally grown edible nuts, it was not until 1840 that Jaubert, a French colonist of Cape Verde, suggested its importation into Marseilles as an oil seed. The first to mention the plant was Fernandez de Oviedo y Valdes who lived in Haiti from 1513 to 1525

and reported that Indians widely cultivated the *mani* – a name for *Arachis* still used in South America and Cuba.
Description Annual herbaceous legume, 25–50 cm tall; stems slightly hairy; leaves consist of 2 pairs of leaflets, oval, 5 cm long. Yellow

flowers possess long calyx tube; after flowering the stem bearing the ovary elongates, bends towards the ground and forces the young pod beneath the soil. Pod oblong, 2.5 cm long, containing 1–4 irregularly ovoid seeds.
Distribution South American native. Widely cultivated, especially Africa, India, China, and America.
Cultivation Unknown in the wild state; grown on a large scale commercially and horticulturally in tropical and subtropical countries.
Constituents Peanut or arachide oil, consisting of the glycerides of 4 fatty acids.
Uses (seed, oil expressed from seeds) Nutritive: the seed is an important foodstuff. Used as a substitute for olive oil. Employed in the manufacture of soap.

Arbutus unedo L ERICACEAE
Strawberry Tree Cane Apples
Known to Dioscorides and early Arabian physicians, but never widely employed; it deserves modern investigation, however.
Arbutus is an ancient name, while *unedo* is from the Latin phrase *unum edo* or I eat only one, after the supposed unpleasantness of the fruit.
Description Erect evergreen shrub or tree 3–10 m tall. Young bark reddish. Leaves alternate, petiolate, serrate, oblong to obovate, shiny above, 5–10 cm long. Flowers creamy-white or pinkish, urceolate, in nodding panicles 5 cm long, appearing late autumn to mid-winter, followed by scarlet, warty berry.
Distribution Native to south Europe, eastern France and Ireland. Introduced elsewhere. In damp situations often in woodland.
Cultivation Wild, locally abundant. Grown horticulturally in warm regions on well-drained soils; requires wind protection. Propagate by seeds and cuttings of half-ripened wood in autumn under glass; also by layering.
Constituents Tannins; arbutoside; ethyl gallate,

the latter possessing strong antibiotic activity against the Mycobacterium bacteria.
Uses (bark, root, leaves, fruit) Antiseptic; anti-inflammatory; astringent; diuretic.
May be used to treat diarrhoea and biliousness, and possibly of use in arteriosclerosis. A decoction provides an excellent antiseptic wash, gargle or poultice. Formerly employed in certain kidney and liver complaints. The flower has weak diaphoretic properties.
Fruit can be used with discretion in alcoholic drinks or preserves such as marmalade. The bark was once used in leather tanning. The wood provides good quality charcoal, and is suitable for turning and marquetry.

Arctium lappa L COMPOSITAE
Greater Burdock Beggar's Buttons/Lappa
A herb with dock-shaped leaves, and fruiting heads covered with hooked spines or burrs, from which characteristics the name is derived. It also resembles Rhubarb, and several common names such as Gypsy's Rhubarb, Pig's Rhubarb and Snake's Rhubarb refer to this. Still widely employed in folk medicine for skin problems, and cultivated commercially in Japan for use as a vegetable.

Description Biennial or short-lived perennial to 2 m; 5 cm thick hairy stems. Vertical roots 1 m long. Large leaves, ovate and petiolate with undulate margins. Small tubular flowers red to purple, consisting of disc florets only, in spherical capitula of 3–5 cm diameter. Fruit surrounded by hooked bracts (burr). Appearing late summer to mid-autumn.
Distribution European native. North America. Prefers weedy sites and roadsides, on loamy, nitrogen-rich soil.
Cultivation Wild plant; cultivated commercially from seed in Japan.
Constituents Inulin; bitter principle; volatile oil; resin; several antibiotic substances.
Uses (root, fresh or dried – from first year plants; fruits, rarely the leaves) Diuretic. Increases resistance to infection. Of use in various skin diseases, especially psoriasis and eczema.
Stalks, before flowering, may be eaten as salad or boiled as vegetable.
Stalks are candied in the same way as angelica. Chopped root cooked and eaten.

Arctostaphylos uva-ursi (L) Spreng.
ERICACEAE
Bearberry Uva-ursi/Mountain box
This herb's common name comes from the Greek *arkton staphyle* signifying 'bear's grapes'. It was used in the thirteenth century by the Welsh physicians of Myddvai, described in detail by Clusius in 1601, and officially recognized to be of medical importance in 1763 by several German physicians working in Berlin. Although use of the herb declined, recent research has shown that it possesses effective antiseptic properties.
Description Trailing or creeping evergreen shrub; to 15 cm high, forming mats of dark green, leathery, ovoid leaves 1–2 cm long. Small flowers, white or pink in terminal clusters of 3–12, followed by red fruit of 5 mm diameter. Appearing early spring to mid-summer.

Distribution Cool regions of northern hemisphere. In coniferous woodland, moors, alpine mats, on porous acid humus-rich soils.
Cultivation Wild plant.
Constituents Arbutin and methylarbutin, which produce antiseptic substances related to phenol. Also flavonoids; tannins; gallic and egallic acids.
Uses (dried leaves) Diuretic; antiseptic. Specifically used in kidney and bladder infections. Once used for bronchitis and urinary incontinence.
Used for leather tanning. Ash coloured dye. Grouse feed.
Added to smoking mixtures.
Contra-indications Prolonged use results in constipation.

Areca catechu L ARECACEAE
Areca Nut Betel Nut
Areca is also known as Betel Nut since it is a constituent of the 'betel' chewing mixture which is a widespread habit in the East. The mixture consists of Areca, a little lime and leaves of the Betel plant (*Piper betle*). As early as 140 B.C. Chinese conquerors of the Malayan archipelago returned with samples of the Areca palm and nuts, which became known as pin-lang after the Malay word, *pinang*, for them. Asians chew small pieces of the nut to sweeten the breath, strengthen gums and improve digestion.
Description Elegant palm; straight smooth trunk 12–30 m high, 50 cm circumference. Numerous feathery leaflets 30–60 cm long, upper confluent and glabrous. Flowers on branching spadix, male above and numerous; female usually solitary and below. Fruit ovoid 5 cm long, orange or scarlet, in bunches of up to 100.
Distribution Maritime Malaysian native; cultivated in India, Ceylon, Malaya, Burma, East Africa. Introduced into American tropics as an ornamental. Prefers coastal sites.
Cultivation Collected from wild, and cultivated in coastal areas.
Constituents Tannin; gallic acid; oil; gum; four alkaloids, one of which resembles pilocarpine; also areca red.

Uses (fruit – ripe or unripe) Astringent; stimulant; taenicide. Once used in human urinary tract disorders, and for the expulsion of tapeworms. Use now restricted to veterinary medicine.
Dentifrice, using the charcoal made from the nut. Chewed as a masticatory in combination with a little lime and a *Piper Betle* leaf. Stains lips and teeth red.
Contra-indications Toxic in large doses; medical use restricted to veterinary.

Aristolochia clematitis L ARISTOLOCHIACEAE
Birthwort Birchwort
The fact that the herb was at one time considered important in childbirth is emphasized by its common and Latin names. *Aristolochia* is derived from the Greek *aristos* meaning best and *locheia* meaning childbirth. William Turner, the father of English botany, gave the herb its common name in the sixteenth century. The herb has not been subjected to modern investigation and is rarely employed.

Description Perennial on long rhizome; stem erect or slightly twining to 50 cm high; heart-shaped dark green leaves with long petioles. Flowers axillary, 3 cm long, yellowish-green appearing from early summer to mid-autumn.
Distribution Europe and temperate North America, Japan. In thickets, vineyards, weedy edges of fields, in warmer situations on calcareous soil.
Cultivation Wild plant.
Constituents Aristolochine, which is similar to colchicine.
Uses (dried root-stock, entire fresh flowering plant) Diaphoretic; emmenagogue; oxytocic; stimulant. Once used in rheumatism and gout. Juice from stems once used to induce childbirth.

Aristolochia serpentaria L ARISTOLOCHIACEAE
Virginia Snakeroot Birthwort/Serpentary
The earliest belief concerning this herb was that it would give protection from poisoning. Specimens from Virginia were growing in London in 1632, and were described by Thomas Johnson. Serpentary was introduced into European medical usage via the London Pharmacopoeia of 1650, and as late as 1741 Geoffroy was praising its effectiveness as a remedy for rattlesnake and rabid dog bites. A century after this it was only being used as a diaphoretic, and then often in combination with Cinchona bark. It is now seldom used even in folk medicine.

Description Perennial herb 25–40 cm high, with erect, slightly branched stems bearing heart-shaped pointed leaves 7.5 cm long; roots fibrous. Dull purple to brown flowers arising singly on short stalk coming from the stem base.
Distribution East Central and southern United States; in shady woods.
Cultivation Wild plant.
Constituents Essential oil; resin; aristolochine.
Uses (dried root-stock) Stimulating tonic; diaphoretic; anodyne; nervine; once used for treating snake bites. Used in early stages of infectious diseases. Small doses stimulate appetite.
Contra-indications Large doses act as irritant, and cause vomiting and vertigo. Respiratory paralysis may also occur.

Armeria maritima (Mill.) Willd.
PLUMBAGINACEAE
Thrift Sea Pink
Sea Pink now belongs to the genus Armeria which consists of at least 100 closely related species and many more subspecies and varieties which are often exceedingly difficult to differentiate. This genus was formerly called *Statice* (*A. maritima* was known as *Statice armeria* L) and is closely related to the Sea Lavender genus – also once called *Statice* but now known as *Limonium*. The American Sea Lavender (*Limonium vulgare* Mill.) has similar antiseptic properties, but like Thrift it is now very rarely used for medicinal purposes.
Thrift has most widely been used as an edging

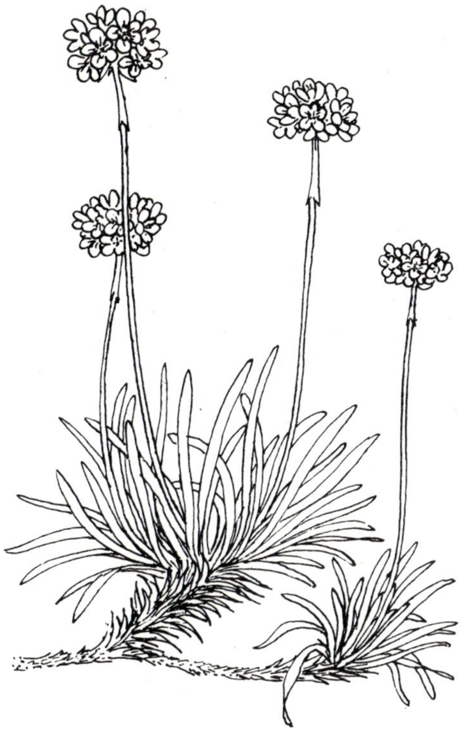

plant in formal gardens, and from the sixteenth to the eighteenth centuries few species were as popular for this purpose.
Description Grass-like perennial on branched woody root-stock forming basal rosette of narrow (3 mm) linear, 1-nerved (occasionally 3-nerved), acute or obtuse, fleshy and glandular leaves, 2–15 cm long, ciliate at the edges. Flowers stalked, rose-pink (or occasionally white), corolla 8 mm diameter, in dense globular heads, 1.5–3 cm diameter, on leafless, downy scape 20–55 cm tall. Appearing mid-spring to mid-autumn. Variable in form.
Distribution Native to Europe, Asia and North America; on dry sandy somewhat acidic soils in sandy turf, coastal salt-marshes, cliffs and mountain pastures to 1400 m altitude.
Cultivation Wild; frequently found growing in dense evergreen masses. Propagate from seed sown in spring on light, dry, well-drained soil, in full sun or partial shade; or by division of clumps, replanting every 2 years, 25 cm apart.
Constituents A napthaquinone, plumbagone; mineral salts comprising mainly iodine, bromine, and fluorine; mucilage. Antibiotic action due to plumbagone.
Uses (dried flowering plant) Antibiotic; anti-obesic. Once used in the treatment of obesity, certain nervous disorders, and urinary infections. Cannot be employed as an antiseptic poultice as it may cause dermatitis or local irritation. Rarely used, even in folk medicine. May be employed horticulturally as an excellent, low, evergreen edging plant for formal arrangements.

Armoracia rusticana Gaertn, Mey et Scherb.
CRUCIFERAE
Horseradish
Linnaeus gave Horseradish the botanical name, *Cochlearia armoracia*, after *cochleare*, an obsolete name for a spoon which its leaves were thought

to resemble, and *armoracia*, the Roman name for a wild Radish which cannot be identified with certainty as Horseradish. Gerard gave the herb its present common name, but before him it was known in English as Red Cole or Redcol. Certainly the plant appears to have been more popular in Scandinavia and Germany and otherwise did not find much use in western Europe until the middle of the seventeenth century. The French called it *moutarde des allemands*, and druggists knew it as *Raphanus rusticanus*.
Description Perennial to 1.5 m high on stout, tapering, fleshy taproot to 60 cm long and 5 cm thick; large basal leaves, 30–100 cm long, coarse, lanceolate with dentate margins and long petioles. Erect flowering racemes 50 cm–1 m high bearing clusters of white flowers and, beneath, stem leaves with short petioles. Appears mid-summer to mid-autumn.
Distribution South-east European native; introduced and cultivated elsewhere; tolerates most dampish soils.
Cultivation Wild plant. Cultivated commercially and horticulturally. Propagate by root division in spring or autumn, planting at 50-cm intervals, or sow seed in early spring and thin later. Grows vigorously.
Constituents Fresh root contains a glycoside, sinigrin, which is decomposed in the presence of water by the enzyme myrosin, producing mustard oil – allyl isothiocyanate; vitamin C; antibiotic substances.
Uses (fresh root) Stimulant; rubefacient; weak diuretic.
May be taken internally as a syrup for bronchitis, bronchial catarrh, coughs, and to stimulate digestive organs. Applied externally as sliced root on boils or as a rubefacient poultice in rheumatism.
Most widely used for culinary purposes, especially in sauces and vinegars; complements fish, poultry, and beef.
Contra-indications May be vesicant to some skins; large internal doses produce inflammation of the gastro-intestinal mucosae.

Arnica montana L COMPOSITAE
Arnica Mountain Tobacco
When grown at high latitudes such as in Arctic Asia or America, a form of this herb is produced which is characterized by narrow leaves; although this was once renamed by Vahl as *Arnica angustifolia*, it is really a variant form of *Arnica montana*. The herb was known by Matthiolus and other botanists, and was widely used in sixteenth-century German folk medicine. Largely as the result of exaggerated claims by a Viennese physician, it enjoyed short-lived popularity among the medical profession in the late eighteenth century.
Description Aromatic perennial with creeping rhizome, producing a basal rosette of 4–8 downy leaves 4–7 cm long in the first year. Flowering stem usually unbranched, hairy, 30–60 cm high, with only 1–2 pairs of opposite leaves. Flowers golden-yellow, daisy-like, appearing mid-summer to early autumn.
Distribution Central and northern regions of the northern hemisphere. Prefers sandy acid soils, rich in humus, in a sunny position.
Cultivation Root division in spring; or seed sown in spring in cold frame and transplanted in early summer. Seed may be slow to germinate, occasionally as long as 2 years. Wild plant, but protected in parts of Europe.
Constituents Polyacetylenic compounds in volatile oil; flavones; arnicin; phulin; inulin; unknown substances acting on the circulatory system which initially lower the blood pressure, and later raise it. Also substances which increase biliary secretion.
Uses (dried flower-heads, dried rhizome) Stimulant; diuretic; rubefacient. It is an irritant to the digestive tract and kidneys, and hence only of use externally – in bruising, sprains and dislocations. Homeopathic doses are effective in epilepsy, seasickness and possibly as hair growth stimulants. Used as a gargle for treating inflammations of the throat.
Contra-indications POISONOUS: can be toxic if taken internally. Repeated external use may cause skin irritation.

Artemisia abrotanum L COMPOSITAE
Southernwood Lad's Love/Old Man
In common with other members of the Artemisia family this is a strong-smelling herb which has the ability to repel insects. For this reason it was called *garde robe* by the French who used it to protect clothes from attack by moths. It was also considered effective against infection and employed in nosegays by court-room and jail officials. The name Southernwood is derived from the Old English *sutherne-wudu* meaning a woody plant from the south, since it is a native of southern Europe. At one time herbalists considered the herb an aphrodisiac, which led to the common name Lad's Love.

Description Perennial subshrub to 90 cm high; with branched feathery grey-green leaves 6 cm long, finely divided and somewhat downy. Flowers very small, inconspicuous, yellowish-white, in loose panicles, appearing late summer to early autumn.
Distribution Southern European native; introduced and widespread in temperate zones as garden plant. Naturalized in North America.
Cultivation Easily propagated from young, green cuttings in summer, or heeled cuttings from old wood in autumn. Prefers full sun and light to medium soil with added compost. Needs hard clipping in mid-spring to prevent straggling growth. May not flower.
Constituents Essential oil, mainly absinthol.
Uses (dried whole plant) Stimulant; emmenagogue; antiseptic; antihelmintic. Once used as a powder mixed with treacle to treat worms in children. Used in aromatic baths and poultices for skin conditions.
Leaves discourage moths.
Stems yield yellow dye. Foliage used in floral decorations.

Artemisia absinthium L COMPOSITAE
Wormwood Absinthe/Green Ginger
Several species of *absinthium* are mentioned by Dioscorides, and many of them were employed for the removal of intestinal worms. Although one of the most bitter herbs known, it has for centuries been a major ingredient of aperitifs and herb wines. Both absinthe and vermouth obtain their names from the plant, the latter being an eighteenth-century French variation of the German *Wermut* which was also the origin of the English name Wormwood. The herb contains several substances which may adversely affect the body if taken in excess (including the hallucinogen, santonin) and for this reason it produces some of the strongest, and most dangerous, alcoholic drinks.

Description Perennial undershrub 0.75–1 m high; hairy stems bearing highly aromatic bipinnate and tripinnate leaves covered in down. Flower-heads 3–4 mm diameter, with grey-green bracts and numerous minute yellow florets, appearing late summer to late autumn.
Distribution Central Europe, North America, Asia. Widely introduced garden plant. Found on waste-ground, especially near the sea, in warm regions.
Cultivation Wild plant. Propagated by seed sown outside in late spring, thinned to 30–60 cm apart. Often slow to germinate. Cuttings taken in summer; root division in spring or autumn. Prefers medium soil in full sun or slight shade.
Constituents Bitter principle and volatile oil which stimulate secretions and promote appetite; also a glucoside; resins and starch; antihelmintic action due to santonin.
Uses (whole flowering plant, leaves) Anthelmintic; antipyretic; antiseptic; stomachic. Used to aid digestion, stimulate digestion or for abdominal colic. The tincture was formerly used in nervous diseases. Used in liniments. Used in vermouth, in absinthe, as a tea, and for stuffing geese. Some countries ban its use in wine.
Contra-indications Habitual use causes convulsions, restlessness and vomiting. Overdose causes vertigo, cramps, intoxication, and delirium.

Artemisia dracunculoides L COMPOSITAE
Tarragon Russian Tarragon
Unlike French Tarragon the flavour of this variety improves as the plant ages, although never achieving the delicacy of *Artemisia dracunculus*. The Latin name is derived from *dracunculus* meaning 'little dragon' after a herbalist's description of the coiled serpent-like root. Artemisia was the Greek name for Diana who was regarded as the discoverer of the *Artemisia* group of herbs. Russian Tarragon is also called *Artemisia redowskii.*
Description Perennial 1.5 m high with erect, branched stems bearing smooth, pale green entire leaves 3–6 cm long, and clusters of greyish-white woolly flowers in late summer.
Distribution Asia and Siberia. Introduced elsewhere.
Cultivation Wild, and cultivated as garden plant. Seed sown under glass in mid-spring or in the open in early summer. Root division in spring or autumn; cuttings in spring. Hardy during winter and tolerates any soil.
Constituents Essential oil identical to Anise, largely lost during drying.
Uses (dried or fresh herb) Fresh herb promotes appetite.

Similar uses to French Tarragon (*Artemisia dracunculus*) but of inferior flavour.

Artemisia dracunculus L COMPOSITAE
Tarragon French Tarragon
An essential component of French cuisine, plants of the 'true' French Tarragon are difficult to obtain and almost as difficult to maintain. Even under ideal circumstances the delicate flavour of this variety tends to revert

to the coarser flavour of Russian Tarragon. Similarly unless it is dried carefully an inferior product results. The common name is derived from the Arabic *tarkhun*, via the Spanish *taragoncia*.
Description Perennial 90 cm high with slim, erect, branched stems, bearing smooth, dark shiny entire leaves 3–5 cm long, and clusters of greyish-green or white woolly flowers, appearing mid-summer to late summer.
Distribution Southern Europe. Introduced elsewhere as garden plant or for commercial cultivation.
Cultivation Cultivated commercially in Europe and the United States. Cannot be propagated from seed. Divide roots in spring or autumn or take cuttings in spring. Renew every 3 years from young cuttings. Protect in warm situation during winter, especially when young. Prefers a richer soil than Russian Tarragon, and may require the addition of peat. Can be grown indoors as a pot herb. Will not tolerate wet soil.
Constituents Essential oil.
Uses (dried or fresh herb) No modern medicinal use – formerly used in toothache. The herb promotes appetite.
Widely used as flavouring for salads, steak,

fish, preserves, pickles, shellfish, lobster, herb butter, vinegars, and is best known for its use with chicken.
Used in some perfumes and liqueurs.

Artemisia vulgaris L COMPOSITAE
Mugwort Felon Herb/St John's Herb
An ancient magical plant, deeply respected throughout Europe, China and Asia, and once known as the Mother of Herbs (*Mater Herbarum*). It was one of the nine herbs employed to repel demons and venoms in pre-Christian times. Although used to flavour drinks, and especially beer, the common name is derived from the Old Saxon *muggia wort* meaning 'midge plant' after its ability to repel insects.
Description Erect sparsely pubescent perennial; stems grooved with reddish-purple colouring, angular, reaching 1.75 m. Leaves 2.5–5 cm long, dark green above, whitish and downy on the underside; pinnate or bipinnate with

toothed leaflets. Flowers brownish-yellow to red, numerous, small, arranged on panicles and appearing late summer to mid-autumn.
Distribution Asia, Europe. Naturalized in North America. Common on various soils, especially if they are nitrogen-rich. In wastelands, hedgerows and near rivers and streams.
Cultivation Wild and cultivated. Seed sown in spring. Root division spring and autumn. Grows quickly and needs restricting in gardens. A variegated form also exists.
Constituents Volatile oil; resin; tannin; a bitter principle, absinthin, which stimulates digestion.
Uses (dried flowering shoots, leaves, roots) Diuretic; emmenagogue. Used as an aid in irregular menstruation, for lack of appetite, and weak digestion. Chinese employ the cones of the leaves (moxas) for rheumatism, in the therapeutic method known as moxibustion. Used as a tea. A culinary herb for stuffing geese, duck or other fatty fish or meat.
Repels flies and moths. Leaves may be used in tobaccos.
Formerly used for flavouring and the clarification of beer.
Contra-indications Large prolonged dosage injures the nervous system.

Arum maculatum L ARACEAE
Cuckoopint Lords and Ladies/Arum
Because of the obvious sexual symbolism of the erect spadix of this attractive plant, almost all its European common names have some sexual connotation. Even Dioscorides suggested that the herb was an aphrodisiac. It may have been for this reason that large quantities of the tubers were processed and sold as a foodstuff in the eighteenth and nineteenth centuries. The herb was also called Starchwort, and root starch obtained from it was employed to starch ruffs in the sixteenth century, even though the practice often caused blisters on the hands of those who used it.
Description Perennial plant arising from ovoid tuber 2 cm diameter; arrow-shaped leaves to 25 cm long, plain dark green or with dark brown-purplish spots. Flowers occur at base of purplish club-shaped spadix which is enclosed in characteristic 15-cm long leafy greenish-

white bract (spathe). Flowers appear late spring to early summer, followed by scarlet fruits.
Distribution Central and western Europe, north Africa, introduced elsewhere. Found in porous loamy soils, in warm damp sites, hedgerows, woods.
Cultivation Wild plant.
Constituents Aroine, an unstable skin and mucosa irritant, which is largely broken down on drying; starch; gums; saponin; sugar.
Uses (fresh or dried leaves, dried tubers) Diuretic; strong purgative; no longer employed internally. Bruised fresh plant applied externally in rheumatic pain. Used homeopathically for sore throats.
Well-baked tubers are edible, nutritious and harmless.
Root starch, after roasting or boiling, and then drying and powdering, produces an arrowroot substitute used for starching.
Contra-indications All parts of fresh plant are POISONOUS.

Asarum canadense L ARISTOLOCHIACEAE
Wild Ginger Canadian Snakeroot
As the name suggests the root-stock may be used as a substitute for root Ginger. American colonists found the herb was an effective stimulant when taken as a tea, and American Indians believed a decoction of the root-stock to be an effective contraceptive.
Description Stemless ginger-smelling perennial, with round, fleshy root and branched, hairy, root stalks each bearing 2 kidney-shaped leaves, dark green above, pale green beneath, 10–20 cm wide. Flowers single, bell-shaped, dull brownish-purple, appearing close to the ground in summer.
Distribution Canada and northern United

States, Russia, Far East. In rich woodland on moist shaded sites.
Cultivation Wild plant.
Constituents Volatile oil; resin; a bitter principle; asarin; sugars; alkaloid.
Uses (root-stock) Stimulant; tonic; diuretic; diaphoretic; carminative. Tea used in flatulence and indigestion. Thought to exert direct influence on the uterus.
May be used as a substitute for root Ginger.
Oil used in perfumery.
Dried root used as snuff to relieve headaches.
Contra-indications Large doses cause nausea.

Asarum europaeum L ARISTOLOCHIACEAE
Asarabacca Hazelwort/Wild Nard
An inconspicuous herb with nut-shaped flowers and cyclamen-shaped leaves, it was called *asaron* and introduced into medicine by Dioscorides. Herbalists of the Middle Ages incorrectly called the plant *baccharis*, a name given by Dioscorides to another herb which was probably a true cyclamen. Sixteenth-century apothecaries joined the names and described the Hazelwort as Asarabacca. Most members of the family Aristolochiaceae are climbing woody plants from South America.
Description Herbaceous perennial bearing 2 kidney-shaped, leathery, long-stalked leaves on short pubescent stems. Inflorescence arises from thick root-stock and flowers on soil surface or leaf mould. Single purplish flower appears early summer to early autumn.
Distribution Europe, Siberia, Caucasus; in woods and shady sites. Introduced elsewhere in temperate zones as a garden plant.
Cultivation Wild plant. May be propagated by root division in autumn; prefers moist, calcareous soil, rich in humus and shaded.
Constituents Volatile oil; bitter principle; alkaloid; sugars; resin.
Uses (dried root and leaves) Emetic; purgative; sternutatory; stimulant in small doses.
Produces copious mucus flow if taken as snuff.
Once an ingredient of tobacconists' 'head-clearin' snuff'.

Asclepias tuberosa L ASCLEPIADACEAE
Pleurisy Root Butterfly Milk Weed
Once officially recognized and included in the United States Pharmacopoeia and long used as an important medicinal herb, it is still employed in European and American folk medicine. Appalachian Indians made a tea from the leaves to induce vomiting during certain religious ceremonies. Several species of Asclepias are grown in warm climates as attractive garden plants.
Description Attractive perennial to 1 m; fleshy white root-stock supporting few stout hairy stems, bearing hairy alternate, lanceolate leaves 5–15 cm long and darker green above. Numerous erect, beautiful orange-yellow flowers in terminal umbels appearing mid-summer to mid-autumn, followed by long, narrow seed pods.
Distribution North American native; common in dry, sandy or gravelly soils on roadsides.
Cultivation Wild plant – propagate by division of root-stock in spring.
Constituents Glycosides, including asclepiadin; resins; volatile oil.
Uses (dried root-stock) Diaphoretic; antispasmodic; carminative; expectorant. Specially of use in infections of the respiratory tract such as pleurisy. Powdered roots used as a poultice on open sores.
Young seed pods and root-stock may be boiled and eaten.
Contra-indications Very large doses cause diarrhoea and vomiting. Fresh leaf tea causes vomiting.

Aspalathus linearis (Burm. fil.) R. Dahlgr.
LEGUMINOSAE
Rooibosch Red Bush Tea
Rooibosch was traditionally used by South African Bushmen and Hottentots and its popularity was noted by the botanist Carl Thunberg when he visited the Cape in 1772.
The common name derives from the red colour of the leaves and shoots which develops, together with a distinctive aroma, during the fermentation process necessary to obtain the tea.
Commercial exploitation of the tea, which is now gaining in popularity in Europe, began in the early twentieth century after successful experiments to improve seed germination and cropping techniques.
Description Shrub or shrublet, decumbent or erect to 2 m. Branches bearing thin (0.4–1 mm wide), glabrous leaves, 1.5–6 cm long, and short, leafy shoots in the leaf axils. Small, bright yellow flowers, often with violet tinge; followed by 1.5 cm long pod.

Distribution South African native; especially in western Cape, on well-drained, sandy but moisture-retaining, non-acidic soils.
Cultivation Wild. Cultivated commercially in South Africa from seed sown 10 mm deep in late winter or early spring in seed-beds; seedlings transplanted in mid or late summer when 10–20 cm tall. Later trimmed to promote branching. Plantations replaced every 6 or 7 years.
Constituents Vitamin C; tannin (1–3%); mineral salts; quercitin; unknown substances.
Uses (dried fermented young leaves and branches) Anti-spasmodic; tonic.
Of benefit in vomiting, diarrhoea, and other mild gastric complaints. Clinically untested but traditionally is considered of use in certain allergic disorders – especially milk allergy.

Mostly employed as a hot or cold beverage: also used as a culinary herb, and as a flavouring in baking.

Asparagus officinalis L LILIACEAE

Asparagus Garden Asparagus/Sparrow Grass

Known as Sperage or Sparrow Grass in the sixteenth century, the Garden Asparagus (*Asparagus officinalis* subsp. *officinalis*) has been cultivated as a delicacy for over 2000 years. It became an 'official' medicinal herb due to its laxative and diuretic properties, and some herbalists claimed it also increased the libido. In parts of eastern Europe Asparagus grows wild and is eaten by cattle. The name is from the Greek word meaning 'to sprout'.

Description Perennial with short root-stock 5 cm long, producing in spring the young fleshy shoots which are eaten as a vegetable. If they are left, they mature into many branched stems 1–3 m high which bear insignificant leaves in the axils of which are clusters of needle-like modified branches (cladodes) 1 cm long. Small bell-shaped whitish-green flowers appear in cladode axils early summer to mid-

summer. Bears fruit of red or orange berries 1 cm in diameter.

Distribution Coasts and sandy areas; woods and hedges; Great Britain to Central Asia.

Cultivation Wild plant; cultivated commercially and horticulturally on a wide scale. Production of the vegetable requires 3-year-old plants. Beds last 12 years. Seed sown in late spring, 7.5 cm deep, 2–3 seeds per hole on deep rich sandy loam in open position. A subspecies *A. officinalis* subsp. *prostratus* is also found wild.

Constituents Volatile oil; glucoside; gum; resin; tannic acid.

Uses (root, young fresh stem) Diuretic; diaphoretic; laxative, due to high fibre content. Once recommended for treatment of dropsy, gout and rheumatism.

Wide culinary use as a vegetable.

Asperula odorata L RUBIACEAE

Woodruff Sweet Woodruff/Waldmeister Tea

This attractive low-growing herb which is frequently found carpeting beech woods makes useful ground cover in shady places or beneath

roses in formal beds. It was widely used as a fragrant herb in earlier times as it develops, when dried, a strong scent of new mown hay; for this reason it was one of the main strewing herbs for home and church floors. The Latin name *asperula* refers to the roughness of the wheel or ruff-like leaves.

Description Perennial with creeping root-stock from which many quadrangular smooth, slender stems arise, 15–30 cm high. Leaves in whorls of 6, dark green, lanceolate, 3 cm long, rough-edged. Small white funnel-shaped flowers appear on long stalks early summer to mid-summer. Plant has a strong characteristic smell.

Distribution Asia, Europe, North Africa. Introduced elsewhere; cultivated in United States. Prefers porous loamy soil, rich in nutrients, especially in mixed woodland.

Cultivation Wild plant; may be propagated from ripe seed sown in late summer to early autumn, or root division after flowering. Ideal herb for underplanting in borders.

Constituents Coumarinic compounds which release coumarin as the plant dies down; also tannin.

Uses (dried herb) Carminative; diuretic; tonic. Once used for biliary obstructions. Source of coumarin for anticoagulant drugs. Tea relieves stomach pains.

Flowers and leaves make a delicious tea.

Used in certain wines as a flavouring.

In perfumery and pot-pourris, and for scenting linen. Repels insects.

Contra-indications Large quantities can produce dizziness and symptoms of poisoning.

Atropa belladonna L SOLANACEAE

Deadly Nightshade Dwale

Although a plant with such powerful sedative and poisonous properties was undoubtedly widely used for sinister purposes, it cannot be identified with certainty in classical writings, and the first definite report of its use is found in the *Grand Herbier* (1504) printed in Paris. The herb was known by various names during the sixteenth and seventeenth centuries including *Strygium, Strychnon, Solanum somniferum,*

and *Solatrum mortale*, the latter – the apothecaries' name for it – being translated as 'deadly nightshade'. Matthiolus stated it was the Venetians who first called the plant *Herba bella donna* after the practice of ladies who used a distilled water of it to dilate the pupils.

Description Perennial with leafy, smooth, branched stem 50–200 cm tall on thick creeping root-stock. Leaves dull green, unequal sized pairs to 20 cm long, bearing solitary bell-shaped purplish-brown drooping flowers 3 cm in diameter in the axils. Appearing mid-summer to early autumn, followed by shiny black berries.

Distribution Native to Europe, Asia; naturalized and introduced elsewhere. Found especially in woods and wasteland on calcareous soils.

Cultivation Wild plant. Widespread commercial cultivation from seed or by root division.

Constituents Hyoscyamine; atropine; traces of other alkaloids mainly in root-stock. Action due to these affecting the autonomic nervous system.

Uses (root-stock and leaf) Narcotic; mydriatic; sedative. Reduces salivary and sudorific gland secretions. Employed in treatment of biliary and intestinal colic. Formerly used in nervous diarrhoea and enuresis. Used in heart arrythmia. Externally as a liniment in gout or rheumatic inflammation.

Contra-indications All parts extremely POISONOUS; only to be used under medical supervision.

Avena sativa L GRAMINEAE

Oats Groats

One of the dozen members of the grass family which together provide the staple diet for most of the world's population. *Avena* is the old Latin name for the plant.

Description Annual tufted erect grass, 1–1.25 m high, with broad leaves 4 mm – 1 cm wide,

15–30 cm long, flat and scabrous. Short ligules. Terminal panicle 15–25 cm long, open and spreading; lemma without hairs.
Distribution *Avena sativa* is a cultigen possibly derived from *A. fatua*, *A. sterilis* or *A. barbata*, which originate from southern Europe and east Asia.
Cultivation Widespread commercial cultivation; often found growing wild, having escaped from cultivation.
Constituents Starch; protein; gluten; albumen; salts; gum oil; tocopherol.
Uses (dehusked seed, starchy seed endosperm) Nutritive; antidepressant; thymoleptic. Of use in depressive states and in general debility; highly nutritious.

Ballota nigra L LABIATAE
Black Horehound Stinking Horehound
This generally unattractive herb is distinguished only by its strong and objectionable odour, which caused Turner in 1548 to describe it as the 'stynkyng horehound'. Dioscorides gave the plant the name *ballote* which is probably derived from the Greek word meaning 'to reject' since it is normally rejected by cattle. Although the plant is of some medicinal value, it is now grown in herb gardens only because it is regarded as one of the traditional herbs.
Description Strong smelling perennial with angular branched hairy stems, 40–100 cm high, bearing heart-shaped leaves, crenulated, 2–5 cm long, opposite and often turning black after flowering. Whorls of typical labiate purple flowers borne in axils. Appearing midsummer to late autumn.
Distribution Natives of temperate Europe and much of the eastern hemisphere. Found on wasteland, hedgerows and on walls; prefers nitrogen-rich, moist, rather loose soil.
Cultivation Wild plant. Propagate by root division in mid-spring or sow seed in late spring, later thinning to 40 cm apart.
Constituents Flavonoids.
Uses (dried flowering herb) sedative; anti-emetic; especially used to counteract vomiting during pregnancy.

Berberis vulgaris L BERBERIDACEAE
Barberry European Barberry/Sowberry
A useful shrub cultivated in medieval times near monasteries and churches. It was used in dyeing, and as a medicine, and its delicious berries were used for jam, jelly and candied sweets. Now relegated to hedgerows, it is becoming scarce. Barberry is a host plant of the wheat rust and long before plant diseases were understood farmers accused the plant of 'blighting' wheat.
Description Erect deciduous shrub to 2.5 m tall, bearing rod-shaped branches tinged yellowish-red. Leaves obovate 2.5–4 cm long in clusters, greyish beneath with 3 sharp spines at the base. Flowers small, yellow, in clusters appearing late spring to mid-summer, and followed by oblong scarlet to purple fruit.
Distribution Native from Europe to East Asia; naturalized in eastern North America. Prefers light deciduous woodland on chalky soils. Once common in hedgerows but becoming scarcer due to infection by black rust fungus disease.
Cultivation Wild plant. Propagated by layering of suckers in early autumn; seed sown in late spring or early autumn; or cuttings taken in early autumn and planted in sandy soil. Horticultural varieties include *var. atropurpurea*.
Constituents Alkaloids comprising berberine, oxyacanthine and chelidonic acid. Fruit rich in vitamin C.
Uses (root bark, stem bark, ripe fruit) Cholagogue; specifically used in the treatment of gall-stones and other liver diseases.
Wood used in the manufacture of tooth-picks and bark as a yellow dye for wool, linen and leather. Fruit made into jelly and eaten with mutton, candied and pickled for use in curries.

Betula pendula Roth. BETULACEAE
Silver Birch
Although birch timber is poor, the tree has nevertheless been of use to man for a considerable time; Birch bark rolls have been found in Mesolithic excavations and North American Indians still use the bark for domestic purposes. The tree has also long been considered magical and reputedly has the ability to repel enchantment and evil. Its employment as a form of whip or 'birch' predates the Roman lictors who used *Betula* species in the *fascis* they carried. Now widely grown horticulturally as an attractive garden tree.
Description Deciduous tree to 20 m high; white bark, smooth and peeling in horizontal strips. Pendulous slender branches bearing resinous, rough and scaly glands. Leaves bright green 4–7 cm long, irregularly serrate, heart-shaped to triangular. Flowers consist of male and female catkins.
Distribution Common throughout central and northern Europe, the mountainous parts of southern Europe and Asia Minor. Also found in Canada and the northern United States. Tolerates all soil types and situations.
Cultivation Wild plant. Grown horticulturally.
Constituents Volatile oil; a saponin; a flavonoid; resin.
Uses (dried young leaves) Diuretic, with mild antiseptic action, thus used in urinary tract infections. Formerly used for gout and rheumatism.

A beer can be made from the bark. The tree sap is made into birch wine and vinegar.
Birch wood seldom used commercially as timber; but employed for broom handles.
Bark once used as candles and the oil extracted from it was used to cure leather, and also in medicated soaps for skin conditions.

Bidens tripartita L COMPOSITAE
Bur-Marigold Water Agrimony
The herb is unrelated botanically to the common Agrimony and it scarcely deserves the name marigold with its inconspicuous brown-yellow flowers. Flies and insects are repelled when the herb is burned.
Description Erect annual 15–60 cm high, with smooth or downy branched stems; leaves 5–15 cm long, opposite, dark green, mostly with 3 or sometimes 5 leaflets. Flowers brownish-yellow, inconspicuous, somewhat drooping. Late summer to mid-autumn.
Distribution European native. Common on river banks, in ditches, near ponds. Prefers muddy soil.
Cultivation Wild plant. Propagate from seed sown in spring.
Constituents Volatile oil.
Uses (dried flowering herb) Astringent; diaphoretic; antihaemorrhagic. Formerly used in a variety of conditions, but now rarely used except for antihaemorrhagic purposes.
A weak yellow dye is obtained from the flowers.

Borago officinalis L BORAGINACEAE
Borage Burrage
Almost all the historical descriptions of Borage refer to the herb's abilities to bring happiness and comfort and drive away melancholia. Even Pliny called the plant *euphrosinum* because it made men joyful and merry. Certainly it was widely used in a variety of alcoholic drinks, and it is still a vital ingredient of summer wine cups. As Borage is very attractive to bees, its bright blue star-shaped flowers are always covered with the insects.
Description Annual or sometimes biennial herb, with erect hairy stems to 60 cm, bearing ovate, alternate, rough leaves, hairy on both surfaces, 3–11 cm long and up to 2.5 cm wide, usually without petioles. Bright blue, drooping star-shaped flowers 2 cm wide appear from early summer to mid-autumn on sparsely flowered racemes.
Distribution Native to mediterranean region; naturalized and introduced elsewhere; found especially as garden escape.
Cultivation Wild plant and prolifically self-seeding. Thrives on ordinary well-drained soil in full sun. Sow seed in shallow drills in late spring or late summer.
Constituents Mucilage; tannin; volatile oil; various mineral acids. Active principles not fully understood, but they act as a mild diuretic and sudorific.
Uses (dried flowering plant, fresh leaves) Mild diuretic; once used for kidney and bladder inflammations. Used externally as a poultice on inflammations. Taken as a tisane for rheumatism and for respiratory infections. Said to stimulate the flow of milk in nursing mothers.
Candied flowers used for cake decoration. Fresh leaves and flowers added to salads, and fresh flowers used to decorate wine cups. Roots flavour wine.

Brassica nigra (L) Koch CRUCIFERAE
Mustard Black Mustard
The powerful flavour of old-fashioned Mustard was due largely to its content of Black Mustard. The plant, however, does not lend itself well to mechanical harvesting as it is often 2–3 m in height, and readily sheds its seed when ripe. As a result it has almost completely been replaced with the shorter Juncea or Brown Mustard (*Brassica juncea*) which is much less pungent. The word 'mustard' is thought to derive from the Latin – *mustum ardens*, or 'burning must' since the French originally ground the seed with grape must.
Description Much branched annual 1–3 m high, smooth above and slightly hairy below; grass-green leaves of varying shapes, generally narrow or lobed with serrate margins. Flowers small, bright yellow, in twig-like racemes, appearing mid-summer to early autumn. Seed dark reddish-brown in colour, in smooth pods.
Distribution Whole of Europe except far north; northern Africa, Asia Minor, China, western India, North and South America.
Cultivation Wild plant; formerly cultivated commercially on a wide scale – this now restricted to southern Italy, Sicily, Ethiopia. Seed sown in drills in spring preferably on rich soil.
Constituents Glycoside (comprising sinigrin) and an enzyme (myrosin) which react in the presence of water to form allyl isothiocyanate (or essential oil of mustard) which is responsible for the smell, taste and inflammatory action of mustard. Also contains proteins; mucilage; and non-volatile oil.
Uses (seed, leaves) Stimulant; irritant; emetic. Mainly used as a rubefacient poultice for rheumatism, local pain and chilblains. Added to hot water as a foot bath. Used as an ingredient of the condiment Flour of Mustard. Young leaves occasionally used in salads.
Contra-indications May blister tender skins. Should be used sparingly when taken internally.

Bryonia dioica Jacq. CUCURBITACEAE
White or Red Bryony/English Mandrake
The common name is derived from the Greek word *bruein* – meaning to grow luxuriantly; another name, the wild vine, emphasizes the vigorous growth of the annual stems which rapidly cover hedgerow shrubs. The herb is also called English Mandrake since the enormous root-stock is similar in appearance to the legendary Mandrake (*Mandragora officinarum*) and was once used as a substitute for it. Bryony roots carved into human form were often used as shop signs by English herbalists in the eighteenth century.
Description Climbing perennial arising from large white tuberous root 75 cm long, 7.5 cm thick. Long stem, branching near the base reaching 4 m tall, and supported by coiled tendrils. Leaves palmate, 5-lobed and rough. Male plants bear pale green flowers on long

stalks; female plants bear greenish flowers in umbels of 2–5 on short stalks and single red berries; both plants appear early summer to early autumn.
Distribution Mediterranean native; widely distributed in Europe and Western Asia; introduced elsewhere. Prefers a well-drained and chalky or loamy soil.
Cultivation Wild plant.
Constituents Resin comprising the glycoside bryonin; tannin; volatile oil; other glycosides and alkaloids. Purgative action due to resin.
Uses (fresh or dried root) Irritant; once employed to allay coughs in pleurisy, now rarely used due to its violent purgative action. Berries of use as a dye.
Contra-indications All parts POISONOUS.

Buxus sempervirens L BUXACEAE
Box Box Tree
Although once used for medicinal purposes the slow growing and somewhat peculiarly smelling Box Tree is now mainly sought after for its timber which is used in the manufacture of chess pieces and turned boxes. At one time Box woods were widespread in Europe but the demand for the wood – which is twice as hard as oak – led to extensive felling. Close clipped Box hedges make excellent edgings to formal herb gardens.
Description Slow growing evergreen tree or shrub, 2–7 m tall; bark greyish, leaves dark green above and shiny, pale beneath, oblong 1–3 cm long. Flowers minute, yellow-green in axillary clusters appearing mid-spring to early summer.
Distribution Native to Europe, North Africa, western Asia. Cultivated widely; prefers chalk or limestone.
Cultivation Wild plant. Cultivated from cuttings in sandy soil taken in spring.
Constituents Alkaloids (buxine, parabuxine, parabuxonidine); oil; tannin.
Uses (leaves, wood) Not used medicinally; but formerly used for syphilis and as a sedative. A volatile oil from the wood was once used in the treatment of epilepsy, piles and toothache. Perfume once made from the bark. Leaves and sawdust were formerly used to dye hair auburn. Box wood is as durable as brass and is therefore used in instrument manufacture. Leaves once used as a substitute for Hops.
Contra-indications Animals have died from eating the leaves.

Calamintha ascendens Jord. LABIATAE
Common Calamint Mountain Balm/Mountain Mint
An ancient medicinal herb which once had such a good reputation as a heart tonic that it was named after the Greek for excellence – *kalos*. Although an 'official' herb of the Middle Ages it now has no place in either orthodox or folk medicine.
Description Hairy perennial; stems square, arising from creeping root-stock, to 30 cm high; leaves stalked, toothed and broadly ovate, 2–3 cm long. Typically labiate flowers, pale purple, in dense whorls of 10–20, appearing late summer to early autumn.
Distribution European native; prefers dry woodland and waste places on chalky soil.
Cultivation Wild plant. Propagated by cuttings of side-shoots taken in spring; seed sown in early spring; root division late autumn and late spring.
Constituents Volatile oils.
Uses (dried flowering herb) Diaphoretic; expectorant. An infusion is a useful tonic. The leaves may be used as a poultice for bruises. A peppermint flavoured tisane can be made from the leaves.

Calendula officinalis L COMPOSITAE
Marigold Garden Marigold
This well-known garden plant is probably one of the most useful of all herbs. It has valuable medicinal properties, yields a yellow dye, and can be used as a culinary herb and for cosmetic purposes. It has been used in the Mediterranean region since the ancient Greeks, and it was known to Indian and Arabic cultures before the Greeks. The botanical name comes from the Latin *calendulae* or *calends* meaning 'throughout the months', which was intended to emphasize the very long flowering period of the Marigold.
Description Annual; biennial rarely; branching, angular stem to 50 cm; leaves oblong or lanceolate, hairy on both surfaces, 5–15 cm long; flower-heads large, yellow or orange, double-flowered (tubular florets absent), appearing mid-summer to late autumn.
Distribution Mediterranean native; distributed throughout the world as a garden plant.
Cultivation Not found wild. Tolerates any soil in full sun, although prefers loam. Seed sown mid-spring, but once established is generally self-sown.
Constituents Volatile oil; a yellow resin; calendulin; saponins; a bitter principle; all of which aid bile secretion and promote wound healing.
Uses (entire flower-heads, individual florets, rarely the entire flowering plant) Cholagogue;

styptic; anti-inflammatory; vulnerary; antiseptic; possibly emmenagogue.
Specifically of use in inflamed lymphatic nodes, duodenal ulcers, and some inflammatory skin lesions. Used externally for treatment of leg ulcers, and in conjunctivitis as an eye lotion.
Petals are substitutes for Saffron, and may be added to salads and omelettes or used to colour cheese and butter.
Young leaves added to salads.
Petals are also used as tea.
Used in skin and cosmetic preparations, and as a hair rinse.
Yellow dye obtained by boiling flowers.

Calluna vulgaris (L) Hull ERICACEAE
Heather Ling
A common herb long used in European folk

medicine whose generic name is from the Greek meaning to sweep, after the use of its branches in brooms.
Description Evergreen subshrub from 15 cm–1 m tall. Leaves grey-green, later reddish, very small, sessile, overlapping in 4 rows. Flowers 3 mm long, pink in terminal one-sided racemes, appearing late summer to late autumn.
Distribution Native to Europe, Asia Minor. Introduced to eastern North America. On acidic sandy soils, or peat bogs. In woodland, dry hillsides, mountainous districts, to 2500 m altitude.
Cultivation Wild. Numerous horticultural cultivars exist for rock-garden use. Dislikes limestone soils. Propagate by young wood cuttings under glass.
Constituents Citric and fumaric acids; arbutin; tannins; an oil, ericinol; a resin, ericoline; flavonoid glycosides, quercitrin and myricitrin; carotene. The combined action is predominantly antibacterial.
Uses (fresh flowering tops) Antiseptic; diuretic; astringent.
Of use in the treatment of kidney and urinary tract infections, diarrhoea. Frequently included in cleansing mixtures such as acne remedies. May possess a weak sedative action. Can be used as a tea substitute.

Cannabis sativa L CANNABACEAE
Hemp Cannabis
Recorded in the fifth century B.C. in the Chinese herbal Rh-ya but now subject to considerable medical and legal reappraisal. Hemp has long been of economic importance to man. John Gerard described it in the sixteenth century as the Indian Dreamer. *C. sativa* L is considered now to be synonymous with *C. indica* L, although the herb is variable

both in constituents and appearance depending upon region and method of cultivation.
Description Coarse strong-smelling dioceious annual, 90 cm–5 m tall. Leaves long-petioled thin, alternate, palmate; 3–11 leaflets, narrowly lanceolate, toothed, 7.5–12.5 cm long. Male flowers in panicles 23–40 cm long; female sessile leafy spikes 2 cm long. Variable.
Distribution Native to central and western Asia; introduced to many temperate and tropical countries. To 3000 m altitude.
Cultivation Wild and cultivated commercially, in temperate regions for oily seed and fibre (Soviet Union and central Europe, for example) and in tropical regions for the drug (Africa, India, Far East). In many countries it can be cultivated only with a government permit.
Constituents A resin, cannabinone, comprising various compounds; pharmacological action probably due to isomers of tetrahydrocannabinol.
Uses (fibre, seed, oil, female and male dried flowering tops – the latter only rarely) Cerebral sedative; narcotic; analgesic; antispasmodic.
Medicinal use and attitude to the drug varies according to country. Considered of benefit in glaucoma, spasmodic cough, neuralgia, asthma and migraine.
Stem fibre provides 'hemp' for rope, sail-cloth etc. Seed is a bird-feed, and source of a drying oil, 'hemp-seed oil'. Dried flowering tops illegally smoked as a narcotic (marijuana).
Contra-indications Possession is illegal. Physical and psychological effects, ranging from change in blood pressure and impotence to hallucination, vary enormously depending on personality. Medical use only.

Capparis spinosa L CAPPARACEAE
Caper Caper Bush
The unopened flower buds of the Caper Bush, pickled in wine vinegar, have been used as a condiment for at least 2000 years, and have always been known as either *capparis* or

kapparis. Dioscorides suggested a medical use for them, but they have never widely been used for anything except culinary purposes. The best known substitute for capers is pickled, green nasturtium seeds.
Description Straggling spiny shrub 1 m high; leaves tough, roundish or oval 2–5 cm long, with short petiole and 2 spines at the base. White or pink single flowers 2.5 cm long with 4 petals, and numerous purple stamens hanging below them, appearing from early summer to early autumn and lasting only 24 hours.
Distribution Mediterranean region and North Africa to the Sahara.
Cultivation Wild plant; cultivated in warmer climates (when the bush is often spineless). May be grown in greenhouses in temperate zones.
Cuttings in summer most successfully rooted with the help of mist propagation (requiring very high humidity).
Constituents Capric acid, which develops on pickling the buds, and which is responsible for the characteristic flavour.
Uses (unopened flower buds) Numerous culinary uses: caper sauce, tartare sauce, vinaigrette, butter, in Liptauer cheese, and as a garnish with hors d'oeuvres, fish, meat and salads.

Capsella bursa-pastoris (L) Medic. CRUCIFERAE
Shepherd's Purse Shovelweed
In almost all European languages the common names of this herb allude to the strange shape of the fruit, which are very similar to the purses or pouches which were once commonly hung from belts. The Latin name also simply means the 'little case of the shepherd'.
Shepherd's Purse can be found growing in Greenland at sites where it was introduced by Norsemen 1000 years ago. It was, and in some places is still, extensively eaten as a spring vegetable.

Description Annual, or generally biennial; smooth or slightly hairy stem, branched, to 50 cm; arising from basal rosette of dentate or variable leaves. Upper leaves entire and narrow. White flowers 2.5–4 mm diameter, in loose racemes appearing throughout the year, and followed by triangular shaped fruit called siliculae.
Distribution Widespread in temperate zones; common weed on gravelly, sandy or loamy soils, especially those which are nitrogen-rich.
Cultivation Wild plant.
Constituents Choline; acetylcholine; and other amines – acting as vasoconstrictors and haemostatics.
Uses (dried flowering plant; fresh plant) Anti-haemorrhagic; the herb acts as a vasoconstrictor and is therefore of use in certain haemorrhages especially profuse menstruation. Thought to assist contraction of the uterus during childbirth. Spring leaves eaten as cabbage in many countries.

Capsicum annuum L SOLANACEAE
Chili Peppers Capsicum/Sweet Peppers
All species of Capsicum are of American origin and were unknown before 1494 when Chanca, the physician to the fleet of Columbus in his second voyage to the West Indies, briefly described their use by the natives. Today there are scores of varieties in cultivation, ranging in shape, size, colour, flavour, and degree of

pungency, and the plants are grown commercially in all tropical and subtropical countries. Some varieties grow in the cooler parts of Europe and America. Chili is dried and ground to form Cayenne Pepper; it is also blended with several varieties of Capsicums, herbs and spices to make Chili powder.
Although the origin of the cultivated varieties is uncertain, experts believe all come from one original species. For this reason the botanical classification of these plants is somewhat muddled, and *C. annuum* is often described as *C. frutescens*.
Description Herbaceous annual or biennial; 30–90 cm high; leaves 2.5–12 cm long, acuminate, often narrowing towards the petiole; white flowers, solitary, 5 mm–1 cm wide, or much larger. Fruit from 1.5–30 cm long, varied in colour (yellow, brown, purple, often bright red), in shape and degree of fleshiness.
Distribution Grown in all tropical and subtropical countries; Europe and America.
Cultivation Not found in wild state, but closely related to the Bird Pepper (*Capsicum microcarpum* (*D.C.*). Seed sown under glass in early spring; later transplanted. Best sown in pots or under glass in cool climates to ensure ripening of fruit.
Constituents Capsicin; capsaicin; alkaloids; vitamin C; palmitic acid.
Uses (fresh or dried fruit) Spasmolytic; nutritive and stimulant. Aids digestion; of use in diarrhoea.
Mainly employed as a condiment and a vegetable.

Capsicum frutescens L SOLANACEAE
Tabasco Pepper Cayenne Pepper
Cayenne was classified as *C. minimum* by Roxburgh, but is generally known as *C. frutescens*. It is the species which is used medicinally, and it is still included in many national pharmacopoeias. Traditionally it came from Cayenne in French Guiana.
Description Perennial shrub to 2 m; trunk becoming woody, 7.5 cm diameter. Leaves various, usually elliptical, 2 cm long; flowers white in groups of 2 or 3, 5 mm–1 cm wide. Fruit small and oblong.
Distribution Tropical and subtropical countries.
Cultivation Wild in parts of South America and southern India; cultivated elsewhere.
Constituents Capsicin; capsicain; alkaloids; vitamin C; palmitic acid.
Uses (dried ground fruit) Stimulant; spasmolytic; antiseptic; rubefacient. Used in flatulence, colic and to improve both the peripheral circulation and digestion. Occas-

ionally employed as a liniment in neuralgia or rheumatism. Weak infusion of benefit as throat gargle.
Contra-indications Large doses are an extreme irritant to the gastro-intestinal system.

Cardamine pratensis L CRUCIFERAE
Lady's Smock Cuckoo-flower/Bittercress
Lady's Smock is one of the first wild flowers to appear in spring, and is characteristic of moist meadows in Europe and America. It is rich in vitamins and minerals and was formerly cultivated and used as a common salad herb, often being found on market stalls. It has, unfortunately, now fallen into disuse. Cardamine is an ancient Greek name for Cress, and refers to its supposed heart-benefitting properties.
Description Slender erect perennial on short root-stock, to 25–50 cm. Leaves pinnately subdivided, consisting of 3–7 segments, oblong or rounded, 1 cm long. Basal leaves broader and form a rosette. Pale lilac or white flowers, 4 attractive petals 1 cm long, in terminal racemes appearing spring to early summer, and followed by 2.5 cm long fruit pod. Double flowers occasionally occur.
Distribution Native in temperate zones of northern Europe and America; prefers loamy soil saturated with water, beside streams, in damp meadows and moist woodland.
Cultivation Wild plant; once cultivated. May be raised from seed sown, when ripe, on damp

loamy soil.
Constituents Vitamins, especially C; minerals; mustard oil.
Uses (fresh leaves, flowering tops) Stomachic; nutritive. Infusion may be taken to promote the appetite, or in indigestion.
Eaten raw in salads, or cooked as vegetable; added to soups. Flavour similar to Watercress.

Carlina acaulis L COMPOSITAE
Carline Thistle Dwarf Thistle
Carlina is possibly derived from the name Charles (a king who traditionally protected his army from the plague with this plant); more certainly *acaulis* means 'stemless'.

Known in France as Baromètre because it closes at the approach of rain.
Description Stemless or short-stemmed perennial to 5 cm on taproot. Bearing oblong 30 cm-long pinnate leaves, divided into numerous spiny segments. Flower-head large (to 12.5 cm) solitary, creamy-white, composed entirely of disc florets; appearing late summer to mid-autumn.
Distribution Native to south and central Europe. In heathland, meadowland, on poor, dry, stony calcareous soils in warm positions to 2800 m.
Cultivation Wild plant.
Constituents Essential oil; resin; tannins; inulin; antibiotic substances, carlinoxide and carlinene.
Uses (dried root) Cholagogue; diuretic; antibacterial; vulnerary; stomachic.
Of benefit in dropsy and urine retention; in skin complaints such as acne and eczema; in some liver disorders, or as a stomachic tonic. The decoction may be used to clean wounds or as an antiseptic gargle. Used in veterinary medicine to stimulate appetite of cattle.
Contra-indications Purgative and emetic in large doses.

Carum carvi L UMBELLIFERAE
Caraway Caraway Seed
Both the common and Latin names of this herb stem directly from the ancient Arabic word for its seed *karawiya*, which are known to have been used by man as medicine and as a flavouring since the early Egyptians. Caraway cultivation is mentioned in the Bible, and the seed has been found among the remains of food at Mesolithic sites – it has thus been widely used for 5000 years, and it is still extensively cultivated for use as a flavouring and as a carminative.
Description Typical umbelliferous biennial; rosette of bipinnate or tripinnate feathery leaves in first year followed by erect slender branched stem 20–100 cm bearing few pinnate leaves and umbels of numerous minute white flowers. Appearing mid to late summer. Fruit when ripe (late summer to late autumn) 3–5 mm long, oblong, strongly ribbed.
Distribution Native to mid-East, Asia, Central Europe; very widely distributed and naturalized. Prefers waste-grounds.

Cultivation Wild plant. Commercially and horticulturally cultivated on a wide scale, especially in Germany and Holland. Tolerates most soils; sow late summer for seed harvesting the following summer.
Constituents Volatile oils, which prevent flatulence and promote secretion of gastric juices.
Uses (ripe fruit, young fresh leaf, fresh roots) Carminative; aromatic. Of much benefit in flatulent indigestion, lack of appetite, diarrhoea. Safe to use with children.
Seed has wide culinary use as flavouring.
Young leaves added to salads; root boiled as vegetable.
Used to flavour liqueurs such as Kümmel.

Cassia angustifolia Vahl. LEGUMINOSAE
Senna Tinnevelly Senna
Senna is well-known for its effectiveness in cases of constipation, and the herb is still officially recognized by inclusion in most national pharmacopoeias. It was first brought into medical usage by Arabian physicians of the ninth century when the best sort was considered to come from Mecca. Another species, *Cassia acutifolia*, provides the slightly inferior 'Alexandrian senna'.
Description Perennial shrub or undershrub to 75 cm with pale erect angled branches. Leaves subdivided into 4–8 leaflets, oval-lanceolate, smooth, 2.5–6 cm long, 7–8 mm wide; flowers on erect racemes, small, yellow, numerous. Followed by fruit, 15–17 mm broad.
Distribution Native to Arabia and Somaliland; introduced in southern India, especially Madura, Mysore and Tinnevelly.
Cultivation Wild plant. Cultivated commercially in India, and to a lesser extent in Arabia and Somaliland.
Constituents Anthraquinone derivatives, especially rhein, aloe-emodin, kaempferin, isorhamnetin; also beta-sitosterol; kaempferol; myricyl

alcohol and resin. Purgative action due to anthraquinone substances acting on lower bowel wall and nerves (Auerbach's plexus) in the wall.
Uses (dried fruit, dried leaflets) Cathartic. Widely used alone or more commonly in combination with aromatics to treat constipation. May be taken as a tea with slices of Ginger or Coriander Seed.
Contra-indications Not to be used in spastic constipation or colitis. Large doses of the leaf cause nausea, griping pain and red coloration of the urine.

Castanea sativa Mill. FAGACEAE
Sweet Chestnut Spanish or Eurasian Chestnut
Kastanea was the classical name for this attractive tree which produces the largest and best nuts only when grown in a mediterranean climate. These nuts, once known as *kastana*, are now called *marones* and traditionally make the best stuffing for turkey.
Description Tree to 30 m; thick dark brown corrugated bark with spiral fissures; large buds 4–5 mm wide, ovoid; leaves oblong-lanceolate 10–25 cm long, coarsely serrated, dark green above, light green and glabrous beneath. Flowers (catkins) 12–20 cm long, appearing late spring to early summer, followed by a burr enclosing 1–3 nuts, 2.5 cm wide.
Distribution Native to western Asia, south Europe and North Africa. Introduced into America and Europe. Tolerates most soils, prefers deep sandy loam.
Cultivation Wild plant; widely grown and hundreds of varieties now exist, some of which are cultivated for food. Best propagated by grafting.
Constituents Tannin; albumin; gum; resin; alkaloids.
Uses (nuts) Nutritive. The fresh leaf was once taken as a decoction in whooping-cough, and the bark was formerly employed as an antipyretic.
Nuts boiled, roasted, ground into flour, and used in pâtés, tarts, bread and soups.
Good quality timber obtained from the tree.

Caulophyllum thalictroides (L) Michx.
BERBERIDACEAE
Blue Cohosh Papoose Root
Eighty years ago this herb was included in the United States Pharmacopoeia and was considered worthy of detailed study and use in obstetric and gynaecological conditions. American Indian women drank an infusion of the root for two weeks prior to childbirth, which was usually comparatively painless. The herb is also called Blue or Yellow Ginseng. Its use is now restricted to herbal medicine.
Description Erect perennial to 1 m on contorted branched root-stock; stem terminated in large sessile tripinnate leaf. Other leaves 2 or 3 pinnate; leaflets being oval, usually 2–3 lobed, 2.5–10 cm long. Flowers 6-petalled, yellowish-green (occasionally purplish) appearing late spring to mid-summer on peduncle arising

from base of upper leaf. Fruit 1 cm diameter, blue-black.
Distribution United States and Canada; especially in moist woodland and mountain glades.
Cultivation Wild plant.
Constituents Saponin; green-yellow colouring matter; resins; starch; salts; unknown substances acting on voluntary and involuntary muscle – especially the uterus.
Uses (dried rhizome and root) Oxytocic. Once used to facilitate childbirth and treat chronic rheumatism. Also used in fevers but only weak diaphoretic action has been shown.
Contra-indications Powder is irritant, especially to mucous membranes. May cause pain to fingers and toes.

Celastrus scandens L CELASTRACEAE
False Bittersweet American or Climbing Bittersweet
A member of the spindle-tree family and a

common plant found growing beside roads in the American Appalachians. This and related species such as *C. orbiculatus* are useful plants to grow as trellis or wall covers. Now rarely used even in folk medicine.
Description Twining shrub to 8 m. Leaves 5–12.5 cm long, ovate to ovate-lanceolate, serrated. Flowers very small, numerous, greenish, on terminal racemes 10 cm long, followed by orange-yellow seed capsules, 1 cm diameter.
Distribution Canada and United States from Quebec to New Mexico. Prefers dense moist thickets and roadsides.
Cultivation Wild plant.
Constituents Active principles unknown.
Uses (dried root bark) Emetic; diuretic; cholagogue; diaphoretic.
Used formerly in biliary obstruction, to promote menstruation and to treat skin cancer.
Attractive orange fruits used in flower arrangements.

Centaurea cyanus L COMPOSITAE
Cornflower Bluebottle/Bachelor's Button
Once common in cornfields but in parts of Europe now becoming much rarer because of changing agricultural methods; the Cornflower gained its name by the translation of the apothecaries' term for the drug – 'flos frumenti'. Before the sixteenth century it was called Blue Bothem or Bluebottle. Both this and another species (*C. montana* L), growing in the mountainous areas of Europe, are considered excellent eyewashes for tired eyes. Tradition maintains they are most effective for blue eyes while a completely different plant – *Plantago major* (the Greater Plantain) – is believed to be best for brown eyes.
Description Annual herb on erect wiry stem 20–90 cm high; leaves grey, downy, alternate, linear-lanceolate, usually less than 5 mm wide, 7.5–15 cm long. Bract fringes silvery. Flowers on large solitary capitulae 2.5–4 cm wide, bright blue (occasionally white, pink or purple). Only disc florets present. Appearing midsummer to early autumn.
Distribution Native to south and east Europe, naturalized in parts of North America. Intro-

duced elsewhere. Found especially on wastegrounds on porous nutrient-rich soil.
Cultivation Wild plant (becoming rare or less common). Widely cultivated horticulturally from seed sown in spring on sunny site.
Constituents Sterols; cyanin; cyanin chloride; fragasin.
Uses (dried flower-head) Diuretic; tonic; mild astringent. A decoction may be used as an eyewash in eye inflammation and fatigue. A blue ink was formerly made from the flower juice.
Flowers used in pot-pourris.

Centaurium erythraea Rafn. GENTIANACEAE
Centaury Lesser or Common Centaury/Century
Common Centaury is named after the centaur Chiron who treated himself with the herb after suffering an arrow wound. The plant is also called Gentian since it has similar properties to the true Gentian (*Gentiana lutea*) and is used for the same purposes. It was considered a lucky plant by some of the Celtic peoples of Europe. Centaury was widely grown in the Middle Ages, and it is still used today as an ingredient of vermouth.
Description Biennial or annual 2–50 cm high; stems erect, glabrous, branching to form inflorescence. Basal rosette of elliptic leaves 1–5 cm long, 8–20 mm wide; stem leaves shorter, linear, oval, glabrous with 5 veins. Flowers sessile, pale red, 1 cm long, borne on apical corymbs of 6–10 flowers. Appearing late summer to mid-autumn.
Distribution Central European native; distributed from western Europe to western Siberia; introduced elsewhere. Prefers dry slopes, woodland and roadsides.
Cultivation Wild plant. Cultivated commercially on a small scale in North Africa and central Europe. Seed sown in spring or autumn.
Constituents Glycosidic bitter principles and related compounds which stimulate gastric and salivary secretions.
Uses (dried flowering plant) Aromatic; bitter; stomachic. Stimulates appetite and bile secretion; of benefit in weak digestion. Widely used as a tonic. Has an insignificant antipyretic effect.
Important constituent of gastric herbal teas; used in bitter herb liqueurs.

Centranthus ruber (L) DC VALERIANACEAE
Red Valerian Red-spurred Valerian/Fox's Brush
The Red-spurred Valerian has none of the medicinal properties of the closely related 'official' Valerian (*Valeriana officinalis*). Both Gesner and Linnaeus classified the herb botanically as *Valeriana ruber*, and Gerard called it Red Valerian or Red Cow Basil.
Description Perennial on woody based stems to 1 m; leaves ovate to lanceolate 10 cm long, sessile, entire, occasionally toothed at base. Flowers 5 mm wide, red or pink, the corolla is tubular and spurred at the base. Appears late spring.
Distribution Europe to south-west Asia; prefers old walls, cliffs, chalky sites.
Cultivation Wild plant; limited horticultural use. A white variety, *C. ruber* var. *albus*, exists. Propagated by root division in spring or autumn.

Constituents Unknown.
Uses (fresh leaves and root-stock) No medical use.
Used in salads (bitter), cooked as a vegetable. Root-stock used in soups.
Attractive garden plant.

Cephaelis ipecacuanha (Brot.) A. Rich.
RUBIACEAE
Ipecacuanha
Ipecacuanha – known as *poaya* in its native Brazil and long used there for medical purposes – did not reach Europe until 1672 and was not botanically identified until 1800. Its use for dysentery was proven and promoted by a Parisian physician called Helvetius who in 1688 sold the secret of his success to the court of Louis XIV.
The drug's effectiveness is emphasized by its current inclusion in all national pharmacopoeias except the Chinese.
Description Small straggling shrub on creeping fibrous roots initially smooth becoming enlarged and annulated (banded). Stem continuous with root-stock, smooth, green, angular to 30 cm, bearing few opposite, ovate, entire leaves. Flowers white in heads on terminal solitary peduncles, appearing late winter to early spring. Bears clusters of dark purple berries.

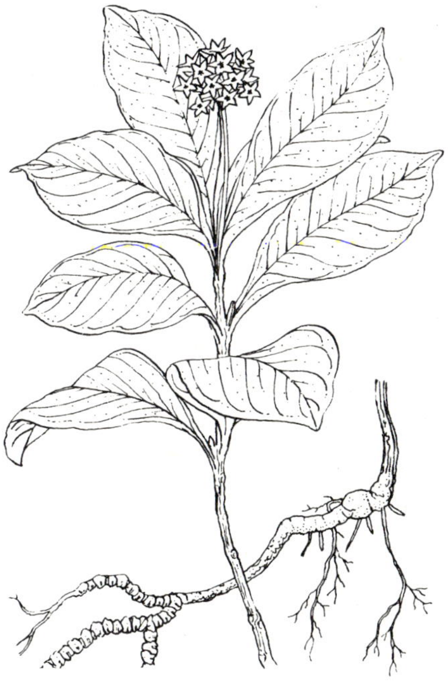

Distribution Indigenous to Brazil; introduced elsewhere. Grows in clumps in moist and shady forests.
Cultivation Wild plant; cultivated in Brazil, India (Bengal), Malaysia, Burma.
Constituents Alkaloids comprising mainly emetine and cephaeline, together with psychotrine, methyl-psychotrine and emetamine. Also a glycoside; ipecacuanhin; starch, ipecacuanhic acid.
Uses (dried root) Emetic; powerful expectorant. Used in acute and chronic bronchitis. Prevents cyst formation in amoebic dysentery. Useful in acute dysentery and as a diaphoretic.

Contra-indications Dangerous in large doses as it irritates the whole gastro-intestinal tract, causing serious vomiting and diarrhoea. Powder irritates skin and mucous membranes causing violent sneezing and coughing. To be used by medical personnel only.

Cereus grandiflorus Mill. CACTACEAE
Night Flowering Cereus
Although many cacti provide food and drink, comparatively few are proven effective medicinally. One exception is the Night Flowering Cereus which is characterized by its exceedingly large and beautiful scented flowers. The plant is commonly grown as a house plant.
Description Perennial succulent shrub; stem 5 or 6 ribbed, simple or rarely branched, 1–4 cm diameter, dark green, prickly. Flowers white, terminal or lateral, very large 20–30 cm in diameter. They bloom in the evening, last 6 hours, and die. Fruit ovate, scaly, orange-red.
Distribution West Indian native; tropical America, Mexico.
Cultivation Wild plant; grown horticulturally as a house plant in sharp, sandy soil.
Constituents Resins; alkaloids; unknown substances. The method of action is not fully understood.
Uses (fresh or dried flowers, young stems)

Cardiac stimulant; increasing the force of myocardial contractions. Used in cardiac arrhythmias and heart failure. Once used in cases of dropsy.

Cetraria islandica (L) Ach. PARMELIACEAE
Iceland Moss
This is not a moss but a lichen and it has long been used as a foodstuff in the cold northern countries where it flourishes. It is still employed in folk medicine largely because of its nutritive properties, although Linnaeus recommended its general use in medicine for pulmonary diseases. It was once called 'muscus catharticus' which suggests wrongly that it possesses purgative properties.
Description Lichen, consisting of erect dichotomously branched, curling thallus 3–12 cm high; upper surface olive-brown or grey, paler lower surface with depressed white spots;

fruits rare, apical, rounded, rust coloured to 1 cm diameter.
Distribution Abundant in high northern latitudes, especially coniferous forests, mountainous parts of central Europe, North America. Also in Antarctica.
Cultivation Wild plant.
Constituents 70% mucilage, comprising lichenin and isolichenin, which acts as a demulcent; also bitter organic acids, including fumaroprotocetraric acid, which stimulate gastric secretions.
Uses (entire dried plant) Demulcent; mild tonic; nutritive; weak antituberculous agent. Stimulates appetite. Specifically of benefit in debilitating diseases associated with vomiting. May be ground and made into flour for baking bread or boiled in milk. Edible jelly made by boiling soaked plant to remove bitterness.

Chamaemelum nobile (L) All. COMPOSITAE
Chamomile Roman, Common or Double Chamomile
This is one of the best known of all herbs and has been in continuous use from the time of the Egyptians (who dedicated it to their Gods), until today when it is widely available prepacked in tea bags. Its name derives from the Greek *chamaimelon* meaning 'apple on the ground' since all parts of the herb are strongly apple-scented.
Description Aromatic perennial to 30 cm with creeping root-stock, low growing, hairy stems, branched and supporting leaflets divided into many segments. Flowers consist almost entirely of yellow-white ligulate florets, 15 mm–3 cm wide, born singly on long erect stems. From mid-summer to mid-autumn.
Distribution Indigenous to southern Europe; introduced and widespread elsewhere; prefers

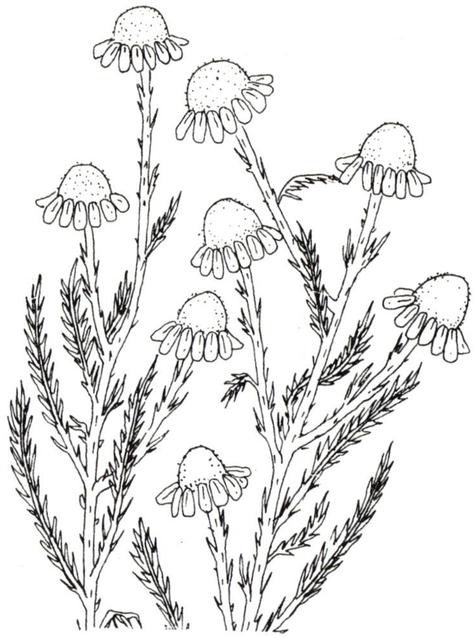

dry, sandy soil in full sun.
Cultivation Commercially grown in central Europe. To ensure double flower-heads, propagate vegetatively by root-stock division in early spring. The non-flowering clone 'treneague' ideal for lawns; 100 plantlets cover 2.5 sq.m., planted at 15 cm spacings. Succeeds on any free-draining soil even in part shade.
Constituents Volatile oil, comprising azulene, esters of angelic and tiglic acids, anthemal, anthemene. Action antiseptic; anti-inflammatory; anti-spasmodic. Improves appetite. Also inositol, and a bitter glycoside, anthemic acid.
Uses (dried flower-heads) Spasmolytic; sedative; carminative. Relieves painful menstruation, dyspepsia, vomiting and nausea. Excellent in flatulent dyspepsia taken as tisane. Whole herb used in beer manufacture.
Used to lighten hair.
Contra-indications Excessive dosage produces vomiting and vertigo.

Chelidonium majus L PAPAVERACEAE
Greater Celandine
The fact that Greater Celandine is commonly found on waste-ground near to habitation indicates that this is yet another herb once cultivated and now forgotten. It is still used in herbal medicine however, chiefly for liver problems, but no longer for its traditional ability to improve poor sight. Dioscorides called the herb *chelidonion* (from *khelidon* – a swallow) since it was supposed to flower when swallows were migrating.
Description Perennial 30–90 cm high; stem branched, slightly hairy, leaves pinnate, finely hairy or glabrous, with 5–7 ovate or oblong leaflets crenated or toothed, blue-green underneath; flowers yellow, 4-petalled, 2–2.5 cm diameter, appearing early to mid-summer. Followed by erect thin green capsules 3–5 cm long.
Distribution Native to Europe, naturalized in eastern North America, introduced elsewhere.

Found on waste-ground, wood edges, paths and walls primarily near habitation.
Cultivation Wild plant. Propagate by root division in spring.
Constituents Acrid orange coloured latex containing several alkaloids, especially chelidonine and chelerythrin; a bitter principle, chelidoxanthin; citric, malic and chelidonic acids; saponin. Acts as an antispasmodic on smooth muscle, such as gall bladder and bladder.
Uses (fresh or dried flowering plant, fresh latex) Cholagogue; narcotic; purgative; antimitotic. Principally used in inflammations of biliary duct and gall bladder, such as gall stones and cholecystitis. Fresh juice formerly used externally on warts.
Contra-indications Large doses POISONOUS; side-effects include sleepiness, skin irritation, respiratory tract irritation causing violent coughing and dyspnoea. Urine stained bright yellow. May cause ulcers.

Chelone glabra L SCROPHULARIACEAE
Turtle-head Balmony
This beautiful swamp plant possesses odourless flowers whose shape resembles that of a turtle's head (*chelone* is Greek for tortoise). It has long been a favourite tonic in North American folk medicine, but has not been scientifically examined.
Description Perennial to 1.5 m; stem erect smooth, square, bearing opposite, sessile or shortly petiolate dark green shiny leaves, 7–15 cm long, narrow and pointed, somewhat serrate. Flowers white or rose-tinged, 2.5 cm long, in terminal or axillary spikes. Appearing late summer to mid-autumn.
Distribution North America from Newfoundland to Florida and Texas. Found on low wet ground, stream margins, wet forests and thickets.
Cultivation Wild plant.
Constituents No analysis available.
Uses (dried flowering plant) Cholagogue; laxative; anthelmintic. Used in general intestinal disorders as a tonic. Of benefit in anorexia, indigestion, constipation and cholecystitis. Once used as an ointment to relieve irritation of piles.

Chenopodium album L CHENOPODIACEAE
Fat Hen White Goosefoot/Common Pigweed
The Chenopodiaceae or Goosefoot family (from the Greek *khenopodion* meaning goose foot which is the shape of the leaves of some species) includes 1500 species of rather unattractive plants, many of which are important edible plants, for example, spinach and beet. Fat Hen and the closely related Good King Henry (*Chenopodium bonus-henricus*) were eaten from neolithic times until the nineteenth century, and the fatty seed from *C. album* was included in the ritualistic last meal of Tollund Man, sacrificed in Denmark in 100 B.C.
Description Annual to 1 m consisting of short, often reddish, branched stem, bearing bluish-green lanceolate toothed variable-sized leaves, and mealy white inflorescence. Flowers small, greenish-white, in clusters, appearing mid-summer to mid-autumn.
Distribution European native; found in nitrogenous weedy places, often one of the first plants to appear on disturbed soil.
Cultivation Wild plant.

Constituents Rich in iron, calcium, vitamins B_1 and C.
Uses (fresh young leaf, seed) Nutritive. No common medicinal use, although mildly laxative.
Seed can be ground and used as flour.
Leaf eaten as cooked green vegetable or raw. It is more nutritious than spinach or cabbage.
Produces a red to golden-red dye.
Can be used as animal fodder.

Chenopodium ambrosioides var. *anthelmintium* L CHENOPODIACEAE
American Wormseed Mexican Tea
Although indigenous to Mexico this herb has become thoroughly naturalized as far north as New England, and it was introduced into Europe in 1732. Mexican Tea was once included in the United States Pharmacopoeia, but is now restricted to American folk medicine.
Description Strong smelling annual reaching 1.25 m, branching profusely from ground level; leaves alternate, oblong-lanceolate, 12.5 cm long; flowers greenish, small, arranged on leafless spikes appearing late summer to late autumn.
Distribution America, especially tropical central America; widely naturalized. On dry waste

places and previously cultivated land.
Cultivation Wild plant.
Constituents Volatile chenopodium oil.
Uses (fruit, entire flowering plant) Anthelmintic, especially for roundworm and hookworm, and used in both humans and animals. Tea from leaf reported to stimulate milk flow and to relieve pain after childbirth. Main use as the source of chenopodium oil for incorporation into anthelmintic preparations.
Contra-indications POISONOUS. Large doses cause vertigo, deafness, paralysis, incontinence, sweating, jaundice, and death.

Chionanthus virginicus L OLEACEAE
Fringe Tree Snowdrop Tree/Old Man's Beard
All the common names of this beautiful tree refer to its spectacular appearance when in flower, for which reason it has of course been

widely cultivated. From a distance the flowering tree appears to be covered with snow, and the name *chionanthus* is from the Greek meaning snow flower. The Fringe Tree belongs to the same family as the olive, lilac, jasmine and forsythia.

Description Deciduous shrub or tree to 8 m; leaves smooth or downy, oblong or oval, 7.5–20 cm long, opposite. Flowers delicate, fringe-like, numerous, white, 2.5 cm long, on long stems, in panicles 10–20 cm long. Appearing late spring to mid-summer and followed by fleshy, purple, ovoid drupes (berries).

Distribution Native to North America from Pennsylvania to Florida and Texas. Found in woods and thickets, on rich moist soils.

Cultivation Wild plant; cultivated as ornamental tree.

Constituents Saponins; phyllyrin; a lignan glycoside.

Uses (dried root bark, fresh trunk bark) Antipyretic; diuretic; cholagogue; hepatic stimulant. An infusion once used as a general tonic after debilitating disease, especially of hepatic origin. Of benefit in skin inflammations, cuts, ulcers and bruises when applied as a poultice.

Chondrus crispus (L) Stackh. GIGARTINACEAE

Carrageen Irish Moss

Irish Moss is unimportant medically and is not mentioned at all in classical writings. It was briefly promoted in 1831 by Dr Todhunter in Ireland, but it attracted little attention and is now largely of use in the food and cosmetic industries.

Description Cartilaginous seaweed, yellow-green to purplish-brown when fresh, white to yellow and translucent after drying. Thallus (fronds) 10–30 cm long, arising from subcylindrical stem, becoming flattened, curled and sometimes bifid. Fruiting bodies (cystocarps) small, oval, appearing on the branches of the thallus.

Distribution Coasts of north Atlantic Ocean on mainly rocky shores.

Cultivation Wild plant; collected in Ireland, Brittany and Massachussetts.

Constituents Mainly mucilage; proteins; iodine. When Irish moss is boiled, the soluble sub-

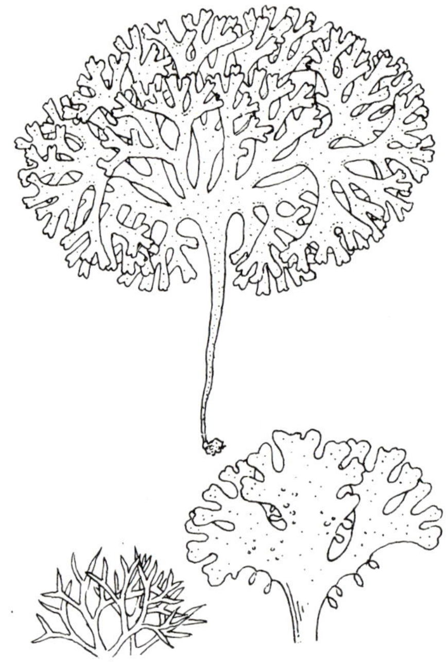

stances extracted are called carrageenin.

Uses (dried plant) Demulcent; nutritive. Formerly used to treat coughs.

Used mostly as a gelatin substitute in jelly manufacture; as an emulsifying agent for cod-liver and other oils; in the food industry as a suspending and gelling agent.

Once used for dressing cotton, stuffing mattresses, fining beer, feeding cattle, and as a colour thickener in cloth printing.

Chrysanthemum balsamita L COMPOSITAE

Alecost Costmary/Bible-leaf Mace

The most obvious characteristic of this ancient herb is its pleasant balsam-like scent from which it is known in several languages as the Balsam Herb. The common English names also refer to this aroma by their incorporation of the Greek word *kostos*; *kostos* was an old Asian herb used in perfumery which had a similar odour to *C. balsamita*. Alecost is famous as the pre-eminent Middle Ages agent for flavouring and preparing ale.

Description Hardy aromatic perennial to 1 m; leaves ovate 5–15 cm long, finely serrate, often with pair of small lobes at the base; greyish-green. Flowers 1 cm broad, yellow, button-like, appearing late summer to early autumn.

Distribution Western Asian native; naturalized in North America, Europe. Tolerates any soil; prefers sunny position.

Cultivation Wild plant; once widely cultivated as a garden plant. Propagate by root division spring or autumn, or by seed sown in spring. It cannot be raised from seed in cool climates. If grown in the shade it will not flower.

Constituents Volatile oil.

Uses (fresh and dried leaf) Stomachic. Rarely used medicinally; an ointment once used as a salve in burns and stings.

Wide culinary uses; including spring salad, flavouring home-made beer, soups, cakes, poultry.

Formerly a cosmetic water was made from the leaf.

Chrysanthemum cinerariifolium (Trevir) Vis. COMPOSITAE

Pyrethrum Flower Dalmatian Pyrethrum

C. cinerariifolium is the source of the best-known natural insecticide, pyrethrum, which is renowned for its possession of an extremely rapid paralyzing effect and toxicity to a wide range of insects. It is non-toxic to mammals, however. For this reason it is used as a spray to kill the vectors of certain insect-transmitted diseases in aircraft. Recent work has shown that the flower-heads possess weak antibiotic activity, although the herb is not used medicinally.

Description Herbaceous perennial 30–75 cm tall with slender, hairy stems; leaves 15–30 cm long, petiolate, oblong or oval, subdivided into linear segments. Flowers solitary on long slender peduncles, white, appearing early summer to early autumn.

Distribution Indigenous to parts of Yugoslavia

and adjacent coastal islands; prefers littoral zones but also found inland including mountainous areas.
Cultivation Wild plant. Cultivated commercially in Japan, Kenya, South Africa, parts of central Europe. Propagation by seed sown in autumn, thinning out in the following mid-spring.
Constituents Pyrethrins, comprising the keto-esters cinerin I and II, pyrethrin I and II; also chrysanthine and chrysanthene; all possess insecticidal properties.
Uses (dried and powdered flower-heads) No medicinal action; used only as a non-toxic insecticide for control of the bedbug, mosquito, cockroach, domestic fly and other pests.
Contra-indications Prolonged human contact may lead to allergic dermatitis, allergic rhinitis and asthma.

Chrysanthemum parthenium (L) Bernh.
COMPOSITAE
Feverfew Featherfew
There is evidence that Feverfew was used as a general purpose tonic in previous ages, its common name being derived from the Latin *febrifugia* meaning a substance which drives out fevers. The old herbalists' term 'febrifuge' – from the same stem – has now been replaced with the medical description, antipyretic, but strangely the herb is rarely employed in folk medicine to treat fevers. It is an attractive, robust and vigorously growing garden plant.
Description Perennial, sometimes biennial, to 90 cm; much branched with yellow-green, strongly scented pinnate leaves, the 1–2 leaflets not exceeding 7.5 cm long. Many flowers, 1–2 cm wide consisting of yellow disc florets, white ray florets, in tight clusters, appear mid-summer to mid-autumn.
Distribution South-east European native; introduced elsewhere. Prefers dry sites on any well-drained soil.
Cultivation Wild plant, propagated by root division, cuttings and seed sown in early to mid-spring. Double-flowered variety grown horticulturally.
Constituents Volatile oils.

Uses (dried leaf, dried flowering plant) Bitter; aperient; tonic.
An infusion is of benefit in indigestion, as a general tonic and to promote menstruation. Once used as a mild sedative.
Small quantities added to food 'cuts' the grease.
Employed as a moth repellent.

Cichorium intybus L COMPOSITAE
Chicory Succory/Wild Succory
The use of Chicory can be traced back to the Egyptians, who – like the Arabians – used the blanched leaves as a salad, a custom continued to this day on a commercial scale in Belgium and horticulturally throughout Europe. Sometimes the blanched winter salad leaves are known as Endive, which is derived from the Arabic word *hendibeh*: the specific botanical name comes from the same source. Dickens in his *Household Words* described the extensive cultivation of 'chiccory' in England for the root which was ground and roasted to be used

as a coffee substitute.
Description Deep rooted perennial reaching 1.5 m; stem bristly or hairy bearing rigid branches. Upper parts practically leafless with small bract-like leaves; lower leaves entire, broadly oblong or lanceolate, partly clasping and bristly beneath. Flowers in large capitula of 4 cm diameter, azure blue and consisting only of ray florets. Appearing from late summer to mid-autumn. Flower-heads close by midday.
Distribution European native; introduced elsewhere; naturalized in the United States. On roadsides, field edges, on nitrogenous, calcareous and alluvial soils.
Cultivation Wild plant; widely cultivated horticulturally and commercially. Seed sown in well-manured soil from late spring to mid-summer, thinned to 15–20 cm apart in mid-summer to late summer. Forced blanched salad heads best obtained from the variety *Witloof*: lift the root in late autumn, shorten to 20 cm, remove all side-shoots and leaves and stack in dry sand in the dark. For coffee substitute, use roots of the varieties *Magdeburg* and *Brunswick* or *Witloof*. White and pink horticultural races also exist.
Constituents Inulin; sugar; mineral salts; lipids; vitamins B, C, K and P; bitter principles (sesquiterpenoid lactones) chiefly lactucine and lactupicrine.
Uses (fresh leaf, root) Diuretic; weak tonic; laxative. Of little medical use; formerly employed as an aid in jaundice, and may protect the liver from the effects of excessive coffee drinking. Increases glandular secretions slightly.
Root roasted and ground as a coffee substitute or additive; can be boiled or baked, or used as flour. Forced leaves used as a winter salad; young leaves added to summer salads.
Leaves produce a blue dye.
Contra-indications Excessive and continued use may impair function of the retina.

Cimicifuga racemosa (L) Nutt.
RANUNCULACEAE
Black Cohosh Black Snakeroot/Bugbane
Linnaeus described this herb in his *Materia Medica* of the eighteenth century as *Actaea racemis longissimus*, but it was first called *Christophoriana canadensis racemosa* by Plukenet in 1696. It is an American herb, introduced into medical practice in America in 1828 by Garden, and used briefly in Europe from 1860. Now only employed by Anglo-American herbalists of the Physiomedical school.
Description Graceful perennial 1–2.5 m high on thick, gnarled, blackish root-stock bearing smooth, furrowed stem with alternate leaves subdivided into 2-, 3- or 5-ovate, toothed leaflets, 4–7.5 cm long. Inflorescence 30–100 cm long, consisting of foetid, creamy-white flowers with numerous long stamens, on a terminal raceme; appears early summer to early autumn.
Distribution Indigenous to Canada and the eastern United States, especially Massachusetts, Ohio, Indiana and Georgia. Prefers rich open woodland and cleared hillsides.

Cultivation Wild plant.
Constituents Resins and salicylic acid, both acting as anti-rheumatic agents; isoferulic acid; phytosterols; alkaloids; tannic acid; 3 unidenfied crystalline alcohols. (A resinoid impure mixture, cimicifugin, is produced by adding tincture of cimicifuga to water.)
Uses (dried root-stock) Anti-rheumatic; a bitter; mild expectorant; emmenagogue; sedative. Particularly effective in acute stage of rheumatoid arthritis, sciatica, and chorea. Apparently most successfully used in females, and acts specifically on the uterus, easing uterine cramps.
Contra-indications Large doses irritate nerve centres, and may cause abortion.

Cinchona officinalis L RUBIACEAE
Cinchona Quinine Tree/Peruvian Bark
The Spanish conquerors learned of the antipyretic properties of Cinchona Bark from the inhabitants of Peru in the sixteenth century; it is not certain, however, that they used the material themselves, considering it extremely powerful. It was introduced into Spain in 1639, and promoted throughout Europe by the Jesuits who gave the powder to those suffering from fever. Medical opinion varied as to its safety, but by 1677 it was introduced into the London Pharmacopoeia. About 12 species of Cinchona are now used as sources of the bark, which is mainly employed for the isolation of quinine, once used as an antimalarial agent.
Description The Cinchonas are evergreen trees from 6–25 m tall; reduced to shrubs at the limits of their habitat. Leaves extremely variable but often bright green, obovate or lanceolate from 7.5–50 cm long, finely veined with crimson, traversed by prominent midrib, and borne on a brown petiole. Flowers very fragrant, small, deep rose-crimson, clustered on panicles. The useful species are differentiated from others by presence of curly hairs bordering the corolla, by its mode of capsule dehiscence from below upwards and by presence of small pits (scrobiculi) at the vein axils on underside of leaf.

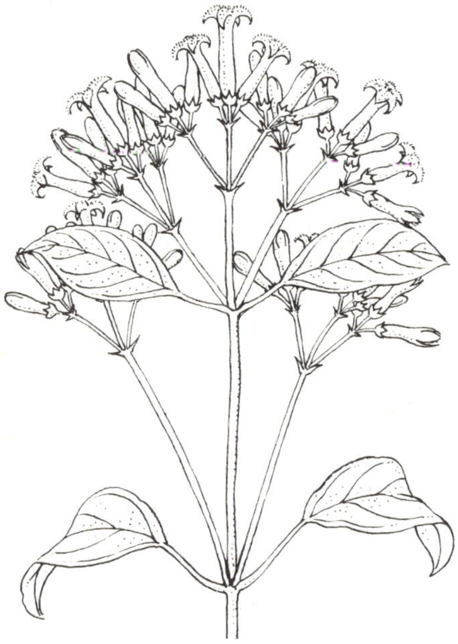

Distribution South American natives, occurring exclusively on the western side of the subcontinent. Also Java, Ceylon, Burma, India, East Africa. Grows only in mountainous regions, most valuable species being found and cultivated from 1500–2500 m.
Cultivation Wild plant; mostly cultivated commercially in Java.
Constituents 20 alkaloids including quinine, cinchonine, cinchonidine, and quinidine; a glycoside; cinchona red; starch; wax; fat; cinchotannic acid; quinic, quinoic and oxalic acids.
Uses (dried stem bark) Antipyretic; bitter tonic; stomachic.
More slowly absorbed and more irritant to the gastro-intestinal tract than quinine in its pure form. Useful astringent throat gargle. Tincture employed for preventative treatment of the common cold; orthodox medicine still employs quinine for the relief of muscle cramps.
Powdered bark used in astringent toothpowders.
May be used as a red dye for fabrics.
Contra-indications May cause vomiting; prolonged usage can cause cinchonism, symptoms of which include deafness and blindness.

Cinnamomum camphora Nees et Eberm. LAURACEAE
Camphor Tree Laurel Camphor
The Camphor Tree was mentioned in the sixteenth-century Chinese herbal *Pun-tsao-kang-muh* and earlier by Marco Polo at the end of the thirteenth century.
The camphor product was certainly known before this and was regarded as one of the most rare and valuable perfumes; it is, however, not certain whether this camphor was derived from *C. camphora* or from *Dryobalanops aromatica*, a Sumatran tree. In 1563 Garcia de Orta wrote that Sumatran Camphor was so superior and costly that none found its way to Europe. Certainly Camphor was known in European medicine by the twelfth century since the German abbess Hildegarde used it – as *ganphora*.
Description Dense topped evergreen tree reaching 12 m, and occasionally even taller; trunk enlarged at base. Leaves camphor scented, alternate, acuminate, smooth and shiny above, whitish beneath, 5–12 cm long. Yellow flowers in axillary panicles appearing early summer.
Distribution Indigenous to China and Japan; introduced elsewhere. Flourishing in tropical and subtropical countries up to an altitude of 750 m.
Cultivation Wild plant; introduced horticulturally.
Constituents Obtained by distillation of 24–40-year-old wood. Camphor, white oil of Camphor, both comprising safrole, acetaldehyde, terpineol, eugenol, cineole, d-pinene, phellandrene.
Uses (Camphor; oil of Camphor) Weakly antiseptic; stimulant; carminative; mild expectorant; mild analgesic; rubefacient; parasiticide.

Used internally (rarely) for sedation in hysteria. Commonly employed externally as a counter-irritant in inflamed rheumatic joints, fibrositis, and neuralgia. Small doses stimulate respiration. Often used in combination with other substances.
Contra-indications Large internal doses toxic to children, causing respiratory failure.

Cinnamomum cassia Blume LAURACEAE
Cassia Bark Tree Chinese Cinnamon
Cassia and Cinnamon are confused in early

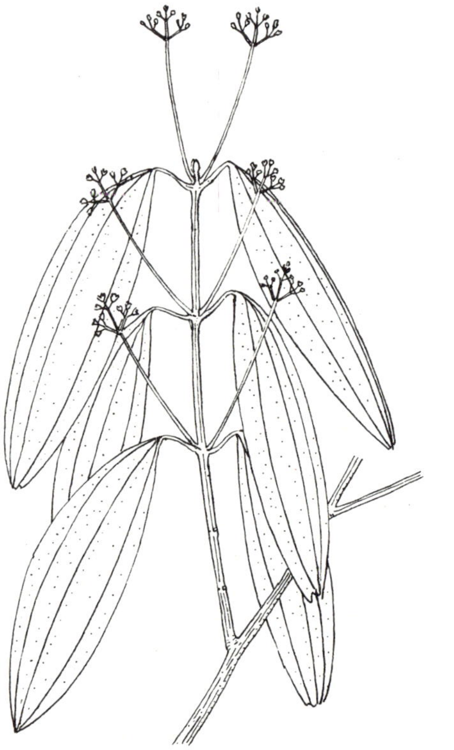

writings, and it is probable that the terms were sometimes used to describe different grades of the same or closely related plants. The spice is called *kwei* in the earliest Chinese herbal by

Shen-nung (2700 B.C.). It reached Europe in classical times via Arabian and Phoenician traders, and is frequently still used as an inferior substitute for Cinnamon.
Description Attractive evergreen tree to 7 m, white aromatic bark and angular branches; leaves oblong-lanceolate 7.5–10 cm long, on slender 6–8 mm long petiole. Flowers small on slender panicles, 7–12 cm long, appearing early summer.
Distribution Native of China; cultivated in China and Burma.
Cultivation Wild plant; also cultivated commercially.
Constituents Volatile oil; resin; tannin; lignin; bassorin; colouring matter. Oil of Cassia comprises largely cinnamaldehyde.
Uses (dried bark) Aromatic; carminative; astringent; stimulant.
Used as a powder or infusion in flatulence and nausea in a similar manner to Cinnamon, which it sometimes replaces. May be used alone or in combination to treat diarrhoea.

Cinnamomum zeylanicum Nees LAURACEAE
Cinnamon Tree Ceylon Cinnamon
Cinnamon was considered by the ancients as one of the most important aromatic spices available and is mentioned in the Old Testament in the same context as Myrrh, Olibanum, gold and silver. It is doubtful, however, whether the species *C. zeylanicum* was known before the thirteenth century, since the spice is not mentioned as a product of Ceylon – to which it was indigenous – until 1275, when it was documented by an Arab writer, Kazwini. The Portuguese occupied Ceylon in 1536 mainly to obtain supplies of Cinnamon, and the Dutch began its cultivation there in 1770 with such success that the total European demand was far exceeded, and for years large quantities had to be burned.
Description Medium-sized evergreen tree 6.5–10 m tall, with thick, smooth and pale bark; leaves opposite or rarely alternate, hard, 7.5–20 cm long and 4–7.5 cm wide, ovate or ovate-lanceolate, shiny above and paler beneath. Numerous yellowish-white flowers, disagreeable odour, in silky loose panicles longer than leaves on long peduncles.

Distribution Native of Ceylon, wild in southern India and Malaya; cultivated in Ceylon, India, Jamaica, Brazil, the Seychelles, and other tropical countries. In forests to 1000 m.
Cultivation Wild plant; cultivated commercially in coppices.
Constituents Volatile oil, whose action is carminative and antiseptic; also tannin and mucilage.
Uses (dried bark; volatile oil) Aromatic; astringent; stimulant; carminative.
Used as an intestinal stimulant and astringent to treat vomiting and nausea.
Widely employed as a spice; oil used in flavouring and in cordials. Limited use in perfumery.

Citrus aurantium var. *amara* (L) Link
RUTACEAE
Bitter Orange Seville Orange/Bigarade
Known to the early Greeks, this was probably also the first orange grown in Europe in about the twelfth century. The Sweet Orange was not known until the mid-fifteenth century. The

Bitter Orange is usually only employed in the food and perfume industry.
Description Glabrous evergreen tree to 8 m; branches spiny. Leaves alternate, ovate-oblong to 8 cm long, sinuate or crenate, petiole broad-winged. Flowers fragrant, white or pink, axillary, single or few; followed by 7.5 cm diameter globose orange to reddish fruit.
Distribution Asian native. Introduced and naturalized in south Europe, Florida, United States and elsewhere.
Cultivation Wild and cultivated commercially. Used as stock for the Sweet Orange. Easily raised from seed.
Constituents (flowers) Oil of neroli, a complex volatile oil. (fruit and rind) Volatile oil comprising limonene (to 90%); vitamin C; flavonoids; bitter compounds including naringine.
Uses (flowers, leaves, fruit, fruit rind) Aperitif; antispasmodic; sedative; cholagogue; tonic; vermifuge.
Neroli oil in vaseline is used in India as a preventive against leeches. Leaves and flowers in infusion act as sedative stomachics. Orange-flower water is used to flavour medicines. Employed in perfumery.
Used in conserves, and for flavouring.

Citrus limon Burm. RUTACEAE
Lemon
The Lemon is a household fruit today, but it was unknown in ancient Greece and Rome. The wild Lemon is probably a native of northern India, and is known in Hindustani as *limu* or *ninbu*, which passed into the Arabic *limun*.
European cultivation of the Lemon was carried out with Arabian knowledge and plants, and probably started in the thirteenth century in Spain or Sicily. Numerous varieties now exist.
Description Small glabrous tree 3–6 m high, with stout stiff thorns; leaves pale green, oblong to elliptic-ovate, 5–10 cm long, on short petioles with very narrow margins. Flowers 8–16 mm long, white inside and pink outside, clustered in the axils. Sour fruit 7.5–12.5 cm long, light yellow, oblong to ovoid terminating in a nipple.
Distribution Native to Asia; wild in India. Cultivated commercially especially in Mediterranean countries.
Cultivation Wild plant; extensive horticultural and commercial cultivation.
Constituents Citric acid; pectin; hesperidin; vitamins A, B and C; citral; citronellol; d-limonene; phellandrene; sesquiterpene.
Uses (fresh fruit, dried peel, juice, oil) Antiscorbutic; tonic; refrigerant; carminative; stimulant; aromatic.
Fresh juice employed as a household remedy

for the common cold; Lemon oil was once used as a carminative, and the peel is still employed as a bitter.
The widest use is for culinary purposes as a flavouring agent and as an antioxidant.
Used for cosmetic purposes as astringent, skin tonic, in scents.

Claviceps purpurea (Fried.) Tulasne
ASCOMYCETES
Ergot Ergot of Rye
Ergot is best known as the cause of a serious and spectacular human disease characterized by symptoms of hallucination and madness. It is now known as ergotism and arose in epidemic proportions throughout Europe from at least as early as the sixth century and lasted until 1816. The disease was called by a variety of names the most common being *Ignis sancti Antonii* or St Anthony's Fire, and was eventually discovered to be caused by eating flour or bread containing a high proportion of the Ergot fungus.
It was found to be of obstetric value in the 1550s by Lonitzer of Frankfurt and is retained to this day in many pharmacopoeias, including the British, French and German.
Description Ergot is the dried sclerotium, or resting stage, of a fungus which develops in the ovary of the rye plant (*Secale cereale* (L)), and other grasses belonging to the genera Agropyrum, Alopecurus, Anthoxanthum, Avena, Brachypodium, Calamagrostis, Dactylis, Hordeum and Triticum.
The sclerotium externally is dark violet to black, usually 1–3 cm long and 1–5 mm broad, fusiform, often tapering towards both ends, brittle. Internally whitish-pinkish to white with a faint odour. Appears in the autumn.
Distribution In all the cereal producing countries in areas or years of high humidity and then often at edges of rye fields.

Cultivation Wild; cultivated commercially by artificial inoculation of rye plant heads with the fungal spores.
Constituents Extremely complex, containing a number of alkaloids; carbohydrates; lipids; quaternary ammonium bases; sterols; dyes; amino-acids and amines. Six isomeric pairs of alkaloids have been isolated, including ergocistine, ergotamine, ergocryptine, ergocornine, ergosine and ergometrine. Most are derivatives of lysergic acid or iso-lysergic acid; action on the uterus is largely due to these alkaloids.
Uses (dried fungus) Uterine stimulant, haemostatic; circulatory stimulant; emmenagogue.
Most effectively employed as a preventative against post-partum haemorrhage and as a stimulant to arrest bleeding in menorrhagia and metrorrhagia. Also used in neurology.
Contra-indications Large doses may induce abortion in pregnant women. Increases blood pressure. To be used by medical personnel only.

Cnicus benedictus L COMPOSITAE
Blessed Thistle
Carduus sanctus or *carduus benedictus* (the Sacred or Blessed Thistle) is still cultivated as a medicinal herb in certain European countries and has long enjoyed a reputation as an effective remedial plant. At one time considered a

cure-all its use now is generally restricted to inclusion in herbal tonics. *Cnicus* is the Latin name for Safflower which was once the name given to the thistle family.
Description Thistle-like branched annual to 70 cm; leaves lanceolate, dentate, with spines on each tooth, dark green, white-veined, 5–15 cm long. Flowers partially concealed within spiny bracts, yellow 3–4 cm wide, and appearing mid-summer to early autumn.
Distribution Mediterranean native; naturalized in United States; introduced elsewhere. Tolerates most soils.
Cultivation Wild plant; cultivated commercially. Easily raised from seed sown in spring or autumn, preferably on well-manured soil.

Constituents Volatile oil; a bitter principle, cnicin, which aids digestion.
Uses (dried flowering plant) Tonic; emetic; diaphoretic. Used as a weak infusion it stimulates the appetite and is said to act as a galactagogue. The flowering tops were once used to treat worms.
Mixed with wine to make an aperitif.
Young leaves used to be eaten in salads, flowerheads eaten in the manner of Artichokes, and root boiled as a pot herb.
Contra-indications Large doses strongly emetic.

Cocos nucifera L PALMAE
Coconut Palm
A well-known tree of enormous economic and nutritional importance in many tropical countries. Many parts of the palm are exploited, but the fruit or coconut is most useful; for this reason cultivated varieties have been bred which produce 100 to 200 coconuts each year. The generic name *Cocos* is from the Portuguese for monkey, as the nut looks like a monkey's face; *nucifera* means nut-bearing.
Description Palm tree to 25 m; trunk usually curving to one side and regularly ringed with leaf scars. Leaves in a terminal crown, very long (5 m) on a yellowish petiole which is deeply embedded in loose fibre surrounding the trunk; deeply pinnate and pendulous. Flowers followed by ovoid nuts 20 cm long, usually in bunches of 10 to 20.
Distribution Native to Malaysia and Polynesia; widely distributed throughout tropical zones. In coastal situations or occasionally inland.
Cultivation Wild. Widely cultivated commercially.
Constituents Oil, comprising the glycerides, trimyristin, trilaurin, triolein, tristearin and tripalmitin; also the glycerides of caprylic, capric and caproic acids.
Uses (oil, kernels, seed, leaves, sap) Nutritive;

anthelmintic. The seed is sometimes used as an anthelmintic in tropical countries. Fractionated coconut oil (containing medium chain triglycerides) is used in certain diets for conditions such as cystic fibrosis and steatorrhoea where patients are unable to absorb normal fats completely.

The oil is used as an ointment base, and in massage creams and certain medicated shampoos. Also used in sea-water soaps, and formerly in margarine.

Wide culinary use of the kernel as a food and flavouring, particularly in Indonesian cuisine; and the apical bud or 'cabbage' of the tree is eaten as a delicacy. The fermented sap is employed in palm wine and spirit manufacture.

Leaves are extensively used in basket, mat and rope manufacture; the husk fibre from the nut is similarly used in coconut matting and rope.

Coffea arabica L RUBIACEAE

Coffee Common or Arabian Coffee

The Coffee plant forms wild forests in parts of the Sudan and Abyssinia and for centuries the berry has been eaten raw by natives as a stimulant.

The habit of drinking Coffee probably originated with the Abyssinians, from whom the use

of Coffee spread into Arabia.

Rauwolf, the botanist, mentioned Coffee for the first time in 1573 when travelling in the Levant, and Prosper Alpinus described it more fully in 1591. European Coffee drinking began in Venice at the beginning of the seventeenth century, and was fashionable in England by 1652 and France by 1669.

It is thought that all the Coffee now exported from Brazil and the West Indies stems from the propagation of a single plant introduced to the Celebes in 1822.

Description Evergreen shrub 3–5 m high, initially with a single main trunk, later developing others from this; leaves dark green and glossy, thin, opposite, 7–12 cm long; 2.5–4 cm wide, abruptly acuminate with a point 15 mm long. White star-like flowers, fragrant, followed by 2-seeded deep red berry (beans) 15 mm long.

Distribution Native to tropical Africa; early introduction to Arabia. Introduced to tropical countries, especially abundant in the Americas. Prefers jungle conditions and partial shade.

Cultivation Wild and extensively cultivated commercially in plantations, often under artificial shading. Horticultural variegated forms exist; grown indoors as a house plant.

Constituents Caffeine (1–2%), acting as a stimulant upon the central nervous system; volatile oils; colouring matter; tannin; traces of theobromine and its isomer, theophylline.

Uses (freshly roasted ground kernel) Stimulant; diuretic.

Taken as a general tonic stimulant, especially useful in narcotic poisoning. Decoction employed as a flavouring agent in pharmaceutical preparations.

Very wide use as a beverage, for colouring and flavouring purposes, and in liqueur and confectionery manufacture.

Contra-indications Excessive intake may cause insomnia, muscle tremor, restlessness, palpitations and tachycardia.

Cola acuminata (Beauv.) Schott et Endl. STERCULIACEAE

Cola Nut Kola/Goora Nut

The Cola Nuts commercially available consist of the cotyledons, fleshy and white before drying, obtained from the 5 to 15 seeds of the large fruit of the Cola tree.

Fresh Nuts are seldom found outside Africa, where they are consumed raw before meals to promote digestion. They are also considered to improve the flavour of food.

Cola Nuts, described as *colla* were first seen in the Congo by Father Carli in 1667. The dried product does not contain the same properties as the fresh Nut, and most of it is used in soft drinks. It is still used in folk medicine as a stimulant.

Description Evergreen tree to 15 m high; leaves leathery, acute, entire, obovate, 10–20 cm long; yellow flowers of 15 mm diameter, in panicles, calyx tube green. Fruit 10–15 cm long, containing red or white seeds 4–5 cm long, and consisting of cotyledons 2–5 cm long.

Distribution Native to north-west African coast, especially Sierra Leone and the Cameroons. Introduced elsewhere. Prefers coastal and estuary sites in forests.

Cultivation Wild plant; cultivated in West Africa, Java, Brazil and the West Indies.

Constituents Caffeine (1.5%), combined with kolatin in the fresh state, and unbound when dried; also theobromine; kola red; fat; sugar; starch.

Uses (dried cotyledons) Stimulant; anti-depressive.

Particularly employed in debilitated, exhausted and depressive conditions; in melancholia, anorexia and migraine.

A flavouring for soft drinks, cordials, ice creams and wines. Used in the manufacture of cola-type beverages.

A red dye is obtained from the Cola Nut.

Colchicum autumnale L LILIACEAE

Autumn Crocus Colchicum/Meadow Saffron

The Autumn Crocus is a rare example of a plant known since the early Greeks which was not introduced into medical practice until quite recently. Most of the ancient and medieval writers, except the Arabic physicians, considered Colchicum too poisonous to use, although it did appear briefly in the London Pharmacopoeia from 1618 to 1639.

Its modern use derives from the research of Wedel (1718) and Storck (1763) on the treatment of gout, for which purpose it is retained to this day in many countries.

Description Perennial; solitary pale purple flower, 6 petals on 20-cm long white 'stalk' which is actually an elongated corolla tube, appearing in the autumn from a corm 15 cm

below ground; 6 stamens, 3 styles; fleshy, lanceolate leaves 30 cm long first appear in the following spring, and enclose the seed-filled brown capsular fruit by mid-summer.

Distribution European native; prefers deep clay and nutrient rich loam in damp meadows and fen woodland.

Cultivation Wild plant; cultivated from seed collected in late summer, or from corms.

Constituents Several toxic alkaloids, largely

colchicine to which its action is due; also starch; gum; sugar; fat; tannin.
Uses (dried corms, seeds) Anti-rheumatic. Used to relieve the pain and inflammation of acute gout and rheumatism.
Contra-indications All parts highly POISONOUS, causing diarrhoea and sometimes death. Only to be used by medical personnel.

Commiphora molmol Engler BURSERACEAE
Myrrh Gum Myrrh/Myrrha
Used from the earliest times as a constituent of perfumes, unguents and incense, the modern name is directly derived from the old Hebrew and Arabic word *mur*, meaning bitter.
The ancient Greeks knew of Myrrh and a liquid form called *stacte* which is no longer found, but is thought to be a natural exudation of the Myrrh tree or a closely related species. Myrrh was highly prized in the Middle Ages and is still used as a mouthwash and in folk medicine.

Description Low stunted bush or small tree to 2.75 m high; trunk thick and bearing numerous irregular, knotted branches and smaller stout clustered branchlets, the latter spreading at right angles and terminating in a sharp spine. Few leaves, 1–1.5 cm long, at ends of short wart-like branchlets; trifoliate, the lateral leaflets minute, the terminal 1 cm long, obovate-oval, narrowed at the base, entire, glabrous.
Gum discharged through the bark naturally or after wounding.
Distribution Arabia; Somaliland. On basaltic soil in very hot areas.
Cultivation Wild plant.
Constituents Oleo-gum-resin, comprising 25–35% resin, 2.5–6.5% volatile oil, 50–60% gum.
Uses (dried oleo-gum-resin) Carminative; antiseptic; mildly expectorant; diuretic; diaphoretic.
Astringent to mucous membranes, and used as a gargle and mouthwash in inflammations of the mouth and pharynx. Tincture is applied to ulcers. Stimulates natural resistance of the body in septicaemia. Small doses effective in dyspepsia.
A constituent of some tooth-powders.
Used in veterinary medicine for wound treatment.
Employed in incense, and when burned repels mosquitos.

Conium maculatum L UMBELLIFERAE
Hemlock Poison Hemlock/Mother Die
Hemlock is best known historically as the principal, if not the only, ingredient of the Athenian State poison used as a method of execution for, among others, Thermanes, Phocion and Socrates. Dioscorides introduced it as a medicine mostly for the external treatment of herpes and erysipelas, and both Pliny and Avicenna considered it effective in the treatment of tumours. The old Roman name

for the herb was *cicuta*, a term found in tenth-century Anglo-Saxon works.
The poisonous nature of the plant varies considerably. Carpenter in 1850 claimed that Hemlock growing in London was harmless, and others maintain that it is less poisonous in colder climates than warmer ones. It must, however, always be treated as a dangerously poisonous plant.
Description Erect biennial herb, smelling of mice, arising from a forked root, and reaching 1.5 m; much branched, stems speckled and purple towards the base. Foliage dark and finely cut, 2–4 pinnate, glabrous; umbels of small white flowers appearing mid-summer to mid-autumn.
Distribution European native; extensively distributed in temperate zones. Found in weedy places especially in moist, warm sites by streams or field edges in loamy soil.
Cultivation Wild plant.
Constituents Several alkaloids, chiefly coniine, to which the intense toxicity of all parts of this plant is attributed; also methylconiine; conydrine; paraconine; oil of conium; conic acid.
Uses (unripe seed, fruit) Anodyne; sedative; antispasmodic.
Once used in neurological conditions such as epilepsy, mania and chorea, and in ancient times externally to treat breast tumours. Never employed today, not even in folk medicine. Although cooking is said to destroy the toxic constituents, this herb should never be eaten.
Contra-indications All parts, and especially the seed, are intensely POISONOUS.

Convallaria majalis L LILIACEAE
Lily-of-the-Valley May Lily
A flower which is frequently found in country gardens and which was shown as early as the sixteenth century to possess strong therapeutic action. It was known as *lilium convallium* to sixteenth-century apothecaries. Like the Foxglove, with which it shares similar heart-assisting properties, the herb did not previously enjoy wide medicinal use. Today, however, it is an important drug in some national pharmacopoeias.
Description Perennial fragrant plant 10–20 cm high producing annually a pair of oblong-oval petiolate leaves 10–20 cm long, 3–7.5 cm wide, deeply ribbed longitudinally; 5–10 bell-shaped white flowers 10 mm wide, borne on leafless peduncle, appearing early summer, and followed by round, red berries containing 2–6 seeds.
Distribution Native to Europe, East Asia, North America; introduced elsewhere. Prefers damp, calcareous, porous soil in woods, in some alpine locations, often forming dense areas of growth.
Cultivation Wild; introduced horticulturally, cultivated races bearing larger flowers. Propagated by root division in the autumn; prefers some shade may spread rapidly.

Constituents Cardio-active glycosides (cardenolides) similar to foxglove glycoside, especially convallatoxine, also convalloside, convallotoxole and convallotoxoside; a saponoside, convallamarine.
Uses (dried flowers) Cardiac tonic; emetic; diuretic.
Regulates heart action in a similar manner to the Foxglove and is considered to be safer and as effective. Seldom used outside eastern European countries.
Flowers provide a perfume base.
Dried ground roots were formerly an ingredient of snuff.
Contra-indications POISONOUS. To be used by medical personnel only.

Coriandrum sativum L UMBELLIFERAE
Coriander
Cultivated for over 3000 years Coriander is mentioned in all the medieval medical texts, by the Greeks, in the scriptures, by early Sanskrit authors – who called it *kustumburu* – and even in the Egyptian Ebers papyrus. Its

name is derived from *koris*, the Greek for bedbug, since the plant smells strongly of the insects.
Description Small glabrous solid-stemmed hardy annual plant from 30–60 cm tall on a thin, pointed root, lower leaves pinnate, cleft and lobed, the upper bipinnate and finely dissected. Small, flat, compound umbels of white and reddish flowers appear from mid-summer to early autumn, followed by brownish orbicular fruit with an unpleasant smell before they ripen, then becoming spicy and aromatic.
Distribution Indigenous to mediterranean and Caucasian regions; now widespread weed in many temperate zones. Prefers dry soil and full sun.
Cultivation Unknown in the wild state, cultivated commercially and horticulturally throughout the world. Seed sown in late spring or early summer in drills 2 cm deep; need thinning later. Germination may be slow.
Constituents Volatile oil, comprising borneol, coriandrol, d-pinene, β-pinene, terpinene, geraniol, and decyl aldehyde.
Uses (dried ripe fruits, leaf and root) Aromatic; carminative; stimulant.
Mostly used to prevent griping caused by other medication, such as Senna or Rhubarb. Chewing the seed stimulates secretion of gastric juices. Bruised seed is applied externally as a poultice to relieve painful joints in rheumatism. Root can be cooked and eaten as a vegetable.
The fresh leaf is probably the most widely used of all flavouring herbs throughout the world.
The seed is employed in baking, as a spice or condiment, in liqueur manufacture, and in confectionery.
May be added to pot-pourris.

Crataegus monogyna Jacq. ROSACEAE
Hawthorn May/Whitethorn
The botanical name of Hawthorn, *Crataegus*, comes from the Greek meaning strength which describes the strength of the wood, while the plant's common names in several European languages refer to the fact that this is a thorny bush producing fruit, the haw.
Much of the Hawthorn's previously considered powerful magical properties are now forgotten, although as with lilac and peacock's feathers, some people still refuse to bring the flowers indoors.
Medicinally the herb is very important and is widely used in orthodox Eastern and unorthodox Western medicine for the treatment of hypertension.
Description Shrub or small tree to 9 m; spreading branches with thorns 1.5 cm long; leaves glabrous, broad-ovate or obovate, deeply lobed, 15 mm–5 cm long; flowers white 1–1.5 cm across, in clusters of 5–12; 20 stamens with red anthers; appearing early summer to mid-summer followed by ovoid scarlet false fruits of 8–10 mm diameter, subglobose, which each contain 1 stony fruit.
Distribution Europe, North Africa, western Asia; introduced in other temperate zones. In hedges and open deciduous woods.

Cultivation Wild plant. Often planted as hedge.
Constituents Flavone glycosides; catechins; saponins; vitamin C; several unidentified constituents. Combined action improves blood flow in coronary arteries. It appears to act as an adaptogenic agent.
Uses (fresh or dried fruits) Hypotensive. Of specific use in hypertension associated with myocardial weakness, arteriosclerosis, paroxysmal tachycardia, and angina pectoris. Prolonged treatment is necessary.
Liqueur once manufactured from the berries.
Timber formerly used for small boxes.

Crithmum maritimum L UMBELLIFERAE
Samphire Peter's Cress/Rock Samphire/Sea Fennel
Samphire has long been collected from the rocks of its natural habitat for shipment in barrels of brine to urban areas or for local use. Surprisingly it was also grown as a kitchen herb. Gerard described its cultivation in 1598 in England, and Quintyne described it in France in 1690. The English particularly

favoured the seed pods for inclusion in sauces and pickles. It was cultivated in American gardens from 1821, but is now rarely seen anywhere.
Description Bushy, aromatic, perennial, umbelliferous plant reaching 30 cm; smooth, bright green and much branched on woody base, fleshy and somewhat spiky leaf segments, and greenish-yellow flowers appearing mid-summer to mid-autumn. Numerous bracts and bracteoles.
Distribution Growing upon rocks on the southern European Atlantic seaboard and on the shores of several mediterranean countries.
Cultivation Wild plant, may be grown horticulturally on well-drained soils.
Constituents Mineral salts; oils; volatile oil; iodine; vitamin C.
Uses (fresh young leaves) Used for culinary purposes as a boiled spiced pickle, as a salad, a buttered vegetable or as a condiment. Said to stimulate the appetite.

Crocus sativus L IRIDACEAE
Saffron Crocus Saffron
The Saffron Crocus has been considered an important trade item from the earliest times, and has long been employed as a medicine, dye, perfume and condiment. Its earliest name was probably the Hebrew *carcom*.
It was cultivated in many countries and exported from Persia and India to China as

early as the Yuen dynasty (A.D. 1280–1368); the Chinese called it *Sa-fa-lang*.
Records suggest the Saffron Crocus was cultivated in Spain in the ninth century, in France, Italy and Germany in the twelfth, and in England by the fourteenth. Such was the standing of the drug that severe penalties were suffered by those who adulterated Saffron: Hans Kölbele, for example, was buried alive in Nuremberg in 1456 with his impure drug.
Description Typical crocus, producing blue, lilac or purple fragrant flowers in the autumn arising from a corm 3 cm in diameter. Numerous narrow, linear leaves to 45 cm long, grey-green. Yellow anthers longer than filaments, blood-red style branches.
Distribution Originally from Asia Minor, now widespread in temperate zones. Prefers sunny, well-drained sites.
Cultivation Now unknown in the wild. Cultivated in the mediterranean, Middle East, Persia, India and China. Propagation by corms planted in rows 10–15 cm apart in late summer.
Constituents Oil 8–13%; essential oil; a bitter glycoside, picrocrocin; crocin, the glycoside of the colouring matter crocetin.
Uses (dried stigma) Stomachic; antispasmodic; sedative.
No longer used medicinally except to colour medicines. Formerly considered an aphrodisiac.
Employed in many culinary dishes both for taste and colour and in some liqueurs.
Cannot be used to dye fabrics as it is readily water-soluble.

Croton tiglium L EUPHORBIACEAE
Croton Croton Seed
Oil from Croton Seeds is one of the most violent purgatives known, and should never be used by non-medical personnel. The seeds were described first by Christoval Acosta in 1578 and called *pinones de Maluco*. They were regarded as 'official' in the seventeenth century

but fell into disuse from then until 1812 when English medical officers in India reintroduced the oil into medicine.
Description Small tree or shrub to 6 m with few branches bearing alternate, smooth ovate or acuminate leaves, dark green above, paler beneath and with a strong, disagreeable odour. Inconspicuous flowers in erect terminal racemes 7.5 cm long, appearing early summer. Brown, capsular, 3-celled fruit, each containing a single seed 1.5 cm long.
Distribution Indigenous to the Malabar coast, south-west India, and Tavoy in Burma.
Cultivation Wild and cultivated as a garden plant in many parts of the East. Commercial cultivation in China and south Asia.
Constituents Fatty oil 60%; croton oil comprising the following acids: palmitic, stearic, myristic, lauric, acetic, butyric, formic, oleic, tiglic, linoleic and valeric. The active constituent is croton-resin, a lactone, which is also responsible for the vesicant activity.
Uses (oil expressed from seed) Powerful cathartic; counter-irritant; vesicant; rubefacient.
Formerly administered as a purgative to violent mental patients; now rarely used internally and only for extremely obstinate constipation. May be used externally with great care, in diluted form, as a counter-irritant in gout and neuralgia.
Contra-indications Powerful gastro-intestinal irritant; capable of causing death. May induce severe external blistering.

Cuminum cyminum L UMBELLIFERAE
Cumin
Although indigenous to the upper regions of the Nile, the seeds of this herb ripen as far north as Norway. The *fructus cumini* or Cumin seeds were known as early as the prophet Isaiah, and, later, Dioscorides. They found wide use in Europe from the Middle Ages. The Romans used ground Cumin seed in the same way that we use Pepper. In the last 300 years, however, it has been discarded from European cooking and is now chiefly used in Indian cooking.
Description Slender, glabrous, annual herb 15 cm high; stems branched above; leaves with few filiform divisions 15 mm–5 cm long; sparsely flowered umbels, white or rose-coloured with simple involucral bracts, appearing late spring. Fruit 7 mm long, bristly.
Distribution Indigenous to Egypt and the mediterranean. Widespread distribution. Tolerates most well-drained soils in sunny situations.
Cultivation Wild plant. Cultivated on North African coast, Middle East, India, Malta and China. Seed sown in late spring in sandy soil in a warm situation, or in the greenhouse. Thin out, harden off and plant 20 cm apart. Keep free of weeds.
Constituents Essential oil, 2.5–4%, which comprises cumaldehyde, terpenes, cuminic alcohol, pinenes; also fatty oil and pentosan.
Uses (dried ripe fruit) Stimulant, carminative. Useful in diarrhoea and dyspepsia.
Commonly used in curries, for pickling, and also for flavouring liqueurs and cordials.
The oil is used in perfumery.
Oil chiefly employed in veterinary medicine.

Curcuma longa L ZINGIBERACEAE
Turmeric Turmeric root or rhizome
Turmeric was once much more highly esteemed than it is today; it fell into disuse in the Middle Ages having previously held a position at least equal to that of Ginger to which it is closely related. Dioscorides called it *cyperus*, and in the sixteenth century it was known as *crocus indicus*, *turmeracke* and *curcuma*. Several types exist of which Bengal Turmeric is considered the best for dyeing. The yellow robes of Buddhist

monks were often dyed with it.
It is similar to another ancient spice, Zedoary (*C. zedoaria Roscoe*), which is today even less well-known in the West.
Description Tall perennial herb arising from large ovoid rhizome with sessile cylindrical tubers, orange coloured within. Leaves very large, lily-like, in tufts to 1.2 m long; oblong-lanceolate blades tapering towards the base, long petiole. Pale yellow flowers, clustered in dense spikes 10–15 cm long; peduncle 15 cm long and enclosed in a sheathing petiole. Pale green bracts. Appears late spring to mid-summer.
Distribution Native to south-east Asia; distributed and introduced elsewhere. Prefers humid conditions and rich loamy soils.
Cultivation Wild and cultivated in many tropical countries; propagation by root division in autumn.
Constituents Volatile oil 5–6%; a terpene, curcumen; starch 24%; albumen 30%; colouring due to curcumin or diferuloyl methane.
Uses (dried rhizome) Aromatic, stimulant. Employed in eastern medicine externally for bruising and internally in certain blood disorders, to relieve catarrh, and in purulent opthalmia. A pharmaceutical colouring agent. Main use is as a condiment and culinary colouring agent in curries and Piccalilli.

Cynara scolymus L COMPOSITAE
Artichoke Globe Artichoke
The Globe Artichoke is not only a delicacy, but an important medicinal herb which was known to the medieval Arabic physicians as *al-kharsuf*. Its name *Cynara*, from the Latin *canina* or canine, is derived from the similarity of the involucral spines to the dog's tooth. It has proven remedial effects on the liver. The plant was one of the Greek cultivated garden herbs, and still enjoys wide horticultural use.
Description Thistle-like perennial usually 1–1.75 m tall, leaves large and deeply pinnatifid, greyish, green above, whitish beneath; very rarely spiny. Large capitula with enlarged fleshy receptacle, broad involucral bracts and numerous purple flowers, appearing mid to late summer.
Distribution Native to North Africa; in most temperate and subtropical zones. Preferring well-manured, moisture-retaining soil, rich in humus.
Cultivation Wild only as an escape; a close relative of the Cardoon (*C. cardunculus*). Cultivated commercially and horticulturally either from seed or preferably from suckers arising from the root-stock, retaining a portion of the parent plant. The 'heels' are planted in rich moist soil 75 cm apart in late spring or early summer. Give plenty of water, some protection in cold weather may be required. Optimal cropping is reached in the third year, and plants should be replaced in the fifth season.
Constituents Cynarine, a bitter aromatic substance; polyphenolic acidic substances; flavonoids; tannins; several enzymes including catalases, peroxydases, cynarase, oxydases, and ascorbinase; also provitamin A. The combined action is diuretic and stimulant to liver cell regeneration and action.
Uses (fresh receptacle, leaves, root) Cholagogue; diuretic.
Of proven value in jaundice, liver insufficiency; anaemia and liver damage caused by poisons. Stimulates and aids digestion; anti-dyspeptic. Considered to be prophylactic against arteriosclerosis. A major constituent of proprietary

digestive tonics.
Fleshy receptacle eaten as a delicacy; the blanched central leaf stalks may be cooked as a vegetable.
Flower-heads employed in floral decorations.

Cynoglossum officinale L BORAGINACEAE
Hound's Tongue Gipsy Flower
All the usual names of this herb refer to the fact that its leaves look like a dog's tongue; it smells, however, more of mice, and is called Rats and Mice in some parts of western England. The medieval name was *lingua canis* and the Greek, *kunoglosson*. It is rarely used in folk medicine today, but is still occasionally employed homeopathically.
Description Annual or biennial herb with unpleasant smell, reaching 30–90 cm; bearing grey leaves covered with silky hairs, the lower to 30 cm long, lanceolate to ovate, stalked, the upper generally without stalks. Flowers dull red-purple, occasionally white, 1 cm diameter, arranged on branched cymes 10–25 cm long, appearing mid-summer.
Distribution European native; on light dry grassy soils, wood fringes, walls and ruins, in particular near to the sea.

Cultivation Wild plant.
Constituents Two alkaloids, cynoglossine and consolidine; essential oil; resin; tannin; gum.
Uses (dried root, dried whole herb, fresh leaves) Anodyne; demulcent.
Effective soothing sedative in coughs and diarrhoea. Administered internally and as a poultice for haemorrhoids. Formerly considered a narcotic and prescribed in combination with Opium, Henbane, and aromatic herbs.
The bruised leaf may be rubbed on insect bites. Used in homeopathic medicine as a tincture.
Contra-indications Incompletely studied therapeutically and therefore to be used with caution; may cause dermatitis.

Cypripedium pubescens Willd. ORCHIDACEAE
Lady's Slipper Yellow Lady's Slipper/Nerve Root
Cypripedium was included in the United States Pharmacopoeia a century ago, and was considered at that time worthy of further investigation. It has continued to be used to the present day in folk medicine for the same purpose that American Indians have always used it, as a sedative. It has been called the American Valerian, and was introduced to European medicine by Rafinesque in the eighteenth century.
Description Perennial orchid on fleshy root-

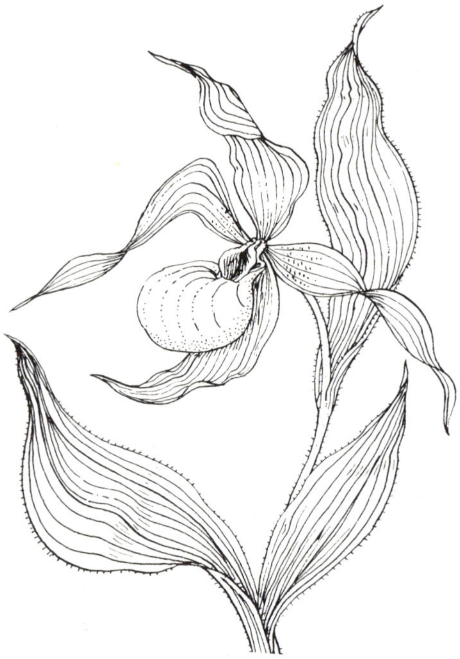

stock producing several 5–20 cm long, many-nerved, acuminate, alternate leaves; on glandular hairy stems 10 cm–1 m high. Flowers distinctive, dull cream to golden yellow, spotted magenta-purple, with lower lip forming the shape of an inflated sac; appearing early to late summer. The plant is variable in shape and degree of fragrance.
Distribution Native to eastern United States, especially the north; prefers shady areas, moist meadows, bogs, woods, rich soils.
Cultivation Wild plant; cultivated in parts of eastern Europe. Very closely related to, and often confused with, *C. calceolus* (L). *C. pubescens* (Willd.) is also named *C. calceolus* var. *pubescens* (Correll), and both orchids are known commercially as Lady's Slipper.
Constituents Volatile oil; glucosides; 2 resins; tannin; gallic acid. The combination of these root constituents, which are not water-soluble, form a resinous complex known as cypripedin.
Uses (root-stock) Sedative: spasmolytic.
Effective in and specifically used for anxiety neurosis associated with insomnia, hysteria or nervous headaches. Formerly taken in sugar water to promote sleep.
Contra-indications Large doses may cause hallucinations. Fresh plant may cause dermatitis.

Daphne mezereum L THYMELAEACEAE
Mezereon Spurge Olive
An attractive winter-flowering shrub of great decorative use in herb gardens. It was known to Arabian physicians as *mazariyun* and considered of similar use as the substance, *euphorbium*, from *Euphorbia resinifera*. It is uncertain if the Greeks used the plant, but it was known as *daphnoides* and *thymelaea* to medieval botanists and herbalists. Tragus (1546) called it *mezereum germanicum*.
Description Perennial deciduous shrub; to 1.25 m; bearing on erect branched stem, alternate, oblong or oblanceolate leaves, 5–7.5 cm long; leaves thin and glabrous. Flowers rose-pink or rose-violet, 10–15 mm long; strongly fragrant and appearing in sessile clusters of 2–5 along previous year's branches before leaves develop. Appearing late winter to early spring; followed by red berries.
Distribution Native to Europe and Western Asia; introduced elsewhere. Found in deciduous mixed woodland and on rich calcareous soil.
Cultivation Wild. Cultivated as garden plant. Propagate from cuttings taken in early summer. A white variety, *D. mezereum* var. *alba* (West.) is in existence.
Constituents An acrid resinous poisonous substance, mezerine; a glucoside, daphnin; also coccognin.
Uses (root bark, bark) Alterative; stimulant; sudorific; vesicant; rubefacient.
Formerly used internally as an alterative in the treatment of venereal, scrofulous and rheumatic conditions, or as a purgative. Bark applied externally as poultice as a counter-irritant or vesicant in certain ulcerative skin conditions. Now only employed homeopathically for some skin complaints.
An excellent horticultural herb.
Contra-indications POISONOUS and fatal; not to be taken internally.

Datura stramonium L SOLANACEAE
Thorn Apple Jimsonweed
The Thorn Apple is indigenous to the shores of the Caspian Sea, and was distributed throughout Europe by the end of the first century A.D. It is doubtful whether the Greeks or Romans used the herb, but it was traditionally smoked by Nubians for chest complaints. Gerard the herbalist cultivated the plant in London in 1598, and Störck (1762) introduced stramonium into wide medicinal use. It is now little used in folk medicine.
Description Strongly and unpleasantly scented annual, from 30 cm–1.5 m high; erect and straggly, bearing glabrous or pubescent, ovate and petiolate leaves 7.5–20 cm long, broad and with irregular acute lobes. Flowers 5–8 cm long, erect, funnel shaped, terminal and white or pale blue. Appearing late summer to late autumn; followed by prickly capsules, 5 cm long.
Distribution Native to the Near East; naturalized in North America, and throughout Europe; on waste-ground, roadsides, forest edges, walls, preferring porous nitrogen-rich soil in sunny situations.
Cultivation Wild; cultivated commercially in Europe by seed sown in late spring.
Constituents Alkaloids, comprising mainly hyoscyamine, hyoscine, atropine, whose action relieves spasms of the bronchioles during asthma.
Uses (dried leaves) Antispasmodic; narcotic; anodyne.
Of benefit in bronchial asthma, either as a tincture or smoked in the form of a cigarette. Also controls muscular spasm and salivation in postencephalitic parkinsonism. May be applied externally as a poultice to reduce local pain.
Contra-indications POISONOUS, hallucinogenic.

Daucus carota L UMBELLIFERAE
Wild Carrot
Daucus is the old Greek name for a wild plant still to be found in the hedgerows of Europe,

and which has long been of service as food and medicine. *Carota* is the Latin name for the same plant.

Several subspecies exist, the root crop being developed by German horticulturalists in the sixteenth century from *D. carota* ssp. *sativus*. Both this and *D. carota* ssp. *carota* are used medicinally.

Description Erect biennial on solid, striate or ridged stem 30 to 100 cm tall; leaves pinnately compound; segments pinnatifid, lobes 5 mm long. White flowers in compound umbels 3–7 cm diameter, flat or convex, with usually one blackish-purple flower in the centre, appear mid-summer.

Distribution Native to Europe, west Asia, North Africa; prefers semi-dry, sandy, or stony soil near to the sea.

Cultivation Wild plant. Wild relative of the common carrot.

Constituents Volatile oils; carotene; B vitamins; an alkaloid daucine; vitamin C; potassium salts.

Uses (dried herb) Diuretic; antilithic. Specifically employed in the treatment of urinary stones; often in combination with other antilithic remedies. Weakly anthelmintic. Decoction of the seed may be employed in flatulence and stomach acidity, as may Carrot juice.

Contra-indications Do not drink excessive quantities of Carrot juice, as it induces hypervitaminosis A.

Delphinium consolida L RANUNCULACEAE
Larkspur Field or Forking Larkspur

A member of the Buttercup family and the Northern European equivalent of the historically much more well-known *Delphinium Staphisagria* (L), or Stavesacre, which was known to the Romans as *Staphisagria* or *herba pedicularia*. There is no evidence that the specific name of Larkspur refers to any power of consolidating wounds, which it does not. It is probably a pre-Linnaean name referring to the consolidated petals. Like Stavesacre, it is effective against skin parasites.

Description Annual herb reaching 1 m, arising from slender taproot. Stem glabrous, forking and diffuse, bearing petiolate and sessile, finely divided, simple leaves 3–4 cm long. Flowers few or scattered, blue or purple, growing in sparse terminal racemes and distinguished by an upward curving spur behind the corolla. Appearing mid-summer.

Distribution European native; introduced in other temperate zones especially on chalky, loamy soil in weedy places, compost sites, and cornfields.

Cultivation Wild plant. The common garden Larkspur is *D. ajacis*. Propagated from seed sown 1 cm deep in early summer.

Constituents Delphinine; unknown substances.

Uses (seed, flowering plant) Purgative, anthelmintic, anti-parasitic.

Formerly used internally for a variety of conditions, its only certain effect being violently purgative.

A strong tincture of fresh seeds may be applied externally to head and pubic hair to destroy human parasites.

Blue ink may be prepared from the fresh petals. Useful garden ornamental.

Contra-indications POISONOUS.

Dianthus caryophyllus L CARYOPHYLLACEAE
Clove Pink Gillyflower/Carnation

The true Gillyflower (*gilly* was the Old English for July and was so named probably because of its appearance in July), is rarely seen in gardens today, having been replaced by the more showy but far less aromatic Carnations. Its specific name reflects the old term for Cloves, *caryophyllon*.

Description Much branched glabrous perennial 30 cm to 1 m high; stems hard with conspicuous nodes, bearing thick linear leaves 7.5–12.5 cm long, obtuse and keeled. Flowers 3 cm in diameter, 2–5 per stem, very fragrant especially at night, rose-purple or white; appear late summer to early autumn.

Distribution Native to southern Europe and India. In open sunny position on old walls, ruins. Calcareous.

Cultivation Wild plant and widely cultivated commercially. All modern horticultural Carnations derive from *D. caryophyllus*; the modern Pink derives from *D. plumarius*.

Constituents Volatile oils comprising eugenol, which are responsible for the clove-like scent.

Uses (fresh flower) No medicinal use, although tonic cordials were made from a conserve of the flowers.

Mainly used as a flavouring agent for beverages, liqueurs, wine cups, cordials, and vinegars.

The fresh flowers decorate soups, stews, sauces, salads, and open sandwiches. A syrup, prepared by steeping petals in a hot sugar solution has culinary applications.

Dried petals added to pot-pourris, scented sachets, cosmetic products.

Digitalis purpurea L SCROPHULARIACEAE
Foxglove Common Foxglove

For all its fame and importance in medicine in the last two centuries, the Foxglove does not seem to have been described by Greek and Roman physicians, nor did it have a classical name. Fuchs in 1542 first called it *digitalis* after the finger-like shape of its flowers, but he considered it a violent medicine, and it was not until William Withering investigated (1776–9) the use of Foxglove tea in Shropshire for dropsy that the herb entered wide medical use. The common name probably derives from the Anglo-Saxon 'foxes-glew' or 'fox-music' after the shape of an ancient musical instrument.

Description Biennial, occasionally perennial; reaching 2 m. Leaves rugose and downy arising in a rosette; radical leaves long, stalked and ovate to ovate-lanceolate, stem leaves short-stalked or sessile. Stem rarely branched and bearing a one-sided raceme 30–40 cm long. Attractive purple flowers, often spotted internally; appearing mid-summer to mid-autumn.

Distribution Western European native, preferring acid soil in sunny situations on rough land. Now cultivated widely.

Cultivation Wild; very widely cultivated both commercially and horticulturally. Many garden variants exist; var. *campanulata*, var. *alba*, var. *maculata*. Propagated from seed which

should be sown in late spring.
Constituents Several glycosides including digitoxin, gitoxin, and gitaloxin, which act directly on heart muscle increasing the output in patients with congestive heart failure.
Uses (dried leaves) Cardiac tonic.
Acts as a cardio-active diuretic in conditions of oedema due to heart failure.
May be used externally as a poultice to aid healing of wounds.
Contra-indications POISONOUS. Only to be used by medical personnel.

Dryopteris filix-mas (L) Schott
POLYPODIACEAE
Male Fern
The Male Fern is an effective remedy for tapeworms which it kills and expels from the intestines. It is, however, an irritant in large doses and must be used only by those medically trained.
It was well known to the ancients, and was also a constituent of secret 'worm remedies' of the eighteenth century, particularly those made by German apothecaries. Frederick the Great purchased the secret of one such mixture for his personal use.
Other ferns, however, seem to be equally or more effective as taenicides; *Dryopteris spinulosa* O. Kuntze, for example, is twice as effective as *Dryopteris filix-mas*.
Description Perennial fern on dark-brown rhizome 20–50 cm long, 10 cm diameter; foliage growing in a crown, fronds arranged spirally, 60 cm to 1.5 m high, 2-pinnate, oblong-lanceolate in outline, leaflets alternate, subdivided, and with rounded segments. Spore-bearing sori, greenish white, later brown, appear from summer to autumn.
Distribution Widespread in temperate zones, to 1600 m altitude.
Cultivation Wild plant; extensively collected.
Constituents Oleoresin; filicin and related taenicidal substances; desaspidin; albaspidin; flavaspidic acid; volatile oil.
Uses (dried rhizome, frond bases, apical buds) An effective agent for removing tapeworms.
Poultice may be applied externally to aid tissue healing.
Contra-indications To be used under medical supervision only: large doses may cause blindness or death.

Ecballium elaterium (L) A. Rich CUCURBITACEAE
Squirting Cucumber Elaterium Fruit
An appropriately named herb both from the point of view of its action, as a strong purgative, and from its violent method of seed dispersal which involves ejaculation of the contents of the ripe fruit to a distance of 10 m. The generic name derives from the Greek meaning expel. It was certainly well-known to Theophrastus and Dioscorides who described the manufacture of Elaterium, and it was cultivated throughout Europe in the sixteenth century. Constituents of Elaterium are now mostly employed for scientific research into cytotoxicity.

Description A coarse, fleshy, trailing perennial, lacking tendrils and borne on a thick white root. Leaves triangular-ovate, downy, 7.5–10 cm long, with sinuate margins. Flowers 3 cm diameter, followed by an ovoid-oblong fruit, 4–5 cm long, rough-haired due to a covering of numerous short, fleshy prickles, green becoming yellowish when mature. Contains a mass of oblong seeds and bitter succulent pulp, which is forcibly ejected up to 10 m.
Distribution Mediterranean native; preferring dry, sandy soil in sunny situations.
Cultivation Wild and cultivated commercially to a limited extent.
Constituents Cucurbitacins B, D, E, and I. The action of cucurbitacin B is that of a powerful hydragogue – purgative; also cytotoxic.
Uses (dried sediment, *elatarium*, deposited in the juice) Purgative.
Once administered to patients suffering from dropsy as a purgative, especially those with kidney complaints. The preparation is very variable from season to season.

Echinacea angustifolia DC COMPOSITAE
Purple Coneflower Black Sampson
This stark and attractive herb is one of several outstanding examples of plants deserving modern examination. The United States Dispensatory stated a century ago that the tincture increased resistance to infection, and the experience of folk medicine supports this claim.
It was formerly classified as *Brauneria angustifolia*, but the present generic name reflects the shape of the sharp-pointed bracts of the receptacle, after the Greek *echinacea*, meaning hedgehog.
Description Coarse perennial reaching 45 cm. Leaves sparse, lanceolate to linear; 7.5–20 cm long, entire with slender petioles. Flower-head solitary on stout terminal peduncle, consisting of spreading ray florets 3 cm long, purple or rarely white, and 3 cm long conical erect disc florets, also purple. Appearing mid-summer to early autumn.

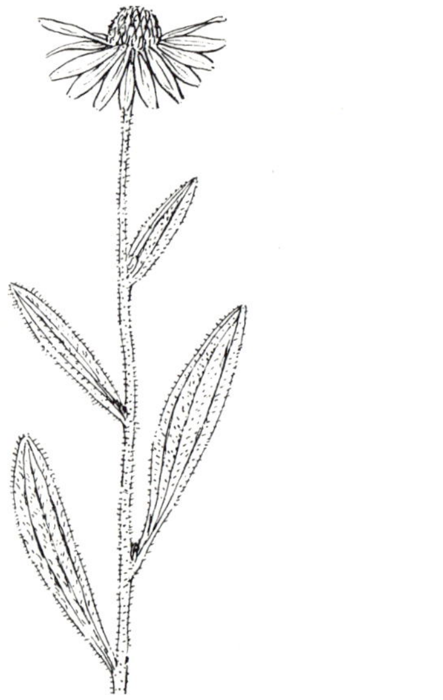

Distribution Native to central and south-western United States; on dry open woodland and roadsides.
Cultivation Wild plant. Propagated by root division in spring and autumn.
Constituents Resins, sugars, mineral salts, fatty acids and inulin which act in combination.
Uses (dried root-stock) Antiseptic, digestive. Particularly effective remedy for boils, acne, pharyngitis, tonsilitis, abscesses and septicaemia; useful externally and internally. Dilates peripheral blood vessels.

Echium vulgare L BORAGINACEAE
Viper's Bugloss Blue Weed
This is not a true Bugloss, that term being reserved for *Lycopsis arvensis*, nor is it the plant known to Dioscorides as the Viper Plant – *echion*. Nevertheless, medieval proponents of the Doctrine of Signatures noticed that the brown stem pustules looked rather like a snake's skin, and that the seed is shaped like a viper's head. It is regarded as a weed in some parts of America, and is of doubtful medical use.

Description Rough hairy biennial, 30–90 cm tall. Stem erect and branched with stiff hairs arising from white or brown pustules. Leaves oblong to linear-lanceolate, 5–15 cm long, sessile, or with short petioles only. Inflorescence loose, flower buds pink, flowers blue to violet-purple, 15 mm long, with longer stamens. Appears mid-summer.
Distribution Native to Europe and Asia; on light porous or stony soils, or semi-dry grassland.
Cultivation Wild plant. Traditionally cultivated in herb gardens.
Constituents Tannins; an alkaloid.
Uses (dried herb) Weak diuretic; weak diaphoretic.
A simple mild tonic infusion is useful in treating nervous headaches or the common cold.
Formerly one of the most respected plants employed for the treatment of vipers' venom.

Elettaria cardamomum var. *miniscula* Maton
ZINGIBERACEAE
Cardamom Lesser Cardamom
As Cardamoms thrive in shady mountain forests ideally with a mean rainfall of 3.5 m and mean temperature of 23°C (73°F), they are not easy to cultivate or harvest, and for this reason are expensive. The best type is the Malabar Cardamom, and others of good quality are Mysore, Ceylon, Aleppi and Madras. Seed pods from related members of the Ginger family are frequently offered as Cardamom, especially *Amomum cardamon* L, but they are inferior. *Elettari* was the Malabar name for the plant.
Description Perennial arising from fleshy thick rhizome bearing from 8–20 smooth erect green stems to 2.7 m. Leaves alternate, oblong-lanceolate, sheathed, 30–60 cm long, 7.5 cm wide. Flowers arising from near the stem base on a long peduncle, arranged in a panicle 30–60 cm long, and are followed by an ovoid 3-celled capsule.
Distribution Indigenous to south and west India; in rich moist forests and in wooded hillsides. Wild in Burma. Introduced in other

tropical countries.
Cultivation Wild plant. Commercial cultivation in many tropical countries in Asia and the Americas.
Constituents Volatile oil (3–8%), comprising terpinene and terpineol; also cineol; starch; gum; yellow colouring matter.
Uses (dried fruit and seed) Carminative.
Employed in flatulent dyspepsia, to allay griping caused by purgatives, and to flavour other medications.
A flavouring agent in some mixed spices, curries and pickles. Also used in mulled wine and in Coffee, especially Persian.
Limited use in scented domestic articles, and for cosmetic purposes.

Ephedra gerardiana (Wall.) Stapf.
EPHEDRACEAE
Ephedra Ma-Huang
Ephedra is a Gymnosperm and hence, like the

Horsetail, primitive in evolutionary terms. It has been used for thousands of years in the East in the treatment of bronchial asthma, and yet today the herb is included in only the British, Indian, Japanese and Chinese pharmacopoeias.
Other species used for the same purpose include *E. sinica*, *E. equisetina* and *E. nebrodensis*. It is rarely available commercially.
Description Tufted, rigid shrub 15 cm–1.2 m high on woody gnarled stem. Green ascending branchlets smooth and striate, with leaves reduced to small sheaths at branch nodes, 2 mm long. Bearing 2–3 male spikes of 4–8 flowers, and solitary female spikes of 1–2 flowers; latter followed by ovoid, edible red fruit, 10 mm long.
Distribution Native to the dry temperate regions of the alpine Himalayas at altitudes 2250–4500 m; also China.
Cultivation Wild plant.
Constituents Alkaloids comprising mainly ephedrine, to which the hypertensive and bronchodilatory action is due; pseudoephedrine, benzyl methylamine; ephidine.
Uses (dried stem) Anti-asthmatic; stimulant. Primarily of use in bronchial asthma and hay fever; also employed in enuresis, urticaria, serum sickness, and in the treatment of myasthenia gravis.
A commercial source of the ephedrine alkaloids.
Contra-indications Not to be used in patients suffering from hypertension, coronary thrombosis or thyrotoxicosis.

Epigaea repens L ERICACEAE
Trailing Arbutus May Flower/Gravel Plant
The botanical name reflects the fact that this aromatic plant clings very closely to the damp mossy banks of its natural habitat: *epigaea* from the Greek meaning upon earth and *repens* meaning creeping. Also known as Moss Beauty because of the attractiveness of its rust leaves and small, pink, scented flowers.

Description Fragrant prostrate evergreen branching shrub, spreading to 50 cm diameter on the ground; with hairy, rounded stems of rust colour, arising from tangled red-brown fibrous roots. Leaves alternate, oval to orbicular 3–7.5 cm long, 1–3 cm wide, entire, and hairy beneath. The apical or axillary inflorescence consists of pink, deep rose and occasionally, white flowers 15 mm long, appearing mid-spring to early summer.
Distribution Native to central and eastern North America, on rich, damp, acid soils in shady protected sites.
Cultivation Wild plant; may be propagated easily by layering any part of the stem.
Constituents The glucosides urson, ericolin, and arbutin; formic acid; gallic acid; tannic acid and an aromatic oil, ericinol; the combined action being antilithic and antiseptic.
Uses (whole dried plant, fresh leaf) Urinary antiseptic; diuretic; antilithic.
Although rarely used, even in folk medicine, this is one of the most effective remedies for cystitis, urethritis, prostatitis, bladder stones and particularly acute catarrhal cystitis.
Horticulturally the herb offers useful fragrant ground cover in shady situations thriving with some protection and little light.

Equisetum arvense L EQUISETACEAE
Horsetail Bottlebrush/Shave Grass
Horsetails have an almost prehistoric appearance, and indeed have hardly evolved since the coal seams were laid down. They were known to medieval apothecaries as *cauda equina*, and were an article of trade from the Middle Ages until the eighteenth century, being used to polish pewterware and woodwork. The herb has continued in cultivation in some eastern European countries and plays a useful role in folk medicine.
Description Perennial on thin creeping rhizome, producing 20 cm long grey-brown, simple, fertile shoots with 4–6 sheaths in the spring; the shoots die after the spores are shed, and are then followed by green sterile shoots 20–80 cm long, erect, or decumbent, bearing whorls of segmented solid lateral branches at each node.
Distribution European native; abundant on moist waste-ground.
Cultivation Wild plant: limited cultivation in eastern Europe.
Constituents Silicic acid and water-soluble silicic compounds; saponins; phytosterol; flavonoids; aconitic acid; traces of the alkaloids, nicotine, palustrine and palustrinine.
Uses (dried sterile stem, fresh juice) Diuretic; vulnerary; genito-urinary astringent; weak anti-haemorrhagic.
A poultice may be applied externally to aid the healing of wounds, sores or ulcers; the tisane is effective as a mouthwash in aphthous ulcers or gingivitis, and can be used as a douche in leucorrhoea or menorrhagia. Also employed in prostatic disease, enuresis and incontinence.
Dried stems may be used to polish pewter or fine woodwork.
Employed in cosmetic preparations to strengthen finger nails.

Erigeron canadensis L COMPOSITAE
Canadian Fleabane
The Canadian Fleabane has received almost universal abuse as an unwanted weed with little to commend it beside extraordinary powers of survival and distribution. Originally from eastern and central North America, it was introduced into Central France in 1653, became naturalized in that country within 30 years, and rapidly spread through Europe, Asia, Australia and several of the Pacific Islands.
The Latin name indicates not only its original home, but also its hoary appearance; from the Greek *erigeron* signifying 'old man in spring'.
Description Annual with stiff, erect stem from 8–100 cm tall depending on soil type. Very leafy and varying from sparsely hairy to glabrous; all leaves sessile; basal leaves obovate-lanceolate, stem leaves linear-lanceolate, 1–4 cm long, entire. Inflorescence in terminal panicle, capitula small, cylindrical, 3–5 mm diameter. Ray florets whitish, disc florets pale yellow; appearing late summer to early autumn.
Distribution North American native; introduced and naturalized elsewhere. Common on dry, weed-covered roadsides, walls, dunes, waste-ground; preferring warm, light, sandy soil, but tolerating most conditions.
Cultivation Wild plant.
Constituents Volatile oil, comprizing mainly a terpene, acting as a styptic; also gallic and tannic acids, acting as astringents.
Uses (whole dried herb, oil) Astringent; tonic; diuretic; styptic.
The tisane or tincture was formerly employed in the treatment of a range of urinary and renal disorders; it appears effective in diarrhoea. The oil soothes sore throats and relieves associated swollen glands, and has been employed in haemoptysis, haematemesis, and haematuria.

Eruca vesicaria ssp. *sativa* (Mill.) Thell
CRUCIFERAE
Rocket-salad Rocket
Although described as a 'good salat-herbe' by

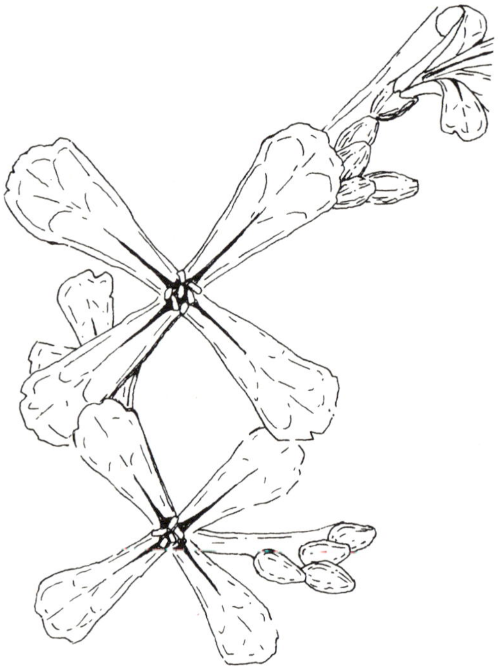

John Gerard and in almost continuous cultivation from the Romans until the seventeenth century, Rocket (from the Latin name *eruca* via the Italian diminutive *ruchetta*) was seldom grown in north-west Europe after 1800. It is, however, still an important and useful salad in Italy, Egypt and France, and deserves wider use.
Description Half-hardy annual, 30–70 cm tall; much branched. Upper leaves sessile, lower long petioled, large-toothed or pinnatifid. Flowers to 3 cm long, creamy-yellow or whitish, with purplish veins; appearing mid to late summer.
Distribution Native to mediterranean region and western Asia. Introduced horticulturally elsewhere. In waste areas or on cultivated land in warm positions.
Cultivation Wild. Grown as a salad herb, especially in south-east mediterranean, southern France and Italy. Propagated from seed

sown in spring or autumn on rich, moist soil; may run to seed in summer. Harvest leaf within 8 weeks and keep cutting. Cultivated herb is milder flavoured than the wild plant *E. vesicaria* L.
Constituents Essential oil; heterosides.
Uses (fresh young leaf and stalk) Tonic; mild stimulant; stomachic.
Only used as a constituent of mixed salads.

Eryngium maritimum L UMBELLIFERAE
Sea Holly Eryngo
The striking prickly nature and coastal habitat of this herb led to it being named, quite obviously, as Sea Holly. In fact, unlike most herbs, it has few other names, and Eryngo is a popularization of the old generic term *eryngium* which signifies a thistle-like herb.
The plant's virtues and uses centre mostly on the sexual organs; even the extremely long roots have been given aphrodisiacal qualities, a fact explaining why they enjoyed widespread sale in Europe for 250 years.

Description Attractive bluish and glaucous biennial or perennial, much branched plant, on 1.5 m long root, forming hemi-spherical bushes 30 cm high. Leaves fleshy, very stiff and deeply veined, ovate, 3-lobed, 5–10 cm long, broad, spiny and long-petiolate. Flowers in spherical umbels, 3 cm diameter, pale blue, appearing mid to late summer.
Distribution European native; introduced elsewhere. On sand dunes and ideally requiring a sandy saline soil.
Cultivation Wild plant; sometimes cultivated on light soils horticulturally, and propagated by root division in the autumn, or from seed sown in the autumn.
Constituents Saponins; unknown substances.
Uses (fresh or dried root) Aromatic; tonic; diuretic.
The herb was formerly considered of use in genito-urinary irritation and infection, especially local inflammations of mucous membranes and painful urination. The powdered root applied externally as a poultice aids tissue regeneration.
Once an important culinary flavouring, the roots being parboiled and candied prior to incorporation in sweet dishes. Young flowering shoots can be boiled and eaten in the same way as Asparagus.

Erythroxylum coca Lam.
ERYTHROXYLACEAE
Coca Leaf
Coca was well-known in pre-Columban days and revered as a magical plant; small bags of the leaves have been found in the graves of Incas. It is still widely employed as a means of maintaining endurance by South American peoples, and is cultivated commercially for cocaine extraction. The generic name refers to the bright red colour of the fruit.
Description Small hardy shrubby tree to 5 m; but pruned to 2 m in cultivation; leaves oval 4–8 cm long, 2.5–4 cm wide, glabrous and entire, with prominent reddish-brown midrib projecting as a small apex (apiculus). Fruits red or reddish-brown.
Distribution Peru and Bolivia. Introduced to Taiwan and Indonesia. On steep valley sides in well-drained, light, humus-rich soil.

Cultivation No longer known in wild state; cultivated commercially in South America, Taiwan, and Indonesia. Propagated from fresh seed sown in shaded humus-rich seed-beds and planted out 2 m apart.
The cultivation of this herb is subject to worldwide constraint.
Constituents Several alkaloids, the most important being cocaine; also cinnamyl-cocaine, α- and β-truxilline; cocatannic acid; vitamins; proteins; mineral salts.
Uses (fresh or dried leaf) Stimulant tonic.
The leaf is chewed in combination with a little lime or the ash of certain *Chenopodium* species as a general stimulant, to reduce fatigue, allay feelings of hunger, to relieve gastric pain, nausea, and vomiting, and as a cerebral and muscular stimulant.
Contra-indications Dangerous; hence not obtainable.

Eucalyptus globulus Labill. MYRTACEAE
Tasmanian Blue Gum Eucalyptus
The genus *Eucalyptus* consists of 300 species of trees indigenous to Australasia of which the most successful in terms of economic importance and distribution is *E. globulus*. In the last century the tree has become well established as a source of timber, oil, shade, and as a means of soil drainage in Africa, the Americas, Southern Europe, and India. The name is derived from the Greek *eucalyptus* meaning a well and a lid, since the sepals and petals fuse forming a cap, which resembles a well with a lid. 'Globulus' or 'little globe' signifies the shape of the fruit.

Description Tree reaching 70 m. Trunk smooth and grey or bluish following natural loss of bark; leaves leathery, lanceolate, glaucous, whitish, sessile and usually opposite; covered with oil-bearing glands. Flowers, 4 cm wide, either single or 2–3 on short flat peduncles, followed by 3-cm wide fruit, surrounded by woody receptacle.
Distribution Native to Australasia; introduced in semi-tropical countries.
Cultivation Wild; extensively cultivated and grows rapidly.
Constituents Eucalyptus oil, chiefly comprising cineol; also pinenes; sesquiterpene alcohols; aromadendrene; cuminaldehyde.
Uses (oil, occasionally leaf) Antiseptic; deodorant; stimulant; counter-irritant.
Widely used in proprietary medicines for external application in burns, colds, and for antiseptic purposes. Vapour inhaled to relieve cough in catarrhal colds and chronic bronchitis. Occasionally taken internally in small doses on sugar for catarrhal inflammation of the respiratory tract.
Limited use in perfumery; leaves included in dry pot-pourris.
Employed in veterinary medicines.
Contra-indications Large doses toxic, leading to delirium, convulsions and death.

Euonymus europaeus L CELASTRACEAE
Spindle Tree European Spindle Tree
This herb is also described as *Evonymus europaeus, Evonymus europaea* and *Euonymus europaea*. Its common name is derived from the Dutch practice of spindle (and peg) manufacture from the strong wood.
Description Deciduous shrub or small tree 2–6

m tall; somewhat bushy. Young twigs square-stemmed. Leaves blue-green, opposite, decussate, dentate, ovate or oblong-lanceolate, 3–8 cm long, yellow-red in autumn. Pale green flowers, up to 6 in axillary panicles, appearing early to mid-summer followed by attractive, deeply 4-lobed, red-orange or pink capsule of 15 mm diameter.

Distribution Native to Europe and western Asia. In open woodland, clearings, hedgerows, close to water, on deep moist loam.

Cultivation Wild. Several cultivars including *Aldenhamensis* and *Burtonii* are used as garden ornamentals. Tolerates most positions and soils. Raise from seed in spring and from hardwood cuttings or layering in summer.

Constituents Vitamin C; lipids; tannins; cardiotonic heterosides including euonoside, to which the toxicity is due; organic acids and esters; several pigments including physaline and phyllorhodine.

Uses (dried seed and fruit, fresh leaves) Emetic; purgative; insecticide; cholagogue.

Effective when used externally against scabies, pediculoses (head, body or pubic), ticks and other skin parasites.

Contra-indications POISONOUS; not to be used internally.

Eupatorium cannabinum L COMPOSITAE
Hemp Agrimony Water Hemp

An attractive plant which in some parts of England is called Raspberries and Cream because of the appearance of its flowers.

Its leaves are similar to those of Hemp (*Cannabis sativa* L) hence its common, Latin, and old botanical (*Cannabina aquatica*) names. It has not, however, been employed in the manufacture of rope or cloth, and no longer enjoys wide use.

Description Perennial on woody base, reaching 30–120 cm. Stems erect, downy, bearing petiolate, oblanceolate, basal leaves and ovate or lanceolate branch leaves. Most leaves subdivided into 3 leaflets. Flowers in cymose capitula, each with 5–6 mauve or whitish florets and 10 purple involucral bracts, appearing mid to late summer.

Distribution European native, found on damp calcareous soil which is rich in nutrients. In marshes and fens or less frequently in mixed deciduous woodland.

Cultivation Wild plant. May be cultivated by root division in the autumn, but only on moist soils.

Constituents Tannin; resins; volatile oil; inulin; iron; bitter principle.

Uses (dried herb) Cholagogue; diaphoretic; emetic; expectorant.

In small doses the herb acts as a bitter tonic or aperitif suitable for those disposed to biliousness or constipation. Often combined with other remedies as a tonic.

In large doses it is laxative and emetic.

Eupatorium perfoliatum L COMPOSITAE
Boneset Thoroughwort

Although it is a less imposing herb, Boneset is closely related to Gravel Root as it possesses similar chemical constituents.

This herb played a role in the American domestic economy during the nineteenth century at least equal to that now enjoyed by hot lemon tea in the treatment of coughs and colds. It is certainly more effective. It was first introduced into Europe in 1699.

Description Perennial herb reaching from 50 cm to 1.5 m; pubescent stem which is stout and cylindrical, branched above, bearing 10–20 cm long lanceolate leaves united at the base around the stem; dark and shiny green above, cotton-like beneath and fine-toothed. Inflorescence of 10–16, small white or, rarely, blue flowers, on a dense corymbose cyme. Appearing late summer to mid-autumn.

Distribution Indigenous to North America from Dakota to Florida and Texas; prefers open marshy regions.

Cultivation Wild plant.

Constituents A glucoside, eupatorine; also tannin; volatile oils; resin; gum; sugar; gallic acid. Diaphoretic action probably due to the glucoside and volatile oil.

Uses (dried flowering plant) Diaphoretic. Although the cold decoction is tonic and stimulant in small doses and emetic in large, the widest use is for the common cold or similar feverishness, taken as a hot infusion it is practically unequalled in its effectiveness.

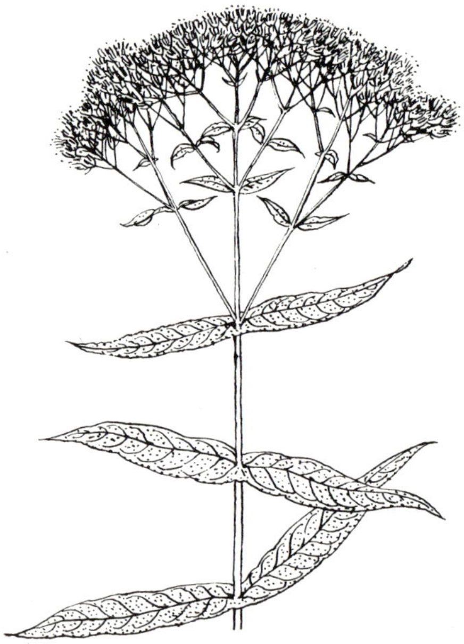

Eupatorium purpureum L COMPOSITAE
Gravel Root Joe-pye Weed

This enormously tall North American herb with its mass of purplish-white flowers makes such a splendid sight when in flower that it has been given the name Queen of the Meadow. Indians used the plant for dyeing and to induce perspiration to break a fever, uses which were quickly adopted by European settlers. Still used by British and American herbalists.

Description Perennial of a variable nature, reaching from 75 cm–3 m high, but typically

tall and graceful. Stem rigid, generally hollow, tinged with purple above the nodes, bearing oblong-lanceolate vanilla-scented, roughish leaves, in whorls of 2–5 leaves, 30 cm long. Flowers creamy white, often tinged with purple, arranged in clusters of 5 or 10 on very numerous dense terminal compound corymbs. Appearing late summer to mid-autumn.
Distribution North American native; preferring rich calcareous woodland soils, either dry or moist.
Cultivation Wild plant; may be propagated by root division in late spring or autumn.
Constituents Resin; volatile oil; a flavonoid, euparin; an oleoresin, eupurpurin, is produced by pouring the tincture into cold water – it has the same action as that of the whole root.
Uses (dried root-stock) Astringent tonic; diuretic; stimulant; antilithic; anti-rheumatic.
Specifically of use in the treatment of renal or urinary calculi (stones), caused by excess uric acid. Hence also useful in gout and rheumatism.
The fruit yields a pink or red textile dye.

Euphorbia hirta L EUPHORBIACEAE
Euphorbia Asthma Weed
The Spurge family consists of several thousand species distributed worldwide; most of the 1000 species of the genus *Euphorbia* exude an acrid milky latex which ranges from irritant in its action to extremely poisonous. *E. heptagona* (L), for example, is used in Ethiopian arrow poisons. The common name for the family indicates the widest use for Euphorbias, that of purgatives – from the Latin *purgatoria*, the purging herb. The dried latex of *E. resinifera* (Berg.), known as *euphorbium* in honour of Euphorbus, physician to Juba II (died A.D. 18), was used continuously from ancient times until the last century. Asthma Weed, however, is one of the few species still considered safe to use.
Description Annual, 15–50 cm high; stems erect covered with stiff yellow hairs, considerably branched. Leaves dark green above, paler beneath, obovate-lanceolate, acute, and dentate; opposite, 1–4 cm long, 5 mm–1.5 cm

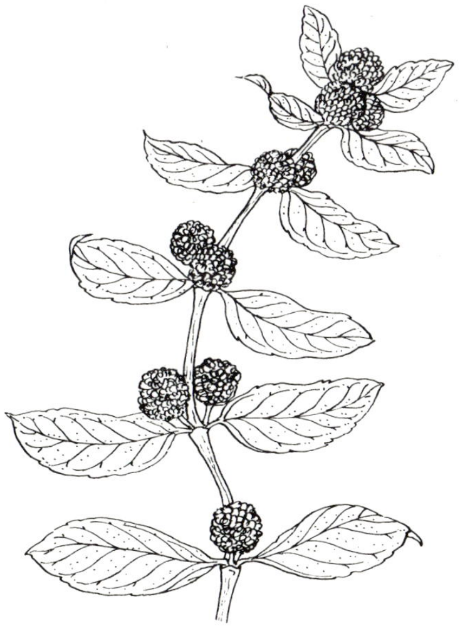

wide. Flowers small, numerous, crowded on 1 cm diameter globose cymes; followed by 3 celled capsular fruit.
Distribution Native to tropical India; introduced and naturalized in most tropical and subtropical countries.
Cultivation Wild plant.
Constituents An ill-defined glycoside and alkaloid; phytosterol; melissic acid; euphosterol; tannin; a phenolic substance; quercetin; gallic acid; sugar.
Uses (dried flowering plant) Expectorant; antasthmatic; anti-amoebic.
Chiefly employed in the treatment of intestinal amoebiasis; also effective in bronchitic asthma and laryngeal spasm since it causes relaxation of the bronchi by central depressant action. The fresh latex is applied externally in the treatment of warts.
Contra-indications Large doses cause gastro-intestinal irritation, nausea and vomiting.

Euphrasia rostkoviana Hayne
SCROPHULARIACEAE
Eyebright Meadow Eyebright
Eyebright is the best known of all herbs used to treat eye conditions. Although its name is

derived from the Greek meaning gladness, it appears unknown to ancient physicians prior to the Middle Ages – when it was introduced by Hildegarde.
The flower certainly gives the appearance of a bloodshot eye. Apothecaries knew the plant as *ocularia* and *ophthalmica*, and its use has been retained to this day in folk medicine. Linnaeus classified it as *Euphrasia officinalis*, but his type species consists of a mixture of a number of species. *E. officinalis* is, therefore, an ambiguous name which has no standing. Only Eyebright species possessing glandular hairs on the calyx have medicinal value.
Description Small attractive annual on erect, usually branched, stems from 5–30 cm high, bearing opposite, ovoid, downy and crenate-serrate leaves 0.5–1 cm long, and spikes of 1 cm long white flowers in the axils of upper leaves. Calyx and leaves close to the inflorescence bear glandular hairs; flower also has purple stripes and yellow flecks. Appears from mid-summer to late autumn.
Distribution European native, on poor meadow land and turf. Calcifugous, and found to 3000 m altitude.
Cultivation Wild plant; cannot be cultivated easily as it is a semiparasite on certain grass species requiring a close physical association with the grass roots, from which it obtains nutrients.
Constituents Tannin; resin; saponin; volatile oils; a glycoside, aucubine. The combined action is anti-inflammatory for mucosae.
Uses (dried flowering plant) Anti-inflammatory; weakly astringent; weak vulnerary.
Almost exclusively employed as a mild eye lotion for use in conjunctivitis. Also as a nasal douche in nasal catarrh, head colds and sinusitis. Externally in poultices to aid wound healing.
A constituent of herbal smoking mixtures.

Ferula foetida Regel UMBELLIFERAE
Asafetida
Asafetida is a strongly foetid brownish gum, hence its name. In small quantities, however, it gives food a particular flavour and has long been used as a condiment by Indians in vegetable dishes.
In the second century A.D., a tax was levied on the drug in Alexandria, and it was used by the Arabian physicians of the Middle Ages who called it *hiltit* The thirteenth-century Welsh Physicians of Myddvai considered it an important medicinal substance; it is now rarely used in Europe.
Description Herbaceous monoecious perennial, 1.5–2 m high, bearing large bipinnate radical leaves, and developing a massive fleshy root-stock 14 cm thick at the crown, which is covered by coarse fibres. The inflorescence is usually produced in the fifth year of growth on

a 2.5–3 m high, to 10 cm thick, naked, flowering stem. Flowers yellow in umbels appearing mid-spring.
Distribution Native to eastern Persia and western Afghanistan, on rocky hillsides.
Cultivation Wild plant; the resin is collected commercially from plants which must be at least 5 years old.
Constituents Volatile oil (10%); resin (50%); gum (25%); ferulic acid. The volatile oil contains terpenes, disulphides and pinene, and is responsible for the therapeutic action.
Uses (dried oleo-resin-gum, obtained by incision of living root-stock) Nervine stimulant; powerful antispasmodic; expectorant; carminative.
Very effective in hysteria and some nervous conditions, and in bronchitis, asthma and whooping-cough. Once employed in infantile pneumonia and in the treatment of flatulent colic.
A condiment commonly used as an ingredient of Indian sauces, pickles, Worcestershire Sauce, and vegetable dishes; also with fish.

Ferula galbaniflua Boiss. et Buhse UMBELLIFERAE
Galbanum
Galbanum was an important ingredient of the incense used by the Israelites who called this plant product *Chelbenah*. It is obtained from this and other species of *Ferula*, notably *F. rubricaulis* (Boiss.), either by collecting the milky-white tears of gum-resin which naturally exude from the stem, or by severing the plant's root crown. *Ferula* is from the Latin, to strike. Both Hippocrates and Theophrastus mentioned its medicinal properties, and Pliny called it *bubonion*. It was known by the Arabic term, *kinnah*, to the physicians of the School of Salerno. Previously imported from Persia, but now only from the Near East.

Description Umbelliferous perennial on solid stem reaching 1.5–1.75 m high, bearing greyish tomentose leaves, yellowish-white flowers in flat umbels appearing in mid-spring, and thin flat fruits.
Distribution Indigenous to Persia.
Cultivation Wild plant.
Constituents Volatile oil (10%), resin (60%); gum (20%).
Uses (semi-hard gum-resin obtained from stem or root crown) Stimulant; expectorant.
Once used in chronic bronchitis as a stimulating expectorant, often in combination with other remedies. May be incorporated in plasters for application on ulcers.
A constituent of incense.

Ficus carica L MORACEAE
Fig Common Fig
Known to the Romans as *ficus*, figs were valued as a food by the ancient Hebrews, and, with the vine, signified peace and plenty in the writings of the scriptures. The plant was so extensively cultivated that even in Pliny's time several different varieties existed, of which the best was considered to be that flourishing in Caria in Asia Minor; hence the modern botanical classification *F. carica*.
Charlemagne promoted its cultivation in central Europe in the ninth century, and today it is still an official plant in the British Pharmacopoeia.
Description Deciduous tree to 9 m, much branched, soft-wooded, with large rough leaves, 10–20 cm long, broad-ovate to orbicular, 3–5 deep lobes and pubescent beneath; forming mass of attractive foliage. Leaves entire in some cultivated forms. Flowers uniquely hidden within a hollow fleshy receptacle (syconus) and therefore never visible. Receptacle 3–7.5 cm long, single, axillary and often pear-shaped, or variable. Appearing early summer to mid-autumn.
Distribution Indigenous to Mediterranean region, widely distributed.
Cultivation Wild; several forms grown for fruit, shade and ornament, of which the best is the variety Brown Turkey. Easily cultivated in full sun; to ensure good harvest, root growth must be severely restricted by planting in 50 cm diameter pot, sunk in the soil. Propagate from cuttings.

Constituents Grape (invert) sugar, gum, sucrose.
Uses (fresh and dried fruit) Mild laxative; nutritive.
Most widely known medicinally as a folk remedy for constipation: taken as syrup of figs. Also used in combination with stronger purgatives like Senna. Once used externally as a demulcent poultice for boils and ulcers.
Wide culinary use in confectionery, in jams, and used to flavour some coffees. May be used in home wine manufacture.

Filipendula ulmaria (L) Maxim ROSACEAE
Meadowsweet Queen of the Meadow
Queen of the Meadow is this herb's most modern common name, and it seems to have been the more popular in several European languages. It is certainly apt, for when the plant is fully established, it may completely dominate a low-lying damp meadow.
Meadowsweet is simply derived from the earlier 'meadwort', since it was once used to flavour mead. Botanically, the herb was classified by Linnaeus as *Spiraea ulmaria* since the fruit consists of small spiral achenes

twisted together. This generic name has been immortalized in the word Aspirin (meaning, from Spiraea), because it was from the flower-buds of Meadowsweet that salicylic acid was first discovered in 1839 – and from which Aspirin was later synthesized.
Description Stout perennial herb 60–120 cm tall on thick, pink aromatic root-stock. Stems erect, reddish, bearing alternate, acute, ovate leaves, irregularly pinnate with 2–5 pairs of leaflets, 2–8 cm long, glabrous above and whitish and tomentose beneath. Faintly aromatic flowers white or cream, small (2–5 mm), 5-petalled, with numerous long stamens, in dense but irregular paniculate cymes on glabrous stems; appearing mid-summer to early autumn.
Distribution European and Asian native. Intro-

duced and naturalized in North America. On wet, nutrient-rich, but not too acidic, sandy or loamy soils near streams and rivers in fens, marshland or wet woodlands, to 1000 m altitude.
Cultivation Wild, often growing in profusion in suitable habitat. Propagate from seed sown in spring or from root division in spring; thin or plant to 40 cm apart. A damp, rich soil in partial shade is required; water well in dry weather.
Constituents Tannins (10%); volatile oil comprising, salicylaldehyde (to 10%) also methyl salicylate; vanillin, heliotropin, ethyl benzoate; also flavonoid glycosides including spiraeoside; salicyclic glycosides, comprising gaultherin and spiraein; vitamin C; sugars; mineral salts.
Uses (dried flowers, dried root-stock) Antipyretic; anti-rheumatic; astringent; weak antispasmodic; diuretic; antiseptic.
The root is employed specifically in the treatment of diarrhoea, while the flowers are of benefit in influenza, fluid retention, rheumatism and arthritis. They are probably the most effective of all plant remedies for the treatment of hyperacidity and heartburn. Useful therefore in the control of peptic ulcers and gastritis. The infusion also has an effect in certain urinary tract infections.
Formerly used in mead and wine cups.
A black dyestuff has been obtained from the plant, using a copper mordant.
May be used in scented articles.

Foeniculum vulgare Mill. UMBELLIFERAE
Fennel Sweet Fennel
The appearance of dried Fennel leaf, which is rather like coarse, crumpled hair, gave rise to both the common and botanical names being derived from the Latin *faeniculum*, meaning little hay.
It has been used for culinary purposes for at least 2000 years, and was formerly prized more for its succulent stems than for its seed, which is the part now commonly employed. Special varieties have been developed supplying swollen bulbous stalk bases (Finnocchio or Florence Fennel), large stalks (Carosella), and foliage for decorative purposes (Bronze Fennel). The seed flavour also varies considerably from the Bitter or Wild Fennel and the less bitter Saxon or German Fennel to the Sweet Roman or Sweet Fennel. It is traditionally considered one of the best herbs to use with fish dishes.
Description Hardy biennial or perennial, often cultivated as an annual; erect blue-green stem, 70 cm to 2 m high, bearing fine, 3–4 pinnately compound leaves, often almost filiform, to 4 cm long, on broad and clasping petioles. Small yellow flowers, on large umbels of 15–20 rays, succeeded by fruit, bluish turning grey-brown. Appearing mid-summer to mid-autumn.
Distribution Native to mediterranean region, introduced and naturalized in other places; prefers wasteland on well-drained soil in sunny locations.
Cultivation Wild, and extensively grown horticulturally and commercially in all temperate

zones. Propagated in any soil except heavy clay, from seed sown in autumn. Remove flower-heads if seed is not required. Different races produce seeds of varying flavour.
Constituents Volatile oil, comprising mainly anethole and also fenchone, d-pinene, limonene, dipentene, phellandrene and anisic acid. Carminative action due to the oil.
Uses (fresh and dried leaf, oil, dried ripe fruit, rarely roots) Carminative; aromatic; weak diuretic; mild stimulant.
The oil is added to purgative medication to prevent griping and intestinal colic; aids flatulence and allays hunger. Once used to promote lactation. Thought to aid in slimming.
All parts of culinary use; leaves traditionally garnish fish, and are added to salads, soups, sauces and pork dishes. Root and stalks may be boiled and eaten as a vegetable; seed used in liqueur manufacture and as a condiment.
Contra-indications Very large doses disturb the nervous system.

Fomes officinalis (Vittadini) Bresadola POLYPORACEAE
Agaricus Purging Agaric
This fungus has also been known as *Polyporus officinalis* Fries., *Boletus laricis* Jacq. and *Ungulina officinalis*. Owing to the difficulty of classification of the fungus group, it cannot be identified with certainty in ancient writings and probably the related species *Fomes fomentarius* (L) Fries. was used more frequently and as a styptic agent in fresh wounds. *F. fomentarius* is only occasionally available, known as Amadou, and is used as a cigar lighter.
Because of its bitter taste *F. officinalis* was once used to flavour confectionery and it was also used as an ingredient of the *Tinctura antiperiodica* or Warburg's Fever Tincture, a compound medication whose composition was published in 1875 by Dr Warburg after years of secrecy. The fungus is not an edible mushroom, and it is now very rarely used.

Description A variably shaped, soft, fleshy, whitish fungus with yellowish spots and pores; to 50 cm long and 30 cm wide. The surface is dry and marked by irregular furrows; it has an aroma of flour.
Distribution Southern Tyrol and French Alps to Russia, in larch forests.
Cultivation Wild plant. Growing on various species of Larch (*Larix* spp.) especially *Larix sibirica* Led., *L. europaea* DC, (*Larix decidua* Mill.). Formerly collected in early autumn.
Constituents Riconoleic acid; phytosterol; agaric acid; agaricol; resins.
Uses (dried whole fungus) Astringent; bitter; purgative.
Formerly used in compound antipyretic medicines, and either alone or in combination with other remedies to treat diarrhoea, excess lactation and fevers.
Also once used as the source of crystalline agaricin which was used for similar medical purposes.
Formerly employed as a bitter flavouring in confectionery.
Contra-indications Large doses cause vomiting and purgation.

Fragearia vesca L ROSACEAE
Wild Strawberry Wood Strawberry
Numerous varieties have been developed since cultivation of the Strawberry began in the early sixteenth century, but it was this species which was gathered wild from the woods of Europe for centuries. *Fraga* was the Latin name, and probably refers to the fruit's fragrance.
Description Perennial 5–25 cm tall, on stout, woody root-stock, producing long, rooting runners. Leaflets ovate, bright green above, pale beneath, silky, toothed, 1–6 cm long. Lateral leaflets sessile, terminal, short-stalked. Flowers white, 15 mm diameter, erect, 3–10 per peduncle; appearing early to mid-summer, followed by red (or white) ovoid, false fruit.

Distribution Native to Europe, western Asia, North America. In woods, scrubland, preferably on moist, somewhat calcareous soils; to 800 m altitude.
Cultivation Wild plant. Propagate by transplantation of daughter plants produced on runners.
Constituents (leaves) Tannins; flavonoids. (fruit) Organic acids; vitamin C; mucilage; sugars.
Uses (fresh fruit, leaves, root-stock rarely) Astringent; diuretic; antiscorbutic; tonic; laxative.
The root decoction was formerly used to treat gonorrhoea, and as a diuretic; it also acts as a weak, bitter tonic. Leaf and root-stock can be used to treat diarrhoea, while the fruit is laxative.
The dried leaf can be used as a tea substitute.
Contra-indications Strawberries may produce an allergic response.

Frangula alnus Mill. RHAMNACEAE
Alder Buckthorn
This medicinal plant is so named because it bears a superficial foliage similarity to the Alder (*Alnus glutinosa* (L) Gaertn.), with which it shares a predilection for wet environments and because it has the same purgative qualities as *Rhamnus catharticus*, which was known as *cervi spina* (buck's thorn) to the early apothecaries.
The quite thornless Alder Buckthorn does not appear to have been used until the beginning of the fourteenth century when the Italian Pierre Crescenzi introduced it. German physicians were to make most use of it in subsequent years.
Since it has similar properties to Cascara sagrada (*Rhamnus purshiana* D.C.), but can be collected locally, it is retained in several European pharmacopoeias.
Description Small tree or deciduous shrub to 6 m; usually 1–4 m. Branches supple, smooth, erect towards the base, young branchlets red-brown at the tips, later darkening to grey-black. Leaves alternate, acute, entire, or sometimes undulate, obovate to oblong, 3–4 cm long, dark green and shiny above. Flowers small, bisexual, greenish, borne in umbelliform cymes. Appearing late spring to mid-summer; followed by globose fruit 7.5 mm diameter, red then black or blue-black.
Distribution Native to Europe, Central Asia, North Africa; introduced and naturalized in eastern United States. On acidic, often heavy soils, in open, damp, deciduous or coniferous woodland, especially near streams, to 1000 m altitude.
Cultivation Wild. Commercial plantations are being established in Eastern Europe. Collected commercially in Russia, Holland, Poland and Czechoslovakia.
Constituents Anthraquinone glycosides, comprising frangulin (produced during drying and storage), frangula-emodin, frangularoside, chrysophanic acid, an iso-emodin; also tannic acid; bitter principles; mucilage.
Purgative action due to the presence of emodins, which act on the large intestine causing peristalsis.
Uses (12-month old stem and inner branch bark) Purgative; choleretic.
Almost exclusively used in the treatment of constipation, often in combination with other remedies. Very small doses may be used to stimulate bile secretion. Once applied externally to aid the healing of wounds.
Contra-indications Fresh bark contains anthrone glycosides which cause severe catharsis, emesis and cramps.
The fruit is POISONOUS.

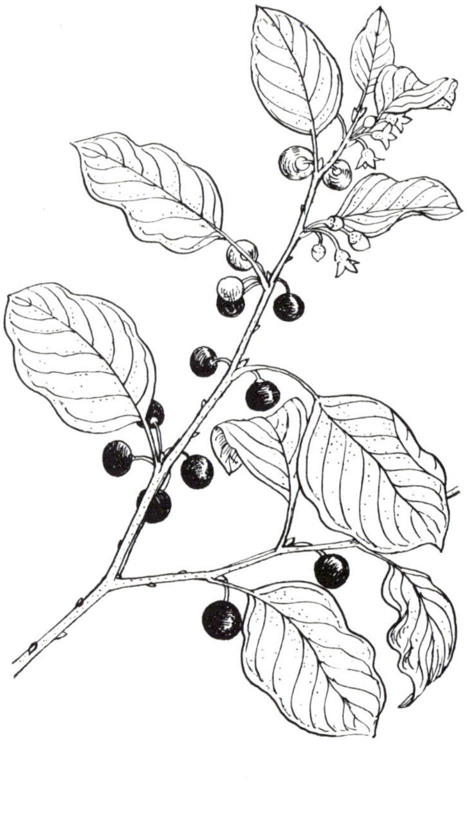

Fraxinus ornus L OLEACEAE
Manna Flowering Ash
According to the Bible, Manna was the substance miraculously supplied to the Israelites during their progress through the wilderness to the Holy Land, and the name has been applied to several substances both real and imaginary, thought to provide spiritual nourishment. Prior to the fifteenth century, Manna was imported from the East and its provenance is uncertain, but from the middle of the sixteenth century most Manna was the dried sugary juice obtained by incisions in the bark of the Flowering Ash grown for the purpose in Sicily and Calabria in southern Italy. Now rarely obtainable in Europe.
Description Deciduous tree 10–20 m. Rounded in shape, and with great variation in leaflet and fruit shape. Leaves 20–25 cm long with 7–11

leaflets, usually ovate or oblong, somewhat pubescent. Flowers dull white, on numerous dense feathery panicles, 7.5–12.5 cm long appearing early to mid-summer, and followed by linear or lanceolate fruit 3 cm long.
Distribution Native to southern Europe and western Asia. Introduced into central Europe, North America and elsewhere.
Cultivation Wild, and cultivated as an ornamental tree and for commercial purposes.
Constituents Various sugars, chiefly comprising mannitol, mannotriose, mannotetrose and dextrose; also mucilage; aesculin and fraxin. Laxative action due to fraxin.
Uses (the yellow-white saccharine exudation obtained by bark incisions during the flowering season) Mild laxative. Exclusively of service as a gentle laxative for children and pregnant women, taken in quite large dosage either alone or in combination with Rhubarb. Nutritive and therefore useful during convalescence.
Contra-indications May cause flatulence.

Fucus vesiculosus L FUCACEAE
Bladderwrack Kelp
Although commonly called Kelp, this is a term usually applied to species of *Laminaria*, which are somewhat larger algae. It is one of several seaweeds long used both as food and medicine,

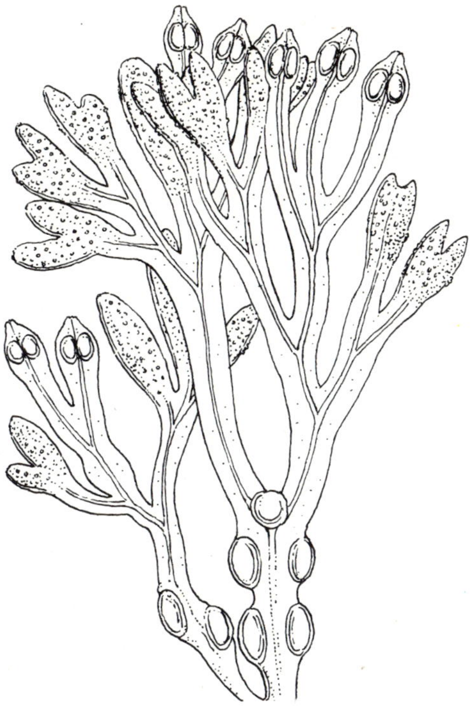

and sometimes as a cheap manure. Iodine was first discovered by distillation of *Fucus* in the early nineteenth century, and for about 50 years most commercial supplies of Iodine were obtained in this way. Its common name is derived both from the typical bladder-like air vesicles on the thallus, and from an ancient word signifying something which is driven ashore.

Description Perennial seaweed consisting of a thin, leathery, branching, brownish-green or yellowish thallus, 18 mm wide and 1 m long. Woody stipe attached to rocks by discoid hold-fast; margins entire, midrib broad and distinct, running the length of the plant, along which air vesicles are borne in pairs. Terminating in strong globose fructifications consisting of ovoid receptacles 3 cm in length.

Distribution Common on north-west Atlantic coastlines, especially west Scotland, Norway, and North America; attached to rocks.

Cultivation Wild plant; collected commercially.

Constituents A gelatinous substance, algin; mannitol; iodine; a volatile oil; β-carotene; zeaxanthin; various inorganic substances.

Uses (dried whole plant) Anti-obesic; anti-hypothyroid.

Specifically of use in obesity which is associated with hypothyroidism. A decoction of the whole fresh plant may be applied externally in rheumatism and rheumatoid arthritis.

An excellent source of manure for horticultural purposes; one of the commercial sources of alginates.

Fumaria officinalis L FUMARIACEAE

Fumitory

Much legend surrounds this herb, including the belief that it arose not from seed but from emanations in the ground, and that its smoke when burned repelled evil spirits. Both its common and botanical names derive from the Latin word for smoke, probably because at a

distance the wispy grey-green leaflets look smoky.

From the earliest times Fumitory was considered effective in conditions of intestinal obstruction leading to skin diseases, but today it is rarely used.

Description Annual; variable in form, the stem being erect, bushy or trailing, from 15–70 cm long; leaves grey-green 1 cm long, pinnate, petiolate, with lanceolate leaf segments. Flowers 8 mm–1.2 cm long, pinkish-purple, dark red at the tips, borne in racemes 5–7 cm long, appearing mid-summer to late autumn.

Distribution European native; naturalized in America and parts of Asia. Common in weedy areas of gardens, fields, vineyards, rarely cornfields. Prefers loamy soils.

Cultivation Wild plant.

Constituents 7 alkaloids, chiefly fumarine; tannic acid; fumaric acid; potassium salts.

Uses (dried flowering plant) Laxative; stomachic; tonic; weak diuretic.

Formerly chiefly employed in the treatment of various skin complaints including eczema, exanthema and dermatitis. Also once considered of benefit in arteriosclerosis.

The flowers produce a yellow wool dye.

Dried leaves may be added to smoking mixtures.

Contra-indications POISONOUS.

Galanthus nivalis L AMARYLLIDACEAE

Snowdrop Bulbous Violet

The Snowdrop is well known as the first flower of the year, and its name *galanthus* is derived from the Greek meaning milk flower after its snow-white appearance.

It is very rarely mentioned in the herbals and has never attracted attention as being of medicinal use except for a poultice of the crushed bulbs which may be applied externally in cases of frostbite. Recent research in Europe, however, suggests that the plant may possess the ability to stimulate the regeneration of some nerve cells.

Description Perennial reaching 10–20 cm tall; leaves linear and glaucous, 7 mm wide, fleshy, basal, ridged, on bulbs growing in compact masses. Pedicel slender, usually less than 25 cm long, bearing single flower; outer segments white, 15 mm–3 cm long, inner segments white and green. Appearing early spring.

Distribution Native to central and south Europe, to the Caucasus; introduced elsewhere. Prefers soils rich in humus and nutrients in mixed deciduous woodland.

Cultivation Wild plant; cultivated as a garden plant and found as an escape. Propagate by division in the autumn. A giant form, *G. Elwesii* (Hook) exists.

Constituents Alkaloids, chiefly in the bulb, comprising tazettine, lycorine, galanthamines.

Uses (bulb) Emetic.

The plant is rarely used medicinally, but in eastern Europe a preparation known as 'nivaline' has been promoted as being of benefit in a range of conditions characterized by nervous tissue degeneration, for example, poliomyelitis.

Contra-indications POISONOUS.

Galega officinalis L PAPILIONACEAE

Goat's Rue French Lilac

The ability of Goat's Rue to promote the flow of milk, by as much as 50% in some animals, is reflected in its name *galega* from the Greek for milk. The most effective galactogenic preparation is an infusion of the fresh plant.

Description Attractive bushy perennial to 1 m on hollow stem bearing leaves consisting of 11–17 oblong or oblong-ovate glabrous, mucronate, leaflets 1–4 cm long. Purplish-blue flowers 1 cm long in racemes slightly longer than the leaves; appear mid-summer to mid-autumn and are followed by 3–4 cm long red-brown pods.

Distribution Native to Europe and western Asia; introduced elsewhere. Prefers slightly moist positions in fields.

Cultivation Wild and occurs as an escape from garden cultivation. *G. officinalis* var. *albiflora* (Boiss.) has white flowers, and *G. officinalis* var.

Hartlandii (Hort.) has lilac flowers and variegated leaves. Propagate by division of roots in spring or autumn, planting in deep soil.
Constituents Alkaloids, chiefly galegine and especially in the seed; a glucoside, galuteoline; tannic acid; saponin; vitamin C; bitter principles.
Uses (dried flowering plant, seeds) Galactogogue; hypoglycaemic; diuretic; diaphoretic.
A tea of Goat's Rue has supportive antidiabetic action and is used to promote milk flow in both women and animals.
The fresh juice clots milk and may be used in cheese-making.

Galipea cusparia St Hilaire RUTACEAE
Angostura Cusparia Bark
First used in 1759 in Madrid by Mutis, Angostura was introduced into England by Brande in 1788 who was the apothecary to Queen Charlotte. Until the end of the nineteenth century Angostura was considered an effective tonic, and it was originally introduced by Dr Siegert as a medical recipe for the treatment of fever. 'Angostura bitters' no longer contains extract of angostura bark, this having been replaced by Gentian root.
Angostura is the former name for Ciudad Bolivar, a town in Venezuela.
Description Small tree 4–5 m tall, 7.5–12.5 cm in diameter, the trunk being straight, irregularly branched and with a smooth bark, covered externally with a yellowish-grey corky layer.
Leaves smooth and glossy, alternate and petiolate, divided into 3 leaflets which are oblong, pointed, 4 cm long. Flowers strongly scented, arranged in terminal peduncled racemes.
Distribution Tropical South America, especially Venezuela. Mostly abundant in mountainous districts.
Cultivation Wild plant.
Constituents Volatile oil; glucoside; alkaloids, chiefly angosturine; a bitter substance, cusparine.
Uses (stem bark) Stimulant tonic.
Employed locally in South America for dyspepsia, chronic diarrhoea and dysentery.
Once considered a valuable tonic, and used in fevers in preference to Cinchona Bark. In combination with sliced Lemon and sugar, Angostura bitters was used for hiccups.
Formerly an ingredient of some commercial bitter liqueurs.
The bark acts as a fish poison.
Contra-indications Large doses cause diarrhoea.

Galium aparine L RUBIACEAE
Goosegrass Cleavers/Clivers
Many of the common names refer to the clinging nature of the stems of this common weed of roadsides and hedgerows, a character shared also by the globular seed capsules which assist in the distribution of the plant via animal coats. The Greeks called it *philanthropon* meaning love man because the leaves and fruit cling to the clothes. It has been widely used in folk medicine for centuries, generally being considered of most benefit in the treatment of various skin conditions.
Description Annual herb with straggling habit, the trailing, quadrangular, rough, stem attaining 120 cm in length. Leaves prickly, cuneate, in whorls of 6 or 8, coarse-haired on the leaf margins. Flowers very small, white, or greenish-white on 2–3 cm long inflorescences borne on leaf axils and extending longer than the leaves.
Distribution European native; prefers moist nutrient-rich loamy soils, in weedy sites, particularly field and garden edges and hedgerows.
Cultivation Wild plant.
Constituents A glycoside, asperuloside.
Uses (dried flowering plant, freshly expressed juice) Vulnerary; weak diuretic.
Used externally to treat wounds and ulcers, and internally in painful urination associated with cystitis; in enlarged lymph glands, and in psoriasis. The herb reduces body temperature and blood pressure slightly. Also employed homeopathically.
The dried plant may be drunk as a tea, and the roasted seeds provide an excellent coffee substitute.

Galium verum L RUBIACEAE
Ladies' Bedstraw Cheese Rennet/Yellow Bedstraw
The pleasant honey scent of the flowers and hay-like aroma of the dried leaves and stems made this an admirable herb for stuffing mattresses in medieval times. It was commonly mixed with bracken or some aromatic or flea-repelling herb for this purpose. Dioscorides knew it as *galion* or the milk plant, and it was used throughout Europe from the time of the Greeks until the 1800s as a means of curdling

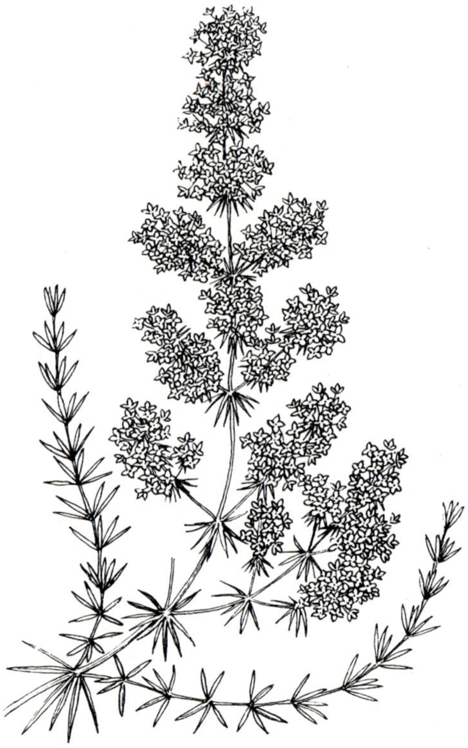

milk in cheese manufacture.
Description A perennial herb with erect or decumbent somewhat woody stems, round with 4 prominent edges or almost square, glabrous, slightly branched and from 20–80 cm tall. Leaves white and slightly hairy on the underside, recurved, bristle-tipped, in whorls of 8–12, linear, 1.5–2.5 cm long, 1–2 mm wide. Flowers 2–3 mm wide, smelling of honey, on terminal panicles, golden-yellow, appearing early summer to mid-autumn.
Distribution European native; now a weed in the eastern United States. On semi-dry or dry grassland.
Cultivation Wild plant.
Constituents Silicic acid; saponin; an enzyme, rennin.
Uses (dried flowering plant) Weak diuretic; styptic.
Formerly employed as a diuretic for dropsy and in epilepsy. Applied externally to wounds and some skin eruptions.
Strong decoctions curdle milk when boiled, and may be used in cheese manufacture; the herb also colours cheese a greenish-yellow.
A red dye can be obtained from the lower stem.

Gaultheria procumbens L ERICACEAE
Wintergreen Checkerberry/Mountain Tea
Most commercial oil of Wintergreen now consists of synthetically produced methyl salicylate. It was formerly obtained largely from young birch trees (*Betula lenta*), and before that it was isolated from the Wintergreen plant. Wintergreen was once mentioned in the United States Pharmacopoeia but has never attracted much medical attention, nor is it widely used in folk traditions. It is named after Dr Gaultier, a physician practising in Quebec in about 1750.
Description Evergreen shrub with creeping stems and erect stiff branches to 15 cm tall, bearing at the top oval leaves, 3–5 cm long, glabrous and shiny above, paler beneath, petiolate and apiculate; white flowers 7.5 mm long, solitary and drooping, appearing from the leaf base in mid and late summer, and followed by scarlet berries 7 mm in diameter.
Distribution North American native, from Newfoundland to Georgia. On poor soils.
Cultivation Wild plant.
Constituents Arbutin: ericolin; urson; tannin; a volatile oil (oil of gaultheria or oil of wintergreen) is obtained by distillation of the leaves and comprises chiefly methyl salicylate, and an alcohol, a ketone and an ester.
Uses (leaves, oil) Stimulant; astringent; tonic; aromatic; counter-irritant.
An infusion of the leaves may be used as a throat gargle, as a douche and for headaches.
The oil is readily absorbed by the skin and is employed in various aches and pains, including rheumatism. It is occasionally used internally as an emulsion against hookworm.
Leaves may be used as a tea substitute.
The oil is a flavouring agent in various dental preparations.
Contra-indications The pure oil may irritate skin; it must not be used internally without medical advice.

Gelidium spp. RHODOPHYCEAE
Agar-Agar Japanese Isinglass
The use of Agar as a semi-solid medium for the cultivation of bacteria and fungi by Robert Koch in the 1880s revolutionized bacteriological research and made it possible to cultivate and identify many of the bacteria responsible for human and animal disease. Today most of the Agar produced is employed for this purpose, and although Japanese Agar made from various species of *Gelidium* is considered the finest and has the greatest gel strength, other seaweeds also provide Agar; British Agar is from either *Chondrus crispus* or *Gigartina stellata* or a combination of the two, the New Zealand variety from *Pterocladia lucida*, and Australian from *Gracilaria confervoides*.
Description Perennial seaweed to 25 cm long; the thallus develops from a persistent basal portion each growing season, is cylindrical or flattened, pinnately subdivided and of a tough consistency. The spherical fruit appear in the late autumn and winter months.
Distribution Gelidium amansii Kutz., *G. elegans* Kutz. and *G. polycladum* Sond. are found in the maritime zones of Japan and *G. cartilagineum* (Gaill.) in the maritime zones of South Africa and United States.
Cultivation Wild marine plant; collected commercially and sometimes encouraged to grow on poles driven into the sea bed.
Constituents Chiefly composed of a calcium salt, of a sulphuric ester of a carbohydrate complex; also a trace of protein, and mineral salts.
Uses (dried Agar; greyish-white translucent strips obtained by drying the liquor resulting from boiling the seaweed for 6 hours in the presence of dilute sulphuric acid) Bulk laxative; emulsion stabilizer.
Unlike gelatine Agar-Agar has no nutritive or

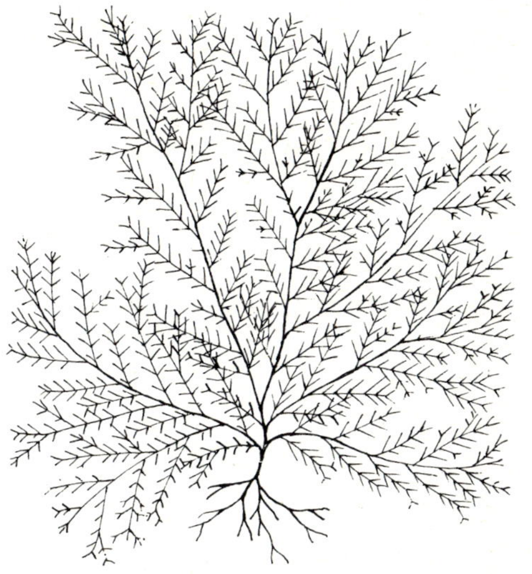

therapeutic value, but it is used medically as a mild evacuant since it absorbs water in the intestine, increases the faeces bulk, and thus promotes peristalsis. Also used to stabilize emulsions of other laxatives. Mostly employed as the basis of bacteriological culture media, and as a thickening agent in some foodstuffs, both commercially and domestically.
Employed as the physical base for certain air purifiers.

Gelsemium sempervirens Ait. LOGANIACEAE
Yellow Jessamine Yellow Jasmine Root
Gelsemium is derived from the Italian *Gelsomino* the name of the true Jessamine or Jasmine. It was introduced to medicine accidentally in the early nineteenth century after a Mississippi planter mistakenly took a tea made from the plant to cure bilious fever. The first tests were made in 1852, and it eventually entered the United States Pharmacopoeia, and the British Pharmaceutical Codex. Until quite recently it was used in various mixtures for migraine treatment, but it is toxic even in quite small doses and now seldom used.
Description Perennial evergreen vine to 10 m on woody purplish-brown rhizomes; stem slender, woody, bearing opposite lanceolate to ovate-lanceolate, short-petioled leaves 2.5–10 cm long, entire, shiny dark green above, and paler beneath. Flowers yellow, 2.5–4 cm long, highly fragrant, 1–6 on axillary or terminal cymes, appearing from mid-spring to mid-summer.
Distribution Native to southern United States, Mexico, Guatemala; in moist woodlands.
Cultivation Wild plant; sometimes cultivated horticulturally as cover, or in greenhouses. Propagate from cuttings or from divisions of root-stock in the late spring.
Constituents Alkaloids: gelsemine, sempervirine and gelsemicine; phytosterol; resin; fixed oil; emodin monomethyl ether; β-methylaeculetin. Action largely due to the alkaloids which depress the central nervous system.
Uses (dried rhizome and roots) Sedative; nervine. Formerly employed in the treatment of neuralgia, sick headache, menstrual and rheumatic pains and particularly migraine and trigeminal neuralgia. A perfume can be

made from the flowers.
Contra-indications All parts POISONOUS; toxic effects include double vision, giddiness, respiratory depression and death. Gelsemium is more strongly depressant than Hemlock.

Genista tinctoria L LEGUMINOSAE
Dyer's Greenweed Dyer's Broom
As the common name suggests this herb was an important dyeing plant, and was often combined with Woad to produce a green wool dye. It is closely related to *Sarothamnus scoparius* which in the Middle Ages was itself called Genista, but unlike this plant Dyer's Greenweed does not possess very strong medicinal qualities and is now mainly employed in homecraft dyeing.
Description Perennial herbaceous shrub, prostrate or decumbent, to 1 m, usually 30–50 cm

tall. Bearing glabrous or pubescent forked branches and 1.5–3 cm long, oblong-elliptic or oblong-lanceolate, alternate, nearly sessile, glabrous, simple leaves. Flowers 15 mm long, golden yellow, in racemes 3–7.5 cm long, appearing mid-summer to early autumn, and followed by long narrow pods.
Distribution Native to Europe and western Asia; naturalized in North America. Introduced elsewhere. On dryish loamy or sandy soils in light woodland, pastures, heaths and meadows.
Cultivation Wild plant.
Constituents The alkaloids, sparteine, cytisine and methyl-cytisine; a flavone, genistein; a yellow glycoside, luteolin. The combined action weakly cardio-active and vasoconstrictive.
Uses (flowering plant, seeds, leaves) Emetic; purgative; diuretic; weakly cardio-active.
Formerly used as a diuretic and purgative; in dropsy, rheumatism and as a prophylactic against hydrophobia.
The young buds may be pickled and used as a caper substitute.
The flowering plant furnishes a yellow-green dye.
Contra-indications Not to be used internally during pregnancy or hypertension.

Gentiana lutea L GENTIANACEAE
Gentian Yellow Gentian
Yellow Gentian root is the most bitter plant material known, and has been used for centuries as a bitter tonic. Several other *Gentiana* species native to Europe and North America have been employed for the same purpose, and it is not certain which of the European species was known to the Greeks. The name *gentiana*, however, is derived from Gentius, King of Illyria (180–167 B.C.) who, according to Dioscorides, introduced the herb to medicine. It has been widely employed ever since. Some plants survive as long as 50 years.
Description Herbaceous perennial to 110 cm on thick taproot reaching 60 cm long. Stems simple and erect, glabrous, bearing oval, 5–7 veined, shiny leaves 30 cm long and 15 cm wide; lower leaves on short petioles, upper leaves sessile. Bright yellow flowers, 2.5–3 cm long, on long peduncles in 3–10 flowered axillary clusters, appearing late summer to early autumn on plants at least 10 years old.
Distribution Native to Europe and Asia Minor; introduced elsewhere. Common in mountain pastures, and thinly wooded mountain forests, on calcareous soils which are porous but often moist.
Cultivation Wild and cultivated commercially in Eastern Europe and North America.
Constituents Unsaturated lactones (gentiopicrosides), amarogentine and gentiopicrine, which are partially or totally converted (depending upon the method of drying) to the bitter glycosides, gentiin and gentiamarine; volatile oil; sugars; mucilage; tannin.
The combined action stimulates secretion of bile and its release from the gall bladder.
Uses (dried root, and dried fermented root) Cholagogue; choleretic; stomachic; promotes

salivation.
Acts as a tonic on the gastro-intestinal system; particularly useful in anorexia associated with dyspepsia. In small doses it stimulates the appetite, and should be taken an hour before eating.
Formerly used externally for cleaning wounds, also used as a powder in veterinary medicine to improve appetite.
The fermented root is used as a bitter preparation in alcoholic drinks.

Geranium maculatum L GERANIACEAE
American Cranesbill Wild Geranium
The specific name of American Cranesbill is derived from *macula* meaning spotted, since the leaves become blotched with whitish-green when they age. *Geranium* is from the Greek word for the crane after the beak-like shape of

the fruit; hence also the herb's common names. This was a favourite herb of the American Indians, once official in the United States Pharmacopoeia, but now restricted to folk medicine.
Description Erect hairy perennial to 60 cm; stem solitary, but occasionally forking, on stout rhizome. Some leaves arise from root and are long-petioled. Stem leaves opposite, 7.5–15 cm wide, 5-lobed, deeply incised and cut at the end, hairy. Flowers rose-purple, large, 2.5–4 cm wide, on 2.5 cm long peduncles, 2–3 flowers arising in the axils, appear late spring to late summer.
Distribution North American native.
Cultivation Wild plant.
Constituents Tannic and gallic acids, 10–25%, which produce astringent action; oleo-resin.
Uses (dried rhizome) Astringent; styptic. Useful in diarrhoea, in haemorrhage of the upper gastro-intestinal tract, haemorrhoids, peptic ulcers and aphthous ulcers. Formerly recommended in dysentery and cholera. Used as a douche in leucorrhoea, as a gargle for sore throats, and in the powdered form externally to stop wound bleeding.

Geranium robertianum L GERANIACEAE
Herb Robert Red Robin
A common herb in Europe and an old medicinal plant which was once official in the Middle Ages, and ascribed to St Robert or Pope Robert, hence the medieval name *herba sanctii ruperti*. It is probable that the plant was commonly associated with magic and goblins in earlier times, a fact reflected in the range of names it has been given in various European countries. Still used in folk medicine in many parts of the world.
Description Unpleasantly smelling annual or biennial, on erect or decumbent, glandular-pubescent, reddish stems to 45 cm. Leaves opposite, palmate with 3–5 leaflets with deeply cut divisions, on long petioles, deep green and red tinged. Flowers pink or rose, 5 mm–1 cm wide, in pairs or peduncles arising in terminal axils. Petals have 3 longitudinal white stripes. Appear early summer to late autumn.

Distribution Native to North America, Eurasia and North Africa; common on rocky soils, walls, mixed and deciduous woodland edges, preferring moist and nitrogenous soils.
Cultivation Wild plant.
Constituents Volatile oil; tannin; a bitter substance, geraniine.
Uses (fresh flowering plant, dried plant) Styptic; astringent; weak diuretic; sedative.
Of most use externally for treatment of skin eruptions, stomatitis, bruises and erysipelas. The leaves may be chewed or used as a gargle in inflammations of the mouth and throat. Formerly used in diarrhoea and applied externally as a poultice to relieve inflammations; also used as an eyewash.

Geum urbanum L ROSACEAE
Avens Herb Bennet/Wood Avens
Avens is also known as Herb Bennet or Benedict's herb; names which derive directly from the medieval name *herba benedicta* from the Latin meaning the blessed herb, since the strongly aromatic roots were thought to drive away evil spirits.
For this reason amulets of the herb were worn, and it was also kept in homes.
The botanical name also reflects the roots' scent: *geum* is from the Greek meaning to produce an agreeable smell. The fragrance is unfortunately lost on drying. It is rarely used today except in folk medicine.
Description Perennial herb on clove-smelling rhizome 3–7 cm long, 1–2 cm thick, bearing richly branched downy stems to 30 cm. Leaves 3-lobed, the terminal leaflets largest, irregular, crenate or dentate; upper leaves palmate and sessile. Pale yellow flowers, 5-petalled, 5–7 mm diameter, in loose open panicles, appearing early summer to late autumn. Variable in form.
Distribution European native; common in thickets, wasteland, wood edges, hedgerows, mixed and deciduous woodland; prefers moist nitrogenous soil.
Cultivation Wild plant.
Constituents Volatile oil, comprising mainly eugenol, the latter being combined as a glycoside (geoside) in the fresh plant; tannin; bitter principles.
Uses (dried rhizome, fresh flowering plant) Astringent: styptic; bitter; tonic; anti-inflammatory.
Useful in diarrhoea, and as an aromatic bitter tonic to promote appetite following illness. Applied to wounds to reduce inflammation, and employed as a gargle for sore gums or in halitosis.
The dried rhizome was formerly used as a substitute for Cloves; used as a pot herb in broths and soups, and hung with clothes to repel moths.
Also used to flavour ale.

Glechoma hederacea L LABIATAE
Ground Ivy Gill Over The Ground/Field Balm
In the second century A.D. Galen was aware of the use of Ground Ivy for treating inflamed eyes, and it is probable that the herb was a popular folk remedy from the earliest times.
The plant was also employed in clarifying ale to impart flavour to it and to improve its keeping qualities. *Glechoma* was used much earlier than hops were, being widely employed until the early 1600s.
It is also known as Alehoof or Tunhoof from an old English word for the herb, *hofe*, and from the process of mashing and fermenting the brew known as tunning.
Description Pubescent perennial, strong-smelling with long creeping or decumbent stems which form a dense mat. Leaves hairy, long petioled and rotund or reniform to 4 cm wide, coarsely crenate and deeply cordate at the base. Flowers in clusters of 2–3 borne in the terminal leaf axils, bluish or pink, appear mid-spring to early summer.
Distribution Native to Europe, north Asia; naturalized in North America. Common on damp grassland in open woods and fen wood-

land, preferring moist, nitrogenous soil.
Cultivation Wild plant; a variegated variety is grown horticulturally as ground cover. Propagate by division in the autumn.
Constituents Essential oil; tannin; a bitter compound, glechomine.
Uses (fresh flowering plant) Tonic; diuretic; vulnerary.
Formerly mostly used to soothe coughs, and as a gentle stimulant tonic following digestive disorders. Also once applied externally as a poultice for the treatment of bruises, contusions, and sore eyes. Taken as snuff to relieve headache.
Used to clarify beers and ales.
Drunk as a tea known as Gill tea.

Glycyrrhiza glabra L LEGUMINOSAE
Liquorice Licorice
Liquorice has been used medicinally for 3000 years and was recorded on Assyrian tablets and Egyptian papyri. It was known as Scythian root to Theophrastus and the old names *glycyrrhiza* and *radix dulcis* reflected the sweet taste of the roots.
Liquorice is a corruption of the medieval *gliquiricia*, itself from *glycyrrhiza*.
Now grown on a wide scale, it does not appear to have been cultivated in Central or Western Europe until the fifteenth century, and it was first introduced to the Pontefract district of England by the Dominican Black Friars.
Description Herbaceous perennial, 50 cm–1.5 m tall, on primary taproot 15 cm long which subdivides into 3–5 subsidiary roots 1.25 m in length and several horizontal stolons which may reach 8 m. Erect stem bearing 4–7 pairs of leaflets 2.5–5 cm long, ovate, glutinous beneath. Inflorescence of 20–30 lilac-blue flowers 1 cm long in loose racemes 10–15 cm long, arising in leaf axils. Appearing mid to late summer, followed by reddish-brown pod, 1–2.5 cm long.
Distribution Europe to West Pakistan. On deep sandy rich soils, preferably in river valleys.
Cultivation Wild plant, although rarely wild in central and western Europe and more common in eastern Europe. Introduced to temperate zones, and extensively cultivated in Russia, Persia, Spain and India. Propagated by root division in autumn; roots harvested from 3–4-year-old plants in early winter. Several varieties exist, the commonest are var. *typica* and var. *glandulifera*.
Constituents Glycyrrhizin (5–10%), comprising calcium and potassium salts of glycyrrhizic acid; flavonoid glycosides, liquiritoside and isoliquiritoside; sucrose and dextrose (5–10%); starch (30%); protein; fat; resin; asparagin; volatile oil; saponins.
Uses (dried root-stock, dried extract) Demulcent; expectorant; laxative; spasmolytic; anti-inflammatory.
Of value in coughs and bronchitis, and in the treatment of gastric ulcers; also has a mineralocorticoid action in treatment of Addison's disease. Once used as an eye lotion for use on inflamed eyelids.
Used as a sweetening agent and flavouring in pharmaceutical preparations, and once in the powdered form as a base in pill manufacture. Used to flavour some beers such as Guinness. Large quantities are employed in tobacco flavouring (some tobaccos contain 10% Liquorice), in snuff manufacture, and in confectionery.
Root pulp incorporated in insulating mill board, and mushroom compost.
Contra-indications Large doses may cause sodium retention and potassium loss leading to water retention, hypertension, headache and shortness of breath.

Gnaphalium uliginosum L COMPOSITAE
Marsh Cudweed Everlasting/Low Cudweed
As its name indicates, Marsh Cudweed is an inhabitant of wet situations; the specific name *uliginosum* derives from the Latin *uliginosus* meaning of marshy places. *Gnaphalium* is from the Greek *gnaphalon* meaning a flock of wool, from its woolly appearance.
The herb has never achieved wide use even in folk medicine, and is rarely mentioned in classical writings. Although it possesses useful properties, it is still rarely used.
Description Annual, 5–20 cm tall, with woolly, ascending or decumbent stems, much branched at the base; bearing narrow, spirally arranged, simple, oblong, woolly leaves 1–5 cm long. Small flower-heads in terminal clusters, yellow, 4 mm wide, with brown bracts, and overtopped by the terminal leaves. Appearing late summer to early autumn.
Distribution European native. On damp, acidic, sandy soils – especially wet heathland.
Cultivation Wild plant.
Constituents Volatile oil; resin; tannic acid; the combined action being antiseptic and astringent.
Uses (dried flowering plant) Astringent; antiseptic; antitussive; weak diaphoretic.
Specifically used as a gargle and mouthwash in aphthous ulcers, quinsy and tonsillitis. Also of benefit in diarrhoea, pharyngitis and laryngitis. A poultice may be applied externally to cuts, bruises or ulcers.
Once used in smoking mixtures.

Gossypium herbaceum L MALVACEAE
Cotton Cotton Root
The plant has been cultivated in India since the earliest times as a source of Cotton fibre, and its botanical name *gossypium* is the ancient Latin name for the Cotton-producing plant. The method of cultivation was introduced to China and Egypt from India in about 500 B.C., and in 1774 *G. herbaceum* was taken to the United States.
This species of Cotton is also called Levant Cotton; many other species and varieties are employed today in cotton manufacture including American Upland Cotton (*G. hirsutum* L), Chinese Cotton (*G. arboreum* L) and Sea Island Cotton (*G. barbadense* L).
The species *G. peruvianum* was probably grown in Peru before Cotton was cultivated in Egypt.
Description Herbaceous annual, in warm climates biennial or perennial, forming a subshrub to 1.5 m with branching stems, hairy or occasionally glabrous, bearing reticulate, coriaceous and cordate leaves, with 5–7 acute and lanceolate lobes. Flowers yellow with purple centre, followed by 18 mm long 3–4 celled capsule containing about 36 seeds covered with greyish trichomes, lint.
Distribution Originally native to East Indies, and now to Arabia and Asia Minor; prefers rich sands and loams, especially alluvial soils.
Cultivation Wild plant; widely cultivated in United States, India and Egypt. Seed sown in rows 1–1.5 m apart, later thinning to 30–60 cm apart; manure applied in early stages of growth, and plants are treated as annuals to prevent insect and disease attacks.
Constituents (root bark) acid resin; dihydroxy benzoic acid; salicylic acid; fatty acids; ceryl alcohol; betaine; sugars; phytosterol; phenolic substances.
Uses (root bark, seed oil) Abortifacient; emmenagogue.
Formerly used in the treatment of metrorrhagia. Cotton seed oil is used similarly to olive oil for external applications, but internally as a lubricant cathartic. Emulsions of the oil have been administered intravenously in cases of severe nutritional deficiency, or where nitrogen-free diets are required.
Seed once used as a food.
The oil is employed in soap manufacture.
The seed trichomes are a major source of

cotton fibre.
Contra-indications No part of the plant should be used internally without medical advice.

Gratiola officinalis L SCROPHULARIACEAE
Hedge Hyssop
Hedge Hyssop belongs to the same family as Foxglove and possesses similar cardio-active properties. It was introduced to northern Europe in the Middle Ages and used as a purgative; its employment has been described as 'heroic' since it was so powerful, and, indeed, it was probably responsible for several deaths. Nevertheless it was described as *Gratia* or *Gratia Dei* meaning thanks-be-to-God in appreciation of its effectiveness.
After the sixteenth century its use declined, but it has recently been introduced into homeopathic practice.
Description Perennial, on white, scaly, creeping rhizome, from which arise erect or decumbent, square, simple or occasionally branched stems to 35 cm. Leaves opposite and decussate, sessile, finely serrate, glabrous, and lanceolate.

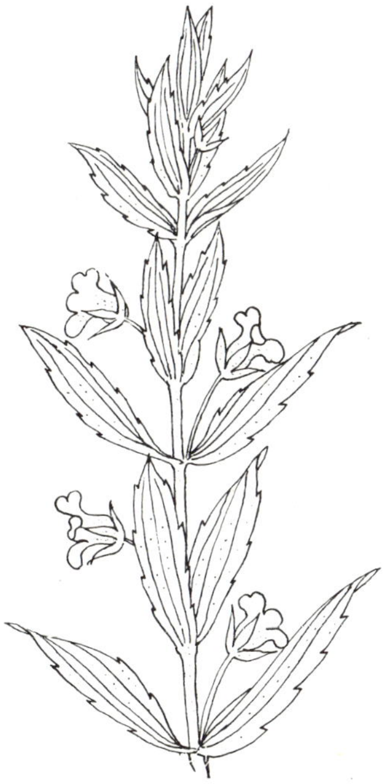

Flowers 1.5 cm long, white or pink, with yellowish corolla tube on short peduncles; appear singly in leaf axils from late summer to early autumn.
Distribution Native to southern Europe; introduced to north and west Asia and North America. On marshy fields, in ditches, peat bogs, river-banks, beside slow-flowing or stagnant water. Prefers wet calcareous soils, but will stand summer drought.
Cultivation Wild plant.
Constituents Cardio-active glycosides (cardenolides), gratioline and gratiotoxin; a bitter principle.
Uses (dried flowering plant, root) Emetic; cathartic; cardiotonic diuretic.
Formerly used as a violent purgative and emetic, and as a diuretic in dropsical conditions. Also in liver disorders such as jaundice and as a heart tonic. Many other uses have been ascribed to the plant. Still used homeopathically.
Contra-indications Highly toxic and drastically purgative. Large doses may cause death.

Guaiacum officinale L ZYGOPHYLLACEAE
Guaiacum Wood or Resin
Guaiacum Wood was first exported from the island of St Domingo in the Carribean in 1514 after Oviedo had learnt of the drug *guayacan* from the local inhabitants.
The Wood, then known as *lignum vitae*, achieved a considerable reputation in the sixteenth century for the treatment of 'Frenche pockes' or syphilis. Its success was possibly due to the method of administration: patients were given massive doses of the Wood decoction, tightly wrapped up in bed and shut in a hot room. In 1932 it was demonstrated that raising a patient's body temperature to 42°C was a partially effective method of destroying the syphilis bacterium. Guaiacum Resin was introduced to the London Pharmacopoeia in 1677, but the drug was gradually relegated to being merely a constituent of the proprietary blood-purifying mixtures of the eighteenth and nineteenth centuries known as Compound Alterative Mixtures, often combined with sarsaparilla, which had no effect in syphilis treatment.
Description Low to medium sized evergreen tree reaching 18 m; trunk covered with greenish-brown furrowed bark; leaves pinnate with ovate very obtuse leaflets, in pairs. Blue flowers and a 2-celled capsule-shaped fruit.
Distribution Native to Carribean islands, north coast of South America; especially on arid plains.
Cultivation Wild plant. Collected commercially and exported either as the wood or as the resin which is extracted by heating the logs.
Constituents Resin (20–25%), comprising α- and β-guaiaconic acid (20%), guaiaretic acid (10%), guaiacic acid; guaiac-β-resin; guaiac yellow; vanillin; guaiacsaponin and guaiacsaponic acid; guaiaguttin.
Uses (heartwood, resin) Local stimulant; irritant; mild laxative; anti-inflammatory.
Formerly frequently prescribed as a preventative in gout and in the treatment of rheumatoid

arthritis. Taken as a hot decoction it is mildly diaphoretic; also useful in sore throats when applied as a lozenge.
Guaiacum tincture is used as a colour test to detect the presence of oxidizing agents which will turn it blue.
The hard wood was once used in the manufacture of such articles as rulers, pulleys and bowling alley balls.
The resin is employed as an antioxidant for edible fats and oils.

Hamamelis virginiana L HAMAMELIDACEAE
Witch Hazel
A well-known garden ornamental and source of the distilled commercial preparation also known as witch hazel. Forked Hamamelis branches were employed as divining rods by water diviners in North America, and Indians brought the medicinal virtues of the plant to the notice of European settlers. *Hamamelis* was included in the United States Pharmaco-

poeia of 1882, and the leaves are still included in some national pharmacopoeias today. The name *hamamelis* is from the Greek words for apple and together, since the flowers and fruit are produced at the same time.
Description Small tree or spreading shrub, from 1.5–2.5 m tall, stem usually single and to 10 cm in diameter. Bark smooth and brown. Leaves elliptic to obovate 7.5–12.5 cm long, coarsely crenate-dentate, downy pubescent when young. Flowers bright yellow externally, brownish-yellow inside, 2 cm long, strap-like, appearing in the late autumn when leaves have fallen.
Distribution North American native; common and profuse in damp woods from Nova Scotia to Nebraska and Georgia.
Cultivation Wild plant; cultivated horticulturally as a hardy garden ornamental; prefers lime-free soil and flowers best in the open, although can be grown in semi-shade.
Constituents Tannin, comprising hamamelitannin (bark 6%, leaves 12%); gallic acid; calcium oxalate; and traces of volatile oil, saponin and flavenoid pigments. Leaves also contain phlobatannin. Distilled witch hazel is prepared from witch hazel brush, the young flower-bearing twigs. It consists entirely of a volatile oil, to which 13 to 15% ethyl alcohol is added.
Uses (bark, leaves, flower-bearing twigs) Astringent; haemostatic.
Once employed in haemorrhages from the rectum, nose and uterus; now externally in the treatment of haemorrhoids and varicose veins. Distilled witch hazel is applied to bruises and sprains, as is the diluted tincture. Very dilute distilled witch hazel may be used in eye lotions. A constituent of proprietary haemorrhoid ointments and cosmetic preparations – specifically as an astringent.
Contra-indications Distilled witch hazel must not be confused with the tincture made from bark or leaves; the latter may be extremely astringent and may cause disfigurement to the skin.

Hedera helix L ARALIACEAE
Ivy Common Ivy/English Ivy
The Ivy has never been widely accepted as having great medicinal value, yet it was once much respected as a magical plant protecting against evil spirits and symbolizing fidelity.
It was also dedicated to Bacchus, possibly because an infusion of the leaves in wine was considered an effective preventative and treatment for drunkenness. For the same reason an Ivy bush painted above tavern doors symbolized the good quality of the wine served therein. No modern work has been undertaken to test this ancient belief.
Some Ivy plants may reach more than 500 years of age.
Description Woody evergreen perennial, climbing by means of adventitious roots and often reaching great heights. Young leaves usually 3–5 lobed, margins entire or nearly so, varying from triangular-ovate to reniform, and from 2–18 cm long; veins often light-coloured. Upper leaves and those on fruiting branches unlobed, narrowly ovate. Flowers small, green-

ish, appearing mid to late autumn on 10-year-old plants; followed by black, globose, 6 mm diameter fruit.
Distribution Native to Europe; widely naturalized in temperate zones and very common, although rarer in coniferous woodland.
Cultivation Wild plant; extensively grown horticulturally with approximately 40 foliage forms recognized.
Constituents Saponin, hederacoside; hederegenine.
Uses (young leaves) Antispasmodic.
Once used internally in the treatment of whooping-cough, neuralgia, rheumatic pain, bronchitis. The berries, though toxic, were formerly considered an effective purgative. Leaves may be applied externally as a poultice for some skin complaints, sores and rheumatic pain. For toothache the mouth may be rinsed with a decoction of leaves in vinegar; the decayed teeth were formerly plugged with the black gummy resin produced by the plant. A varnish was made from the gummy resin.
Contra-indications The whole plant is POISONOUS and should only be used externally. The berries may cause blisters and the leaves dermatitis.

Helianthus annuus L COMPOSITAE
Sunflower Common Sunflower
The aptly named Sunflower is well-known as the source of a fine salad oil, and is cultivated commercially in several countries for this and other purposes. Its origins are uncertain, but the plant is most probably indigenous to Mexico where it is called *chimalati*. American Indians have long cultivated the Sunflower for its seed, often growing the plant in the same field as maize.
It was once believed that growing Sunflower near to one's home gave protection against malaria, which may be explained by the fact that an infusion of the flowers has weak insecticidal properties.
Description Robust annual from 30 cm to 5 m tall; stems erect, sometimes mottled, rounded and rough, bearing opposite leaves below and alternate long-petioled, ovate, acute or acuminate leaves above, 10–30 cm long and 10–20 cm wide.
Peduncles long, thickening towards the involucre. Flower-heads 7.5–15 cm in diameter, and up to 35 cm in diameter in cultivated forms, appearing late summer to early autumn. The central disc is brownish-purple and the ray florets are chrome-yellow.
Distribution Native to Central America and western North America; introduced and widespread in many countries; tolerates most soils in full sun.
Cultivation Wild; often found as a garden escape. Cultivated commercially, particularly Rumania, Bulgaria, Russia, Hungary, United States, Mexico, Argentina and parts of Africa. Grown horticulturally in sunny position from seed sown in late spring to early summer – they should not be transplanted. Several hybrids exist including some with double heads, and with colours ranging from a dull white to

chestnut brown.
Constituents Seed contains an unsaturated fixed oil (30%); albumin; lecithin; betaine; choline; plant contains potassium nitrate; potassium carbonate; tannins; a flavonic glycoside, quercimetrin.
Uses (seed, seed oil, occasionally leaf and flowers) Nutritive; expectorant; diuretic.
Formerly the seeds were considered useful in treating coughs and bronchial infections; and leaves and flowers were used in malaria. Used externally on bruises, and a homeopathically prepared tincture is employed in constipation. Sunflower oil is widely used in foodstuffs as a salad and margarine oil, and pharmaceutically as a substitute for olive or ground-nut oils.
Seed is roasted and eaten, used as a Coffee substitute, ground into meal for cakes and soups. Unopened flower buds are boiled and eaten with butter in the same way as Artichokes.
It has excellent burning qualities and may be used in old-fashioned oil lamps.
Leaves provide animal fodder, and when dried may be used as a substitute for cigar tobacco. Seed receptacles and stalk pith may be used in paper manufacture.

Helleborus niger L RANUNCULACEAE

Black Hellebore Christmas Rose

Helleborus is the classical name for a closely related species *Helleborus orientalis*, and was a term also applied to the White Hellebore and other Hellebores by the Greeks.

Many of the Hellebores have similar actions, and several species such as *H. viridis* L and *H. foetidus* L, the Green and Stinking Hellebores respectively, were employed by herbalists in the Middle Ages – largely for their purgative effect, but also in the treatment of certain skin complaints. Outside homeopathy, their use is now confined to horticulture.

Description Perennial to 30 cm; on slowly creeping, tangled, blackish-brown root-stock. The true stem does not rise above ground; basal leaves have long petioles, are leathery and evergreen, serrate, and deeply divided into 7 or more oblong leaflets. Flowering stem simple or occasionally forked, bearing single white or purplish flowers 3–8 cm wide, appearing mid-winter to mid-spring.

Distribution European native; especially southern and central mountainous regions. In mountain forests, open woodland, on stony, humus-rich, calcareous soils only.

Cultivation Wild. Cultivated as a garden plant. Propagate by division of root-stock, or from seed sown as soon as ripe, in the open or under a cold-frame. Well-drained shady positions on chalky soil are ideal. Horticultural varieties include var. *Altifolius* (Hayne) and Potters Wheel; both have large flowers.

Constituents A cardenolide, hellebrigenine; saponosides, comprising helleboreine and helleborine; also protoanemonine. The combined action of the cardenolide and saponosides is cardio-active and purgative.

Uses (dried root-stock) Powerful hydragogue cathartic; cardio-active; local irritant.

Once used as a purgative; emmenagogue; heart tonic; local anaesthetic; abortive and in many other conditions. Now obsolete except in homeopathy which employs a tincture for treating certain psychoses.

The powdered root-stock was once a constituent of sneezing powders.

Contra-indications All parts POISONOUS; produces violent inflammation of the gastro-intestinal mucous membranes, and of the skin if applied locally.

Heracleum sphondylium L UMBELLIFERAE

Cow Parsnip Hogweed

A common weed, dedicated to Hercules (hence its generic name, *Heracleum*) after its robustness; related species have long been used both as human and animal foodstuffs. Particularly favoured by Scandinavian peoples.

Description Stout, erect biennial or perennial 50–200 cm tall, with ridged, hollow stems bearing hairy, large (15–60 cm), pinnate to palmately lobed leaves. Flowers white in umbels of 5–15 cm diameter, appearing mid-summer to mid-autumn. Variable in form.

Distribution Native to Europe, northern Asia,

western North America. In woodland, grassland, roadsides, on nutrient-rich, moist soils, to 1800 m altitude.

Cultivation Wild plant.

Constituents Pimpinellin; sphondrin; a complex oil; bergapetene, a furo-coumarin to which the photosensitization is due.

Uses (young shoots, seed, leaves) Stimulant; stomachic; hypotensive; emmenagogue; mild aphrodisiac.

Leaf is of benefit in combination with other remedies in hypertension. Once used to treat epilepsy. Now used homeopathically. The seeds have a substantiated aphrodisiacal action. Young shoots can be cooked and eaten, or used in certain east European beers. Young stems are peeled and eaten raw.

Contra-indications Percutaneous photosensitization (blisters and possibly permanent purple pigmentation) may follow ingestion or handling of juice with subsequent exposure to sunlight.

Hibiscus sabdariffa L MALVACEAE

Roselle Sudanese Tea/Red Tea/Jamaica Tea

Hibiscus is the old Latin name for this plant which was introduced to Jamaica and used as an acid flavouring at least as early as 1774; the calices being the parts used. It is now being used in other parts of the world, and is especially popular in Switzerland where it is called *karkade* and is used in wines and sauces.

Other parts of the plant are used medicinally, and the stem yields an excellent fibre known as rosella hemp.

Description Bushy annual reaching 2 m, forming a broad growth by branching at the base. Stems reddish and almost glabrous. Basal leaves undivided and ovate; stem leaves 3-lobed, 7.5–10 cm wide, lobes 2.5 cm wide and crenate. Flowers borne in the leaf axils,

solitary, and almost sessile; consisting of red calyx and yellow corolla and followed by 2-cm long ovoid fruit.

Distribution Native to tropical Asia; introduced to Sudan and Mexico. Needs a tropical environment.

Cultivation Wild, and cultivated commercially in Ceylon, Egypt, Asia and Mexico. Can be grown horticulturally from seed sown in the early spring. Red and white forms also exist.

Constituents Organic acids, comprising tartaric, citric, malic and hibiscic acids; red pigment comprising gossipetin and hibiscin; vitamin C; also glucosides and phytosterolin.

Uses (dried young calices) Diuretic; weak laxative; antiscorbutic.

Used in Africa and Asia as a cough remedy, wound dressing and diuretic. Mostly employed as an acid flavouring for sauces, jams, jellies, drinks, wines, curries and chutneys.

A pleasant tea which can also be used as a red colourant for other herb teas.

Hieracium pilosella L COMPOSITAE

Mouse-ear Hawkweed Mouse Bloodwort

The botanical name *Hieracium* is from the Greek for hawk after the tradition that hawks

improved their vision by using the plant's sap. Because of this early belief, herbalists employed it for some eye complaints, but it has now largely fallen into disuse. The common name Mouse-Ear is from the apothecaries' term *auricula muris*, being a description of the shape of the leaves.
Description Perennial on creeping leafy runners, forming a basal rosette of hairy leaves, 4–7 cm long, entire, oblong, white or grey on the underside; leafless stem. Flowers usually solitary, occasionally 2–4, reaching 10–40 cm high on hairy or bristly scape; flower-heads consist of capitula of ray florets only, sulphur yellow, appearing early summer to mid-autumn. Very variable in form.
Distribution European native; introduced to other temperate zones. On dry waste-ground, dry grassland, rocky screes, preferring moderate sunshine and tolerating most soils.
Cultivation Wild plant.
Constituents Volatile oils; tannic acid; flavones; an umbelliferone; antibiotic substances.
Uses (dried flowering plant) Weak diuretic; astringent; cholagogue; antibacterial.
Formerly used in the treatment of liver disorders, enteritis and diarrhoea. Possesses weak antipyretic action and was used in the treatment of intermittent fever. The powdered herb arrests nose bleeds. Various claims have been made for its effect in eye conditions. Possesses antibiotic action, and is an effective gargle.

Hordeum vulgare L GRAMINEAE
Barley Big Barley/Bere/Six-rowed Barley
Barley was the first cereal crop to be cultivated and its use has been traced back to Neolithic times. The Egyptians believed it was introduced by their goddess Isis, while the Greeks considered it was a sacred grain. Besides its use as food and medicine, many civilizations from the early Egyptians have enjoyed beer obtained from fermented Barley. The Greeks and later generations grew a closely related species, *H. distichon* L, which itself was the parent of many other cultivated forms.
Description Stout erect annual grass, to 90 cm; leaves 7 mm–2 cm wide, short and tapering. The terminal spike is 7.5–10 cm long, erect or occasionally nodding, topped by many long, stout beards.
Distribution Temperate cereal crop.
Cultivation *H. vulgare* is a cultigen derived from an oriental wild grass, either *H. spontaneum* (Koch) or *H. ischnatherum* (Schulz.). Wide commercial cultivation.
Constituents Starch (75–80%); proteins; fat; vitamins B and E; mucilage.
Uses (seed, germinating seed) Nutritive; demulcent. Barley water is a soothing preparation for inflammations of the gastro-intestinal system, and a nutritive demulcent in convalescence. Cooked Barley is a useful poultice for sores. The germinating grain contains an alkaloid, hordenine, whose action resembles ephedrine and it is thus of use in bronchitis.
A well-known cereal with many culinary uses in soups and stews.

Humulus lupulus L CANNABACEAE
Hops Hop Bine
The use of Hops revolutionized brewing since it enabled beer to be kept for longer, yet although the plant was grown by the Romans Hop gardens were not widespread in France and Germany until the ninth and tenth centuries. Bavarian Hops were famous in the eleventh century, but the English only introduced Hops as a replacement for traditional bitter herbs (such as Alehoof and Alecost) in the sixteenth century. Pliny called the plant *lupus salictarius* or 'willow wolf' after its habit of twining tightly around willows and other trees in its damp natural habitat. *Humulus* is a medieval latinization of the Anglo-Saxon term,

humele.
Hops were once grown as a kitchen herb.
Description Dioecious perennial; rough-stemmed and twining clockwise to 6 m tall. Leaves opposite usually 3-, sometimes 5- or 7-lobed, broad terminal lobe, coarsely serrate and long-petioled.
Flowers indistinct, in greenish-yellow catkins, the female enclosed in a conical inflorescence (strobilus) 2 cm in diameter; appear late summer to mid-autumn.
Distribution Native to northern temperate zones; in hedgerows, thickets, alder, willow and osier groves, on damp humus-rich soils in warm situations.
Cultivation Wild; cultivated commercially, especially in northern Europe, United States and Chile. Propagate from cuttings taken in the early summer.
Constituents Volatile oil (0.3–1%) comprising humulone, cohumulone, adhumulone, lupulone, colupulone, adlupulone and xanthlumol; tannins (5%); bitter principles; resin.
Uses (dried female strobilus) Mild sedative; weak diuretic; weak antibiotic; bitter.
Employed alone or in combination with other herbs as a soporific in insomnia and restlessness. Aids nervous indigestion and may be applied externally to ulcers. Once used in the treatment of certain prostate disorders.
Young shoots and male flowers may be eaten in salads.
The oil is used in some perfumes.
Stems once used in basket and wickerwork.
Most widely employed in brewing.

Hydrastis canadensis L RANUNCULACEAE
Golden Seal Orange Root/Ground Raspberry
Golden Seal was once common in the damp shady forests of North America and was used both as a dye and a medicine by the Indians. It entered the United States and British Pharmacopoeias as a treatment for uterine mucosa inflammation, and was so extensively

collected in America that by the beginning of the twentieth century it was necessary to devise methods of commercial cultivation. Now it is a very expensive herb which still finds considerable use in folk medicine.
The name *hydrastis* is derived from the Greek meaning water-acting after its effect on the secretion of mucous membranes.
Description Low herbaceous perennial from 15–30 cm tall; on knotted, gnarled, tortuous, sub-cylindrical rhizome which grows horizontally or obliquely and is 1–6 cm long and 4–15 mm thick, yellowish-brown outside and bright yellow internally. Flowering stem erect, sub-cylindrical, hairy, bearing two sessile, rounded, doubly-serrate leaves reaching 20 cm wide, each consisting of 5–9 lobes. Occasionally a single 24-cm wide root-leaf arises on a tall petiole from the root-stock. Single flower, greenish-white, without petals, 7.5 mm wide, appearing late spring to early summer; followed in late summer by raspberry-shaped, inedible berry.
Distribution Native to Canada and eastern United States; in shady woods and the edges of woodland on rich moist soil.
Cultivation Wild, and becoming rarer. Cultivated commercially on damp humus-rich soil under artificial shading from root buds or divided root-stock; planted 20 cm apart in early autumn.
Constituents Alkaloids, hydrastine (1–3%), berberine (2%), canadine (trace); fixed oil; volatile oil; resin; starch; also mineral salts.
Uses (dried root-stock) Bitter tonic; stomachic; laxative; smooth-muscle stimulant; nervine stimulant; anti-haemorrhagic; hypoglycaemic.
Used internally in atonic dyspepsia, anorexia or gastritis. Also in dysmenorrhoea and menorrhagia. Its main action (due to the alkaloid hydrastine) is on mucous membranes – especially those of the uterus. Large doses cause over-secretion of these membranes, while therapeutic doses aid in catarrhal conditions. The powdered root-stock was once used topically on mouth ulcers and as a snuff in nasal catarrh. A weak infusion is employed in conjunctivitis, as eardrops, and acts as an antiseptic mouthwash.
The root tea was formerly drunk as a tonic. Produces a yellow or orange cloth dye.
Contra-indications POISONOUS in large doses; not to be used in pregnancy.

Hydrocotyle asiatica L UMBELLIFERAE
Indian Pennywort Centella/Indian Water Navel Wort
Indian Pennywort was employed traditionally in the Indian and African continents as an important treatment of leprosy, and modern research has now shown that the plant does possess some action against the leprosy bacteria. The herb is called *brahmi* in the Indian Ayurvedic medical system which still employs it. In Europe it was last mentioned in the French Pharmacopoeia of 1884.
Hydrocotyle is attributed with many other medicinal properties and one which has recently attracted attention is its supposed general beneficial tonic effect; this, however, remains to be proved.
Description Slender trailing umbelliferous plant with reddish prostrate stems, rooting at the nodes, from which also arise 1–3 petioles to 15 cm tall bearing glabrous, entire, or crenate, cupped, orbicular-reniform leaves, 7–15 cm long. Flower-heads bear 3 or 6 reddish, sessile flowers.
Distribution Indigenous to subtropical zones such as India, Ceylon, southern Africa, southern United States, Malaysia. Also found in eastern Europe. On marshy sites to a 600 m altitude.
Cultivation Wild plant.
Constituents A heteroside (saponoside), asiaticoside, which is antibiotic and also assists in the formation of scar tissue; triterpene acids, including indocentoic acid; a glycoside, indocentelloside; an alkaloid, hydrocotylin; resin; pectic acid; vitamin C; a bitter compound, vellarin; tannin (9%); sugars; volatile oil.
Uses (fresh or dried plant) Diuretic; tonic; purgative.
Used in India and Africa for 'blood-purifying' purposes in venereal conditions and tuberculosis. The active principle, asiaticoside, appears to exert a direct effect on the bacterium (*Mycobacterium leprae*) involved in leprosy (possibly by dissolving the protective waxy coat around the bacterium), and also assists in scar healing – for which purpose it is used in ointments. Also formerly used in fevers, rheumatism and gastric complaints, including dysentery. There is some evidence it may act as a general tonic.
Used in Africa as a snuff.
Contra-indications POISONOUS. Large doses narcotic, producing vertigo and possibly coma.

Hyoscyamus niger L SOLANACEAE
Henbane
Henbane has a long medicinal history which runs from the Assyrians to the present day, and which derives from the sedative, analgesic and spasmolytic properties of the leaf's powerful constituents. At various times it has been considered as a love potion, a magical herb, and an ingredient of witches' brews.
Its name *Hyoscyamus* comes from the Greek meaning hog bean, a term which is still retained in some areas. The herb has had several other names including Symphoniaca, Jusquiamus, Henbell, Belene, Hennibone, and Hennebane.
Description Strongly smelling, erect, coarse annual or biennial; the former less robust and shorter than the biennial form which reaches 30–150 cm on a stem covered with long, jointed hairs. Leaves pale-green, ovate-oblong, coarsely dentate, hairy and slightly sticky, 5–30 cm long. Flowers on short stalks in leaf axils, or sessile in terminal unilateral panicles; funnel-shaped, 3–4 cm long, yellow-brown or cream, usually marked with purple veins, particularly at the petal base. Appearing late summer to early autumn (annual) or early to mid-summer (biennial).
Distribution Indigenous to Europe; widely distributed throughout Eurasia and introduced to North America, Asia, Australia and Brazil. On waste-ground and roadsides, and in well-drained sandy or chalky soils.
Cultivation Wild and cultivated, or collected, on a small scale. Seed sown in sunny position in early summer (annual) or early autumn (biennial), and the soil kept moist until germination.
Constituents Alkaloids, hyoscyamine, atropine and hyoscine – to which the narcotic and sedative actions are due.
Uses (fresh or dried leaves) Sedative; anti-spasmodic; analgesic.
Formerly used in a wide range of nervous or painful conditions which required sedation

and analgesia, but due to its poisonous nature it is now generally only employed internally in homeopathic dosage; it is retained, however, in several South American and European pharmacopoeias as an aid in spasm of the urinary tract, or to alleviate the griping caused by strong purgatives.
Oil of Henbane or a poultice of the fresh leaves may be applied externally to relieve rheumatic pain.
Contra-indications POISONOUS. To be used only under medical supervision.

Hypericum perforatum L HYPERICACEAE
Common St John's Wort
St John's Wort has been closely associated with supposed magical properties since the Greeks gave it the name *hypericon*. This indicated that the smell was strong enough to drive away evil spirits, and it was believed to purify the air. The oil glands when crushed certainly release a balsamic odour similar to incense. In addition the yellow flowers turn red when crushed due to the release of the red fluorescent pigment hypericine – and this was undoubtedly an important factor in the development of the folklore which surrounds the herb – red signifying, of course, blood. As St John was beheaded, and the herb is in full flower on St John's Day (24 June), it became known as *herba Sancti Ioannis* and, later, as St John's Wort – the herb of St John.
Besides the magical attributes which predate Christianity, *Hypericum* has real and effective medicinal properties and it is still widely used in European folk medicine.
Description Perennial; rapidly spreading from many long runners produced at the base. Stem erect with 2 raised edges along its length, branched at the top, reaching 30–60 cm; bearing oblong or linear leaves 1.5–3 cm long, opposite, entire, glabrous, and marked with numerous translucent oil spots. Flowers 2–3 cm wide, yellow, consisting of 5 petals dotted with small black oil glands, and carried on many flowered terminal cymes, appearing late summer to mid-autumn.
Distribution Native to temperate zones of Europe and western Asia; naturalized in the Americas and Australasia. In open situations, on semi-dry soils of various sorts, but particularly calcareous soils.
Cultivation Wild plant. May be propagated by division in autumn, and efforts are being made to cultivate it commercially.
Constituents Volatile oil, called red oil; resin; a red pigmented glycoside, hypericine; a polyphenolic flavonoid, hyperoside; tannin (8–9% in the whole herb and 16% in the flower); carotene; vitamin C.
Uses (fresh or dried flowering plant, fresh flower, fresh leaves) Vulnerary; weakly diuretic; sedative; anti-inflammatory; anti-diarrhoeic; cholagogue; antidepressant; antiviral; antibiotic; astringent.
Many virtues have been ascribed to this plant ranging from the antipyretic and anthelmintic properties reported by the most ancient writers, to modern suggestions of antiviral activity. Certainly when taken internally the herb stimulates both gastric and bile secretions, and is effective in irregular menstruation. It has been shown to improve the blood circulation and to be of use in some conditions characterized by neurosis and disturbed sleep patterns.
It is one of the most effective agents for assisting in the healing of wounds or burns when applied externally, especially where nervous tissue has been damaged; it is also applied to haemorrhoids and bruises. The plant contains an antibiotic which has been patented as a possible food preservative. Leaves once used as a salad herb.
An alcoholic extract of the flowers dyes silk and wool a violet-red, but does not colour cotton.
Contra-indications If eaten by light-skinned animals, the herb may cause photosensitization, leading to swelling of the face, generalized skin irritation of unpigmented areas, and possible death.

Hyssopus officinalis L LABIATAE
Hyssop
The genus Hyssopus consists of this single species, and the herb's common name is practically identical in all European languages. Hyssop is a very ancient name and can be traced back almost unchanged through the Greek *hussopos* to the Hebrew *esob*.
Whether *Hyssopus officinalis* is in fact the Hyssop frequently referred to in the Old Testament is doubtful, however – this was probably a marjoram – and how it came to be given the biblical name is not known.
The herb was once much respected as a medicinal plant being mentioned by Paulus Aegnita in the seventh century, and was also used both for cosmetic and strewing purposes. Gerard (1597) described 3 varieties and Mawe (1778) 6 varieties.
Hyssop has had a mixed fortune as a culinary herb due to its strong flavour, and is now mostly employed for decorative purposes especially as a low hedge in herb gardens.
Description Aromatic perennial subshrub with erect branched herbaceous stems 20–60 cm long, covered with fine hairs at the tips. Leaves linear to oblong, 2.5 cm long and 4–9 mm wide, sessile or nearly so, opposite and tomentose. Blue flowers 7.5–15 mm long in one-sided whorls in leaf axils, the terminal inflorescence being 10 cm long; appear late summer to early autumn. Violet, red, pink or white forms occasionally occur.
Distribution Native to central and southern Europe, and temperate western Asia; introduced into North America. On rocky, calcareous dry soils in sunny situations.
Cultivation Wild in native habitat; occasionally wild elsewhere as a garden escape. Cultivated commercially in Europe, Russia and India. Wide horticultural employment as an ornamental; propagate by seed sown in spring, root division in spring or autumn, or cuttings taken in late spring or early summer. Plant out 30 cm apart in full sun on well-drained light soil, and clip occasionally. Replace after 4 or 5 years.
Constituents Volatile oil (0.2–1%); a flavonoid glycoside, diosmin; tannin (8%).
Uses (dried flowering tops, fresh leaf) Tonic; stomachic; expectorant; carminative; sedative; weak diaphoretic; weak diuretic; astringent; mild spasmolytic.
Specifically employed in bronchitis and the common cold; to improve appetite and stimulate gastric secretions; and as a gargle to soothe sore throats. The herb also reduces perspiration and may be applied externally to cuts or bruises around the eyes. Once used to treat hysterical conditions, but its action is weak.
A constituent of some herb teas.

Small quantities may be used to flavour meats or soups.
The oil distilled from the flowering tops is employed in the liqueur and perfumery industries.

Ilex aquifolium L AQUIFOLIACEAE
Holly Common Holly/English Holly
Although Holly is no longer considered of any importance medically, it has retained an important role in the traditions associated with Christmas and in northern Europe red Holly berries and branches are symbolic of Christmas-time – perhaps representing drops of blood and a crown of thorns.

The plant was not called Holly until the seventeenth century, previously having been known as Holy Tree and earlier as Holme; the latter being derived from the old English plant name *holen*. Its botanical name *Ilex* was the ancient name for the Holm or Holly Oak (*Quercus ilex*), while *aquifolium* is from the Latin meaning point and leaf after the well-known shape of its leaves.
Description Evergreen shrub or tree usually 2–5 m, occasionally to 12 m tall; with many spreading glabrous branches forming an oblong-shaped plant. Leaves shiny, leathery, ovate or oblong-ovate, 4–7.5 cm long, margins wavy and spiked with 6-mm long spines, short-petioled. Small unisexual or bisexual, dull white, scented flowers produced in axillary clusters on previous year's growth, appearing early to mid-summer.
Distribution Native to Europe and widely distributed from western Asia to China; introduced elsewhere. Common in deciduous woodland, less so in mixed or coniferous woodland; on most soils but preferably humus-rich, acid, moist well-drained types.
Cultivation Wild. Cultivated horticulturally for decorative purposes and as hedging; avoid planting in frost-prone sites.
Constituents Leaves: tannin; a bitter substance, ilicine; theobromine; unknown substances. Bark: tannin; pectin; a yellow pigment, ilixanthine.
Uses (leaves) Antipyretic; weak diuretic; tonic. Once used in the treatment of fevers, bronchitis and rheumatism. Occasionally employed in diarrhoea, and as a tonic tea.
Wood used for engraving.
Contra-indications Berries are purgative and toxic.

Ilex paraguariensis St Hil. AQUIFOLIACEAE
Maté Yerba Maté/Paraguay Tea/Hervea
Maté has been taken as a refreshing stimulant tonic drink by South American inhabitants long before the Jesuits recorded the habit in the sixteenth century. Although in many South American countries it is drunk more frequently than any other beverage, 'Jesuits' tea' as it was first called has only recently become known in Europe as an alternative to Indian or Chinese tea.
Description Evergreen shrub or tree to 6 m, often kept low in cultivation; branches glabrous bearing glossy, obovate, crenate-serrate, short-petioled, alternate leaves, 4–10 cm long; flowers white and axillary, followed by rounded, reddish 7-mm diameter fruit.
Distribution Brazil, Argentina, Chile, Peru, Paraguay; frequently in mountainous areas.
Cultivation Wild, and cultivated commercially in Paraguay.
Constituents Caffeine (0.2–2%); chlorogenic acid (10–16%); neochlorogenic acid; theobromine catechols; the combined action being tonic.
Uses (dried leaves) Tonic; nervine; diuretic; stimulant.
Almost entirely employed as a tonic tea in the manner of Indian or Chinese tea, but devoid of any undesirable stimulant effect.

Ilex verticillata (L) Gray AQUIFOLIACEAE
Black Alder Winterberry/Feverbush
North American Indians were the first to use this attractive plant for medical purposes and it was once included in the United States Pharmacopoeia; it was also used homeopathically. Other remedies have now replaced it, even in folk medicine, and it is rarely found in use as other than a garden ornamental. It was formerly classified as *Prinos verticillatus* L. The specific epithet *verticillatus* means whorled or clustered around the stem, after the arrangement of the flowers and fruit.
Description Upright and spreading deciduous shrub 1.2–3 m tall, with thin obovate, oval or

oblanceolate, acute to acuminate, serrate leaves, 4–7.5 cm long, pubescent on lower veins; petiolate and alternate. Flowers dioecious, white, small, in groups of usually less than 10, on short peduncles in umbels, appearing in leaf axils in late spring and early summer. Followed by bright red globose berry 7.5 mm in diameter.

Distribution North American native, from Canada to Florida and Wisconsin; introduced elsewhere. Usually in woodland thickets on wet, marshy, rich soils or beside rivers and lakes.

Cultivation Wild plant. Cultivated as a garden ornamental for its attractive berries which remain until mid-winter on the bare branches. Requires rich soil in damp, preferably shady, site.

Constituents Tannins (to 5%); bitter principles; resins; unknown substances.

Uses (fresh bark, rarely dried bark, fruit) Astringent; antipyretic; bitter; tonic.

The bark may be employed as an infusion or decoction in the treatment of diarrhoea, or as a tonic following severe diarrhoea or feverish complaints. It acts as a carminative and promotes both the appetite and the digestion. Due to its astringent action it was once used externally as a wash in skin complaints such as herpes and ulcers. The berries possess slight antihelmintic and laxative action, but should not be used as the effective dose is slightly toxic.

Illicium verum Hook. f. MAGNOLIACEAE

Star Anise Chinese Anise

The oil obtained by steam distillation of the fruit of Star Anise is now an important substitute for expensive European aniseed oil, and is widely used in commercial preparations requiring aniseed flavour.

It has long been used as a spice in the East, but was not seen in Europe until 1588 when Candish brought a sample from the Philippines to London. Clusius first described it in 1601, but even in 1694 when the Dutch used it to flavour tea it was rare in Europe.

The Latin name *illicium* means that which entices from the very pleasant scent of the tree and fruit. It is also classified as *I. anisatum* (L). A closely related species *I. religiosum* (Siebold) or Japanese Star Anise, which in the East is sometimes found as an adulterant of the Chinese Star Anise, has poisonous leaves and fruit due to their content of sikimitoxin. This plant is called the 'mad herb' in China, but in Japan it is revered and used at funerals. Fruit of the plant cannot be used, and may be distinguished by their lack of aniseed smell, unlike the Chinese variety.

Description Small tender evergreen tree or shrub to 5 m; leaves aromatic, alternate, entire, shiny, 7.5 cm long, elliptic and acuminate; magnolia-like attractive greenish-yellow solitary, unscented flowers with many petals. Followed by 4-cm wide, 8-rayed star-like fruit consisting of one-seeded follicles which are collected when green, and then sun-dried until they are woody and reddish-brown.

Distribution Indigenous to south and south-west China and north Vietnam; introduced elsewhere. On well-drained soils, frequently above a 2500-m altitude.

Cultivation Wild and cultivated in south China and parts of eastern Asia. Prefers sheltered sunny situations on well-drained, moisture-retaining soils.

Constituents Volatile oil (to 10%), comprising 80–90% anethol; fixed oil; sugar; resin; tannin.

Uses (dried fruit) Carminative; slightly stimulant; mild expectorant.

Chiefly employed as an aniseed flavouring agent, and as a carminative for digestive disorders. Used in cough remedies as an expectorant and considered to benefit the bronchial mucous membranes.

Used in the East as a spice, particularly with duck and pork; added to tea and coffee in China. The oil is of commercial importance as an aniseed flavouring for drinks and liqueurs.

Inula helenium L COMPOSITAE

Elecampane Scabwort

Elecampane is still employed in folk medicine as a favourite constituent of cough remedies and has always been popular both as a medicine and a condiment. Its use as a flavouring in sweets continued until the 1920s, and it was traditionally cultivated in herb gardens.

Much controversy surrounds the origin of the plant's names, but *helenium* is from Helenus, the son of Priam – a somewhat obscure association – while *elecampane* is derived from the ancient Latin name *inula campana* via the French *énule-campane*. It was commonly used both by the early Anglo-Saxons and Celts as well as by the Greeks and Romans; the Welsh called it *marchalan* in the thirteenth century.

Description Tall attractive perennial to 2 m; on thick 15-cm long taproot. Stems hairy, erect, bearing large, alternate, elliptical leaves to 45 cm long and 15 cm wide, velvety beneath, hairy above, dentate-serrate, the lower leaves petiolate, others partly clasping. Flower-heads large, to 7 cm in diameter, solitary or corymbose, yellow, the ray florets numerous, long, slender, and arranged in a single row, appearing mid-summer to mid-autumn.

Distribution Native to central and southern Europe and north-west Asia, naturalized in United States; introduced elsewhere. On damp

soils near ruins (probably because they were once cultivated near monasteries, etc.), or roadsides and woodland edges.

Cultivation Wild. Limited cultivation in central Europe; on rich moist soil from seed sown in spring or by division of root-stock in autumn. Plant in semi-shaded position at back of the border.

Constituents Inulin (40%); essential oil, comprising a mixture of lactones, chiefly alantolactone; resin; a complex camphor, elecampane camphor; mucilage.

Uses (dried root-stock) Bactericidal; antitussive; expectorant; tonic; weak cholagogue.

Almost exclusively employed in the treatment of respiratory disorders, especially bronchitis, coughs, and catarrh. Also used to promote appetite as it acts as an aromatic tonic. Once used in the treatment of skin diseases and in veterinary medicine for the same purposes – hence its other name, Scabwort. The herb is strongly antibacterial.

Formerly candied and eaten as a sweetmeat; used in the flavouring of certain sweets.

Still employed in some wines and liqueurs in central Europe.

Iris foetidissima L IRIDACEAE

Stinking Iris Gladdon/Scarlet-seeded Iris

Most Iris species possess substances in the fresh root-stock which act as purgatives, and when purging was a popular form of medicinal treatment Stinking Gladdon was commonly used.

The name Gladdon is derived from the Latin *gladiolus* meaning a little sword after the shape of its leaves; while the term stinking is an inaccurate description of the roast-beef smell of its crushed leaves.

Description Slow growing perennial on slender

horizontal rhizome; producing 60–90-cm tall branched stems which bear glossy dark green, narrow (3 cm) leaves, 30–45 cm long. Leaves remain during winter, and are sometimes variegated. Flowers inconspicuous, purple-grey with purple veins, beardless, appearing early to mid-summer and followed by 4–5-cm long capsule containing scarlet-red globose seeds.
Distribution Native to North Africa, west and south Europe. Prefers rich moist soils by rivers or ponds in a semi-shaded position.
Cultivation Wild. Cultivated horticulturally by root-stock division in late spring or early summer. Requires humus-rich wet soil.
Constituents Acrid resin; unknown substances.
Uses (fresh root-stock) Purgative.
Once used as a purgative by drinking a macerate of the fresh root in ale. No longer employed medically.
Chiefly cultivated for the use of its attractive ripe flower capsules and seeds in dried flower arrangements.

Iris germanica var. *florentina* Dykes IRIDACEAE
Orris Florentine Iris
The Greek word *iris* means the rainbow and is used to describe the variable colouring of the members of this genus.
Orris, derived directly from *iris*, is the descriptive term for the violet-scented, powdered root-stock which has been used in perfumery since the Egyptians and ancient Greeks. Several species or hybrids are used as the source of Orris of which the most important are *I. germanica* L (especially *I. germanica* var. *florentina* Dykes), *I. pallida* Lamk. and *I. florentina* L. Due to the variation and hybridization of this group, some authorities believe that *I. florentina* L is not a distinct species and should be considered a variety, *florentina*, of *I. germanica*; others consider *I. florentina* is a synonym of *I. spuria*, while some feel it is a true species with its own, pure white, variety – *I. florentina* var. *albicans*.
The white Florentine Iris became associated with Florence in the early Middle Ages, and the plant's cultivation there was described by Petrus de Crescentiis in the thirteenth century. It is still represented on the heraldic arms of the city.
Description Perennial on stout rhizome bearing 45 cm tall, 3–4 cm wide, sword-shaped leaves, and flowering stalk reaching 60 cm–1 m. Terminal flower-head usually 2-flowered, sessile; the flowers unscented, white tinged with violet and with a yellow beard, or pure white and beardless. Appearing early to mid-summer. Variable in the form and colour of the flowers.
Distribution Native to southern Europe; naturalized in central Europe, Persia, north India; introduced elsewhere. Tolerates most well-drained soils, but prefers sunny, stony, dry, hilly situations.
Cultivation Wild. Cultivated commercially in Italy, Persia, India and Egypt. Propagate by division of root-stocks in late spring or early autumn, planting in deep, rich, well-drained soil in sunny position.

Constituents Essential oil (0.1–0.2%) comprising myristic acid (85%) and methyl myristate; oleic acid; a ketone, irone, which develops on drying and storage; resin; tannic acid; starch; sugars.
Uses (dried root-stock) Stomachic; diuretic; aromatic; weak expectorant.
Formerly used in mixed remedies for the treatment of chest complaints such as bronchitis and asthma. The fresh juice was once used as a powerful purgative. It is now rarely used even in folk medicine.
Used as a bitter flavouring in certain liqueurs. Widely employed as a violet scent in the perfume industry, and as a fixative in pot-pourri manufacture. May be used in some tooth powders or dusting powders.
Contra-indications Fresh root-stock may be violently purgative. Large doses of the powdered root-stock cause vomiting. The powder may cause allergic reactions.

Iris versicolor L IRIDACEAE
Blue Flag Flag Lily
Blue Flag is a common American herb which was employed by both the Indians and early settlers as a remedy for gastric complaints. It was once included in the United States Pharmacopoeia and is still believed in folk medicine to be a blood purifier in eruptive skin conditions.
In some places the plant is known as Liver Lily because of its particular effect on that organ.
The herb may be a hybrid between the closely related *I. virginica* (L) and another Iris.
Description Perennial bog plant on thick branched creeping root-stock bearing erect, stout, coarse stem 30 cm–110 cm tall, and sword-shaped leaves 20 cm–1 m long, 15 mm–

3 cm wide.
Attractive blue or violet flowers, marked with yellow, 2–6 per plant, on short peduncles, appearing early to mid-summer, followed by globose, leathery capsule.
Distribution North-east North America; in wet places on peaty soils.
Cultivation Wild plant.
Constituents An acrid resinous substance, irisin; volatile oil; fixed oil; starch; tannic

acid; an unidentified alkaloid.
Uses (dried root-stock; leaves) Purgative; diuretic; sialagogue; emetic.
Chiefly employed in eruptive skin conditions caused by a sluggish gastro-intestinal system and constipation. It stimulates the flow of saliva, bile and gastric secretions, acting particularly on the liver and pancreas. Leaves applied externally on bruises.
Contra-indications Large doses cause nausea, vomiting and facial neuralgias. Handling the plant may cause dermatitis.

Isatis tinctoria L CRUCIFERAE
Woad Dyer's Weed
Woad was cultivated as the source of a blue dyestuff for over 2000 years in Europe and was only superseded 50 years ago by indigo, which was first extracted from subtropical *Indigofera* species.
Isatis is an ancient name for a healing herb, which was described by Dioscorides as being an excellent styptic. Doubtless the habit adopted by ancient Britons of painting their bodies with a paste of the leaves served the dual purpose of frightening their enemies and healing the wounds of battle.
The herb is now mainly of historical interest, although as its blue colour is more permanent than *Indigofera indigo* it is in demand by homecraft dyers.
Description Biennial from 45 cm to 130 cm tall; produces in the first year a rosette of entire or toothed, oblong or obovate leaves from which arises stout, erect stems branching near the top, bearing lanceolate to linear glaucous sessile leaves, 10 cm long at the base and 4 cm long near the flowering top. Small yellow flowers, very numerous, in 45 cm wide panicled racemes, produced in early to mid-summer, and followed by pendulous black seeds that persist on the stem for weeks.

Distribution European native; introduced elsewhere. On humus-rich, well-drained chalky waste places in sunny situations.
Cultivation Wild. Cultivated in western Europe until the 1930s. Propagate from seed sown in sunny position on well-drained, very rich soil, in late summer. Thin to 40 cm apart by transplanting in early spring.
Seeds itself readily, but acts as a short-lived perennial if the unripe flower-heads are removed.
Constituents Indigo (developed by fermenting leaves).
Uses (fermented leaves, rarely fresh leaves) Vulnerary; styptic.
Once employed externally to stop bleeding and assist in the healing of wounds and ulcers. Too poisonous and astringent to be used internally. Traditionally the source of a blue dye obtained by fermenting, drying and refermenting the crushed leaves, and adding lime-water to the final product.
Contra-indications POISONOUS. Not to be used internally.

Jateorhiza palmata Miers MENISPERMACEAE
Calumba Colombo
Calumba remains a favourite tonic for the treatment of gastric disorders in Africa and India, and retains a place as a bitter in some European pharmacopoeias. In East Africa it is known as kalumb or koamwa and has long been used as a treatment for diarrhoea and as a general tonic, as well as being used as a dye. The Portuguese introduced it to Europe in the seventeenth century when it was considered an antidote to poisons, but it was generally neglected until Percival promoted it in 1773. By 1781 it was valued at $12 a kilo and in 1788 it was included in the London Pharmacopoeia. Lamarck first described the plant in 1797 and called it *Menispermum palmatum*.
Description Tall dioecious twining perennial vine; often reaching the tops of trees. Large fleshy tuberous root. Annual stems herbaceous, hairy and bearing large, membranous, alternate, palmate-lobed, long-petioled leaves, and insignificant greenish-white flowers, which are followed by a moon-shaped stone contained within a globose drupe. Male flowers in panicles 30 cm long.
Distribution Indigenous to East Africa, especially northern Mozambique; introduced elsewhere, for example, Brazil. In forests.
Cultivation Wild. Some small-scale cultivation in East Africa.
Constituents Volatile oil (0.07–1.15%), comprising mainly thymol; 3 yellow alkaloids, columbamine, jatrorrhizine, palmatine; bitter principles, chasmanthin and a lactone, columbin; traces of the sapogenins, diosgenin and kryptogenin; mucilage; starch.
Uses (dried root) Stomachic; bitter tonic. Chiefly employed as an aqueous infusion in vomiting during pregnancy or atonic dyspepsia associated with hypochlorhydria. In Africa it is used as a remedy for diarrhoea and dysentery, and in India as an antipyretic and anthelmintic.

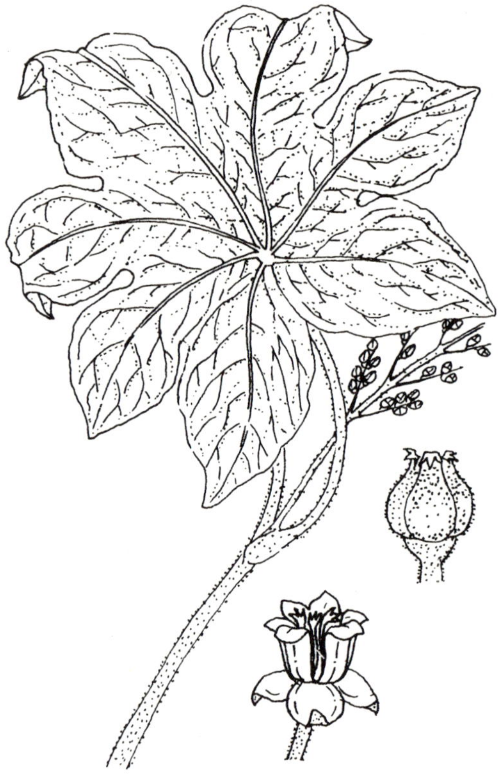

The alkaloids present in the root have been shown to increase the intestinal tone and lower the blood pressure. An excellent bitter tonic. Used as a yellow dye.

Juglans cinerea L JUGLANDACEAE
Butternut White walnut/Oil-nut
The walnut family derive their generic name, *Juglans*, from the Latin *Iovis glans* meaning the nut of Jupiter after the ancient belief that the gods ate walnuts.
Most of the names of this tree, in fact, refer to its nut, for example, butternut, Oil-nut and Lemon nut, indicating both the oily nature and shape of the fruit. This species is described as both white and as *J. cinerea* after the light colour of its bark, the botanical name being derived from the Latin *cinereus* meaning ash-coloured. It is thus distinguished from the closely related black walnut, *J. nigra*.
Oil from the nut was once used as a strongly flavoured seasoning in America.
Description Tree from 12–30 m tall; bark light grey, deeply furrowed with broad ridges; branches pubescent, bearing 11–19 opposite leaflets, 5–12.5 cm long, irregularly serrate, acuminate, short-petioled and oblong lanceolate. Flowers in drooping catkins. Fruit elongated, pointed, 4 cm long in groups of 2–5, externally sticky and strong smelling, containing an edible nut.
Distribution North American native, from New England to Georgia and Maryland. Introduced elsewhere. In rich damp woods or close to rivers, on well-drained soils.
Cultivation Wild.
Constituents Fixed oils; a complex resin, called juglandin, containing nucin.
Uses (inner root bark; ripening fruit, leaves) Cathartic; anthelmintic; weak rubefacient.

The bark was formerly used as a domestic remedy for constipation. The oil from the fruit was employed to remove tapeworms. It is now rarely used even in folk medicine.
Ripening fruit can be pickled.
The sap produces a syrup similar to maple syrup.
Root bark, leaves and fruit provide a brown wool dye.

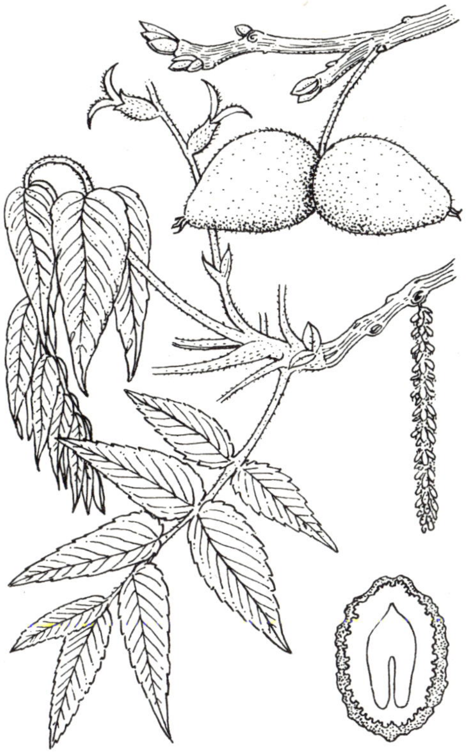

Juglans regia L JUGLANDACEAE
Walnut Persian Walnut
This tree bears the name *regia*, meaning royal, both because of its attractive appearance and its historical importance as a source of timber and food. It was known to Theophrastus as *karuon*, and Pliny – who believed it entered Europe from Persia – first described the use of the shells for dyeing white hair brown. He suggested that the green husks be boiled with lead, ashes, oil and earthworms, and the mixture applied to the head!
Both the green walnut husks and fresh leaves have been used as a brown hair dye for centuries, remaining as the main constituent of proprietary hair tints until the beginning of the twentieth century.

Description A number of varieties exist, and the form of the tree is variable. Tree to 30 m; bark silvery-grey. Usually 7 or 9 glabrous leaflets, entire, acute, oblong-ovate, 5–12.5 cm long. Male flowers in drooping catkins appear late spring to early summer. Indistinct female flowers followed by almost globular, glabrous fruit singly or in groups of 3.
Distribution Native to western Asia, south-east Europe, China and the Himalayas. Introduced elsewhere. In open woodland.
Cultivation Wild. Widely cultivated for its timber.
Constituents Fruit: Fixed oils; vitamin C. Leaves: A bitter compound, juglone; hydrojuglone; tannic acid; unknown substances.
Uses (dried leaves, fresh fruit) Tonic; astringent; anti-inflammatory; weakly hypoglycaemic.
Leaves considered of benefit in a wide range of eruptive skin conditions, and used both internally and externally. Also employed homeopathically for the same purposes.
Ripening fruit can be pickled. The ripe nuts are of commercial importance. Oil expressed from the nuts provides a cooking oil, and is occasionally employed in non-drying artists' paints.
Timber used in furniture.
Leaves yield a brown dye.

Juniperus communis L CUPRESSACEAE
Juniper Common Juniper
Juniperus is the classical name for this variable and widely distributed plant of the northern temperate zones, which has remained in use from the Greek and Arabic physicians to the present day. Although no longer generally considered as a spice, it is still an important flavouring for certain preserved meats, liqueurs and especially gin. The English word gin is derived from an abbreviation of Hollands Geneva as the spirit was first called – which, in turn, stems from the Dutch *jenever* meaning Juniper. Only 1 kilogram of the berries is used to flavour over 400 litres of gin.
Description Variable, from a dense procumbent shrub to a 12 m tall tree; evergreen. Leaves needle-like, 5–13 mm long, in whorls of 3, spreading from the branchlets, bluish-white on upper surface. Flowers indistinct, axillary, dioecious, greenish-yellow, appear late spring to early summer; followed by 7.5–10 mm diameter blue-black, fleshy, 3-seeded berries.
Distribution Native to Mediterranean region; also Arctic Norway to Soviet Union, north-west Himalayas, North America. On heaths, moorland, open coniferous forests and mountain slopes.
Cultivation Wild. Berries collected commercially. Other forms may be used, for example, *J. communis* ssp. *nana* Syme, *J. communis* ssp. *hibernica* Gard., *J. communis* cv. *prostrata* Beissen.
Constituents Essential oil (0.5–2%), comprising terpene hydrocarbons (α-pinene, β-pinene, limonene) sesquiterpenes (α-caryophyllene, cadinene, elemene), bitter substances, alcohols, and a monocyclic cyclobutane monoterpenoid, junionone; resin (10%); sugar (30–33%); organic acids.
Uses (dried fruit, leafy branchlets) Antiseptic; diuretic; stimulant; carminative; rubefacient. Used internally as a urinary antiseptic, specifically in cystitis; also promotes gastric secretions and improves the appetite. Applied externally to relieve rheumatic pain, to counteract alopecia, as a styptic and to wounds. Used homeopathically and in veterinary medicine.

Berries are used to flavour meats, gin and liqueurs. Once used as a spice and substitute for pepper, and when roasted as a coffee substitute.
Contra-indications Not to be used in pregnancy or when the kidneys are inflamed.

Juniperus sabina L CUPRESSACEAE
Savin Savin Tops
Savin has a long history as a stimulant veterinary drug in Europe, and was applied to the wounds and ulcers of animals. Due to its toxicity, however, it has never been widely used as a medicine for humans.
Description Evergreen shrub, usually low-growing and of spreading habit, to 2 m tall; sometimes a small tree, to 7.5 m. Young leaves opposite, acute and pointed; older leaves scale-like, closely adhering to branchlets, bright green. Flowers indistinct, greenish-yellow, dioecious, appearing late spring followed by 7 mm diameter brownish-purple, 2-seeded berries on pendulous pedicels.
Distribution Native to central and south Europe; distributed from the Caucasus to south Siberia. Also in North America. On sunny mountain slopes.
Cultivation Wild. Grown horticulturally as a hedge-plant, for which purpose *J. sabina* var. *tamariscifolia* Ait. and *J. sabina* var. *variegata* Laws. are also used.

Constituents Volatile oil (1–4%), similar to that of *J. communis*; tannic acid; resin.
Uses (young green shoots) Powerful uterine stimulant; emmenagogue; irritant.
Now only used externally, with care, as a stimulant dressing for blisters, wounds, ulcers, and to remove warts. Employed in veterinary medicine.
Contra-indications POISONOUS and occasionally fatal. Causes severe gastro-intestinal irritation, haematuria and hallucinations. To be used only under medical supervision.

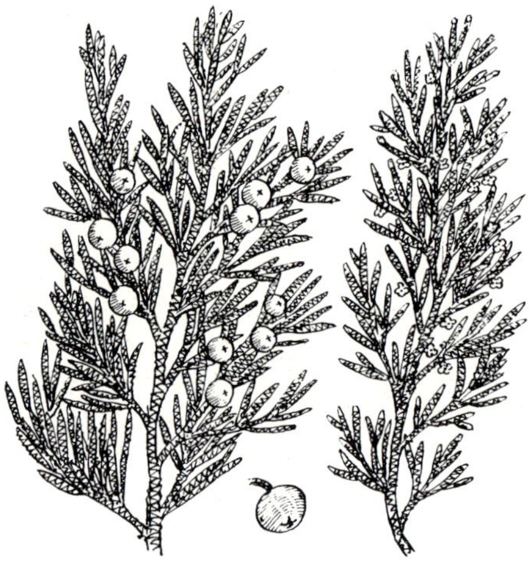

Lactuca virosa L COMPOSITAE
Wild Lettuce Greater Prickly Lettuce
In the nineteenth century this, and a closely related species *L. scariola* L, was cultivated on a small scale in western Europe as the source of lactucarium – the dried latex which exudes from the cut surface of the plant's stem. It was introduced to medical practice in 1771 by Collin and called 'lettuce opium' by Coxe in 1799.
Although its action as a sedative is fairly weak, it was used as an adulterant of true opium and entered the Edinburgh and other European pharmacopoeias as a cough suppressant. The common Garden Lettuce, (*L. sativa* L), was also once used as a source of lactucarium, but by breeding out the bitterness of this salad herb modern cultivars only contain a trace of the complex.
Description Strongly smelling biennial, producing a rosette of obovate, undivided leaves 12–30 cm long in the first year, and an erect stout, cylindrical, pale green branched stem to 1.5 m high in the second. Stem-leaves dark green, clasping, scanty, alternate, ovate-oblong.
Numerous flower-heads, arranged in panicles, short-stalked, pale yellow, appearing late summer to mid-autumn.
Distribution European native. On dry nitrogen-rich soils, in wasteland and hillsides.
Cultivation Wild. Formerly cultivated on a small scale.
Constituents Lactucarium, comprising bitter substances (lactucine, lactucopicrin, lactucic acid); crystalline substances (including lactucerin); sugar; caoutchouc; traces of a mydriatic alkaloid; and other substances.
Uses (dried latex, dried leaves occasionally) Mild sedative; mild hypnotic.
Formerly used as a constituent of remedies employed in the treatment of irritable coughs. May be used in insomnia or restlessness.
Contra-indications The latex is very irritant to the eyes.

Lamium album L LABIATAE
White Dead-Nettle Blind Nettle
This is not a true nettle, nor is it botanically related to the nettle family, but *L. album* does bear a superficial similarity to nettles and is often found growing close to or among them. The common name Dead-Nettle reflects the fact that it does not possess any sting, while its generic name *Lamium* is from the Greek word for throat after the shape of the plant's flower.
Not of importance historically, but nevertheless a useful medical plant particularly for menstrual problems.
Description Perennial 20–60 cm tall, spreading by underground stolons; stems rigid, square, bearing opposite, decussate, stalked or sessile, downy, deeply dentate, nettle-shaped leaves, 4–6 cm long. Flowers off-white, usually 5–8 (or occasionally to 16) in axillary whorls, the calyx consisting of 5 long, toothed projections. Appearing early summer to late autumn.
Distribution European native; introduced elsewhere. On rich soils in waste places, preferably in sunny positions.
Cultivation Wild.
Constituents Traces of essential oil; mucilage; tannic acid; flavonic heterosides, (kaempferol, isoquercitin); potassium salts; histamine; tyramine; and unknown substances.
Uses (flowering plant) Astringent; expectorant; diuretic; vulnerary; anti-inflammatory. Useful internally in cystitis, leucorrhoea and particularly metrorrhagia; as a bowel regulator, it can be used to treat either diarrhoea or constipation; in respiratory or nasal catarrh.

Applied externally to wounds it is both styptic and healing. It may also be applied to haemorrhoids and burns.
Young leaves may be boiled and eaten as a green vegetable, or added to soups.

Lapsana communis L COMPOSITAE
Nipplewort
In the sixteenth century this was called *papillaris* by the apothecaries, after the Latin *papilla* meaning nipple, since the herb was traditionally employed to treat cracked nipples – a use which may originally have been

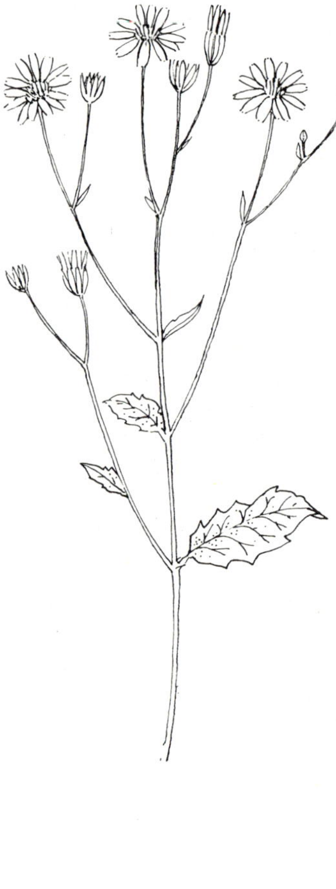

suggested by the nipple-shaped unopened flower buds.

In some parts of Europe ointments made from the fresh juice are still used for this purpose.

Description Annual 20 cm–120 cm; stem hairy, much branched near the top, bearing three types of alternate leaves, the lower lyre-shaped, the middle oval and petiolate, the upper small, sessile and lanceolate. Flowers composed entirely of ray florets, yellow, in small capitula, arranged in panicles, appear early summer to mid-autumn.

Distribution From Europe to northern Asia; naturalized in America. On humus-rich moist soils on wild or cultivated land, wood edges, and in thickets, to an 1800 m altitude.

Cultivation Wild.

Constituents Unknown.

Uses (fresh leaves, fresh juice) Laxative; vulnerary.

Traditionally used externally to treat cracked nipples or to promote the flow of milk from the breast. Considered useful in constipation associated with liver problems. Supposed, but unproven, antidiabetic agent. May be applied to wounds or cuts.

Young radish flavoured leaves eaten in salads, or boiled as a green vegetable.

Laurus nobilis L LAURACEAE

Bay Tree Sweet Bay/Sweet Laurel

This is an ancient aromatic plant, once dedicated to Apollo, and for thousands of years it was considered to be a powerful antiseptic. It is a vital ingredient of the genuine bouquet garni.

Its botanical name emphasizes the respect with which the ancients held the plant; *laurus* from the Latin meaning to praise, and *nobilis* meaning renowned or famous.

This was the leaf used to make the victor's crown of laurels in classical times – and the tree was once called the *baccae lauri* or noble berry tree, from which by direct association with the victor's crown the modern French educational term *baccalauréat* is derived.

Description Evergreen tree to 15 m; with grey shiny bark. Usually grown as a bush to 2 m. Leaves leathery, dark green, shiny above, lanceolate to oblong-lanceolate, 3–7.5 cm long. Flowers small, yellowish, in groups of 3–4 in the leaf axils, appearing late spring to early summer and followed by 15 mm-diameter dark purple berries.

Distribution Native to Asia Minor and Europe; introduced elsewhere; in sheltered sunny mountain valleys on rich soils.

Cultivation Wild plant. Grown horticulturally on a commercial scale as a garden ornamental, especially in Holland and Belgium. Plant bushes in late spring or mid-autumn, in sunny frost-free sites, on rich soil; or in tubs filled with rich soil which should be kept moist, and protected in winter. Propagate from cuttings in autumn, or by layering of lower branches in late summer or early autumn.

Constituents (leaves) Volatile oil (1–3%), comprising geraniol, cineol, eugenol, terpenes; tannic acid; bitter principles. (berries) fat (25–30%), comprising glyceryl laurate; volatile oil (1%), with similar composition to that of the leaf, comprising mainly cineol.

Uses (berries, leaves, oil expressed from berries) Antiseptic; stimulant; stomachic; weak insecticide. Formerly used to stimulate digestion. Once used externally to relieve rheumatic pain and as an antiseptic. Employed in stimulant liniments in veterinary medicine.

A flavouring in some liqueurs.

Most widely used as a culinary herb (the freshly dried leaf). Can be used in both savoury and some sweet dishes and confections.

Lavandula angustifolia Mill. LABIATAE

Lavender English Lavender

One of the most popular and well-known of the traditional herbs. This species has also been classified as *L. vera* DC and *L. officinalis* Chaix., and is closely related to *L. latifolia* Vill. with which it is sometimes confused. The latter, however, (which is also called *L. spica* L) produces an inferior oil, called spike lavender oil.

In classical writings these species are not clearly differentiated and it is probable that French Lavender has been used longer for medicinal purposes, although *L. angustifolia* was a popular strewing and cosmetic herb from at least the twelfth century.

Many horticultural varieties were developed in the eighteenth and nineteenth centuries, but some of these are now difficult to obtain.

Description Aromatic perennial subshrub to 80 cm; on woody stem. Leaves opposite, entire, very narrow, lanceolate or oblong-linear, 2–5 cm long, the smaller often clustered in axils, grey-green and tomentose. Flowers usually grey-blue, 6–15 mm long, in spikes on peduncles from 10–20 cm long; appearing mid-summer to early autumn.

Distribution Native to mediterranean region; widely distributed in southern Europe; introduced elsewhere. Often on poor, well-drained soils.

Cultivation Wild. Cultivated commercially in southern Europe. Very wide horticultural use as garden ornamental. Propagate from seed sown in pans in late spring, later planting out 45 cm apart (germination may be slow). Or use green cutting, 10 cm long taken in spring, or hardwood cuttings taken between early spring and late summer.

Constituents Volatile oil, comprising an alcohol, linalol, and linalyl acetate; a hydroxycoumarin, herniarin eucalyptol; limonene; cineole; geraniol.

Uses (dried flowers; oil of lavender) Carminative; rubefacient; sedative; antispasmodic; antiseptic; stimulant; weak diuretic.

Still used in folk medicine internally as a mild sedative and cough suppressant, or in gastric disturbances characterized by flatulence. Externally the oil is stimulant and is occasionally employed to counteract rheumatic pain, or in tonic embrocations.

Lavender oil vapour is traditionally inhaled to prevent vertigo and fainting.

May also be used as an antiseptic lotion for cuts.

The oil is used as an insect repellent; to mask unpleasant odours in ointments; in perfumery and as a flavouring agent.

Dried flowers are employed in scented pillows, sachets, moth repellents and pot-pourris.

Lavandula dentata L LABIATAE

Fringed Lavender French Lavender

This is one of the least hardy lavenders and is best grown indoors or as a winter flowering pot plant under glass.

Its botanical name *dentata* refers to the attractive fern-like leaves which are quite different

from those of English Lavender. The aroma of Fringed Lavender is also different – being a sweet blend of Rosemary and Lavender.
Description Aromatic perennial, usually shrubby from 30–80 cm tall; leaves 3–4 cm long, linear, light green or grey, pubescent, pinnately dentate, truncately toothed. Deep lavender flowers, 6–15 mm long on small, long peduncled spikes, 7.5–20 cm long, appear winter.
Distribution Native to the mediterranean region as far east as Malta; introduced elsewhere.
Cultivation Wild. Grown horticulturally as a garden plant in warm climates, and as a greenhouse or indoor pot plant elsewhere. Propagate from cuttings in sandy, slightly alkaline soil; prune to prevent straggling growth or cut back to produce a bushy plant. Requires full sun and feeding occasionally with liquid manure if grown in pots.
Constituents Volatile oil.
Uses (dried flowering plant, dried leaves) Cultivated as a winter-flowering ornamental. Dried flowers and leaves used in floral arrangements and in scented sachets and pot-pourris.

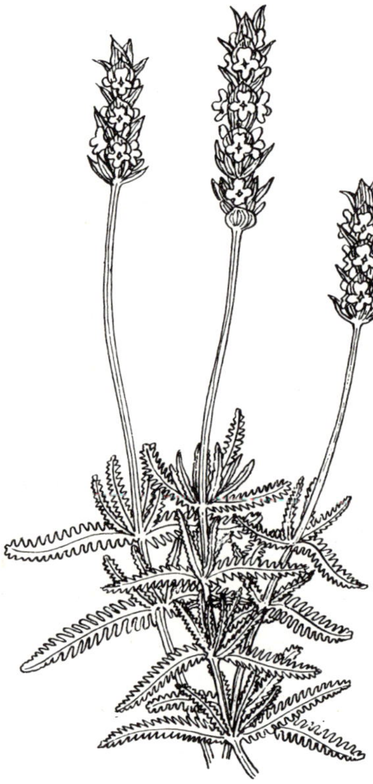

Lavandula stoechas L LABIATAE
French Lavender Spanish Lavender
This is the lavender species which was best known and possibly most widely used by the ancient Greeks, Romans and Arabs – usually as an antiseptic and sweet-smelling herb for inclusion in bath and other washing water.
The generic name *lavandula* is derived from the latin *lavare* meaning to wash. Like *L. dentata*, the scent is somewhat balsam-like and a mixture of Rosemary and Lavender.
It continued to be used medicinally (known as *Flores stoechados, sticadore* or *stoechas arabica*) until the eighteenth century, and was even included in the London Pharmacopoeia of 1746. Gradually, however, it was replaced by the hardier *L. angustifolia* Mill.
Description Perennial subshrub, 30 cm–1 m tall. Leaves linear, narrow, hairy, entire, grey-green, 1.5–4 cm long. Flowers 3 mm long, dark purple, specked with orange, in short wide spikes on 3 cm long peduncle. Flowers surmounted by attractive purple bracts one-third or one-quarter the length of the spike; appearing mid-spring to early summer.
Distribution Native to the mediterranean region; also the Canary Islands, Turkey and Asia Minor; introduced elsewhere. In coastal sites on sandy soils.

Cultivation Wild plant. Grown horticulturally as a garden ornamental in warm countries, and occasionally in cooler temperate zones in very warm protected sites. May be propagated from seed sown under glass in spring or from cuttings taken in spring or summer. Also cultivated indoors as a pot plant; requires a dry, sandy, well-drained soil, full sunlight, and occasional feeding with liquid manure.
Constituents Volatile oil.
Uses (dried flowers, dried leaves, dried flowering plant) Antiseptic; antispasmodic; carminative; vulnerary; stimulant; insect repellent. Formerly used in a wide range of complaints; now only employed in southern Europe as a mild sedative, antiseptic and remedy for nausea and vomiting. The flowers may be used in conserves.
Dried flowers and leaves employed in scented articles such as sachets.

Lawsonia inermis L LYTHRACEAE
Henna Mignonette Tree/Egyptian Privet
Henna, or Al Kenna as it is called in Arabic, has played an important role in religion and mysticism in the East for centuries. The red colouring produced from the leaf was considered to represent the fire and blood of the earth, and to link mankind with nature. For this reason it has long been used to dye the nails, hands, feet and hair – and the Berbers still colour both corpses and young babies with the dye, as well as using it in marriage ceremonies. The shrub now has a very wide distribution and commercial henna varies greatly in composition and quality – often being adulterated with Lucerne leaves or powdered *Acacia catechu*, Catechu. The variety now considered finest for use as a hair dye comes from Persia. Green Henna gives the deepest red tones and is made from young shoots, while so-called 'compound henna' consists of inferior leaf and synthetic dyes. The botanical name *Lawsonia* is named after the Surveyor-General of North Carolina, who was burned to death by Indians in 1712.
Description Shrub to 6 m with glabrous branches bearing greenish brown, opposite, shortly petiolate, oblong or broadly lanceolate leaves, 1.5–5 cm long, 1–2 cm wide. Small highly scented, white, light red or deep red flowers to 7.5 mm diameter in a corymbose terminal panicle, followed by spherical fruits 7.5 mm diameter.
Variable in form.
Distribution Indigenous to Arabia, Persia, India, Egypt and Australia; naturalized in tropical America; introduced elsewhere.
Cultivation Wild. Grown horticulturally as an ornamental and cultivated commercially for the leaves, mainly in India, Egypt, China, Morocco and Iran.
Constituents Fats; resin; mannitol; volatile oil; fixed oil; a yellow pigment, lawsone (hennotannic acid or oxynaphthochinon).
Uses (dried leaves, dried green shoots, dried twigs) Astringent; stimulant.
Used for the treatment of leprosy in African folk medicine; the powdered leaf has also been used to treat intestinal amoebiasis.
Most widely used as a hair, skin and nail dye.

Ledum groenlandicum Oed. ERICACEAE
Labrador Tea Marsh Tea
This aromatic herb, (synonym *L. latifolium* Jacq.) is named after Greenland where it grows in profusion.
It is rarely used today, perhaps because of its slightly narcotic qualities, but during the American War of Independence it was one of several herbs used as a substitute for tea.
Labrador Tea may be grown horticulturally in cold, wet, exposed sites.
A closely related plant, *L. palustre* L is also called Marsh Tea and has similar properties.
Description Evergreen shrub to 90 cm; bearing aromatic, alternate, entire leaves 3–5 cm long on short petioles. Leaves folded back at the edges, green above and rust-coloured beneath. Flowers small (to 12 mm wide), scented, white, and carried on thin pedicels in terminal clusters; appearing in spring.
Distribution Native to Greenland and Canada. In sphagnum bogs and wet peaty soils in colder parts of the northern hemisphere.
Cultivation Wild. May be cultivated in cold wet situations; propagate by root division in mid-autumn.
Constituents Tannic acid; arbutin; resin; essential oil, comprising ledol; mineral salts.
Uses (leaves, fresh or dried) Astringent. Once used to treat dysentery and diarrhoea.
Now rarely used as a tea.
Formerly added to beer to increase its intoxicant properties.
Contra-indications Evidence suggests excessive use of the tea may cause delirium or poisoning.

Leonurus cardiaca L LABIATAE
Motherwort
Several *Leonurus* species from various parts of the world, which include *L. sibiricus*, *L. glaucescens*, *L. deminutus* and *L. heterophyllus*, have been shown in animal experiments to possess hypotensive and sedative properties. The European species *L. cardiaca* has the same properties and was used since the early Greeks to treat pregnant women for anxiety – hence its name Motherwort.
Its action on the heart led to the specific name *cardiaca*, from the Greek *kardiaca* meaning heart, while the generic term, *Leonurus*, is from the Latin *leo* or lion and the Greek *oura* or tail, since it was thought that the tall, leafy stem resembled a lion's tail.
Once commonly grown in herb gardens but now rare, even in the wild.
Description Strongly smelling erect perennial 90–150 cm tall; on stout stem, square in section, branching below and hairy. Leaves pale green beneath, darker above, long petioled, serrate, the lower leaves deeply palmately lobed, the upper leaves less deeply 3-lobed. Flowers pale pink to purple, very hairy, small,

arranged in whorls of 6–12 in leaf axils; appearing mid-summer to mid-autumn.
Distribution European native; introduced elsewhere. Usually rare or localized on waste-ground and roadsides near ruins. On well-drained, light, calcareous soils in sunny situations.
Cultivation Wild. May be propagated by root division in mid-autumn or late spring. Self-seeds easily.
Constituents Tannic acid; essential oil; an alkaloid, leonurinine; glucosides; a bitter principle, leonurine. The combined action is sedative.
Uses (fresh or dried flowering plant) Sedative; antispasmodic; emmenagogue; cardiotonic; hypotensive; slightly astringent.
Formerly used in the treatment of bronchitis, diarrhoea, asthma, and rheumatism. Now considered of benefit in amenorrhoea and dysmenorrhoea, and specifically useful in tachycardia.
May be of use in anxiety. Employed homeopathically.
Contra-indications May cause contact dermatitis.

Levisticum officinale Koch UMBELLIFERAE
Lovage Love Parsley
With its interesting and unusual flavour Lovage has a wide culinary potential, but it is not widely used except as a soup flavouring.
The Greeks, who called it *ligustikon*, chewed the seed to aid digestion and relieve flatulence – a medicinal use which was promoted in the Middle Ages by Benedictine monks.
The common name is derived from the fact that in many European countries the herb had a traditional reputation as a love charm or aphrodisiac. The botanical name is a corruption of the earlier name *Ligusticum*, after Liguria, Italy, where it once grew in abundance.
Description Glabrous aromatic perennial on stout fleshy root-stock to 2.20 m. Stem stout and hollow, bearing large dark green long-petioled, ovate-cuneate, to 3-pinnate leaves, 70 cm long and 50 cm wide near the base, smaller at the top. Flowers small, greenish yellow, in umbels 5–7.5 cm wide, appearing summer, followed by 7.5 mm long oblong fruit.
Distribution Southern European native; naturalized in Asia Minor and eastern United States; introduced elsewhere. Tolerates most soils except heavy clay.
Cultivation Very rarely wild, and then usually as a garden escape. Cultivated commercially on a small scale in central Europe, and widely as a garden herb. Seed sown as soon as ripe or in spring in well-manured, moist, but well-drained soil; transplanting 60 cm apart. Also propagate by root division in autumn or spring, replanting 5 cm deep. Full size is reached in 3–5 years.
Constituents Essential oil comprising mainly umbelliferone and butyl phthalidine; resin; starch; sugars; tannin; gum; vitamin C; coumarin.
Uses (dried root, fresh or dried plant, seed) Diuretic; stomachic; emmenagogue; expectorant.

Formerly used as a diuretic, in the treatment of rheumatism and migraine, and for bronchial catarrh. Of use in flatulence and to promote the appetite.
Sometimes employed externally to treat some simple skin problems.
The powdered root was once used as a pepper.

The leaf may be used as a flavouring in soups, sauces and salads, and as a vegetable; the seed in biscuits and with meat.
Young stems may be candied like Angelica. Stems and leaf stalks can be blanched and eaten in the same way as celery.
Contra-indications Large quantities should not be taken by pregnant women or by people suffering from kidney disease.

Liatris odoratissima Willd. COMPOSITAE
Deer's Tongue Vanilla Plant
Deer's Tongue, so called because of the shape of its leaves, is one of 40 species in the North American Blazing Star or *Liatris* genus. The group is difficult to classify botanically due to hybridization between species, but is characterized by attractive flower-heads which persist for weeks.
This species possesses coumarin in its leaves which is responsible for its attractive scent.
Description Glabrous perennial on thick tuberous root-stock, to 1.2 m. Leaves alternate, clasping, narrow, entire, spoon-shaped and fleshy to 25 cm long. Flowers bright purple on spikes 35 cm long; appearing early to late autumn.
Distribution North American native. On damp soils in meadows and open woods.
Cultivation Wild. Propagate by root division in early spring.
Constituents Coumarin; unknown substances.
Uses (dried root, fresh or dried leaf) Diuretic.

Once used as a diuretic, but it is rather too strong for this purpose.
Leaves once employed as a tobacco flavouring.
Largely cultivated as an attractive late flowering garden herb, and as a source of vanilla-scented leaves for use in pot-pourris.

Liatris spicata Willd. COMPOSITAE
Blazing Star Dense Button Snakeroot
The botanical name, *Liatris*, is of unknown origin, while *spicata* refers to the spikes on which the flowers are carried.
Although now rarely used medicinally it is

still found as a horticultural plant, (sometimes called *L. callilepis*). A related species, *L. chapmannii*, also called Blazing Star, contains a substance (liatrin), which has been shown to possess anti-cancer properties.
Description Nearly glabrous erect perennial on tuberous root; stem 30 cm–2 m, bearing alternate linear, punctate leaves, 30 cm long and 10 mm wide. Flowers dark blue, 4–8 mm diameter, in groups of 5–13, in dense spikes 40 cm long, appearing from early to late autumn.
Distribution North American native from Massachusetts to Florida and Arizona. On rich, damp meadow soils or near marshes.
Cultivation Wild. May be propagated by root division in early spring, planting in well-manured, damp soils. A white variety *alba* exists.
Constituents Coumarin; unknown substances.
Uses (root, fresh plant) Diuretic; antibacterial.
Formerly used in New England as a treatment for venereal diseases, particularly gonorrhoea.
The decoction is of use as a gargle for the treatment of sore throats.
Powdered root and leaf may be employed in scented sachets and pot-pourris.
The leaf was once used to flavour tobacco.
The powdered root and leaf may also be used as an insect repellent.
The herb may be employed horticulturally as a hardy late flowering plant.

Ligusticum scoticum L UMBELLIFERAE
Lovage Sea Parsley
This herb is so called because it was particularly collected and used as a culinary herb in Scotland, where it is known as *shunis*.
North American Indians also ate it, peeling the stem and eating it raw. Because of its viatmin C content, the plant was also popular with sailors and fishermen suffering from scurvy. It was once cultivated, but has long ceased to be of medicinal or culinary importance.
Description Coarse perennial to 60 cm on branched root-stock. Stem red below, bearing dark green, long stemmed, ternate leaves with

few segments, 3–5 cm wide, toothed on upper half only. Flowers yellowish white, in umbels, appearing late summer to early autumn, followed by fruit with prominent ridges.
Distribution Sub-arctic Atlantic coasts; occasionally inland. Especially on rocky shores and river estuaries.
Cultivation Wild. May be propagated from fresh seed, and grown in damp, slightly shady situations.
Constituents Essential oil, comprising umbelliferone; starch; vitamin C.
Uses (root, fresh plant, seed) Diuretic; aromatic; carminative.
Once used medicinally as an aromatic flavouring and in the treatment of rheumatism.
Young leaves and stems may be eaten raw as a salad, or cooked as a vegetable. Stems can be candied like Angelica, and they may also be eaten in the same way as celery.
The seed may be powdered and used like Pepper.
The root was formerly chewed as a tobacco substitute.
Bath water may be scented by the root.

Linum usitatissimum L LINACEAE
Flax Linseed
Flax has been of exceptional economic importance to man and has been grown since 5000 B.C. It was used by Mesopotamians and and by early Egyptians who wrapped their mummies in cloth made from it.
Unknown in the wild state, it is thought to have been derived from the Pale Flax, *L. bienne*

Mill. by selection and cultivation.
Today several cultivars exist, some with large seeds which are used for oil extraction, and the small seeded types which are used in linen and cloth manufacture.
Flax has been described in detail in all the classical writings of the Egyptians, Hebrews, Greeks and Romans, and was promoted in northern Europe first by the Romans and later by Charlemagne; Irish linen manufacture, however, was not reported until A.D. 500.
Description Thin annual, branching at the base, from 30–130 cm tall; stems erect, usually glabrous with narrow, sessile, linear or lanceolate alternate glaucous green leaves, 3–5 cm long, and marked with 3 veins.
Flowers 5-petalled, blue or occasionally white or red, 3 cm diameter, on erect terminal panicles, appearing mid to late summer and followed by globose capsules somewhat longer than the calices. Variable in form depending upon variety and environment.
Distribution Originally Asian; widely distributed through temperate and subtropical zones, often as escape from cultivation.
Especially on well-drained wasteland in sunny situations.
Cultivation Unknown in the wild state.
Different cultivars are commercially grown for seed (Holland, England, Argentina, North Africa), oil (United States, Morocco, USSR), and fibre (United States, USSR, India, Middle East). Some varieties are biennial. Seed is sown in drills in late spring or early summer, on dryish, well-drained soils.
Constituents (seed) Fixed oil (30–40%) comprising the glycerides of linoleic, linolenic and other fatty acids, and stearic and palmitic acids; mucilage (6%); a cyanogenic glycoside, linamarine; vitamin F; pectin; other nitrogenous substances. The laxative action is due to the oil and mucilage content.
Uses (stem, seed, seed-oil, powdered oil-exhausted seed) Laxative; demulcent; anti-inflammatory. Seed is of value internally as a mild laxative; it is sometimes combined with other anti-inflammatory medicinal plants for the treatment of respiratory and gastro-intestinal inflammatory disorders.
Both the seed and powdered seed may be applied externally as a poultice to relieve pain and heal skin wounds, certain skin conditions and suppurations.
Seed may be roasted and eaten, and unripe capsules can be eaten raw. The oil has been used for culinary purposes. It is of importance in paint and varnish manufacture. Fibre from the stems is very widely used in linen and cloth manufacture.
Although linseed oil is rarely used internally as a purgative in humans, it is used in veterinary medicine for this purpose.
Exhausted seed pulp is utilized as cattle fodder.

Lobelia inflata L LOBELIACEAE
Indian Tobacco Lobelia
Indian Tobacco is so called because it was formerly smoked by North American Indians to relieve asthma and related conditions. Early settlers used it for a wide variety of complaints, and some early American herbalists considered it almost a panacea. Samuel Thomson, who was an important figure in the physiomedical school of herbal medicine, particularly promoted Lobelia in the early nineteenth century, but was charged with murder after poisoning one of his patients with it. Cutler examined its anti-asthmatic properties in 1813, and the herb was introduced to British medicine in 1829. It is now rarely used. The generic name, *Lobelia*, is after the Flemish botanist Matthias de L'Obel (1538–1616),

while *inflata* refers to the way in which the seed capsule inflates during ripening.
Description Hairy, erect, somewhat angled stem from 20–70 cm, branching near the top, containing an acrid latex, and bearing oval or ovate-lanceolate, alternate, sessile, toothed leaves. Flowers pale blue externally, often violet within, small (4–6 mm long), irregular, on loose terminal spike-like racemes; followed by 2-celled capsule which inflates to a 1 cm long oval, glabrous structure.
Distribution Native to North America from Labrador to Georgia. Introduced elsewhere.
Cultivation Wild. Propagated from seed sown on the surface of rich soil, in the autumn.
Constituents Alkaloids (0.3–0.4%) comprising, lobeline, lobelidine, lobelanine, isolobelanine; also lobelic acid; inflatin; resin; fat; fixed oil; caoutchouc (India rubber). In small doses the combined action dilates bronchioles and relaxes bronchial muscles.
Uses (dried fruiting plant) Expectorant; anti-asthmatic; emetic; diaphoretic.
Of benefit in chronic bronchitis with associated dyspnoea and in bronchial asthma.
Formerly used to induce vomiting and in the treatment of whooping cough, croup and tetanus. May be applied externally to relieve pain and irritation caused by rheumatism, bruises, bites and certain skin conditions.
Contra-indications POISONOUS – may be fatal. Large doses cause purgation, vomiting, convulsions, medullary and respiratory depression.

Lonicera caprifolium L CAPRIFOLIACEAE

Perfoliate Honeysuckle

Honeysuckle receives its common name from an old habit of sucking the sweet honey-tasting nectar from the flowers, while this species – most common in southern Europe – is also called perfoliate because its upper leaves surround the stem.

Now widely used as a climbing or hedge plant.

Description Climbing deciduous shrub. Stems glabrous to 6 m. Leaves opposite simple, oval, 5–10 cm long, green above glaucous beneath; the upper 2 or 3 leaf pairs united at their base forming a cup (connate). Flowers fragrant, pale yellow, 4–5 cm long, corolla not glandular, borne in terminal whorls of 2–3. Bracts large. Appearing early to mid-summer and

followed by orange berries.

Distribution Native to central and southern Europe and western Asia; introduced elsewhere. On well-drained loamy soils. Calcifugous.

Cultivation Wild. Cultivated horticulturally: propagate from woody cuttings taken in early autumn and rooted in peat and sand mix; or by layering in late summer.

Constituents Mucilage; an amorphous glucoside; salicylic acid; sugars; invertin.

Uses (flowering plant) Diuretic; antiseptic; emetic; expectorant.

Similar actions to Honeysuckle (*L. periclymenum* L).

Contra-indications POISONOUS berries. External use only.

Lonicera periclymenum L CAPRIFOLIACEAE

Honeysuckle Woodbine

This is the taller growing of the two common European honeysuckles, and may live for 50 years. It is often found bound tightly around

trees – hence its alternative name Woodbine.

The generic name, *Lonicera*, refers to a sixteenth-century German physician, Lonicer (or Lonitzer).

Description Climbing, twining, deciduous shrub; stems to 9 m. Leaves opposite, simple, ovate to oblong-ovate, 4–7.5 cm long; dark green above, often glaucous or pale beneath; upper leaves not united.

Flowers fragrant, yellow, 4–5 cm long, corolla glandular, borne in many-flowered, peduncled, terminal clusters. Bracts small. Appearing mid-summer to mid-autumn and followed by red berries.

Distribution Native to Europe, western Asia and North Africa; introduced elsewhere. Especially on porous sandy or loam soils, in mixed woodland. Calcifugous.

Cultivation Wild. Cultivated horticulturally; propagate from woody cuttings taken in early autumn and rooted in peat and sand mix; or by layering in late summer. The varieties *var. Aurea* and *var. Belgica* are garden plants.

Constituents Mucilage; an amorphous glucoside; salicylic acid; sugars; invertin.

Uses (flowering plant) Diuretic; antiseptic; expectorant; emetic; slightly astringent.

Formerly used internally for several conditions; but now recommended only for external use as an application for skin infections.

Contra-indications POISONOUS berries: external use only.

Lycopodium clavatum L LYCOPODIACEAE

Club Moss Stags-Horn Moss

Club Moss, known to apothecaries as *muscus clavatus*, is so called because of the club-shaped fruiting bodies which it carries.

It has also been called vegetable sulphur, not only because of the yellow colour of the moss's spores, but also because they burn brightly in a similar manner to powdered sulphur.

The generic name, *Lycopodium*, means fox or wolf foot – another allusion to the shape of the plant.

This and closely related species, such as *L. selago* L (the Fir Club Moss), were once widely used medicinally, especially in North America and continental Europe. The use of the spores in treating wounds, which was introduced by German apothecaries in the seventeenth century, continues to this day in several parts of the world.

Description Procumbent evergreen perennial moss, reaching at least 100 cm long; rooting along the branching stem which is thin and

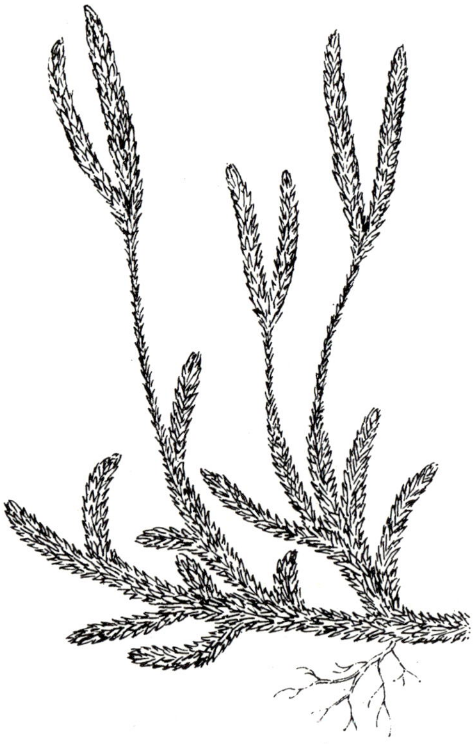

densely covered with bright green, smooth, narrow, pointed, bristled leaves, 3–5 mm long. Spores yellow, minute, carried in large numbers in yellow-green cones, usually 1 or 2 (rarely 3), which are borne at the ends of stalks extending from aerial branches, to 15 cm long. Spores ripe from early to mid-autumn.

Distribution World-wide distribution on acidic or silica-containing soils; on moorland, coniferous woodland and grassland, especially in mountainous districts.

Cultivation Wild plant.

Constituents (spores) Fixed oil (50%) comprising glycerides of palmitic, stearic, arachitic and lycopodium oleic acids; phytosterin; sporonine; lycopodic acid (2%); hydrocaffeic acid; a carbohydrate, pollenin (45%).

(whole plant) in addition to the above, contains alkaloids (0.12%) comprising clavatoxine, clavatine and lycopodine.

Uses (spores) Vulnerary; haemostatic; aperient; weak antispasmodic.

Formerly used internally in the treatment of kidney, liver and bladder inflammatory disorders, and in urinary incontinence. Use now is confined to its external application as a soothing dusting powder for wounds and in skin irritations such as in eczema. Also employed homeopathically. Hypoglycaemic action has been demonstrated experimentally.
It was also used to coat pills to prevent their adhesion when stored.
Once used as a basis for medicinal snuffs and as a vehicle for the application of powdered herbs to the nose and ears.
Still employed in firework manufacture.
Contra-indications The whole plant is toxic; only the spores may be used internally. The powder may ignite explosively if introduced to a flame.

Lycopus europaeus L LABIATAE
Gipsywort Gypsyweed
Called Gipsywort because it was supposed gypsies stained their skin with the herb. More certainly the plant has been of use as a cloth dye for centuries.
Although quite closely related to the mints this herb lacks aroma almost entirely.
Description Perennial on creeping rhizome. Stems erect, simple or branched from 30–100 cm tall; bearing opposite, shortly petiolate, ovate-lanceolate to elliptic leaves up to 10 cm long. Lower leaves pinnate, upper leaves crenate. Flowers, 3 mm diameter, white and dotted with purple, numerous, in dense whorls in upper leaf axils. Appearing late summer to mid-autumn.
Distribution Native to Europe, western Asia; introduced to North America. On many soil types, but especially those which are flooded; river margins, marshland and ditches.
Cultivation Wild.

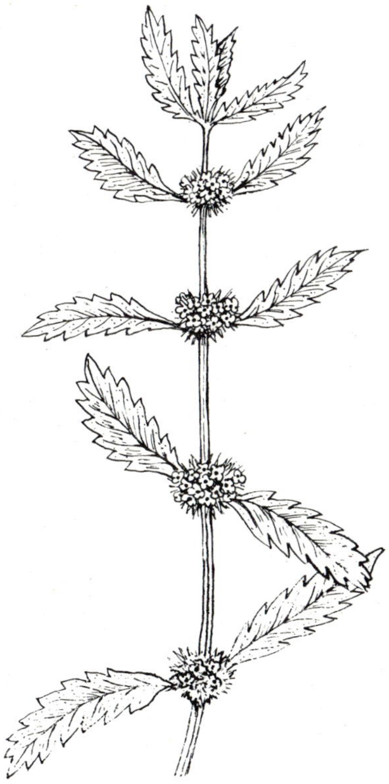

Constituents Tannic acid; essential oil; a bitter, lycopine; flavone glycosides.
Uses (fresh or dried flowering plant) Sedative; anti-haemorrhagic; cardioactive; antithyroidic.
Many uses have been ascribed to this herb; it has been used in the treatment of tuberculosis, haemoptysis and other forms of haemorrhage including menorrhagia.
It is a sedative, as it reduces the pulse rate in conditions involving an overactive thyroid gland.
The fresh juice provides a black dye, which is permanent on wool and linen.

Lycopus virginicus L LABIATAE
Bugle Weed Virginia Bugle Weed
Virginia Bugle Weed is very similar to the European Gipsywort (also known as Gypsyweed), and is itself sometimes called Gypsyweed. Its action was investigated originally in the latter half of the nineteenth century and its effectiveness in the treatment of internal haemorrhages and other conditions led to its inclusion in the United States Pharmacopoeia. It is now rarely used outside folk medicine.
This species is slightly more active than Gipsywort (*L. europaeus*) when used medicinally.
Description Perennial from 15–60 cm tall. Stem erect, glabrous or nearly so, producing stolons at the base, and bearing ovate or oblong-lanceolate, shortly petiolate, coarsely serrate leaves. Flowers whitish, sometimes heavily marked with purple, small, in loose axillary whorls; appearing late summer to mid-autumn.
Distribution North American native; from Labrador to Florida and British Colombia. On rich, damp soils, in shady situations, especially marshy land and moist forests.

Cultivation Wild.
Constituents Tannic acid; essential oil; a bitter, lycopine; flavone glycosides.
Uses (fresh or dried flowering plant) Sedative; anti-haemorrhagic; cardio-active; antithyroidic; hypoglycaemic.
Action the same as that of *L. europaeus*. It has also been employed in the treatment of diabetes.

Lythrum salicaria L LYTHRACEAE
Purple Loosestrife Spiked Loosestrife
This is still popular in European folk medicine, and was once used in tanning leather. Pliny described a purple-red *Lysimachia* which Matthiolus thought was this species. The generic name, *Lythrum*, is derived from the Greek for blood after its haemostatic properties. *Salicaria* refers to the Willow-like (*Salix* means willow) appearance of the leaves.
Description Erect, somewhat downy perennial 50–175 cm tall, on creeping rhizome; stem square and branched at the top. Leaves mostly

opposite, cordate below, lanceolate above to 10 cm. Flowers purple in whorled clusters on tall, leafy terminal spikes; appearing midsummer to mid-autumn.
Distribution Native to Europe and western Asia, Russia. Introduced and naturalized in other temperate zones. In reed-beds, ditches, fenland, beside stagnant or flowing water; to 1500 m altitude.
Cultivation Wild. Horticultural cultivars exist; may be propagated by seed or by division in spring.
Constituents Tannins; pectin; essential oil; provitamin A; calcium oxalate; a glycoside, vitexin. The combined action is antibacterial and haemostatic.
Uses (fresh or dried, whole flowering plant) Astringent; haemostatic; antibacterial; tonic. An excellent gargle, douche and wound cleanser, and of benefit in diarrhoea or gastro-intestinal disorders such as mild food poisoning. Rapidly stops bleeding. Once used in diluted form as an eye-wash.

Mahonia aquifolium (Pursh.) Nutt.
BERBERIDACEAE
Mountain Grape Barberry
This is known as *Mahonia aquifolium* after the American horticulturalist Bernard McMahon. The herb was introduced into Europe in 1823, and is now often grown because of its attractive foliage and fruit.
Description Fast growing evergreen shrub to 2 m; leaves consisting of 5–9 ovate leaflets 2–7 cm long, dark green and glossy, lighter beneath. Flowers yellowish-green, heavily scented, in terminal racemes. Bears purple-blue smooth berries.
Distribution Indigenous to mountainous regions of British Columbia. Distribution from British Columbia to Oregon. Introduced elsewhere.

Cultivation Wild plant. Cultivated as garden plant and now naturalized in temperate zones.
Constituents Alkaloids comprising mainly berberine, berbamine and oxyacanthine.
Uses (dried rhizome and root) Used in digestive complaints and for skin diseases – especially psoriasis. Combined with *Cascara sagrada* for use in constipation.

Malva sylvestris L MALVACEAE
Common Mallow
The Common Mallow was once highly respected as a medicinal plant and foodstuff, and from the days of the Romans was cultivated as a garden herb. In the sixteenth century it was given the name *omnimorbia*, meaning a cure-all – probably because of its gently purgative action; a practice which in itself was thought to rid the body of disease.
The common name Mallow is from the Latin *malva* for soft and emollient, after the feel, and properties respectively, of the leaves.
For medicinal purposes it has largely been replaced by the more effective Marshmallow.

Description Usually perennial, occasionally biennial. Stem hairy, erect or decumbent, branched, 30–150 cm tall; bearing tomentose, reniform or round-cordate, long-petioled leaves, 4 cm diameter, with 5–7 crenate lobes. Few pinkish-violet flowers, 4 cm diameter, 5-petalled, in clusters in leaf axils; appearing early summer to mid-autumn.
Distribution Native to Europe, western Asia, North America; on porous nutrient-rich soils, especially hedge banks, field edges, and waste-land; in sunny situations.
Cultivation Wild. Once grown as a garden plant; propagate from seed sown in late spring, later thinning to 75 cm apart.
Constituents Mucilage; volatile oil; tannin; vitamins A, B_1, B_2, C.

Uses (dried leaves and flowers, occasionally roots) Demulcent; anti-inflammatory; laxative; slightly astringent.
Useful in irritation of the gastro-intestinal system. Taken for the treatment of coughs and bronchitis.
Large doses are gently purgative.
Externally may be used as a soothing poultice. Its supposed sedative effect is unproven. Leaves were once cooked as a vegetable; and seeds and capsules (known as cheeses) may be eaten raw in salads.

Mandragora officinarum L SOLANACEAE
Mandrake
Mandrake is the most commonly cited example of the former abuse of medicinal plants by those obsessed with magical rites and orgiastic ritual with which some hallucinogenic and narcotic herbs became closely associated in the dark ages.
It was protected by the early Greek collectors who invested the root with such fictitious harmful attributes as the ability to kill a man who pulled it out of the ground.
Certainly Mandrake, like Henbane and Belladonna, was an ingredient of witches' brews and poisons, but it was also used by the Greek and Roman physicians as an anaesthetic and employed in early surgery.
It continued to be included in many European pharmacopoeias until the nineteenth century, and an official homeopathic preparation was introduced in 1877.
Description Perennial on thick, branching, tuberous root; practically stemless. Leaves reaching 30 cm long, ovate and undulate, basal or nearly so, dark green. Flowers greenish-yellow or purplish, 3 cm long, single or clustered within the leaves; appearing mid to late spring and followed by orange, globose, fleshy, many-seeded fruit.
Distribution Native to Himalayas and south-eastern mediterranean region. On poor thin, sandy soils in full sun.
Cultivation Wild plant. Rarely cultivated horticulturally in historical gardens or in botanic drug collections. Requires warm situation and winter protection in north Europe. Propagated from seed sown as soon as ripe, or by division.
Constituents Alkaloids, including atropine, scopolamine and hyoscyamine, to which the action is due.
Uses (dried root, fresh leaves rarely) Sedative; hallucinogenic; purgative; emetic; anodyne. No longer used medicinally owing to its high

toxicity. The leaves were once applied externally to ulcers, while the root formerly had wide application in the relief of pain, in the treatment of nervous disorders and as an aphrodisiac.
Contra-indications POISONOUS and dangerous; not to be used internally or externally.

Maranta arundinacea L MARANTACEAE
Arrowroot Maranta Starch
Arrowroot was first noticed on the West Indian island of Dominica at the end of the seventeenth century, and it was subsequently grown in Jamaica where it was employed both as a source of starch and as a poison antidote.

The common name is thought to be derived from the fact that a poultice of it was applied to arrow wounds. Its Brazilian name, however, is *araruta*, which may indicate a different etymological origin.
Supplies of Arrowroot first reached Europe from Jamaica at the beginning of the nineteenth century, but by 1840 it was being grown in India, and by 1858 *Maranta* was a commercial crop in Georgia, in the United States. The generic name is after B. Maranta, sixteenth-century Venetian botanist and physician; *arundinacea* refers to the reed-like shape of the plant.
Although it is still used, it was much more popular before the 1914–1918 war.
Description Herbaceous perennial on creeping rhizome and fleshy tubers; stems 60 cm–2 m tall, thin, reed-like, branched, bearing ovate-oblong, petiolate, glabrous, 15–30 cm long and 4–10 cm wide leaves; the petioles sheathing around the stem. Few small, white flowers on long thin peduncles.
Distribution Native to tropical America, from Brazil to Mexico. Introduced to Africa, India and south-east Asia.
Cultivation Wild. Cultivated commercially by lifting it at harvest time and replanting a portion of the rhizome that has buds on it.
Constituents Starch; small quantities of gum and fibre.
Uses (starch, occasionally rhizome) Nutritive; demulcent.
The powdered rhizome was applied to poisonous bites and wounds in some tropical countries.
Of benefit as a soothing food-stuff following diarrhoea or illness. Once employed in pill manufacture, and in barium meals for X-ray of the gastro-intestinal system.
It may be candied as a sweet. It can also be used in cooking as a thickener.

Marrubium vulgare L LABIATAE
White Horehound
White Horehound has been used as a cough remedy from the time of the Egyptians to the present day. The herb is still included in the Austrian and Hungarian pharmacopoeias as an expectorant, and it remains a popular domestic and folk medicine. Wherever European emigrants have travelled they have taken this plant and grown it in herb and cottage gardens, thus widely distributing it. The generic name, *Marrubium*, was first used by Pliny and refers to the bitter taste; the common name is derived from the Old English *har hune* meaning a downy plant.
Description Faintly aromatic woody perennial, almost entire plant is woolly. Branched near the base; stems erect, nearly square, 30–60 cm tall, bearing wrinkled, dentate, ovate, opposite leaves 1.5–5 cm long; tomentose beneath and long-petioled. Flowers whitish, 5–8 mm long, numerous in axillary whorls; followed by nutlets. Appearing mid-summer to mid-autumn.
Distribution Native to southern and central Europe, North Africa, Asia; introduced elsewhere, often widespread. On dry grassland or pastures, field edges and wasteland, in warm situations.
Cultivation Wild. Cultivated commercially on a small scale by root division in mid-spring. May also be grown from seed sown in late spring, thinning to 30 cm apart, or from cuttings taken in summer.
Constituents Tannins; volatile oil, comprising marrubiol; mucilage; resin; sterols; a bitter principle, marrubin; vitamin C.
Uses (dried flowering plant, dried leaves) Expectorant; emmenagogue; weak diuretic; spasmolytic; weak diaphoretic.
Useful in many respiratory disorders, but specifically in bronchitis and coughs. Promotes bile flow and stimulates the appetite. Considered of benefit in disorders of the gall bladder and stomach, and acts as a stomach tonic. Formerly used to treat menstrual pain. Possesses some weak sedative action, suitable for use in conjunction with other herbs in nervous tachycardia.
May be applied externally to minor cuts and certain skin conditions. Laxative in large doses. Leaves may be used powdered as a bitter condiment, or whole as a tisane and in the manufacture of the confection, Horehound candy.

Matricaria recutita L COMPOSITAE
German Chamomile Wild Chamomile
German or Wild Chamomile was previously called *M. Chamomilla*, but in botanical terms it is not a true chamomile and it is also sometimes called Sweet False Chamomile. Although now considered slightly inferior to Roman Chamomile (*Chamaemelum nobile*) – even its aroma being somewhat less pronounced – there is no certainty which of the chamomiles was meant by the *chamaimelon* of Dioscorides. Today both *C. nobile* and *M. recutita* are used for similar purposes. The name, *Matricaria*, is either from the root word *mater* meaning mother or from *matrix*, the Latin for womb, after its use for treating female complaints.
Description Aromatic glabrous annual to 60 cm; stems erect, much-branched, bearing 2–3 pinnate leaves with almost filiform segments. Flower-heads pedunculate, single at branchlet apices. Flowers to 2 cm wide, ray florets (10–20) white; disc florets yellow; receptacle hollow and conical. Appearing early summer

to mid-autumn or sometimes later.
Distribution Indigenous to Europe, northern Asia, naturalized in North America; widespread on wasteland, farmland and in gardens.
Cultivation Wild. Cultivated and collected commercially in central Europe. Propagate from seed sown thinly in the autumn, or with less success in the spring.
Constituents Volatile oil (0.3–0.75%) comprising azulene (chamazulene), farnesene, α-bisabolol, sesquiterpenes, palustrine, quercetol, methoxycoumarin, furfural; also apigenin; salicylic acid; choline; phytosterol; triacontane; fatty acids and flavonic heterosides. The anti-inflammatory action is due mainly to α-bisabolol, but also to chamazulene; spasmolytic action due to dicyclic ether; antiseptic action due to several components.
Uses (dried flower-heads) Anti-inflammatory; antiseptic; antispasmodic; carminative. Of great benefit as an aromatic bitter for gastric disorders, promoting bile and gastric secretions and increasing the appetite. In large doses it is emetic.
Promotes sweating and is used to treat the common cold; a weak infusion acts as a tonic. Although formerly used to treat painful menstruation, it is not very effective.
May be applied as an antiseptic douche; used as a gargle for aphthous ulcers; applied to haemorrhoids; or used as a poultice or compress for cuts, bruises, ulcers and skin disorders.
A flavouring in certain alcoholic drinks. Employed as a tisane.
Widely employed as an anti-allergic agent in cosmetic preparations.
A constituent of some liquid and dry hair shampoos, and lotions. Highlights and lightens fair hair.

Medicago sativa L LEGUMINOSAE
Lucerne Alfalfa
The name, *Medicago*, is derived from Medea in North Africa where this important plant was thought to have originated.
Certainly the Arabs have used Lucerne fodder for centuries to feed their horses, and it has been in cultivation for so long that, like Flax, it exists in many different forms.
The plant was not known in north-west Europe until the seventeenth century however, when it was given the name *lucerna* meaning lamp, after the bright shiny appearance of the seeds. The specific name *sativa* means cultivated.
Lucerne has few traditional medicinal uses outside the veterinary field, but recent investigation has shown that it is of great nutritional importance and contains, for example, four times as much vitamin C as citrus juice, measured weight for weight.
Description Glabrous perennial 30 cm–1 m; on deep, thick taproot; much-branched stem often forming dense bushy growth. Leaves pinnate, with 3 denticulate leaflets to 3 cm long, obovate-oblong. Flowers 1.5–3 cm long, violet-blue, on axillary racemes, appearing late summer to mid-autumn; followed by pubescent spiralled seed pod.
Distribution Originally native to mediterranean region and western Asia; naturalized in North America. Now worldwide in distribution, especially on dry, light or chalky soils.
Cultivation Wild as an escape. Many strains exist and the form of the plant depends on the variety grown. Very widely cultivated as fodder and for commercial purposes. Seed sown in late spring after risk of frost has passed, preferably on calcareous loam, which is free of weeds and prepared to a fine tilth. When grown commercially, seed is usually inoculated with a specific nitrogen-fixing root nodule bacterium to ensure growth. Replace after 5–7 years. Very drought resistant.
Constituents Protein (16%); fat (3%); vitamins C, B_1, B_2, D, E, K_1; provitamin A; several mineral salts, including potassium, calcium and phosphorus; choline; trimethylamine; betaine; alfafa saponin; an alkaloid, stachydrine; a bitter principle; a hormonal

substance, coumestrol.
Uses (fresh or dried leaf, occasionally seed) Nutritive; diuretic; anti-haemorrhagic.
The seed was once used by Indians as an abortifacient. Of benefit as a tonic and nutritive herb; an infusion taken regularly promotes appetite and leads to weight increase. A very rich source of vitamin C, when used fresh.
May be applied externally to aid wound healing.
Used as a beverage.
The leaf is employed as a salad herb, or cooked as a vegetable.
The seed is sprouted indoors and eaten as a rich source of vitamins and amino-acids.
Of considerable veterinary importance as a food-stuff; in cows it increases milk yield. One of the major commercial sources of chlorophyll; also a source of vitamin K_1.
The seed provides a yellow dye. Formerly used as a diluent to adjust the strength of powdered medicinal plants such as *Digitalis*.

Melaleuca leucadendron L MYRTACEAE
Cajuput Tree Punk Tree
Cajuput oil is extracted by steam distillation from the leaves of a number of related Australasian trees or shrubs, all of which are members of the Bottle Brush group. *Melaleuca leucadendron* is the most important commercial source. The characteristic flowering spike with its numerous long creamy-white stamens led to the specific name *leucadendron* meaning white tree, while *melaleuca* is from the Greek for black and white, after the trunk and bark colours of one of the species.
The word Cajuput is derived directly from the local Malaysian name *kayu-puti* which means white wood – another reference to the colour. The oil was first noticed by Rumphius in the

late seventeenth century who described the use of the plant by Malaysians.
Lochner, a physician to the German Emperor, and von Wittneben, promoted its use in the early eighteenth century particularly in Germany, where it was called *Oleum Wittnebianum*.
Description Large tree with spongy, shiny and peeling bark; branches usually pendulous, bearing oblong tapering strongly-veined leaves, 1.5–2 cm wide and 5–10 cm long. Flowers creamy white, small, with numerous stamens extending 15 mm, borne on terminal spikes to 15 cm long, which themselves terminate in a tuft of leaves; followed by brown capsules.
Distribution Native to Australasia and Malaysia; introduced elsewhere in tropical situations, especially swamps.
Cultivation Wild. Limited cultivation; propagate from cuttings.
Constituents Oil comprising cineole (60%), terpineol, l-pinene, aldehydes, including those of benzoic, valeric and butyric acids.
Uses (oil, occasionally leaves and twigs) Carminative; antispasmodic; antiseptic; stimulant; rubefacient; antihelmintic; expectorant.
Formerly used internally in the treatment of chronic bronchitis and tuberculosis (the oil is excreted via the lungs), as a gastro-intestinal antiseptic, and for the removal of roundworms. Of benefit internally in some digestive disorders. Used externally in stimulant-rubbing oils for rheumatic pain; in various liniments; to treat scabies; and in tooth cavities to relieve pain.
A tea is made from the leaves.
Oil and leaves repel insects.
Contra-indications All essential oils should be used only in very small quantities.

Melilotus alba Medic. LEGUMINOSAE
White Melilot White Sweet Clover/ Bokhara Clover
This is the taller of the common melilots and although of little benefit to man directly it is of great importance as an agricultural fodder crop, honey plant and cover crop for green manuring. Spoiled White Sweet Clover may sometimes cause cattle poisoning due to the presence of large quantities of dicoumarol, which delays blood coagulation and leads to severe, often internal, haemorrhage. Evidence suggests the cultivated races of the herb have lower concentrations of dicoumarol.
Description Sweet smelling erect, branched, annual or biennial from 1–2.5 m tall. Stems ribbed longitudinally, glabrous, bearing pinnate leaves with oblong, denticulate leaflets 1.8–4 cm long. Flowers white, honey-scented, small (4 mm long), numerous, on long thin, erect, terminal racemes; appearing midsummer to early autumn and followed by small pods.

Distribution Native to Asia and Europe. Naturalized in North America, especially the eastern states; varieties introduced elsewhere. In weedy wastelands, especially on stony and nitrogenous soils in sunny situations.
Cultivation Wild. An annual variety of this, herb, *M. alba* var. *annua* Coe, also called Hubam Clover, developed as a drought-resistant, high weight yielding fodder and honey yielding crop, is grown worldwide – from seed sown in spring.
Constituents Coumarin and related substances; occasionally dicoumarol (melitoxin); fixed oil. Dicoumarol acts as a vitamin K antagonist, thus reducing prothrombin synthesis which delays blood coagulation.
Uses (cured fresh plant, occasionally flowering plant) Nutritive; aromatic; stimulant; vulnerary.
Rarely used medicinally, but used in Central America as a stimulant. May be employed in ointments to promote the healing of skin complaints. Possesses weak antibacterial activity. Formerly used homeopathically.
Of greatest importance as cattle fodder, and honey plant.

Melilotus officinalis (L) Pall. LEGUMINOSAE
Common Melilot Yellow Sweet Clover
This member of the Laburnum family (which is also called Wild Laburnum) is a very old medicinal plant from which an antithrombotic preparation is now made commercially. It is also of commercial importance as a flavouring for cheese and tobacco and was once used in beer manufacture. Its botanical name, *Melilotus*, means honey-lotus or honey clover, and reflects the sweetness of its nectar. The hay-like smell of the substance coumarin develops only when the plant is dried, and it was for this aromatic property that Common Melilot was once used as a strewing herb.
Known to the apothecaries as *corona regis*, or the kings crown, it is not now used very widely.
Description Straggly biennial to 130 cm; stems glabrous or pubescent, ribbed, erect or decumbent, branched. Bearing trifoliate leaves, and obovate or oblanceolate, 1–2 cm long, denticulate leaflets. Flowers yellow, honey-scented, small (4–6 mm long) borne on long, narrow axillary racemes, appearing midsummer to early autumn.
Distribution Eurasian native; naturalized in North America. Especially on nitrogenous wasteland, embankments and fields.
Cultivation Wild plant. Collected commercially.
Constituents Coumarin and related substances, released on drying; a glycoside, melilotoside; fixed oil; melilotic acid.
Uses (dried flowering plant) Aromatic; carminative; expectorant; antithrombotic; antispasmodic; antibiotic.
Formerly used in a wide range of conditions.

May be taken regularly to help prevent thrombosis; also to treat bronchial catarrh and flatulence. Externally applied to wounds and skin inflammations and can be used with care on inflamed eyes. The seeds possess antibiotic activity.
Formerly used in herb beer; flowers and seeds used to flavour Gruyère cheese, snuff and smoking tobacco.
May be employed in some meat dishes, for example, rabbit.
Limited cosmetic use where hay-like aroma is required. Repels moths and is used to protect clothes.
Contra-indications Large doses are emetic.

Melissa officinalis L LABIATAE
Balm Lemon Balm/Common Balm
Although Balm has been cultivated in the mediterranean region for over 2000 years, it was for almost half this period considered important only as a bee plant, and until the fifteenth century was known as either *melissophyllon*, Greek for bee leaf, or *apiastrum*, Latin for bee plant. Its modern botanical name, *Melissa*, reflects this early association.
The Arabs introduced it as a medicinal herb specifically of benefit in anxiety or depression, and it has been used as a sedative or tonic tea ever since. Balm has frequently been incorporated in proprietary cordials or liqueurs, and its popularity in France led to its name *Thé de France*. Balm is an abbreviation for balsam after its sweet aroma, but this aroma is rapidly lost, together with much of its therapeutic value, on drying and storing.
Description Sweet-smelling perennial, on slightly hairy square stem, branching near the top, from 30–80 cm. Leaves opposite, petiolate, ovate, greenish-yellow, dentate or crenate-dentate, to 7.5 cm long; lemon scented. Flowers whitish, occasionally pinkish or yellow; small (0.75–1.5 cm long) in scanty axillary clusters; appearing late summer to mid-autumn.
Distribution Native to southern Europe; mediterranean region; central Europe; introduced and widespread in northern temperate zones, often as a garden escape. Especially common on nutrient-rich soils in sunny position.
Cultivation Wild. Cultivated commercially and horticulturally; from seed sown in mid to late spring (slow germination) or by root division in spring or autumn. Prefers rich, moist soil in sunny position with some shade; some shelter required in cooler climates, as it is susceptible to frost. A variegated form exists.
Constituents (fresh plant) Essential oil (0.1%) comprising citral, linalol, citronellal and geraniol; tannins (5%); a bitter principle; resin; succinic acid.
Uses (fresh or dried leaves, occasionally flowering tops, oil) Carminative; diaphoretic; antispasmodic; sedative.
Of use in aromatic waters or as a tea for the treatment of minor gastric disturbances, nausea and headaches. Also used in conjunction with other remedies to treat nervous tachycardia and restlessness. Some hypotensive action. Fresh leaf is soothing when rubbed on insect bites.
Oil once used alone as a diaphoretic, but is slightly toxic.
Wide culinary potential where delicate lemon flavour is required.
An important constituent of several liqueurs, including Benedictine and Chartreuse. Useful in wine cups and cold drinks. Taken alone as a tisane.
A useful bee plant.
May be used in pot-pourris, herb pillows, and in herb mixtures for aromatic baths.

Mentha aquatica L LABIATAE
Water Mint
A very variable plant which is sometimes considered to exist in distinct varieties. This species hybridizes readily with other mints, producing a large array of varieties.
It is strong-smelling and not as pleasant as most common mints, although in the Middle Ages Water Mint (then called *menastrum*) was used as a strewing herb. The related *Mentha spicata* L is used as a commercial source of oil of Spearmint.
Description Strong-smelling perennial; variable in form. Angular, glabrous or pubescent, much-branched stem to 1 m, on stolons. Leaves opposite, serrate, decussate, ovate, petiolate, and rather crisp; 2–6 cm long. Flowers lilac or red, in rounded terminal inflorescence, 4 cm diameter, with usually only 1 (rarely 2) axillary whorls of flowers beneath this. Appearing late summer to late autumn.
Distribution Native to Europe and naturalized in many northern temperate zones. On wet soils, beside streams, in ditches and on regularly flooded land.
Cultivation Wild. May be propagated by stolon division in spring. Plant in water or keep very wet.
Constituents Volatile oil (poco oil, to 0.85%) comprising menthofuran, linalol acetate, limonene, L-carvol; also betaine; choline; succinic acid; glucose; menthyl pentose; dotricontane; aquaticol; tannins.
Uses (fresh herb, occasionally root bark and oil) Carminative; antispasmodic; cholagogue; slightly astringent.
Of benefit as a warm infusion in disturbances of the gastro-intestinal system, particularly diarrhoea, and intestinal spasms. Also useful in the treatment of the common cold and in painful menstruation. In Africa the root bark is employed in the treatment of diarrhoea and colds.
May be taken as a tisane.
May be employed with discretion in scented articles.
Once used as a strewing herb.
Contra-indications Large doses may be emetic.

Mentha x *piperita* L LABIATAE

Peppermint

Peppermint is now one of the best known of all herbs, but it was not definitely recorded until 1696 when the botanist, Ray, published a brief description of a pepper-tasting mint which had, near to that date, first been observed by Dr Eales in Hertfordshire, England.

In his *Historia plantarum* (1704) Ray called the mint Peper-mint or *Mentha palustris*, and although the latter correctly refers to the marsh-loving nature of the plant, no satisfactory explanation can be given for his erroneous description of the plant's taste; the common name has nevertheless been retained. Peppermint's medicinal value was soon recognized and within 25 years of its description the herb was included in the London Pharmacopoeia – it is still retained in many national pharmacopoeias.

Botanically the herb represents a hybrid between *M. spicata* and *M. aquatica* and by some authorities is thought to exist as two main varietal forms called Black (*forma rubescens*), and White (*forma pallescens*) Peppermints.

Description Aromatic perennial on root-stock producing runners. Stem square, erect, somewhat branched above, slightly hairy, either purple (Black Peppermint) or much less so (White Peppermint), from 30 cm–1 m tall; variable. Bearing petiolate green or purple-green, lanceolate, or ovate-lanceolate, acute, deeply dentate leaves, 4–8 cm long and 1–2.5 cm wide. Flowers mauve (occasionally white) irregularly arranged on a conical terminal spike 3–7.5 cm long; appearing late summer to mid-autumn.

Distribution European native; widely distributed and often naturalized. In sunny or partially shady conditions on rich damp soils; hedgerows, ditches and it is also found near habitation.

Cultivation Wild only as an escape, and seldom established permanently. Cultivated commercially and horticulturally in many parts of the world. Divide stolons in autumn and replant 30 cm apart, 5 cm deep. Water well in ordinary garden situations; replace after 5 years. Does not breed true if raised from seed.

Constituents Volatile oil (to 2%) comprising menthol (50%), menthone, menthyl isovalerate, cineole, jasmone, phellandrene, amyl alcohol, acetaldehyde, cadinene; tannins; bitter compounds.

Uses (fresh or dried plant, oil) Aromatic stimulant; carminative; antiseptic; antispasmodic; anti-inflammatory; cholagogue.

May be employed in a variety of gastro-intestinal disorders where its antispasmodic, anti-flatulent and appetite-promoting actions are required. Particularly useful in nervous headaches and agitation. Used in conjunction with other remedies for the common cold. Both the herb and the oil may be used externally in baths to treat cuts and skin rashes.

Wide cosmetic, dental and confectionery use of the oil where a mint flavouring or cold-taste is required.

Well-known culinary uses.

Also employed to flavour some liqueurs.

Contra-indications The oil may cause allergic reactions.

Mentha x *piperita* var. *citrata* (Ehr.) Briq. LABIATAE

Bergamot Mint Eau de Cologne Mint/ Orange Mint

This mint is one of the most attractively scented of all herbs and should occupy a place in every herb garden. The aroma is, however, somewhat intangible and it is variously described as lemon, orange, bergamot, lavender and eau de Cologne mint – the latter being the most widely used. Its former botanical name, *M. odorata*, is therefore rather more accurate than the present one, which suggests only a lemon scent.

Description Very aromatic decumbent, glabrous perennial from 30–60 cm tall, on overground leafy stolons. Stems branched, bearing dark green, purple-tinged, smooth, ovate or elliptic, petiolate leaves 1.5–4 cm long. Mauve flowers in rounded dense terminal spikes or in upper leaf axils, appearing from mid to late autumn.

Distribution European native, naturalized elsewhere. On rich, moist soils in conditions of partial shade.

Cultivation Wild. Cultivated horticulturally by division of stolons in spring; planting 5 cm deep.

Constituents Volatile oil.

Uses (fresh or dried leaves) Not used medicinally. Used sparingly in tisanes, jellies, cold drinks, or salads.

May be employed in a range of scented and cosmetic articles.

Mentha pulegium L LABIATAE

Pennyroyal Pudding Grass

Pennyroyal was held in very high repute for many centuries throughout Europe and was the most popular of all the members of the mint family, being used both for a wide range of medicinal purposes and in various ancient ceremonies.

Pliny is regarded as the originator of its name *pulegium* which is derived from *pulex* meaning flea, since both the fresh plant and the smoke from the burning leaves were used to eradicate the insects.

This association with fleas has been retained in the botanical name given to the plant by Linnaeus. Before his scientific classification the superficial appearance and unusual aroma of the herb led to it being considered as a thyme. *Puliol* was an old French name for thyme and this plant was designated the royal thyme – hence *puliol royale* and thus the corruption, Pennyroyal. The modern French name is *la menthe Pouliot* – from *puliol*. Although long considered an abortifacient, it has been found that this effect is usually only possible with a dose of the oil which is highly toxic and leads to irreversible kidney damage.

The plant can therefore be used as a flavouring agent, but only when the concentration of pulegone does not exceed 20 mg in 1 kg of the final product being flavoured.

The American Pennyroyal (*Hedeoma pulegioides* (L) Pers.) has similar properties and uses.

Description Aromatic perennial with much branched prostrate or erect stems to 30 cm tall; on overground runners. Leaves dark green, slightly hairy, petiolate, oblong or oval crenate or serrate, 0.8–2 cm long. Flowers mauve-blue, in rounded dense axillary whorls, along upper half of the stem. Appearing late summer to early autumn.

Distribution Native to Europe, North Africa and western Asia; introduced elsewhere. On nutrient-rich, moist but sandy soils. Prefers sunny situations.

Cultivation Wild. Commercial cultivation

limited. Grown horticulturally; the prostrate form as a lawn (var. *decumbens*) or for aromatic ground cover. Sow seed in late spring under glass in cool zones, planting out in early summer on open, friable, loamy soil 15–20 cm apart. Keep well watered in dry weather, and protect from hard frosts. Propagate also by root division in autumn or spring, or from cuttings taken in the summer.
Constituents Volatile oil (0.5–1%) comprising a ketone, pulegone (80–90%), to which the action is largely due; also menthone; β-caryophyllene; methylcyclohexanol; iso-menthone; tannins.
Uses (fresh or dried flowering plant) Emmenagogue; antispasmodic; carminative.
May be used in minor gastric disturbances, flatulence, nausea, headache, and menstrual

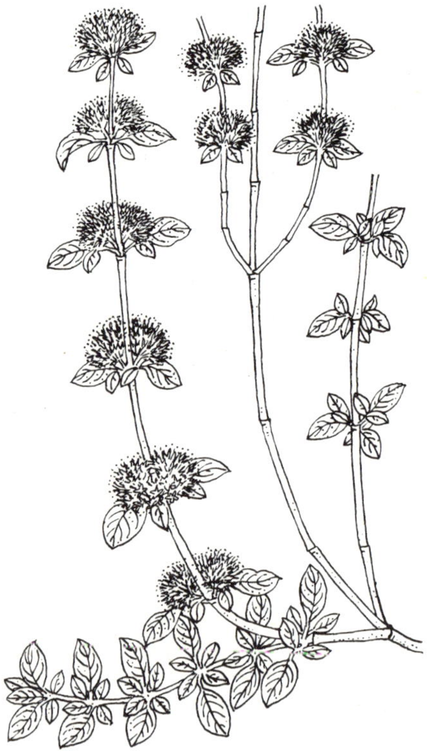

pain. In combination with other remedies it is of benefit at the onset of the common cold. Fresh leaves may be applied externally to skin irritations and insect bites, as it acts as a rubefacient.
May be taken, weak, as a tea (Organy tea). Formerly used as a flavouring in puddings.
Useful in scented articles, particularly clothes drawer sachets.
The oil may be used in cosmetics as an insect repellent.
In the eastern mediterranean region it has been used as a dye plant.
Contra-indications Somewhat irritant to the genito-urinary tract possibly causing reflex uterine movements; not to be used in pregnancy, or in kidney disease.
May cause contact dermatitis.

Mentha rotundifolia (L) Huds. LABIATAE
Apple Mint Round-leaved Mint
Apple Mint is so-called simply because its aroma is a combination of mint and apples. It is more subtle than most mints and may therefore be employed far more widely in the kitchen.
Bowles Mint (also sometimes incorrectly called Apple Mint) is a hybrid between this species and *M. spicata*, but is usually known as *M. rotundifolia* 'Bowles Variety. An attractive variegated form of Apple Mint is commonly grown as a garden ornamental.
Description Aromatic pubescent perennial on

leafy stolons, bearing erect, somewhat branched, thin stems to 90 cm. Leaves green, white and velvety beneath, sessile, oblong to round, crenate-serrate, 3–10 cm long. Flowers white, cream to pink, on dense irregularly flowered, somewhat pointed terminal spikes, from 3–6 cm long; appearing early to mid-autumn.
Distribution European native; widely naturalized; on damp soils in ditches and waste places.
Cultivation Wild. Widely cultivated horticulturally. Propagate by stolon division in autumn.
Constituents Volatile oil; tannins.
Uses (fresh leaf) Not used medicinally.
Many culinary uses, including meat and fish, egg dishes, fruit dishes, jellies, hot and cold beverages, sauces and vinegars.
Once used in confectionery manufacture.

Mentha spicata L LABIATAE
Spearmint Garden Mint/Pea Mint
Spearmint was formerly known as *Mentha viridis* L; the specific name *viridis* meaning green emphasized the bright green colour of the herb. The modern botanical name, and the common name, reflect the spear or spike-like shape of both the inflorescence and the leaves. In the sixteenth century the plant was called Spere mynte and even then, as today, it was the most commonly used of all mints.
The Romans were responsible for its distribution throughout north and west Europe.
Besides important culinary and flavouring uses it is still retained in the Hungarian Pharmacopoeia for its medical use.
Description Aromatic nearly glabrous perennial on leafy underground stolons. Stems erect, square, somewhat branched, from 30–60 cm tall. Leaves smooth and green, opposite, almost sessile, lanceolate or ovate-lanceolate and curled, margin deeply serrate, to 6 cm long. Flowers pale lilac, on cylindrical, irregularly flowered terminal spikes 5–10 cm long, appearing early autumn.
Distribution Native to southern Europe. Widely naturalized, especially in damp, shady sites near habitation.
Cultivation Wild. Very widely cultivated commercially and as a garden plant. Propagate from stolon division in the autumn; plant 5 cm

deep and water well. Replace after 4 years. Rarely grown from seed since it does not breed true.
Constituents Volatile oil comprising menthol, carvone, limonene; vitamin A; tannins.
Uses (fresh or dried leaf, oil) Carminative; aromatic; antispasmodic; weak emmenagogue.
Similar uses to Peppermint.
Wide culinary use in sauces, jellies, hot and cold beverages, and for garnishing and general flavouring.
The oil is used as a flavouring agent in toiletries and confectionery.

Menyanthes trifoliata L MENYANTHACEAE
Buckbean Marsh Trefoil/Bog Bean
Menyanthes is the old Greek name for an attractive and distinctive herb, common locally and sometimes extensive in shallow water in many cooler parts of the northern hemisphere. Its Greek name means flower of the month, which reflects not only the duration of its beautiful shaggy flowers, but also its beneficial effects on menstrual pain. At one time Buckbean was considered in Germany to be a panacea and was used to treat many ailments from gout to scurvy and rheumatism. The Swedes, Norwegians, Icelanders and Scots also particularly favoured this bitter tasting plant. It is now generally considered to be a useful substitute for Gentian Root.
The common name, Bog Bean, is less than 200 years old and is derived from the German *Bocksbohnen* meaning goat's beans, which in English became Buckbean.
Description Glabrous, aquatic perennial on black, creeping, thick horizontal root-stock; bearing alternate, basal, trifoliate leaves with pale prominent midribs, sheathing at the base,

on petioles to 25 cm high. Petioles thicker at the base and surrounded by bracts. Leaflets obovate or oblong, entire, sessile, terminal, 4–7.5 cm long, dark green. Flowers white; pinkish or purplish externally with shaggy petals, 15 mm long, 10–15 per terminal raceme on long scapes; appearing early to mid-summer.

Distribution Native to northern temperate zones, from North America to Siberia including Iceland and Greenland. In ditches, fresh-water marsh and bog, reed-beds and meadows which are always wet and consist of acidic, peaty soils.

Cultivation Wild plant. May be grown as a pond or bog plant by division of root-stock in spring or autumn.

Constituents A glycoside, menyanthin; bitter principles, loganine, sweroside, meliatine; flavone heterosides; inulin; vitamin C; choline; resin; malic acid.

Uses (dried leaves, occasionally dried whole plant) Bitter tonic; emmenagogue; stomachic. The fresh plant was formerly used as a cathartic. Now of greatest benefit as a gastro-intestinal tonic; stimulates gastric and biliary secretions, and hence promotes appetite. It has a direct beneficial effect on the liver; it is of

value in amenorrhoea, and possesses some anti-helmintic activity. The root has been used externally to treat obstinate skin complaints. Leaves once used in brewing and baking and may be taken as a tonic tea.

Leaves used as a tobacco substitute.

Contra-indications Not to be used in the treatment of diarrhoea. Large doses of the whole plant may cause vomiting and diarrhoea.

Monarda didyma L LABIATAE

Red Bergamot Bee Balm/Oswego Tea

Red Bergamot has become widely cultivated as a garden ornamental for its combination of orange scent and attractive flowers. It is called Bergamot because of its scent which resembles that of a Bergamot orange. Several varieties now exist of which the best-known is Cambridge Scarlet; other types are salmon, rose, purple, or white in colour – but the wild, red *M. didyma* is the most aromatic.

Red Bergamot belongs to the *Monarda* or Horsemint genus, named after the sixteenth-century Spanish medical botanist Nicholas de Monardes, and is closely related to Wild or Purple Bergamot (*M. fistulosa* L) which is also called Oswego Tea – and which has long been used by American Indians for medicinal purposes. Oswego derives its name from the Oswego River district near Lake Ontario in the United States where the herb grew in abundance and from where most supplies originally came. After the Boston Tea Party, 1773, a protest at the tea duty imposed on the colonies, Oswego Tea replaced Indian tea in many American households.

Description Aromatic, usually glabrous perennial from 40–100 cm tall; stems erect, acutely quadrangular, bearing opposite, serrate, ovate to ovate-lanceolate dark green, often red-tinged, leaves to 15 cm long. Flowers scarlet-red, 4–5 cm long, usually in solitary terminal whorls, with slightly hairy calyx. Appearing late summer to mid-autumn.

Distribution North American native, from Ontario to Georgia; naturalized in South America. On moist nutrient-rich soils preferring shade but tolerating full sun; especially deciduous woodland.

Cultivation Wild. Cultivated throughout the world as a horticultural plant; occasionally wild as an escape. Many horticultural forms exist. Propagate from seed sown in spring or by root division in spring; succeeds best on light soils and may be a vigorous grower. Cut back each autumn and replace after 3 years.

Constituents Volatile oil comprising compounds related to thymol; tannic acid.

Uses (fresh or dried flowering plant; sometimes root and oil) Carminative; stimulant; rubefacient; weak diaphoretic; weak emmenagogue; expectorant.

May be used as a tea to relieve nausea, flatulence, menstrual pain, vomiting and, with less success, headaches and colds. It is also taken internally and by inhalation of the water vapour (pouring on boiling water) for bronchial catarrh and sore throats.

Formerly used externally as an ointment for skin problems.

May be taken as a tea, and used sparingly in salads.

Useful in a very wide range of scented articles.

Once an ingredient of hair preparations. The oil is sometimes used in perfumery.

Morus nigra L MORACEAE

Mulberry Black or Common Mulberry

Morus and *morarius* were the classical Latin names for the Mulberry and come from the Latin verb meaning to delay after the tree's habit of delaying spring bud formation until the cold weather had passed. The Greeks knew it as both *moron* and *sukamnos* – from its sweetness; the fruit being only slightly less sweet than the sweetest fruits known to them, namely

the fig, grape and cherry. Until the fifteenth century *M. nigra* was important as a medicinal plant, and its leaves were used for silkworm rearing, but after this date it was mostly replaced by the oriental species *M. alba* L. The tree is now becoming quite scarce in parts of Europe.

Description Bushy tree to 10 m; branches dark coloured, bearing thick, alternate, cordate-ovate, pointed leaves, 5–20 cm long; margins serrate, somewhat variable. Flowers unisexual catkins; the female, numerous, consisting of green perianths and 2 stigmas. Fruit to 3 cm long, purplish red.

Distribution Native to western Asia, Persia and the Caucasus; introduced to other temperate zones.

Cultivation Wild. Cultivated as a fruit-tree in areas that are protected from cold winds and frost. Propagate from cuttings taken in early spring or by layering in autumn. Slow growing. Requires a loamy soil in warm position.

Constituents (fruit) Sugar (10%); malic acid

(2%); pectin; gum; vitamin C.
Uses (fresh fruit, root bark and occasionally leaves) Nutritive; laxative; antipyretic; anthelmintic.
Until recently the leaves were employed in the Balkans as an hypoglycaemic agent for use in diabetes. The root bark was formerly used as a cathartic and to remove tapeworms.
Once used to colour medicines.
Now usually employed as a food, and in the home manufacture of wines, jams, and conserves.
May be used as a dyestuff.

Myrica cerifera L MYRICACEAE
Wax Myrtle Bayberry/Candleberry
Both the specific and common names of this fragrant North American plant indicate the fine yellow or light green wax (strictly an edible fat) which is produced on the berries as they ripen. This substance, called bayberry tallow or myrica wax, was once widely collected on the East Coast of the United States and was used in soap and candle manufacture. Related members of the *Myrica* genus are used throughout the world for various domestic and medicinal purposes; in South Africa, for example, *M. cordifolia* L is both a source of berry wax and a valuable anti-diarrhoeic remedy. *M. cerifera* is now unused outside folk medicine except as a constituent of some proprietary domestic cold cures such as Composition Powders.
Description Fragrant perennial evergreen (occasionally semi-deciduous or deciduous) dioecious shrub (1–3 m) or evergreen tree (to 10 m), much branched with pubescent, somewhat rough branchlets bearing glandular, entire or occasionally serrulate oblong-lanceolate to lanceolate, acute leaves 3–7.5 cm long. Flowers consist of short, conical or globular scaly catkins, either sterile or fertile; followed by grey, waxy, spherical, 1-seeded berries. Appearing late spring to mid-summer.
Distribution North American native, especially on the East Coast from New Jersey to Florida. On poor, sandy, well-drained soils, but frequently near swamps or marshland. In coniferous woodland and thickets near the sea.
Cultivation Wild.
Constituents (berries) Myrica wax, comprising glycerides of palmitic, stearic and myristic acids; lauric acid; unsaturated fatty acids.
(root bark) Volatile oil; tannic acid; gallic acid; an acrid resin, myricinic acid; an astringent resin; gum; starch. Action largely due to the resin content.
Uses (root bark, berries' wax, occasionally fresh leaves) Astringent; weak diaphoretic; tonic; sialogogue. Principally employed as a gargle, douche and poultice in the treatment of sore throats, leucorrhoea and ulcers respectively. May be used internally for mucous colitis, diarrhoea, the common cold and feverish conditions. Powdered bark formerly taken as a snuff in the treatment of nasal catarrh. Small pieces of bark may be chewed to promote salivation, aid gingivitis, and reduce toothache.
Once taken as a tonic tea.
Wax used in candle and soap manufacture.
Contra-indications Large doses emetic; may cause flatulence.

Myrica gale L MYRICACEAE
Bog Myrtle Sweet Gale
Bog Myrtle was once one of the many important herbs used in northern Europe to flavour beer, and was both widely collected and protected by law.
The herb's ability to repel and destroy insects, such as fleas, led to the now obsolete common name Flea Wood, and the plants' domestic employment in mattresses and linen drawers. Small quantities can be used as a flavouring in meat dishes.
Description Deciduous shrub to 1.5 m tall; branchlets reddish and growing almost vertically, bearing grey-green oblanceolate, glandular-pubescent, aromatic, obtuse leaves 3–6 cm long. Brown and yellowish-green unisexual flowers borne in dense apical catkins to 15 mm long; appearing late spring to early summer, and followed by numerous small flattened berries.
Distribution Native to north-west Europe; north America as far south as Virginia; Asia. Introduced elsewhere. Especially in thickets on wet heathland or fens. To 600 m altitude.
Cultivation Wild. May be propagated from suckers, by division or from cuttings. Requires a damp, acidic soil in a shady position.
Constituents (berries) Myrtle or Myrica wax; similar to *M. cerifera* (Wax Myrtle). (leaves) Aromatic volatile oil.
Uses (berries' wax, occasionally leaves and bark) Aromatic; insecticide.
Formerly used externally to treat scabies.
Dried leaves may be employed with discretion as a spice in soups and stews. Berries can be similarly used.
Leaves formerly flavoured beer (Gale beer), and may also be used as a tea.
Wax may be used in the manufacture of aromatic candles. Roots and stem bark dye wool yellow.
Repels fleas and may thus be used in scented sachets.

Myristica fragrans Houtt. MYRISTICACEAE
Mace Nutmeg
The early history of the use of Mace (the outer covering of the seed of the plant) and Nutmeg (the seed itself) is not known with certainty, but it is improbable that these spices were used by the Greeks and Romans. By the sixth century, however, both Indians and Arabs were obtaining them from the Far East, and they were known in Europe by 1191. In that year they were one of several fumigant strewing aromatics used in the streets of Rome during the coronation of Emperor Henry VI.
Around 1300 an Arabian writer, Kazwini, had named the Molucca Islands as the source of both materials, but it was not until 1506 to 1512 that the Portugese took possession of the Islands and began a spice monopoly which was to be continued by the Dutch and English until the beginning of the nineteenth century.
It has been recognized for centuries that moderate doses of Nutmeg cause a feeling of unreality and visual illusions. These effects have now been shown to be caused by a proto-alkaloidal constituent, myristicin, which is a psychotropic with structural similarities to mescaline – found in the Peyote Cactus.

Description Tall, dioecious, bushy, glabrous, evergreen tree to 12 m. Leaves yellowish, coriaceous, petiolate elliptic – or oblong-lanceolate, 5–12 cm long. Flowers 6 mm long, in axillary umbels; followed by nearly globular or pear-shaped, red or yellow, pedunculous fruit which splits on maturing to release the ovoid seed (Nutmeg) surrounded by a scarlet aril (Mace).
Distribution Indigenous to the Molucca Islands; introduced and widespread in the tropics. Frequently on volcanic soils in shade and high humidity.
Cultivation Wild; now cultivated in East and West Indies, Zanzibar, Brazil, Ceylon and India. Trees first produce seed in ninth or tenth year of growth and may last 80 years. Outside the tropics may be grown as an ornamental hothouse plant, in humus-enriched soil with high ambient temperature and humidity.
Propagate from woody cuttings in a peat and sand mix.
Constituents (kernel) Volatile oil (5–15%) comprising eugenol and iso-eugenol; fixed oil (25–40%) yielding nutmeg butter and comprising myristic acid (60%), oleic, palmitic, lauric and linoleic acids; also terpineol, borneol and terpenes.
Action mainly due to volatile oil, acting as a carminative.
Uses (seed, aril, occasionally oil) Carminative; aromatic; stimulant.
Used in small doses to reduce flatulence, aid digestion, improve the appetite and to treat diarrhoea, vomiting and nausea.
Both Mace and Nutmeg may be used in a range of sweet and savoury food-stuffs. Mace is less strongly aromatic, and Nutmeg particularly complements milk and cheese dishes.
The oil is employed as a flavouring agent and in some rubefacient liniments and hair lotions.
Contra-indications POISONOUS. Use very sparingly. Even moderate doses overstimulate the motor cortex causing disorientation, double vision, hallucination, tachycardia, and possibly epileptiform convulsions.

Myrrhis odorata (L) Scop. UMBELLIFERAE
Sweet Cicely British Myrrh
Sweet Cicely was once cultivated as a pot shrub in Europe. It is among the first garden herbs to emerge after winter and is almost the last to die down, and it was therefore considered a useful plant. Its aniseed-like aroma is responsible for the botanical name – *myrrhis* meaning perfume, and *odorata* meaning fragrant, while many of its common names are prefixed 'sweet' because of the taste of the leaf. Until the sixteenth century it was known as Seseli, a name first used by Dioscorides although not necessarily for this particular species.
Description Strongly smelling hirsute-pubescent perennial on grooved, hollow, branching stems 60–100 cm tall. Leaves bright green, pale beneath, soft, thin, 2 or 3-pinnate to 30 cm long, with oblong-ovate, narrow-toothed segments. Stem-leaf petioles sheathing. Flowers small, white, in umbels 1–5 cm diameter, appearing early to mid-spring; followed by large (2–2.5 cm long) ridged brown fruit.
Distribution European native. Introduced to some temperate regions, locally naturalized. On grassy soils, in hedgerows, often in mountainous regions; prefers shady sites, but tolerates full sun.
Cultivation Wild. Cultivated commercially on a small scale in Western Europe, and elsewhere as a garden herb. Propagate from seed sown in mid or late spring on well-drained, but humus-rich, soil in partial shade; transplant to 45 cm

apart. Taproots may be lifted, cut into sections each having a bud, and replanted 5 cm deep in either spring or autumn. Often self-sown and may become rampant when established.
Constituents Essential oil, comprising anethole.
Uses (fresh or dried leaf, occasionally seed and root) Weak diuretic; tonic; hypotensive; weak antiseptic. Rarely used medicinally. Once an ingredient of wound-healing ointments. May be used as a sugar substitute by diabetics.
Fresh leaf and chopped green seed may be used in salads; leaves may be boiled as a vegetable or added to soups. They may also be used as a sugar substitute in sweet conserves and tart fruit dishes.
Roots were once boiled, cooled, and eaten in salads.
A useful honey plant.
An anise flavouring used in certain liqueurs.

Myrtus communis (L) Herm. MYRTACEAE
Myrtle Common Myrtle
Myrtle is frequently mentioned in the Old Testament, the writings of ancient poets and in the works of the Greeks and the Romans, to whom it was known as *myrtos*. *Myrtus* is directly derived from this old name, while *communis* means common.
It was almost certainly because the aromatic leaves bear a resemblance to the female pudenda that Myrtle has been dedicated to Venus, that it has been considered as an aphrodisiac, and carried by Israeli brides, for example, at their weddings.
Every part of the shrub is highly scented and in southern Europe it is used in a number of home-made cosmetic recipes.
Description Aromatic evergreen shrub 1–3 m high; occasionally taller. Highly branched, bearing glossy dark green, opposite, entire, acute, ovate to lanceolate leaves, 3–5 cm long and dotted with transparent oil glands. Petioles short. Flowers pure white, but often rose coloured, very fragrant, 5-petalled to 2 cm wide, numerous golden stamens; on long thin pedicels in pairs in leaf axils; appearing mid to late summer and followed by 12-mm diameter bluish berries.
Distribution Native to mediterranean region and western Asia, growing to 800 m altitude; introduced elsewhere.
Cultivation Wild. Cultivated as a garden plant against south-facing walls in all except the warmest south European sites. Requires full sun and well-drained, medium rich soil. Propagate from woody cuttings, taken in summer, under glass in a sand and peat mix. Usually slow growing in cool regions.
Constituents Volatile oil; malic acid; citric acid; resin; tannic acid; vitamin C.
Uses (fresh or dried leaves, dried fruit, dried flower-buds, fresh flowers, occasionally oil) Astringent; antiseptic. Rarely used medicinally, but a leaf decoction may be applied externally to bruises and haemorrhoids. An infusion was once used as a douche in leucorrhoea, and it was formerly employed internally for psoriasis and sinusitis. The fresh fruit juice has been used as a drink to stimulate the mucous membranes of the stomach.
Dried flower-buds and fruit may be crushed and used as a spice in the same way as peppercorns.
The leaves can be added to roast pork for the final 10 minutes of cooking.
Fresh flowers once added to salads. Formerly used in the manufacture of toilet water called *Eau d'ange*.

Nasturtium officinale R.Br CRUCIFERAE

Watercress

Watercress is so common that its valuable medical and dietic values are often forgotten, even though for centuries it was an official medicine. *Nasturtium* is from the Latin *nasi tortium* or distortion of the nose, after its pungent taste.

Description Aquatic perennial, either floating or creeping with freely rooting, succulent stems; leaves dark green to bronze, entire, ovate, or cordate; pinnate when older, the terminal leaflet largest. Flowers small, white, in pedicelled racemes, appearing early summer to mid-autumn.

Distribution European native; world-wide introduction and widespread naturalization. In ditches, streams to 2500 m altitude.

Cultivation Wild, and world-wide commercial cultivation as a salad herb. Easily propagated by stem or root cuttings, taken at any time and rooted in water. May be cultivated in rich, moist garden soil with frequent watering, but the pungency then increases.

Constituents Vitamins A, B_2, C, D, E; nicotinamide; a glucoside, gluconasturtin; volatile oil comprising phenylethylisothiocyanate; minerals including manganese, iron, phosphorus, iodine and calcium.

Uses (leafy stems) Stimulant; diuretic; antipyretic; stomachic; irritant.

Numerous medicinal attributes from many countries including use as a contraceptive, aphrodisiac, purgative and asthma remedy. It is an excellent cough remedy when mixed with honey.

May be eaten raw or cooked and as a delicious summer soup.

Nepeta cataria L LABIATAE

Catnip Catmint/Catnep

Although this herb possesses what many consider to be a disagreeable mint-like aroma, it is relished by cats and for this reason commonly used to stuff toy mice. Cats frequently damage the plant in gardens, which is unfortunate since their attractive light grey foliage and long persistant flowers are suitable for formal displays.

Catmint is now very rarely used for medicinal purposes even in folk medicine.

It was once used by hippies as a mild hallucinogen.

Description Strongly smelling, branching, pubescent, erect perennial 40–100 cm tall. Leaves 3–7 cm long, coarsely serrate, whitish beneath, grey-green above, ovate or oblong-ovate, petiolate. Flowers white, dotted with purple, or purple, 6 mm long, in crowded terminal whorls and spiked axillary whorls. Appearing midsummer to mid-autumn.

Distribution Native to Europe, East and West Asia. Introduced and often naturalized in other temperate zones. On moist calcareous soils, especially road or railway sides, hedgerows, in open situations.

Cultivation Wild. May be propagated from cuttings taken in summer and rooted in a peat and sand mix under glass or by root division in spring or autumn.

Constituents Volatile oil comprising thymol, carvacrol, nepetol, nepetalactone and nepetalic acid; also tannic acid. Antispasmodic action due to the oil content.

Uses (dried – or occasionally fresh – flowering plant) Antispasmodic; anti-diarrhoeic; carminative; stomachic; weak emmenagogue. The tea is of benefit in the treatment of a number of gastro-intestinal complaints but particularly infantile colic and diarrhoea. It is also of value in the common cold, irritability and delayed menstruation. Externally it may be applied to cuts, abrasions and bruising. Combined with ground Cloves and Sassafras bark it was formerly applied to aching teeth.

Leaves may be used with discretion as a flavouring (mint-like) in sauces, and as a mildly stimulant tea.

Once smoked to relieve chronic bronchitis – but this may cause hallucinogenic effects.

Contra-indications A mild hallucinogen when smoked.

Nymphaea alba L NYMPHAEACEAE

White Water Lily

Although controversy surrounded the supposed anaphrodisiac qualities of this attractive aquatic herb, it is now considered that *N. alba* and some related plants may depress sexual activity. The Chinese have coincidentally used two other members of the family Nymphaeaceae – *Nelumbium nucifera* Gaertn. and *Euryale ferox* Salisb. – for precisely similar purposes indicating their possession of similar chemical constituents.

Nymphaea is from the Greek *nymphae* meaning water nymphs, while the pre-sixteenth century name Nenuphar (still retained as the modern French common name) was derived from the Arabic *niloufar* and Sanskrit *nilotpala* – terms first used for the Indian Blue Lotus.

N. odorata Aix is the similar, but more fragrant, American White Pond Lily; it has similar properties and uses.

Description Perennial aquatic herb with stipulate, round or heart-shaped, floating leaves 10–30 cm in diameter; on horizontal, black, branched, rhizome. Leaves reddish when young, later dark green, smooth and shining. Flowers white, 20-petalled, 5–20 cm diameter, stamens numerous and golden. Appearing mid-summer to early autumn, followed by 15–40 mm diameter obovoid fruit which opens under water.

Distribution Native to Europe and North America; introduced elsewhere. On rivers, lakes, ponds to 800 m altitude.

Cultivation Wild. Cultivated as an ornamental aquatic. Propagate in spring from rhizomes planted under water not deeper than 50 cm. In cold situations the flowers and leaves are much reduced in size.

A red variety, *N. alba* var. *rubra* Lönnr. is the parent of most water lily hybrids in cultivation.

Constituents Alkaloids, especially nupharine; tannins as nymphaea-tannic acid; a cardenolide, nymphaline; mucilage.

Uses (rhizome, occasionally seeds) Weak astringent; antiseptic; antispasmodic; anaphrodisiac.

A decoction may be used as a gargle for sore throats, a douche in leucorrhoea, and externally for ulcers or, much diluted, as an eyewash. Rarely used internally but acts as a sedative cardiac tonic, and is considered of benefit in spermatorrhoea. Once taken to reduce libido.
Well-cooked leaves once eaten as a vegetable.
Fresh root once used as a soap substitute.
Provides a dark brown dyestuff.

Ocimum basilicum L LABIATAE
Basil Sweet Basil
Basil was introduced to Europe from the East in the sixteenth century as a culinary herb and

is still popular with cooks who utilize its sweet, pungent flavour. Unfortunately the dried herb is not comparable with the flavour of leaves freshly picked from the garden. Several forms are in cultivation, including a lettuce-leaved variety, and the flavour varies with the volatile oil content; one type has a peppermint-like taste.
Both this species and the smaller Bush Basil originally from Chile (*Ocimum minimum* L), make excellent pot or window-box herbs, and can only be grown indoors in cooler, temperate climates in winter.
The common name is an abbreviation of *basilikon phuton*, Greek for kingly herb. A related plant, *Ocimum sanctum* L, is still considered kingly or holy by the Hindus.
Description Much-branched aromatic annual 30–60 cm tall, with glabrous entire or slightly serrate ovate leaves 3–5 cm long; often slightly reddish in colour. Flowers small, white, or purplish, in whorls of 6 flowers on open terminal racemes. Appearing mid-summer to mid-autumn.
Distribution Native to southern Asia, Iran, Middle East. Naturalized in parts of Africa and some Pacific Islands. Introduced elsewhere in subtropical zones.
Cultivation Rarely wild. Cultivated commercially in central and southern Europe, North Africa, Asia, and in subtropical America. Wide horticultural cultivation as a culinary herb. Propagate from seed sown in early summer, or after frost danger, on moist, well-drained, medium-rich soil in full sun. Varieties exist with somewhat different aromas.
Constituents Essential oil comprising mainly estragol (present also in French and Russian Tarragons); also eugenol, lineol and linalol; sometimes thymol; tannins; basil camphor. Antispasmodic and other actions due to the oil content.
Uses (fresh leaf) Antispasmodic; galactagogue; stomachic; carminative; mild sedative.
May be employed in a wide range of simple gastro-intestinal complaints; particularly for stomach cramps and vomiting. Its weak sedative action may be used in the treatment of nervous headaches or anxiety.
Mainly used for culinary purposes in soups, salads, fish and meat dishes; particularly compatible with tomatoes.
Dried powdered leaf once taken as snuff. Basil oil, obtained by steam distillation, is used as a commercial flavouring and in perfumery as a substitute for mignonette scent.

Oenothera biennis L ONAGRACEAE
Evening Primrose Evening Star
Evening Primrose has recently received attention from pharmaceutical concerns who discovered that it possesses a compound capable of reducing the rate of blood clotting or thrombus formation, and hence possibly acting as a prophylactic against some forms of heart attack.
This is an American native introduced to Europe in 1619 via the Padua Botanic Garden, and is now well established in parts of Europe. It has never been extensively used even in folk medicine.
The name *Oenothera* is of uncertain provenance but it may come from an older Greek plant name which signified that its roots were eaten to promote the appetite for wine. As late as the nineteenth century in Germany, pickled *O. biennis* roots were still eaten as an aperitif.
The less well-known common name Evening Star is derived from the fact that the petals emit phosphorescent light at night.
Description Biennial, or occasionally annual, producing, on thick yellowish conical root, compressed rosette of obtuse basal leaves to 60 cm diameter, from which arise much-branched reddish, rough stems to 1.25 m bearing alternate, lanceolate to ovate, entire, shortly petiolate leaves 4 cm long. Flowers very fragrant, 3–5 cm diameter, yellow, erect on spikes, 4-petalled, opening in the evening. Appearing mid-summer to mid-autumn.
Distribution North American native. Introduced and naturalized in Europe. In wastelands especially on dry, sandy or stony soils such as railway embankments.
Cultivation Wild. May be propagated from seed sown as soon as ripe, usually in late summer, in a permanent position. Tolerates most soils in a sunny position. Readily self-sown. Several varieties exist including large-flowered and hairy forms.
Constituents (seed) Unsaturated fatty acids;

unknown anticoagulant substances.
(whole plant) Tannins; mucilage; resin; bitter principle; potassium salts.
Uses (fresh whole plant, fresh root, seeds) Antispasmodic; nutritive; demulcent; weak astringent; vulnerary; anticoagulent. May be applied externally as a poultice or in ointments in the treatment of minor wounds or skin eruptions, and used internally for coughs, colds, gastric irritation and intestinal spasm. A direct effect on the liver is suspected but not proven.
Young roots can be boiled or pickled, and can be eaten hot or cold; all parts of the plant are edible.

Olea europaea L OLEACEAE
Olive
The Olive is well known from frequent references in the Bible and in the writings of the Greeks and Romans, to whom it symbolized peace.
It has been in cultivation for more than 3000 years and for this reason many different varieties now exist; some providing oil and others the large fruit so frequently used in salads and with drinks.
The ancient Egyptians called the plant *bak*, while the Romans knew it as *olea* from *oleum* meaning oil, after the large quantity of this important commodity which may be extracted from the fruit.
Description Evergreen tree usually to 8 m, and occasionally to 12 m. Branches pale grey, thin, thornless, bearing opposite, entire, lanceolate or oblong leaves, dark green above and lighter beneath; 3–7.5 cm long. Flowers fragrant, numerous, off-white, borne on short panicles in leaf axils, followed by dark purple fruit (drupe) 1.5–4 cm long.
Distribution Native to mediterranean region; introduced elsewhere.

Cultivation Wild only as an escape. The wild parent of the Olive is considered to be *Olea europaea* var. *oleaster* DC, which may be differentiated by its thorny branches, wider leaves and smaller fruit. Cultivated commercially and domestically on a wide scale in the Iberian Peninsula, North Africa, southern France, Greece, Italy and the Middle East. Propagated by grafting or from suckers; fruiting begins in the second year of growth.
Constituents (fruit) Oil (to 70%) comprising mainly glycerides of oleic acid, also glycerides of palmitic, stearic, myristic and linoleic acids; protein; mineral salts, particularly calcium; organic acids; vitamins A B_1 B_2 and PP (nicotinamide or B_3).
Uses (oil, fruit, occasionally fresh leaves) Nutritive; demulcent; mildly purgative; antiseptic; weakly astringent.
The oil is used internally as a physical laxative in chronic constipation, and as it reduces the flow of gastric secretions it has been used to

treat peptic ulcers. Externally it may be applied as a liniment or embrocation for a variety of purposes, particularly as the vehicle for more active substances.
The leaves possess antiseptic activity and have been used in a decoction for wound treatment. They may also have some antipyretic and hypotensive activity.
For medicinal purposes the oil should be extracted by the 'cold press' method to retain its active ingredients.
The fruit is of considerable commercial importance in the food industry.
The oil is of culinary importance and is also used in soap manufacture.

Ophioglossum vulgatum L OPHIOGLOSSACEAE
Adder's Tongue
Both the common and botanical names refer to the distinctive shape of this small fern's leaves from the Greek *ophis* meaning snake and *glossa* meaning tongue. Once famous as a wound-healing herb it is now only of historical interest.
Description Fern, on small, yellow, fibrous root-stock; to 20 cm tall. Stem solitary, arising from root-stock crown, round, hollow and succulent, expanding at 5–10 cm above ground level into broad, leathery, concave,

oval leaf blade which sheaths the stalk of the fertile spike; the latter usually 2–5 cm long and rising above the leaf blade. Spores ripen early to mid-summer.
Distribution Europe, North Africa, Asia and America. On grassland, pastures, scrub and fens.
Cultivation Wild plant.
Constituents Unknown.
Uses (fresh leaf, fresh juice) Vulnerary.
Formerly an ingredient of wound healing ointments, and once used internally for the same purpose. Not used today.

Origanum majorana L LABIATAE
Sweet Marjoram Knotted Marjoram/ Annual Marjoram
Also classified botanically as *Majorana hortensis* Moench. it has been cultivated in Europe for many centuries for its culinary and medicinal value. *Majorana* or *maiorana* is a very old name of unknown derivation by which the plant was known when first introduced to Europe in the Middle Ages. The common name Knotted Marjoram refers to the unusual knot-like shape of the spherical, clustered flower spikes. This plant is one of the most important of all western culinary herbs and its use in meat flavouring is emphasized by the German name *Wurstkraut* or sausage herb.
Description Spicy aromatic perennial (usually grown as an annual or biennial), 30–60 cm tall, with square, branched, tomentose stems; sometimes occurring as a subshrub. Leaves elliptic, entire or toothed, petiolate, opposite, greyish-pubescent, 0.75–3 cm long. Flowers small and insignificant, white to pink, in spherical clustered spikes, 3–5 per cluster. Appearing late summer to mid-autumn.
Distribution Native to North Africa, Middle East, parts of India. Introduced and naturalized in south-west Africa, mediterranean region, central Europe and North America. On dryish or well-drained, nutrient-rich soils, in sunny positions.
Cultivation Wild. Impermanently established in parts of central Europe. Cultivated commercially in Asia, America, central Europe and the mediterranean region. Grown horticulturally

as a perennial in warm regions or as a half-hardy annual in cooler temperate zones; sensitive to frost. In north-west Europe and North America sow seed in late spring or early summer, on medium-rich, finely prepared soil, later thinning to 25 cm apart; or raise under glass and plant out when hardened off.
Constituents Essential oil (to 2%) comprising terpineol, borneol and other terpenes (to 40%); mucilage; bitter substances; tannic acid.
Uses (fresh or dried flowering plant) Weak expectorant; antispasmodic; carminative; choleretic; aromatic; weak hypotensive; antiseptic.
Useful in most simple gastro-intestinal disorders, and an excellent digestive aid. Similar external uses to Oregano (*Origanum vulgare*).
Very wide culinary use; particularly in meat dishes, but must be added only in the last 10 minutes of cooking.
Employed as a tisane.
May be used in domestic cosmetic waters, and scented articles.

Origanum onites L LABIATAE
Pot Marjoram
This is also known as *Majorana onites* Benth. from the classical name *onitin* used by Pliny in the first century. This species was not cultivated very widely in north-west Europe or America, and was only introduced to Great Britain in the eighteenth century. Pot Marjoram is inferior to Sweet Marjoram and is now only cultivated as an alternative in areas too cold for *O. majorana*, or where the decorative perennial variegated variety is required for ornamental purposes.
Description Aromatic perennial on erect tomentose or hirsute stems to 30 cm tall; leaves serrate, sessile, tomentose and usually ovate, 0.75–2.5 cm long. Flowers small, white to pink, in numerous ovoid spikelets arranged in a

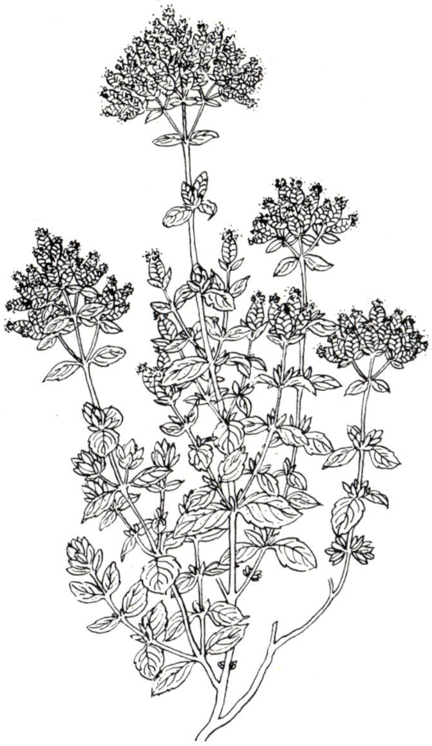

cluster. Appearing late summer to mid-autumn.
Distribution Native to Sicily, south-east Europe, Syria and Asia Minor. Prefers full sun and light well-drained soils in open positions and hillsides. Tolerates most conditions.
Cultivation Wild. Cultivated in cooler climates as a semi-hardy alternative to *O. majorana*; from cuttings in early summer, root division in spring or autumn, or from seed sown 1 cm deep in light, dry soil in late spring (germination may be slow or poor). Variegated forms exist. In very cold positions grow in pots and keep in a cool greenhouse during winter.
Constituents Essential oil (to 1%), comprising terpenes; also bitter substances; tannic acid.
Uses (fresh or dried flowering plant) Not used for medicinal purposes.
Employed in cooking as a substitute for Sweet Marjoram, although its flavour is inferior. Variegated forms may be used as garden ornamentals.

Origanum vulgare L LABIATAE
Oregano Wild Marjoram
Although Wild Marjoram is now cultivated commercially in some parts of the world, most supplies are still collected from the wild in the mediterranean region, and particularly in southern Italy. The nature of both the volatile oil composition and to some extent the plant's appearance depends on where it is cultivated. The southern European product is far more pungent and bears little resemblance in flavour to that from the cooler north.
The generic name *Origanum* is from the Greek *oros* and *ganos* meaning mountain glamour, or joy of the mountain, after the attractive appearance and aroma of the bushy flowering plant; *vulgare* means common.
Description Erect hairy aromatic perennial, frequently bushy, on horizontal root-stock, to 75 cm tall. Leaves glabrous, opposite and decussate, entire or obscurely toothed, petiolate, pointed, broadly ovate 1.5–4.5 cm long, upper leaves often reddish. Flowers rose-purple, sometimes pink to whitish, 6–8 mm long, bracteoles purple, borne on short spikes or corymbose clusters, appearing late summer to mid-autumn.
Distribution European native; also in Iran, Middle East and Himalayas. Introduced to Far East. On dry, usually calcareous or gravelly but nutrient-rich soils in warm positions; especially hedgebanks, woodland clearings and peripheries, roadsides; to 2000 m altitude.
Cultivation Wild. Collected commercially in southern Italy, cultivated commercially in North America. Propagate from seed sown in late spring on warm site, later thinning to 30 cm apart. Several forms exist including a variegated form with golden leaves.
Constituents Essential oil (0.5%) comprising thymol (to 15%), origanene, carvacrol; bitter principles; tannic acid; resins.
Uses (dried flowering plant, occasionally oil) Expectorant; antiseptic; antispasmodic; carminative; tonic; stomachic; anti-inflammatory.
Useful specifically for gastro-intestinal or respiratory disorders; particularly coughs associated with upper respiratory tract infection, and colic or indigestion. May be used externally in baths, inhalants or poultices where an antiseptic action is required. Weakly sedative and of some benefit in nervous headaches or irritability. Aids digestion.
Wide commercial and domestic culinary use as a flavouring, especially in meat dishes and stuffings.
Oil and herb used in cosmetic industry.
May be used as a tisane (*Thé Rouge*); once used to flavour beer.

Oxalis acetosella L OXALIDACEAE
Wood Sorrel Irish Shamrock
Oxalis is from the Greek for sour, after the taste of this small attractive herb which contains quite high concentrations of oxalic acid and its salts. It was cultivated from at least the fourteenth century as a major sauce herb, but it was displaced after the introduction of the unrelated French Sorrel (*Rumex scutatus* L).
Description Stemless perennial on scaly rhizome,

reaching 5–8 cm. Pale green leaves composed of 3 obcordate leaflets on long petiole. Flowers 5-petalled, white tinged with purple veins and yellow flecks at corolla base, solitary on long peduncles; appearing late spring to early summer.
Distribution Native to Europe, north and central Asia, Japan; introduced elsewhere. On acidic, humus-rich moist soils in mixed or deciduous woodland shade, to 2000 m.
Cultivation Wild plant. Cultivated by root division in spring.
Constituents Oxalic acid and potassium oxalate, to which the taste is due; mucilage; vitamin C.
Uses (fresh leaves and root-stock) Diuretic; weakly antipyretic.
Once used internally as a spring tonic (especially in Iceland), in fevers, and after excess alcohol consumption. Now principally used as an external application for the treatment of scabies, and as a gargle. Small quantities only of the leaves may be used in salads or sauces.
Contra-indications Large quantities are POISONOUS. To be avoided by those predisposed to gout, rheumatism or renal calculi.

Paeonia officinalis L PAEONIACEAE
Peony Common Peony
The Peony was first used very early in medical history and is named after Paeon, the physician of the Greek gods. Known as *paeonia*, it was included in many very early medicinal recipes and one, accredited to Pliny, combined this herb with Mint (*Mentha* spp.) and Chick Pea (*Cicer arietinum* L) for the specific treatment of both kidney and bladder stones, which, it was claimed, the mixture would dissolve.
After the sixteenth century the medicinal status of *P. officinalis* declined rapidly in Western folk medicine, but the herb is still retained in Chinese traditional medicine today.
Description Perennial on thick, knotted, dark, root-stock, producing stout succulent stem 60 cm–1 m tall. Leaves biternate or ternate, with ovate-lanceolate leaflets, 3 cm wide, dark green above and lighter beneath. Single red, or occasionally pink or whitish, flower; large and attractive and composed of 8 petals and 5 petal-like sepals, to 20 cm diameter. Appearing early summer to early autumn.
Distribution Native to southern Europe from France to Albania, and western Europe. Widely introduced as garden ornamental elsewhere.
Cultivation Wild. Propagated by division of root-stock in early autumn or from seed sown in spring on deeply-dug, well-manured soil. Once established, it must not be moved. Several forms exist, including *Alba plena*, *Rubra plena* and *Rosea plena*.
Constituents Benzoic acid (5%) l-asparagin; essential oil; an alkaloid; a ketone, paeonol; a heteroside. The alkaloid is vasoconstrictive; stimulates uterine contractions, and may increase blood coagulation.
Uses (dried root-stock) Vasoconstrictor; antispasmodic; diuretic; sedative; emmenagogue. Formerly used specifically in the treatment of both renal and gall-bladder calculi. Also once used for a variety of other conditions including those of a nervous origin, gastric disorders, varicose veins and haemorrhoids. May be effective in the latter condition, but now rarely used.
Contra-indications POISONOUS, the flowers especially so. Only to be used by medical personnel.

Panax pseudoginseng Wallich ARALIACEAE
Ginseng
Ginseng is so well known in both the East and West that it has become the most widely used of all medicinal herbs. The Koreans and Chinese have employed it as a panacea for centuries. This is reflected in its botanical name, *Panax* from *pan* meaning all, and *akos* meaning remedy. It was so highly prized in the Orient that not only did emperors monopolize the rights to harvest the roots, but wars were fought over them.
The word *Ginseng* is derived from *Jin-chen* or *Schin-seng*, meaning man root or like a man, after the peculiar human shape of the root. In commerce various grades exist depending on shape, age and colour. Red Korean Ginseng is one of the most expensive and sought-after types, and Ginseng production in Korea is carefully controlled by the government.
The wide range of effects on human physiology claimed by Chinese physicians have only recently been tentatively acknowledged by Western pharmacologists who have created a new term, adaptogen, to explain the normalizing effect of the active ingredients.
Panax pseudoginseng was formerly classified as *P. ginseng* C. A. Mey and *P. schinseng* Nees. Russian scientists claim that another member of the Araliaceae family, *Eleutherococcus senticosus* or Siberian Ginseng, possesses similar adaptogenic properties to Ginseng.
A related species, *Panax fruticosum* L, is used in some Polynesian Islands as both a food and medicine.
Description Perennial 60–80 cm tall on aromatic, frequently bifurcated, spindle-shaped root-stock; bearing persistent fleshy scales at stem base. Single erect stem, unbranched and reddish, bearing whorl of 3 or 5 palmate leaves, the leaflet thin, finely serrate, gradually acuminate, 8–13 cm long. Flowers greenish-yellow, small, few, in single terminal peduncled umbel; appearing mid to late summer and followed by bright red drupe-like berry on elongated peduncle.
Distribution Native to China (Manchuria) and Korea. In damp, cool, humus-rich woodland.
Cultivation Wild, but becoming rare. Cultivated on an increasing scale commercially in Korea and China, from seed and carefully selected seedlings, by a complex horticultural procedure involving specially prepared seed-beds, transplantation and shading. Harvested up to 9 years after planting.
Constituents Volatile oils, comprising sapogenin and panacen (stimulating the central nervous system); a saponin, panaxin; panax acid; ginsenin (with hypoglycaemic activity); a glycoside, panaquilon (acting as a vasoconstrictive stimulant); ginsennosides; phytosterols; hormones; vitamins B_1 and B_2; mucilage; several other substances; all combining to produce a complex total effect.
Uses (dried root) Tonic; adaptogenic.
Used in a very wide range of conditions, but particularly of benefit where increased mental

and physical efficiency is required, or where the patient is exposed to internal and external physiological stress factors – such as ageing, surgery or disease.
Contra-indications Large doses may cause depression, insomnia and nervous disorders. Do not combine with any herbal remedies containing iron, or with Indian or China teas (*Camellia* spp.).

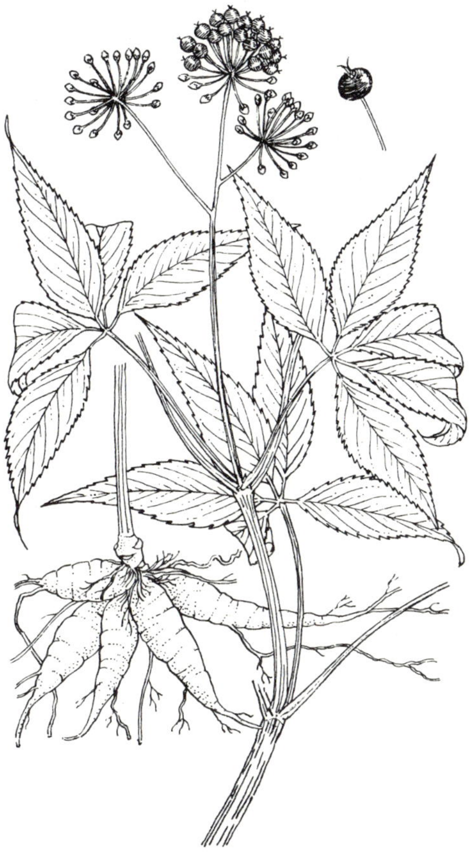

Panax quinquefolium L ARALIACEAE
American Ginseng
This has the same general properties as *Panax pseudoginseng*, its Oriental relative, and from 1718, when first exported to China by Canadian Jesuits, until the end of the nineteenth century it was so heavily collected that it is now practically unknown in its natural wild habitat. Most supplies are today cultivated in Wisconsin and exported to the East; some probably return to the United States and Europe fraudulently described as the more expensive Chinese or Korean root. There is little evidence that any North American Indian tribes beside the Chippewas or Ojibwas used the herb to the same extent as the Chinese.
Description Perennial 12.5–45 cm tall on aromatic, occasionally bifurcated, spindle-shaped root-stock, bearing thin scales at stem base which are shed during growth. Stem simple, erect, unbranched and reddish, bearing whorl of 3 or 5 palmate leaves; the leaflets obovate, thin, coarsely serrate, abruptly acuminate, 8–13 cm long. Flowers pink, small, few, in single terminal, peduncled umbel; appearing late summer and followed by a cluster of red drupe-like berries on elongated peduncle.

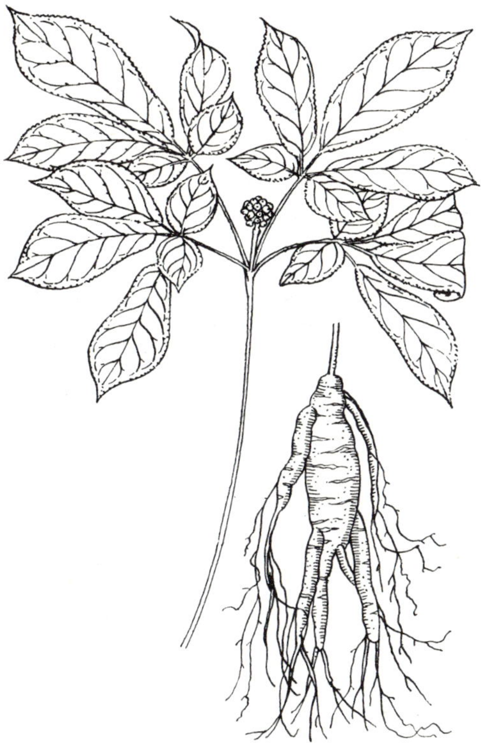

Distribution North American native from Quebec to Minnesota. Exclusively in cool, humus-rich woodlands.
Cultivation Formerly wild. Now extremely rare. Cultivated commercially in the same way as *Panax pseudoginseng*.
Constituents Similar to *Panax pseudoginseng* Wallich.
Uses (dried root) Tonic; adaptogenic. Similar to *Panax pseudoginseng* Wallich.

Papaver rhoeas L PAPAVERACEAE
Corn Poppy Field Poppy/Flanders Poppy
Corn Poppy petals have been collected as a colouring agent since at least the fifteenth century, and were employed from the earliest times as a medicine. *P. dubium* L is often substituted for this species, its action being similar.
Description Slender erect branched annual to 90 cm; hairy stem bearing deeply pinnate, sessile, short leaves with lanceolate segments. Flowers to 5 cm diameter, solitary, deep red with purplish flecks at the base (occasionally white), on long peduncles. Appearing early to late summer, followed by ovoid capsule.
Distribution Native to Europe and Asia, naturalized in North America and introduced elsewhere. In fields, arable land, on roadsides, especially after soil disturbance. On either chalky soils or loam, in warm positions; to 1700 m altitude.
Cultivation Wild plant.
Constituents (flower) Pigments comprising the anthocyanins, mecocyanin and cyanidol; mucilage; traces of the crystalline alkaloids, rhoeadine, rhoeagenine and rhoearubine.
Uses (fresh, dried flowers rarely) Sedative; antispasmodic; diaphoretic.
Of benefit in colic, anxiety, tonsillitis, bronchitis and particularly irritable coughs.
Principally used as a colouring agent for medicine and wine.
Seed is sprinkled on bread, biscuits and cakes.
Poppy seed oil is used in cooking.

Papaver somniferum L PAPAVERACEAE
Opium Poppy
The abuse of this medicinal plant and its products has caused considerable human misery and a great deal of governmental effort has gone into controlling its cultivation and distribution.
America and other nations have recently attempted to dissuade Turkish farmers, for example, from cultivating it on so large a scale, for it presents a formidable problem of drug abuse – and is therefore an extremely lucrative crop.
The Opium Poppy has, however, provided the greatest of all pain killers, morphine – a substance which has not been artificially synthesized – and opium which has been employed in medicine in the eastern mediterranean, the Middle East and western Asia, since the earliest times. Extraction of the opium or latex is achieved by cutting the green capsule with a small sharp implement and scraping off the soft material which will exude within the following 24 hours.
Opium syrup was particularly advocated in the treatment of coughs by an eleventh-century Arabian physician, Mesue, and as late as the seventeenth century this preparation was still widely known as *Syrupus de Meconio Mesuae*.
The plant's specific name *somniferum* means sleep inducing.
Description Glaucous annual from 60 cm–1.25 m tall; stem rigid, seldom branched and then

only at the base, sometimes slightly hairy; bearing glossy, cordate, unequal, coarsely dentate leaves, 10–25 cm long, the upper leaves usually clasping. Flowers 4-petalled, 7.5–10 cm wide, entire, of variable colour; usually white or lilac with pink or purple markings. Sometimes red or purple. Appearing late summer to early autumn and followed by ovoid, glabrous, then woody, capsules.

Distribution Native to Middle East, south-east Europe, western Asia. Introduced elsewhere. On shallow loamy or chalky soils in sunny situations; especially wasteland as escape.

Cultivation Cultivated plant, especially in Turkey, India and China. Occasionally wild as an escape. Possibly derived from *Papaver setigerum* and developed by centuries of cultivation. Seed is mixed with 4 parts of sand and sown from mid-autumn to late spring; thinning to 25 cm apart.

Constituents (capsules) At least 25 alkaloids mainly comprising morphine (0.1–0.3%), also codeine, papaverine, narcotine, meconic acid, thebaine, narceine. (latex) 25% alkaloid content, and 12% morphine; (seeds) Oil (to 60%); lecithin.

Uses (dried latex, ripe seeds, seed oil) Narcotic; sedative. Opium has traditionally been used in the relief of pain, diarrhoea and certain forms of cough, and is now the source of purified morphine and other pain-killing alkaloidal drugs. An infusion made from powdered capsules of the Poppy was once applied externally to sprains and bruises.

Ripe seed (which does not contain harmful substances) may be used in curries or sprinkled on bread and cakes. The seed oil provides two products: a culinary oil (olivette), and an artists' oil.

Dried capsules are used in dried flower arrangements.

Contra-indications DANGEROUS. To be used only by medical personnel.

Parietaria diffusa Mert. & Koch URTICACAE

Pellitory of the Wall Pellitory

This plant has been used for centuries and was described as a medicinal plant by Pliny and as a vegetable by Theophrastus.

It is commonly found on ruins and old walls, hence its name *parietaria* from the Latin *paries* meaning a wall. As it was a favourite of the apothecaries and herbalists – who used it almost exclusively for urinary complaints – it was formerly an official herb and therefore classified as *P. officinalis* L.

Pellitory contains an unusually large quantity of sulphur.

Description Perennial with reddish, hairy stems, erect and spreading or sometimes decumbent; 20–75 cm tall. Leaves alternate, petiolate, entire, ovate to lanceolate, mostly acuminate, softly hairy. Flowers greenish, unisexual, female terminal, male lateral; appearing mid-summer to mid-autumn.

Distribution European native. Beneath or in the crevices of old walls; occasionally in hedgerows. To 700 m altitude.

Cultivation Wild. May be grown on low stone walls. Divide root-stock in mid-spring, plant in cracks with peaty soil.

Constituents Sulphur; tannic acid; bitter principles; flavones; potassium and calcium salts; mucilage. Diuretic action due to the presence of potassium salts and flavones.

Uses (dried or fresh flowering plant) Demulcent; diuretic.

Employed in the treatment of cystitis, with or without bladder stones, and less frequently in pyelitis. The fresh plant is much more effective than the dried herb.

Contra-indications To be avoided by hay fever sufferers; this is one of several species shown to cause allergic rhinitis and possibly hypersensitivity pneumonitis.

Passiflora incarnata L PASSIFLORACEAE

Passion Flower Maypop

Passiflora species are predominantly of subtropical American origin, and several have been employed traditionally for a variety of complaints. This herb was introduced in 1867 in the United States for its effective sedative properties, and has been retained in certain national pharmacopoeias; it is also a popular folk medicine and constituent of some proprietary herbal sedative preparations.

Passion-flower, from the Latin, *passiflora*, is named after the supposed symbolic association between the anatomical and numerical arrangement of the flowers and the elements of the crucifixion.

Description Perennial vine on strong, woody, hairy stem 6 m to 10 m tall, climbing by means of axillary tendrils. Leaves serrate, 3-lobed, cordate, petiolate, 7.5–12.5 cm long. Flowers attractive, white, with pink or purple calyx, 4–7.5 cm wide, appearing early to late summer and followed by edible, yellow, ovoid fruit 5 cm in diameter.

Distribution Native to southern United States. Introduced to Bermuda and elsewhere. On

loamy, nutrient-rich soils in full sun.
Cultivation Wild. Occasionally cultivated; the commercial sources of the edible passion fruit or Granadilla are *Passiflora edulis* Sims, or less commonly *P. ligularis* Juss. *P. caerulea* L is the most common species grown as a climbing shrub in warmer temperate zones.
Constituents (fruit) Ascorbic acid; flavonoids; citric and malic acids; amylopectin; fixed oil. (flowering plant) Alkaloids comprising harmine, harmol, passiflorine; a cyanogenic heteroside; flavonoids; passiflortannoid; maracugin.
Uses (dried fruiting and flowering tops, fruit) Antispasmodic; sedative; anodyne.
Principally of benefit in the treatment of nervous tachycardia, anxiety and insomnia; also used in certain types of convulsion or spasmodic complaints such as epilepsy. Its anodyne effects are employed in various neuralgias.
The fruit is edible, refreshing, tonic and employed in commercial drinks in some countries.
Contra-indications Sedative. To be taken only under medical supervision.

Pastinaca sativa L UMBELLIFERAE
Parsnip Wild Parsnip
The Parsnip (a fourteenth-century name) was once a major Roman foodstuff being called *pastinacea* after the Latin word *pastus* for food. It was largely replaced by the Carrot in the eleventh century, probably because of dangers of mistaking it for related but poisonous species of the Umbelliferae family.
Description Thick-rooted biennial, 50–120 cm tall, with hairy, robust, grooved stem becoming hollow. Leaves pinnate or bipinnate with ovate or oblong, sessile, toothed leaflets 5–10 cm long. Greenish yellow flowers in compound umbels appearing mid to late summer.
Distribution Eurasian native. Naturalized in

New Zealand, Australia, North America and Uruguay and introduced elsewhere. In deep nitrogenous or calcareous soils on wasteland and meadows. To 1000 m.
Cultivation Wild plant. Extensive commercial cultivation for the edible root, especially the cultivar *P. sativa* var. *sativa hortensis* Ehrh. Requires deeply dug loamy soil. Sow seed in spring and lift root in autumn.
Constituents (root): Protein; starch; vitamin C (0.03%); pectin; essential oil; a furo-coumarin, bergaptene (to 0.2%).
Uses (fresh leaf, root) Diuretic; aromatic; nutritive; mild sedative.
Traditionally employed in urinary disorders as a diuretic, and to promote appetite.
Principally used as a root vegetable; the leafy tops may be cooked and eaten. Root extract employed to flavour schnapps.
Contra-indications May cause photodermatoses; gloves should be worn when handling leaves.

Pelargonium graveolens L'Hérit GERANIACEAE
Rose Geranium Pelargonium
In the rose-scented geranium group the species most commonly cultivated in temperate gardens and homes is *P. graveolems*. Other species which are grown commercially as sources of oil of Geranium include *P. capitatum*, *P. radens* and *P. odoratissimum*; and these may be employed for similar domestic and culinary purposes.
Almost all scented Geraniums – or more correctly Pelargoniums – are South African natives. They were introduced to England from Cape Province in 1632 but were largely unknown until 1847 when their potential in perfumery was recognized by the French. Oil of Geranium is an essential ingredient of certain perfumes for men, and some of the finest quality used for this purpose comes from Rhodesia and Réunion.
Pelargonium is derived from the Greek for stork's bill after the fruit's shape.
Description Bushy aromatic perennial, becoming woody, to 1 m. Leaves long-petioled, hairy, 5–7 lobed, circular to cordate-ovate, margins dentate. Flowers 2.5 cm wide, pink, unscented, sessile or nearly so, on short-peduncled, dense umbels.
Distribution South African native. Introduced elsewhere. On dryish, well-drained, loamy soils in full sun.
Cultivation Wild. Widely cultivated as a house plant. Cultivated commercially in the warmer south-west mediterranean region, central and southern Africa and Réunion. In cooler temperate zones grow as tender perennial, sinking pots in the garden during the summer, and bringing plants indoors before threat of frost. Easily propagated from cuttings taken in late summer and struck in a peat and sand mix. Several cultivars exist, and the aroma varies from lemon to apple.
Constituents Volatile oil, comprising mainly geraniol, also linalol, geranyl tiglate, citronellol, citronella forminate and iso-menthone.
Uses (fresh or dried leaf, oil) Aromatic; astringent. Not used medicinally in Europe: in Africa the roots of certain *Pelargonium* species are employed in the treatment of diarrhoea.

Fresh leaves can be added to cakes before baking; to sweet fruit dishes, and cold summer dishes.
The oil is of importance in the perfumery industry, and is often used as a substitute for oil of Rose.
Dried leaves may be employed in a variety of scented articles, and cosmetic bath preparations.
An attractive house plant.

Petasites hybridus (L) Gaertn., May & Scherb. COMPOSITAE
Butterbur Bog Rhubarb
The botanical name is derived from the Greek *petasos*, meaning a large Greek hat that was thought to resemble the shape of the Butterbur leaf. In French the plant is known as *chapeau du diable* – devil's hat.
The common name Butterbur may indicate that butter was once wrapped in these large leaves.
In 1685 Schröder described several preparations from this plant for use against the Plague: they included the juice extracted from the root; an alcoholic extract; the fresh leaves and flowers; and an oil distilled from the whole plant. Butterbur is now only seldom used in folk medicine.
Description Semi-aquatic perennial on thick, creeping, pinkish rhizome. Flowers appear before the leaves, from mid-spring to early summer, on 10–40 cm long, stout, scaly, hollow, purplish stems. Male and female flowers appear on different plants; both flowers are a pinkish violet on spike-like racemes, but the former are 7–12 mm wide and short-stalked, and the latter are 3–6 mm wide and long-stalked. Leaves, appearing towards the end of flowering, are large, 10–90 cm wide, long stalked, woolly underneath, deeply cordate and roundish.
Distribution European native; on wet, calcareous and stony soils, beside streams, rivers, in ditches or flooded pasture.
Cultivation Wild.
Constituents Inulin; helianthenine; tannic acid; mucilage; an essential oil; petasine and

petasitine; an alkaloid.
Uses (dried rhizome, occasionally fresh or dried flowers and leaves) Vulnerary; astringent; weak diuretic; expectorant; antispasmodic; weak emmenagogue.
Principally used homeopathically in the treatment of neck pains and headache. Fresh leaves and flowers may be applied as a poultice to wounds. Rhizome may be employed in combination with other inulin-containing remedies for certain eruptive skin conditions. Once used as an antispasmodic in coughs, urinary tract infections and for stammering.

Petroselinum crispum (Mill.) Nyman
UMBELLIFERAE
Parsley
The Greeks differentiated between Marsh Celery or Smallage (*heleio selinon*) and Rock Celery or Parsley (*petros selinon*). Both types were associated with death and funerals and only later on in Roman times were they used as food. Pliny stated that every sauce and salad contained what was then known to the Romans as *apium* – or Parsley. Today Parsley is the best known of all garnishing herbs in the West, and a number of varieties exist. Columella (A.D. 42) was the first to mention a curly form – the type now favoured in English-speaking countries. It lacks, however, the hardiness of plain-leaved varieties, though it is less likely to be confused with the highly poisonous Fool's Parsley (*Aethusa cynapium*). At least three other forms are commonly cultivated: the Neapolitan or celery-leaved; the fern-leaved; and the Hamburg or turnip-rooted. Parsley root is still retained in the Portugese, Yugoslavian and Czechoslovakian pharmacopoeias, and the seed is found in Swiss, French and Portugese pharmacopoeias. The botanical name for this herb has changed several times; it has previously been classified as *Petroselinum hortenso* Hoffm., *P. sativum* Hoffm., *Apium petroselinum* L, *A. crispum* Mill., and *Carum petroselinum* Benth.
Description Biennial or short-lived perennial on stout vertical taproot; stems solid, branching, to 75 cm tall (usually 30 cm). Leaves deltoid, pinnate, segments 1–2 cm long, cuneate-ovate, stalked, much curled (depending on cultivar). Flowers small, greenish-yellow or yellowish, in flat-topped, 2–5 cm wide compound umbels, appearing mid-summer to early autumn; followed by 2.5 mm long, ribbed, ovoid fruit.
Distribution Native to northern and central Europe. Introduced and naturalized elsewhere, including some subtropical zones (such as the West Indies).
Cultivation Wild. Extensively cultivated horticulturally and commercially. Propagate from seed sown in drills in early spring to early summer. Remove flower-heads to encourage leaf growth. Requires rich, moist, open soil in partial shade or full sun; a good watering during hot weather and protection under cloches during winter. Germination is often poor and slow (to 8 weeks) and may be encouraged by pouring boiling water in drills immediately after sowing. The plain-leaved varieties tolerate extremes of cold and dryness better than the curly-leaved varieties.
Constituents Essential oil comprising apiol, apiolin, myristicin, pinene; flavonoids; a glucoside; apiin; provitamin A; ascorbic acid. Action largely due to the apiol content of the essential oil, which stimulates the appetite and increases blood-flow to the digestive tract, uterus and mucosae.
Uses (fresh or dried leaves, dried root, dried seed, occasionally oil) Diuretic; emmenagogue; stomachic; carminative.
Effective in dysmenorrhoea, amenorrhoea, as a diuretic, anti-flatulent and to stimulate the appetite.
The use of the leaf for culinary purposes is well known. The leaf was formerly used as a tea (Parsley tea). May be chewed to destroy garlic odour on the breath. Dried stems of use as a green dye.
Contra-indications The oil should only be used under medical supervision. Very large doses of either the oil or the leaf may cause abortion. They may also cause polyneuritis. Apiol and myristicin can induce fatty degeneration of the liver, and gastro-intestinal haemorrhages.

Petroselinum crispum var. *tuberosum* Crovetto
UMBELLIFERAE
Turnip Rooted Parsley Hamburg Parsley
This variety of Parsley was probably first developed in Holland since it was once called Dutch Parsley. Fuchs described it as *oreoselinum* in Germany in the mid-sixteenth century, and the name Hamburg Parsley was used by Mawe in 1778. Philip Miller (1691–1771), the curator of the Chelsea Physic Garden, introduced it to England in 1727, but it was only

popular there for a century – from 1780 to 1880. The plant is still frequently found in France and Germany in vegetable markets.
It is also described botanically as *P. crispum* var. *radicosum* Bailey and *P. sativum* var. *tuberosum* Bernh.
Description Similar to *P. crispum* but leaf segments usually not curled or crisped, and taproot is fleshy, 5 cm wide and 12.5 cm long.
Distribution North and east European cultivated plant.
Cultivation Cultivated horticulturally and commercially particularly in Holland, France and Germany.
Seed is sown in early spring on deep, rich, well-dug soil; watered well during dry weather; and roots harvested from mid-autumn onwards. Frost resistant.
Constituents Similar to *P. crispum*; the root also contains bergapten.
Uses (cooked root) Not used medicinally. Cooked as a vegetable; or used in soup mixes. Flavour resembles both Celery and Parsley.

Peumus boldus Molina MONIMIACEAE
Boldo Boldu
This native of the Chilean Andes is still retained in several South American and European pharmacopoeias, and is employed predominantly for liver disease. The leaves, which are the only parts used in medicine, were first tested in Europe in 1869 by the French physician Dujardin-Baumez.
Other botanical names for Boldo, which is the local Chilean name, included *Boldoa fragrans* Gay and *Ruizia fragrans* Pavon.
Description Aromatic, dioecious, evergreen shrub 5–6 m tall; leaves shortly petiolate, grey-green, coriaceous, entire, somewhat revolute, ovate or elliptical, upper and lower surfaces slightly pubescent, upper surface covered with small papillae. Flowers small, pinkish, on open terminal racemes.
Distribution Chilean native. Introduced elsewhere. Especially on sunny slopes.
Cultivation Wild. Limited cultivation in Morocco and elsewhere.
Constituents Volatile oil (to 2%) comprising mainly eucalyptol, also ascaridol; alkaloids, comprising mainly boldine (to 0.1%); a glycoside, boldin (boldoglucin or boldina). Cholagogue action due to the presence of boldine. Antihelmintic action due to ascaridol.

Uses (dried leaves, occasionally bark) Cholagogue; choleretic; stomachic; sedative; diuretic; sternutatory; antihelmintic. Formerly used as a tonic where quinine was contra-indicated; in rheumatism; and in certain urinary tract infections, including gonorrhoea. Of benefit in the treatment of hepatic congestion and gallstones; used to stimulate the secretion and release of bile, and hence to aid digestion, and as a tonic in gall-bladder disease. The powdered leaf may be used to induce sneezing.
The aromatic fruit pulp can be eaten.
Bark was once used in tanning.
Contra-indications Large doses cause vomiting.

Physalis alkekengi L SOLANACEAE
Bladder Cherry Chinese Lantern
Dioscorides called the herb *phusalis* or *strychnos halikakabos* and considered it a sedative. Although several other *Physalis* species are used for jams, they are now seldom of medicinal interest.
Description Perennial (often grown as annual) on creeping rhizome, reaching 20–110 cm. Leaves entire, ovate, petiolate to 8 cm. Flowers solitary, whitish, nodding, appearing early summer to late autumn and followed by red globose berry enclosed in paper-thin, orange-red calyx.
Distribution Native from central and south-east Europe and western Asia to Japan. On dry calcareous soils in vineyards and wasteland, to 1500 m altitude.
Cultivation Wild; frequently as a garden escape. Cultivated as an ornamental from seed sown as early as possible, or under glass. Requires warm position. Also propagated by division.
Constituents (fruit) Vitamin C; organic acids including malic and citric; a bitter substance, physaline; pectin; pectinase; glucose.

Uses (fruit, rarely leaves) Diuretic; antipyretic; mild sedative; nutritive; laxative. Formerly employed in the treatment of renal calculi, rheumatism, arthritis and gout. The fruit may be eaten in small quantities or used in jams, and the whole plant (except the root) is used in certain diuretic wines.
Contra-indications Large quantities may cause diarrhoea.

Physostigma venenosum Balfour LEGUMINOSAE
Calabar Bean Ordeal Bean/Esere Nut
Calabar Bean is named after the area in south-east Nigeria, and near to the modern Port Harcourt, where the plant is most commonly found.
It is known locally as *esere*, hence one of its common names – Esere Nut. The plant's cotyledons were once used in trials by ordeal in Africa in which the accused had to drink the powdered bean. An explanation for the fact that the innocent generally survived and the guilty died is that in the former case the entire quantity was drunk thereby inducing violent vomiting and purging which removed much of the poison; while the guilty person sipped the potion, allowing rapid absorption of the alkaloids from the gastro-intestinal tract and therefore subsequent death from cardiac arrest.
It was introduced to Europe in 1840 by Daniell, and its medicinal properties were recognized in 1860. The plant has no place in modern medicine, and physostigmine (its chief constituent) has now largely been replaced by neostigmine.
Description Perennial on climbing woody stem (to 5 cm thick) reaching 15 m tall. Leaves large, ternate, pinnate; flowers purple, 3 cm wide, produced on long pendulous axillary racemes, each possessing 30 or more flowers; appearing early to mid-spring, and followed by a dehiscent oblong pod 16 cm long, and containing 2 or 3 seeds to 3 cm long.
Distribution Native to west coast of Africa, especially Nigeria, Cameroun, Togo, Dahomey; introduced to Brazil and other tropical countries. On swampy river banks.
Cultivation Wild, and collected commercially in West Africa. Ripe seed germinated and plant grown in greenhouses in temperate zones.
Constituents Alkaloids comprising mainly eserine (physostigmine) to 0.3%, also calabarine; starch (to 50%); proteins (to 23%).
Uses (cotyledons from ripe seed) Miotic. Now used exclusively in opthalmology – to contract the pupil in the eye, and decrease intro-ocular

pressure in glaucoma. Formerly employed in tetanus and rheumatism. Used as a source of physostigmine, a parasympathomimetic alkaloid used in some of the above conditions and in the treatment of myasthenia gravis (a neuro-muscular disease), and to induce peristalsis in post-operative gastro-intestinal debility. Calabarine and physostigmine exert opposite effects; the action of the seed is therefore frequently different from that of pure alkaloids. Once used in veterinary medicine.
Contra-indications Very POISONOUS. Death may be caused by cardiac arrest or respiratory paralysis.

Phytolacca americana L PHYTOLACCACEAE
Poke Weed Poke Root/Pigeonberry
Phytolacca is derived from the Greek *phyton* meaning plant and the French *lac* (a reddish pigment), reflecting the berries' ability to produce a crimson dye.
The herb was introduced to American settlers by Indians to whom it was known as *pocan* or *cocum* and from which the name Poke Weed originates. Traditionally Poke Weed was used as an emetic and as a remedy for venereal

diseases, but by 1830 Geiger had discovered other medicinal attributes.
Because of its complex chemical constituents the herb has received considerable scientific attention, and among other things it has been shown to possess a mitogenic phytohaemagglutin called Poke Weed mitogen factor (PWM) which is employed for immunological purposes in modern medicine.
Another factor, which has the ability to destroy snails, is being examined in Africa as a possible agent to control the carrier of Bilharzia, a disease caused by a parasite which invades and destroys many body organs and which is contracted by washing in water containing certain snails.
Description Perennial with thick, smooth hollow purplish stem, 1.25–3.5 m tall, on large fleshy branched root. Leaves unpleasantly scented, petiolate, alternate, entire, ovate-lanceolate or oblong, 10–30 cm long, acute at both ends. Flowers white or sometimes pinkish, 7.5 mm wide, bisexual, on many-flowered terminal, then lateral, racemes from 5–20 cm long. Appearing late summer to mid-autumn and followed by purple-red, globose berries to 1 cm diameter.

Distribution North American native, from New England to Texas and Florida. Introduced elsewhere, particularly in the mediterranean region. Especially on rich, light soils in newly cleared land, field edges, roadsides.
Cultivation Wild. Cultivated on a market-garden scale in Carolina and elsewhere in the United States. Propagated from seed sown in spring or from root division in spring or autumn. Prefers sunny situation on deeply-dug, nutrient-rich, well-drained soils. A winter crop of vegetable leaf may be obtained by lifting roots in late autumn and planting closely in a box of damp peat, kept indoors; leaf may be cut when 15 cm long.
Constituents (root) Neutral principle, phytolaccin; alkaloidal substance, phytolaccine; phytolaccic acid; phytolaccatoxin (cyanchotoxin) and a hydrolysis product, phytolaccagenin; jaligonic acid; carboxy and dicarboxy oleanenes; various steroids and saponins; potassium salts. (berries) Saponins (to 25%); mucilage; tannic acid; phytolaccinic acid; red pigment, caryophylline. (leaf) Anti-viral protein, called PAP and similar to interferon; rubber; fatty oil. Note: the exact chemical status and nature of phytolaccin and phytolaccine are not fully known.
Uses (dried root, occasionally young cooked leaves) Emetic; purgative; narcotic; sternutatory; molluscicidal; spermicidal; fungicide; anti-rheumatic; anti-catarrhal. Root principally used internally in the treatment of throat infections associated with swollen glands; acting particularly on the lymphatics. Also used in chronic rheumatism and upper respiratory tract infections. Externally it is applied as an ointment or poultice in fungal infections, ulcers, haemorrhoids and scabies. Juice from the berries was once applied externally to ulcers and tumours, but it is not very effective. In Hungary the root is employed as an abortifacient, and in Mauritius it is considered to be a sedative.
After special treatment the berries may be used to colour wine and confectionery. They have also been used as a colouring in artists' paint.
Contra-indications Toxic and dangerous; it should only be used by medical personnel. To remove harmful substances it is important to soak in salt water, and cook well with 2 changes of water. The use of the young cooked plant, however, is not advised. When handling the mature plant gloves should be worn. May cause haematological abnormalities, violent emesis and possibly death.

Picea abies (L) Karst. PINACEAE
Norway Spruce
Picea is the ancient Latin name for a tree which is now the most commonly planted conifer in North America and Europe. It yields a light but strong timber. Norway Spruce is locally employed in the manufacture of spruce beer by fermenting with yeast the leaves and twigs in a sugar solution.
Description Monoecious evergreen tree to 40 m tall; bark reddish brown, branches pendulous, pubescent or glabrous, bearing quadrangular leaves 14–18 mm long. Female cones cylindrical-oblong to 18 cm, woody and pendulous. Male cones catkin-like.
Distribution Central and north European native. Introduced elsewhere.
Cultivation Wild. Extensively grown for timber. Numerous horticultural cultivars used as ornamentals.
Constituents Resin comprising α – and β – piceapimarolic, piceapimarinic and piceapimaric acids and juroresene; also volatile oil.
Uses (resin, Burgundy pitch, wood) Burgundy pitch was formerly used in counter-irritant plasters for the treatment of lumbago, rheumatism and chronic bronchitis.
Young tips (the spray) used in beer manufacture in north Europe.
The timber, white deal, is of great economic importance and a main source of paper pulp.

Picrasma excelsa (SW.) Planchon SIMARUBACEAE
Quassia Jamaican Quassia/Bitter Ash
Quassia was a generic name given by Linnaeus to *Quassia amara* L in honour of a Guyanan slave called Quassi who had used the wood from this 2 m-high shrub to treat fevers. *Quassia amara* L or the Bitter Wood of Surinam (Surinam Quassia) was therefore introduced to Europe (1756) and entered the London Pharmacopoeia in 1788.
By 1791 however the much larger, but closely related, West Indian tree, *Picrasma excelsa* (then known as *Quassia excelsa* Swartz) had been shown to possess very similar properties and this so-called Bitter Wood of Jamaica was imported to England. It replaced Surinam Quassia in the London Pharmacopoeia of 1809, but in several other countries – including Holland and Germany – *Quassia amara* has remained to this day the official Quassia. The Indians use another related plant, *Picrasma quassioides* Benn. for exactly the same purposes.
Description Ash-like tree to 20 m tall; leaves opposite, entire, unequally pinnate; the leaflets pointed at both ends, ovate. Flowers inconspicuous, greenish, appearing late autumn to early winter; followed by shiny black drupes.
Distribution Native to West Indies, particularly Jamaica (on lower mountains and plains), St Vincent and Antigua.
Cultivation Wild. Trees felled and sawn into logs 2 m long for export for quassia chip manufacture and for local pharmaceutical processing.
Constituents Resin comprising α- and β-piceasin, isoquassin (picrasmin) and neoquassin, to which the action is due.
Uses (stem wood) Bitter tonic; stomachic; insecticide. A powerful non-astringent bitter of benefit in loss of appetite due to gastric

debility. Stimulates the gall-bladder and gastric secretion. Once used as an enema to eradicate threadworm, and as an ingredient of lotions to destroy pediculi and other parasites. Roasted, powdered wood once employed as a Hop substitute to render ale bitter.
Infusions of Quassia chips, sweetened with sugar, or used alone, may be used as a fly killer. Of service as a horticultural insecticide destroying red spider, woolly aphids and greenfly.
Contra-indications Large doses irritate the stomach and cause vomiting.

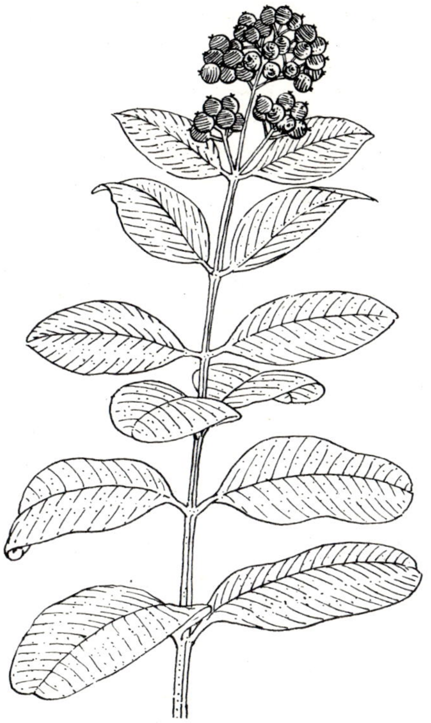

Pimenta dioica (L) Merr. MYRTACEAE
Allspice Pimento/Jamaica Pepper
Most of the European supplies of Allspice come from Jamaica where plantations of natural woodland consisting predominantly of these trees are called Pimento walks. The berries are harvested by hand when green and unripe, and then either sun or kiln-dried.
The name Pimento derives from the Spanish *pimienta* or *pimiento* meaning pepper, after the similarity in shape to peppercorns. *Pimienta* itself comes from the medieval term *pigmentum* meaning spicery.
The spice was first imported to Britain in the early seventeenth century and variously called *Pimienta de Chapa* and *Pimienta de Tabasco*, before Ray in 1693 described it as Allspice because of its combination of the flavours of cinnamon, nutmeg and cloves.
Botanically it has been classified as *Myrtus dioica* L, *M. pimenta* L, *Eugenia pimenta* DC, and *Pimenta officinalis* Lindl. – the last name emphasizing that the plant was included in the official British Pharmacopoeia from 1721 to 1914.
Description Aromatic evergreen tree to 12 m, resembling a large Myrtle; leaves petiolate, entire, glossy and leathery; oblong-lanceolate to 12.5 cm long. Flowers small (to 7.5 mm wide) white, in many-flowered cymes borne in the upper axils. Appearing mid-summer to early autumn and followed by dark brown, globose, 6 mm wide, 2-celled berries.
Distribution Native to Central America, Mexico, West Indies. Introduced to Indonesia. Prefers hilly environments on calcareous soils.
Cultivation Wild. Cultivated commercially in Central America; collected commercially in Jamaica. May be propagated by cuttings or layering, but in northern zones only grown as a non-flowering greenhouse ornamental.
Constituents Volatile oil (to 4.5%) comprising mainly eugenol (to 65%), also cineole, phellandrene, caryophyllene.
Uses (dried unripe berries, oil) Carminative; aromatic stimulant. Used as the source of oil of Pimento, which was once employed as a carminative. Powdered berries are of benefit in flatulence, dyspepsia and to disguise the taste of disagreeable medicines. They may also be incorporated in stimulant lotions and plasters. Principally used as a flavouring in rice, curries, puddings and cakes, and in pickling.
The tree provides wood which was once much used in the manufacture of umbrella handles and walking sticks.

Pimpinella anisum L UMBELLIFERAE
Anise Aniseed
Aniseed is one of the most ancient of spices and was cultivated by the Egyptians and later by the Greeks and Arabs. The early Arabic name was *anysum* from which was derived the Greek *anison* or *anneson* and the Latin *anisum*. Dioscorides considered that Egyptian Aniseed was second only to that grown in Crete.
In the Middle Ages it was largely used as a spice and as a carminative medicine, but it also entered into the composition of several classic aphrodisiac mixtures. In recent years its use as a flavouring has declined because of its high cost, and it is often replaced by Chinese Anise (*Illicium verum* Hook).
Description Aromatic, pubescent annual on thin root, to 75 cm tall. Stems erect, bearing long-petiolate, simple, coarsely-toothed, reniform lower leaves, 2.5–5 cm long, and 2 or 3 lobed, cuneate, entire or toothed upper leaves. Flowers whitish, small, numerous in open, thin, compound umbels; appearing late summer to early autumn, and followed by brownish, ribbed, aromatic, ovate fruit.
Distribution Indigenous to Egypt, the Levant and parts of the eastern mediterranean. On dry poor soils in sunny situations.
Cultivation Wild, or occasionally wild as an escape. Widely cultivated commercially in many warm countries, particularly India, Turkey, south mediterranean region, Mexico, Chile and Soviet Union. Propagate from seed sown in spring, later thinning to 30 cm apart; cannot be transplanted successfully. Will not produce ripe seeds in cold northern zones.
Constituents (seed) Volatile oil (to 3.5%) comprising mainly anethole (to 85%), methyl chavicol (estragol) (to 15%); also fixed oil (to 20%); starch; choline; sugars; mucilage. Action mostly due to volatile oil content.
Uses (ripe seed, fresh leaf, occasionally oil) Mild expectorant; carminative; galactagogue; weak diuretic; laxative; antispasmodic.
Especially effective in flatulence or flatulent colic. Aids digestion and improves the appetite by promotion of gastric secretions. Stimulates the mammary gland secretions and acts as a cough suppressant. Used in the treatment of bronchial catarrh. Used in combination with other laxatives. Once employed in asthma powders.
The oil may be combined satisfactorily with

liquorice in cough lozenges, or used alone as an antiseptic.

Important in manufacturing industries as a flavouring for food, liqueurs. Fresh leaf may be used in salads. Seed is added to vegetable curries, or chewed to sweeten the breath. It is occasionally used in perfumery, for example, as a constituent of eau de Cologne.

Pimpinella saxifraga L UMBELLIFERAE

Burnet Saxifrage

This somewhat variable herb is widely distributed throughout much of Europe but was not certainly used by the ancients – although it may be the *kaukalis* which Dioscorides referred to in his writings.

German physicians used it particularly from the Middle Ages onwards and it appeared in a number of pharmacopoeias including those of Augsburg (1640), Württemberg (1741) and Prussia (1799–1829).

In seventeenth-century Germany is was an ingredient of 'magic powders'.

Description Perennial on unpleasantly smelling taproot. Stem 30–100 cm tall, strong, slightly hairy, finely furrowed; bearing few 1 or 2-pinnate leaves, with ovate to lanceolate segments, 1–2.5 cm long. Flowers white or pink in compound umbels to 5 cm diameter. Appearing late summer to early autumn.

Distribution Native to Europe, Middle East and Siberia. Introduced and naturalized in New Zealand and the United States. On dry, grassy, shallow, stony and calcareous soils in warm situations to 2500 m altitude.

Cultivation Wild.

Constituents Volatile oil (to 0.4%) comprising coumarinic substances including isopimpinellin and pimpinellin; saponosides; bitter principles; resin; tannic acid.

Uses (dried root, occasionally fresh root) Expectorant; vulnerary; diuretic; stomachic; antiseptic; weak galactagogue; weak sedative. May be used in combination with other remedies for genito-urinary infections. Alone it is of benefit in the treatment of respiratory tract catarrh, upper respiratory tract infections and throat infections – in the latter case it may be used as a gargle. It promotes gastric and mammary gland secretions when taken internally.

Formerly employed as a mild sedative and externally as a poultice or bath to treat wounds. The young fresh leaf can be included in salads. The oil has limited use in certain liqueurs as a bitter flavouring.

Pinus mugo var. *pumilio* (Haenke) Zenari PINACEAE

Dwarf Mountain Pine

This variety of Mountain Pine is the source of a pure essential oil which is variously described as Pumilio Pine Oil, Pine Needle Oil and Oleum Pini Pumiliones. The oil is retained in the Swiss, Rumanian, Yugoslavian, Hungarian, Austrian and Czechoslovakian pharmacopoeias, and it is especially popular in Swiss, Italian and Hungarian medicinal use.

Pumilio Pine Oil is produced by distillation of the fresh young needles (which are shown in the illustration, below). It has been used since at least the seventeenth century.

In Britain, Dr Prosser James described its beneficial action in 1888 for certain respiratory diseases, and suggested its use in an atomizer to disinfect sickrooms.

Description Low prostrate shrub with glabrous, dark brownish, erect branchlets, and a grey somewhat scaly bark. Leaves to 3.5 cm long, stiff, needle-like, crowded in clusters or fascicles, bright green. Cones dark brown to yellowish, almost sessile, deciduous and dehiscent, ovoid to 4 cm long.

Distribution Native to the mountains of southern and central Europe. Rarely introduced elsewhere. Often on light, sandy or rocky soils.

Cultivation Wild plant infrequently cultivated horticulturally as an ornamental.

Constituents (oil) Esters (4–10%) comprising mainly bornyl acetate. (leaves) Esters; resins; small quantities of glycosides; unknown substances.

Uses (fresh leaves) Stimulant; counter-irritant and sometimes appears to possess slight anaesthetic properties. Inhaled as steam, the oil is of benefit in the treatment of coughs, laryngitis, chronic bronchitis, catarrh, asthma and other respiratory diseases since it exerts dilatatory action on the bronchi, the oil may be taken internally in small doses in the form of lozenges, syrups, or on sugar. The infusion of leaves is inhaled in the treatment of similar respiratory disorders.

Piper betle L PIPERACAE

Betel Betel Leaf

Betel chewing is a habit among Malays almost as popular as tobacco smoking among Europeans. The method consists of rolling up a slice or Areca Nut (*Areca catechu* L) with a little Lime (Chunam) (made by burning seashells), inside a leaf of Betel, and then slowly chewing the mixture – called a quid.

Chavica siriboa Miq. is sometimes used as a substitute for Betel Leaf.

Description Shrub, climbing by adventitious rootlets; stems semi-woody, enlarged at nodes, bearing entire, or undulate, thick, glossy, broadly ovate, slightly cordate leaves on 2.5 cm long petioles. Flowers yellowish in dense pendulous cylindrical spikes to 5 cm long; followed by fleshy fruit.

Distribution Indigenous to India, Ceylon and Malaysia. Introduced elsewhere. Requires hot and moist environment, in partial shade.

Cultivation Wild. Cultivated in India and the Far East.

Constituents Essential oil (0.2–1.0%) comprising cadenene, chavicol, chavibetol and sesquiterpenes; also sugars; starch; tannic acid;

acid; diastase (to 2%).
Uses (leaves, oil) Stimulant; antiseptic; carminative; sialogogue; tonic; stomachic.
Leaves commonly employed as a masticatory in the East; they act as a general tonic, promote salivary and gastric secretions, aid digestion, decrease perspiration and increase physical endurance.

Piper cubeba L PIPERACEAE
Cubeb Cubebs/Tailed Pepper
Cubeb was the East Indian name for this spice

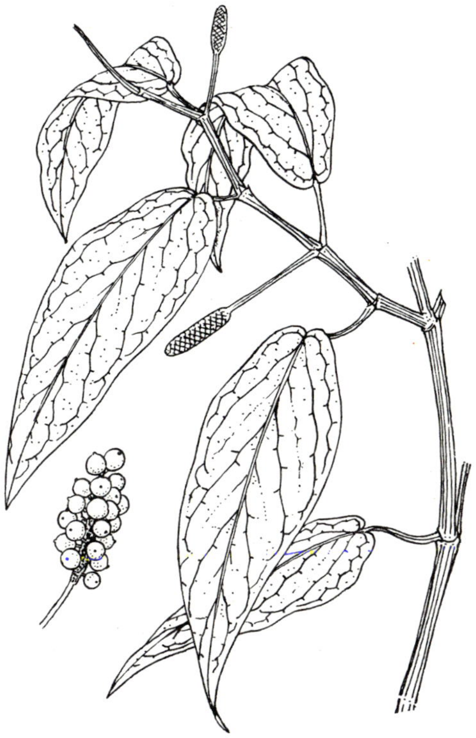

which as early as the tenth century was recognized by the Arabs to be a product of Java. Some authorities consider that the Arabic word *kababe* was a collective term which referred to a number of similar cubeb-like fruit. Indeed, even in modern times the peppercorn-like berries are frequently adulterated with inferior Piper species such as *Piper crassipes*, *P. ribesioides*, *P. mollissimum* and *P. muricatum*. The spice has enjoyed varying popularity. In the thirteenth century it was commonly found in Europe as a medicine and as a condiment, but by the end of the seventeenth century it was both uncommon and expensive. In England it had fallen into almost complete disuse by the early nineteenth century, but was reintroduced in 1815 after verification of its therapeutic effects by Army medical officers serving in the Far East.
Description Climbing perennial or shrub; stems smooth and flexuous, bearing glabrous entire, acuminate, petiolate, oblong or ovate-oblong, coriaceous and obliquely cordate leaves. Flowers dioecious, in spikes, and followed by brownish globose fruit to 6 mm diameter.
Distribution Native to south-east Asia, especially Sumatra and Java. Introduced elsewhere.
Cultivation Wild. Cultivated commercially in Ceylon, India and the East Indies.
Constituents Volatile oil (5–20%) comprising cubebic acid (to 1%), cubebin, cadinene, several terpenes and sesquiterpenes; resin; fixed oil; starch; calcium and magnesium malate. Action largely due to cubebic acid which has a local irritant and stimulant effect on mucous membranes.
Uses (dried unripe fruit, occasionally oil) Antiseptic; diuretic; stimulant; expectorant; stomachic; carminative. Once used in the treatment of genito-urinary tract infections, including gonorrhoea. May be of benefit in cystitis, indigestion, and if incorporated in lozenges, can be used for coughs, bronchitis and respiratory complaints. Formerly employed in the United States in asthma cigarettes. Principally of use as a condiment; the flavour resembles Allspice, and is suitable for sauces and fruit dishes.

Piper nigrum L PIPERACEAE
Pepper Black Pepper
Historically one of the most important spices which has been very highly prized since the earliest days of East-West trade. It has been used as a form of currency: during the siege of Rome (A.D. 408) part of the city's ransom was paid in Pepper berries, and a thousand years later 'pepper rents' were commonly paid to landlords. The quest for Pepper by European nations led them to discover a maritime route to the East. During the Middle Ages much of the wealth of Venice was derived from its Pepper trade.
In England the control of the spice trade was in the hands of the Guild of Pepperers (or *Piperarii* – derived from *Piper* or Pepper) from as early as 1154; this Guild was later to become incorporated with the Grocers Company, which in turn eventually lost its control over drugs and spices to the apothecaries. *P. nigrum* is also the source of White Pepper. Instead of picking the unripe berries and drying them to produce the Black variety, the fruit is allowed to ripen on the vine and then soaked to remove the dark skin (pericarp). White Pepper was known to Theophrastus and his Greek contemporaries but by the Middle Ages it had lost its popularity. Although still used most White Pepper is now, in fact, decorticated Pepper in that the outer layer is incompletely removed by machinery.
Description Perennial climbing shrub; stem strong and woody bearing glossy, prominently nerved, ovate-oblong to orbicular leaves, to 18 cm long and 12 cm wide, on 2 cm long petioles. Flowers white, usually dioecious, on glabrous spikes from 5–15 cm long. Followed by 6 mm diameter globose, yellow and then red, fruit.
Distribution Native to southern India; introduced to tropical Asia, Malagasy Republic, Brazil. In tropical forests; requires shade and high humidity.
Cultivation Wild. Cultivated commercially in Indonesia, South India, West Indies, Brazil and China; frequently in mixed plantations with other lucrative crops such as Coffee. Will yield a crop for approximately 10 years.
Constituents Volatile oil (to 2.5%), comprising

the alkaloids piperine, piperidine and chavicine; a yellow compound piperettine which hydrolyzes to piperidine and piperettic acid; traces of hydrocyanic acid; resins (to 6%); starch (to 30%).
Uses (dried unripe fruit) Stomachic; carminative; aromatic stimulant; antibacterial; insecticide; diaphoretic.
Stimulates taste-buds and thus causes reflex stimulation of gastric secretions. Employed in atonic dyspepsia. Also stimulates mucous membranes and part of the nervous system, and raises body temperature. May be used as a gargle, and externally as a rubefacient. East Africans use it as an abortifacient. They also consider that the body odour resulting from eating the fruit repels mosquitoes.
Mostly employed as a stimulating condiment and food preservative, as, for example, in sausage meats.

Plantago major L PLANTAGINACEAE
Greater Plantain Rat-tail Plantain/ Waybread
This and some closely related *Plantago* species such as *P. major* var. *asiatica* Decne. and *P. lanceolata* L have a long traditional use in the treatment of sores which has recently been vindicated by modern examination of the plant's action.
The unattractive and tenacious Plantains are the scourge of gardeners, but many are still highly respected in folk medicine from Africa to Vietnam.
Description Perennial. Leaves entire or slightly toothed, long petioled, ovate to elliptic, 5–20 cm long, forming a basal rosette. Leaves prominently 7-veined and no more than twice as long as the petiole. Flowers inconspicuous 3 mm wide, numerous, yellowish-green, with lilac and then yellow anthers; on cylindrical spike 5–40 cm long. Appearing early summer to mid-autumn.
Distribution Native to Europe. Introduced to other temperate zones. Widely distributed on cultivated land, wasteland and roadside. Prefers moist sandy or loamy nutrient-rich

soils, but tolerates most conditions.
Cultivation Wild plant. In eastern Europe commercial cultivation of *P. lanceolata* L. has recently begun.
Constituents (leaf) Mucilage; a pentacyclic triterpene, oleanolic acid; a glycoside, aucubin (rhinanthin); the enzymes emulsin and invertin; potassium salts (to 0.5%); citric acid. (seed) Oil (to 22%); a trisaccharide, planteose; aucubin; choline; various organic acids.
Uses (dried leaves, seed) Vulnerary; diuretic; expectorant; astringent; bacteriostatic.
Principally of use as a poultice, ointment or in decoction for the external treatment of wounds, ulcers and bites. Also used as a gargle and as an eye-wash in blepharitis and conjunctivitis.

The plant has the ability to destroy a wide range of micro-organisms, and stimulates the healing process (epithelization).
The leaf may be employed internally to treat diarrhoea, and conversely the seed is of benefit in constipation.
Formerly used to treat various haemorrhages including post-partum haemorrhage; also bronchitis, bronchial catarrh and coughs. An effective diuretic. Employed homeopathically. The young leaf was once used as a pot-herb.

Plantago psyllium L PLANTAGINACEAE
Psyllium Flea Seed
Seeds from several *Plantago* species which have the ability to swell in water due to their high mucilage content have been used for medicinal and other purposes.
P. psyllium and *P. indica* L. seeds are rich in mucilage and both are commercially known

as Psyllium. They have been used since Dioscorides' day, and the specific name is derived from the Greek for flea (*psylla*) – an allusion to the seed's appearance. Apothecaries called the seed *Pulicariae*, from the Latin for flea.
In India *P. ovata* Forskal, commonly known as Ispaghula, is used for precisely the same purposes, and may therefore replace Psyllium.
Description Annual with erect thin hairy stems 10–35 cm tall, bearing sessile, long thin (acicular) grey-green glandular leaves; opposite or in whorls of 3–6 leaves. Flowers small, numerous, white, in globose spikes borne on long peduncles; appearing late spring to late summer, and followed by 2–3 mm long, dark brown glossy seeds.
Distribution Native to the mediterranean region; especially France, Spain and North Africa. On poor, dry sandy soils in full sun.
Cultivation Wild. Cultivated commercially from seed sown in the spring.
Constituents Oil; mucilage (to 10%), comprising xylose, arabinose, galactose, and galacturonic acid, to which its therapeutic action is due.
Uses (seeds) Emollient; laxative.
Used in the treatment of chronic constipation; the seed's mucilage swells considerably in water and the gelatinous mass acts as a bulk purgative. The emollient action makes this herb also suitable for use in severe diarrhoea. It can be used as a soothing eye lotion.
Young leaves may be added to salads.
Employed industrially to dress muslin.
An ingredient of certain cosmetic preparations, such as face masks.

Podophyllum peltatum L BERBERIDACEAE
American Mandrake Podophyllum/Common May-apple
The name May-apple is derived from the fact that the juicy and acidic fruits are sometimes eaten, and, despite their laxative effects, they were once on sale in some American markets. All other parts of the plant must, however, be considered as poisonous, and the powerful nature of the dried rhizome is emphasized by the size of the therapeutic dose – 0.12 of a gram. American Mandrake was long used as an emetic by the Indians; but its purgative effect was introduced to medicine by Schöpf (1787) who was the physician to German soldiers fighting in the American War of Independence. It first entered the United States Pharmacopoeia in 1820 and is also in the Spanish and Portugese pharmacopoeias – although now only as the source of Podophyllum resin.
The generic name is derived from the Greek for foot-leaf; while *peltatum* means shield-shaped.
Description Perennial on reddish-brown, long (to 2 m), cylindrical rhizome 5–15 mm diameter. Stems simple, erect to 45 cm, bearing 1 or 2, 7–9 deeply lobed drooping leaves, to 30 cm wide. Flowers white, borne singly on nodding peduncle in the stem bifurcation between 2 leaves. Petals fleshy, 6 or 9; stamens 12 or 18; corolla to 5 cm wide. Appearing early summer

and followed in early autumn by 3–5 cm long, ovoid, yellow edible fruit.
Distribution North American native from Texas to Florida and Quebec. On damp nitrogenous soils in open woodland, pastures and near streams.
Cultivation Wild. Collected commercially in eastern North America. May be propagated by division of root-stock in the autumn, or from seed sown in the spring. Requires damp, humus-rich soils, and partial shade.
Constituents Podophyllotoxin and related substances such as picropodophyllin; podophylloresin; quercetin; α- and β-peltatin; starch; flavonoids. Purgative action due to the podophyllotoxin and podophylloresin content.
Podophyllin or podophyllum resin is produced by adding the alcoholic tincture to water.
Uses (rhizome, Podophyllum resin) Powerful purgative; gastro-intestinal irritant; antihelmintic; anti-mitotic. Used locally externally on soft venereal warts and on other warts. Both resin and rhizome have been employed as a purgative in cases of chronic constipation with associated liver complaints, although actual choleretic action is not substantiated. Normally combined with less drastic remedies.
Contra-indications POISONOUS. May cause severe gastro-intestinal irritation or polyneuritis. External application must be carefully restricted to abnormal tissue only; systemic absorption has been shown to cause poisoning. Not to be used during pregnancy. Only to be used by medical personnel.

Pogostemon patchouli Pellet LABIATAE
Patchouli
Patchouli oil has one of the strongest and most distinctive perfumes known and for this reason was traditionally used to scent Indian linen, to distinguish material of Indian origin. Several of the 40 species in the genus *Pogostemon* are now used as a source of Patchouli oil, which has therefore become of somewhat variable quality. Besides *P. patchouli* Pell. (which is also known as *P. heyeanus* Benth. and *P. cablin* (Blanco) Benth.), Patchouli is mostly derived from the Javanese species *P. comosus* Miq. Alternative sources from different genera

include *Microtaena cymosa* Prain and *Plectranthus patchouli* Clarke.
Description Aromatic perennial to 1 m tall; stems erect, square, slightly hirsute, bearing opposite, ovate or triangular leaves approximately 3–5 cm long. Flowers whitish, often marked with purple, arranged in groups on terminal and axillary spikes.
Distribution Native to south-east Asia and India; introduced to West Indies and parts of South America. Requires tropical or subtropical conditions.
Cultivation Wild. Cultivated commercially and horticulturally from seed sown in the spring, or by division of root-stock in spring or autumn, or from cuttings taken in late spring. May be grown as a greenhouse plant in temperate zones. Use a rich or medium-rich potting compost, and strike heeled cuttings in high humidity.
Constituents Oil comprising cadinene, stearoptene and related compounds. Obtained from leaves by distillation.
Uses (dried leaves, oil) Antiseptic; insecticide. Not commonly used for medicinal purposes. Once considered to act as a stimulant.
Principally of use as a perfume. The oil may be employed in a wide range of cosmetic preparations, including soaps. It is also used in incense. Leaves can be incorporated in potpourris, scented sachets and other scented articles.

Polemonium caeruleum L POLEMONIACEAE
Jacob's Ladder Charity/Greek Valerian
Polemonium is an ancient name of uncertain origin for a herb which has now largely fallen into disuse. It was known to Dioscorides as *polemonion* and the root was once administered in wine in cases of dysentery, toothache and against the bites of poisonous animals.
As late as 1830 the herb, then called *Herba Valerianae graecae,* was still retained in some European pharmacopoeias and was employed predominantly as an antisyphilitic agent or in the treatment of rabies.
The common name refers to the ladder like shape of the leaves.
Description Perennial from 30 cm to 1 m tall; stems erect bearing short, petiolate or sessile, alternate, pinnate leaves. Basal leaves from 7.5–12.5 cm long, long-petiolate, the petioles being winged; 11–21 lanceolate leaflets larger than stem leaves, from 15 mm to 2 cm long. Flowers blue, 5-petalled, 3 cm diameter, in drooping panicles, appearing late to mid-summer.
Distribution European native. Introduced to temperate zones.
Prefers damp soils near streams in the partial shade of woodland.
Cultivation Wild, usually rare and localized. Found as a garden escape. Cultivated horticulturally from seed sown in spring or by division in the autumn. Requires rich, moisture-retaining soil and the addition of lime.
P. caeruleum var. *lacteum* Benth. has white flowers; *P. caeruleum* var. *himalayanum* Baker has larger lilac-blue flowers. Both may be found in cultivation as Jacob's Ladder.
Constituents Unknown.
Uses (dried flowering plant, dried root) Weak diaphoretic. Once considered to possess blood-purifying qualities, but now no longer used for medicinal purposes.
Principally of horticultural use in formal and historical gardens.

Polygala vulgaris L POLYGALACEAE
Common Milkwort
In chalky areas and in continental Europe the very similar Bitter Milkwort (*P. amara* L) is the species commonly found; it has the same properties as *P. vulgaris* but it is more bitter and hence acts as a bitter tonic. Early writers decided that *P. vulgaris* was the *polygala* and *polugalon* of Pliny and Dioscorides respectively – both from the Greek meaning much milk – but this cannot be certain and several Milkwort's now retain the traditional virtue of being galactogogues.
Description Perennial 10–30 cm tall, with erect or decumbent stems. Leaves alternate, evergreen, obovate to lanceolate, 5–35 mm long. Flowers usually blue, occasionally pink or whitish, in loose racemes; appearing early summer to early autumn.
Distribution Native to Europe; on grassland, heathland, mountain pastures, in sandy, well-drained, but humus-rich soils to 2000 m altitude.
Cultivation Wild. Propagate from seed sown in spring on the soil surface; do not cover with soil or germination will be poor.
Constituents Essential oil, comprising gaultherine and other compounds; saponins; polygalic acid and senegine; mucilage; resin.
Uses (dried whole plant, dried root) Expectorant; diuretic; laxative; stomachic.
Traditionally considered to be a galactogogue, but this is unsubstantiated. Of use in bronchitis and pulmonary complaints, often combined with other remedies; but not effective in asthma as once supposed.
The leaves and root make a crude soap which is similar to *Saponaria officinalis* but less effective.

Polygonum bistorta L POLYGONACEAE
Bistort Snake Root/Snakeweed
Bistort belongs to the knotweed genus, many members of which are characterized by their swollen or jointed stems. *Polygonum* itself means many-kneed from the stem's shape.

Bistorta describes the rhizome and is from the Latin for twice twisted, after the snake-like shape of the underground parts. It used to be known as *Serpentaria* or *Serpentaria rubra* (after the red colour within the blackish rhizome) which has led to some confusion since both *Artemisia dracunculus* L and *Arum maculatum* L were also called *Serpentaria* in the sixteenth and seventeenth centuries.

There are over 200 species of *Polygonum* and this one was not introduced into medical practice until the Renaissance; the leaf, however is still included in the Swiss Pharmacopoeia and the rhizome in the pharmacopoeias of France and Russia.

It was certainly an important food in the spring in northern countries from earliest times – sometimes even being cultivated as a garden herb.

Description Perennial on thick, somewhat flattened and twisted S-shaped rhizome; stem erect 25–50 cm or occasionally to 1 m tall. Radical leaves broadly ovate or lanceolate, lighter and hairy beneath, 5–15 cm long, outline wavy; stem leaves sparse, smaller, triangular-acuminate. Petioles variable in length and triangular in section; leaves folded longitudinally before opening. Flowers pale pink or rarely white, numerous, small (4 mm diameter), in dense solitary, cylindrical terminal spikes of 10–15 mm diameter. Appearing mid-summer to early autumn.

Distribution European native. On moist siliceous nutrient-rich grassland, mixed woodland, fenland and alpine mats. Particularly on higher ground, and frequently near water.

Cultivation Wild plant.

Constituents Tannic acid (to 20%); oxalic acid; vitamin C; starch; action due to the astringency of the tannins.

Uses (dried rhizome) Strong astringent; anti-inflammatory; vulnerary.

Useful in decoction or infusion for diarrhoea or as a gargle in aphthous ulcers, stomatitis and gingivitis. Applied externally to cuts or sores and to haemorrhoids. The powdered rhizome acts as a styptic. Once used in the treatment of tuberculosis (action uncertain).

The root is edible after it has been soaked in water and then roasted.

Young shoots and leaves may be boiled and eaten as spring greens.

Used in veterinary medicine.

Polypodium vulgare L POLYPODIACEAE
Polypody Root Common Polypody/
Brake Root

Both the generic and common names of this fern refer to the branching habit of the rhizome; the Latin *polypodium* means many-footed.

Dioscorides knew the drug and prescribed it as a purgative. He also used the pulverized fresh mucilaginous root as a poultice for sprained or fractured fingers. It is now rarely used and in the past it was usually only used for its expectorant action, which is weak. A related Peruvian Polypody, *P. calaguala* Ruiz – whose

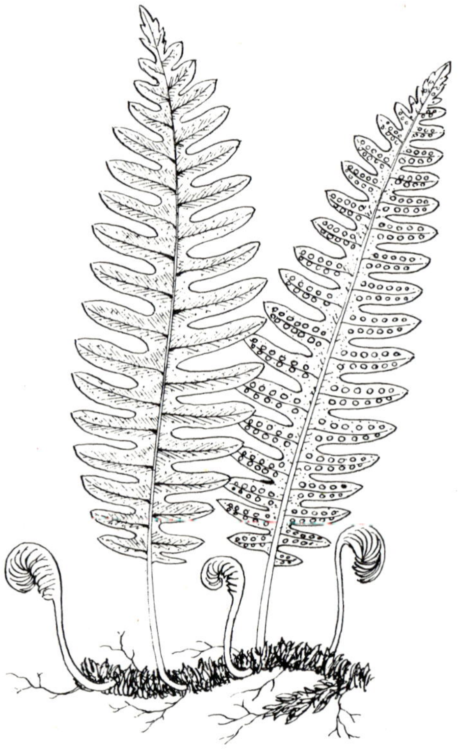

common name is Calahualae – was shown in the 1930s to possess better expectorant qualities than this species.

Description Perennial fern on long creeping somewhat flattened rhizome to 10 mm thick, bearing numerous brown scales, and from which the stipes grow to 10–50 cm. Leaves smooth, deeply pinnate, with 20–40 lanceolate, alternate and opposite, obtuse or semi-acute sometimes curved, segments; midribs prominent. Sporangia in light brown circular sori arranged either side of main segmental nerve.

Distribution Native to Europe, western Asia; introduced to North America and other temperate regions. Frequently found on old walls, rocky ground, woodland, ruins and old decaying tree trunks. Requires damp, shady sheltered conditions.

Cultivation Wild. Several varieties cultivated for horticultural purposes; most of these forms being characterized by attractive foliage.

Constituents Essential oil; mucilage; sugars; tannic acid; bitter resins; a saponoside, polypodine; various mineral salts. Cholagogue action largely due to polypodine.

Uses (dried rhizome) Cholagogue; expectorant; laxative; antihelmintic.

Small doses promote the appetite; stronger decoctions are useful in the treatment of chest infections, coughs, and bronchial catarrh. Large doses act as a mild laxative and antihelmintic with some action against tapeworms.

Populus candicans Ait. SALICACEAE
Balm of Gilead Poplar Buds

The descriptive term Balm of Gilead has been used for a number of different plants. One of the first and possibly the original Balm of the Bible was the oleo-resin obtained from *Balsamodendron opobalsamum* Kunth. – also called the Balm of Mecca. Miraculous properties were once attributed to this aromatic substance but it is now obsolete in Europe and most authorities consider it is extinct in its former Indian and Egyptian homes, although it may survive locally in the Middle East.

Canada Balsam from *Abies balsamea* Marshall was also once called Balm of Gilead, but the commercial product is now derived from *P. candicans* (which is also known as *P. balsamifera* var. *candicans* Gray and *P. gileadensis* Rouleau) and from the Balsam Poplar, *P. balsamifera* L. (also called *P. tacamahacca* Mill.). It is probable that several other substitutes from the Poplar family (such as *P. tremuloides* Michx.) are known as Balm of Gilead.

Description Tree to 20 m (occasionally to 30 m), spreading with open and irregular top; leaves

dark above, lighter and hirsute beneath, cordate, alternate, petiolate, broad-ovate or deltoid, 10–15 cm long. Flowers in drooping scaly catkins to 15 cm long. Winter leaf buds sticky, resinous and highly aromatic.
Distribution Uncertain origin. Introduced and naturalized in several temperate countries. Frequently beside rivers.
Cultivation Wild. Cultivated horticulturally as aromatic garden ornamental.
Constituents Oleo-resin; salicylic compounds including salicin and salicin benzoate; buds yield to 40% of an alcohol-soluble extractive.
Uses (dried or rarely fresh leaf buds, occasionally oleo-resin) Antiseptic; rubefacient; expectorant.
Used internally in the treatment of upper respiratory tract infections, particularly coughs, laryngitis and bronchitis. May be employed in ointments for external application to relieve the local pain and irritation of arthritis, cuts and bruises. An excellent gargle for sore throats.
The buds can be used in a range of scented articles where a heavy resinous balsamic aroma is required.

Portulaca oleracea L PORTULACACEAE
Purslane Wild Purslane/Yellow Portulaca
Purslane has long been used as a foodstuff in India and the Middle East, and was introduced into cultivation in Europe in the Middle Ages. It was first grown in England in 1582 but was probably well-known in Italy and France long before this as Ruellius described both the wild and erect cultivated garden form in 1536.
It is still collected from the wild in Africa, India and the Far East and used for culinary and medicinal purposes. The related plant *P. quadrifida* L is used in South Africa as an emetic by the Zulu.
Description Annual or biennial with fleshy prostrate or decumbent stems to 15 cm; somewhat pinkish, and bearing opposite, fleshy, spatulate, sessile leaves 1–2 cm long. Flowers small (7.5 mm), yellow, sessile, single or in groups of 2 or 3, appearing in late summer; the petals soon fall and reveal a small seed capsule.

Distribution Native from Greece to China. Introduced elsewhere. On dry, sandy, nitrogen-rich weedy soils in full sun.
Cultivation Wild. Cultivated horticulturally for centuries in the Middle and Far East. A number of varieties and cultigens have been developed from this wild species. Propagate from seed sown successively from late spring to early autumn on light, well-drained soil; water well and harvest 6–8 weeks after sowing. Leaves of the cultivated varieties may be less sharp than the wild plant.
Constituents Vitamin C (700 mg per 100 g fresh plant); potassium salts (1% in fresh, 70% in dry plant); urea; oxalic acid; carotenoid pigments; alkaloids (0.03%); glucoside; β-sitosterol; volatile oil; resins; organic acids (to 1%); sacchariferoid (2%). The combined action being predominantly diuretic and tonic.
Uses (fresh herb) Diuretic; tonic; anti-scorbutic. Due to its high vitamin C content the plant was once an important remedy for scurvy. It has also been used in a variety of pulmonary and skin diseases. The seed and root are reported to be antihelmintic but this has not been proved. It is a useful diuretic when used fresh and may be incorporated with other remedies for the treatment of urino-genital infections. The leaf has vasoconstrictive properties, and in conditions of low blood pressure can be used to induce more vigorous contractions of the heart.
Extensively used in several subtropical countries as a cooked vegetable and a salad herb.

Portulaca oleracea var. *sativa* (L) DC. PORTULACACEAE
Garden Purslane Green Purslane/Kitchen-garden Purslane
Garden Purslane was popular in north-west Europe from the end of the sixteenth century until the end of the eighteenth century, but in English speaking countries it is now rarely grown.
Several varieties were developed from the Wild Purslane of which the Green, Golden and large-leaved Golden were the best known. Only the Green and Golden varieties are now easily obtained, the latter sometimes erroneously being described as a separate species, *P. sativa* or the Yellow Purslane. The true Yellow Purslane is *P. lutea* Soland and is found in New Zealand.
The common name is from the old Latin name for the plant *porcilacca*; while *oleracea* means a vegetable garden herb used in cooking.
Description Annual. Similar to *P. oleracea* L but a taller plant reaching 50 cm, with thicker stems and bright green succulent spatulate leaves.
Distribution Widespread in temperate and subtropical zones. Probably developed in the Middle East or southern Europe. Prefers nitrogen-rich, well-drained dryish soils in full sun.
Cultivation Only found in the wild as a garden escape. Propagate as for *P. oleracea* L. Plant 15–20 cm apart in rows 30 cm apart. If sufficient water is given, 2 or 3 gatherings will be possible from each plant. A winter and early

spring crop can be obtained by successive plantings on hotbeds or in frames. Grown semi-commercially in France, Italy and Holland.
Constituents Similar to *P. oleracea* L.
Uses (fresh herb) Not used for medicinal purposes. Principally eaten cooked but may also be used sparingly in salads; it has a sharp taste. The stem and leaves are pickled for winter use. A traditional ingredient of the French soup *bonne femme* and the Middle East salad, *fattoush*.
The attractive golden-leaved variety may be used for horticultural purposes in formal herb gardens.

Potentilla anserina L ROSACEAE
Silverweed Wild Tansy
There are more than 300 species in the genus *Potentilla*, most of which are found in the northern temperate zones, and Silverweed is one of the most easily recognized with its silky-silver leaf undersides. This characteristic led to both its current common name and the earlier names *Argentina* and *Argentaria* (from *argent* meaning silver).
The generic name is from the Latin *potens* meaning powerful after the medicinal action of the group, most of which contain high percentages of tannin and are thus strong astringents.
Anserina comes from the Latin *anserinus* meaning pertaining to geese, since the birds were thought to be particularly partial to the leaves; many animals are happy to graze on the plant. The Silverweed has been identified as the *Myriophyllon* of Dioscorides who suggested boiling the plant in salted water for the treatment of haemorrhages.
Description Silky perennial 20–40 cm tall, on short, thick root-stock from which arise long creeping stolons (to 80 cm long) which root at the nodes. Radical leaves 5–25 cm long, compound, pinnate, silvery-white and hairy beneath; 14–24 leaflets, 1–6 cm long, alternately large and small, oval, deeply dentate.

Flowers 5-petalled, golden yellow, to 2 cm diameter, borne singly on long stems arising from the basal rosette. Appearing mid to late summer.

Distribution European native. Introduced elsewhere. On nitrogen-rich, loamy, undisturbed damp soils; roadsides, railway embankments, damp pastureland to 1500 m altitude.

Cultivation Wild.

Constituents Tannins; choline; resins; flavones; an alcohol, tormentol; starch.

Uses (dried flowering plant, dried leaves, occasionally root-stock) Astringent; antispasmodic; tonic; stomachic.

Used in the treatment of diarrhoea, painful menstruation (weak action), and as a digestive aid in indigestion. Formerly used to treat various haemorrhages including those arising from haemorrhoids; as a douche in leucorrhoea, and for uterine spasms. Externally it may be applied to cuts and wounds, and it is of use as a gargle in mouth complaints such as ulcers. Employed homeopathically. The roots may be roasted, boiled or eaten raw.

Potentilla erecta (L) Raüsch. ROSACEAE

Tormentilla Common Tormentil

The red colouring matter found in the root-stock of this herb appears to be identical with a substance known as ratanhia-red present in the root-bark of *Krameria triandra* Ruiz and Pav. or Peruvian Rhatany, an astringent plant which was introduced to Europe in 1796 by Hipolito Ruiz and which has now largely replaced Tormentilla in several official preparations. Many authorities have noted that Rhatany is preferred only for economic reasons, since the plants possess similar actions. It is coincidental that Rhatany was brought to the notice of Ruiz by the women of Lima who used it to preserve their teeth, while Tormentilla was long used as an astringent tooth powder. *P. erecta* was apparently not widely used in medicine until the sixteenth century when it first found favour in the treatment of colic; the name Tormentilla is derived from the Latin *tormina* meaning colic.

It is still employed widely in European folk medicine, and occasionally in the manufacture of artists' colours.

Description Perennial, 10–40 cm tall on thick (to 3 cm), woody, long (to 20 cm) rhizome, reddish internally. Stems prostrate or more usually erect, thin, branched, bearing sessile, 5-lobed stem leaves, with 1–2 cm long, narrow leaflets and long stalked, 3-lobed, broadly ovate, basal leaves, with 5–10 mm long leaflets. Flowers yellow, only 4-petalled, 10–15 mm wide, carried singly on long (10–30 cm) thin peduncles, arising from stem-leaf axils. Appearing from early summer to early autumn.

Distribution Native to Europe, West Asia and Siberia; rarer in the mediterranean region. On light, acidic, damp soils, particularly heathland, fenland, open deciduous and coniferous woodland, and often in hilly regions. To 2200 m altitude.

Cultivation Wild plant.

Constituents Catechol-tannins (to 20%), which on storage convert to phlobaphenes; an alcohol, tormentol; a glycoside, tormentilline; starch; sugars; a bitter, chinovic acid (or quinovic acid) also found in Cinchona bark.

Uses (dried root-stock) Astringent; haemostatic; anti-inflammatory; vulnerary.

A powerful remedy in severe diarrhoea, largely due to its high tannin content. Principally used to much benefit externally as an infusion on cuts, wounds, abrasions and burns, including sunburn. The plant promotes epithelization. It is also used as a lotion for topical applications to haemorrhoids, frostbite, and as a gargle in throat and mouth inflammations. The powdered root-stock is an excellent styptic.

A root extract is used in certain forms of schnapps.

The roots provide a red dye.

Once used in tanning.

Contra-indications A powerful astringent; must be used internally with care. Prolonged contact with the skin should be avoided, as it may cause scarring.

Poterium sanguisorba L ROSACEAE

Salad Burnet Garden Burnet

It has been cultivated as a salad herb at least since Lyte recorded it in *Dodoens' Herball* of 1578, but was also known as *Sanguisorba minor* from the time of Fuchs (1542). The Great Burnet (*Sanguisorba officinalis* L) was preferred as the official medicinal plant, probably because it is larger; both species, however, possess similar properties.

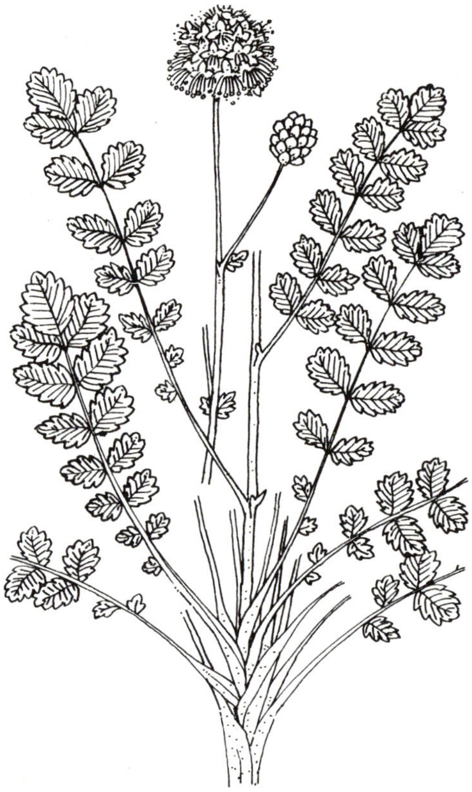

Sanguisorba means either blood-ball or blood stopping after both the appearance and action of the inflorescence and whole plant.

Description Perennial on woody root-stock 20–70 cm tall, forming a clump of branching grooved stems bearing leaves subdivided into 7–11 serrate lobes, oblong or orbicular. Flowers greenish or reddish brown, small, in a dense rounded terminal panicle to 15 mm diameter; appearing early to mid-summer.

Distribution Native to Europe and Asia; introduced and somtimes naturalized elsewhere. On dryish porous calcareous grassland, woodland edges, roadsides, in warm situations to 1700 m altitude.

Cultivation Wild. Cultivated as a salad herb from seed sown in spring or autumn. Remove the flowers to encourage production of leaf. Suitable as an edging plant in formal herb garden designs.

Constituents Vitamin C; essential oil; tannins; flavones; a saponoside.

Uses (whole fresh or dried plant, fresh leaf; rarely dried root-stock) Astringent; vulnerary; haemostatic; carminative; digestive.

Chewing the leaf assists digestion, while infusions of the whole plant are of use in treating haemorrhoids or diarrhoea. The root decoction is an excellent haemostatic and can be used on all cuts and wounds. Traditionally considered of benefit in the menopause, but this is unsubstantiated.

Primula veris L PRIMULACEAE

Cowslip Paigle

The Cowslip obtained its name by corruption of 'cowslop' from the old English *cu-sloppe*, signifying its occurrence in meadows fre-

quented by domesticated animals. Changing agricultural practices, however, have led to its rapid disappearance in parts of Europe, and attempts to cultivate it on a commercial scale in eastern Europe have proved uneconomic.
Tradition maintains that the Cowslip arose from the ground where St Peter dropped his keys, hence the English, French and German common names, Keys of Heaven, *Clef de St Pierre* and *Schlüsselblumen*. The generic name Primula is from the Latin *primus* meaning first after its early flowering in the spring.
Description Soft-pubescent perennial on short, stout rhizome surrounded by leaf bases and producing long thin rootlets. Leaves obtuse, ovate-oblong, finely hairy and crenate, 5–20 cm long, narrowing at the base into a winged petiole, equally long as the leaf blade. 1–30 deep yellow flowers marked with orange, 10–15 mm diameter, on a nodding umbel surmounting a 10–30 cm long stalk (scape). Appearing late spring to late summer.
Distribution Native to northern and central Europe, Iran. Introduced and sometimes naturalized elsewhere. On porous calcareous soils in meadows and pastures, mixed or deciduous woodland; preferably in warm dryish situations. To 2000 m altitude.
Cultivation Wild. May be propagated from seed sown as soon as ripe, or by division of root-stock in autumn. The Oxlip *P. elatior* (L) Hill is frequently mistaken for the Cowslip but may be distinguished by its lack of orange marking and its possession of a seed capsule longer than the calyx.
P. veris var. *Kleynii* Hort. is found in cultivation; it has darker yellow to salmon coloured flowers.
Constituents Vitamin C; saponins (to 10%); flavonoid pigments; a volatile oil, primula camphor; the heterosides primulaveroside and primveroside; enzymes; mineral salts.
Uses (dried root-stock, dried flowers and calices, occasionally dried leaves) Expectorant; antispasmodic; weak diuretic; weak laxative.
Of benefit in inflammatory conditions of the respiratory tract, bronchitis and coughs; frequently used in the form of a syrup. Once used to treat pneumonia and traditionally thought to be a remedy for palsy and paralysis.
The flowers are used as a weakly sedative tea; also in the manufacture of home-made wines, and are candied and used as cake decorations.
Contra-indications Some members of the Primulaceae, but particularly *Primula obconica* Hance, possess the quinone, primin, which causes a particular form of contact dermatitis called primula sensitivity, characterized by a violent vesicular eruption on the fingers and forearms. Allergic individuals should avoid the plants.

Primula vulgaris Huds. PRIMULACEAE
Primrose
The Primrose is so popular in spring that it is now almost extinct close to large urban areas. It has in fact always been heavily cropped by man, not so much as a medicine but rather as a base for home-made drinks, conserves, cosmetics or just for their attractive appearance and subtle smell. They are to the north Europeans the epitome of spring, and are well named since the word Primrose comes from the Latin *prima rosa*, meaning the first rose (of the year).
The genus *Primula* comprises more than 400 species which hybridize readily and are an important horticultural group. This species, for example, hybridizes with *P. veris* L to produce the so-called Common Oxlip.
Description Perennial on short thick root-stock Leaves wrinkled, blunt, obovate-spatulate, hairy beneath, glabrous above, crenulate, 8–20 cm long, narrowed into a petiole shorter than the leaf blade. Flowers pale yellow, occasionally purplish, 3–4 cm wide, solitary on pubescent pedicels to 20 cm long. Appearing early spring to early summer.
Distribution European native. On rich, damp soils in shady woodland, hedgerows, grassland.
Cultivation Wild plant. Propagate by division on heavy or medium loam in semi-shade or sun.
Constituents Saponins; volatile oil.
Uses (dried root-stock, fresh flowering plant) Expectorant; antispasmodic; diuretic; anodyne.
Used as an expectorant in bronchitis and other respiratory infections. The tisane may be of benefit as a mild sedative in anxiety and insomnia. Formerly used in rheumatic disorders and in ointments for skin wounds and blemishes.
Flowers may be candied, used in salads and in Primrose tea.
Leaves once boiled as greens.
Contra-indications The same precautions apply as for *Primula veris*.

Prunella vulgaris L LABIATAE
Self Heal Heal-all/Woundwort
A common weed throughout America and from western Europe to China. Its easy availability led no doubt to its commonest use in stemming blood flow resulting from domestic accidents and fights; hence the common names Carpenter's Herb, Touch and Heal, Sicklewort, Hercules Woundwort, and the plant's historical pre-eminence as a vulnerary herb. It has other uses: the Chinese, for example, discovered its antipyretic and diuretic actions and still use it in gout in conjunction with other remedies.
Sixteenth-century adherents of the Doctrine of Signatures saw the throat in the shape of the flower and introduced it to treat diseases of the throat such as quinsy and diphtheria. Hence its modern generic name *Prunella* which is derived via Brunella and Braunella from the German for quinsy (*Die Braüne*). It is still called *Brunelle commune* and *Gemeine Brunelle* in France and Germany respectively.
Description Aromatic perennial with creeping rhizome on square erect or decumbent stems to 60 cm. Leaves either entire or toothed, petiolate, opposite and decussate, oblong-ovate, 3–7.5 cm long. Flowers violet-purple

(occasionally pink) 8–15 mm long, borne in leaf axils on compact spikes to 4 cm long. Appearing mid-summer to mid-autumn.
Distribution Native to Europe, Asia and North America; introduced elsewhere. On moist, loamy, well-drained soils in grassland, pastures, open woodland; preferably in sunny situations.
Cultivation Wild. Propagate from stem cuttings taken in spring or summer and rooted in a peat and sand mix; or by division of clumps. The pink flowered form is sometimes called *P. vulgaris* var. *rubrifolia* Beckhaus., while a white variety may be found as *P. vulgaris* var. *leucantha* Schur.
Constituents Tannins; volatile oil; an alkaloid; bitter principles; unknown substances.

Uses (dried flowering plant) Vulnerary; astringent; antiseptic; carminative.
Commonly used as a mouthwash, gargle and external wash in the treatment of sore throats, irritation and inflammation of the mouth, ulcers, cuts, burns, wounds and bruises. Once considered a specific against diphtheria. Rarely used internally and then only in cases of mild diarrhoea or flatulence. It acts as a weak bitter tonic.
Strong infusions of the dried powdered herb are effective styptics.

Prunus avium L ROSACEAE
Wild Cherry Common Wild Cherry/Gean
The fruit of *P. avium* are smaller than those of the cultivated Cherry varieties but, unusually for wild European fruits, they are quite sweet. The tree is, therefore, understandably called Sweet Cherry in the United States yet rarely so described in its native home.
It has doubtless long been of domestic importance since its stones have been discovered in Neolithic remains. This species has also provided the stock for the table Cherry while the Morello or Sour Cherry comes from *P. cerasus* L. *Prunus* is an ancient name for the plum, while *avium* is the Latin for bird, which readily eat the fruit. The word cherry can be traced back to an Assyrian base *karsu*; the Greek name for it was *kerasos*.
Description Deciduous tree 10–20 m tall; bark smooth, reddish, peeling off transversely in strips; branches ascending bearing dark green, dentate, alternate somewhat variably shaped leaves, 10–15 cm long, but usually oblong-ovate to oblong-obovate, and pubescent beneath. Flowers white, 5-petalled, 3 cm wide, on long glabrous pedicels to 4 cm; appearing late spring to early summer with the first leaves, and followed by globular or cordate fruit which are first yellow, then red and finally purple.
Distribution Native to Europe, western Asia; introduced elsewhere. In deciduous woodland.
Cultivation Wild – the species from which the cultivated Cherry was developed. It is used for grafting purposes in fruit-tree nurseries. Many different ornamental forms exist with double flowers, variegated leaves, weeping growth and attractive foliage. The variety *P. avium*

var. *Juliana* (L) Schübl. and Martens provides the Heart Cherries, and *P. avium* var. *duracina* (L) Schübl. and Martens the Bigarreau Cherries, of which the best known are Napoleon and Windsor.
Constituents (fruit stalks) Tannic acid; potassium salts; flavonoids. (fruit) Organic acids; provitamin A; tannins.
Uses (fruit, dried fruit stalks) Diuretic; astringent.
Many parts of the tree have traditionally been used for a variety of medicinal purposes. Today only the dried fruit stalks are available commercially, for use in folk medicine as a diuretic.
They also have some effect in cases of mild diarrhoea.
The fruit is used domestically for home-made conserves and commercially in liqueur manufacture (kirsch).
The wood is a valuable timber.

Prunus dulcis (Mill.) D.A. Webb ROSACEAE
Almond
The Almond tree has been in cultivation in Asia for thousands of years and is mentioned in Genesis. It was introduced to Europe by the Greeks who knew of more than 10 kinds of the seed which was then known as *amugdale*, and from which the Latin term *amygdala* was derived. The Romans called them *Nuces graecae* or Greek Nuts, and they have been cultivated in Italy from a very early date. They do not seem to have been grown in France until the eighth century and were not grown in north-west Europe until the late Middle Ages; the first tree was planted in England in the early sixteenth century. Elizabethan cooking, however, used large quantities of the seed, and 'Almond water' was frequently called for and used much as we now use milk in certain recipes. The botanical classification of the plant is complicated and very many different names will be found; *Prunus amygdalus* Batsch. and *Amygdalus communis* L are the commonest, but have now been superseded.
Description Bush or tree from 3–7 m tall, with glabrous light-coloured branches, and narrow, glabrous finely dentate, acuminate, oblong-lanceolate leaves 7.5–10 cm long, with gland-bearing petiole. Flowers pink or white, usually solitary, 3–4 cm wide, sessile, appearing mid to late spring either with or before the first leaves; followed by oblong-ovoid light green pubescent fruit, to 4 cm long containing 2 seeds.
Distribution Native to southern and central Asia, especially Persia. Introduced to south-Europe 2500 years ago; now widespread and frequently naturalized. To 3000 m altitude.
Cultivation Wild. Widely cultivated, and is the original species from which many varieties have been developed. The Bitter Almond is *P. dulcis* var. *amara* (DC) Buckheim (formerly *P. amygdalus* var. *amara* (DC) Focke), and the Sweet Almond is *P. dulcis* var. *dulcis* (DC) Buckheim (formerly *P. amygdalus* var. *sativa* (F.C. Ludw.) Focke). Other varieties and cultigens provide fruit of different shapes and sizes. The tree is somewhat frost sensitive and should be planted on well-drained soil in full

sun in a warm position.
Constituents (seed) Protein (to 20%); edible fatty oil (to 65%); enzymes, mainly emulsin; vitamins A, B_1, B_2,B_3, B_6, E and PP (nicotinamide); mineral salts. (Bitter almond seed contains up to 4% of a toxic glycoside, amygdalin).
Uses (oil, seed) Demulcent; nutritive; emulsifying agent. Sweet Almond oil is predominantly used to prepare emulsions in which other herbal remedies may be suspended, particularly for cough mixtures. The sweet oil is used externally in massage oils and internally as a laxative. Bitter Almond oil was once used as a flavouring in pharmaceutical preparations and externally in demulcent skin and sunburn lotions, and is now used in the perfumery, liqueur and confectionery industries. Almond flour was formerly used in diabetic foodstuffs. Both oils are widely used in cosmetic and toilet preparations.
The seed is used in many sweet and savoury dishes.
Contra-indications The raw Bitter Almond seed contains cyanide derivatives and is POISONOUS.

Prunus laurocerasus L ROSACEAE
Cherry Laurel Cherry Bay/
Common Cherry Laurel
The Cherry Laurel is now most commonly found as an ornamental hedge, and has never been of great importance medically although some Spanish and Swiss physicians once promoted it as a sedative. In Britain it was noticed first by Madden in Dublin (1731) following fatal poisoning by Irish cooks who mistakenly thought it could be used as a Bitter Almond flavouring. Its action is due to the presence of cyanide derivatives, which may be fatal even in small quantities.
The plant was introduced to European botany by Pierre Belon and Clusius between 1550 and 1580.
Description Variable evergreen bush or small tree usually 3–4 m (occasionally 6 m) tall. Leaves shiny, dark green, oblong, alternate, obtuse or occasionally retuse, short-petioled, 7.5–12.5 cm long. Flowers strongly scented, white, in slender racemes to 10 cm long, appearing late spring to early summer and

followed by dark purple conical fruit to 15 mm long.

Distribution Native to south-east Europe, and western Asia to Iran. Introduced and often naturalized elsewhere. Frequently in valleys in hilly regions.

Cultivation Wild. Introduced as an ornamental bush and successfully grown in areas where neither the summers nor the winters are too extreme. Frequently used in hedging, when it should be pruned carefully with secateurs rather than generally clipped. May be propagated by cuttings taken in summer.

Constituents The glycosides prulaurasin (laurocerasin) and prunasin, which are decomposed in water by the enzyme prunase to release hydrogen cyanide, benzaldehyde and glucose. Cherry Laurel water is manufactured from the leaves by distillation.

Uses (Cherry Laurel water, very occasionally leaves) Sedative; antispasmodic.

The water was once used in the treatment of nausea and vomiting, as a flavouring agent, and, much diluted, as an eye lotion. It is now obsolete in most countries. The leaves can only be applied externally in small quantities in a mixed poultice for the temporary relief of pain.

Contra-indications Very POISONOUS. To be used internally only under medical supervision.

Pulmonaria officinalis L BORAGINACEAE

Lungwort Jerusalem Cowslip/Jerusalem Sage

This herb's common names variously refer to the white spots on its leaves, the change in its flower colour from pink to blue, or more frequently to its former application in lung diseases. Hence the generic name *Pulmonaria* which is derived from its medieval Latin name of *pulmonaria*, and, by translation, Lungwort. Lungwort's reputation far exceeded its therapeutic action, however.

Description Hairy perennial on creeping rootstock, reaching 30 cm tall; stems hairy and unbranched bearing few, alternate, sessile, white-spotted, oval and slightly pointed leaves to 7.5 cm long. Flowers blue, pink, purplish or white, primrose-like, to 2 cm long in terminal cymes; appearing spring to early summer. Flowering stem dies down in late summer and is replaced by a rosette of basal, long-petioled, auriculate-cordate leaves.

Distribution Native to Europe; introduced elsewhere. On well-drained calcareous soils in mixed woodland and thickets; to 1000 m altitude.

Cultivation Wild. Propagate by rootstock division in autumn or after flowering.

Constituents Mucilage; tannins; mineral salts, especially potassium and silica; saponins; allantoin.

Uses (dried flowering plant) astringent; diuretic; emollient; weak expectorant. Of use in the treatment of diarrhoea, haemorroids and some gastro-intestinal problems; also of some benefit in respiratory disorders such as bronchial catarrh.

Leaves once used as a pot herb.

Punica granatum L PUNICACEAE

Pomegranate

Pomegranates are mentioned in many ancient writings and have been depicted in various forms of illustration from the days of the Egyptians.

Both the fruit rind and root bark were used medicinally by the ancients, and Pliny and Dioscorides specifically mentioned the root decoction as being effective in the destruction of tapeworms. Yet, although various parts of the plant – such as the fruit rind – can be traced in the writings of the apothecaries and druggists, the valuable root bark apparently fell into disuse for 2000 years until the nineteenth century. In 1807 Buchanan and then Fleming reintroduced it following observations of its use in India.

The generic word *Punica* is derived from the Latin *malum punicum* meaning the apple of Carthage, which is one of its early names while *poma granata* (and hence pomegranate) means apples with many seeds.

Description Deciduous tree or shrub to 6 m tall, with spiny tipped branches; leaves opposite, sub-opposite or clustered, glabrous, entire, oblong or oval-lanceolate with pellucid areas, 2.5–6.0 cm long, narrowing at the base to a very short petiole.

Flowers orange-red, waxy, 4–5 cm long and wide, followed by large brownish-red or yellowish edible fruit (4–8 cm diameter) containing numerous seeds and soft pink pulp.

Distribution Native to Asia, particularly Afghanistan, Persia and the Himalayas. Naturalized in the mediterranean region, India, South America, southern United States, and parts of south and east Africa.

Cultivation Wild. Cultivated commercially and horticulturally. Both this species and a dwarf form, *P. granatum* var. *nana* (Pers.) are grown in temperate zones as greenhouse ornamentals.

Constituents (fruit rind) Yellow bitter colouring matter; gallotannic acid (to 30%). (root bark) Alkaloids (to 0.9%), comprising mainly pelletierine, pseudopelletierine, isopelletierine and methylisopelletierine, to which the antihelmintic action is due; also tannins (to 20%). (leaf) Ursolic and betulic acids; various triterpenes. (fruit) Invert sugar (10–20%); glucose (5–10%); citric acid (0.5–3.5%);

boric acid; vitamin C.

Uses (dried fruit rind, fresh or dried root bark, fresh leaf, fresh fruit) Astringent; antihelmintic; antibacterial. The rind is a powerful astringent which is used in decoction in the treatment of dysentery and diarrhoea, and as an infusion for colitis or stomach ache. Also used as a douche in leucorrhoea. The bark is effective in the removal of tapeworms (more effective when fresh), and has been used as an emmenagogue.

The leaf has antibacterial properties and is applied externally to sores.

The fruit is bitter and refreshing; of commercial importance both as the whole fruit and in fruit drinks.

Pyracantha coccinea M.J. Roem. ROSACEAE

Firethorn Everlasting Thorn

Although closely related to the genus *Crataegus* some of whose species provide valuable heart remedies, the Firethorn is now employed only as an ornamental. *Pyracantha* is from the

Greek for fire and thorn after the red fruit and shiny branches.
Description Much branched evergreen shrub or small tree to 5 m. Leaves dark green, acute, crenate-serrate, narrow-elliptic, 1.5 cm–5 cm long. Small, white flowers in large corymbs, appearing early summer and followed by red or orange berries which last through the winter.
Distribution Native from south Europe to western Asia. Escaped and naturalized in North America and elsewhere.
Cultivation Wild. Cultivated as ornamental or wall shrub, often espaliered. Hardy on well-drained soils. Propagate by ripe wood cuttings under glass, by seed, or by layering. Prune back hard to promote branching. Dislikes transplanting.
Constituents Cyanogenic glycosides.
Uses No longer used for medicinal purposes; the fruit is purgative but toxic.
Of use as a winter ornamental for hedges or walls.

Quercus robur L FAGACEAE
Oak English Oak/Pedunculate Oak
No plant has been of greater symbolic, religious and magical importance in Europe than the Oak tree, and its esteem has been traced back to the earliest Indo-Germanic religions. No other plant has provided more in the construction of buildings, ships, weapons and fine furniture. Oak's strength and durability were unequalled, and as a result the vast Oak forests of Europe have been virtually destroyed. Although its bark provides an excellent astringent medicinal remedy, only herbalists used it to much extent, the apothecaries and others preferring more exotic and costly drugs.
Description Round-topped deciduous tree to 40 m tall; bark first smooth, later developing fissures; leaves 5–12.5 cm long, oblong-ovate with 3–7 lobes each side, petiole short (to 1 cm). Small, greenish-yellow staminate flowers in thin catkins; pistillate flowers in spikes in leaf axils; appearing late spring to early summer, and followed by ovoid or oblong fruit on peduncles 3–7.5 cm long.
Distribution Native to North Africa, Europe and western Asia; introduced elsewhere. In forests, mixed woodland, on clay soils; from lowlands to mountainous regions.
Cultivation Wild plant. Planted commercially on estates and forestry land for timber. The variety *Q. robur* var. *fastigiata* DC has a more columnar appearance while the Durmast or Sessile Oak (*Q. petraea* (Matt.) Lieblein) has a less spreading and less branched growth, and sessile fruit. Several forms of *Q. petraea* exist.
Constituents Tannins (to 20%); a glycoside, quercitrin.
Uses (dried bark, occasionally dried leaves and fruit) Astringent; anti-inflammatory; antiseptic.
Used as a gargle for throat disorders; as a douche in leucorrhoea; externally as a lotion for cuts, burns, abrasions, and for application to haemorrhoids.

Used internally for haemorrhoids, diarrhoea and enteritis. Once used as a tonic tea.
Roasted acorns have been used as a coffee substitute.
Valuable timber.
Bark was once the most important agent for tanning leather; and also provided a variety of dyes, the colour depending upon the mordant used.

Ranunculus ficaria L RANUNCULACEAE
Lesser Celandine Pilewort
The fig-like shape of the swollen root-tubers of this plant led to the specific epithet *ficaria* from *ficus* or fig. Earlier herbalists considered the same structure to resemble piles and by association they were used, with much success, in the treatment of haemorrhoids.
Members of the genus *Ranunculus* are not popular in folk medicine because of their poisonous and acrid nature, and all species should be handled with care and only used externally.

The Latin *ranunculus* means a little frog and it was given this name since many of the 250 species in the group are aquatic or are found in very wet habitats.
Description Perennial with hollow, erect or prostrate branched stem, on several clavate or fusiform root-tubers; 5–25 cm tall. Leaves cordate, occasionally toothed, glabrous, petiolate and sheathed at the base, glossy; 1–4 cm long, the stem leaves being smallest. Flowers yellow, 2–3 cm diameter with 8–12 petals, solitary, appearing mid to late spring on long peduncles.
Distribution Native to Europe, North Africa and western Asia. On rich nitrogenous soils in wet situations; in woodland, meadows, ditches. Prefers shade.
Cultivation Wild plant. Propagate from root-tubers planted in the autumn, 5 cm deep, in damp rich soils.
Constituents Vitamin C; anthemol; tannins.
Uses (fresh herb, occasionally dried herb) Astringent. The plant is specifically used in the preparation of ointments for external application to haemorrhoids.
The acrid and vesicant juices from the sliced tubers were once applied to warts.
Very young leaves were once eaten to prevent scurvy.
Contra-indications POISONOUS in the fresh state; not to be used internally. Handling the bruised plant may cause skin irritation.

Raphanus sativus L CRUCIFERAE
Radish
This well-known salad herb has been in cultivation for so long that its origin is uncertain, but it probably originated in China where many varieties exist today including a long-rooted, winter-harvested Chinese Radish, or Daikon (a Japanese name), which is sometimes cultivated in the West.
Some authorities believe that *R. sativus* (*sativus* means cultivated) is a cultivated variety of the Wild Radish or Wild Charlock (*R. raphanistrum* L), a widespread and troublesome weed.
Radishes have certainly been grown since the time of the Pharaohs, and the Greeks and

Romans knew several varieties including the *syriacan* (or round Radish) and the *radicula* or *radix* (the common long Radish) the latter meaning simply root and being the source of the common name, Radish.
The black Radishes which are the varieties now employed in homeopathic medicine were probably developed in Spain in the Middle Ages.
Description Annual or biennial on fleshy root of variable shape and colour; stem glaucous 60–90 cm bearing lyrate-divided, petiolate leaves with a large terminal segment. Flowers dark-violet, white-veined, in racemes appearing summer and followed by 3–7 cm long fruit (a silique).
Distribution Worldwide on most soil types.
Cultivation Cultivated plant; found wild as an escape. Many cultigens exist, all of which are raised from seed sown thinly on moist, friable soils in an open position. Time of sowing depends on variety; but usually best sown every three weeks.
Constituents An antibiotic glycoside, glucoraphenine; mineral salts; vitamin C; oxalic acid. The seeds contain linoleic and linolenic acids.
Uses (fresh root, fresh leaves, root juice, fresh young seed pods) Antibiotic; bechic; tonic; carminative; choleretic; nutritive.
Of benefit in the relief of dyspepsia and used to promote salivation. Formerly employed in the treatment of coughs and bronchitis. May be used in combination with other remedies in the treatment of liver conditions especially where bile secretion is inadequate. Also used homeopathically.
The root and young leaves are eaten as a salad herb, and the young seed pods may be pickled.

Rhamnus catharticus L RHAMNACEAE
Buckthorn
So common a plant with so drastic an effect as this powerful purgative has doubtless been used for a very long time. The Anglo-Saxons certainly recorded it in the ninth century, when it was known as Waythorn or Hartsthorn, while the thirteenth-century Welsh physicians of Myddvai used its fruit boiled with honey. Three hundred years later Gerard was to recommend boiling them with broth; they are rarely taken alone, and even when Syrup of Buckthorn was first included in the London Pharmacopoeia in 1650 (it had appeared almost a century earlier in the German pharmacopoeias) it was mixed with Nutmeg, Cinnamon, Aniseed and Mastich (the latter a gum from *Pistacia lentiscus* L).
The characteristic spine on the branches has led to most of its names: Crescenzi and Gesner called it *Spina cervina*; Cordus, *Cervi spina*; Matthiolus, *Spinus infectoria*; and Caeselpinus, *Spina cervatis*. Dodoens knew it as *Rhamnus solutivus*.
The plant is now rarely used for medicinal purposes, but home dyers still employ the bark as a golden-brown dyestuff.
Description Deciduous bushy shrub from 2–4 m tall, occasionally to 6 m. Branches spreading irregularly, and often tipped with a spine; bark reddish-brown and glossy. Leaves opposite, acute or obtuse, margins finely dentate, ovate, 3–6 cm long, 2–5 cm wide. Flowers small, greenish-yellow; usually unisexual, in delicate clusters in leaf axils, appearing late spring to mid-summer, and followed by 7.5 mm diameter globose, fleshy, black fruit (drupe).
Distribution Native to north-west Europe, northern Asia, eastern North America. Widespread in scrub, woodland, forests, on calcareous soils to 1200 m altitude.
Cultivation Wild. Planted on farmland as hedging. Cuttings taken in summer are easily rooted.
Constituents Vitamin C; frangula-emodin; shesterine; chrysophanol; rhamnosterin; rhamnicoside; rhamnicogenol; a fluorescent pigment, rhamnofluorin; other yellow pigments.

Uses (2 year old bark, fruit) Purgative; diuretic. Only employed in the treatment of chronic constipation; usually in association with other remedies. Juice from the fruit was once used in veterinary medicine as a laxative.
The fruit and bark can be used as sources of dyes.
Contra-indications Strong purgative action; to be taken with great care.
Do not use fresh bark.

Rhamnus purshiana DC RHAMNACEAE
Cascara Sagrada Sacred Bark
Cascara sagrada means sacred bark and this was the name first given to the tree by Spanish-Mexicans who noted the American Indian use of the bark as a laxative and tonic.
The tree was mentioned in the eighteenth-century American materia medicas but first described botanically in 1814 by Pursh – hence the plant's specific name. Use of the bark in conventional medicine began in 1877 and a year later a nauseous and bitter fluid extract for use in chronic constipation was available pharmaceutically. This extract was exported to Europe and it was not until 1883 that the bark itself was made available outside the United States of America. It has been conclusively demonstrated that the crude bark is

very much more effective as a purgative than any commercial preparation made from the bark; the official dried and liquid extracts are for example only 15 per cent as active. The bark is retained in many national pharmacopoeias.
Description Deciduous tree to 10 m. Bark dark grey, smoothly wrinkled. Leaves in tufts at branchlet tips; 5–15 cm long, elliptic to ovate-oblong, either rounded or acute. Flowers in umbels, stalked, appearing spring and followed by black, globose fruit of 7.5 mm diameter.
Distribution North American native from British Columbia to Washington state. In coniferous woodland, on mountain ridges and canyon walls.
Cultivation Wild plant.
Constituents Anthraquinone glycosides (6–9%), comprising cascarosides A, B, C and D and other glucosides, to which the action is due.
Uses (dried stem bark, at least 6 months old)

Purgative; bitter stomachic. May be used in small doses as an appetite stimulant. In large doses it acts as a laxative or a mild purgative. Sometimes the tincture is applied to childrens' fingernails to deter them from biting their nails.

Rheum officinale Baill. POLYGONACEAE
Rhubarb
This is not the garden species commonly grown for its edible leaf stalks, that one being *R. rhabarbarum* L. The garden Rhubarb was introduced to western Europe in 1608 and was first cultivated at Padua botanic gardens by Prosper Alpinus; it was widely grown by the end of the eighteenth century, but the root has never been used owing to a substance (the glycoside, rhaponticin) which exerts a hormonal effect on humans.
Rheum officinale, however, is one of two main species, the dried rhizomes of which have been important medicinally in China since around 2700 B.C. Both have been imported into Europe since the time of the early Greeks. Dioscorides described the drug as *rheon* or *rha*, hence the modern names. Because the main centre for trading in the drug has changed over the centuries, both this and other species have been variously described as Turkey, East Indian and Muscovitic rhubarbs. The plant was introduced to Europe in 1867 and limited cultivation led to further names such as English, German, Bucharest, Dutch and French rhubarbs.
Description Perennial on thick rhizome, reaching 3 m tall. Leaves to 1 m wide, round-elliptic, basal, 3–7 lobed. Flowers white small, numerous, in panicles on tall, stout, hollow, finely grooved stem. Appearing mid to late summer.
Distribution Native to Tibet and west China, introduced elsewhere. On deep, rich, moist soil at altitudes of 3000–4000 m.
Cultivation Wild. Cultivated in the East.
Constituents Tannins; anthraquinone derivatives of aloe-emodin, chrysophanol, emodin and rhein (to 10%).
Uses (dried rhizome) Mild purgative; astringent; bitter.
Principally employed alone or in combination with other remedies in the treatment of chronic constipation. In small doses it may be used to treat diarrhoea, gastro-intestinal catarrh, and to stimulate the appetite.
Added to tonic wines as a bitter.
Contra-indications Not to be used by individuals with renal or urinary calculi.

Rheum palmatum L POLYGONACEAE
Rhubarb Chinghai Rhubarb
R. palmatum and some varieties such as *R. palmatum* var. *tanguticum* (L) Maxim., and *R. palmatum* var. *palmatum* (L) Maxim., are now, and possibly always were, the main sources of medicinal Rhubarb.
R. palmatum was introduced to European gardens in 1763, earlier than *R. officinale* Baill., and like that species was cultivated commercially. It is still cultivated in Russia and Germany, but the Chinese product is superior. In the Chinese herbal Pen-King (2700 B.C.) the drug was called *Ta-huang*, meaning the great yellow, after its colour and reputation, and this name was retained for 2000 years by the traders who collected it in Tibet and the province of Kansu. *R. palmatum* is now called Chinghai or high-dried Rhubarb.
Description Perennial on thick rhizome, reaching 2 m tall. Large leaves in basal clumps, cordate at base, orbicular and palmately lobed. Flowers reddish to greenish-white, small, numerous, in clusters on tall, stout, hollow, finely grooved stem. Appearing mid to late summer.
Distribution Native to north-east Asia. On deep, rich, moist soils at altitudes of 3000–4000 m.

Cultivation Wild. Cultivated commercially in China, Russia, Germany and Central Europe. Requires moist, deep, well-manured soil; propagated from root division and root cuttings, rarely from seed. Occasionally grown as garden ornamental.
Constituents Tannins; anthraquinone derivatives of aloe-emodin, chrysophanol, emodin and rhein (to 10%).
Uses (dried rhizome) Mild purgative; astringent; bitter.
Principally employed alone or in combination with other remedies in the treatment of chronic constipation. In small doses it may be used to treat diarrhoea, gastro-intestinal catarrh, and to stimulate the appetite.
Added to tonic wines as a bitter.
Contra-indications Not to be used by individuals with renal or urinary calculi.

Ribes nigrum L SAXIFRAGACEAE
Blackcurrant
A well-known fruit formerly collected from the wild in northern Europe and now extensively cultivated commercially and horticulturally. Although it was once used in folk medicine for throat infections it is now not considered to be of medicinal importance and finds greatest use in the food and drinks industries.
Ribes is an old Arabic name and the specific epithet *nigrum* means black, referring to the colour of the wild fruit. Today green, yellow and white forms are grown, and many cultivars have been developed.
Description Aromatic perennial shrub to 2 m, lacking spines and bearing 5-lobed, rounded, long-petiolate, alternate or clustered leaves. Flowers 4–10, greenish-white in pendulous racemes in leaf axils. Appearing late spring to early summer and followed by spherical, soft berries.
Description Native to north and central Europe, and west Asia. Introduced and naturalized in North America. On moist, loamy, slightly acidic soils in woodland.
Cultivation Wild. Cultivated commercially and horticulturally for fruit. Several cultivars exist. Propagation by cuttings taken in autumn. Prefers cool, humid climate and clay soils provided they are well drained. Constant pruning is essential to good cropping.
Constituents Anthocyanin pigments; vitamin C; pectin; sugars; various organic acids; essential oil.
Uses (fresh or dried leaves, fruit) Nutritive; diuretic; astringent; tonic.
The leaves may be used as an infusion to treat

diarrhoea; they are also weakly diaphoretic and have been included in cold remedies, and to treat urinogenital infections.

Once employed in the treatment of rheumatism. The fruit is of value to those suffering from hypertension, or possessing capillary fragility; and can be used in an infusion as a gargle for sore throats. Leaves can be used as a tea substitute. Fruit widely used in conserves, jams, drinks, cordials and liqueurs as well as eaten fresh.

Ricinus communis L EUPHORBIACEAE

Castor Oil Plant Wonder Tree

The Castor Oil Plant was certainly known to the Egyptians who employed the seed oil as an unguent base and also in lamps. Theophrastus, Dioscorides and other Greeks also knew both the plant and the oil, but considered the latter unfit for culinary use and suitable only for external application medically – a tradition maintained for the following 1500 years

and faithfully reproduced in the sixteenth-century herbals of Turner and Gerard. Up to the end of the sixteenth century European supplies of the oil came from the East, notably India, but for a period of 200 years the supply declined for some reason and in much of Europe it was only used infrequently.

The oil was reintroduced to medicine in 1764 by Canvane who had noted its use in the West Indies where it was called *Palma Christi* and *agno casto* by the Spanish, (hence Casto oil, and then Castor oil).

Since the 1780s it has been retained as a purgative in many pharmacopoeias.

Description Very variable annual herb or perennial tree from 2–15 m tall, usually 4 m. Leaves simple, alternate, long-petioled, 5–11 lobed, glossy, to 1 m wide. Flowers monoecious; male below, female above; both without petals and in panicles. Followed by a smooth or spiny capsule, 3 cm in diameter.

Distribution Native to India, tropical Africa; distributed throughout tropical and many temperate regions. On most well-drained soils in full sun.

Cultivation Wild. Cultivated commercially in many countries especially South America, India, Africa, Italy. Grown as a house plant in cool, northern temperate zones, or outside in protected sites. Prefers well-drained clay or sandy loams. Propagate from seed planted in early spring or under glass, transplanting in early summer. Many cultivars exist.

Constituents (seed) Protein (to 26%); fixed oil (to 50%) comprising ricinoleic, oleic, linoleic, stearic and hydroxystearic acids. One of the protein substances in the whole seed is a toxic albuminoid, ricin, to which the poisoning is due.

Uses (seed oil, steam treated seed cake) Purgative.

Principally used to treat chronic constipation but also in acute diarrhoea caused by food poisoning. Applied as an enema to remove impacted faeces.

Used externally as an emollient and a vehicle for various ointments. Soothes eye irritations.

The oil is not suitable for cooking, but is used in the manufacture of paints, varnishes and soap.

The seed cake (steam treatment destroys the poison, ricin) is employed as a fertilizer.

Contra-indications Whole seeds are toxic; not to be used internally. Large doses of the oil may cause vomiting, colic and severe purgation.

Rosa canina L ROSACEAE

Dog Rose Dog Briar

The Rose more than any other flower symbolizes the zenith of beauty in the plant kingdom, and since man started cultivation its scent has been most highly esteemed. The Dog Rose, however, was so common throughout Europe (Pliny thought Britain was called Albion because it was covered with the white rose – *alba* meaning white) that it has generally been treated with familiarity and contempt.

The epithet Dog is only incidentally derogatory, coming originally from the *cynorrodon* of Pliny and *Rosa canina* of the Middle Ages after a supposed ability of the root to cure 'mad-dog bites', or rabies. Apothecaries employed the briar balls or galls of the Dog Rose as a diuretic and the rose-hips were used as a tart fruit from the earliest times. The latter became medicinally important only in the Second World War as a rich source of vitamin C.

Description Climbing and trailing prickly perennial shrub to 3 m. Leaves alternate, ovate to elliptic, to 4 cm long, serrate, acute or acuminate. Flowers aromatic, large, white or pale pink on long pedicels, appearing mid to late summer. Followed by 15 mm-long, fleshy, scarlet false fruits (hips).

Distribution Native to Europe, North Africa, western Asia; introduced and naturalized elsewhere. On porous soil in hedgerows, woodland, thickets to 1600 m in altitude.

Cultivation Wild.

Constituents Vitamin C (to 1.7%); vitamins B, E, K; nicotinamide; organic acids; tannins; pectin.

Uses (rose-hips, leaves) Tonic; laxative; diuretic; astringent.

The leaves may be used as a laxative or in poultices to aid wound healing.

Rose-hips, usually used as a tisane or in the form of the seedless purée, are an excellent source of vitamin C, a tonic, and useful in lethargy. The seeds were once used as a diuretic. The hips are used in conserves and jams.

Rosa eglanteria L ROSACEAE

Sweet Briar Eglantine

This is a vigorous grower and possesses a strong fragrance which can be smelled at a distance, characteristics which led to its use as a hedging plant from early times.

The common and specific names come from the medieval Latin *aculentus* meaning thorny. Formerly classified as *Rosa rubiginosa* agg. and subdivided into two species, *R. rubiginosa* L and *R. micrantha* Borrer ex Sm., but now considered as *R. eglanteria*.

Description Perennial shrub 1–2 m tall. Leaves orbicular to elliptic, to 3 cm long; pubescent

and rusty-coloured beneath. Flowers 1–3, bright pink, strongly scented, to 3 cm wide, appearing mid to late summer and followed by round scarlet false fruit (hip).
Distribution Native to Europe, west Asia, introduced and naturalized elsewhere. In hedgerows and woodland edges.
Cultivation Wild plant. A cultivar, *Duplex*, with double flowers is grown horticulturally.
Constituents Tannins; essential oil.
Uses (flowers) Astringent.
No longer used medicinally. In some countries it is employed in the treatment of diarrhoea and colic.
A useful hedging plant in large gardens.

Rosa rugosa Thunb. ROSACEAE
Japanese Rose Turkestan Rose
This is one of the most hardy of all roses and is in addition both disease resistant and a profuse and continuous bloomer. The scent is rich and

somewhat clove-like and is considered superior to Sweet Briar as a hedge plant. The hips may be used as a source of vitamin C.
Description Perennial to 2 m. Very prickly stems. Leaves subdivided into 5–9 elliptic leaflets to 5 cm long. Flowers scented, white to rose, to 7.5 cm diameter, followed by large red or orange hip to 3 cm diameter.
Distribution Native to Japan and China.
Cultivation Wild. Widely cultivated as a large number of attractive hybrids, and varieties include Max Graf, one of the lowest growing roses, obtained by crossing *R. rugosa* with *R. wichuraiana* Crép.
Constituents (hips) Vitamin B, C, E, K; nicotinamide; organic acids; tannins; pectin.
Uses Rarely used for any purpose other than as a hedge plant.

Rosmarinus officinalis L LABIATAE
Rosemary
The common and generic names are derived from the early Latin *ros maris* or dew of the sea, from its habit of growing close to the sea and the dew-like appearance of the blossom at a distance. From earliest times its medicinal virtues were recognized and it has always been a popular aromatic plant.
The oil was first extracted by distillation in

about 1330 by Raymundus Lullus, and it is still extensively used in perfumery. One of the most famous cosmetic preparations containing the herb was the Queen of Hungary's water. The apothecaries used Rosemary in a wide range of preparations including waters, tinctures, conserves, syrups, spirits and unguents; but today only the oil is included in the pharmacopoeias, while the leaf remains popular in folk medicine.
Description Aromatic, evergreen perennial shrub to 180 cm, usually 100 cm tall. Branches somewhat pubescent when young, becoming woody. Leaves simple, opposite, leathery, tomentose beneath, to 3.5 cm long. Flowers pale blue or rarely white to pink, small, in short axillary racemes, appearing late spring to early summer.
Distribution Native to mediterranean coast.
Cultivation Wild. Collected commercially from the wild and cultivated only as a garden plant. Requires well-drained soil and warm, wind-sheltered position in cooler regions. May be grown in pots. Propagate by stem cuttings or seed. Various cultivars are grown of which the most useful is the prostrate form, (sometimes called *R. prostratus* Hort.).
Constituents Essential oil (to 2%) comprising 2–5% esters (mainly bornyl acetate) and 10–20% free alcohols (mainly borneol and linalol); organic acids; choline; saponoside; heterosides; tannins.
Uses (fresh or dried leaves, oil) Tonic; diuretic; aromatic; stomachic; carminative; antispasmodic; cholagogue; antiseptic; emmenagogue.
A leaf infusion has a wide variety of internal applications as indicated. The oil may be used externally as an insect repellant, in various soothing embrocations, and diluted as an antiseptic gargle. It is particularly effective in neuralgia.
Wide culinary use of the leaf in meat dishes.
The oil is employed widely in the cosmetic industry.
Leaf may be used in bath mixtures and aromatic preparations.
Contra-indications The oil should not be used internally. Extremely large doses of the leaf are toxic, possibly causing abortion, convulsions, and very rarely, death.

Rubia tinctorum L RUBIACEAE
Madder Dyer's Madder
Both the early Greek name *Erythrodanon* and the Latin name *Rubia* come from a stem-word meaning red, since this has traditionally been the source of a brilliant red permanent dye Adrianople Red or Turkey Red, later called alizarin.
By the end of the nineteenth century the process of maddering wool or cotton consisted of various steps including scouring in mild alkali, steeping in oily emulsions, washing in sheep dung, galling with oak galls, treating with alum and finally maddering with powdered and partially fermented roots.
The dried roots were first exported from south-east Europe and Turkey to other parts of Europe, and cultivation then commenced near the cloth centres of France, Holland, Germany and, less commonly, England. Even though it has long since been replaced by synthetic alizarin, it is still grown as a medicinal plant in central Europe and west Asia.
The Wild Madder (*Rubia peregrina* L) provides a rose-pink dye.
Description Climbing perennial, 60–100 cm tall, on long, fleshy, much-branched rootstock. Leaves in whorls of 4–8 on stiff, prickly stem; usually sessile, lanceolate, 5–10 cm long, tipped and spiky at the margins. Flowers small, greenish-yellow, in both axillary and terminal cymes; appearing mid-summer to early autumn, followed by globose, purple-black berry.
Distribution Native to south-east Europe, Asia Minor; introduced to central and north-west Europe, and locally naturalized. On well-drained alkaline soils in full sun or partial shade to 1000 m altitude.
Cultivation Wild. Propagated from seed sown spring or autumn, or by root division. Prefers deep, friable soils.
Constituents Heteroside anthraquinones (comprising mainly ruberythric acid) to which the medicinal action is mainly due; sugars; pectin. The colouring matter includes madder red (alizarin), madder purple (purpurin),

madder orange (rubiacin), and madder yellow (xanthine).
Uses (root, rarely leafy stems) Choleretic; tonic; antiseptic; diuretic; vulnerary; emmenagogue; laxative; antispasmodic.
The powdered root is of much value in the dissolution and elimination of renal and bladder calculi; the remedy also acts as a prophylactic against stone formation. May be used externally to aid wound healing.
The leafy stem in infusion can be used to treat constipation.
Root is employed as a dye.

Rubus fructicosus agg. ROSACEAE
Bramble Blackberry
While the Raspberry was named after a sweet red French wine, *raspis*, the common fruit of the 1000 or more varieties and species grouped under the name *R. fructicosus* were simply blackberries, and the plant itself was the brom or thorny shrub, hence bramble.
In German the plant is still called *Brombeere*. Like raspberries they have been picked and eaten for thousands of years and today in much of industrialized Europe Blackberry picking is now the last ritualistic seasonal collecting of wild plant food still practised.
Description Variable shrub with woody, biennial stems densely covered with prickles. Leaves palmate or ternate, and petiolate. Flowers white to pink in compound inflorescence appearing mid-summer to early autumn and followed by fleshy, black, edible fruit.
Distribution European native; especially in hedgerows, wood edges and gardens. On moist soils to 2400 m in altitude.
Cultivation Wild. Introduced near habitation and often rampant.
Constituents (fruit) Vitamin C; organic acids; pectins. (leaves) Tannins; sugars.
Uses (dried or fresh leaves, fruit, rarely flowers) Astringent; tonic; diuretic.
Leaves may be used in decoction as a gargle or douche and externally on ulcers. They have been accredited with (as yet unsubstantiated) antidiabetic activity.
Wide culinary use of the fruit. The root provides an orange dye.

Rubus idaeus L ROSACEAE
Raspberry
Like so many wild fruits the Raspberry has been known and used since prehistory in Europe, fragments of the berry being found in archaeological excavations of Swiss villages. Cultivation began in the Middle Ages, and the many European raspberry cultivars are all developed from this wild species. Prior to 1866 (at which time over 41 varieties were known in the United States of America) all American types were also from *R. idaeus*. They are now also developed from *R. ulmifolius* Schott, *R. ursinus* Cham and Schlechtend, *R. occidentalis* L. *Rubus* is from the Latin for red, and *idaeus* means 'of Mount Ida', after its abundance on Mount Ida.
Description Upright or bent perennial 90–150 cm tall, with varying degrees of prickles or sometimes entirely lacking them. Leaves glabrous above, grey tomentose beneath, comprising 3 or 5 ovate leaflets. Flowers small, 1–6 in drooping panicles in terminal axils, appearing early to mid-summer, followed by aromatic fleshy cone-shaped red to yellow fruit.

Distribution Eurasian native, introduced and widespread. In woodland clearings and edges, especially deciduous woodlands. On light soil, moist and rich in nutrients, to 2000 m in altitude.
Cultivation Wild. Numerous cultivars propagated by suckers or root cuttings. Canes should be removed after fruiting to allow new ones (primocanes) to develop. Tolerates most soils.
Constituents (leaf) Fragarine and other substances, acting in isolation as both uterine muscle stimulants and relaxants. (fruit) Citric acid; vitamin C; pectin.
Uses (fresh or dried leaves, fruit) Astringent; oxytocic; nutritive; laxative.
The leaf is of proven value during confinement, if taken regularly and in small doses as an infusion – it eases and speeds parturition. In larger doses the leaf is of benefit in painful menstruation and also in diarrhoea. In large amounts the fruit is mildly laxative.
The fruit was formerly employed in a variety of pharmaceutical and herbal products as a flavouring and colouring.
Edible fruit is of economic importance.
Used in wines, liqueurs, vinegars, syrups, and for other confectionery, culinary and some cosmetic purposes.

Rumex acetosa L POLYGONACEAE
Sorrel
All sorrels are acidic and sour-tasting, and in former times were popular ingredients of sauces, especially those for fish. The common name is derived from *sur* meaning sour, via the old French *surele*.
The plant's acidity is due to both its vitamin C and its oxalic acid and oxalate salts (mostly potassium hydrogen oxalate).
These latter substances are responsible for the occasional cases of Sorrel poisoning caused either by *R. acetosa* or by *R. acetosella* L, occurring in both man and animals. The herb has, nevertheless, long been used as a salad and vegetable and was cultivated in the fourteenth century or even earlier. By the eighteenth century, however, it was largely replaced by *R. scutatus* L in horticulture. The plant was known to the apothecaries as *Herba Acetosa* and was included in many dispensatories from the fifteenth to the nineteenth centuries.
Description Perennial 50–150 cm tall, nearly glabrous. Leaves rather thick, oblong-lanceolate to 10 cm long, the upper ones sessile. Flowers small, reddish-brown on slender, loose inflorescence to 40 cm long, appearing early summer to early autumn.
Distribution European native; also found in northern Asia. In meadowland on nitrogen-rich, damp, loamy soils to 2500 m in altitude.
Cultivation Wild plant. May be propagated by root division in autumn.
Constituents (leaf and juice) Oxalic acid and potassium binoxalate (to 1%); tartaric acid; vitamin C. (rhizome) A hyperoside, quercetin-3-D-galactoside; anthracene; oxymethylanthraquinone; tannins (to 25%).
Uses (fresh leaf, rhizome) Diuretic; laxative; tonic; antiseptic; bitter.
The root decoction is used as a bitter tonic and as an astringent in diarrhoea; also as a diuretic; it is not suitable for use in either young or very old people.
The leaf may be employed in poultices to treat certain skin complaints, including acne.

The young leaf is edible fresh or cooked.
Contra-indications Very large doses are POISONOUS, causing severe kidney damage. The herb should not be used by those predisposed to rheumatism, arthritis, gout, kidney stones or gastric hyper-acidity. The leaf may cause dermatitis.

Rumex crispus L POLYGONACEAE
Yellow Dock Curled Dock/Rumex
In ancient writings both this species and another common weed, the Broad-leaved Dock (*R. obtusifolius* L) have been used for the same medicinal purposes, and more recently they have been shown to possess similar chemical constituents.
R. obtusifolius was known as *Lapathum* or *Lapathum acutum* from the fourteenth century, while the Yellow Dock was called *Lapathum crispum*. In the development of physiomedicalism in the early nineteenth century in America, *R. crispus* was used for obstinate skin complaints, while in Europe *R. obtusifolius* was used for the same condition. Today *Rumex* is found in English herbals, and *Lapathum* in European ones.
Description Perennial 50–100 cm tall on stout rootstock. Leaves with undulate edges, lanceolate, large, crispy. Flowers greenish, small, in whorls along a somewhat branched inflorescence, appearing mid-summer to mid-autumn.
Distribution Eurasian native, widely distributed in temperate and subtropical countries as a weed. In any rich, heavy soil in weedy places, to 1500 m altitude.
Cultivation Wild. Propagate from seed.
Constituents (root-stock) Oxymethylanthraquinone (to 0.2%); emodin (to 0.1%); chrysophanic acid; volatile oil; resin; tannins; rumicin; starch; thiamine. The combined action is both astringent and purgative, and is described as tonic laxative.
Uses (root-stock, young leaves, rarely seed) Purgative; cholagogue; tonic; astringent. Of much value both internally and externally in skin complaints, especially where the cause is associated with constipation or liver dysfunction. May be applied to ringworm, scabies and urticaria, the parasites probably being destroyed by the rumicin content.

In small doses it is stomachic and tonic, and in China it is considered antipyretic.
The powdered root-stock in water is employed as a gargle for laryngitis and as a tooth powder in gingivitis.
The seed is highly astringent and may be used in cases of diarrhoea.
Young leaves may be eaten as greens, but water should be changed twice during cooking.
Contra-indications May cause dermatitis. Excessive doses produce nausea.

Rumex scutatus L POLYGONACEAE
French Sorrel Garden Sorrel
While *Rumex alpinus* L or Monk's Rhubarb is the most physiologically active of the European species of *Rumex*, the French Sorrel is probably the least, and since it in addition possesses a mildly sour, lemony taste it has become the most popular of the edible sorrels. Once established its deeply-growing roots may be difficult to eradicate.
Description Perennial, low-growing and glaucous, 10–50 cm tall. Leaves petiolate, hastate, fleshy. Flowers small, reddish, unisexual, appearing mid to late summer.
Distribution Native to Europe and Asia; introduced elsewhere.
Cultivation Wild. Cultivated as a salad herb in any rich, moist soil. Propagate from seed sown in spring, thinning to 30 cm apart and

removing flower-heads to promote leaf. Water well in hot weather. Tolerates partial shade or full sun, and can be grown under cloches to provide leaf throughout the year.
Constituents Oxalates, in small quantities.
Uses (fresh leaf) Diuretic.
Not used medicinally but moderate amounts of the leaf are diuretic.
May be used with discretion in salads.
Contra-indications Not suitable for those predisposed to kidney stones.

Ruscus aculeatus L LILIACEAE
Butcher's Broom Box Holly/Jew's Myrtle
This unusual member of the Lily family was associated with the meat trade from the sixteenth to the nineteenth centuries, first as a crude repellent barrier to vermin and animals,

then as a broom or twitch to scrub chopping blocks, and finally as a decoration for meat at festive times. It bears scarlet berries at Christmas time, and the evergreen twigs are now used in florists' winter decorations.
It is related to Asparagus and starts with young edible shoots which can be eaten in a similar way. The ancient names of Butcher's Broom included *Bruscus*, *Eruscus* and *Hypoglosson*; Dioscorides recommended the rhizome in cases of kidney stones.
Description Erect evergreen perennial 30–90 cm tall. The leaves are minute and bract-like and subtend the 4 cm-long, spine-pointed, ovate, leaf-like cladodes. Flowers whitish or pinkish, minute, solitary or clustered, attached to the cladode midrib, appearing mid-autumn to late spring and followed by red or yellow globose berries reaching 15 mm in diameter.
Distribution Native from the Azores to Iran, including north-west Europe and the mediterranean region. Introduced elsewhere. In woodland thickets on poor, dry soil among rocks. To 600 m in altitude.
Cultivation Wild. Grown horticulturally, and collected on a small commercial scale.
Constituents Essential oil; saponoside; resin; potassium salts.
Uses (dried root-stock, young shoots, rarely leaves) Antipyretic; diuretic; vasoconstrictive. Rarely used medicinally, but of value in some problems associated with venous circulation. Traditionally used in the treatment of haemorrhoids, gout and jaundice.
The young shoots have been used in spring salads in the same way as Asparagus.
Contra-indications Not to be used by individuals with hypertension.

Ruta graveolens L RUTACEAE
Rue Herb of Grace/Herbygrass
Rue is an ancient and important medicinal plant of undoubted effectiveness which deserves wider use by medical personnel; yet, besides folk medicine application and use in Chinese herbal medicine, it is now only retained in the Swiss Pharmacopoeia.
It had wide therapeutic application traditionally and was also included as a major ingredient of the poison antidotes of Mithridates. Its

beneficial effects led to its pre-eminence as a protector against witchcraft and magic; the name was once thought to be derived from the Greek *reuo* meaning to set free after its general effectiveness. The ancients, however, knew it both as *hrute* and *peganon* and Dioscorides further differentiated between a sharper 'mountain peganon' and a 'garden peganon'. *Ruta* is now thought to be derived from *hrute*, and hence the word Rue.

Writers after Dioscorides also emphasized the plant's effect on the uterus and the nervous system, and many, such as Bock in the fifteenth century and Lemery in the eighteenth, differentiated between the wild and garden herbs in medicinal application. Hahnemann introduced its use in homeopathy in 1818.

Since the flavour of Rue is strong and distinctive and the plant has to be used with care, it has not enjoyed popular use in recent times; maintaining the tradition of its employment in the old Mead known as sack, however, it is included in the Italian grape spirit *Grappa con ruta*.

Description Aromatic semi-evergreen perennial, glabrous and glaucous herb or subshrub to 1 m. Deeply subdivided alternate leaves with spatulate or oblong 15 mm long segments.

Flowers yellow in terminal corymbose inflorescence, appearing summer to early autumn.

Distribution Native to southern Europe, as far north as the southern Alps. In sheltered positions on dry rocky or limestone soils.

Cultivation Wild. Collected commercially from the wild. Grown horticulturally and propagated from seed sown in the spring, from cuttings taken in spring, or by careful division. Prefers full sun and well-drained soil. The cultivar *variegata* with variegated leaves, and the variety var. *divaricata* (Ten.) Wilk., with bright yellow-green leaves, are also grown in herb gardens.

Constituents Volatile oil (to 0.6%), comprising various ketones, but mainly methylnonylketone (to 90%), also limonene, cineol, methyl acetate; resin; tannins; the rhamno-glucoside, rutin; coumarin; fixed oil; bergapten; xanthotoxin; alkaloids; ascorbic acid; furo-coumarins; several other active substances.

Uses (dried or fresh leaf, rarely juice) Emmenagogue; abortifacient; antihelmintic; stomachic; diaphoretic.

Principally active on the uterus and in small doses beneficial for the relief of dysmenorrhoea; it acts as an emmenagogue.

Increases blood-flow to the gastro-intestinal system, aids in colic and acts as a stomachic. Of much value in certain autonomic nervous system disorders; traditionally employed in epilepsy. Externally used to treat skin diseases, to aid wound healing, in neuralgia, rheumatism and as an eye lotion. Also as a gargle. Leaves may be used, with discretion, in salads as a flavouring.

The oil is employed in the perfumery industry.

Contra-indications Must be used only by medical personnel. Must not be used at all by pregnant women as it is an abortifacient. Large doses are toxic, sometimes precipitating mental confusion, and the oil is capable of causing death. Handling the plant can cause allergic reactions or phytophotodermatitis.

Salicornia europaea agg. CHENOPODIACEAE
Glasswort Marsh Samphire

A herb of the salt marshes of Europe, especially found in the north and west, and one which – as its common name suggests – was employed as a source of materials used in glass manufacture. It replaced the southern *Salsola soda* L which had been exported northwards up to the sixteenth century. Its other common name indicates it was eaten in the same way as Samphire (*Crithmum maritimum* L).

It is now rarely, if ever, used. It is also known botanically as *S. herbacea* L.

Description Succulent annual or biennial with green leaves, and green or dull red uniformly candelabra-shaped stems, to 10 cm tall. Leaves opposite, joined along their margins forming 'segments'. Flowers minute, greenish, borne on fleshy spikes, appearing early to mid-autumn.

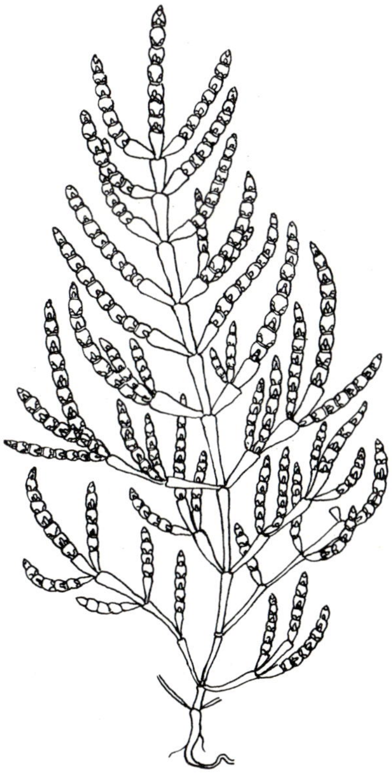

Distribution European native. On salt marshes and mud flats.

Cultivation Wild.

Constituents Large proportion of mineral salts.

Uses (fresh plant) Diuretic.

Rarely used medicinally.

May be eaten either raw, or cooked with a knob of butter.

Salsola soda L CHENOPODIACEAE
Saltwort

Both this species and the closely related *S. kali* L were once important in the manufacture of glass, and large amounts of the mineral-rich

ash were exported from southern Europe and North Africa under the name Barilla. In north-west Europe *Salsola* species were replaced over 300 years ago by the abundant local Salicornias, but in France and Italy they continued to be of both commercial and, to a lesser extent, medicinal importance until the nineteenth century. The herb was never included in German pharmacopoeias, since superior remedies are numerous. The plant is no longer used.

Description Decumbent annual with spreading stems to 60 cm; leaves to 4 cm long, fleshy, sessile, simple and cylindrical; flowers usually solitary, greenish and insignificant. Appearing late summer to mid-autumn.

Distribution Native to mediterranean region. On sandy seashores.

Cultivation Wild plant.

Constituents Mineral salts, particularly large quantities of sodium sulphate; alkaloids, salsoline and salsolidine.

Uses (fresh or dried plant) Diuretic. No longer employed medicinally.

Salvia officinalis L LABIATAE
Sage

The Sage family is a large group of horticultur-

ally important plants which consists of over 750 species widely distributed throughout the world. Some are also of culinary use, others medicinal and at least one central American species is a powerful hallucinogen, traditionally employed in religious and magical rites.
The most important and best known is *Salvia officinalis*, which has been cultivated for millenia. Its ancient names include *elifagus*, *elelisphakon* (the latter named by Dioscorides), *lingua humana*, *selba* and *salvia*. The name *salvia* is from the Latin *salvere*, meaning to be in good health; and the old French *saulje* gives us the modern common name.
At one time Sage was included in a brew called Sage Ale, and Sage tea was also a popular drink. The Chinese once preferred it to their local teas and exchanged their product with the Dutch for Sage tea, bartering on the basis of weight for weight.
Description Subshrub from 30–70 cm tall; stem woody at the base, branched, quadrangular, white and woolly when young. Leaves oblong, 3–5 cm long, usually entire, glandular or rugose, grey-green, petiolate. Flowers violet-blue, to 3 cm long, between 5 and 10 arranged on terminal spikes. Appearing early summer to early autumn.
Distribution Native to southern Europe, notably the mediterranean region. On limestone soils in full sun slopes, to 750 m altitude.
Cultivation Wild. Collected commercially from the wild, especially in Yugoslavia (Dalmatian Sage). Wide horticultural use and several varieties commonly grown. In northern countries Narrow-leaved Sage is grown from seed in late spring, flowering early summer to early autumn. Broad-leaved Sage does not flower in cool regions and cannot be raised from seed; use cuttings taken in late spring or early summer. Red-leaved Sage (Purple or Red Sage), Variegated Sage and Tricolor Sage (variegated and tipped with purple) are all grown from cuttings or by layering. Old leggy plants should be earthed up in spring and rooted cuttings cut off and planted out in autumn. Replace every 4–7 years.
Constituents Volatile oil (to 2%) comprising mainly thujone and cineol but including numerous other substances; also tannins; organic acids; rosmarinic acid; oestrogens; bitter compounds including picrosalvine.
Uses (fresh or dried leaves, oil) Antiseptic; antifungal; anti-inflammatory; astringent; carminative; emmenagogue; choleretic; weak hypoglycaemic.
Wide medicinal application; especially effective as an anti-sudorific in cases of excessive sweating, and also to reduce lactation. Useful in liver disease, respiratory tract infections, and in nervous conditions such as anxiety or depression. Red Sage is an effective antiseptic gargle and may be used as a douche in leucorrhoea, or in baths to treat skin problems. It was traditionally employed in female sterility.
The oil is employed in both the pharmaceutical and culinary industries.

Salvia sclarea L LABIATAE
Clary Clary Sage/Muscatel Sage
Clary Sage is also known as Muscatel Sage since it is now almost exclusively grown commercially as the source of Muscatel oil, which is used in flavouring and in the perfumery industry. The leaves were once mixed

with Elderflower and employed in flavouring wines, and Clary wine itself was a sixteenth-century aphrodisiac. The name Clary comes from the Latin *clarus* after the use of its mucilaginous seeds to clear the eye of grit.
Description Erect biennial 30–120 cm tall, flowering stems bristly. Leaves simple, aromatic, pubescent, petiolate, broad-ovate, 15–22 cm long. Flowers white, lavender and pink, attractive, numerous, on terminal panicles. Appearing early summer to late autumn.
Distribution Native to southern Europe on dry limey or sandy soils, to 1000 m altitude.
Cultivation Wild. Grown commercially and horticulturally from seed sown thinly in spring. For blooming each year allow some plants to self-seed, or plant every year.
Constituents Essential oil (to 0.1%) comprising linalol and esters; choline; saponine; tannins; mucilage.
Uses (seed, fresh or dried leaves, oil) Anti-spasmodic; stimulant; emmenagogue.
The seed becomes mucilaginous in water and may then be used to extract foreign bodies from the eye. The leaves in infusion may be used as a gargle, douche, skin wash for ulcers and cuts, and in small doses may be taken to promote appetite. It reduces sweating. Its principal employment is as the source of the oil, and it is most commonly used in herbal medicine to treat vomiting.
Oil is of value in the perfume and flavouring industries.
A decorative garden plant.

Sambucus ebulus L CAPRIFOLIACEAE
Dwarf Elder Danewort
Of the 20 or so species in the genus *Sambucus* the Dwarf Elder is the most active pharmacologically, and unlike its close relative the Elder (*S. nigra* L) its fruit should be considered as poisonous. The dark purple berries are certainly violently purgative; in the Middle Ages both these and the root or root bark were used as such – although ancient Greek physicians did not recommend their use.
Early names included *chamaiakte*, *atrix* and *ebulus*, the last stemming from the Latin *ebullire* meaning to bubble out, and possibly describing its purgative action.
Grigson in *The Englishman's Flora* traces the origin of the common name Danewort and shows it has nothing to do with the spilled 'blood of the Danes', from which the herb was once thought to grow; it is, in fact, derived from the *danes*, or diarrhoea, caused by the plant.
The Anglo-Saxons and Gauls employed Dwarf Elder berries as a blue dye, and this is now the main use for the herb.
Description Strong-smelling herbaceous perennial to 120 cm, on creeping rhizome. Stems numerous, grooved, bearing long-pointed, oblong, serrate, leaflets 5–15 cm long. Flowers in flat-topped, broad cymes, white to pink; appearing late summer to early autumn and followed by small black fruit.
Distribution Native to Europe, North Africa, Asia; introduced elsewhere. On damp soils,

wasteland, grassland or roadsides, to 1400 m altitude.
Cultivation Wild plant.
Constituents Essential oil; anthocyanins; tannins; organic acids.
Uses (root bark, fresh berries, flowers) Purgative. Rarely used owing to its drastic action. The fruit produces a blue dye.
Contra-indications The berries should not be taken internally.

Sambucus nigra L CAPRIFOLIACEAE
Elder
The Elder has been used continuously since the days of the Egyptians and probably before, and it is still included in certain modern cosmetic preparations as well as retaining its popularity in folk medicine. Elder flowers and Peppermint infusion is the medicine of choice for the treatment of colds in many country homes in Europe.
The plant has several uses, and some believe that every part of the Elder has some use. None is more popular than elderberry wine, while Elder flowers soaked in lemon juice overnight provide a most refreshing summer drink. Probably out of respect for its usefulness, the plant has been attributed with a variety of magical virtues, and many different European spirits were thought to inhabit it. In some

places old people still doff their caps at the plant or refuse to burn it.
It was known to the ancients as *rixus*, *ixus* and *akte*, but mostly as *sambucus* which gives us its modern generic name.
Description Shrub or small tree to 10 m tall; leaves dull green, subdivided into 5 elliptic, serrate acuminate leaflets, 3–9 cm long. Flowers white, 5 mm diameter, numerous, in flat-topped cymes to 20 cm diameter; appearing mid-summer and followed by numerous edible, purple, globose fruit to 8 mm diameter.
Distribution Native to Europe, North Africa, western Asia. Introduced elsewhere. In hedgerows, woodland edges, on nitrogen-rich soils. To 1000 m altitude.
Cultivation Wild plant. Usually propagated by suckers or cuttings. Prefers moist soils.
Some horticultural varieties exist, such as white, golden-yellow, variegated, or deeply dissected forms.
Constituents Essential oil comprising terpenes; the glucosides, rutin and quercitrin; alkaloids; tannins; vitamin C; mucilage; anthocyanins. The combined action is predominantly diaphoretic.
Uses (fresh or dried flowers, fruit, leaves, root bark, stem pith) Diaphoretic; laxative; antispasmodic: diuretic; emollient.
Mostly of use in combination with Peppermint and Yarrow in the treatment of colds and nasal catarrh, or alone as a gargle in throat infections.
Also of value with other remedies in constipation, haemorrhoids, rheumatism, bronchitis and cystitis. The flowers are sometimes used as an ingredient of eye lotions. Young buds can be pickled, and the flowers can be eaten raw or used in various drinks including wines. Fruit valuable in conserves, pies, jams and also wines. They can be used in home dyeing.
Wide cosmetic use of the flowers.

Sanguinaria canadensis L PAPAVERACEAE
Bloodroot Red Puccoon/Tetterwort
Another common name for this small pretty herb is Indian Paint since it was one of the body stains (and clothing dyes) used by the Red Indians.
Introduced to medicine via folklore, it was used as a domestic remedy for gastric complaints. It was described by Geiger (1830) as having an action similar to Foxglove (*Digitalis purpurea* L), and a century later in the *Hager-Handbuch* as an emetic similar to Ipecacuanha. These are powerful properties for a domestic remedy, and the rhizome should not be used except under medical supervision, since in large doses it can be fatal.
Sanguinaria describes the red colour of the rhizome and juice. It is the only species in the genus.
Description Perennial to 30 cm on thick rhizome; one leaf, basal, palmately lobed, petiolate, and only appearing when flower dies. Stem is a smooth scape to 20 cm, terminated by white, sometimes pinkish, flower. Solitary flower to 4 cm wide, appears mid-spring to early summer, followed by 3 cm-long oblong capsule.
Distribution North American native. On moist, rich soils in woods and woodland slopes in the shade.
Cultivation Wild. Introduced as a shady wild garden ornamental. Propagate by division in the autumn. A cultivar 'multiplex' with double flowers is found horticulturally.
Constituents Alkaloids comprising sanguinarine, protopine, chelerythrine, α- and β-homochelidonine, also chelidonic acid; an orange resin; gum; starch; sugars.
Uses (dried rhizome) Expectorant; emetic; antipyretic; spasmolytic; cardio-active; stimulant; topical irritant; cathartic; antiseptic.
The fresh juice is caustic (escharotic) and has been used against warts. The powdered drug has also been used externally to treat certain skin complaints and as a snuff in nasal polyps.

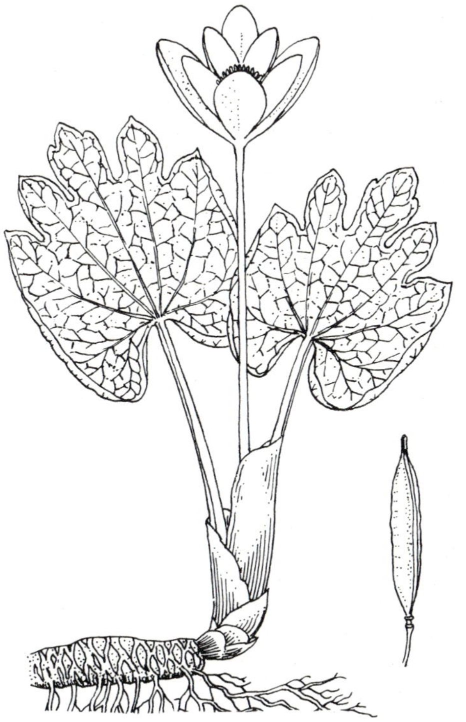

Principally employed in chronic bronchitis as an expectorant, and in cases of deficient capillary circulation.
May be used, much diluted, as a gargle in sore throats.
Contra-indications POISONOUS. Medical use only. The therapeutic dose is very small; large doses are toxic, causing violent vomiting, and possibly death.

Santolina chamaecyparissus L COMPOSITAE
Lavender Cotton Cotton Lavender/French Lavender
This southern European native was introduced to cooler northern climates (which it tolerates well) in the sixteenth century, largely to be used in the low, clipped hedges of formal knot gardens. It was also valued as an ingredient of scented sachets to repel moths in clothes drawers. Other than this the herb has not received much attention, although its vermifugal properties have been recognized from the earliest times.

The Greeks knew it as *abrotonon* and the Romans as *habrotanum*, both referring to the tree-like shape of the flowering branches – a characteristic also indicated in the modern specific name.
Description Perennial evergreen shrub 20–50 cm tall; much branched with silver-grey, tomentose leaves to 4 cm long, subdivided into small, thin segments. Flowers bright yellow, numerous, but in solitary rounded capitula at the tips of branchlets; appearing mid-summer to early autumn.
Distribution Spain to Albania; North Africa; introduced elsewhere and locally escaped. On dry rocky soils in full sun, to 1000 m altitude.
Cultivation Wild. Cultivated horticulturally from cuttings taken late summer, autumn or early spring, and rooted under glass in a peat and sand mix. Well-drained soil in full sun is required in cool climates. Clip in mid-spring to shape.
Constituents Essential oil; bitter principles; unknown substances.
Uses (dried flowering stems, leaves) Vermifuge; antispasmodic; weak emmenagogue.
Rarely used medicinally.
Leaves may be included in insect-repellent sachets.
Principally of use as a decorative evergreen garden shrub. Especially suitable as a low hedge.

Saponaria officinalis L CARYOPHYLLACEAE
Soapwort Bouncing Bet
As both the common and generic names suggest, the boiled leaves and roots of this herb may be used as the source of a somewhat astringent lather suitable for cleaning woollen fabrics. How long the herb has been used as a natural soap (its cleaning properties being due to the presence of saponins in the plant) is uncertain. It is not known how widely it was employed, but it may have been known to the Assyrians and is certainly still used both in the Middle East and rarely in the West for cleaning old and delicate tapestries.
Dioscorides probably knew *Saponaria officinalis* as *Struthion* while in the Middle Ages it was variously called *Herba Philippi, Sapanaria* or *Herba fullonis*. The latter name indicates that those who fulled cloth (that is, the fullers who cleaned and thickened it) used it as a cleaning agent, and from this William Turner in his *The Names of Herbes* (1548) called it 'Soapwort'.
Soapwort has to be treated in special ways before it can be used medicinally and it has been implicated in the poisoning of both animals and man, a property once recognized in its use as a fish poison.
Description Perennial, sparingly branched, on rhizome bearing erect, finely pubescent stems 30–40 cm tall. Leaves opposite, ovate-lanceolate, usually 7 cm long, 3-veined. Flowers pink or whitish to 4 cm wide in dense terminal clusters; appearing mid-summer to mid-autumn.
Distribution Native to Europe and western Asia.
Introduced and naturalized elsewhere.

On moist but well-drained soils in wasteland and roadsides, to 1500 m altitude.
Cultivation Wild. Grown horticulturally from seed sown in mid-spring, or by division. Tolerates poor soils.
Constituents Saponins (to 5%), comprising saporubin and saprubrinic acid; gums; flavonoids; vitamin C; vitexin.
Uses (fresh leaves, dried root-stock) Diuretic; laxative; cholagogue; choleretic; expectorant. Once used in the treatment of certain skin conditions, including psoriasis, eczema, and acne. In India the specially prepared root-stock is considered a galactagogue, and elsewhere it has been employed as an expectorant in respiratory complaints. Fresh leaf is principally used as the source of a soap to clean old fabrics.
Contra-indications To be used internally only under medical supervision.

Sarothamnus scoparius (L) Wimmer ex Koch PAPILIONACEAE
Broom Scotch Broom
Formerly classified as *Cytisus scoparius* (L) Link and known as *Genista* in the early herbals, this useful medicinal herb was employed by all the major European schools of medicine and is still in demand in folk medicine. It was the emblem of the Norman conquerors of England. *Cytisus* was the Greek name for a type of clover, which, in fact, it hardly resembles at all.
Description Deciduous shrub to 3 m; with many erect slender glabrous 5-angled branches bearing short-petioled obovate or oblanceolate acute leaves, 5–10 mm long. Flowers usually appear alone in the axils, pale or bright yellow, 2-lipped, 2.5 cm long, appearing spring and summer.
Distribution Central and southern European native; naturalized in the United States. On wood fringes, roadsides, in clearings to 500 m altitude. Calcifugous.
Cultivation Wild plant; grown horticulturally, the variety *Andreanus* has yellow flowers with dark crimson wings.
Constituents Several alkaloids, including sparteine; flavonoid pigments; a glycoside, scoparin; mineral salts; bitter principles; tannin; volatile oil. Action largely due to sparteine

which lessens irritability and conductivity of cardiac muscle.
Uses (dried flowering herb) Diuretic, purgative, anti-haemorrhagic.
Of use in the treatment of tachycardia and functional palpitation, especially when the blood pressure is lowered. Some oxytocic activity, and therefore cannot be used in pregnancy. Constricts peripheral blood vessels, and of benefit in profuse menstruation.
Seeds once served as a Coffee substitute, and the flowers and buds were pickled and eaten as Capers.
Twigs used for basket manufacture.
Bark yields fibre suitable for manufacture of paper and cloth.
Formerly used to tan leather, and leaves yield a green dye.
Contra-indications Large doses paralyze the autonomic ganglia; to be avoided in pregnancy and hypertension.

Sassafras albidum (Nutt.) Nees LAURACEAE
Sassafras
This tree is considered by many authorities to

have provided the first of the American medicinal plant drugs to reach Europe. Its action was noticed by Monardes during an expedition to Florida (1564), and in 1574 the wood was imported to Spain.
It was known firstly by the native Indian name *pavame*, and also the French *sassafras*. From 1582 the Germans called it *lignum floridum* and Fennel Wood, as well as *lignum pauame* after its origin and the fennel-like aroma of the bark. The tree was grown in England as early as 1597. An Italian, Angelus Sala, first extracted the Sassafras oil by distillation, and it was this product which in modern times has been used most frequently. It is now under scrutiny for possible toxicity problems, and in many countries it has been withdrawn as a flavouring.
Description Aromatic deciduous tree to 30 m tall. Leaves variable, lobed or entire, alternate, ovate to 12 cm long, darker above. Flowers greenish yellow, on clustered racemes to 5 cm long; followed by dark blue fruit with fleshy red pedicel. Leaves attractively coloured in autumn.
Distribution North American native from central to southern states.
Cultivation Wild.
Constituents (oil, to 3%) comprising safrole (to 80%), phellandrene and pinene.
Uses (root wood, root bark, oil rarely) Aromatic; carminative; stimulant; diaphoretic; diuretic. The inner root bark in decoction is mildly aromatic and carminative and has been used for gastro-intestinal complaints, and in association with purgatives in constipation. The wood shavings were formerly administered with Guaiacum and Sarsaparilla (*Smilax ornata*) in decoction to induce sweating.
The oil is rubefacient and destroys lice, although safer remedies for both purposes are preferred. Pith from the stem forms a demulcent mucilage in water and can be used in eye lotions.
Oil is used in food flavouring (now under review), tobacco flavouring and perfumery.
Sassafras tea is made from the wood shavings.
Contra-indications Oil should not be used internally as it causes liver and kidney damage. May irritate the skin if used externally.

Satureja hortensis L LABIATAE
Summer Savory
This is sometimes incorrectly named as *Satureia hortensis*. It is now most commonly used as a culinary herb, the name Savory emphasizing its culinary use. It has been employed in food flavouring for over 2000 years and probably longer than Sage. The herb also possesses effective medicinal properties including a stimulant effect which led to its former use as an aphrodisiac. Some authorities believe that this effect was the origin of the old name *Satureia* meaning satyr. The Italians were among the first to introduce this as a garden herb, and it has been in cultivation since the ninth century.
Description Annual, 30–40 cm tall, pubescent, erect and branched. Leaves acute, entire, 3 cm long. Flowers rose, lilac or white, in a sparsely-flowered inflorescence, appearing late summer to mid-autumn.
Distribution Native to eastern mediterranean region, and south-west Asia, introduced to South Africa, America and elsewhere. On dry chalky soils, rocky hills, roadsides; to 800 m altitude.
Cultivation Wild. Collected commercially from the wild. Cultivated from seed sown in spring.
Constituents Essential oil (to 1.5%) comprising mainly carvacrol and cymene; phenolic substances; resins; tannins; mucilage.
Uses (fresh or dried leaves, dried flowering tops) Antiseptic; expectorant; carminative; stomachic; stimulant; antihelmintic; diuretic. Principally of use in gastric complaints, to aid digestion or stimulate appetite. Possesses a beneficial antihelmintic action, and can also be used as an antiseptic gargle. Once considered an effective aphrodisiac although this is probably only due to its stimulant effect.
The oil is used commercially as a flavouring, as is the leaf which is an important constituent of salami.

Satureja montana L LABIATAE
Winter Savory
This has the same properties and uses as Summer Savory and is collected commercially both for the leaf and for the oil extracted from the leaves. The flavour of Winter Savory is, however, both coarser and stronger, but it has the advantage of being a hardier plant and a perennial evergreen, thus providing fresh leaf for winter flavouring in warmer climates.
Winter Savory is also called Mountain Savory, hence its specific name *montana*.
Description Shrubby evergreen perennial 10–40 cm tall, woody at the base, branched and forming a compact bush. Leaves sessile, entire, oblong-linear or oblanceolate, 15–30 mm long. White or pink flowers, in terminal flowering spikes appearing early summer to early autumn.
Distribution Native to south-east Europe and North Africa; introduced elsewhere. On dry chalky soils, rocky hills and mountains to 1500 m altitude.
Cultivation Wild. Collected commercially from the wild. Grown from seed sown in poor, well-drained and chalky soils in early to mid-autumn; or propagated by division in spring or autumn.
Constituents Essential oil (to 1.5%) comprising mainly carvacrol and cymene; phenolic substances; resins; tannins; mucilage.
Uses (fresh or dried leaves, dried flowering tops) Antiseptic; expectorant; carminative; stomachic; stimulant; antihelmintic; diuretic. Principally of use in gastric complaints, to aid digestion or stimulate appetite. Possesses a beneficial antihelmintic action, and can also be used as an antiseptic gargle. Once considered an effective aphrodisiac although this is probably only due to its stimulant effect.
The oil is used commercially as a flavouring, as is the leaf which is an important constituent of salami.

Scrophularia nodosa L SCROPHULARIACEAE
Knotted Figwort
Figwort is an interesting medicinal plant which deserves closer modern examination. Like the Foxglove, which is also a member of the Scrophulariaceae, it possesses cardio-active substances which lead to increased myocardial contraction. It is not used in heart therapy however, and its main employment in folk medicine is a dermatological one, where its action on the liver is traditionally considered to benefit skin problems. Nineteenth-century research also indicated a hypoglycaemic action, and for a time the root was included as an antidiabetic agent. The plant's names indicate still older, traditional uses. Figwort and the apothecaries' name *Ficaria major* refer to the ancient application against the *ficus* (Latin for fig) or piles; while *Scrophularia* is from *scrophula* (Latin for goitre and tuberculosis of the cervical lymph nodes), since it was used in complaints characterized by swelling, such as tumours and mastitis.
Description Square-stemmed, strong-smelling perennial, 40 to 120 cm tall, on tuberous rhizome; leaves opposite, undivided, decussate, ovate and glabrous. Flowers greenish-brown, to 1 cm long in panicles appearing mid-summer to mid-autumn.
Distribution European native. In wet woodland,

fenland hedgerows, ditches, near streams. To 1700 m altitude. On nutrient-rich loamy, but porous, soils.
Cultivation Wild plant.
Constituents Cardio-active glycosides; saponins, comprising mainly diosinine; hesperetin; vitamin C; palmitic and malic acids; unknown substances.
Uses (dried root-stock, dried flowering tops) choleretic; diuretic; cardio-active; vulnerary; weak hypoglycaemic.
Used in poultices for the external treatment of wounds, burns, ulcers and haemorrhoids. Formerly used externally and internally in glandular disorders, mastitis and tumerous conditions. Also used externally and internally in chronic skin diseases such as eczema.
Contra-indications Owing to its action on the heart it should only be used under medical supervision.

Sedum acre L CRASSULACEAE
Biting Stonecrop Yellow Stonecrop or Wall-pepper
The Wall-pepper, named after its habitat and taste, has never been considered of much medicinal importance, and even some of the ancient writers warned against its internal use. It was, however, included in some sixteenth-century apothecaries' remedies for intestinal parasites, and was known then as *vermicularis*. Similar, related plants were used for the same purpose and by 1741 the Württemberg Pharmacopoeia specified '*Vermicularis flore flavo*', the yellow-flowered *Vermicularis*. In 1830 its possible employment in epilepsy had been recognized, but it was rarely used for this purpose because the irritant substances it contains caused blisters.
Description Fleshy perennial on creeping or decumbent stems forming mats 5–20 cm tall. Leaves 3–4 mm long, thick, sessile, numerous, cylindrical, arranged closely along the stem. Flowers yellow, to 15 mm wide, sparse, in terminal cymes; appearing mid-summer to early autumn.
Distribution European native; introduced elsewhere. On poor, dry, warm, calcareous or stony soils, or sand; especially on old walls,

rubble, embankments and roofs.
Cultivation Wild.
Constituents Alkaloids including semadine; glycosides; mucilage; unknown substances.
Uses (fresh leaves) Rubefacient; hypotensive; irritant.
Use of the fresh plant must be restricted to external application for local treatment of warts and corns; it should be diluted with water to aid wound healing. The plant cannot safely be used in the treatment of hypertension. May be employed homeopathically.
Contra-indications Not to be used internally. External use may cause blistering.

Senecio aureus L COMPOSITAE
Golden Ragwort Liferoot/Squaw Weed
Senecio aureus is also called Female Regulator and indeed most of its uses were traditionally concerned with female complaints. American

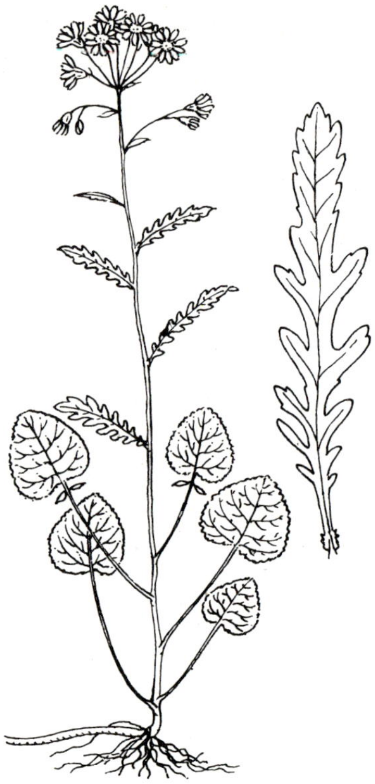

Indian women formerly made a tea from the plant which they used before or during childbirth, and to treat conditions such as leucorrhoea. The herb never attracted much attention however, and it was only included in the early nineteenth-century American *Eclectic Materia Medica*; Hale introduced a homeopathic preparation, however, of the fresh flowering plant in 1875. The plant contains toxic substances which have been implicated in cattle poisoning, and it is, therefore, now seldom used.
Description Perennial on thick horizontal root, reaching 30–60 cm tall. The stem is grooved, erect and brown-streaked; basal leaves alternate, long petioled, obtuse, toothed, 3–15 cm long. Stem leaves oblong or lanceolate, lyrate or pinnatifid. Flowers golden-yellow to 2 cm wide, in corymbs, appearing early to mid-summer.
Distribution North American native; on nutrient-rich wet soils, near to streams, in marshland.
Cultivation Wild.
Constituents Alkaloids; tannins; resin; unknown substances.
Uses (fresh or dried flowering plant and root) Emmenagogue; diaphoretic; tonic; diuretic; anti-haemorrhagic.
Once used in the treatment of certain internal haemorrhages, especially pulmonary haemorrhage; in female complaints and in childbirth; in genito-urinary tract infections. Considered to be a tonic in debility following illness.
Contra-indications To be used only by medical personnel. May prove toxic.

Senecio vulgaris L COMPOSITAE
Groundsel
This common weed is known to most European gardeners as an unwelcome intruder in the vegetable plot, or wherever soil has been disturbed. Dioscorides called it *erigeron* and considered it had cooling properties, a statement echoed 1600 years later by Culpeper who thought the herb of value in all diseases caused by 'heat'. In the sixteenth and seventeenth centuries Groundsel was frequently used in various conditions, but it evidently fell out of fashion, since in 1780 Hagen wrote that 'it had formerly been used . . .'. Dr Finazzi reintroduced the herb in 1824 for liver diseases, and a century later its folk medicinal application included it being used in amenorrhoea and dysmenorrhoea. It is now known that, like its American relative *S. aureus*, it possesses toxic alkaloids which after prolonged or large dosage damage the liver.
The English name Groundsel, (from the old English ground swallower) and the French name *Toute-venue*, emphasize the weed's vivacity.
Description Annual 4–60 cm tall; stems erect, succulent, purple at the base. Leaves pinnatifid, with irregularly toothed lobes, short-petioled or half-clasping. Flowers yellow, the flower-heads to 4 mm diameter in cylindrical involucre, on terminal dense corymbose clusters; appearing throughout the year.
Distribution European native, introduced else-

where. Widespread and common on wild and cultivated soils, to 2000 m altitude.
Cultivation Wild.
Constituents Alkaloids including senecionine; mucilage; tannins; resin; various mineral salts; unknown substances.
Uses (entire flowering plant) Emmenagogue; astringent; vulnerary; haemostatic. Used in homeopathy. Once used in various conditions associated with blood circulation or haemorrhages, and in problems of menstruation. Now very rarely employed, except externally as a wash for cuts.
Popularly used to feed caged birds.
Contra-indications Large doses are dangerous and can damage the liver; to be used only under medical supervision.

Serenoa repens (Bartr.) Small PALMAE
Saw Palmetto Sabal
The generic name *Serenoa* is named after Sereno Watson, an American botanist (1826–1892); *repens* means creeping, and refers to the habit of the stems. This habit leads to dense stands of Saw Palmetto growing along the coastal plains of Florida and Georgia in the United States of America.
American Indians used the ground-up seed as food and considered the fruits were sedative and tonic. They were, therefore, included in some orthodox pharmacopoeias from 1830 for about 100 years, but their use is now restricted to folk medicine. Saw Palmetto refers to the saw-toothed edges of the leaves of the palm. It was formerly known as *S. serrulata* (Michx.) Hook.
Description Palm, usually low and shrubby, 1–2 m tall, sometimes to 6 m tall, with prostrate and creeping, branching stem, often underground. Leaves very deeply divided (to 20 segments), 75 cm wide, green or glaucous. Flowers inconspicuous, on a branched cluster, followed by succulent purple drupes (fruit) soon drying, darkening, and shrinking to 18 mm long.
Distribution North American native, on coastal

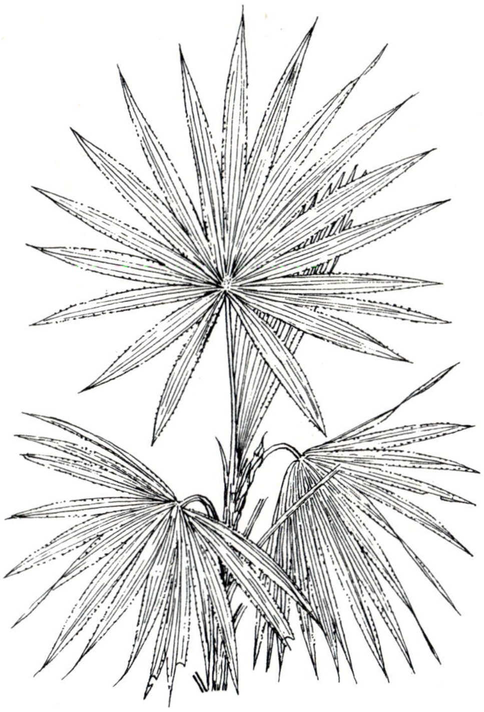

plains from Florida and Texas to South Carolina. In swampy, low-lying land on well-drained soils.
Cultivation Wild. Sometimes transplanted as a garden cover plant.
Constituents Fixed oil (to 1.5%) to which the action is due.
Uses (partly dried ripe fruit) Tonic; stimulant; expectorant; nutritive; sedative. Although the general action is mildly sedative, the fruits have a local stimulant action on the mucous membranes of both the respiratory and genito-urinary systems. The overall action is considered tonic, especially following illness. Principally used therefore in chronic and sub-acute cystitis, bronchitis, catarrh, and as a tonic tea. Considered to be of benefit in sexual debility and atrophy of the testes, but this is unsubstantiated.

Sesamum indicum L PEDALIACEAE
Sesame Benne/Gingelli
Sesame is still widely cultivated for its seed which yields the valuable Sesame or Gigelly oil – an edible oil with similar properties to those of Olive oil. The name Sesame can be traced back through the Arabic *Simsim* and Coptic *Semsem* to the early Egyptian *Semsemt*, a name mentioned in the Ebers Papyrus (*c.* 1800 B.C.) which indicates how long man has known and used the herb.
Description Erect, strongly smelling, finely pubescent annual to 90 cm tall. Leaves variable, simple above, lanceolate or oblong, alternate or opposite. Flowers purple to whitish, to 3 cm long, sub-erect or drooping, solitary, axillary. Followed by 3 cm-long capsule containing numerous flat seeds.
Distribution Native to the tropics.
Cultivation Widely cultivated in Africa, Asia and America, on sandy loam; the seed being sown broadcast and harvested within 4 months. *S. indicum* L yields white or yellowish seed and the expressed oil is suitable for both culinary and medicinal purposes. The black or brown seed from *S. orientale* L (now classified as a cultivar of *S. indicum* L) gives an oil which is considered suitable for industrial purposes.
Constituents Fixed oil (to 55%) comprising glycerides of palmitic, stearic, myristic, oleic and linoleic and other acids; a phenolic substance, sesamol; sesamin; choline; lecithin; nicotinic acid; calcium salts.
Uses (seed, seed oil, fresh leaves rarely) Nutritive; laxative; emollient; demulcent. Fresh leaves may be used as a poultice, as may the seeds. The ground seed when mixed with water can be used to treat bleeding haemorrhoids, and can be taken for genito-urinary infections when combined with other remedies.
Seeds are of benefit in constipation, and Indians consider a decoction acts as an emmenagogue.
The oil has wide medical, pharmaceutical and culinary application.
Sesame seed paste (tahini) is used in spreads, sauces, casseroles and pâtés.
The seed is used to decorate and flavour bread.

Silybum marianum L Gaertn. COMPOSITAE
Milk-thistle Marian Thistle/ Wild Artichoke
Dioscorides described this herb as *silybon* but from early Christian times both Latin and common names have normally included the name of the Virgin Mary, after an old tradition that the white veination on the leaves came from her milk. From this there arose the belief that the plant affected lactation – for which there is no modern evidence. The herb is

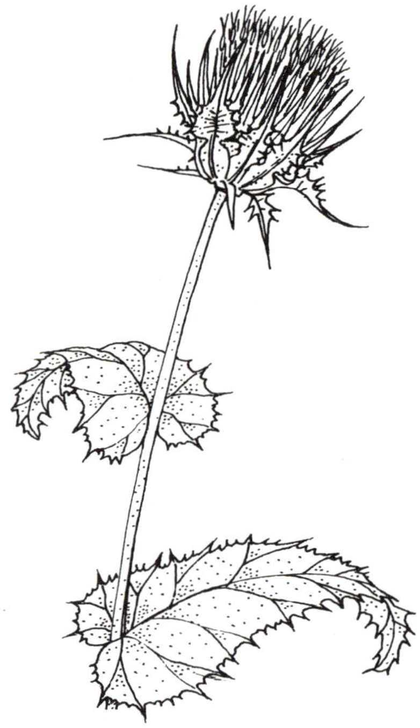

effective upon the liver, however, a property it shares with another species of the Compositae Family, the Artichoke; and, like the Artichoke, the flower receptacle can be eaten.

Milk Thistle was formerly cultivated quite widely, not only for the receptacle but also for the young stalks, leaves and roots – the latter resembling Salsify (*Tragopogon porrifolius* L). In the eighteenth century the young shoots were thought to be superior to the best cabbage.

Medicinally the herb was often used in place of the Blessed Thistle (*Cnicus benedictus* L) and for a long time the seed was considered a specific for stitches in the side.

Description Annual or biennial; 30–150 cm tall with erect, prominently grooved, seldom branched stem. Leaves large, oblong, shiny, variegated and very spiny; sessile or clasping. Flowers violet-purple, thistle-like in a hemispherical capitula to 5 cm long; usually solitary and surrounded at the base by long spiny appendages.

Appearing late summer to early autumn.

Distribution Native to central and west Europe; introduced and naturalized in California and elsewhere. On dry rocky or stony soils in wastelands, fields and roadsides to 600 m altitude.

Cultivation Wild plant. Easily grown from seed; prefers sunny situation and well-drained soil.

Constituents Essential oil; tyramine; histamine; bitter principles; a flavonoid, silymarine.

Uses (powdered seed, fresh and dried leaves, whole and dried flowering plant, fresh root, fresh young stems and shoots, fresh receptacle) Choleretic; cholagogue; bitter tonic; hypertensive; diuretic.

The whole herb is of value in the stimulation of appetite and to assist digestion. The powdered seeds taken in emulsion are markedly choleretic and of use in certain cardiovascular disorders. They also act prophylactically against travel sickness. Formerly used in the treatment of leg ulcers and varicose veins.

Young leaves, shoots, peeled stems, receptacles and roots can be cooked and eaten.

Contra-indications The seed should be used only by medical personnel.

Sinapis alba L CRUCIFERAE

Mustard White Mustard

The ancient Greeks and Romans used Mustard as a spice, usually ground up and sprinkled over food. The development of the now universally known condiment began in France in the seventeenth century, and today over half the world's supply comes from Dijon. White Mustard is closely related to the Wild Charlock (*Sinapis arvensis* L), and is much less pungent than Black Mustard. There was no medicinal differentiation between the various types of Mustard seed until the London Pharmacopoeia of 1720.

Description Branched annual to 1 m high; slightly hairy stems; leaves generally oval and lobed. Flowers small, bright yellow, appearing mid-summer to early autumn. Seed yellowish in colour, in bristly pods.

Distribution Native to southern parts of Europe and western Asia. Introduced elsewhere.

Cultivation Wild plant. Cultivated commercially on wide scale.

Constituents A glycoside comprising sinalbin; an enzyme, myrosin, which interact in the presence of cold water when the seed is crushed.

Uses (seed, leaves) Stimulant, irritant, emetic. Less powerful than Black Mustard and used in combination with it for similar purposes. Powerful preservative, effective against moulds and bacterial growth; used for this reason in pickles. Young leaves used in salads.

Sisymbrium officinale (L) Scop. CRUCIFERAE

Hedge Mustard

This herb was the *erysimon* of Dioscorides who prescribed it (combined with honey) against deadly poisons and a host of other diseases and pestilences. The Greek name was retained in the apothecaries' *Herba erysimi*, and even by Linnaeus who classified it as *Erysimum officinale* –

recognizing in that name the fact that Hedge Mustard had long been an official plant, and effective as an expectorant.

Traditionally, and in practice, the herb or juice may be used fresh to restore the voice in hoarseness or in complete loss, and for this reason it became known as the Singer's plant.

Description Annual on branched, erect stem 30–90 cm tall, with 5–8 cm long basal leaves deeply pinnatifid and toothed; stem leaves thinner and hastate. Flowers small, pale yellow on long racemes, appearing early summer to mid-autumn.

Distribution European native; in hedgerows, roadsides, railway embankments, most wasteland and weedy places and occasionally on walls. To 1700 m altitude.

Cultivation Wild. Once cultivated as a pot-herb.

Constituents Sulphur-containing compounds; cardenolides.

Uses (fresh flowering tops, fresh juice) Expectorant; bechic; stomachic; tonic; diuretic; laxative.

Useful in bronchitis, pharyngitis, tracheitis, and as a tonic.

May be used with discretion in sauces; formerly eaten as a vegetable but the flavour is strong and disagreeable in large quantities.

Contra-indications As it has an effect on the heart it is not suitable for the very young, old or those with cardiovascular problems.

Smilax ornata Hook. f. LILIACEAE

Sarsaparilla

Sarsaparilla was introduced to Seville, Spain, between 1536 and 1545 from Mexico, and it soon received attention as a potential remedy for syphilis – particularly following the reports of successful treatment using the herb's roots by Pedro de Ciezo de Leon in the 1540s. The plant was established as an official drug by the mid-sixteenth century and remained official until the early twentieth century.

Initially it was given various names, including Zarzaparilla, Zarza-Parrilla, Salsa Parilla and *Sarmentum indicum*, and by 1685 three main sorts, Mexican, Honduran and that from the province of Quito were being exported to Europe in large quantities.

By the nineteenth century Sarsaparilla was established as a valuable alterative and tonic for use in rheumatic, syphilitic, scrophulous, and chronic dermatological problems, and many different types of root were reaching Europe. These included Honduran, Guatemalan, Brazilian, Jamaican, Mexican and Guayaquil Sarsaparillas. Of these, the so-called Jamaica Sarsaparilla (exported via Jamaica but actually from central America) was the only sort once allowed in the British Pharmacopoeia.

The root is now retained in few national pharmacopoeias, and besides folk medicinal use, it is only employed as a vehicle and flavouring agent for medicines, or as a soft drink flavouring.

Description Dioecious, woody vine climbing by means of paired stipular tendrils. Stems prickly arising from rhizomatous root-stock, from which numerous thin, cylindrical roots also arise. Leaves alternate, variable. Flowers greenish to white, followed by berries.

Distribution Native to Central America, especially Costa Rica. In humid forests, swamps, and river-banks.

Cultivation Wild. The thin rootlets are usually collected from the wild.

Constituents Sarsaponin, a glycoside; sarsapic acid; sitosterol-d-glycoside; fatty acids; sugars; resins.

Uses (root) Alterative; diuretic; tonic. This remedy is ineffective in syphilis and is now considered of low therapeutic value. It does assist in the elimination of urea and uric acid, however, and is thus of value in gout; it is of some benefit in rheumatism. Evidence suggests it is more effective in warmer climates. Employed as a pharmaceutical flavouring agent. Used in soft drinks.

Smyrnium olusatrum L UMBELLIFERAE

Alexanders Black Lovage/Horse Parsley

Because of superficial similarities with other members of the Umbelliferae family, Alexanders is also known as Black Lovage, Wild Celery, and Horse Parsley. A medieval name *Petroselinum Alexandrium* or the Rock Parsley of Alexandria echoes these similarities and gives us the name Alexanders.

It was known to Theophrastus as *hipposelinon* and occasionally as *petroselinon*, the latter name usually being applied to Parsley. A related plant, *S. perfoliatum* L, which had similar properties and uses was given the Greek name *Smyrnion* and from this the generic name of Alexanders is obtained. Both plants were official from the earliest times, and the root

and seed remained so until 1830 in much of Europe.

Alexanders has been most important as a culinary herb however, and its cultivation was described by Pliny and Columella in the first century A.D. Even Galen considered it more important as a food than a medicine. The leaves, the upper part of the roots, stem and shoots were most often used, but the flower buds were also added to salads. Like Celery the herb was blanched to remove bitterness. Due to the whims of fashion, Alexanders largely disappeared from gardens in the mid-eighteenth century, but it is worthy of modern cultivation.

Description Glabrous biennial, 50–150 cm tall on solid, furrowed stem. Lower leaves to 30 cm long, compound, stalked, with broadly ovate segments to 6 cm long. Flowers yellow-green in sub-globose umbels to 10 cm wide appearing early to mid-summer and followed by aromatic black seed.

Distribution Native to west Europe, mediterranean region, and naturalized elsewhere; on moist soils in hedge banks, rocky soils, cliffs, specially close to the sea.

Cultivation Wild plant. Cultivated on most soils in a sunny position from seed sown in the autumn. Its cultivation is similar to Celery.

Constituents Unknown.

Uses (seed, dried and fresh root, fresh stems and leaves) Stomachic; diuretic.

Now rarely used medicinally, the seed soaked in wine was formerly considered an emmenagogue, while the leaves were antiscorbutic in days when vitamin C was unavailable. The root is mildly diuretic and a bitter, thus promoting appetite. The seed is stomachic, and was once thought to be of benefit in asthma. The fresh juice may be used on cuts and wounds.

Seed may be crushed and used with discretion as a condiment.

Leaves, stem, root and shoots may be boiled and eaten. The fresh blanched stem and flower buds can be eaten raw.

Solanum dulcamara L SOLANACEAE

Nightshade Bittersweet/Woody Nightshade

The Solanaceae family consists of over 1700 species, some of which are of considerable economic importance – such as the Egg-plant, Pepino, and Potato. Others are of horticultural interest and several have been employed for medicinal purposes in all parts of the world. Many, such as this species, have very poisonous berries due to their glycoalkaloid content. This irritant substance partially breaks down, however, in solution to yield steroidal alkamine aglycones which have an effect on the nervous system. Various parts of the plant (excluding the berries) have therefore been used appropriately in medicinal practice since as early as the thirteenth century. The specific use of the herb's stem was introduced in Germany in the sixteenth century when it was called *Dulcis amara*, literally sweet bitter, after the taste which is first bitter, then sweet (due to the chemical changes mentioned above).

Its medical use has almost disappeared in the last 30 years although it is included as a food flavouring provided the solanine content in the final food product is not more than 10 mg per kg.

Description Shrubby perennial usually 60–170 cm tall, sometimes climbing or trailing to 4 m tall. Leaves ovate, pubescent, petiolate, entire

2 or more basal lobes; to 10 cm long. Flowers violet, spotted green, with bright yellow anthers; numerous in long-stalked cymes, appearing mid-summer or mid-autumn. Followed by ovoid, scarlet-red fruit to 12 mm diameter.
Distribution Widespread. Native to Europe, Asia, and North America. On wasteland, weedy places, stream edges, and woodland; on damp nutrient-rich soils.
Cultivation Wild plant.
Constituents Alkaloids (to 1%) comprising solaceine, solaneine and solanine; glycosidal and non-glycosidal saponins comprising dulcamaric and dulcamaretic acids.
Uses (dried stems) Expectorant; diuretic. Formerly employed in decoction to treat asthma, catarrh, rheumatism and bronchitis, and especially of benefit in dermatological problems such as eczema, psoriasis and pityriasis. May be used homeopathically.
Contra-indications All parts of the plant are POISONOUS; to be used only by medical personnel.

Solidago virgaurea L COMPOSITAE
Golden Rod
The common name refers to the herb's appearance. It is an attractive plant and has been taken into cultivation as a useful late-flowering ornamental.
The herb is not certainly mentioned in ancient writings and there is evidence that it was particularly promoted by the Arabs in the Middle Ages, since to fifteenth and sixteenth-century Italians it was known as *Erba pagana* and the Germans called it *Consolida Saracenia.* Golden Rod has principally been used as a wound herb, hence the name *consolida* from the Latin to make whole – and hence its generic name. Traditionally it was employed both externally and internally. Clarke introduced an extract of the fresh flowers to homeopathic medicine in 1902, and in 1949 it was discovered by Hager that Brazilians used the closely related herb *S. microglossa* DC as a wound plant, too.
Description Erect perennial to 1 m tall; on knotted rhizome. Stems usually sparsely branched, sometimes unbranched. Leaves alternate, pubescent, the basal ones obovate to oblanceolate and petiolate, to 10 cm long. Upper leaves smaller and becoming sessile. Leaves either dentate or entire. Flowers golden-yellow, to 15 mm wide, arranged in terminal panicles; appearing late summer to late autumn.

Distribution Native to Europe, North Africa and Asia. Introduced elsewhere. In woodland clearings, wood edges, grassland; on deep porous acid and calcareous soils, to 2800 m altitude.
Cultivation Wild plant. Propagated horticulturally by division in spring or autumn, or from seed sown in spring. Prefers open conditions, and soils which are not too rich.
Constituents Essential oil; flavonoids; tannins; saponins; various organic acids comprising mainly citric, tartaric and oxalic acids; unknown substances.
Uses (dried flowering plant) Anti-inflammatory; expectorant; vulnerary; astringent; weakly diuretic.
Of much use applied externally in poultices or ointments to assist tissue healing; used internally for the same purpose, and also in urinogenital inflammations or to treat chronic skin problems.
Formerly taken as an adjuvant (assisting agent) with other remedies, of benefit in asthma, arthritis and rheumatism.
Rarely used in cases of diarrhoea. Its ability to reduce cholesterol levels is not clinically substantiated.

Spigelia marilandica L LOGANIACEAE
Pink Root Carolina Pink/Worm Grass/ Indian Pink
The generic name of this once popular North American Indian remedy for round-worms is taken from Adrian van der Spiegel, a physician from Brussels who died in Padua in 1625, in whose honour it was called *Spigelia.*
The herb was particularly favoured in the southern States by the Cherokees, to whom it was known as *unsteetla.* It was introduced to medicine in the 1750s by Dr Garden and Dr Chalmers; it was included in the United States Pharmacopoeia, and continued to be used in orthodox medicine until 40 years ago. The name Pink Root comes from the internal colour of the root-stock. It was formerly classified as *Lonicera marilandica* L.
Description Perennial on twisted root-stock, from 30–60 cm tall. Leaves opposite, entire, acuminate, sessile, ovate to ovate-lanceolate, somewhat pubescent beneath; 5–10 cm long. Flowers very attractive, 3–5 cm long, deep red outside, yellow inside, carried on erect, one-sided terminal cymes; appearing early to late summer.
Distribution North American native; from southern New Jersey to Florida and Texas; in rich, deep soils at the edges of woods and in woodland clearings.
Cultivation Wild plant.
Constituents An alkaloid, spigeline; bitter principles; resin; volatile oil; fixed oil; tannins; the action is mostly due to the spigeline content, which is a slightly toxic substance.

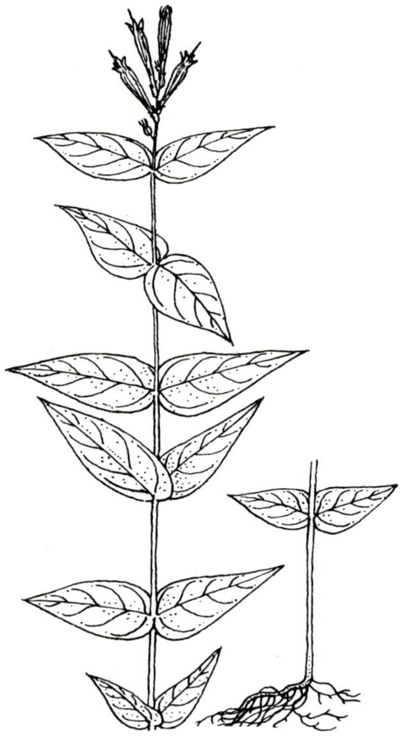

Uses (dried or fresh roots and rhizome, rarely fresh leaves) Antihelmintic; narcotic.
Once specifically used to expel round-worms; the action only being effective when purgation takes place. It was, therefore, usually administered in conjunction with a purgative.
In small quantities the powder is thought to be of use in the treatment of nervous headache. The remedy is incompletely studied, but may be of benefit in certain nervous complaints.
The leaves may be used, with discretion, as a stomachic tea; they do not contain the same quantity of active substances as are found in the root-stock.

Stachys officinalis (L) Trevisan LABIATAE
Betony
This is an interesting example of a herb which was attributed with magical properties from the earliest times when it was used medicinally, and which for some time retained an important place in folk medicine even though its value is now being seriously questioned. The Egyptians were the first to attribute Betony with magical properties, and it was the most important magical plant of the Anglo-Saxons, being mentioned as one of the medicinal plants in the eleventh-century work, the *Lacnunga.* Dioscorides knew it as *kestron* while the Romans called it *vettonica,* from which the old name *betonica* is derived. It was previously known as *Betonica officinalis* L.
Today opinions differ as to its value; some authorities consider it is only an astringent bitter (it was once an ingredient of bitter tonics), while others believe it is sedative. It is, however, now chiefly employed in herbal smoking mixtures and herbal snuffs, as well as occasionally being used in folk medicine.
Description Perennial with square stems; reach-

ing 30–60 cm tall. Basal rosette of cordate, dentate, slightly hairy, long-petiolate and strongly-nerved leaves. Flowers pink or purple, in a dense, terminal spike surmounting a long stalk; appearing mid-summer to mid-autumn.

Distribution European native; on sandy loams in wood clearings, meadowland, to 1500 m altitude.

Cultivation Wild plant.

Constituents Tannins (to 15%); bitter substances; saponosides; glucosides; alkaloids comprising betonicine and stachydrine.

Uses (dried flowering tops, root-stock rarely) Astringent; stomachic; emetic; purgative; vulnerary; sternutatory; bitter; sedative.

The root may cause purgation and is not usually employed.

The herb is an effective bitter tonic and useful in diarrhoea and for external application to wounds.

It may possess a mild sedative action of benefit in headaches and anxiety states, but is best taken with other remedies.

The dried leaves may be used as a tea substitute, and are included in smoking and snuff mixtures.

The fresh plant provides a yellow dye.

Stellaria media (L) Vill. CARYOPHYLLACEAE

Chickweed

Chickweed is this herb's English name, *herbe à l'oiseau* its French name, *Vogelmiere* its German, and in medieval Latin *morsus gallinae* (hen's bite) – all of these emphasizing the association with birds.

It has long been used as a bird feed, and in winter it provides one of the few sources of fresh seed for them. Indeed, it is as a foodstuff for animals and poor country folk that it has received most attention; the ancient writers ignored it and it has few, if any, medicinal applications.

Stellaria is from the Latin *stella* meaning a star, after the flower shape; while *media* serves to distinguish this plant from both larger and smaller relatives as it means middle.

Description Vigorous annual, but rapidly propagating and found throughout the year. Stems much-branched, decumbent and ascending, very straggly, 10–40 cm tall. Leaves

ovate-acute, long-petioled, 3–20 mm long; some leaves ovate and sessile. Flowers small, white, numerous on downwardly pointing stalks. Appearing early spring to mid-winter.

Distribution European native; distributed worldwide, and often naturalized as a weed of importance. On all moist, cultivated land and wasteland to 2000 m altitude.

Cultivation Wild plant.

Constituents Mineral salts including calcium and potassium salts; saponins.

Uses (fresh stems and leaves) Vulnerary.

The crushed plant may be used in poultices; once rubbed on arthritic joints to relieve discomfort. Used homeopathically in the treatment of rheumatism.

Principally used as a salad herb or may be cooked as a vegetable with a knob of butter added.

Stillingia sylvatica Gard. EUPHORBIACEAE

Queen's Delight Queen's Root/Yaw-root

Queen's Delight receives its generic name from Dr Benjamin Stillingfleet, after whom it was named.

The use of the herb as a specific against syphilis was established in the southern United States well before 1828 when it was introduced

to medicine by Dr Symons. It was soon an official drug in the United States Pharmacopoeia, and entered European pharmacopoeias; its action is markedly reduced if old tinctures or roots are employed, and it was found to be a better expectorant than an antisyphilitic. It is still retained in folk medicine and proprietary herbal products as an alterative.

Its leaves are often marked with chancre-like (like syphilitic lesions) spots – which may have originally suggested its use in syphilis.

Description Glabrous, perennial subshrub to 90 cm tall, on thick, creeping root-stock. Stems clustered and regularly branched. Leaves very variable in form; from ovate to oblong or lanceolate, sessile or short-petioled, toothed, green to red, 3–11 cm long. Flowers monoecious, yellow, without petals, in dense, terminal spikes to 12 cm long; male flowers in clusters, female solitary. Appearing late spring to mid-autumn.

Distribution North American native; from Virginia to Florida and Texas. In sandy, light, dry soils in full sun.

Cultivation Wild plant.

Constituents Volatile oil (to 4%); fixed oil; an acrid resin, sylvacrol; tannins; calcium oxalate; cyanogenic glycosides; starch. The combined action is mildly irritant.

Uses (dried or fresh root-stock, not more than 12 months old) Expectorant; emetic; purgative; laxative; sialogogue.

Principally used now as an alterative in chronic skin problems, liver infections and urino-genital infections. In small doses it is laxative, and in large doses it is emetic and purgative.

Of benefit as an expectorant in pulmonary disorders.

Styrax benzoin Dryander STYRACACEAE

Benzoin Gum Benjamin

It was first noted by Ibn Batuta following his visit to Sumatra in 1325 to 1349, and he called it Java Frankincense (or Luban Jawi in Arabic). The Arabic name was altered to Banjawi, Benzui, Benzoin and Benjamin over subsequent centuries.

The resin was imported to Europe following Garcia de Orta's description of the drug (1563), and in the list of taxes levied at Worms in 1582 it was listed as *Asa dulcis* (Sweet Asa) – a name retained until the 1850s.

By 1800 the antiseptic properties of Benzoin had been fully recognized and both Simple and Compound Tinctures of Benzoin were regularly employed as preservatives in a wide range of medicinal and cosmetic preparations, and the resin is still used today in herbal preparations.

Description Tree to 7 m tall; leaves simple, elliptic to orbicular, entire or slightly dentate. Flowers white, several, in drooping clusters on 2 cm long pedicels.

Distribution Native to south-east Asia, especially Sumatra; in mixed forests close to rivers.

Cultivation Wild and cultivated commercially.

The resin is obtained by tapping 7–10 year old trees and scraping off the whitish exudation from the bark. Trees can be so treated for up to

20 years, before they die.

Constituents Balsamic acids (to 60%) comprising esters of cinnamic and benzoic acids; benzoresinol; benzaldehyde; styrol; vanillin; and several related substances. The combined action is predominantly antiseptic.

Uses (resin) Carminative; antiseptic; diuretic; mildly expectorant.

Used internally as a genito-urinary antiseptic, and as an expectorant in chronic bronchitis. Principally of benefit as an antiseptic in poultices and plasters, and also applied directly to the skin as an antiseptic tincture. The tincture is an excellent preservative, suitable for various pharmaceutical and cosmetic preparations.

It can be used diluted as a mouth wash.

Used in incense and aromatic products.

Succisa pratensis Moench. DIPSACACEAE

Devil's-Bit Scabious

The second part of this herb's common name refers to the fact that it has been used in the treatment of scabies and similar skin conditions in which scratching is characteristic. It was formerly classified as *Scabiosa succisa* L.

This may have been introduced through the theory of the Doctrine of Signatures, since most members of the Dipsacaceae have scratchy seed heads; the Fuller's Teasel (*Dipsacus sativus* (L) Honk.) is the most extreme example of this, and the bracts were once used to tease or scratch up the nap on cloth.

Devil's-Bit is an old prefix from a traditional story in which the devil bit part of the root off. The herb is not very effective medicinally and is rarely used today.

Description Perennial on short, erect root-stock; stem erect 15–100 cm tall, usually glabrous. Basal leaves narrowly elliptic to obovate-lanceolate, to 30 cm long, arranged in a rosette; stem leaves narrower and rarely

toothed. Flowers dark blue, occasionally white, numerous, arranged in globular, involucral heads, terminating a long stalk. Appearing late summer to late autumn.

Distribution Native to North Africa; Europe; western Siberia; introduced and naturalized in north-east United States and elsewhere. On moist soils in woods, pastures, fenland, and marshes. To 1800 m altitude.

Cultivation Wild plant.

Constituents Saponins; a glucoside, scabioside; starch; tannins; mineral salts.

Uses (dried root-stock; rarely flowers and juice) Expectorant; diuretic; antihelmintic; vulnerary; astringent; stomachic.

Now rarely used; the root-stock was formerly considered of benefit as an expectorant in bronchitis. A decoction may be used externally to relieve itching of the skin (pruritus) or to aid wound healing or ulcers. Also used homeopathically.

Symphytum officinale L BORAGINACEAE

Comfrey Knitbone

Comfrey has received much attention in recent years both as a medicinal plant (providing a source of vitamin B_{12} and the cell-proliferant allantoin) and as a potential source of protein. Certain strains of the herb contain almost 35 per cent total protein, which is the same percentage as that of soya beans, and 10 per cent more than that of Cheddar Cheese.

Attempts to extract the protein in a form suitable for human consumption and to develop the plant as a food source in underdeveloped countries have so far been unsuccessful.

Comfrey is, however, an important animal feed in some parts of the world, and in Africa, for example, it is increasing in importance. It is also grown as an organic compost and mulch. It is not certain that this species was the *symphiton* of Dioscorides, but it probably was the Roman *conferva* (from the verb meaning to join together), the name from which both the medieval *Consolidae maioris* and common name Comfrey are derived.

Comfrey was once one of the main herbs used in treating fractures and hence the alternative name Knitbone. The pounded root forms a mucilaginous mass which can be bound around a fracture and which, when dry, holds the bone in place.

Description Perennial, 30–120 cm tall, on thick brownish-black root-stock. Leaves and stem erect, with stiff hairs. Lower leaves to 25 cm long, petiolate, lanceolate, hairy beneath. Upper leaves narrower. Flowers purplish, pinkish or yellowish-white, in crowded terminal cymes; appearing early summer to early autumn.

Distribution Native to Europe, Asia; introduced and naturalized elsewhere. On rich, wet soils near rivers, streams, in ditches, on low-lying meadowland. To 1500 m altitude.

Cultivation Wild. Propagated by division in spring and autumn, or by root cuttings from spring to autumn. Tolerates most conditions, but requires regular watering on dry soils.

Constituents Mucilage; allantoin (to 0.8%); tannic acid; resin; traces of alkaloids comprising consollidine and symphyto-cynoglossine; sugars; essential oil; choline. The cell-proliferant action is due to the allantoin content.

Uses (fresh or dried root-stock, fresh or dried leaves) Astringent; demulcent; cell-proliferant; vulnerary; weak sedative.

Root used internally in the treatment of gastric and duodenal ulcers and diarrhoea; leaf used in pleurisy and bronchitis.

For wounds, bruising, ulceration and dermatological complaints the leaves or macerated root are applied as a poultice, lotion or decoction. Considered of benefit in neuralgia and rheumatism, applied externally. Occasionally used externally in the treatment of varicose veins.

Dried leaf is a tea substitute.

Fresh leaf used as a vegetable; in animal feeds; in composting and mulching.

Symplocarpus foetidus (L) Nutt. ARACEAE
Skunk Cabbage Polecat Weed
This herb has an unusual appearance and, as its common names suggest, an awful smell when bruised.
It has been classified botanically in several different genera, notably *Ictodes*, *Pothos*, *Arum*, and *Dracontium*, but it is now included as the only species of the genus *Symplocarpus*. Skunk Cabbage root and seed were introduced to Europe in the early nineteenth century from American folk use, and although included in the United States Pharmacopoeia for a short time they did not attract much attention since superior antispasmodics were available. It is, however, retained in folk medicine.
Description Foetid, hardy perennial on large tuberous root-stock and long rootlets. Stemless. Leaves (produced after the flowers) ovate-cordate, 45 cm long and 30 cm wide, smooth, entire, long-petioled (to 25 cm). Inflorescence is a fleshy ovoid spathe to 15 cm long, purple-brown, mottled with yellow, covering a black oval spadix; appearing early to mid-spring.
Distribution North-eastern North American native; also in north-east Asia; in swamps and boggy land.

Cultivation Wild.
Constituents Resin; fixed oil; volatile oil; sugars; gums; unknown acrid substances.
Uses (dried root and rhizome) Antispasmodic; expectorant; diuretic; emetic; mild sedative.
Of use in the treatment of various respiratory complaints, including asthma, bronchitis, whooping cough, hay fever, respiratory catarrh.
The leaves can be used fresh as a vulnerary. Root-stock formerly employed in the treatment of certain nervous disorders; also used to treat snake bites.
Contra-indications Slightly narcotic; medical use only. The fresh plant may cause blistering.

Syzygium aromaticum (L) Merr. & Perry MYRTACEAE
Clove-tree
The dried unopened flower buds, known as Cloves, are derived from a tree originally growing only on the 5 small islands comprising the Moluccas proper. For this reason they were

first mentioned in the writings of Chinese physicians, and an early custom of the Han dynasty (266 B.C. to A.D. 220) was to retain a Clove in the mouth when addressing the emperor, presumably to counteract halitosis. Pliny mentioned a spice called *caryophyllon*, hence the specific name, and by the fourth century Cloves were widely used throughout Europe. In the seventeenth and eighteenth centuries the spice caused serious trade rivalry between some European countries, and eventually the French began cultivation in Mauritius. It was first grown in Zanzibar in 1800.
Description Attractive pyramidal evergreen tree 10–15 m tall. Leaves ovate-oblong, 5–12.5 cm long, smooth and shiny, leathery, acute, and tapering at the base. Flowers crimson or pale purple, 7 mm wide, in branched terminal cymes. Fresh buds pink, but reddish-brown after sun drying.
Distribution Native to south-east Asian islands, especially the Moluccas. Introduced to West Indies, tropical East Africa, China.
Cultivation Wild; cultivated commercially in tropical maritime countries.
Constituents Volatile oil (15%); gallotannic acid (13%); caryophyllin; action due to volatile oil.
Uses (dried flower buds, oil) Aromatic stimulant; antispasmodic; carminative; rubefacient; counter-irritant.
Used in the treatment of flatulent colic, and as a remedy for toothache. Applied externally in embrocations to relieve neuralgic pain, and in rheumatism.
A constituent of tooth-powders and toothpastes, as a flavouring agent and antiseptic.
Culinary uses include bread sauce, curry, mulled spiced wine, liqueurs and stews. Acts as a preservative in pickles. Used in pomanders.
Contra-indications If applied for toothache, the oil should not have prolonged contact with the gums as this may cause serious irritation.

Tamus communis L DIOSCOREACEAE
Black Bryony
The Black Bryony is thought to be the herb described as the wild or field *Ampelos* (*Ampelos agria*) of Dioscorides – who prescribed his remedy externally to treat bruises.
Certainly by the Middle Ages this plant was called *ampelos melana* (black ampelos), *vitis nigra* (black vine) and finally *brionia nigra*

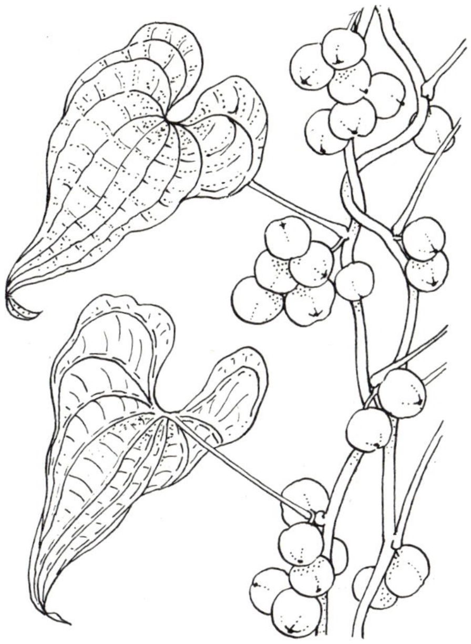

(black brionia) – from which the common name is derived.
Black Bryony is poisonous, and if the root is used internally it is violently purgative and emetic. It has, therefore, never been considered useful medicinally, but Clarke introduced a homeopathic preparation in 1902 to be used in sunstroke and rheumatism.
Description Dioecious perennial, on very large tuber (to 60 cm diameter), producing annual, twining stems. Leaves entire, cordate, broadly-ovate, glossy, to 10 cm long, with very long petioles. Flowers yellowish-green, male stalked, female sessile; both small. Appearing late spring to late summer, and followed by 12 mm diameter globose, red berry.
Distribution Native to central and southern Europe. In hedgerows, woodland clearings, wood margins, scrubland; on moist, well-drained, nutrient-rich soils, to 1100 m altitude.
Cultivation Wild plant.
Constituents (root-stock) Mucilage; gums; histamine-like compound; calcium oxalate; unknown substances.
Uses (fresh or dried root-stock) Rubefacient; resolvent.
Formerly only used externally as a poultice to treat contusions.
Contra-indications POISONOUS; the berries can be fatal to children.

Tanacetum vulgare L COMPOSITAE
Tansy
Tansy is also found classified as *Chrysanthemum vulgare* (L) Bernh. It is now frequently grown in herb gardens for its attractive and long-lasting yellow flower-heads, many of which are used in insect-repelling pot-pourris or other scented articles.
It has traditionally been used as an insecticide or insect repellent, and in the Middle Ages was one of the strewing herbs used on floors. Tansy was also rubbed over meat to keep flies away, and one of its old names *arthemisia domestica* emphasizes its use in the house.
It was also called *athanasia* and *tanacetum*,

names of uncertain association but considered to mean deathless – possibly because the flowers last so long.

Tansy was used until the mid-eighteenth century in certain types of pancakes called tansies. These were eaten at Lent, and the bitterness was meant to remind the eater of Christ's sufferings; they, no doubt, also acted as a useful vermifuge since this has been the herb's main therapeutic use from the days of the first apothecaries.

Description Aromatic, somewhat straggling perennial, 60–120 cm tall, on a rhizome. Leaves pinnate, alternate, to 12 cm long, subdivided into numerous leaflets which are deeply toothed. Several golden yellow flowers, consisting only of disc florets, in a dense flat or hemispherical corymb. Appearing late summer to early or mid-autumn.

Distribution Native to Europe and Asia; introduced and naturalized elsewhere, especially in north-east North America. On wasteland, wood clearings and undisturbed, nitrogen-rich, loamy soils to 1500 m altitude.

Cultivation Wild. May be propagated by division of old clumps in spring or autumn, or from seed sown in spring or autumn. Tolerates most positions provided the soil is not constantly wet. A variety (var. *crispum* DC) with larger and more finely divided leaves is sometimes preferred in herb gardens.

Constituents Essential oil, comprising thujone (to 70%), and borneol; vitamin C; tannins; resin; citric acid; butyric acid; oxalic acid; lipids.

Uses (fresh or dried flowering stems) Antihelmintic; insecticide; emmenagogue.

Small doses are effective in the treatment of round-worms. The herb also aids digestion. May be used in infusion as a gargle in gingivitis. The extracted oil was formerly used externally in the treatment of rheumatic pain.

Employed in a variety of insect-repellent sachets and scented articles.

Contra-indications Large doses are irritant and if taken during pregnancy may induce abortion.

Taraktogenos kurzii King FLACOURTIACEAE
Chaulmoogra

This tree is also classified as *Hydnocarpus kurzii* (King) Warb. It is one of several members of the family Flacourtiaceae which yield seed containing a fatty oil. The oil, and the crushed seed, have long been used in south-east Asia to treat various skin diseases, and it has been shown that the active principles of the oil (hydnocarpic and chaulmoogric acids) are strongly antibacterial. For this reason Chaulmoogra is employed in Hindu medicine to treat leprosy.

Description Tree to 20 m tall; leaves glossy, entire, alternate, leathery and oblong-lanceolate, to 20 cm long. Flowers few, in branched axillary cymes, or appearing singly. Followed by rugose, indehiscent, hard, globular fruit to 10 cm diameter; containing numerous seeds in a pulpy mass.

Distribution Native to Burma and Thailand; and now introduced to other regions of tropical

south-east Asia.

Constituents (seed) Chaulmoogra oil, comprising hydnocarpic acid (to 36%), chaulmoogric acid (to 23%), gorlic acid, oleic acid and palmitic acid.

Uses (oil, seed) Antibacterial; alterative; irritant.

The oil is effective in the treatment of lepromatous leprosy, and is still used in the East. Also useful in the treatment of intestinal worms. Seed used externally and internally in various skin diseases. Usually applied as an ointment. In India the seeds are considered to be an alterative tonic.

Contra-indications The oil is irritant and may cause nausea and vomiting, as well as having a slight depressant action on the cardiovascular system.

Taraxacum officinale Weber COMPOSITAE
Dandelion

Although the Dandelion is generally considered to be a ubiquitous weed, it is in fact one of the most useful of European herbs and all parts of the plant can be employed. It is an extremely effective medicinal plant, being possibly the safest and most active plant diuretic and one of the best herbs known to treat liver complaints. Both the leaves and root have long been eaten as salad material, and in the last century cultivated forms with large leaves have been developed as an autumn and spring vegetable; these usually being blanched in the same way as Endive.

Dandelion roots provide (when dried, chopped and roasted) the best-known coffee substitute, and all parts have been employed in fermented and unfermented beers, wines and tonic drinks. Surprisingly the herb is rarely mentioned by the ancient Greeks and Romans, and it is generally considered that the Arabs promoted its use in the eleventh century.

By the sixteenth century it was well established as an official drug of the apothecaries, who knew it as *Herba Taraxacon* or *Herba Urinaria* – the latter term emphasizing its diuretic effect. It was also called *Denta Leonis* (lion's teeth), after the leaf shape, and from which term the common name is derived via the French *dents de lion.*

It is still retained in the national pharmacopoeias of Hungary, Poland, the Soviet Union and Switzerland. The Russian Dandelion (*T. kok-saghyz* Rodin.) was extensively cultivated during the Second World War as a source of rubber, which was extracted from the latex of the roots. Small quantities of a similar latex are found in *T. officinale.*

Description Variable perennial on taproot, to 30 cm tall. Leaves spatulate, oblong or oblanceolate, entire to runcinate-pinnatifid. Flowers yellow, on hollow scapes, appearing late spring to mid-summer.

Distribution Native to Europe and Asia; introduced elsewhere. On nitrogen-rich soils in any situation to 2000 m altitude.

Cultivation Wild. Propagated from seed sown in spring for use as an autumn salad herb. Blanch by earthing up or placing an inverted flower pot over the plant. Grow as an annual to prevent bitterness developing in the plant.

Constituents Taraxacin, a bitter principle; taraxerin, an acrid resin; taraxerol; taraxas-

terol; 3:4 dioxycinnamic acid; flavoxanthin; inulin; citric acid; phenyloxyacetic acid; riboflavin; sitosterol; sitosterin; stigmasterol; coumestrol; vitamins B, C and provitamin A.
Uses (fresh or dried roots, leaves and flowers) Diuretic; cholagogue; choleretic; laxative; bitter tonic; stomachic.
An excellent bitter tonic in atonic dyspepsia; a mild laxative in chronic constipation; a cholagogue and choleretic in liver disease (especially jaundice, cholecystitis and the primary stages of cirrhosis). Considered of benefit as an anti-rheumatic. As a bitter it promotes appetite and improves digestion. A very effective diuretic.
Leaf and root used as a salad; root is a coffee substitute. Flowers used in Dandelion wine, and leaves in Dandelion beer and tonic drinks. The plant is safe to use in large amounts.

Teucrium chamaedrys L LABIATAE
Wall Germander Germander
The genus *Teucrium* consists of about 300 species, many of which are native to the mediterranean region. For this reason it has not been possible to identify definitely this particular species with the *Khamaidrys* of Dioscorides, and it is now considered most probably to be the same as his *Teukrion*.
Both these Greek names have, however, been combined to give the botanical name, and for much of the Middle Ages the herb was known as *Herba chamaedryos*. Germander was also called *Quercula maior* or *Quercula* – names which (like *chamaedryos*) mean ground or little oak, after the shape of the leaf. The common name is derived from *gamandrea* the latinization of *khamaidrys*.
The herb was once a popular medicine used predominantly in digestive or feverish complaints, but it was also much employed in formal herb and knot gardens as an edging plant. There is very little modern information available on Germander, however, and it is little used other than as an ingredient of liqueurs and tonic wines.
Description Small, shrubby, practically evergreen perennial, 10–30 cm tall. Stem erect or decumbent, hairy, marked with purple, bearing oblong to obovate-oblong, toothed leaves,

2 cm long. Flowers purple, rose or rarely white, typically labiate but lacking upper lip, in either loose or dense terminal spikes; appearing early summer to mid-autumn.
Distribution Native to Europe and south-west Asia; introduced elsewhere. On dry chalky soils, in dry thickets, woodland, rocky screes, and old walls. To 1500 m altitude.
Cultivation Wild. Cultivated as an edging plant. Propagated from seed sown in spring; division in autumn; or cuttings from spring to summer. The dwarf cultivar *T. chamaedrys* cv. Prostratum is useful as a carpeting herb.
Constituents Tannins; an essential oil; bitter principles probably including picropulin; sugars including stachyose and raffinose; unknown substances.
Uses (dried flowering plant) Choleretic; antiseptic; antipyretic; tonic; aromatic; diuretic. Principally of use in gall-bladder and digestive disorders. The infusion can be employed to promote the appetite, aid digestion, and dispel flatulence.
Once used in feverish conditions and formerly considered effective in the treatment of gout, although this is unsubstantiated.
Used in the manufacture of liqueurs, vermouths and tonic wines.
May be used effectively as a horticultural edging plant.

Theobroma cacao L BYTTNERIACEAE
Cacao Cocoa-Plant
The Spanish were the first to describe the seeds of this now important economic plant. In the sixteenth century Valdes reported their use as a form of exchange instead of coins (in the Yucatan), and the trees have long been cultivated in northern South America as a source of chocolate. The name itself comes from the Mexican *chocolatl* while *cacao* is from *cacauatl* in the same language.
Both the seed and chocolate itself were known in much of Europe by 1600, and Cacao butter was prepared in 1695 by Homberg in France. The medicinal applications of Cacao butter were promoted by the French and it was soon popular in various cosmetic preparations. It is still retained as a base for medical pessaries, bougies, and suppositories, and forms a vehicle for certain cosmetics – its main value being that it does not go rancid quickly. Both Cocoa and chocolate consist of the fermented and roasted plant seed; they differ in the quantity of sugar and type of additional flavouring (such as vanilla) added to the product.
Description Evergreen tree to 7 m tall. Leaves simple, alternate, glossy and leathery, oblong to 30 cm long, red when young. Flowers small, yellowish-pink, long-stalked in clusters carried directly on branches or the trunk, followed by 30-cm long yellow to brown fruit containing 20–40 3 cm-long seeds.
Distribution Native to Central and South America; introduced elsewhere. In lowland tropics or wet soils.
Cultivation Wild. Cultivated commercially in many tropical countries, especially Brazil and the west coast of Africa. Usually given arti-

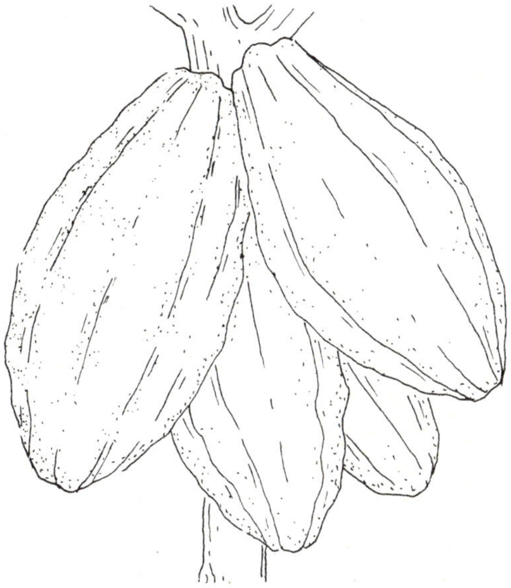

ficial shading or planted under higher trees. Propagated from seed.
Constituents (seed) Fat called Cocoa butter or Theobroma oil; theobromine (1–3%); sucrose and glucose (2.5%); caffeine; mucilage. (fat) Comprises 55% oleopalmitostearin.
Uses (Fat – Cocoa butter, seed products – cocoa and chocolate) Emollient; nutritive; diuretic.
Any medicinal actions of the seed products are due to their theobromine and caffeine content, which act as a mild stimulant and diuretic. Theobromine has no stimulant effect on the central nervous system.
Cocoa and chocolate are now used pharmaceutically to mask unpleasant flavours. The fat is used in pessaries, ointments and as a massage lubricant.
Very wide culinary and confectionery use of the seed products.
The fat is used in cosmetics.

Thymus x *citriodorus* (Pers.) Schreb. ex Scheigg. & Körte LABIATAE
Lemon Thyme
Of the many species and cultivars of Thyme which are available for use in a scented herb garden, one of the most popular is the true Lemon Thyme.
Since it is a cross between *T. pulegioides* L and *T. vulgaris* L there is often confusion with other lemon-scented Thymes, notably some varieties of *T. vulgaris*.
Lemon Thyme is variable in form. It is often found as the silver-variegated cultivar, Silver Queen, which itself ranges in degree and colour of variegation.
Because of its mild flavour Lemon Thyme is a popular culinary herb.
Description Aromatic lemon-scented bushy shrub to 25 cm tall. Leaves glabrous and revolute, varying in colour from dark to light, or silver-variegated, lanceolate to ovate, to 9 mm long. Flowers pale lilac, in small, oblong inflorescence; appearing mid to late summer.
Distribution Cultivated world-wide.
Cultivation Found horticulturally only; propagate from cuttings spring to autumn, or by

division in spring. Requires well-drained soil in a warm position. Winter protection under glass may be necessary for some cultivars in northern climates.
Constituents Essential oil.
Uses (fresh or dried leaves) Not used medicinally.
Widely used as a culinary herb. Used horticulturally as an aromatic ornamental and edging plant.

Thymus serpyllum L LABIATAE
Wild Thyme
As the common name suggests this herb is found wild. It is extensively distributed in Europe and Asia and is found as far north as Iceland. Wild Thyme has been used since the earliest times, and Dioscorides called it *herpyllos*; the Romans knew it as *serpyllum*. Both ancient names refer to the prostrate, snake-like growth habit of the plant. Wild Thyme exists in many forms with variations in colour, growth habit and leaf size; many different varieties are, therefore, found as Wild Thyme, but all are suitable as a quickly spreading aromatic carpeting herb for the garden. *T. serpyllum* is also described as Mother of Thyme, Creeping Thyme and, confusingly, Lemon Thyme.
Description Extremely variable, prostrate, mat-forming, aromatic perennial 10–40 cm tall; woody at the base and sometimes a semi-shrub. Flowering stems erect to 10 cm tall bearing 8 mm-long linear to elliptic, almost sessile leaves and pink to purple small flowers arranged in an ovoid, short, terminal infloresence. Appearing late summer to early autumn.
Distribution Native to Europe, north-west Asia; introduced and naturalized elsewhere. On well-drained sandy soils or sandy loams in dry turf, roadsides, sunny slopes, woodland clearing; to 2600 m altitude.
Cultivation Wild. Propagated by layering in summer or from cuttings taken from spring to autumn.
Constituents Essential oil (to 0.3%) comprising mainly thymol and carvacrol; tannins; saponoside; resins; flavones; bitter principles. Composition varies considerably.
Uses (dried flowering tops, rarely oil) Antispasmodic; antiseptic; expectorant; carminative; bitter aromatic.
Principally employed in digestive complaints, including flatulence and indigestion. Useful in coughs and respiratory tract infection.
May be used as a disinfectant mouth wash, external poultice on wounds, for rheumatic pain, and as a douche.
The oil (Oil of Serpolet) is used commercially in certain pharmaceutical and cosmetic products.
Dried leaves can be taken as a tea, and are used for culinary purposes.

Thymus vulgaris L LABIATAE
Garden Thyme Common Thyme
Thyme is one of the best known and most widely used of the culinary herbs, and to satisfy the demand it is not only collected from the wild in mediterranean areas, but is also cultivated commercially in central and eastern Europe.

The generic and common names come from the Latin *thymum* which in turn derives from the Greek names *thymbra* or *thumon*. It is however, most unlikely that this species was the main one used by the ancient Greeks, more probably they used *Thymus capitatus* Lk.
It is also uncertain when Thyme was first cultivated in northern European countries; some believe the Romans took it to Britain, while there is stronger evidence that it became popular north of the Alps between A.D. 850 and 1250. Certainly by the sixteenth century it was in general cultivation being grown as an annual in the far north.
The German apothecary Neumann first isolated the plant's essential oil in 1725, and this powerfully antiseptic substance is still used in pharmacy and various commercial preparations.
Description Aromatic perennial sub-shrub on somewhat gnarled or tortuous woody stems, 10–30 cm tall; leaves grey-green, opposite, small, entire, linear to elliptic, petioled or sessile, tomentose, to 15 mm long. Flowers lilac to white, small, in dense or loose many-flowered terminal inflorescences, characterized by somewhat larger leaves than those on non-flowering stems. Appearing early summer to late autumn.
Distribution Native to the western mediterranean region and southern Italy; introduced elsewhere. To 2500 m in altitude. On dry soils, either rocky or well-drained, in sunny positions.
Cultivation Wild. Collected commercially from the wild in south-west mediterranean countries; cultivated commercially in Europe, especially Hungary and Germany.
Widely grown as a horticultural or culinary plant. Propagated from seed sown in early summer, by division in spring, or by cuttings or layering from mid-spring to early summer. Grown as an annual in very cold climates. Very variable plant.
Constituents Essential oil (to 2.5%), comprising thymol (to 40%), carvacrol, borneol, cymene, linalol, *l*-pinene, bornyl-acetate; acid and neutral saponins; thiamine; ursolic acid; caffeic acid; tannins; bitter compounds; other active components.
The combined action is antiseptic, and mostly due to the thymol content.
Uses (dried flowering plant, oil) Antiseptic; carminative; vermifuge; rubefacient.
Thyme can be used in a wide range of conditions where its antiseptic properties are required. Particularly beneficial in gastro-intestinal and respiratory complaints.
The oil may be used as an antihelmintic, particularly to destroy hookworm.
Wide use of the oil in commercial, pharmaceutical, flavouring, and cosmetic preparations.
The plant is of great importance as a flavouring and kitchen herb.

Tilia cordata Mill. TILIACEAE
Small-Leaved Lime
The Lime, like the Oak and certain other European plants, was sacred to the Indo-Germanic peoples, and the name Lime is

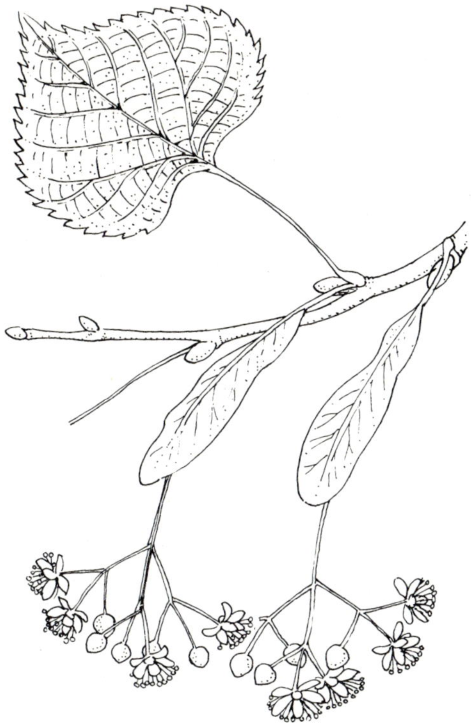

derived from the German base *lind.* A tea made from the flowers is still called Linden Tea. In America the so-called American Linden (*T. americana* L) provides a similar drink – the Basswood Tea (which should, however, only be taken sparingly since it can cause nausea). The Latin name for this and related species was *Tilia*, hence the generic name and the modern French, Italian, and Spanish names *Tilleul, Tiglio* and *Tilia*.

The tree has long been planted around houses and in towns as a decorative or shade-plant. It is the lightest European wood in weight as well as being one of the easiest to work in carving. The inner bark fibre was also once used in rope manufacture.

Besides the use of its blossom in a pleasant herbal tisane, Lime has an important place in folk medicine and eastern European medicine as a remedy for high blood pressure. For this purpose the flowers of *T. platyphyllos* Scop. (Large-leaved Lime) and *T. x europaea* L (a hybrid between *T. platyphyllos* and *T. cordata*) are also collected for medicinal application.

Description Deciduous tree or, rarely, shrub 15–40 m tall. Trunk straight, smooth when young. Leaves to 6.5 cm, orbicular, petiolate, serrate. Flowers aromatic, yellowish, in either erect or pendulous cymes of 5–10 flowers, appearing mid to late summer, followed by globose fruit.

Distribution European native, in mixed or deciduous woodland especially in sandy or stony soils in warm position; to 1600 m altitude.

Cultivation Wild. Introduced in towns as an ornamental tree. May reach 1000 years old.

Constituents Volatile oil (to 0.02%) comprising several compounds including farnesol; mucilage; manganese salts; flavonoid glycosides; saponins; polyphenols; tannins; other unknown active substances.

Uses (dried flowers and bracts, bark, fresh leaves). Antispasmodic; sedative; diaphoretic; diuretic; expectorant; choleretic.

Flowers principally used in combination with Hawthorn (*Crataegus monogyna* Jacq.) and Mistletoe (*Viscum album* L) in the treatment of hypertension.

They are also of much benefit in feverish chills, respiratory catarrh, indigestion, anxiety states and migraine, and in combination with other remedies in urinary infections. Small doses assist digestion. An infusion can be made for external use on skin rashes, as a gargle, or as a soothing bath. The bark decoction is of benefit in liver disease. Flowers used as a tisane – Linden Tea.

Fresh leaves may be eaten.

Wood used for carving and is also used in charcoal manufacture.

The tree is used (often clipped to shape) as a roadside ornamental.

Toxicodendron toxicaria (Salisb) Gillis
ANACARDIACEAE
Poison Ivy Poison Oak/Hiedra

The genus *Rhus* contains more than 150 species, some of which are grown as orna-

mentals. Recently six species (each commonly known as Poison Ivy or Poison Oak) have been transferred to the genus *Toxicodendron*, and *Toxicodendron toxicaria* was formerly classified as *Rhus toxicodendron* L. It is frequently confused with the closely related *R. radicans* L (now *T. radicans* (L) O. Kuntze) which is considered by some authorities to be a variety of *T. toxicaria*, and having the same properties. Poison Ivy is best known as an agent causing a violent allergic response in susceptible individuals. This allergy occurs either on contact with the plant or simply by standing close to it.

Its medicinal use was discovered in 1794 by Anderson and Horsfield in America, and it was introduced to Europe by Du Fresnoy in 1798. The leaves and a tincture have been included in various pharmacopoeias and materia medicas until as late as 1941. Now only used homeopathically.

Description Perennial shrub to 2 m containing milky juice. Leaves compound, comprising three thin, acute, rounded and dentate or crenate leaflets, downy beneath. Flowers small, several, greenish, in open axillary, racemose panicles; appearing mid-summer, followed by pale brown globose fruit.

Distribution Native to eastern North America in thickets.

Cultivation Wild plant.

Constituents Tannins, as rhoitannic acid; toxicodendric acid; unknown substances.

Uses (leaves, juice) Narcotic; irritant.

Once used in the treatment of chronic skin problems, rheumatism and paralysis. No longer employed, except in homeopathy.

The juice was formerly used as an indelible ink, and in shoe-creams.

Contra-indications May cause severe contact dermatitis. Not to be used internally.

Tragopogon porrifolius L COMPOSITAE
Salsify Vegetable Oyster/Oyster Plant

The Greek name for Salsify was *tragopogon* which means goat's beard; this gives both the generic name for this species and the family, as well as the English common name for a different herb, *Tragopogon pratensis* L. The French name for *T. pratensis* is, however, *Salsifis des prés*, or Meadow Salsify (although *barbe de bouc* or goat's beard is also used), thus adding to and emphasizing the confusion that surrounds international names.

The medieval names for Salsify were *oculus porci* or pig's eye (which might be a reference to the colour and appearance of the broken root) and *herba salsifica* from the Italian *sassefrica* (meaning the plant which accompanies stones – after its predisposition for rocky land).

The Italians were the first to cultivate Salsify as a vegetable, doing so in the early sixteenth century. By the seventeenth century it had not only been introduced as a vegetable in northern Europe, but also as a flower.

Salsify was largely ignored by nineteenth-century gardeners in favour of the Spanish Scorzonera (*Scorzonera hispanica* L), although both are now used commercially.

The herb has never been of medicinal interest.

Description Attractive hardy biennial to 110 cm, on 25 cm-long edible taproot. Leaves clasped, tapering, pointed and grass-like. Flowers purple, attractive, solitary, opening in the morning, ligulate to 8 cm wide. Appearing early to late summer.

Distribution Native to southern Europe; introduced elsewhere. Naturalized as a weed in North America. On stony but moist soils with some loam, in meadowland to 2000 m altitude.

Cultivation Wild. Propagate from seed sown in spring, thinning to 10 cm apart. Requires well-dug, rich and deep soil which is kept well-

watered. Lift roots in autumn or leave during winter in the soil. Readily self-sown.
Constituents Unknown.
Uses (fresh taproot) Nutritive; diuretic; bitter.
Although not used medicinally, the root acts as an appetite stimulant, and there is some evidence that it may have a beneficial effect on the liver.
Roots cooked and eaten as a vegetable.
Leaves may be used sparingly in salads.

Trifolium pratense L LEGUMINOSAE
Red Clover
Red Clover is a short-lived perennial (sometimes incorrectly described in seed lists as an annual or biennial) which is of great importance as a forage and cover crop in agriculture. It is often incorporated in short-term leas (arable land under pasture) with Italian Ryegrass (*Lolium multiflorum* ssp. *multiflorum* (Lam.) Husnot). The herb was known to the ancients as *triphyllon* and *trifolium*, after its 3 leaves, but it was not widely used medicinally, only occasionally being used as a vulnerary.
After its introduction to America it soon became naturalized and American Indians both ate it and used it medicinally – in ointments for external sores and internally in skin disease. It appears to have re-entered British herbal use from American folk medicine in the nineteenth century.
Description Short-lived perennial to 50 cm tall, on large branched root. Stems short and hairy, being ovate to obovate, leaflets to 5 cm long, in long-petioled, trifoliate leaves. Flowers rose-purple or white in ovoid, dense heads to 3 cm long; appearing early summer to early autumn.
Distribution European native; introduced and naturalized elsewhere. Widely distributed in fields, beside roadways, on deep, rich, dry or moderately moist soils.
Cultivation Wild. Grown agriculturally as a fodder crop. Usually sown broadcast on prepared, rolled fields in spring.
Constituents (flower) Salicylic acid; coumaric acid; isorhamnetin; a phytosterol glucoside; trifolianol; a quercitin glucoside; essential oil; a phenolic glycoside, trifoliin; an hydroxymethyloxyflavone, pratol; sugars, including rhamnose; a plant oestrogen, coumestrol.
Uses (dried flower-heads, fresh plant) Alterative; antispasmodic; expectorant; vulnerary.
Flower-heads applied externally in the treatment of ulcers, burns, sores and skin complaints. Used internally to treat chronic skin conditions such as psoriasis and eczema.
Once used in domestic wine-making.
The fresh plant is used for cattle fodder and other agricultural purposes – although it has been known to cause a photosensitive dermatitis in cattle known as trifoliosis.

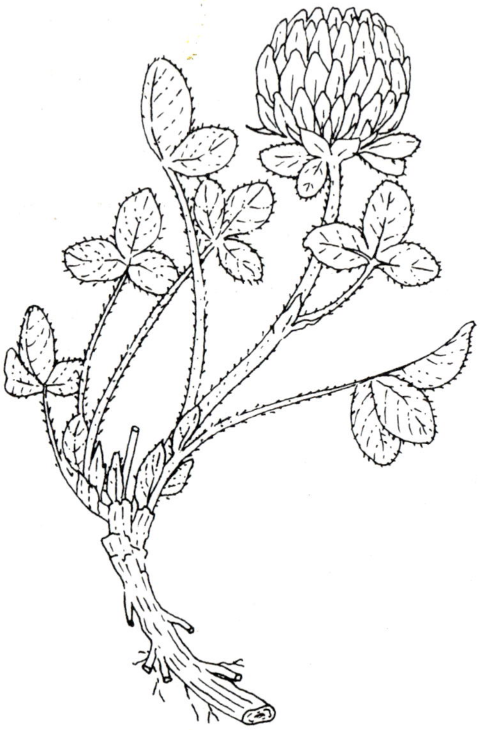

Trigonella foenum-graecum L LEGUMINOSAE
Fenugreek Foenugreek
Like Red Clover (*Trifolium pratense* L) this herb is a fodder crop and the specific name *foenum-graecum* is Latin for Greek hay emphasizing its agricultural use, and the fact that it has been used for this purpose since the earliest times.
Benedictine monks introduced the plant to central Europe and Charlemagne promoted it in the ninth century. It was grown in England in the sixteenth century. The herb has long been a favourite of the Arabs and it was studied at the School of Salerno by Arabic physicians.
Egyptians not only use the seeds for medicinal purposes, but roast them as a coffee and eat both the sprouting seed and the fresh leaves as a vegetable. Indians also use the leaves as a vegetable and consider the seed not only a spice for curries, but as a source of a yellow cloth dye. The name Fenugreek is simply an abbreviation of *foenum-graecum*.
It is now used more in veterinary than human medicine.
Description Smooth, erect annual to 60 cm. Leaves trifoliate; leaflets 2–2.5 cm long, toothed, oblanceolate-oblong. Flowers whitish, solitary or in pairs in axils, petals deciduous after flowering, appearing mid-summer and followed by beaked pod, 5–7.5 cm long, containing 10–20 seeds.
Distribution Native to south Europe and Asia.
Cultivation Wild. Cultivated commercially in the Middle East, India, Morocco and elsewhere. Propagated from seed sown in spring.
Constituents (seed) Mucilage (to 30%); trigonelline; choline; flavone pigment; fixed oil; protein (to 20%); lecithin; phytosterols.
Uses (seed, fresh leaves) Aromatic; carminative; tonic. Seed valuable in dyspepsia and diarrhoea.
Used as a spice, or roasted as a coffee substitute.

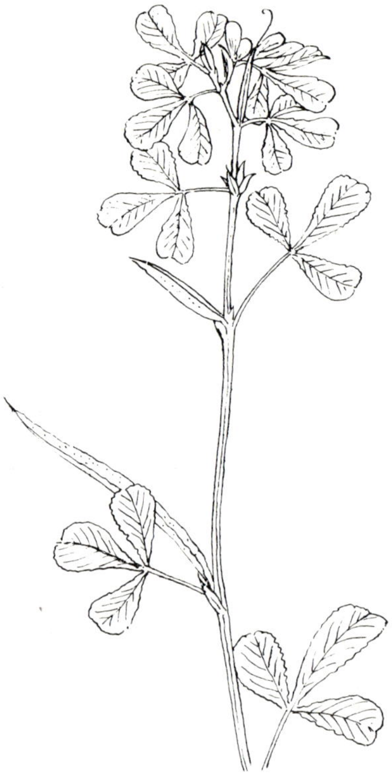

An ingredient of commercial chutneys and the Middle Eastern confectionery, halva. The seeds are celery-flavoured. Fresh leaf may be used in curries, or seed can be sprouted and used as a salad herb.
Seed provides a yellow dye.
Employed as a fodder plant.

Trillium erectum L LILIACEAE
Bethroot Brown Beth/
Squawroot/Stinking Benjamin
The Bethroot (or Wake-Robin) genus consists of about 30 species of attractive spring-flowering liliaceous plants. The generic name refers to the fact that each species produces three leaves and a tripartite flower.
Most are native to North America and traditionally the Appalachian and other Indians used various species to treat a range of female complaints (hence the name Squawroot).
When Rafinesque and others introduced Bethroot to medicine in 1830 it was considered that any species of *Trillium* could be employed, although the Indians considered the white flowering species the most effective.
Millspaugh proposed in 1892 that only *T.*

erectum L be used, which led to some confusion since herb collectors continued to collect several different species and generally called them all *T. pendulum* – a name which is now obsolete. Indians traditionally used the herb as an aphrodisiac. It is now only retained in some folk medicine.
Description Perennial to 50 cm tall, on short, thick root-stock; 3 leaves, sessile, rhomboid, to 21 cm long in terminal whorl, subtending a pedunculate solitary, somewhat nodding, attractive flower to 5 cm wide. The colour ranges from white to brownish purple. Appearing late spring.
Distribution North American native, from Quebec to North Carolina. In shaded woodland, on moist rich soils.
Cultivation Wild.
Constituents Volatile oil; gum; tannins; fixed oil; a saponin, trillarin.
Uses (dried root-stock) Astringent; emmenagogue; antispasmodic; emetic; expectorant. Used in uterine haemorrhages, metrorrhagia, menorrhoea, leucorrhoea. The poultice is applied to ulcers and sores.
Considered to be an astringent tonic and of use post-partum; and an alterative of benefit in chronic skin conditions.

Tropaeolum majus L TROPAEOLACEAE
Garden Nasturtium Indian Cress
Nasturtium is a well-known garden ornamental which is a perennial although it is grown as an annual.
It was introduced to Spain from Peru in the sixteenth century and reached Gerard in London in the 1590s; it was unknown in central Europe, however, until 1684 when Bewerning promoted it as a vegetable and medicine.
The herb was known from its introduction as *Nasturcium indicum* or *Nasturcium peruvianum*; hence it became *Nasturtium indicum* or Indian Cress. The seed, flowers and leaves are now eaten for their spicy taste in salads, and the pickled flower buds provide the best substitute for capers. It is now rarely used medicinally, but it is still collected commercially in some countries.
Description Somewhat succulent perennial, grown as an annual in cool climates. Climbing and twining to 3 m tall – dwarf forms only reaching 40 cm. Leaves reniform to orbicular 5–20 cm wide, entire, glossy, alternate, long-petioled. Flowers spurred, to 5 cm wide, from orange to white, occasionally red or mahogany; appearing from early summer to first frosts.
Distribution South American native, especially Peru and Bolivia.
Cultivation Wild. Cultivated widely as an ornamental, and rarely as a drug. Propagated from seed sown in late spring to early summer in rich soil in sunny situation. Dwarf and double-flowered cultivars are found. Some double-flowered forms cannot be raised from seed. Harvest seed before pods lose their green colour.
Constituents (seed) A glycoside, glucotropaeoline, which hydrolyzes to yield an antibiotic and an essential oil. Principal action is antibiotic.
Uses (fresh leaves, flowers, seeds, pickled flower buds) Antibacterial; antimycotic.
Used in infections of the genito-urinary and respiratory systems.
Principally employed as a salad herb or as a caper substitute.
Used as a garden ornamental.

Turnera diffusa Willd. var. *aphrodisiaca* (Ward.) Urb. TURNERACEAE
Damiana Mexican Damiana/Turnera
Damiana is principally a tonic tea which has long been used by the Mexicans who call it *hierba de la pastora*.
It was introduced to Europe from American folk medicine in the early twentieth century and recommended as a tonic and aphrodisiac – formerly being incorporated with other supposed aphrodisiacs or agents considered of benefit in sexual debility. It has not been studied extensively but appears to be useful in various disorders such as depression. Related members of the genus *Turnera* are also used as tonics in tropical America and Africa (such as the Yellow Alder, *T. ulmifolia* L) indicating the presence in the group of a tonic constituent or constituents.
Description Aromatic, pubescent, shrubby perennial to 60 cm tall. Leaves simple, petiolate, obovate, pale green, dentate, to 2.5 cm long. Flowers small, yellow, axillary, attractive, appearing early to late summer, followed by small, globular, many-seeded capsule.
Distribution Native to subtropical North America, especially Mexico, California and Texas. On dry, sandy or rocky soils in full sun.
Cultivation Wild plant. May be propagated from seed sown in spring, division in spring or

autumn, and from cuttings taken in summer and rooted in a peat and sand mix.
Constituents Volatile oil (to 1%) comprising damianin; also fixed oil; gum; tannins (4%); starch; two resins.
Uses (dried leaves) Tonic; laxative; mild stimulant.
Principally of benefit as a tonic in depression and similar anxiety neuroses. In atonic constipation the infusion initiates peristalsis and acts as a laxative. It has a specific irritant and hence stimulant, effect on the mucosa of the genito-urinary tract, and therefore possibly acting as an aphrodisiac.
Small doses aid digestion.

Tussilago farfara L COMPOSITAE
Coltsfoot Son-before-father
Named after the leaf shape, Coltsfoot is still one of the most important herbal remedies for the treatment of coughs. The Greeks knew it as *bechion* and the Romans as *tusilago*, both names referring to the 'cough plant' and from which the modern medical terms bechic and (anti-) tussive are derived. Even in the days of Dioscorides Coltsfoot was smoked to relieve coughing, a tradition maintained in its modern

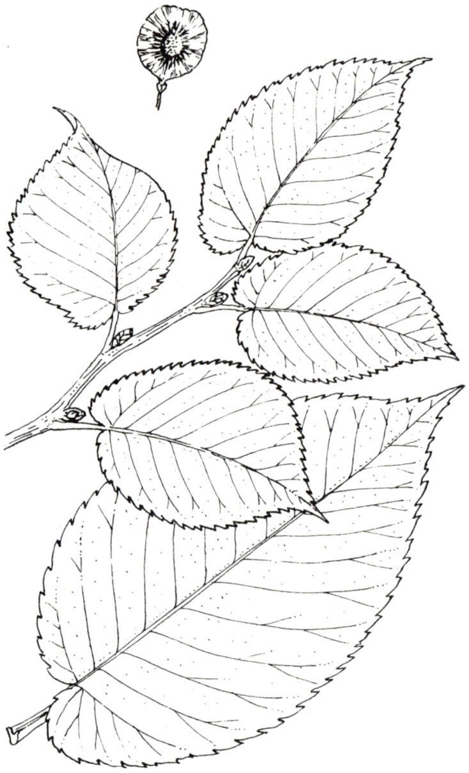

incorporation as the basic ingredients of herbal smoking mixtures. The leaves and flowers are now normally administered in the form of an infusion.
Description Perennial on creeping stolons reaching 8–30 cm tall. Flowers yellow, to 4 cm wide, in solitary capitula, appearing early to late spring on purplish, woolly and scaly scape 12 cm long, later elongating and bearing numerous achenes covered with a pappus of white hairs. Leaves appear from late spring; basal, long-petioled, tomentose beneath, orbicular-cordate, sinuate, 10–18 cm wide.
Distribution Native to Europe, north and west Asia, North Africa; introduced and naturalized in North America and elsewhere. On moist, loamy soils in wasteland and uncultivated places, to 2400 m altitude.
Cultivation Wild. Collected from the wild. Propagated by seed, by root cuttings or division. A moist soil is essential. The herb may become rampant, and care is needed to restrict its growth in gardens.
Constituents Mucilage; tannins; inulin; a bitter glycoside; essential oil; potassium and calcium salts; saponins.
Uses (dried leaves and flowers, rarely fresh leaves, fresh juice) Expectorant; demulcent; anti-inflammatory.
Used in the treatment of irritating coughs and respiratory disorders such as bronchitis and laryngitis; applied externally as a poultice to ulcers and sores.
Fresh leaves eaten as a salad herb rarely.
Fresh or dried flowers used in wine-making.
Leaves formerly smoked to relieve coughing, and now included in herbal tobaccos.

Ulmus rubra Mühlenb. ULMACEAE
Slippery Elm Red Elm
Slippery Elm receives its common name from the feel of the moistened inner bark (the secondary phloem), which is the only part now used medicinally. North American Indians have long used the bark tea as both a laxative and treatment for diarrhoea, and the root tea to assist childbirth. Since the bark has been used as a mechanical abortive it is now only available commercially in the powdered, and hence harmless, form.
Slippery Elm drinks, some including malted constituents, are still popular nutritive medicines following gastro-intestinal illnesses.
Formerly called *U. fulva* Michx.
Description Small or medium-sized tree reaching 20 m tall; leaves dark green, simple, rough above and pubescent below, serrate, 12 cm long, obovate to oblong. Flowers inconspicuous in clusters, appearing spring followed by flat, conspicuous l-seeded samara.
Distribution North American native from Florida to southern Canada. In moist woodland and stream edges; also rarely in dry situations. Prefers poor soils.
Cultivation Wild plant. Inner bark collected in spring.
Constituents Mucilage, on hydrolysis yielding 3-methyl-galactose.
Uses (dried powdered inner bark) Demulcent; emollient.
Used in poultices, or as a decoction for diarrhoea or constipation.
Employed commercially and domestically in nutritive, convalescent drinks.

Urginea maritima (L) Baker LILIACEAE
Squill Sea Onion/White or Red Squill
The Squill is a powerful medicinal plant which has been in almost continuous use from the time of the earliest Greeks to the present. To Dioscorides it was known as *scilla*, hence the common name. There is some evidence that the bulbs were used to beat to death scapegoats or ritual victims in very early Greece in order to placate the gods of fertility. Certainly the large, heavy bulbs have strong magical associations as well as having therapeutic uses. Two varieties were known, the white and red (the colour referring to the bulb scales, not the flowers); both belong to the species *U. maritima*, but the red is more active and preferred by both the early Arab physicians and later French apothecaries. It is now the variety used in certain rat poisons.
White Squill is retained in several national pharmacopoeias, but in view of its action on the heart it is unsuitable for use by other than the medical profession.
Description Bulbous perennial to 150 cm tall; leaves fleshy, glaucous, basal, to 10 cm wide and 40 cm long. Flowers white or rose, in racemes terminating a leafless scape; appearing autumn.
Distribution Native to mediterranean region from Spain to Syria; also Canary Islands and South Africa. On dry sandy soils specially near to the sea, in full sun; but also to 900 m altitude.
Cultivation Wild plant.
Constituents (red and white varieties) Glycosides (mainly scillarin A and B) to which the action is largely due; mucilage (to 11%); a carbohydrate, sinistrin; and other substances. Red Squill, in addition, contains the rat poison scilliroside.
Uses (dried bulb) Expectorant; emetic; irritant; cardio-active.
Used in the treatment of chronic (but not acute) bronchitis.
Employed as a constituent of rat poisons.
Contra-indications Very POISONOUS; to be used only by medical personnel.

Urtica dioica L URTICACEAE
Stinging Nettle Nettle/Common Nettle
The Nettle is now a common and painful stinging weed which appears wherever land is disturbed by man and left derelict. In the past, however, it has variously been used in cloth manufacture, as a food, and medicinally. It was once even cultivated in Scotland, Denmark and Norway.
The use of the plant in cloth manufacture only stopped in the first quarter of the twentieth century but can be traced back to the Bronze Age – and is recorded in the common name, nettle, from an old word meaning to twist (and hence make fibre).
Greeks knew it as *akalyphe* and Romans as

urtica – but the ancients probably used the annual *U. pilulifera* L (or Roman Nettle) rather more, since it is native to southern Europe. Both this species and the Small Nettle (*U. urens*), which is also an annual, have the same values as *U. dioica*.

Description Dioecious perennial, from 80–180 cm tall, stems bristly, sparsely branched, bearing opposite and decussate, acuminate, deeply serrate, petiolate and ovate leaves to 14 cm long. Flowers minute, in pendulous axillary racemes, appearing mid-summer to mid-autumn.

Distribution Widespread; Eurasian native. On wasteland, especially damp and nutrient-rich soils which have previously been disturbed by man; to 2700 m altitude.

Cultivation Wild plant. Cultivated only rarely for medicinal purposes, and as a source of commercial chlorophyll.

Propagated from seed, or by root division in spring.

Constituents (leaves) Histamine; acetylcholine; formic acid; gallic acid; tannins; 5-hydroxy-tryptamine; vitamins A and C; mineral salts including calcium, potassium, silicon, iron, manganese and sulphur; other active substances; unknown components.

Uses (fresh or dried leaves, root-stock rarely) Astringent; anti-haemorrhagic; diuretic; galactagogue.

The Nettle has many therapeutic applications, but is principally of benefit in all kinds of internal haemorrhages; as a diuretic; in urticaria, jaundice, haemorrhoids; a laxative; and it is used in dermatological problems including eczema.

The powdered leaf used as a snuff stops nose bleeds.

It has been shown to lower the blood-sugar level and also to lower the blood pressure slightly.

Used to promote hair growth rarely, and fresh branches applied externally in rheumatism.

Young shoots and leaves cooked like Spinach.

A commercial source of chlorophyll.

Used in paper and cloth manufacture.

Vaccinium myrtillus L ERICACEAE

Bilberry Whortleberry/Huckleberry

The genus *Vaccinium* includes several species which are grown as ornamentals as well as others which provide such edible berries as the Blueberry, Cranberry and Bilberry.

V. myrtillus has many common names and there is much confusion in the genus (which contains about 150 species) because of the free exchange of the same common name between various species. It is not possible, therefore, to identify definitely this species in ancient writings, but it was an official medicinal plant from the sixteenth century and known then as *vaccinia* and *mora agrestis*. The specific name refers to the Myrtle-shaped leaves.

The fruits have long been a popular food, and are still collected for this purpose.

Description Subshrub 30–60 cm tall, deciduous and glabrous on thin creeping and rooting stems. Leaves alternate, bright green, finely dentate, oval, to 3 cm long. Flowers pale greenish-pink, small, solitary, appearing in leaf axils from late spring to late summer, followed by globose purple fruit.

Distribution Native to Europe and northern Asia; in humus-rich, acidic, damp soils in woodland, forests, moorland and fenland, to 2600 m altitude.

Cultivation Wild. Propagated as ground cover in shady positions on damp and acidic soils – either peaty or sandy. Grown from rooted cuttings.

Constituents (fruit) Organic acids; pectin; sugars; mineral salts; tannins; vitamins A and C; arbutin; anthocyanin pigments.

Uses (fresh fruit, leaves rarely) Astringent; antiseptic; tonic.

Fruit used in the treatment of diarrhoea. Leaves have a weak hypoglycaemic action, and have been used in combination with other remedies in the treatment of diabetes.

Principally employed as a nutritive, rather tart fruit in conserves and syrups, or eaten raw. Also distilled to flavour certain liqueurs.

Valeriana officinalis L VALERIANACEAE

Valerian Common Valerian/Garden Heliotrope

Several different species of *Valeriana* have been used in European medicine of which *V. officinalis* L, *V. celtica* L, *V. dioica* L and *V. phu* L, were the most important. The latter species was probably the herb known as Phu to the ancients while *V. celtica* was referred to as *Nardus celticus*.

Valeriana officinalis was particularly promoted by the Arab physicians and the name Valeriana first appears in the tenth century.

Tincture of Valerian was employed in the First World War to treat shellshock, and the rhizome and roots are still retained in several national pharmacopoeias. The root was once included in various recipes and was also used to scent linen.

Description Glabrous perennial 20–150 cm tall, on aromatic root-stock. Stems lightly grooved. Leaves pinnate to 20 cm long, leaflets either entire or toothed, lanceolate. Flowers white or pinkish, small, in terminal inflorescence appearing mid-summer to early autumn.

Distribution Native to Europe and west Asia; naturalized in North America. In grassland, ditches, damp meadowland, close to streams, on nutrient-rich soils to 2000 m altitude.

Cultivation Wild. Propagated by division of root-stock in spring or autumn, or from seed sown in spring.

Constituents Essential oil (to 1%) comprising various components (which include monoterpene valepotriates) and which in combination are sedative and antispasmodic.

Uses (dried root-stock) Sedative; stomachic; antispasmodic; carminative.

Of benefit in the treatment of a wide range of nervous disorders and intestinal colic. Used in combination with other remedies in the treatment of hypertension. Useful in insomnia and migraine, nervous exhaustion and anxiety

states. The root was once used, in small quantities, as a culinary flavouring.
Contra-indications The drug should not be taken in large doses for an extended period of time.

Vanilla planifolia Andrews ORCHIDACEAE
Vanilla
Vanilla was introduced to Europe by the Spanish in the early sixteenth century following their observation of its use in Mexico by the Aztecs for flavouring chocolate. Early names included *Araco aromatico*, *banillen* and *vainillen*.
It was employed in the seventeenth century, chiefly in France, both for chocolate manufacture and scenting tobacco, and in the eighteenth century it was included for the first time in several pharmacopoeias – as an aromatic carminative. Vanilla pods are now mainly employed in flavouring. West Indian Vanilla is from *V. pompona*.
Description Epiphytic orchid with stout stems, and oblong-lanceolate leathery, fleshy, short-petioled leaves to 20 cm long. Flowers yellow and orange to 5 cm long, followed by aromatic fruit to 18 cm long.
Distribution Native to tropical America; introduced and cultivated elsewhere.
Cultivation Wild. Widely cultivated in Mexico, Madagascar and elsewhere; in high humidity under shade, on poles or tree trunks.
Constituents Vanillin (to 2%); aromatic substances.

Uses (dried cured seed-pods (Vanilla beans)) Aromatic carminative.
Rarely used for medicinal purposes other than as a pharmaceutical flavouring.
Principally employed as a culinary and commercial flavouring and in cosmetics.

Veratrum viride Ait. LILIACEAE
American White Hellebore
Green Hellebore
Veratrum viride was formerly classified as *V. eschscholtzii* A. Gray. The European White Hellebore is *V. album* L. Both these species and another European plant, *V. nigrum* L (the Black Hellebore) have long been used as arrow poisons as they are very toxic.
The Red Indians used *V. viride* as an ordeal poison, and it was introduced to American medical practice in the late eighteenth century when British supplies of *V. album* were cut off by the War of Independence. Green Hellebore was once an American domestic remedy for removing lice from the hair – combing it through in the form of a strong decoction.
The herb contains alkaloids which drastically depress the action of the heart and reduce blood pressure. Its use is now strictly limited to veterinary practice.
Description Rhizomatous, unbranched perennial to 2 m, on thick root-stock. Leaves alternate, ovate to elliptic, to 30 cm long. Flowers in terminal panicles, greenish, to 2.5 cm wide, appearing late spring to late summer.
Distribution North American native, on wet soils in woodland, beside streams, or on low-

lying meadowland.
Cultivation Wild plant. Propagated by root-stock division in spring or autumn.
Constituents Several alkaloids (to 1.5%) including veratrine, jervine and veratrosine; glycosides.
Uses (dried rhizome) Hypotensive; toxic; emetic; purgative.
Rarely used for any medicinal purpose. Once employed to reduce blood pressure associated with toxaemia during pregnancy. A decoction is anti-parasitic and can be used by veterinary personnel for animal use.
Contra-indications Very POISONOUS; only to be used by medical personnel.

Verbascum thapsus L SCROPHULARIACEAE
Mullein Aaron's Rod
The common name, Mullein, is derived from the Latin *mollis* meaning soft, after the large ear-like leaves – the herb is also variously known as Donkey's Ears, Bunny's Ears and Bull's Ears.
Mullein's tall, spire-like flowering stem was once used as a taper, having first been dried and then dipped in tallow. There is evidence that at one time it was one of the supposed magical herbs of the ancients.
Various species of *Verbascum* have been employed medicinally, the most important, historically, being *V. thapsiforme* Schrad. and *V. phlomoides* L. Mullein is now grown mostly as a decorative plant.
Description Erect, very soft and woolly biennial, to 2 m tall. Leaves grey-green, forming a basal rosette in the first year, eventually reaching 30 cm tall. Flowers yellow, sessile, in clusters, on dense, erect 2.5 cm-wide spikes appearing mid-summer to early autumn.
Distribution Eurasian native; naturalized in some temperate zones. On stony, shallow, well-drained, nitrogen-rich soils in wasteland and woodland clearings.
Cultivation Wild. Propagate from seed sown as soon as ripe or in the spring. Will not tolerate cold, wet conditions.
Constituents Mucilage; essential oil; saponosides.
Uses (dried or fresh leaves, dried flowers) Emollient; weakly sedative; expectorant.
Principally employed with other remedies in the treatment of respiratory disorders.

The leaves have been included in herbal smoking mixtures, and used in domestic cosmetic preparations.
The flowers provide a pale yellow dye. An attractive horticultural ornamental.

Verbena officinalis L VERBENACEAE
Vervain
Like Betony, Vervain has a long and well-documented history of association with the magic and sorcery of the Celtic and Germanic peoples of Europe. It also seems to have been considered sacred by the Greeks and Romans however, being known as *Herba sacra* and *Herba veneris*. Not surprisingly for a herb with alleged magical properties, Vervain was used in numerous complaints and it became an official drug. By 1830, however, Geiger stated that in Germany it was seldom used. It still has a place in folk medicine.
Description Perennial 35–80 cm tall, glabrous or nearly so, on erect, ribbed, angular stem; loosely branched and only sparsely leafy. Leaves petiolate, ovate, some pinnatifid, to 6 cm long. Flowers small, lilac, at the tips of long stalks. Appearing summer to late autumn.
Distribution Native to the mediterranean region; established elsewhere. On roadsides, wasteland, on nutrient-rich soils to 1500 m altitude.
Cultivation Wild. Propagated from seed sown in spring. Requires full sun.
Constituents Mucilage; tannins; saponins; essential oil; verbenaloside; the glycosides, verbenaline and verbenine; unknown substances.
Uses (dried flowering plant) Tonic; astringent; diuretic; diaphoretic; galactagogue; emmenagogue; vulnerary; antispasmodic.
Used in the treatment of nervous complaints such as depression, and with other remedies in chronic skin complaints. Considered to have a specific benefit to the uterus, but this is unsubstantiated.
Used externally to treat wounds.

Veronica beccabunga L SCHROPHULARIACEAE
Brooklime Water Pimpernel
Brooklime has a similar (but more bitter) taste to Watercress, and in former times was eaten as a salad herb. Its sharpness may have led to another common name Mouth Smart – or more probably this English name was a translation of the Flemish *beckpunge* and German *Bachbunge* which mean the same.

To the apothecaries it was known as Herba Beccabunga (hence the modern specific name) and *Anagallis aquatica* or Water Pimpernel – from the similarities between Brooklime's flowers and those of the Scarlet Pimpernel (*Anagallis arvensis* L) although they differ in colour.
Description Semi-aquatic succulent perennial, 10–60 cm tall, with hollow, creeping, easily rooted stems. Leaves opposite, short-petioled, oblong to ovate, to 5 cm long, crenate-serrate. Flowers small, blue, in loose short, axillary racemes, appearing early summer to mid-autumn.
Distribution Native to Europe, Asia, North Africa; introduced elsewhere. In streams and ditches to 2600 m altitude.
Cultivation Wild plant.
Constituents Tannins; a glucoside; unknown substances.
Uses (fresh or dried flowering plant, fresh leaves) Diuretic; stimulant; weakly antipyretic; bechic; stomachic.
Rarely used medicinally. Formerly used in liver problems, haemorrhoids, gastro-intestinal complaints, and applied externally to ulcers. Fresh leaves may be eaten sparingly.

Veronica officinalis L SCROPHULARIACEAE
Speedwell Fluellen
Fluellen is probably the older of the two common English names, and it is derived from the old Welsh *llysiau Llywelyn* – the herb of St Llywelyn.
The name Speedwell is given to the entire family, as well as to this species. In America it is also known as Low Speedwell and Gypsyweed – one of many herbs with the latter name.
As *Herba Veronica majoris* this plant became official in the Middle Ages and had a reputation as a healing herb – including the ability to treat a variety of skin complaints. It was also used in a wide range of syrups and elixirs, for respiratory and stomach problems; it became less important by the mid-nineteenth century and it was then mostly used as a tea substitute. The French give it the name *thé d'Europe* – European Tea.

Description Low-growing pubescent perennial, often forming mats of prostrate rooting stems. 10–40 cm tall. Leaves opposite, serrate, ovate or oblong, to 4 cm long, with short petioles or sessile. Flowers pale blue, small, attractive, in dense, erect racemes. Appearing early to late summer.
Distribution Native to Europe, Asia, North America; in scrubland clearings, moorland, coppices, hedgerows, heaths; on acidic, sandy or loamy soils, to 1000 m altitude.
Cultivation Wild.
Constituents A glycoside, aucuboside; resins; bitter principles; tannins; unknown substances.
Uses (dried flowering plant) Expectorant; stomachic; vulnerary; galactagogue; diuretic.
All the actions are weak and the plant is no longer of medicinal interest.
Principally employed as a tea substitute in herbal tea mixtures.

Veronicastrum virginicum Farwell
SCROPHULARIACEAE
Culver's Root Black Root/Physic Root
Formerly classified as both *Veronica virginica* L and *Leptandra virginica* Nutt., this tall American herb is closely related to the Speedwell family or Veronicas.
Its popularity as an Indian remedy is reflected in another common name, Bowman's Root; the Seneca Indians once used its root as a tea to cause vomiting for ritualistic and medicinal purposes.
Although it was formerly included in the United States Pharmacopoeia it is not now widely used.
Its botanical name *Veronicastrum* is derived from *veronica* (which itself was named after St Veronica) and *astrum* or star – after the arrangement of the leaves.
It was first introduced to Europe in 1714.
Description Perennial to 2.25 m on horizontal blackish rhizome. Stem erect, smooth and unbranched bearing 15-cm long lanceolate, or oblong-lanceolate, dentate, and shortly petiolate flowers in whorls of 3–5 or occasionally 9. Flowers white, pink or blue, 7 mm long, numerous, on short pedicels, arranged in dense terminal spike-like racemes. Appearing mid-summer to mid-autumn.

Distribution North American native from Massachusetts to Florida and Texas, on a variety of soils from dry to rich and wet; but especially in moist meadows and river banks.
Cultivation Wild. May be propagated by division of rhizomes after flowering in late autumn, or in mid-spring. A purple variety is also known.
Constituents Gum; resin; a phytosterol, verosterol; volatile oil; citric acid; mannitol; a saponoside; a volatile alkaloid; a bitter principle; leptandrine, to which the action is largely due.
Uses (dried rhizome and root) Purgative; emetic; cholagogue; tonic.
Small doses are valuable as a stomachic tonic, in diarrhoea, dyspepsia and atony of the gastro-intestinal system. Promotes the flow of bile from the gall bladder. Boiled in milk it acts as a laxative; larger doses are purgative or emetic.
Contra-indications In large doses or when used fresh it acts as a drastic purgative and may cause vertigo and bloody stools.

Viburnum opulus L CAPRIFOLIACEAE
Guelder Rose Cramp Bark/
Cranberry Tree
This is an attractive plant and several cultivars are found as horticultural ornamentals. As the name Cranberry Tree suggests, the fruit have been used like Cranberries but they do not really compare in quality and they must be cooked before they are eaten – the raw fruit contains a substance, viburnine, which can cause severe gastro-intestinal disorders.

In Norway and other Scandinavian countries a liquor has been distilled from the fruit. *V. opulus* has numerous common names: Guelder Rose is from the Dutch *Geldersche roos* since the tree was introduced from Guelders, on the German border, to England in the sixteenth century. Strictly, Guelder Rose is *V. opulus* var. *roseum* L (or *V. opulus* L var. *sterile* DC) and is a sterile, thus non-fruiting, ornamental (found in horticultural lists as the Snowball Tree). The herb was rarely employed in north and west European medicine, but it was popular in the early nineteenth century in America – it is still included, however, in the Polish, Rumanian and Russian pharmacopoeias.
Description Shrub to 4 m tall, branches glabrous and erect; leaves 3–5 lobed, opposite, petiolate, dentate. Flowers white, in pedunculate cymes to 9 cm wide, appearing early to mid-summer; followed by scarlet, then purple, fruit.
Distribution Native to Europe, North Africa, northern Asia; introduced elsewhere, often as an ornamental. In woodland clearings, on wet loamy soils to 1200 m altitude.
Cultivation Wild plant. Propagated from seed or hardwood cuttings; several cultivars are grown as ornamentals.
Constituents (bark) Tannins; isovalerianic acid; resin; viburnine.
Uses (dried stem bark) Sedative; spasmolytic. Of benefit in functional uterine disorders, as a uterine sedative; menopausal metrorrhagia, miscarriage, and dysmenorrhoea.
Fruit may be cooked and eaten, or used as a dye.
Contra-indications Fresh berries are POISONOUS.

Viburnum prunifolium L CAPRIFOLIACEAE
Black Haw Sweet Viburnum/Stagbush/
American Sloe
V. prunifolium has similar constituents, properties and uses to *V. opulus* L, but differs in that the part used medicinally is usually the root bark rather than the stem bark. Its fruit are also sweeter than those of *V. opulus* – hence the name Sweet Viburnum. Black Haw continues to be used in folk medicine and is retained in several pharmacopoeias; other species are similarly used, besides *V. opulus*, and they include *V. nudum* L. (the Possumhaw Viburnum) and *V. rufidulum* Raf. (the Southern Black Haw) – the latter being found in the Mexican Pharmacopoeia.
Description Deciduous shrub to 5 m tall; branches spreading. Leaves dull-coloured,

opposite, petiolate, ovate to elliptic, finely toothed to 7.5 cm long. Flowers small, white, in sessile cymes to 10 cm wide, appearing late spring to early summer, and followed by purple oval fruits.
Distribution Native to North America from Connecticut to Florida.
Cultivation Wild plant.
Constituents (root bark) Tannins; isovalerianic acid; resin; viburnine.
Uses (dried root bark) Sedative; spasmolytic. Of benefit as a uterine sedative in dysmenorrhia, and threatened miscarriage. Once taken as a tonic tea, and considered to be of benefit in asthma.
Contra-indications Uncooked fruit is POISONOUS.

Vinca major L APOCYNACEAE
Greater Periwinkle Periwinkle
The Periwinkle family consists of about 12 species of trailing evergreen shrubs. The genus Vinca (from the old Latin name *Vinca peruinca* from which the common name is derived) formerly included the Madagascan Periwinkle, *Vinca rosea* L, (now classified as *Catharanthus roseus* (L) G. Don) which is an important medicinal source of anti-leukaemic drugs. Both the Greater and the Lesser Periwinkle (*V. minor* L) have long been considered as magical and medicinal plants, but *V. major* was generally preferred, and it is still used in folk medicine.
Various cultivars of *V. minor* are grown as garden ornamentals.
Description Trailing evergreen perennial 30–90 cm tall. Long prostrate stems bearing dark green, shiny, ovate, short-petioled, obtuse or acute leaves to 4 cm long. Flowers pale blue to 4 cm wide, solitary on hollow stalk appearing mid to late spring.
Distribution European native, in mixed woodland in loamy calcareous soils, well-drained, to 1200 m altitude.
Cultivation Wild. Used as ground cover in shady positions; propagate by division or stem cuttings taken in spring or autumn.
Constituents Tannins; alkaloids, including pubescine, vinine and vincamine; flavonoids; pectin; organic acids; several mineral salts; vitamin C; rubber; ursolic acid. The flower contains robinoside.
Uses (flowering plant) Hypotensive; vasodilator; hypoglycaemic; astringent; vulnerary; sedative.
Generally used to stop bleeding, both externally and internally, as in metrorrhagia and menorrhagia. Also used in nervous conditions such as anxiety states and subsequent hypertension.
The herb possesses many other uses. It reduces blood pressure and dilates both coronary and peripheral blood vessels. There is also a marked effect on smooth muscle. Can be used as a tonic, bitter and in catarrh. Employed traditionally in Africa to treat Diabetes mellitus. Note: diabetes must only be treated by medical personnel.

Viola odorata L VIOLACEAE
Sweet Violet
The name Sweet Violet describes both the smell and colour of the flowers, and the plant has been cultivated for over 2000 years as both a colouring agent for drinks and syrups, and as a source of perfume. It is still grown in southern France for the perfume industry. At the turn of the century Violet Water and other Sweet Violet perfumes were one of the most popular of all scents in England (although Violet-scent was also obtained from *Iris germanica* L).
Early names included *viola purpurea*, *viola glaucia* and the Greek *ion agrion*. (The aromatic principle is known as ionine or irone.) The generic name is taken directly from the old Latin name.
Various parts of the plant are still used medicinally but their actions differ. The rootstock is now the part most commonly employed.
Description Perennial on long stolons, 10–15 cm tall, on short rhizome. Stemless. Leaves reniform to cordate-ovate, petiolate. Flowers attractive, scented, to 2 cm wide, usually violet, also white or pink; appearing mid to late spring.
Distribution Native to Asia, North Africa, Europe; introduced elsewhere on damp calcareous soils in shady woodland, scrubland, hedgerows, wood clearings; to 1000 m altitude.
Cultivation Wild. Propagated from offsets replanted in late winter or early spring in a peat and sand mix, under glass; or divide in spring. Requires shade, rich soil and moisture. Various cultivars may be found.
Constituents Saponins; a glycoside, violarutin; methyl salicylate; mucilage; vitamin C; an alkaloid, odoratine; anthocyanin pigments; an aromatic substance ionine or irone; salicylic glycosides.
Uses (dried leaves and flowers, fresh flowers, dried root-stock) Emetic; purgative;

hypotensive; expectorant; diuretic.
Leaves and flowers are principally employed in the treatment of respiratory disorders, especially chronic naso-pharyneal catarrh and bronchitis. Used in cough mixtures, and once employed in the treatment of rheumatism. Used as a gargle in inflamed buccal mucosae. Flowers used to colour medications; candied in confectionery, and used widely in perfumery.
Contra-indications In large doses the root is emetic and purgative.

Viola tricolor L ssp. *arvensis* Murr. VIOLACEAE
Heartsease Wild Pansy/Field Pansy
This herb with three-coloured petals (white, yellow and purple) became the *Herba Trinitatis* of the Middle Ages, and was later given the similarly descriptive specific name *tricolor*.
Heartsease is still official in some eastern European countries and remained so in Germany until 1926; it is now no longer cultivated medicinally. Various cultivars do however remain important horticultural ornamentals as edging plants. The name Pansy is from the French word *pensée*, meaning thought or remembrance, and Wild Pansy is still called *Pensée sauvage* in France. In the traditional language of flowers the purple form meant memories, the white loving thoughts and the yellow souvenirs. Hence Heartsease was a plant received in happy memory to ease the heart-break of separation.
Description Variable, annual or short-lived perennial, somewhat straggly and branched to 25 cm tall. Leaves opposite, ovate to lanceolate, dentate, with lobed stipules. Flowers purple, white, yellow or a combination of these colours. Most frequently yellowish in the wild plant. Appearing mid-spring to late autumn.
Distribution European native. Naturalized in North America. Introduced elsewhere. On wasteland, in fields, hedgerows, rarely in mountain pastures; on acidic soils. To 2000 m altitude.

Cultivation Wild. This species is one parent of the cultivated Garden Pansy (*V.* x *wittrockiana* ssp. *tricolor*) which is found in several forms. The herb hybridizes readily with related plants. Propagate from seed sown in spring or as soon as ripe. Requires rich, damp soil.
Constituents Salicylic acid and salicylates; saponins; flavonic glycosides including violaquercitin; a blue chromoglucoside, violanin; a bitter principle, violin (which acts as an emetic); rutin and related rutins; traces of volatile oil.
Uses (dried flowering plant, fresh juice, dried flowers) Diuretic; antipyretic; tonic; laxative; anti-inflammatory.
Used as a blood-purifying agent especially in chronic skin complaints and rheumatism. Stimulates the metabolism and induces perspiration, and therefore employed in feverish conditions. Of benefit in indigestion and urino-genital inflammatory conditions. Used as a gargle or lotion to aid wound healing, ulcers and sores. A valuable horticultural plant.
Contra-indications Large doses or prolonged use may cause allergic skin reactions.

Viscum album L LORANTHACEAE
Mistletoe
The Loranthaceae family comprises 20 genera and almost 1500 species of mostly parasitic plants which are widely distributed around the world. The species of medicinal interest in Europe is *V. album*, although since the plant is collected from the wild the resultant drug may also contain other species – notably *V. album* L ssp. *abietis* (Wiesb.) Abrom., *V. album* ssp. *album* L, *V. album* L ssp. *austriacum* (Wiesb.) Vollm., and *Loranthus europaeus* L.
The parasite, Mistletoe (which contains chlorophyll) is found on different deciduous trees and commonly the Apple. It has been shown that the constituents of the Mistletoe may vary according to the host plant on which it is found. This may explain the ancient druidic belief that the drug from the Oak was most valuable (itself thought to be magical by the Druids).
Mistletoe is currently being examined for possible anti-cancer effects. It contains substances called lectins which may combine with certain cancer cells; the chemistry and pharmacology of the plant is very complicated, however, and no definitive results have yet been demonstrated in humans.
Description Woody perennial evergreen; stems to 1 m long and regularly branching. Leaves leathery, light green, blunt, narrow and obovate, to 8 cm long. Flowers sessile, unisexual, in short, almost sessile axillary inflorescence, appearing mid-spring to early summer and followed by 1-cm diameter white, sticky fruit.
Distribution Native to several regions from north-west Europe to China, including Iran and parts of the mediterranean region; rarely found on conifers, but common on some deciduous trees.
Cultivation Wild. Semi-cultivated in some places by the inoculation of tree bark (in Apple orchards, for example) with the squashed ripe fruit.
Constituents 11 proteins; a lectin (with a D-galactosyl specificity); a toxin, viscotoxin; alkaloids; many other supposedly active compounds.
Uses (dried branches and leaves) Hypotensive; cardio-active; diuretic; sedative.
Used in combination with other remedies to treat hypertension, and associated, nervous complaints. Considered anti-neoplastic (demonstrated in some animals but not humans). Used pharmaceutically in certain preparations.
Employed in winter decorations.

Vitex agnus-castus L VERBENACEAE
Chaste Tree Monk's Pepper/Agnus Castus
Vitex agnus-castus is also called Indian Spice, Sage Tree, Hemp Tree and Wild Pepper – the latter reflecting the name *piper agreste* of the Middle Ages (*agreste* meaning wild). It was also called *viticis* and *agnus-castus* from which the botanical name is derived.
Athenian women used to put the leaves in their beds, and later monks in Europe used the ground-up seed as pepper – in both cases the purpose was to ensure chastity (hence Chaste Tree and Monk's Pepper). It is now known that the seeds contain hormone-like substances which reduce libido in the male and are of benefit to women with certain hormonal problems. Chaste Tree is now included in several gynaecological formulations. The branches are used in basket making in southern Europe.
Description Aromatic shrub or small tree to 6 m tall. Leaves opposite, palmately compound, divided into 5–7 lanceolate leaflets, each to 10 cm long. Flowers small, lavender or lilac, in dense cymes to 15 cm wide, in panicles to 30 cm long.
Distribution South European native; introduced and often naturalized in warm regions. On sandy or loamy, well-drained soils in full sun.
Cultivation Wild. Propagated from seed sown in spring, by layering in spring to summer, or from young woody cuttings under glass. Several cultivars are grown for decorative purposes, including the white variety *Alba* Westn.
Constituents Several hormonal substances.
Uses (dried fruit) Anaphrodisiac (in males)

Principally employed in gynaecological conditions including depression in menopause. May be used sparingly as a condiment.

The drug was introduced in 1849 by King following long use by Red Indians as a local and general stimulant. It was once included in remedies for alcoholism, but is now used only in folk medicine.
Sometimes incorrectly found classified as *Xanthoxylum*.
Description Aromatic shrub or small tree to 3 m. Leaves to 30 cm long, subdivided into 5–11 ovate leaflets. Flowers greenish-yellow appearing in late spring before the leaves; arranged in axillary clusters.
Distribution North American native especially in the east. Usually in rich woodland on moist soils.
Cultivation Wild.
Constituents Resins; alkaloid-like substances; a phenol, xanthoxylin.
Uses (dried stem and root bark, rarely fruit) Stimulant; counter-irritant; diaphoretic; carminative.
Used in atonic dyspepsia; in combination with other remedies in respiratory catarrh, and more frequently with other remedies of value in chronic skin disease and rheumatism. Decoction used externally on ulcers.

Zanthoxylum americanum Mill. RUTACEAE
Prickly Ash Toothache Tree
Several *Zanthoxylum* species have a medicinal action, notably Prickly Ash and the Southern Prickly Ash (*Z. Clava-Herculis* L.). They are called Prickly because of their stem and petiole spines; and the other common name refers to the Red Indian use of the bark for toothache. In this respect the therapeutic use seems to be that of a powerful counter-irritant, and it is not a cure.

Zingiber officinale Roscoe ZINGIBERACEAE
Ginger
Before Roscoe reclassified this well-known plant, it had been called *Amomum zingiber* L, a name reflecting the old Arabic name *Amomum Zerumbeth*. The term *amomum* had been used to describe certain aromatic spices – the Round Cardamom, for example, is still called *Amomum compactum* Soland. ex Maton.
Ginger was long known as Zingiberis however, and the Greeks had imported the rhizome from the east for centuries before Dioscorides described its medicinal uses. In the Far East it had also long been employed; in China it was, and still is, an important drug, and Green Ginger in syrup was a delicacy from the fifteenth century. Ginger is now grown commercially throughout the tropics – from Australia to Jamaica – and many types and grades are available. The Spanish were importing Ginger from Jamaica before the mid-sixteenth century, and Jamaican Ginger is still considered the best for culinary use.
Description Perennial, creeping plant, on thick tuberous rhizome, producing an erect annual stem 60–120 cm tall. Leaves 1–2 cm wide, 15–30 cm long, lanceolate to linear-lanceolate. Flowers greenish marked with purple, in radical spikes (to 7 cm long) on 30 cm-long peduncles.
Distribution Native to south-east Asia; introduced and widespread in several tropical countries. To 1500 m altitude.
Cultivation Cultivated plant. Propagated from rhizome cuttings, planted on rich, well-drained loam.
Constituents Volatile oil (to 3%), comprising camphene, phellandrene, zingiberine, and many other substances; resin; starch; gingerol; shogaol – the latter two substances being pungent.
Uses (fresh or dried rhizome) Stimulant; carminative; aromatic; sialogogue; anti-emetic. Very valuable in flatulent colic, dyspepsia and atonic dyspepsia. Often used as an adjunct to other remedies for general tonic or stimulant purposes, or to purgatives to prevent griping. Rubefacient when applied externally in the fresh state.
Very wide culinary uses in many domestic and commercial preparations.
Contra-indications Large doses should be avoided by patients suffering from any skin complaint.

Glossary

ABORTIFACIENT A substance causing expulsion of the foetus; hence an agent which induces an abortion.
ABORTIVE (bot.) Undeveloped; barren; immature; faulty; coming to a premature end; (med.) cutting short the course of a disease; ending without completing.
ABSOLUTE Relating to alcohol (ethanol or ethyl alcohol); that which does not contain less than 99% pure alcohol by weight.
ABSORPTION The passage of substances through body membranes and tissues from one body compartment to another.
ACETYLCHOLINE The substance which transmits cholinergic nerve impulses.
ACHENE (bot.) A dry, indehiscent, one-seeded pericarp or fruit.
ACICULAR (bot.) Needle-shaped.
ACID (chem.) A substance which forms hydrogen ions in solution, and which contains replaceable hydrogens. Opposite to alkali.
ACTIVE SUBSTANCE A substance which, either in combination with other substances or in the isolated form, exerts a physiological or pharmacological effect on living tissue.
ACUMINATE (bot.) Describing the acute apex of a leaf, the sides of which are concave and taper to a protracted point. The point of such a leaf is called the acumen.
ACUPUNCTURE A system of medicine, originated in China, in which needles are inserted into specific tissues and/or organs at predetermined points thereby relieving pain, inducing anaesthesia, or assisting in the healing process.
ADAPTOGEN A term introduced by Professor Israel Brekhman to describe a new class of drug (of which Ginseng is the prime example) which is ineffective and harmless in the absence of stress, but which returns body processes to normal when faced with stress or damage. (Similar in meaning to the herbalists' term, alterative.)
ADJUVANT A substance which modifies the effect of another.
ADRENALIN A hormone secreted by the adrenal glands. One of the substances which transmits sympathetic nerve impulses.
ADRENERGIC Describing either a substance which acts like (nor)adrenalin or the type of physiological action characteristic of (nor)adrenalin.
ADVENTITIOUS ROOT (bot.) A root that appears casually or in an unusual place on a plant, and is not a part of the main root system.
AERIAL VEGETATIVE PART Any part of a plant which exists above ground.
AGLYCONE The non-sugar part of a glycoside molecule. (See *Glycoside*.)
ALBUMEN Egg white; comprised chiefly of albumin.
ALBUMIN One of a group of protein substances; soluble in water and coagulable by heat.
ALDEHYDES A class of organic chemicals intermediate between alcohols and acids.
ALGAE (bot.) A group of largely aquatic plants which lack roots, stems and leaves and which do not flower. They range in size from large seaweeds to minute organisms, and are of great importance as the primary source of organic matter in the food chains of seas, rivers and lakes.
ALIMENTARY TRACT The digestive tract, from the mouth to the anus.
ALKALINE (chem.) A substance which forms ions in solution, and usually referring to the soluble hydroxides of metals. Opposite to acid.
ALKALOIDS A group of naturally occurring basic organic compounds which contain at least one nitrogen atom in a ring structure in the molecule. They are usually of plant origin, physiologically active, insoluble in water, and often found as salts of organic acids.
ALKYL RADICAL Hydrocarbon radical derived particularly from those of the paraffin series.
ALUM Potash alum or crystalline potassium aluminium sulphate, a chemical substance occurring naturally and used for a number of purposes, including as a mordant in dyeing.
ALVEOLAR DUCTS The minute air passages in the lung which lead from branched bronchioles to alveolar sacs.
ALVEOLAR SACS The terminal branches of alveolar ducts comprising alveoli.
ALVEOLUS An air cell of the lung.
AMENORRHOEA Absence of menstruation.
AMINO-ACIDS The basic constituents of proteins, consisting of organic compounds.
AMMONIA A characteristically pungent-smelling gas with the formula NH_3. It is very soluble in water, forming an alkaline solution of ammonium hydroxide.
AMOEBIASIS Infection of the gut and liver by *Entamoeba histolytica*, a parasitic protozoan.
AMYGDALIN A cyanogenic glycoside found in peach stones, for example.
ANABOLISM That aspect of metabolism which is concerned with the building up of complex substances from simpler material; the conversion of nutritional compounds into those of which living matter is composed.
ANAEMIA A reduction in the normal level of the red blood cells and/or haemoglobin content of the blood.
ANALGESIC A substance which produces insensibility to pain without loss of consciousness.
ANDROECIUM The male organs of a flower.
ANGIOSPERMS Plants which have their seed enclosed in a seed vessel.
ANNUAL (bot.) A plant whose life-cycle from germination to maturity and death lasts only one growing season.
ANODYNE A substance that relieves pain.
ANOREXIA NERVOSA A condition characteristically found in young women usually in which intense aversion to excess weight leads to great restriction in food intake and subsequent emaciation and nutritional deficiencies; often the emaciated patient is convinced she is fat. The condition is associated with emotional conflict.
ANTHELMINTIC See antihelmintic.
ANTHER (bot.) The part of the stamen which contains pollen.
ANTHOCYANIN One of the flavonoid glycosides which comprise the soluble colouring matter of certain plant material, such as the purple and red of autumnal leaves, and the violet, red and blue of flowers.
ANTHRAQUINONE GLYCOSIDE A glycosidic derivative of anthraquinone, usually possessing a cathartic action.
ANTHRAQUINONE NUCLEUS Complex aromatic compound. (See *Aromatic*.)
ANTICHOLINERGIC Acting as or relating to a cholinergic blocking agent, hence blocking the action of cholinergic nerves or acetylcholine.
ANTI-COAGULANT A substance that slows or prevents the clotting of blood.
ANTIDOTE A substance which counteracts or neutralizes a poison.
ANTIHELMINTIC A substance which destroys or expels intestinal worms.
ANTI-MITOTIC A substance which inhibits the division of cells.
ANTI-NEOPLASTIC A substance that inhibits or destroys tumours (neoplastic cells).
ANTIPYRETIC A substance which prevents or reduces fever.
ANTISCORBUTIC A substance which prevents or cures scurvy.
ANTI-SUDORIFIC A substance which stops or reduces perspiration.
ANTI-TUSSIVE An agent which reduces or relieves coughing.
APERIENT Laxative.
APHRODISIAC A substance which stimulates sexual excitement and sometimes ability.
APHTHOUS ULCER White oral sore or ulcer of unknown cause.
APICAL BUD (bot.) The bud nearest to the top of a shoot.
APOTHECARY An archaic term for those who prepared and sold drugs and who at one time administered to the sick. The modern apothecary is, strictly speaking, a general medical practitioner, but the term may also be applied to pharmaceutical chemists and druggists.
AQUEOUS SOLUTION A solution in water.
ARABINOSE A sugar which is found in plant material. It is also called pectin sugar and pectinose.
ARACHIDIC Relating to the Peanut, *Arachis hypogaea*.
ARACHNOID (bot.) Soft entangled hairs, like a cobweb.
ARECA RED A red dye obtained from the fruit of the Betel Palm, *Areca catechu*.
ARIL (bot.) An outer wing on a seed or appendage to a seed, growing out from the hilum or funiculus.
AROMATHERAPY The use of essential oils in the treatment of medical and cosmetic problems; the oils are considered to act at a spiritual or emotional level. The subject was promoted by René-Maurice Gattefossé in the 1920s and is not accepted as a legitimate branch of herbal medicine.
AROMATIC (chem.) Organic compound derived from benzene; also called aromatic compound; (herb.) having a fragrant and/or spicy taste and smell.
ARRHYTHMIA (med.) Irregularity or absence of rhythm of the heart
ARTERIOSCLEROSIS Hardening of the arteries.
ARTIFICIAL (chem.) Man-made substance.
ARYL RADICAL Radicals derived from aromatic compounds. (See *Aromatic*.)
ASCORBIC ACID Vitamin C.
ASTHMA Difficulty in breathing, due to constriction or spasm of air passages and caused by increased responsiveness of the bronchi and trachea to various stimuli, particularly allergy.
ASTRINGENT A substance that causes contraction, shrinkage or firming of living tissues, often mucous membranes, and which in so doing reduces or stops the function of those tissues thereby affecting haemorrhages, secretions, diarrhoea, etc. The term is often applied to cosmetic preparations which tighten the skin.
ATROPINE An alkaloid obtained from

Atropa belladonna (Deadly Nightshade) and other members of the Solanaceae family. It is a parasympatholytic agent which is used mainly for its spasmolytic action on smooth muscle and for its action in reducing secretions.
AURICULATE Ear-shaped, particularly referring to the shape of leaves.
AXIL (bot.) The upper angle formed between a petiole or peduncle and the stem carrying it.
AXILLARY BUD A bud formed in an axil, the angle of the leaf with its stem.
AXIS (bot.) The main stem or root of a plant.

B

BACTERIA An enormous group of unicellular or sparsely cellular micro-organisms which are neither animal nor plant, but which possess a wide range of structural and biosynthetic ability. They range from free living soil and water organisms to human parasites which have never been cultivated. Some forms are able to photosynthesize in a manner similar to that of green plants but they do not produce oxygen.
BALLAST MATERIAL Those substances, naturally occurring in medicinal herbs, which modify the physiological activity of a plant or extract.
BECHIC A substance that soothes a cough.
BIENNIAL (bot.) A plant whose life-cycle from germination to maturity and death takes two growing seasons.
BIFURCATION Forking or branching.
BILE A secretion of the liver which is stored in the gall-bladder. It is rich in fats, pigments and various salts which aid digestion.
BILHARZIA Bilharziasis or Schistosomiasis. One of the most important debilitating diseases of man, contracted in tropical and subtropical regions of the world. A parasitic worm permeates the circulatory system, as part of its life-cycle.
BILIARY COLIC Acute paroxysmal pain caused by the movement of gallstones down the bile duct.
BILIARY OBSTRUCTION Reduction in the flow of bile from the gall-bladder down the bile duct due to physical obstruction.
BILIOUS Sometimes called Bilous. Either relating to bile itself or to disorders caused by excessive production and release of bile into the intestinal system.
BILIOUSNESS A disorder associated with poor digestion and characterized by general discomfort, headache, constipation and nausea. It may or may not be related to bile secretion, and the term is medically inexact.
BINOMIAL (biol.) Describes the system of nomenclature of animals and plants in which two names are applied to a specific organism; the first (genus) groups the organisms into closely related types, and the second (specific epithet) specifies a distinct species.
BIOCHEMICAL Relating to physiological or biological chemistry; the chemicals associated with living matter.
BIOSYNTHESIS The production of chemical substances by a living organism.
BIRD-LIME A glutinous substance manufactured from various plant materials which was traditionally applied to sticks to capture birds.
BITERNATE (bot.) Leaflets in a compound leaf, arranged in threes, in which one group is borne on a secondary but similarly arranged petiole.
BITTER A substance characterized by a bitter taste. Often applied to alcoholic drinks containing bitter substances, or to botanical drugs with bitter constituents, which are used to promote the appetite.
BLEPHARITIS Inflammation of the eyelids.
BLOOD-BRAIN BARRIER A functional barrier between the tissue of the brain and the brain capillaries which effectively controls the movement of substances from the blood to the central nervous system, allowing some to pass freely while inhibiting or completely preventing the movement of others.
BRACT (bot.) A much reduced and often scale-like leaf that bears a flower or inflorescence in its axil.
BRACTEOLE (bot.) A small bract.
BRONCHIOLE A branch of a bronchus which is less than 1 mm in diameter.
BRONCHODILATORS Substances which increase the diameter of the pulmonary air passages.
BRONCHUS One of the main branches of the trachea or that within the lung which contains cartilage in the wall structure (pl. bronchi).
BRYOPHYTA (bot.) A division of the non-flowering plants which contains the Liverworts, Hornworts and Mosses.

C

CALCAREOUS Composed of, or containing free lime or limestone.
CALCICOLOUS AND CALCICOLE (bot.) Descriptive of plants which tolerate, or require soils containing chalk or limestone.
CALCIFUGOUS and CALCIFUGE (bot.) Descriptive of plants which will not tolerate soils containing chalk or limestone.
CALCULI Stones in the kidney, gall-bladder or bladder. They are composed of mineral substances and salts, often phosphate or oxalate.
CALYX (bot.) The outer covering of a flower.
CAMBIAL CELLS (bot.) Cells of the cambium.
CAMBIUM (bot.) A secondary meristematic tissue, producing annual growth of vascular tissues, or cork in woody plants.
CAOUTCHOUC India-rubber or Gum Elastic obtained from the juice of many plants.
CAPILLARY The smallest subdivision of blood vessels which connect the smallest subdivision of veins to the smallest subdivision of arteries.
CAPILLARY ATTRACTION That force between the surfaces of narrow tubes which results in the movement of fluids along them.
CAPITULUM (bot.) A flower-head; often referring specifically to those with sessile flowers (pl. capitula).
CARBOHYDRATES A class of organic compounds containing carbon, hydrogen and oxygen. Included in this group are the sugars, starches and cellulose.
CARBON DIOXIDE An odourless and colourless gas with the formula CO_2. Formed in the process of respiration by man and plants, and used in photosynthesis by plants as the starting point for the synthesis of carbohydrates.
CARDIO-ACTIVE Acting on the heart.
CARDIOTONIC SUBSTANCES Agents which increase the contractility of heart muscle; applied loosely to substances which have some beneficial action on the heart.
CARDIOVASCULAR SYSTEM Relating to the heart and blood vessels.
CARMINATIVE A substance which relieves flatulence and colic.
CAROTENES Reddish-yellow pigments in plants which may be converted by animal tissue into vitamin A.
CARPEL (bot.) One of the units composing the gynoecium or the female parts of a flower.
CARTILAGINOUS Related to or containing cartilage.
CATABOLISM That aspect of metabolism concerned with the breaking down of complex substances to simpler ones, with the release of energy.
CATALYST A substance which alters the rate at which a chemical reaction takes place, but itself remains unchanged at the end of the reaction.
CATHARTIC A purgative substance.
CAUDATE (bot.) Having a tail-like appendage or tail.
CELL SAP (biol.) The fluid within plant cells, including that in conducting vessels and the material which can be extracted on crushing and macerating plants.
CELLULOSE (bot.) The carbohydrate structural constituent of the cell-walls of all true plants.
CEREBRAL CORTEX The external grey layer of the brain.
CEREBRO-SPINAL FLUID The fluid which surrounds the brain and spinal cord. Abbreviated as CSF.
CHLOROPHYLL (bot.) The green pigment of plants, vital to the process of photosynthesis.
CHLOROPLAST (bot.) A minute organ (organelle) within green plant cells, containing the green pigment, chlorophyll. The basic processes of food manufacture occur within the chloroplast.
CHOLAGOGUE A substance which stimulates or aids the release of bile from the gall-bladder.
CHOLECYSTITIS Inflammation of the gall-bladder.
CHOLELITHIASIS The presence of stones in the bile duct and/or gall-bladder.
CHOLERETIC A substance which stimulates the production of bile in the liver.
CHOLINERGIC That part of the nervous system which uses acetylcholine as its transmitting substance; or the type of physiological action characteristic of acetylcholine.
CHROMATOGRAPHY The separation of a mixture of substances by various methods, such as selective adsorption or partition between non-mixing solvents, for example.
CHROMOSOMES (biol.) Small bodies found in cell nuclei which carry the genes or inheritable characteristics of the organism concerned. Different organisms often have different numbers of chromosomes. Normal vegetative cells have two sets; reproductive cells have only one.
CILIATE (bot.) Fringed with small hairs.
CILIUM A small hair or whip-like structure attached to some animal and plant cells. (pl. cilia).
CIRRHOSIS A disorder of the liver characterized by increase in fibrous connective tissue, degeneration and regeneration of liver cells. Caused especially by alcohol.
COLIC Acute paroxysmal pain in the abdominal region.
COLON That part of the large intestine which begins at the caecum and ends at the rectum.
COLOSTOMY The surgical formation of an artificial anus in the abdominal wall following lower bowel disease.
COMBUSTION PROCESS Any chemical process which is accompanied by the release of heat.
COMPOUND LEAF (bot.) One made up of

several distinct leaflets.
CONJUNCTIVITIS Inflammation of the conjunctiva, the mucous membrane covering the eye-ball.
CONTUSION A bruise.
CONVERGENT EVOLUTION The separate and independent development of unrelated plants or animals leading to structural or functional similarities or close identity that superficially suggests a close relationship between them.
CORDATE (bot.) Heart-shaped.
CORIACEOUS (biol.) Having a leathery texture.
CORM (bot.) A swollen, rounded underground stem which lasts for one year only, that of the next year being produced on the top of its parent.
COROLLA (bot.) Collective term for the petals of a flower.
CORONARY THROMBOSIS The formation of a clot or thrombus in a coronary artery of the heart.
CORPUSCLE A blood cell or any other small rounded body.
CORTEX (med.) The peripheral portion of an organ – as in the cortex of a kidney; (bot.) the tissue region between the vascular cylinder and epidermis of the stem and root.
CORYMBOSE CLUSTER (bot.) A short and broad, practically flat-topped flower cluster.
CORYMBOSE TERMINAL PANICLE See *Corymbose cluster.*
COTYLEDON (bot.) The leaf or leaves of an embryo, usually differing from the shape of mature leaves, and found already developed within the seed. On germination they either remain in the seed-coat or rise above ground and become green.
COUMARIN A compound found in many plants and responsible for the aroma of new-mown hay which some possess. Ingestion in large amounts can lead to haemorrhage in man and animals.
COUNTER-IRRITANT A substance that causes inflammation of the skin. It is applied for the temporary relief of a deep-seated painful irritation.
CRENATE (bot.) Scalloped or shallowly round-toothed.
CRENULATE The diminutive of crenate.
CROSS-BREEDING and CROSS-FERTILIZATION To fertilize with pollen from another plant of different variety, strain or species.
CULTIGEN A plant deserving species status but which is known only in cultivation, not being found in the wild.
CULTIVAR (hort.) A cultivated or horticultural variety of a plant species which may have originated either in the wild or in cultivation.
CUNEATE (bot.) Triangular or wedge-shaped petals or leaves in which the narrow end is attached to the plant.
CUTICLE (bot.) The water-conserving outer layer of epidermal cells.
CUTIN A wax-like substance found on the surface of the external cellular layers of most plants, which assists in the prevention of excessive water-loss.
CUTTING One of the commonest methods of plant propagation, consisting of the removal of stem, leaf or root portions from the parent plant, before rootlets are formed on them. Portions are rooted in sand, peat, vermiculite or a mixture of these and other materials, often after application of a hormone rooting compound to the cut surface.
CYANOGENIC GLYCOSIDE A glycoside which liberates hydrocyanic (or prussic) acid when broken down. (See *Glycoside*.)
CYCAD A group of evergreen plants belonging to the Gymnosperms, and thus among the most primitive of living seed plants. The Cycads were especially dominant in the flora of the Mesozoic period.
CYME (bot.) A broad, inverted cone-shaped flower-cluster in which the central flowers open first.
CYSTITIS Inflammation of the bladder.
CYTOPLASM The material within cells, excluding the cell nucleus.

D

DECIDUOUS A plant that loses its leaves in autumn.
DECOCTION (herb.) Extract of a herb obtained by boiling a given weight of plant matter in a given volume of water for a given time.
DECOMPOSITION The breaking down of complex substances into simpler ones.
DECUMBENT (bot.) Lying on the ground or bending towards it, but with the apex pointing upwards (as for a plant stem or branch).
DECUSSATE (bot.) Arranged in opposite pairs, each pair being at right angles to the next.
DEFAECATION The action of expelling waste matter from the body.
DEHISCENT (bot.) Opens to shed seeds or spores.
DELTOID (bot.) Triangular.
DEMULCENT A substance that is smooth and soothing when applied to an inflamed or painful surface.
DENTATE (bot.) Having sharp or coarse indentations or teeth that are perpendicular to the leaf margin.
DENTICULATE Very finely dentate.
DERMATITIS Inflammation of the skin.
DESICCATION The complete drying of a substance.
DIABETES A condition characterized by the habitual discharge of an excessive volume of urine and by an associated excessive thirst. Used loosely to describe diabetes mellitus.
DIABETES MELLITUS A disorder of the carbohydrate metabolism characterized by disturbance to the insulin mechanism and resulting in hyperglycaemia or excess of sugar in the blood.
DIAPHORETIC A substance that causes an increase in perspiration. Some are used to treat fevers.
DICOTYLEDON A flowering plant which has two cotyledons.
DILATION (med.) The enlargement or stretching of an organ.
DIOECIOUS Having the male and female flowers on different plants.
DISPENSATORY (1) The early name for a pharmacopoeia. (2) A book in which medicinal substances are listed and their preparation and administration for various conditions are described.
DISTILLATION The process of heating a liquid to convert it to vapour (often doing so under reduced pressure), condensing the vapour, and collecting the condensate or distillate. Components with different boiling points can thus be separated.
DIURETIC A substance that increases the volume of urine, and hence the frequency of urination.
DNA (Deoxyribonucleic acid) Complex molecules containing a deoxyribose sugar and organic bases. DNA is present in chromosomes of all plant and animal cells and carries coded genetic information.
DOUCHE Normally referring to the direction of a flow of liquid into a body cavity; often the vagina for the purpose of washing with a medicinal substance.
DROPSY An old-fashioned term for heart failure, characterized by the abnormal accumulation of serous fluid in body tissues.
DUODENUM The first part of the small intestine following the outlet from the stomach, and containing the pancreatic and common bile ducts.
DYSENTERY Inflammation of the intestine, characterized by diarrhoea containing mucus and blood, pain and painful straining to evacuate the bowels.
DYSMENORRHOEA Painful or difficult menstruation.
DYSPEPSIA Disorder of the digestive process.
DYSPNOEA Difficulty in breathing.

E

ECLAMPSIA A disease occurring during the latter half of pregnancy characterized by a rise in blood pressure, and sometimes convulsions.
ECLECTIC MEDICINE A form of medicine that particularly attracted attention in North America in the late eighteenth and early nineteenth centuries, in which methods and materials were borrowed from different systems of medicine.
ECZEMA An acute or chronic inflammatory disease of the skin of unknown cause. Characterized by a variety of lesions.
EFFLUENT Waste fluid.
EMBALM The treatment of a corpse with antiseptic and preservative substances to resist putrefaction.
EMBROCATION A liquid medication or liniment applied to the body surface by rubbing.
EMESIS Vomiting.
EMETIC A substance that causes vomiting.
EMMENAGOGUE A substance that stimulates the menstrual flow.
EMOLLIENT A substance used internally to soothe inflamed membranes, or externally to soften the skin.
EMPHYSEMA Distention of the tissues by air; especially referring to the lungs in which there is destructive change to the alveolar walls.
ENCEPHALITIS Inflammation of the brain.
ENDOCARP (bot.) The innermost layer of the fruit wall.
ENDOCRINE Relating to the endocrine glands, which are those secreting hormonal substances directly into the bloodstream. Examples include the pancreas, testes and adrenals.
ENDOSPERM The nutrient tissue in the seed of a flowering plant, formed after fertilization of the ovule.
ENEMA The injection of fluid material into the rectum; usually for therapeutic purposes but occasionally to help diagnosis.
ENTOMOLOGY The study of insects.
ENURESIS Incontinence, in the absence of organic causes.
ENZYME An organic catalyst composed mainly of protein found in all living systems and vital for the functioning of biochemical reactions. There are numerous kinds.

EPIDERMIS (bot.) The outermost cell-layer of the primary tissues of a plant.
EPIGEAL GERMINATION Plant germination when the cotyledons are raised above the ground.
EPILEPSY A brain disorder characterized by transient episodes or seizures during which convulsions and psychic dysfunction may occur.
EPILEPTIFORM CONVULSION Convulsion resembling that typical of epilepsy.
EPIPHYTE Plant which grows attached to another plant, but not as a parasite.
EPITHELIUM (med.) Cellular tissue of a variety of types, one of which forms the uppermost layer of the skin.
EPITHELIZATION The growth of epithelium over a raw and damaged surface.
ERGOTAMINE An alkaloid obtained from Ergot, *Claviceps purpurea*. It can be used to treat migraine.
ERYSIPELAS A skin disease characterized by inflammation of the skin, caused by the bacterium *Streptococcus pyogenes*.
ERYTHROCYTE Red blood corpuscle.
ESCHAROTIC A substance that provides a slough on the skin; acting as a caustic substance; corrosive.
ESERINE An alternative name for the alkaloid physostigmine, obtained from the Calabar Bean (*Physostigma venenosum*, Balfour), which is largely responsible for the powerful action of the plant.
ESSENTIAL OIL A volatile oil, obtained from a plant by distillation and having a similar aroma to the plant itself.
EXCRETION The discharge from the body of waste products; not limited to the evacuation of the bowels, and including, for example, the excretion of waste matter via the sweat glands.
EXOCARP (bot.) The outermost layer of the fruit wall (pericarp); also called the epicarp.
EXPECTORANT A substance which promotes the expulsion of fluid or semi-fluid matter from the lungs and air passages, by coughing or spitting.
EXTRACT A product obtained by treating plant material with a solvent or mixture of solvents designed to extract the desired constituents.

F

FALLOWING (agric.) Ploughing ready for sowing; or now, more commonly, allowing land to remain uncropped for a year or more.
FASCICLE (bot.) A bunched tuft of branches, roots or fibres.
FAT-SOLUBLE Soluble in fatty substances.
FATTY ACIDS Acids which with glycerine form fats.
FEBRIFUGE A substance which prevents or reduces fever (now known as antipyretic).
FILAMENT (bot.) The part of the stamen that supports the anther.
FIXATIVE (perfumery) A substance which assists in retaining the aroma of the other substances.
FIXED OIL A non-volatile oil that cannot be distilled or evaporated without decomposition. (See *Essential oil.*)
FLATULENCE A condition in which excess gas is present in the gastro-intestinal system.
FLAVONE A type of flavonoid; a yellow dye.
FLAVONE HETEROSIDE A glycoside with flavone or a derivative as the aglycone.
FLAVONOID A broad class of coloured aromatic substances. (See *Aromatic.*)
FLORET (bot.) Small flower which forms part of a compound flower.
FORMALIN SOLUTION A powerful disinfectant and fixing substance consisting of a 37 per cent aqueous solution of formaldehyde; also called formaldehyde solution.
FRAGMENTATION (bot.) A term loosely applied to a process of natural vegetative reproduction of plants in which portions are variously detached and propagated.
FUMIGANT A disinfectant substance in a vaporized or gaseous state.
FUNGI Non-flowering plants ranging from microscopic moulds to edible mushrooms. They are incapable of photosynthesis and share some other features with the animal kingdom. They provide various antibiotics and are important in the breakdown of organic matter in the soil, but are also responsible for the loss of foodstuff through spoilage and disease.
FUNICULUS or FUNICLE (bot.) The stalk by which an ovule is attached to the ovary wall or placenta.

G

GALACTAGOGUE A substance that can induce or increase the secretion of milk.
GALLIC ACID An astringent substance.
GAMETES (biol.) Sexual reproductive cells.
GASTRO-INTESTINAL TRACT The alimentary system, from the mouth to the anus.
GEL Colloidal solution which sets to a jelly on cooling.
GENES (biol.) The units of heredity controlling one or more inherited characteristics; composed of DNA, and protein.
GENITO-URINARY TRACT The urinogenital (or urogenital) system comprising the urinary organs and the genitalia.
GINGIVITIS Inflammation of the mucous membrane and soft tissues surrounding the teeth.
GLABROUS (bot.) Lacking hairs; but not the same as 'smooth' when used in the botanical sense.
GLANDULAR PUBESCENT (bot.) Hairs and glands mixed on a surface, such as a leaf.
GLOBOSE Almost spherical.
GLUCOSIDE A glycoside which yields glucose when broken down. (See *Glycoside.*)
GLYCEROL Glycerine.
GLYCOALKALOID An alkaloid combined with a sugar.
GLYCOSIDE An organic substance which may be broken into two parts, one of which is always sugar. (See *Aglycone.*)
GONORRHOEA A venereal disease characterized by mucopurulent (mucous and purulent) discharge from and inflammation of the genital tract. Caused by the bacterium, *Neisseria gonorrhoeae.*

H

HAEMOGLOBIN The red oxygen-carrying pigment in the red blood corpuscles.
HAEMOLYSIS The release of haemoglobin from red blood corpuscles following their damage.
HAEMOPTYSIS Spitting of blood, or blood-stained sputum.
HAEMORRHAGE Bleeding; the escape of blood from the blood vessels.
HAEMOSTATIC A substance that stops bleeding.
HALLUCINOGEN A substance which can affect all or any of the senses, producing a wide range of perception and reaction.
HALOPHYTE Salt-tolerant plant, generally associated with the vegetation of salt-marshes and other saline habitats.
HEEL (hort.) Breaking a young shoot away from the parent stem, with a portion (heel) of the parent attached to it, for the purpose of propagation.
HEPATIC CONGESTION Congestion or inefficient functioning of the liver.
HERBACEOUS (bot.) (1) Relating to plants which are not woody and which die down at the end of each year; (2) plant parts which are soft and green with the texture of leaves.
HERBARIUM Formerly a live collection of plants in monasteries, now referring to dried plant specimens.
HERBICIDE (hort.) A substance that kills plants.
HERPES An inflammatory skin disease characterized by the formation of small vesicles in clusters – such as coldsores.
HETEROSIDE A glycoside in which the aglycone is not a sugar.
HIGH ENERGY PHOSPHATE BOND A chemical linkage between phosphorus and oxygen (usually in adenosine triphosphate) which releases a large amount of chemical energy on reaction.
HILUM (bot.) The point of attachment of a seed, denoted by a scar.
HISTAMINE Protective substance present in all tissues of the body, being released into the blood, when, for example, the skin is cut or burnt.
HOMEOPATHY A system of medicine, introduced by Samuel Hahnemann, based on the supposition that minute quantities of a given substance, such as that of a medicinal plant, will cure a condition in which symptoms exist that would be identical to the symptoms produced in a healthy person were he given large quantities of the same substance.
HORMONES (med.) Chemical substance produced by tissues which is introduced into the general blood circulation, and acts as a regulatory agent on different tissues in different parts of the body. (bot.) Chemicals which are produced in small amounts by the plant and control its growth and behaviour.
HUMUS (hort.) The product of the decomposition of organic matter.
HYBRID (biol.) An organism which results from cross-breeding.
HYDROCHLORIC ACID (med.) The acidic substance secreted in the stomach to adjust the stomach contents to the correct degree of acidity for the action of certain digestive enzymes.
HYDROGEN CYANIDE Prussic acid; hydrocyanic acid; an intensely poisonous substance, derivatives of which are found in certain plants.
HYDROLYSIS The chemical fission of a substance by water into two or more parts, in which the water is also decomposed.
HYDROPHYTE An aquatic plant.
HYPERTENSION Excessive tension such as may be found in some nervous individuals often characterized by high blood pressure.
HYPERVITAMINOSIS A A condition caused by the excessive intake of vitamin A.
HYPOGEAL GERMINATION The germination of plants where the cotyledons remain below the ground.
HYPOGLYCAEMIC A substance that lowers the concentration of glucose in the blood.
HYPOTENSIVE A substance that lowers the blood pressure.
HYPOTHALAMUS That part of the brain

which controls the integration of the functions of the endocrine system and the nervous system. (See *Endocrine.*)

I

IMMUNOLOGY The study of the systems whereby living organisms (especially man) respond to foreign matter of a biological nature which, when taken into the body, may cause damage to it; especially of those factors in the blood and lymph that produce resistance to disease.
INDEHISCENT (bot.) Not opening, or not opening regularly.
INFLORESCENCE A flowering branch (or, a group of flowers with a common stalk).
INFUSION The preparation of a dose of a herb by pouring a given quantity of boiling water over a given weight of herb, and infusing for a given time.
INGESTION The act of taking in food or other material through the mouth.
INSULIN A hormone secreted in the pancreas which regulates carbohydrate and fat metabolism; deficiency causes diabetes mellitus.
INTESTINE That part of the gastro-intestinal tract from the distal end of the stomach (pylorus) to the anus. Consists of the duodenum, the jejunum, the ileum, the caecum, the colon, the rectum and the anal canal.
INULIN A complex sugar found in several plants, especially in members of the family Compositae.
INVOLUCRE Bracts or small leaves arranged in a whorl or whorls immediately beneath a flower or flower-cluster.
IODIZED SALT Common salt to which an iodide (or iodine-containing) salt has been added.
ION Electrically charged atom or groups of atoms.
IONIZED In the form of ions.
ISOMERIC Having the same molecular formula but different properties owing to a different arrangement of atoms within the molecule. Hence one compound may be an isomer of another.
ISOPROPYL ALCOHOL (Isopropanol) An alcohol with many applications as a substitute for ethyl alcohol (ethanol); some grades are used in the food industry.

J K

JAUNDICE A condition which is caused by excessive amounts of bilirubin in the blood and is characterized by yellowness of the skin and body secretions.
KERATIN A protein material which characteristically constitutes hair, feathers and nails.
KHELLIN A substance, isolated from *Ammi visnaga*, which is used as a bronchial dilator.
KNOT GARDEN (hort.) A decorative formal garden popular in the sixteenth century and consisting normally of very low hedges in geometric patterns.

L

LACTAGOGUE See *Galactagogue.*
LACTATION The secretion of milk.
LAMINA (bot.) The blade of a leaf or petal.
LANCEOLATE (bot.) Spear-shaped (of leaves) with the widest part near the centre.
LARYNGITIS Inflammation of the larynx.
LEACH The extraction of soluble constituents from a mixture of soluble and insoluble material.
LEAF FALL Loss of leaves.
LEAF MOULD Partially decomposed leaves.
LECITHIN A member of the group of phospholipids; a very complex substance containing phosphorus, found in egg yolk, brain and blood.
LEUCORRHOEA A white discharge from the vagina.
LICHEN (bot.) A member of a group of slow-growing plants that consist of a symbiotic relationship between an alga and a fungus.
LINIMENT A substance, usually medicinal, applied to the skin.
LIPID A fat or fat-like substance insoluble in water and soluble in fat solvents; the group of lipids includes many different but related materials.
LOAM (hort.) A good soil containing at least two of the main soil particle sizes: gravel, sand, silt or clay; designated by the dominant particle – hence a 'sandy loam'.
LYMPH A straw-coloured fluid which circulates many tissues of the body and serves to lubricate and cleanse them.

M

MACERATION The process of extracting substances from a botanical drug by steeping in a solvent.
MEDULLA The central part of an organ, used to distinguish it from the cortex.
MELANCHOLIA (med.) Severe depression, often of a psychotic nature.
MENINGITIS Inflammation of the meninges, the covering of the brain.
MENORRHAGIA Excessive menstrual flow.
MENSTRUATION The periodic, usually monthly, elimination of blood and cellular material from the uterus of sexually mature women.
MERISTEMS (bot.) The formative tissues of plants, distinguished from the permanent tissues by the power their cells possess to divide and form new cells. Primary (apical) meristems are located near the tips of roots and in the buds of stems. Secondary meristems produce lateral growth subsequent to the primary extension growth produced by the primary or apical meristems.
MESOCARP (bot.) The middle layer of a fruit wall.
MESOPHYTE (bot.) A plant suited to a moderately moist climate.
METABOLISM The reactions involved in the building up and decomposition of chemical substances in living organisms.
METABOLISM, PRIMARY Vital processes concerned with the maintenance of life.
METABOLISM, SECONDARY Reactions which result in the formation of complex materials which are not concerned with the maintenance of life. These are often the medicinally active compounds in plant extracts.
MINERAL A natural inorganic substance; often applied to metallic salts and certain elements.
MIOTIC A substance that contracts the pupils.
MITHRIDATE An antidote to poison. (From the second-century B.C. King Mithridates, who studied poisons and their antidotes.)
MOLLUSC A member of the Mollusca, animals without segments or limbs and usually having a shell.
MOLLUSCIDAL A substance that kills molluscs, such as snails.
MONOCARPIC (bot.) Bearing fruit only once, and then dying.
MONOCOTYLEDON A flowering plant that has only one cotyledon.
MONOECIOUS A plant which has unisexual flowers, but with both male and female flowers on the same plant.
MONOSACCHARIDE A simple sugar.
MORDANT A substance used in dyeing which when applied to the fabric to be dyed reacts chemically with the dye thereby fixing the colour.
MORPHOLOGY The study of the arrangement of organs and tissues, including their inner structure and outer form.
MOULD A small fungus of web-like structure.
MUCILAGE A slimy product formed by the addition of gum to water; mucilages occur naturally in many plants and may be applied to irritated or inflamed surfaces to relieve them.
MUCOSAL SURFACE The surface of a mucous membrane.
MUCOUS COLITIS Inflammation of the colon resulting in a mucous discharge.
MUCOUS MEMBRANE Membrane, kept continually moist by a variety of glands, that lines canals and cavities of the body which are exposed to the air: mouth, anus, vagina.
MULCH (hort.) Substances spread around a plant to protect it from weeds, water-loss, heat, cold and in some cases to provide nutrient material. Mulches comprise many materials from sawdust and pine-needles to black plastic, but leaves and old straw are the materials most commonly employed. Mulches should only be applied to moist soil.
MYASTHENIA GRAVIS A condition of weakness and rapid tiredness in the muscles of the skeleton (voluntary muscles) which is caused by a malfunction in the release of acetylcholine.
MYCOPHYTA (bot.) A term used to denote the group of fungi as a separate division of the plant kingdom.
MYCORRHIZAL Referring to any soil fungus which establishes a close symbiotic relationship with the young roots of particular trees and shrubs.
MYDRIATIC A substance which dilates the pupils.

N

NARCOTIC A substance that in small doses produces sleep and relieves pain, but which in large doses may cause poisoning with coma or convulsions.
NASOPHARYNX Cavity extending from the back of the throat to the nose.
NERVINE (herb.) A substance that calms nervous excitement.
NEURALGIA Brief but severe pain along the course of a nerve.
NEUROLOGY The study of the nervous system.
NEUROMUSCULAR Relating to both nerves and muscles.
NEURONE, NEURON A complete nerve cell.
NODULE A small rounded organ.
NUCLEIC ACIDS (biol.) One of a group of substances characteristic of the nuclei and cytoplasm of cells, which yield purine and pyrimidine bases when broken down.
NUCLEUS (biol.) The functional centre of a cell.

O

OBLANCEOLATE (bot.) Inversely lanceolate.
OBLIGATE PARASITE (biol.) A parasite that cannot live without a host.
OBOVATE (bot.) Inversely ovate.
OESOPHAGUS The gullet; passage from the

pharynx to the stomach.
OFF-SET (bot.) A short lateral offshoot of a stem or root of a plant that can be used for propagation.
OLEIC ACID An unsaturated acid found in many fats and oils.
OLEO-GUM-RESIN A resinous substance containing an oil and a gum, obtained from certain plants.
ORBICULAR Disc-shaped or circular.
OSMOSIS The flow of a solvent through a semi-permeable membrane from a dilute solution into a more concentrated one.
OVARY (med.) A glandular organ which produces female eggs. (bot.) The ovule bearing part of the pistil.
OVATE Egg-shaped.
OVULE (bot.) The egg-containing part of the ovary which becomes the seed after fertilization.
OXYTOCIC An agent that hastens evacuation of the uterus by stimulating contractions.

P

PALMATE (bot.) Shaped or divided like a hand.
PANCREAS An abdominal gland which secretes substances responsible for the digestion of carbohydrates, proteins and fats; it also secretes insulin.
PANICLE (bot.) A flower-cluster in which the branches are racemose.
PANICULATE Arranged in a panicle.
PARASITICIDE A substance that destroys parasites, especially those which exist on the skin.
PARASYMPATHETIC NERVOUS SYSTEM (med.) That part of the autonomic nervous system which is concerned with maintaining muscle tone, inducing glandular secretion and dilation of the blood vessels. The sympathetic nervous system generally decreases muscle tone, depresses glandular secretion and contracts the blood vessels.
PARASYMPATHOMIMETIC Substances causing an action in the body similar to that occurring when the parasympathetic nerves are stimulated.
PECTIN A natural carbohydrate substance used as a demulcent or thickening agent.
PECTORAL (med.) Relating to the chest. (herb.) A substance used in the treatment of chest complaints.
PEDICEL (bot.) The stem of one flower in a cluster.
PEDICULOSIS A skin condition caused by lice, characterized by itching and skin lesions.
PEDUNCLE (bot.) (1) The stem of a flower-cluster. (2) The stem of a flower when that flower is the only one remaining in an inflorescence. (3) The stem of a solitary flower.
PEPSIN A digestive enzyme secreted into and part of the gastric juice.
PEPTIC ULCER Tissue loss in parts of the digestive system which are exposed to the acidic juices; characteristically the stomach, lower end of the oesophagus and the beginning of the duodenum.
PERCOLATION The extraction of constituents from a powdered substance by the passage of suitable solvents through a vessel containing the substance.
PERCUTANEOUS That which is performed or applied through the skin.
PERENNIAL (bot.) A plant which survives for three or more years.
PERIANTH (bot.) Collective term for the outer flower parts usually consisting of distinct sepals and petals.
PERISTALSIS The progressive, wave-like contractions of the gastro-intestinal tract or parts of it, whereby matter is moved along it.
PETIOLATE (bot.) Possessing a petiole.
PETIOLE (bot.) The stalk of a leaf.
PHARMACOKINETICS The study of the absorption, distribution and elimination of drugs.
PHARMACOPOEIA A book containing descriptions of and recipes for the manufacture of those therapeutic substances that are officially recognized by a given country or place.
PHARMACY (1) The study of the preparation of therapeutic substances. (2) The place where prescriptions are made.
PHARYNGITIS Inflammation of the pharynx.
PHARYNX The muscular tube from the back of the nose, mouth and larynx extending to the oesophagus.
PHLEGM Thick, elastic mucus secreted by the cells lining the air passages. Originally one of the four humours or cardinal body fluids (the other three being choleric, sanguine and melancholic) in the ancient Greek system of medicine.
PHLOEM (bot.) The principal tissue responsible for the internal transport of substances synthesized by plants.
PHOSPHOLIPIDS Substances widely distributed in nature and comprising lipids, phosphoric acid and fatty acids.
PHOTOSENSITIZATION Becoming sensitive to sunlight following the intake of certain substances.
PHOTOSYNTHESIS The process whereby food substances are formed by green plants in the presence of light, using carbon dioxide and water as the starting materials.
PHYSIOMEDICALISM A system of herbal medicine in which herbs are used to assist the body's natural powers of healing. The system was developed in North America in the early nineteenth century.
PHYTODERMATITIS A skin eruption which is initiated by contact with plants.
PHYTOHAEMAGLUTININ A substance found in plant seeds which possesses specific antibody-like activity to animal cells.
PHYTOSTEROL One of a group of sterols, very similar to cholesterol, which occurs in plants.
PHYTOTHERAPY The medicinal use of plants; herbalism or medical herbalism.
PINNATE (bot.) Formed like a feather; applied to a compound leaf in which the leaflets are arranged either side of the axis in the same way as a feather.
PISTIL (bot.) The ovary of a flower, with its style and stigma.
PLACEBO A pharmacologically inactive substance given as a drug either in the treatment of psychological illness or in the course of drug trials.
PLASMA The liquid part of blood or lymph.
PLUMULE (bot.) The embryonic shoot which emerges from a germinating seed.
PNEUMONITIS Inflammation of the lungs.
POLLEN (bot.) The microspores or grains of a flowering plant which carry the male reproductive cells.
POLYNEURITIS The inflammation of several nerves simultaneously.
POLYPEPTIDE A substance containing amino-acids.
POLYPHARMACY The administration of medication which consists of many different therapeutic substances, as, for example, in herbalism when several different herbs are included in one prescription.
POMADE A perfumed ointment; often applied to those used on the head.
POULTICE (herb.) Warm or hot external application of crushed herbs or extracts of plant contained in cloth such as muslin. Applied locally to contusions, bruises, sprains and inflammations.
PRIMARY PHOTOSYNTHESIZERS The microscopic plants of land and water which constitute the greatest part of the world's photosynthetic ability, that is, the lowest part of the food-chain.
PROPHYLACTIC A substance that helps to prevent disease.
PROTHALLUS (bot.) The sexual generation of the Pteridophytes (which include ferns and clubmosses) which consists of a minute, flat structure bearing the sexual organs.
PROTHROMBIN A precursor (or stage in the development) of thrombin which is formed in the liver; thrombin acts as a clotting agent in bleeding.
PROTOALKALOID A precursor (or stage in the development of) or substance that can be converted to an alkaloid.
PROTO-BOTANY Early development of botanical studies; primary botany.
PROTOZOAN A microscopic, unicellular animal.
PROVITAMIN The precursor of a vitamin.
PSORIASIS A chronic, inflammatory skin condition.
PSYCHOSIS An aspect of serious mental impairment that leads to inability to manage normal affairs, and is characterized by delusions, hallucinations and mental confusion.
PSYCHOTROPIC A substance which affects the mind or psyche.
PTERIDOPHYTA (bot.) A botanical group which contains the ferns and fern allies.
PUBESCENT (bot.) Covered with short, soft hairs.
PUDENDA The external genitalia; usually applied to those of the female.
PULMONARY Relating to the lungs.
PULQUE A fermented Mexican drink obtained from the sap of *Agave americana*.
PURGATIVE A substance that causes evacuation of the bowel.
PYELITIS Inflammation of the kidney.
PYRETHRUM An insecticide made from the powdered flowers of certain of the Compositae family, especially *Chrysanthemum cinerariifolium*.

Q

QUANTUM A small unit of energy.
QUINSY Abscesses surrounding a tonsil.

R

RACEME An elongated inflorescence in which the terminal flowers open last.
RADICAL (bot.) Relating to the root (see also *Radicle*).
RADICALS (chem.) Groups of atoms in a chemical molecule which retain their identity during chemical changes and affect the rest of the same molecule.
RADICLE (bot.) The embryonic root which emerges from a germinating seed.
REAGENT A substance involved in a chemical reaction.
RECEPTACLE (bot.) The upper part of the stem which bears the flowers; it may be

flattened, concave or convex.
RECTUM The lower part of the large intestine.
RENAL ARTERY The artery of the kidney.
RENIFORM Kidney-shaped.
RETARDANT (chem.) Serving to delay or slow down a chemical reaction.
RHINITIS Inflammation of the mucous membranes of the nasal passage.
RHIZOME (bot.) A horizontal underground stem bearing roots, scales and nodes.
RHIZOTOMIST A root and herb collector of ancient Greece.
RINGWORM A fungus infection of the skin or nails producing ring-like lesions.
RUBEFACIENT A substance that causes reddening of the skin.
RUNNER (bot.) An aerial, trailing shoot, the tip of which takes root when it touches the ground.

S

SALICYLIC GLYCOSIDE Glycoside containing as the aglycone salicylic acid, or a derivative.
SALTPETRE Potassium nitrate.
SAMARA (bot.) An indehiscent winged fruit.
SAPONIN A glycosidic substance that foams in water and has a detergent action. Some plants containing saponins have been used as a substitute for soap.
SAPROPHYTE (biol.) An organism that obtains its nutrient material solely from dead or decaying matter.
SCABIES An infectious skin condition caused by a small insect.
SCABROUS (bot.) Rough.
SCURVY A nutritional disorder caused by lack of vitamin C.
SECONDARY MERISTEMS (bot.) Meristematic tissue which produces lateral growth subsequent to the primary extension growth produced by the apical meristems.
SEPALS (bot.) The separate parts of the calyx.
SEPTICAEMIA Bacterial infection in which the organisms invade or multiply in the blood.
SERRATE (bot.) A leaf margin which has forward-pointing, saw-like teeth.
SESSILE Lacking a stalk.
SIALAGOGUE A substance that initiates or increases salivation, the production of saliva.
SILICULA, Silicle or Silicule (bot.) A short, specialized fruit or capsule found in certain Cruciferae, which is usually less than three times as long as it is wide.
SILIQUA, Silique (bot.) A long, specialized fruit or capsule found in certain Cruciferae.
SIMPLE LEAF (bot.) A leaf that is not divided into leaflets.
SITOSTEROL A common plant sterol.
SPASMOLYTIC A substance that counteracts or relieves convulsions or spasmodic pains.
SPERMATORRHOEA The involuntary release of semen, in the absence of orgasm.
SPHAGNUM MOSS A group of related mosses which grow in very wet places.
SPORANGIUM An organ which produces spores. (Pl. sporangia.)
SPORE (bot.) An asexual, unicellular reproductive cell.
SPUTUM Material eliminated from the mouth by spitting, consisting of secretions from the mucous membranes of the buccal cavity which can include pus or blood.
STAMEN (bot.) The pollen-producing part of a flower, consisting of the anther and filament.
STEAM DISTILLATION The distillation of substances with the aid of introduced steam.
STEATORRHEA, STEATORRHOEA (1) Fat in the stools. (2) Increase in the secretions of the sebaceous glands.
STERNUTATORY A substance that causes sneezing.
STEROL A saturated or unsaturated alcohol derived from perhydrocyclopentanophenanthrene, such as cholesterol.
STIGMA (bot.) The part of a pistil which accepts the pollen.
STOLON (bot.) A short, horizontal stem that is normally produced above the soil surface and which gives rise to a separate plant at its tip.
STOLONIFEROUS Bearing stolons.
STOMACHIC A substance that counteracts or relieves cramps.
STOMATA (bot.) Minute openings on leaf surfaces, rhizomes and some stems that allow exchange of gases between the plant and the atmosphere.
STOMATITIS Inflammation of the soft tissues within the mouth.
STYPTIC A substance that stops bleeding, usually by contracting the tissue.
SUBCUTANEOUS TISSUES The loose connective tissues beneath the skin.
SUCROSE Common sugar.
SUDORIFIC A substance that induces sweating.
SUPPOSITORY A substance or substances of therapeutic value introduced into the urethra, vagina or rectum in the form of a body solidified by means of a fatty agent and which melts at body heat.
SYMBIOSIS (biol.) A mutually advantageous relationship between two different organisms.
SYMPATHETIC NERVOUS SYSTEM (See *Parasympathetic nervous system.*)
SYNAPSE The point of communication between nerve cells.
SYNERGISM Potentiating action between two or more substances.

T

TACHYCARDIA Excessive speed of the heart action.
TANNIN Astringent substance related to tannic acid.
TAPROOT (bot.) A persistent primary root, usually swollen with food.
TENDRIL (bot.) A thin, supporting appendage on a plant. A whip-like, modified leaf, sensitive to touch, which supports the plant by coiling around a support.
TERNATE (bot.) In groups of three.
TERPENOID Organic substance derived from mevalonic acid.
THALLUS FRONDS (bot.) Flat, primitive fronds, not distinguished as stem or leaf.
THERIAC An old term for poison antidote.
THYMOL A bactericide and fungicide found in several volatile oils.
THYMOLEPTIC (herb.) An antiseptic substance.
THIAMINE A member of the vitamin B complex. Deficiency affects the nervous system, circulation and alimentary tract.
TILTH (hort.) A prepared soil surface.
TINCTURE A solution of substances (both active and inactive therapeutically) extracted from medicinal plants by the maceration or percolation of the plant with alcohol or alcohol-water solutions. Most herbal tinctures are made with 70 per cent alcohol solutions.
TISANE A drink made by the addition of boiling water to fresh or dried unfermented plant material; usually applied to green leaf.
TISSUE REGENERATION The growth of tissue following damage or loss.
TOMENTOSE (bot.) Having a thick mat of soft, white hairs.
TRACHEA The windpipe.
TRACHEID (bot.) A vascular plant cell with pitted, woody (lignified) walls and oblique end walls.
TRACHEITIS Inflammation of the trachea.
TRANSMITTER (med.) A substance that transmits or passes on; usually applied to substances involved with the transmission of nerve impulses.
TRIFOLIATE (bot.) Bearing three leaves.
TRIFOLIOLATE (bot.) Bearing a leaf subdivided into three equal leaflets.
TRISACCHARIDE A carbohydrate which yields three molecules of monosaccharide when it is broken down.
TUBER (bot.) An underground, rounded storage organ, formed from the stem or root of a plant.
TUMOUR An abnormal swelling resulting from the multiplication of cells.

U V

UMBEL (bot.) An indeterminate, flat-topped, umbrella-shaped inflorescence, in which the flower stalks arise from a common point.
UNGUENT An ointment; formerly a perfumed or scented ointment.
UNICELLULAR (biol.) Consisting of a single cell.
URCEOLATE Shaped like an urn.
URETHRA The duct through which urine passes.
URTICARIA Nettle rash; a skin condition characterized by red weals that itch.
VACUOLE (biol.) A space within a cell.
VALEPOTRIOTE Substances in the rootstock of Valeriana species responsible for the plants' sedative action.
VARIEGATION (bot.) Patches or markings of different colour on a leaf.
VASCULAR CYLINDER (bot.) The tissues constituting the conducting regions of a stem, root or leaf.
VASOCONSTRICTOR A substance that causes the constriction of blood vessels.
VERMIFUGE A substance that expels or destroys intestinal worms.
VERTIGO Sensation of giddiness.
VESICANT A blistering agent.
VIRUS Minute organism, composed of a protein shell and a nucleic acid centre, which is unable to reproduce outside a host. Viruses are responsible for a wide range of diseases in all other living organisms.
VISCERA Normally referring to the organs within the abdominal cavity but strictly also those organs of the cranium, thorax or pelvis.
VISCOUS Sticky or glutinous.
VITRIOL Sulphuric acid.
VOLATILE OIL See *essential oil.*
VULNERARY A substance used to treat or heal wounds.

W X

WHORLS (bot.) Three or more leaves, bracts or flowers arranged at one point in a circle around an axis.
XEROPHYTE (bot.) A plant adapted to arid conditions.
XYLEM (bot.) The tissue responsible for conducting water upwards within plants; also imparts mechanical strength to the plant, and contains cells with food and waste reserves.

Conversion tables

Conversions from imperial to metric are only approximate as exact conversions are unwieldy for quick measurement.

Oven temperatures

The table below is only an approximate guide and the suggested temperatures and timings are those appropriate to the oven of an average-sized domestic cooker.

°F	°C	GAS NO	OVEN HEAT
225°F	110°C	¼	very cool
250	130	½	very cool
275	140	1	cool
300	150	2	slow
325	170	3	moderately slow
350	180	4	moderate
375	190	5	moderately hot
400	200	6	hot
425	220	7	very hot
450	230	8	very hot

Solid measurements

ENGLISH	AMERICAN
8 oz butter or fat	1 cup (solidly packed)
1 oz butter or fat	2 tablespoons
1 lb castor sugar	2⅓ cups powdered sugar
8 oz castor sugar	1 cup plus 3 tablespoons
2 oz castor sugar	4 tablespoons
1 lb plain flour, sieved	4½ cups cake flour, sieved
4 oz plain flour, sieved	1 cup plus 4 tablespoons
2 oz plain flour, sieved	8 tablespoons
12 oz dry, grated cheese	1 cup
8 oz rice, raw	1 cup

Solid measurements

METRIC *grams*	IMPERIAL *ounces*
450	16 (1 lb)
425	15
400	14
375	13
340	12
300	11
280	10
250	9
225	8
200	7
180	6
140	5
110	4
85	3
50	2
25	1
15	½

Liquid measurements

METRIC *millilitres*	IMPERIAL *fluid ounces*	U.S.
1140	40 (2 pints)	5 cups (2½ pints)
1000	35	4¼ cups
560	20	2½ cups (1¼ pints)
420	15	scant 2 cups
280	10	1¼ cups
230	8	1 cup
140	5 (1 gill)	½ cup plus 2 tablespoons
100	4	½ cup
50	2 (4 tablespoons)	¼ cup
30	1	2 tablespoons
15	½ (1 tablespoon)	1¼ tablespoons
7	¼ (1 dessertspoon)	2 teaspoons
5	⅛ (1 teaspoon)	1 teaspoon

8 pts = 1 gal = 4.54 litres

NOTE Measurements for dry ingredients in wine-making are usually by volume. Pack the herbs into a jug and 'bump' to firm. Do not press down.

Organizations

The following organizations offer membership, information and details of suppliers. Those marked(*) offer a regular publication such as a magazine and services of particular benefit to those with an interest in herbalism. A stamped addressed envelope or international reply coupon will usually secure details of what each one offers.

The Herb Society of South Australia Inc.
P.O. Box 140, Parkside, S. Australia, 5063.

The Queensland Herb Society*
23 Greenmount Avenue, Holland Park, Brisbane, Queensland, Australia.

The British Herbal Medicine Association
The Old Coach House, Southborough Road, Surbiton, Surrey, England.

The Garden History Society*
12 Charlbury Road, Oxford, England.

The Herb Society*
34 Boscobel Place, London, SW1, England.

Société de Recherches et de Diffusion de Plantes Medicinales
8 rue St Marc, Paris 2e, France.

Bundesfachverband der Heilmittelindustrie e.V.
D–5000 Koeln, Glockengasstrasse 1, Germany.

Verband der Reformwaren-Hersteller (VRH) e.V.
D–6380 Bad Homburg v.d. H.
Hessenring 73, Postfach 2320, Germany.

The Chinese Medical Practitioners Association
170 Johnston Road, Hong Kong

The Icelandic Nature Health Society
Laufasvegi 2, Reykjavik, Iceland.

Associazione Nazionale Commercianti Produtti Erboristici
Via Massena 20, 10128 Torino, Italy.

Associazione Nazionale Erboristi e Piante Officinali (ANEPO)*
Via E. S. Piccolomini 159, 53100 Siena, Italy.

The Botanical Society of Japan
c/o University of Tokyo, 3 Hongo, Bunkyo-ku, Tokyo, Japan.

The Auckland Herb Society
P.O. Box 20022, Glen Eden, Auckland 7, New Zealand.

The Tasmanian Herb Society
12 Delta Avenue, Taroona, Tasmania, 7006.

The American Horticultural Society*
901 N. Washington Street, Alexandria, Virginia 22314, U.S.A.

The Herb Society of America*
300 Massachusetts Avenue, Boston, Massachusetts 02115, U.S.A.

The Society for Economic Botany
c/o Dr. A. D. Marderosian, Philadelphia College of Pharmacy and Science, Philadelphia, Pennsylvania 19104, U.S.A.

The following organizations offer either training in medical herbalism or include herbalism as part of other courses:

National Herbalists Association of Australia (Queensland Chapter)
Montville Road, Mapleton, Queensland, Australia 4560.

The Academy of Natural Healing Pty Ltd.
7 The Esplanade, Ashfield, New South Wales, Australia 2131.

The General Council and Register of Consultant Herbalists Ltd and
The British Herbalists Union Ltd
93 East Avenue, Bournemouth, England.

The National Institute of Medical Herbalists Ltd
20 Osborne Avenue, Jesmond, Newcastle, England.

The Chinese Medicine and Acupuncture Research Centre
2nd floor, 322–324 Nathan Road, Kowloon, Hong Kong.

Swedish Herbal Institute (Svenska Örtmedicinska Institutet KB)
Bellmansgatan 11, 411 28 Göteborg, Sweden.

American Foundation for Homeopathy
Suite 428–431, Barr Building, 910 17th Street, N. W., Washington D.C. 20006, U.S.A.

National College of Naturopathic Medicine
1327 North 45th Street, Seattle, Washington 98103, U.S.A.

School of Natural Healing
P.O. Box 352, Provo, Utah 84601, U.S.A.

Bibliography

Introduction

Altschul, S von Ries, *Drugs and Foods from Little-Known Plants* (Harvard University Press, Cambridge, Mass. 1973)

Baker, H G *Plants and Civilization* (Macmillan, London 1970)

Brock, A J *Greek Medicine, being extracts illustrative of medical writers from Hippocrates to Galen* (J M Dent, London 1929)

Budge, Sir E W *The Divine Origin of the Craft of the Herbalist* (Culpeper House, London 1928)

Clarkson, R E *Herbs and Savoury Seeds* (Dover Publications, New York 1970)

Crockett, J U and Tanner, O *Herbs* (Time-Life Books, London and New York 1977)

Dawson, W R *A Leechbook or Collection of Medical Recipes of the Fifteenth Century* (Macmillan, London 1934)

Gelfand, M *Medicine and Magic of the Mashona* (Juta & Co., Cape Town 1956)

Genders, R *Scented Flora of the World* (Robert Hale & Co., London 1977)

Giles, W F *Our Vegetables, Whence They Came* (*Royal Horticultural Society Journal*, vol. *69*, 1944)

Grieve, M A *A Modern Herbal* (Penguin, Harmondsworth, Middx. 1974)

Grigson, G *A Dictionary of English Plant Names* (Allen Lane, Harmondsworth, Middx. 1974)

Grigson, G *The Englishman's Flora* (Paladin, St Albans, Hertfordshire 1975)

Hedrick, U P *Sturtevant's Edible Plants of the World* (Dover Publications, New York 1972)

Heffern, R *The Herb Buyer's Guide* (Pyramid Books, London 1973)

Hemphill, R *Herbs and Spices* (Penguin, Harmondsworth, Middx. 1966)

Huxley, A *Plant and Planet* (Allen Lane, Harmondsworth, Middx. 1974; Viking Press, New York 1975)

Kelly, I *Folk Practices in North Mexico* University of Texas Press, Austin, Texas 1965)

Kreig, M *Green Medicine* (Harrap, London 1965; Rand McNally, Chicago, Illinois 1964)

Levy, J de Bairacli *Herbal Handbook for Everyone* (Faber & Faber, London 1972)

Lust, J B *The Herb Book* (Bantam Books, London 1975; Des Plaines, Ill. 1974)

Mabey, R *Food for Free* (Collins, London 1972)

Mabey, R *Plants with a Purpose* (Collins, London 1977)

Mességué, M *Of Men and Plants* (Weidenfeld & Nicolson, London 1972)

Phillips, R *Wild Flowers of Britain* (Pan Books, London 1977)

Pirie, N W *Food Resources: Conventional and Novel* (Penguin, Harmondsworth, Middx. 1969)

Stearn, W T *Botanical Latin* (David & Charles, Newton Abbot, Devon 1973; Hafner Press 1966, distrib. Macmillan, Riverside NJ.)

Swain, T (ed.) *Plants in the Development of Modern Medicine* (Harvard University Press, Cambridge, Mass. 1972)

Thompson, C J S *The Mystic Mandrake* (Rider & Co., London 1934)

Thorwald, J *Science and Secrets of Early Medicine: Egypt, Mesopotamia, India, China, Mexico, Peru* (Thames & Hudson, London 1962)

History

Altschul, S von Ries '*Exploring the Herbarium*' (*Scientific American*, vol. *236*, May 1977)

Arber, A *Herbals, their Origin and Evolution* (Cambridge University Press 1938)

Clair, C *Of Herbs and Spices* (Abelard-Schuman, London, New York, Toronto 1961)

Gerard, J *The Herball or Generall Historie of Plantes*, 1597 edition (Minerva Press, London 1974; Walter J Johnson, Norwood, NJ. 1974)

Goodwin, G '*Which were the magic herbs?*' (*The Herbal Review*, vol. *2*, no. 4, October 1977)

Hadfield, M *A History of British Gardening* (Spring Books, Feltham, Middx. 1969)

Jackson, G *The Making of Medieval Spain* (Thames & Hudson, London 1972; Harcourt Brace Jovanovich, New York 1972)

King, R *The World of Kew* (Macmillan, London 1976)

Le Strange, R *A History of Herbal Plants* (Angus & Robertson, London 1977)

Moldenke, H N and A L *Plants of the Bible* (Ronald Press, Oxford 1952)

Monardes, N *Joyfull Newes out of the Newe Founde Worlde* (W Norton & Co., London 1577)

Sanecki, K N *The Complete Book of Herbs* (Macdonald & Jane's, London 1974; Macmillan, New York 1974)

Singer, C '*The Herbal in antiquity*' (*Journal of Hellenic Studies*, vol. *47*, Macmillan, London 1927)

Smith, A G R *Science and Society in the Sixteenth and Seventeenth Centuries* (Thames & Hudson, London 1972; Neal W Watson, Academic Publications, New York 1972)

Stearn, W T '*The origin and later development of cultivated plants*' (*Royal Horticultural Society Journal*, vol. *90*, 1965)

Biology and chemistry

Armstrong, E *The Simple Carbohydrates and Glucosides* (Longmans, Green & Co., London 1919)

Brook, A J *The Living Plant* (University Press, Edinburgh 1964)

Clapham, A R *et al, Excursion Flora of the British Isles* – 2nd edition (Cambridge University Press, 1959)

de Wit, H C *Plants of the World* – 3 volumes (Thames & Hudson, London 1965; E P Dutton & Co., New York 1969)

Everard, B and Morley, B D *Wild Flowers of the World* (Ebury Press & Michael Joseph, London 1970)

Fahn, A *Plant Anatomy* (Pergamon Press, Oxford, 1969)

Hutchinson, Sir J *The Families of Flowering Plants* – 2 volumes (Oxford University Press, 1973)

Huxley, A *Encyclopedia of the Plant Kingdom* (Hamlyn, London 1976)

Karlson P *Introduction to Modern Biochemistry* (Academic Press, New York 1975)

Martin, W K *The Concise British Flora in Colour* (Ebury Press & Michael Joseph, London 1969)

Polunin, O *Flowers of Europe* (Oxford University Press, 1969)

Roberts, M B *Biology: A Functional Approach* (Nelson, London 1971; Ronald Press, New York 1971)

Sinnot, E W and Wilson, K S *Botany: Principles and Problems* (McGraw-Hill, New York 1963)

Smith, G M *Cryptogamic Botany – Volume I: Algae and Fungi* (McGraw-Hill, Maidenhead, Berkshire, and New York 1955)

Steward, F C *Plants at Work* (Addison-Wesley, London 1964)

Tortora, C J *et al, Plant Form and Function* (Collier-Macmillan, London 1970)

Trease, C E and Evans, W C *A Textbook of Pharmacognosy* (Baillière Tindall, London 1970)

Willis, J C *Dictionary of the Flowering Plants and Ferns* (Cambridge University Press, 1973)

Medicinal uses

British Herbal Medicine Association *British Herbal Pharmacopoeia* (London 1973)

Brooker, S G and Cooper, R C *New Zealand Medicinal Plants* (Unity Press, Auckland 1961)

Bryant, A T *Zulu Medicine and Medicine-Men* (C Struik, Cape Town 1966)

Burlage, H M *Index of Plants with Reputed Medicinal and Poisonous Properties* (Austin Press, Austin, Texas 1968)

Chopra, R N *Indigenous Drugs of India* (Arts Press, New Delhi 1973)

Croizier, R C *Traditional Medicine in Modern China* (Harvard University Press, Cambridge, Mass. 1968)

Culbreth, D M R *A Manual of Materia Medica and Pharmacology* (Lea & Febiger, Philadelphia, Penn. 1927)

Flück, H *Medicinal Plants and their Uses* (W Foulsham, Slough 1970)

Gunther, E *Ethnobotany of Western Washington* (University of Washington Press, Seattle, Wash. 1973)

Gunther, R T *The Greek Herbal of Dioscorides* (Oxford University Press 1934; Hafner Press 1959 – distrib. Collier-Macmillan, Riverside, NJ.)

Huard, P and Wong, M *Chinese Medicine* McGraw-Hill, Maidenhead, Berks., and New York 1968)

Keys, J D *Chinese Herbs; their Botany, Chemistry and Pharmacodynamics* (Charles E Tuttle, Rutland, Vermont 1976)

Kowaro, J O *Medicinal Plants of East Africa* (East African Literature Bureau, Nairobi 1975)

Krochmal, A and C *A Guide to the*

Medicinal Plants of the United States (Quadrangle 1975, distrib. Harper & Row, Scanton, Penn.)
Lewis, W H and Elvin-Lewis, M P F *Medical Botany* (Wiley-Interscience, Chichester, Sussex 1977; John Wiley & Sons, New York 1976)
Martindale, W *The Extra Pharmacopoeia*, 26th edition – ed. N W Blacow (The Pharmaceutical Press, London 1972; distrib. Rittenhouse Book Distributors, Philadelphia, Penn.)
Millspaugh, C F *American Medicinal Plants* (Dover Publications, New York 1974)
Nelson, A *Medical Botany* (Churchill Livingstone, Edinburgh 1951)
Palaiseul, J *Grandmother's Secrets* (Penguin, Harmondsworth, Middx. 1976; G P Putnam's Sons, New York 1974)
Revolutionary Health Committee of Hunan Province, The *A Barefoot Doctor's Manual* (Routledge & Kegan Paul, London 1978)
Schauenberg, P and Paris, F *Guide to Medicinal Plants* (Lutterworth Press, Guildford, Surrey 1977)
Schendel, G *Medicine in Mexico* (University of Texas Press, Austin, Texas 1968)
Schneider, W *Lexicon zur Arzneimittelgeschichte* (Govi-Verlag, Frankfurt 1974)
Selection du Reader's Digest *Secrets et Vertus des Plantes Médicinales* (Paris 1977)
Stary, F and Jirasek, V *Herbs* (Hamlyn, London 1976)
Tschirch, A *Handbuch der Pharmakognosie* – volumes 1–3 (Tauchnitz, Leipzig 1909–1927)
Vogel, V J *American Indian Medicine* (University of Oklahoma Press, Norman, Oklahoma 1970)
Wallis, T E *Textbook of Pharmacognosy* (J & A Churchill, London 1962; Longman, New York 1969)
Watt, J M and Breyer-Brandwijk, M G *Medicinal and Poisonous Plants of Southern and Eastern Africa* (Churchill Livingstone, Edinburgh 1962)
Webb, L J *Guide to the Medicinal and Poisonous Plants of Queensland* (Bulletin 232, Center for Scientific and Industrial Research, Melbourne 1948)
Wilson, A and Schild, H O *Applied Pharmacology* (J & A Churchill, London 1968)
Wren, R C *Potter's New Cyclopaedia of Botanical Drugs and Preparations* (Health Science Press, Holsworthy, North Devon 1973; Harper & Row, New York 1972)

Culinary uses
Apicius: The Roman Cookery Book, eds. Flower, B and Rosenbaum, E (Harrap, London 1974; British Book Center, New York 1975)
Barber, R *Cooking and Recipes from Rome to the Renaissance* (Allen Lane, London, 1974)
David, E *Spices, Salt and Aromatics in the English Kitchen* (Penguin, Harmondsworth, Middx. 1970)
Day, H *The Complete Book of Curries* (Kaye & Ward, London 1975)
Grange, C *The Complete Book of Home Food Preservation* (Cassell, London 1949)
Grieve, M *Culinary Herbs and Condiments* (Dover Publications, New York 1971)
Hartley, D *Food in England* (Macdonald & Jane's, London 1975)
Hayes, E *Herbs, Flavours and Spices* (Faber & Faber, London 1961)
Hogner, D C *Herbs from the Garden to the Table* (Oxford University Press, London and New York 1953)
Loewenfeld, C and Back, P *Herbs for Health and Cookery* (Pan Books, London 1971; Universal Pub. and Distr. Corp., Happauge, NY. 1970
McKenzie, E *Dining with Herbs* (The Herb Society of America, Boston, Mass. 1971)
Medsger, O P *Edible Wild Plants* (Macmillan, New York 1966)
Miloradovich, M *The Art of Cooking with Herbs and Spices* (Doubleday & Co., New York 1950)
Rohde, E S *Culinary and Salad Herbs* (Dover Publications, New York 1972)
Sass, L *To the King's Taste* (John Murray, London 1976; Metropolitan Museum of Art, 1977 – distrib. New York Graphic Society, Greenwich, Conn.)
Sass, L *To the Queen's Taste* (John Murray, London 1977)
Stobart, T *Herbs, Spices and Flavourings*, (David & Charles, Newton Abbot, Devon 1970; International Pubns. Service, New York 1972)
Wilson, C A *Food and Drink in Britain* Constable, London 1973)

Domestic and cosmetic uses
Arlott, J *The Snuff Shop* (Michael Joseph, London 1974)
Audy, J and Fondin, J *Santé et Beauté par les Plantes* (Edita SA, Lausanne 1968)
Brooklyn Botanic Garden Record *Plants and Gardens* (New York 1973)
Buchman, D D *Feed Your Face* (Duckworth, London 1973)
Hériteau, J *Pot Pourris and Other Fragrant Delights* (Lutterworth Press, Guildford, Surrey 1975)
Huson, P *Mastering Herbalism* (Abacus, Tunbridge Wells, Kent 1977; Stein & Day, New York 1974)
Mességué, M *Mon Herbier de Santé* (Opera Mundi S A, Paris 1975)
Plummer, B *Fragrance* (Robert Hale & Co., London 1976)
Poucher, W A *Perfumes, Cosmetics and Soaps* – volumes 1–3 (Chapman & Hall, London 1936)
Redgrove, H S *Scent and all about it* (Heinemann, London 1928)
Rimmel, E *Book of Perfumes* (Chapman & Hall, London 1867)
Ritchie, C *Candle Making* (Hodder & Stoughton, Sevenoaks, Kent 1976)
Uphof, J C T *Dictionary of Economic* Plants (Wheldon & Wesley, Hitchin, Hertfordshire 1970)

Cultivation
Aichele, D *Wild Flowers* (Octopus Books, London 1975)
Bailey, L H *Manual of Cultivated Plants* (Macmillan, London 1949)
Brownlow, M E *Herbs and the Fragrant Garden* (Darton, Longman & Todd, London 1978)
Clarkson, R E *Herbs, their Culture and Uses* (Macmillan, New York 1966)
Day, A *Vegeculture* (Methuen & Co., London 1917)
Eley, C *Gardening for the Twentieth Century* (John Murray, London 1923)
Hay, R and Synge, P M *The Dictionary of Garden Plants* (Ebury Press & Michael Joseph, London 1973)
Herb Society, The *Growing Herbs* (London 1977)
Hewer D G and Sanecki, K N *Practical Herb Growing* (G Bell & Sons, London 1969)
Hunter, B T *Gardening without Poisons* (Hamish Hamilton, London 1965)
Loewenfeld, C *Herb Gardening* (Faber & Faber, London 1964)
Perring, F (ed.) *The Flora of a Changing Britain* (*Botanical Society of the British Isles Conference Report* No. 11, 1972)
Sanecki, K N *Discovering Herbs* (Shire Publications, Aylesbury, Buckinghamshire 1973)
Teetgen, A B *Profitable Herb Growing and Collecting* (Country Life, London 1916)

Periodicals
ACTA PHYTOTHERAPEUTICA, ten editions per year 1954–1972. Scientific journal on botanical medicine. In 1973 merged with the *Quarterly Journal of Crude Drug Research.* Back copies. Swets & Zeitlinger B V, Publishing Dept., 347 b Heereweg, Lisse, The Netherlands.
ECONOMIC BOTANY, quarterly; economic and medicinal plants, including food crops. Available from: The Society for Economic Botany, The New York Botanical Garden, The Bronx, NY 10458, U.S.A.
GARDEN HISTORY, quarterly; historical, horticultural and etymological information; often of relevance to herbalism. Editor: Dr Christopher Thacker, French Studies, The University, Reading, Berkshire, England.
PLANTS AND GARDENS, quarterly; some editions contain data on domestic and horticultural aspects of herbs. Available from: Brooklyn Botanic Garden, Brooklyn, NY 11225, U.S.A.
QUARTERLY JOURNAL OF CRUDE DRUG RESEARCH, quarterly; scientific aspects of crude drugs, both animal and plant, and their derivatives. Articles in English, French and German; published since 1961. Back copies and subscriptions: Swets & Zeitlinger B V, Publishing Dept., 347 b Heereweg, Lisse, The Netherlands.
RIVISTA DI ERBORISTERIA, quarterly; medical herbalism. Editor: Dr Angiolo Severi, Via E S Piccolomini 159, 53100 Siena, Italy.
THE HERB GROWER, quarterly; mainly horticultural aspects. Available from: Herb Grower, Falls Village, Conn. 06031, U.S.A.
THE HERBAL REVIEW, quarterly; all aspects of herbs and herbalism. Available from: The Herb Society, 34 Boscobel Place, London SW1, England.
THE HERBARIST, annually; non-medical aspects of herbalism. Available from: The Herb Society of America, 300 Massachusetts Avenue, Boston, Mass. 02115, U.S.A.

General index

Note Page numbers in *italics* refer to illustrations. Entries in **bold** type refer to recipes.

Index of plants

Note Page numbers in *italics* refer to illustrations. Page numbers in **bold** type refer to the entry in the reference section.

Acknowledgments

We are grateful to Mark Constantine, Ivan Day and Ian Tribe for their kind assistance, and to Michael Stringer and Roberto Campagna for the drawings on pages 142–283.

We are grateful to the following for the pictures on the following pages: 6–7 Iris Hardwick Library; 8 (top) IGDA; 8 (bottom) Bodleian Library; 9 IGDA; 10 Snark International; 11 A–Z Collection; 12–13 Wellcome Institute; 14 Snark International; 15 Mansell Collection; 16 (top) Mary Evans Picture Library; 16 (below left) Mary Evans Picture Library; 16 (below right) Mary Evans Picture Library; 17 Ronald Sheridan; 18 (top) Bodleian Library; 18 (below) Mary Evans Picture Library; 19 Snark International; 20 (top) Mansell Collection; 20 (bottom) Prague National Library Dagli Orti; 21 IGDA; 22 Bodleian Library; 23 (below left) Radio Times/Hulton; 23 (right) Mary Evans Picture Library; 24 Ann Ronan Picture Library; 24–25 Iris Hardwick Library; 26 IGDA; 27 Ronald Sheridan; 28 Bruce Coleman/Stephen Dalton; 30 (top left) C Bevilacqua; 30 (top right) C Bevilacqua; 30–1 Harry Smith Collection; 37 A–Z Collection; 38 Heather Angel; 39 Heather Angel; 41 Dr S F Buczacki; 42 Gene Cox; 43 Paul Brierley/Orbis; 44 Paul Brierley/Orbis; 45 (top left) Paul Brierley/Orbis; 45 (top right) Paul Brierley; 46–47 Michael Holford; 48 (top) Pat Brindley; 48 (below) Snark International; 49 Mary Evans Picture Library; 50 Ronald Sheridan; 51 Mary Evans Picture Library; 52 Iris Hardwick Library; 53 (top) R J Corbin; 53 (below) Pat Brindley; 54 Gene Cox; 55 IGDA; 57 IGDA; 63 A P Paterson; 64 Mike Leale/Orbis; 66 Iris Hardwick Library; 70–71 Mike Leale/Orbis; 72 (left) Mansell Collection; 72 (right) Mansell Collection; 73 Leslie Johns; 74 Zefa; 75 Syndication International; 77 Ann Ronan Picture Library; 78 IGDA; 79 IGDA; 80 Orbis; 81 IGDA; 85 (left) IGDA; 85 (right) A P Paterson; 86 Bernard Alfieri; 87 IGDA; 88 (left) Mansell Collection; 88 (right) Mansell Collection; 89 Brian Furner; 92–93 Orbis; 94 (left) A P Paterson; 94 (other 4) National Museum of Wales; 96 Angelo Hornak; 97 Leslie Johns and Associates; 98 (3) Leslie Johns and Associates; 99 (top) Mansell Collection; 99 (bottom) Ann and Bury Peerless; 101 Michael Holford; 102 IGDA; 104 A P Paterson; 105 A P Paterson; 106 P2/IGDA; 107 (centre) Syndication International; 107 (right) IGDA; 108 Syndication International; 110 (left) Ann and Bury Peerless; 110 (right) IGDA; 111 Mansell Collection; 112 Snark/Edouard Rousseau; 113 H Roger-Viollet; 114–5 Leslie Johns and Associates; 116 Mansell Collection; 119 Paul Miles; 120–121 Brian Furner; 121 A–Z Collection; 125 Ronald Sheridan; 127 (both) Orbis; 128 (left) NRVS; 128 (centre) ICI Ltd; 129 Iris Hardwick Library; 130 Brian Furner; 131 (left) Snark/Edouard Rousseau; 131 (right) Brian Matthew/Royal Botanic Garden, Kew; 140–141 Leslie Johns and Associates; 142 A P Paterson; 143 (left) P2/IGDA; 143 (centre) P2/IGDA; 143 (right) Brian Furner; 144 (centre) Brian Furner; 144 (right) Iris Hardwick Library; 145 Harry Smith Collection; 146 (left) A P Paterson; 146 (centre) Weed Research Organisation; 147 (left) A P Paterson; 147 (centre) A P Paterson; 148 (left) A P Paterson; 148 (right) A P Paterson; 149 (left) Harry Smith Collection; 149 (centre) G E Hyde; 149 (right) A P Paterson; 150 (left) A P Paterson; 150 (centre) A P Paterson; 150 (right) Iris Hardwick Library; 151 (left) A P Paterson; 151 (right) A P Paterson; 152 (centre) A P Paterson; 152 (right) Pat Brindley; 153 (left) Pat Brindley; 154 (left) Pat Brindley; 154 (right) A P Paterson; 155 (left) P2/IGDA; 155 (centre) A P Paterson; 155 (right) A P Paterson; 156 (left) P2/IGDA; 156 (centre) A P Paterson; 157 (centre) A P Paterson; 157 (right) M Bavestrelli; 158 (left) A P Paterson; 158 (centre) M Bavestrelli; 159 (left) A P Paterson; 159 (centre) A P Paterson; 159 (right) M Bavestrelli; 160 (left top) A P Paterson; 160 (left bottom) A P Paterson; 160 (centre) A P Paterson; 161 (left) A P Paterson; 161 (centre) A P Paterson; 161 (right) A P Paterson; 162 (left top) A P Paterson; 162 (left bottom) A P Paterson; 162 (centre) C Bevilacqua; 162 (right) P2/IGDA; 163 (left) A P Paterson; 163 (centre) A P Paterson; 163 (right) G E Hyde; 164 (left top) A P Paterson; 164 (left bottom) Pat Brindley; 164 (right) A P Paterson; 165 (centre) A P Paterson; 165 (right) A P Paterson; 166 (left) A P Paterson; 166 (centre) A P Paterson; 167 (left) M Bavestrelli; 167 (centre) A P Paterson; 168 (left) A P Paterson; 169 (left top) A P Paterson; 169 (left bottom) A P Paterson; 169 (centre) A P Paterson; 170 G E Hyde; 171 (left) A P Paterson; 171 (centre) A P Paterson; 171 (right) A P Paterson; 172 Pat Brindley; 173 (left) A P Paterson; 173 (centre) A P Paterson; 174 P2/IGDA; 175 (left) M Bavestrelli; 175 (right) A P Paterson; 176 (left) A P Paterson; 176 (centre) A P Paterson; 176 (right) IGDA; 177 (left) IGDA; 177 (right) A P Paterson; 178 (centre) A P Paterson; 178 (right) A P Paterson; 179 (left) A P Paterson; 179 (centre) A P Paterson; 179 (right) A P Paterson; 181 (centre) Harry Smith Collection; 181 (right) A P Paterson; 182 (centre) A P Paterson; 182 (right top) P2/IGDA; 182 (right bottom) A P Paterson; 183 (left and right) A P Paterson; 184 (left) A P Paterson; 184 (centre) A P Paterson; 185 (left) P2/IGDA; 185 (right top) A P Paterson; 185 (right bottom) A P Paterson; 186 (left) A P Paterson; 186 (centre) A P Paterson; 187 (left) A P Paterson; 187 (centre) IGDA; 187 (right) G E Hyde; 188 A P Paterson; 189 A P Paterson; 190 A P Paterson; 191 (centre) Pat Brindley; 191 (right) Dr Derek Reid; 192 (left) H Veiller; 192 (right) Iris Hardwick Library; 193 (centre) Giorgio Negri; 193 (right) Leslie Johns and Associates; 194 (left) A P Paterson; 194 (centre) A P Paterson; 196 (left) A P Paterson; 196 (right) Iris Hardwick Library; 197 (right top) A P Paterson; 197 (right bottom) A P Paterson; 198 (left) A P Paterson; 198 (centre) A P Paterson; 199 (left) A P Paterson; 199 (right) P2/IGDA; 200 (centre) Pat Brindley; 200 (right) Pat Brindley; 201 IGDA; 202 (centre) A P Paterson; 202 (right) A P Paterson; 204 (left) A P Paterson; 204 (centre) A P Paterson; 205 (left top) Pat Brindley; 205 (left bottom) A P Paterson; 206 M Bavestrelli; 207 (centre) A P Paterson; 207 (right) A P Paterson; 208 Pat Brindley; 209 (left) A P Paterson; 209 (right) G E Hyde; 210 A P Paterson; 211 (centre) A P Paterson; 211 (right) A P Paterson; 212 A P Paterson; 213 (top) A P Paterson; 213 (bottom) A P Paterson; 214 (centre) Pat Brindley; 214 (right) Harry Smith Collection; 217 (centre) A P Paterson; 217 (right) H Veiller; 218 (left) A P Paterson; 218 (centre) A P Paterson; 218 (right) A P Paterson; 219 A P Paterson; 220 Pat Brindley; 222 (left) Pat Brindley; 222 (right) A P Paterson; 223 (left) A P Paterson; 223 (centre) A–Z Collection; 224 (centre) Pat Brindley; 224 (right) Pat Brindley; 225 (centre) Pat Brindley; 225 (right) A P Paterson; 226 (centre) A P Paterson; 226 (right) Brian Furner; 227 (centre) A P Paterson; 227 (right) R J Corbin; 228 (centre) A P Paterson; 228 (right) A P Paterson; 229 (left) A P Paterson; 229 (right) Brian Furner; 230 (left) A P Paterson; 230 (centre) A P Paterson; 231 A P Paterson; 232 Pat Brindley; 233 A P Paterson; 234 (top) A P Paterson; 234 (bottom) Pat Brindley; 235 G E Hyde; 236 (top) A P Paterson; 236 (bottom) Pat Brindley; 238 A P Paterson; 240 A P Paterson; 241 Brian Furner; 242 (left top) A P Paterson; 242 (left bottom) A P Paterson; 242 (right) A P Paterson; 244 A P Paterson; 245 (left) A P Paterson; 245 (right) A P Paterson; 246 (top) A P Paterson; 246 (bottom) A P Paterson; 247 (left) A P Paterson; 247 (centre) Pat Brindley; 247 (right) A P Paterson; 248 (left) A P Paterson; 248 (right) A P Paterson; 249 (left) A P Paterson; 249 (right) G E Hyde; 250 (centre) Iris Hardwick Library; 250 (right) A P Paterson; 251 (centre) A P Paterson; 251 (right) A P Paterson; 252 (left) Brian Furner; 252 (right) P2/IGDA; 253 (top) A P Paterson; 253 (bottom) A P Paterson; 254 (left) Pat Brindley; 254 (centre) A P Paterson; 254 (right) A P Paterson; 255 (left) A P Paterson; 255 (centre) A P Paterson; 255 (right) Pat Brindley; 256 (left) A P Paterson; 256 (centre) A P Paterson; 256 (right) A P Paterson; 257 Pat Brindley; 258 (left) A P Paterson; 258 (right) A P Paterson; 259 (left) Iris Hardwick Library; 259 (right) Pat Brindley; 260 (centre) A P Paterson; 260 (right) A P Paterson; 261 (centre) A P Paterson; 261 (right) A P Paterson; 262 (left) A P Paterson; 262 (centre) A P Paterson; 264 A P Paterson; 265 (centre) A P Paterson; 265 (right) A P Paterson; 266 A P Paterson; 267 (left) IGDA; 267 (centre) A P Paterson; 268 A P Paterson; 269 (left) A P Paterson; 269 (right) Brian Furner; 270 (left) A P Paterson; 270 (right) A P Paterson; 271 Bernard Alfieri; 272 (left top) Pat Brindley; 272 (left bottom) C Bevilacqua; 273 (centre) A P Paterson; 274 A P Paterson; 275 (left) A P Paterson; 275 (centre) Brian Furner; 276 (left) A P Paterson; 276 (right) A P Paterson; 277 (left) A P Paterson; 277 (right) A P Paterson; 278 Giorgio Negri; 279 A P Paterson; 281 (left) A P Paterson; 281 (right) Harry Smith Collection; 282 (top) A P Paterson; 282 (bottom) A P Paterson; 283 (left) A P Paterson; 283 (right) A P Paterson.